Introduction to
Social Work
in Canada

Introduction to Social Work in Canada

Histories, Contexts, and Practices

Nicole Ives • Myriam Denov • Tamara Sussman

OXFORD
UNIVERSITY PRESS

OXFORD
UNIVERSITY PRESS

Oxford University Press is a department of the University of Oxford.
It furthers the University's objective of excellence in research, scholarship,
and education by publishing worldwide. Oxford is a registered trade mark of
Oxford University Press in the UK and in certain other countries.

Published in Canada by
Oxford University Press
8 Sampson Mews, Suite 204,
Don Mills, Ontario M3C 0H5 Canada

www.oupcanada.com

Library and Archives Canada Cataloguing in Publication
Ives, Nicole, author
Introduction to social work in Canada : histories, contexts and practices / Nicole Ives,
Myriam Denov, Tamara Sussman.

Includes bibliographical references and index.
ISBN 978–0–19–900317–4 (pbk.)

1. Social service—Canada—Textbooks. I. Denov, Myriam S., author II.
2. Sussman, Tamara, author III. Title.

HV105.I94 2015   361.30971   C2014-907920-6

Cover image: paul_june/iStockphoto
Chapter and Part opener images: Part I: © Blend Images/Alamy;
Chapter 1: Makiko Tada; Chapter 2: © moodboard/Alamy; Chapter 3: Wendy Bush;
Part II: © digitalskillet/iStockphoto; Chapter 4: © Angela Hampton Picture
Library/Alamy; Chapter 5: © Jim West/Alamy; Part III: © Bubbles Photolibrary/Alamy;
Chapter 6: Sun Media; Chapter 7: Rocky Mountain Center for Play Therapy, University
of Wyoming; Chapter 8: Port Alberni Friendship Center; Chapter 9: Photo by Katie Hyslop;
Chapter 10: Dax Melmer/The Windsor Star ; Chapter 11: © Howard Barlow/Alamy;
Chapter 12: Dan Janissee/The Windsor Star; Chapter 13: © Joerg Boethling /Alamy

Oxford University Press is committed to our environment.
Wherever possible, our books are printed on paper which comes from
responsible sources.

Printed and bound in the United States

1 2 3 4 — 18 17 16 15

Brief Contents

Contents

From the Publisher

Oxford University Press is delighted to present *Introduction to Social Work in Canada: Histories, Contexts, and Practices*, a comprehensive introductory text designed for students of social work at Canadian colleges and universities. Drawing extensively on Canadian statistics and scholarship, the book begins by examining the historical roots of social work practice in Canada before moving on to discuss contemporary theoretical perspectives, ethics, and research. Practical applications are emphasized throughout, providing students with foundational skills they can apply in a broad range of contexts, from working with families, groups, and communities, to practising social work among children, Indigenous peoples, and people with disabilities.

Key Features

- **An inclusive approach** draws not only on English contributions to Canadian social work practice but also long-neglected Aboriginal and French contributions, providing students with the most diverse and well-rounded introduction to social work on the market.

- **Feature boxes** in every chapter engage students in the everyday world of Canadian social work by highlighting issues, events, and ideas shaping the field today.

Theory in Practice

- **"Theory in Practice" boxes** demonstrate how theories and ideological approaches discussed in the chapter apply to the real world of practice.

Case STUDY

- **"Case Study" boxes** present students with landmark Canadian studies that connect the concepts under discussion to in-the-field contexts.

• **"In Their Own Words" boxes** feature first-person narratives by social workers active in the field, giving students diverse perspectives from across the country in an up-close and personal way.

In Their Own Words

• **"Practical Tip" boxes** offer students advice on topics ranging from writing consent forms to enhancing group facilitation.

Practical TIP

- **Learning objectives and chapter outlines** at the beginning of each chapter provide students with an overview of the concepts to be covered and a preview of the chapter contents.

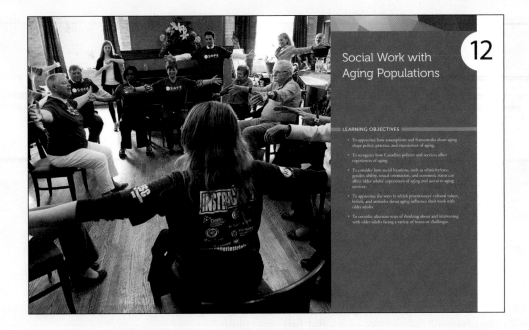

- **Visually engaging photos, tables, and figures** bring topics to life and help students understand concepts and data in approachable ways.

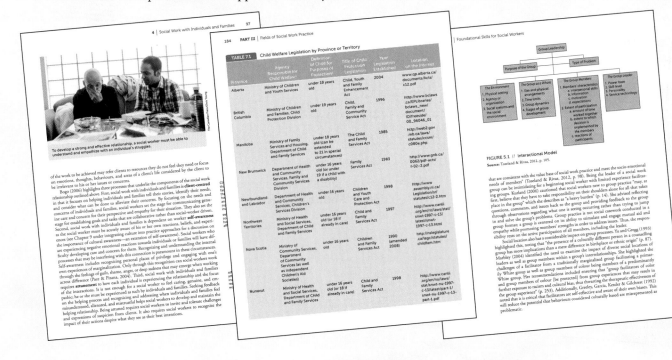

- **Marginal definitions of key terms** reinforce core concepts and provide a quick guide for reference and review as well as appear in the end-of-book glossary.

- **Questions for critical thought** challenge students to engage with the content beyond the chapter pages and further explore the material, issues, and concepts.

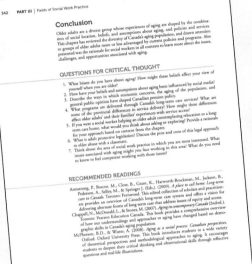

- **Recommended readings and websites** provide links to information and other resources for further study and research relevant to work in the field.

Supplements

Introduction to Social Work in Canada is supported by a comprehensive package of learning and teaching tools that includes resources for both students and instructors.

For Instructors

- A detailed **instructor's manual** provides an extensive set of pedagogical tools and suggestions for every chapter, including overviews and summaries, key concepts, teaching notes, homework assignments, and additional print and online resources.
- Classroom-ready **PowerPoint slides** incorporate graphics and tables from the text, summarize key points from each chapter, and may be edited to suit individual instructors' needs.
- A comprehensive **test generator** enables instructors to sort, edit, import, and distribute hundreds of questions in multiple-choice, short-answer, and true–false formats.

For Students

- The **student study guide** includes chapter summaries, study questions, self-grading quizzes, and explore-and-discuss exercises to help students review textbook and classroom material.

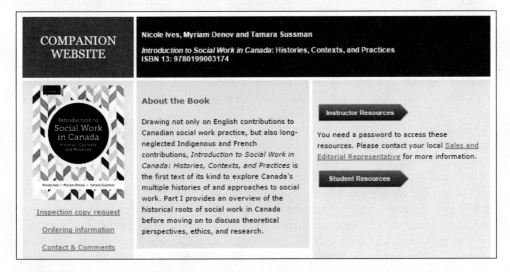

COMPANION WEBSITE

Nicole Ives, Myriam Denov and Tamara Sussman

Introduction to Social Work in Canada: Histories, Contexts, and Practices
ISBN 13: 9780199003174

About the Book

Drawing not only on English contributions to Canadian social work practice, but also long-neglected Indigenous and French contributions, *Introduction to Social Work in Canada: Histories, Contexts, and Practices* is the first text of its kind to explore Canada's multiple histories of and approaches to social work. Part I provides an overview of the historical roots of social work in Canada before moving on to discuss theoretical perspectives, ethics, and research.

Inspection copy request

Ordering information

Contact & Comments

Instructor Resources

You need a password to access these resources. Please contact your local Sales and Editorial Representative for more information.

Student Resources

Acknowledgements

We would like to thank the following reviewers, as well as those who chose to remain anonymous, for their insightful comments and suggestions during the development of *Introduction to Social Work in Canada*.

- Ken Barter, Memorial University of Newfoundland
- Mike Devine, Memorial University of Newfoundland
- Rachelle Hole, University of British Columbia
- Andrew Mantulak, Western University
- Lisa Ondejko, Okanagan College
- Patricia Slade, Redeemer University College

From the Authors

Contemporary Canadian social work draws on foundational knowledge composed of myriad histories, theoretical frameworks, and research-based practices to understand human behaviour in countless social, cultural, political, and economic contexts. This knowledge shapes how social workers conceptualize issues needing intervention, where they locate the "problem," and how they determine their approach to practice. Despite the multiple histories and knowledge bases informing the development of social work practice in Canada, most Canadian texts frame the site of foundational knowledge in the English roots of social work, starting with the Poor Laws of 1601. As a consequence, historical contributions of Indigenous and French Peoples have been largely ignored.

The three of us came together with the idea for this text after teaching introductory social work history and practice skills courses for many years. Frustrated with the often narrow and Eurocentric focus in other Canadian texts, we decided that we wanted to write an introductory textbook that explored the evolution of social work knowledge through the lens of three interwoven histories. We also wanted to problematize how particular paradigms became prominent in the social work knowledge base, and help students learn how to think about and use these multiple knowledge bases to inform their practice with individuals, families, groups, and communities. Our main goal in writing this textbook is to create space for the integration of multiple and diverse histories—English, French, and Indigenous—that have contributed to the development of social work in Canada, addressing directly a criticism of social work texts for providing primarily a Eurocentric perspective that does not adequately reflect the complex political, social, or cultural realities of all who live in Canada.

Thus, we have conceptualized the foundation of social work in Canada as interwoven braids, each braid representing English, Indigenous, and French histories and contemporary approaches to social work practice and policy. Each braid is composed of countless strands, or stories, which reflect Canada's diverse history and relationships among its peoples. Including Canada's multiple histories of and approaches to social work addresses the shortcomings of generalist texts that have tended to privilege one perspective. In addition to the existence of the English, Indigenous, and French traditions, the most recent Canadian census (2006) demonstrates that Canada's demographic landscape has been and continues to be shaped and transformed through international migration. Therefore, in this sense, as the landscape changes, diverse perspectives and approaches form new braids that continue to be woven into the Canadian landscape. Another goal of the book is to address such complexities, opening up opportunities for contributions from multiple communities, whether they are newly arrived in Canada or have been up-to-now un- or underrepresented populations in social work curricula. Although Canada first adopted multiculturalism as official policy in 1971, its historically diverse ethnocultural and religious population is centuries old. Many chapters describe the contexts of diverse ethnic communities that have deep roots in Canada's history and how beliefs, values, and traditions of these communities shape contemporary social work practice. In order to provide relevant, effective services, social work students need to be aware of the historical experiences of diverse groups and communities as well as understand how contemporary manifestations of racism and discrimination continue to shape lives.

Unique Features of This Book

This text has several unique features. First, this book's historical backdrop includes Indigenous, English, and French histories and multicultural practice perspectives. Multiple historical foundations are an important component of Canadian history, and are rarely, if ever, addressed in Canadian social work texts. This book provides an important backdrop of interrelated aspects of Canadian history that will help students appreciate more fully the Canadian context of social work practice. We believe that an inclusive approach to teaching social work history and philosophy is strengthened by the integration of approaches by Canada's founding peoples together with the contemporary realities of the country's multicultural population.

Second, the text focuses on Canadian examples and references. Included are a wealth of examples and references from across the country, making it highly relevant to Canadian social work students. Each chapter contains "In Their Own Words," "Case Study," and "Theory in Practice" boxes featuring examples from cities big and small across Canada, as well as provincial, national, and international illustrations related to the specific content of the chapter. Some chapters also contain "Practical Tips" boxes, containing practice- and research-based suggestions for working with clients. "In Their Own Words" boxes feature short guest editorials written by practitioners working in the field. Great effort was made to include voices from across the country, who share their successes and struggles as they relate to social work practice. Also included in every chapter are "Case Study" boxes that draw attention to significant Canadian studies that illustrate the concepts under discussion. Every chapter includes theoretical linkages to social work practice. This book introduces students to the theoretical bases of the profession *and* outlines how to link theoretical principles and concepts to case material. Theory is addressed in a clear and engaging style, making it accessible to undergraduate students. To underscore the theoretical linkages, each chapter contains "Theory in Practice" boxes that demonstrate application of social work theories and ideological approaches to the real world of practice. To help facilitate the connection of theory to practice, the book also encourages students to engage in a process of reflexivity. The practice examples and "Questions for Critical Thought" are designed to elicit how in-practice knowledge shapes actions and reactions. This practical approach will help students learn how to identify and question the social work knowledge informing their own in-practice actions and reactions—a common challenge for student trainees.

Third, this text interweaves foundational practice skills expected of social workers across settings with specific content. Throughout the book, social work students are provided with an overview of the contexts in which social workers typically work and of the roles they may be called on to play. Particular attention is paid to the iterative processes of reflective practice, and models of reflection that will help students learn how to link the concepts and knowledge base of the profession to case material are offered. As students move through the text, they are taken through a process to help them recognize that what they ask and what they do is tied to what they think. Recent research suggests that critical reflection is a metacompetency on which the effectiveness of many other skills is based.

The Structure of This Book

This book is divided into three sections. Part I focuses on the historical foundations of social work, the theoretical and philosophical frameworks that guide social work practice as well as discussion of ethics in social work practice and research. Part II concentrates on social work practice and foundational skills for social workers. Attention is paid to social work practice with individuals and families and social work practice with groups and communities. Part III is composed of chapters that highlight the multiple fields of social work practice. At the same time, however, each chapter contains examples that illustrate the interconnectedness of these fields. Each chapter ends with questions for critical thought to further engage students in discussion of and reflection on the chapter's content as well as recommended readings and websites. Three chapters are authored by prominent scholars whose areas of expertise cover Indigenous social work practice, social work practice and sexual and gender diversity, and social work with people with disabilities.

Part I

The opening **Chapter 1** establishes the braided theme by tracing the origins and evolution of social work and social welfare in English-speaking Canada. Addressing the historical realities regarding the transition from private charities to public welfare, settlement houses, and the emergence of trained social workers, the chapter also traces the ways in which the English traditions and values have shaped and continue to shape service delivery in English-speaking regions of Canada. This chapter also traces the Indigenous foundations of social work in Canada and addresses Canada's colonial history in relation to Indigenous Peoples, the meaning and development of Indigenous social welfare as well as its impact on social work practice across Canada. Regarding terminology used in this book, all authors, including guest authors, agreed on the interchangeable use of Indigenous and Aboriginal to describe the descendants of peoples living in Canada prior to the arrival of the Europeans. The history of Canadian social welfare cannot be fully understood without addressing its French historical foundations. Such traditions are of particular relevance to innumerable communities living in Ontario, Québec, Manitoba, and New Brunswick. Thus, this chapter includes the unique features of social welfare emerging from the French traditions, with a discussion of the maintenance of French culture and traditions.

Chapter 2 examines key theoretical perspectives that have informed social work thinking and practice over time, beginning with a discussion of the role of theory in social work. It explores theory's multiple meanings and definitions, addresses why theories are useful, their limitations, and the process of selecting theories to guide social work practice. The chapter then summarizes key theoretical perspectives in social work followed by a discussion of four theoretical perspectives that are grouped metaphorically into "onion peeling theories," "faulty-engine theories," "story-telling theories," and "mountain-moving theories." The chapter concludes by addressing the key interconnections between theory and practice and the role of critical reflexive practice in helping to ensure this interconnection.

The Canadian *Code of Ethics for Social Work* requires that social workers have "a responsibility to maintain professional proficiency, to continually strive to increase their professional knowledge and skills, and to apply new knowledge in practice commensurate with their level of professional education, skill and competency, seeking consultation and supervision as appropriate" (CASW, 2005, p. 8). Thus, **Chapter 3** introduces students to the guidelines for ethical behaviour in social work practice and research and the development of contemporary ethical standards. Particular areas of focus include approaches to ethical decision-making and essential ethical considerations in research studies, including ethical frameworks for working with Indigenous Peoples.

Part II

Chapter 4 introduces students to the foundational principles of social work practice with individuals and families. The chapter is divided into two sections: (1) an overview of the different roles social workers play when practising with individuals and families in a variety of contexts and settings, and (2) a review of the stages or phases of the helping process including exploration/assessment, contracting/planning, implementation/intervention, and ending/evaluation and their application to different social work settings. Particular emphasis is placed on the importance of assessment both as a process (i.e., developing rapport; asking critical questions) and as a product (i.e., the written record).

Chapter 5 introduces foundational principles of social work practice with groups and communities. The first section provides an overview of different types of groups (e.g., therapeutic groups, task groups), different group structures (e.g., open ended, time limited) and different models of facilitation (e.g., self-help, professionally led). Also introduced are the stages of group development and how to apply these principles to different group types. The second section provides an overview of different approaches to working with communities and introduces the principles and practices informing community development from multiple perspectives. Woven throughout the chapter is the inclusion of how personal and professional values shape work with groups and communities.

Part III

Chapter 6 is focused on the intersection of social work practice and health. The beginning of the chapter provides an overview of the development and contemporary delivery of health care in Canada. This section illustrates how recent transformations in healthcare delivery have served to threaten the core principles on which the Canadian system has been based. Much of the chapter is then devoted to various issues related to health as explored through a social determinants of health framework.

Social work with children in Canada can be divided into three distinct, but often overlapping areas of practice: child welfare, youth justice, and prevention. **Chapter 7** explores social work practice with children and its surrounding complexities by addressing issues and realities affecting Canadian children, tracing changing conceptualizations of childhood and the history of child welfare in Canada, and exploring social work practice in the context of child welfare. Discussion of preventive social work with children is also included, alongside the dilemmas and tension of practice in relation to child welfare and youth justice.

Chapter 8 is written by Dr Cyndy Baskin. Indigenous and non-Indigenous social work practitioners working with Indigenous individuals, families, and communities need a comprehensive, grounded understanding of Indigenous Peoples in context: their histories, cultures, and political, economic, social, legal, and health issues. This chapter provides an overview of the most significant aspects of what social work is to Indigenous Peoples in Canada. The current challenges that Indigenous Peoples face is discussed in the context of the impacts of colonization and the often ongoing role of social work as an agent of social control. The chapter concludes with what Indigenous Peoples are doing to recreate their original ways of helping within their communities and the successes of doing so.

Changing demographics across Canada have created unique challenges for social workers. **Chapter 9** explores the barriers to economic, social, cultural, and political integration faced by immigrant and refugee groups that require social workers to adapt their practice in order to provide services that are culturally relevant and effective. The chapter introduces social work concepts regarding the particular needs and issues facing refugee and immigrant clients and explores the various ecological contexts in which social workers work with these populations. Intergenerational issues, challenges regarding education and employment, unique challenges for children and youth, and community organizing and direct service delivery to refugee and immigrant individuals and families are highlighted.

Chapter 10 is written by Ed Lee, MSW, and Dr Shari Brotman. Social workers working with two-spirited, lesbian, gay, bisexual, transgendered and queer (TSLGBTQ) individuals require an understanding of the ways in which gender diversity and sexual orientation shape their clients' lives. Homophobia and discriminatory practices persist into the twenty-first century, including in the field of social work. Thus, it is imperative for social work students to analyze and address biased attitudes they may hold towards these historically marginalized communities in an effort to prevent further oppression of these communities and provide effective, relevant services. This chapter introduces students to the everyday realities of TSLGBTQ individuals and to theoretical and practice approaches used by social workers working with these communities.

Chapter 11 is written by Radha MacCulloch, MSW, and Dr Carl Ernst. The chapter begins with a discussion of the different ways in which disability has been conceptualized, ranging from medicalized understandings to social constructions. The prevalence and impact of disability on individuals, caregivers, and the broader society, as well as historical trends in the disability field are discussed. Included within this discussion is the evolution of the disability movement in Canada. Examples used throughout are grounded in the context of contemporary Canadian health and social services.

Increasingly, social workers are being called upon to practise with aging populations in different settings. **Chapter 12** engages students in the study of aging in the Canadian population by introducing them to the strengths and limitations of dominant paradigms in aging, such as the life course perspective and successful aging. Alternate views on aging and their potential to inform research, service delivery, and practice will be presented. An overview of the major health and social service systems that shape the lives of older adults is provided. Discussions of myths and realities in aging assist students in becoming reflective practitioners when working with this diverse population.

International migration, advances in technology and communications, and local social challenges with global implications have continued to reshape the environment in which social workers practice. They have also introduced new responsibilities and novel opportunities for social workers and the profession as a whole. These global trends inevitably shape contemporary social work theory, research, and practice and thus require the establishment of greater awareness, new knowledge, and new approaches to the discipline. **Chapter 13** introduces students to concepts and skills relating to international social work practice, including the challenges of adequately defining international social work as well as the evolving definition of the concept over time. Given the complexities inherent to international social work practice, whether domestic or international in nature, issues of knowledge, values, and ethics are addressed.

Acknowledgements

We would like to acknowledge all the people who have supported us in making this project a reality. We are enormously grateful to the guest authors for their expert contributions: Cyndy Baskin, Shari Brotman, Carl Ernst, Woo Jin Edward Lee, and Radha MacCulloch. We would like to thank Bree Akesson for her comprehensive editorial assistance, technical expertise, and her invaluable feedback on content. Thanks also go to Lindsay Jones, Pamela Weightman, and Sonia Ben Soltane.

To all the contributors who shared their personal and professional experiences for the "In Their Own Words" or "Theory in Practice" sections, we are extremely grateful: Bree Akesson, Christine Anthony, Mitch Case, Grace Chammas, Joanne Dallaire, Mark Demaine, Kathy Dobson, David Este, Jill Hanley, Judi Jacobs, Jenny Jeanes, Lindsay Jones, Joan Keefler, Alison Kent, Emma Larson-Ure, Yvette Lepage, Michael Loft, Fiona

Meyer Cook, Lise Milne, Reanna Mohamed, Evelyn Mondonedo, Doug Nutting, Pamela Orzeck, Maya Roy, Vanessa Scrivens, Raven Sinclair, Lynn Sparks, and Jim Torczyner.

This textbook would not have been possible without the support of Mark Thompson, our developmental editor at Oxford. Mark's steadfast dedication to our vision for our book, insightful feedback on drafts, and supportive reminders to keep our timelines were critical to its completion.

We greatly appreciate the comments and suggestions of the anonymous reviewers whose feedback helped to ensure the accessibility and comprehensiveness of the text.

Nicole Ives, Myriam Denov, Tamara Sussman
January 2015

To my father Syrophine Lamb and mother Faith Lamb-Parker and step-father Judson Parker for passing on their passions for social change, Jeffrey for his support and encouragement, and Sam, Ben, and Luke for putting up with discussions of social work history and practice at home, leaving less room for hockey talk.

—Nicole

To my mother Celia, my father Robert, and my aunt Myna for their constant support and encouragement. To my nieces Amber, Ashlee, Kayla, and Tamara for providing inspiration, insight, and telling me like it is. My deepest gratitude goes to Dédé and Léo for bringing light and laughter to my life. My work on this project would not have been possible without you.

—Myriam

To my late mother Miriam who sparked my initial interest in social work, my father Edmond for his listening ear, Dror for keeping the household going when deadlines approached, and Aviva, Eli, and Dalia, for providing a welcome distraction from writing and inspiring me to work towards social change.

—Tamara

PART I

Historical, Theoretical, and Philosophical Frameworks

Historical Foundations of Addressing Need: Indigenous, French, and English Traditions

LEARNING OBJECTIVES

- To identify the origins of foundational concepts and issues of social work practice in Canada.

- To understand these historical foundational concepts and issues and their application to Canadian social work practice.

- To appreciate the historical contributions of Indigenous, French-speaking, and English-speaking populations to Canadian social work philosophy and practice.

- To envision approaches to social work practice that reflect the myriad heritages of all who live in Canada.

Chapter Outline

social welfare An organized system which provides social services and programs to assist individuals and families.

This chapter focuses on traditions of the three cultures that contributed to the development of Canadian social work by exploring traditional Indigenous approaches to helping and healing, tracing the unique features of **social welfare** emerging from French traditions, and identifying the British roots of social welfare in English Canada as well as values and social contexts from which such traditions emerged. Midgley (1995) defined social welfare as "the degree to which social programs are managed, the extent to which needs are met, and the degree to which opportunities for advancement are provided" (p. 14). Another definition of social welfare incorporates "all societal responses that promote the social well-being of a population: education, health, rehabilitation, protective services for adults and children, public assistance, social insurance, services for those with mental and physical disabilities, job training programs, marriage counseling, psychotherapy, pregnancy counseling, adoption, and numerous other activities designed to promote well-being" (Ambrosino, Ambrosino, Heffernan, & Shuttlesworth, 2012, p. 4).

Canadian social work has been strongly shaped by British and American traditions, although connections with American social work have been the most influential in terms of social work education and formal practice. Even up to 1970, Canadian schools of social work were accredited by the American Council of Social Work Education (CSWE). Faith-based organizations were particularly active in meeting the needs of people living in poverty, particularly in French-speaking Canada and in the Black and Jewish communities across the country. For Indigenous Peoples, traditional ways of addressing communities' needs were greatly disrupted and, in many cases, targeted by colonizing forces. Indigenous Peoples' traditions of helping and healing included bringing needs to community Elders, consulting traditional helpers and healers, and utilizing spiritual ceremonies.

Indigenous Helping and Healing Traditions

While the formal social work profession has had a largely negative history with Indigenous Peoples in Canada (see Chapters 8 and 9), helping and healing traditions have an extensive positive history in Indigenous communities. Addressing social issues effectively within the community was present before colonization, yet the importance of such foundations has been overlooked historically by the social work profession. In order to understand contemporary Canadian social work approaches holistically, the silenced histories of Indigenous Peoples must be included. It is important to acknowledge, however, the fear that many Indigenous Peoples have of the appropriation of Indigenous knowledges by non-Indigenous peoples (Baskin, 2011). History is replete with cases of non-Indigenous peoples exploiting Indigenous resources. The purpose of this section is not to provide a guide to specific teachings, ceremonies, or medicines of Indigenous Nations, but to illuminate healing traditions that have always been present on Turtle Island (what is referred to now as Canada) but, as a result of Eurocentric social work perspectives and practices, have often been ignored. This section discusses traditional Indigenous holistic approaches to healing and helping; Chapter 9 addresses contemporary social work practice in Indigenous communities across Canada in greater detail.

Indigenous Approaches to Holistic Helping and Healing

Although there is great heterogeneity of Indigenous Peoples across time periods, Indigenous scholars in Canada, including Elders, have highlighted common elements of what they have experienced as foundational Indigenous worldviews. These worldviews offer insight into the ways in which Indigenous Peoples have experienced and continue to experience

Participants in an Aboriginal Healing Range home in Stony Mountain, Manitoba, join in a traditional healing circle in their spiritual path to healing.

CP Photo/Winnipeg Free Press - Ken Gigliotti

helping and healing. Michael Hart (2002), a Cree social work scholar, identifies an approach to Indigenous social work using the **Medicine Wheel** which he describes as "an ancient symbol of the universe used to help people understand things or ideas which often cannot be seen physically" (p. 39).

Medicine Wheel An ancient symbol that signifies a holistic method of helping and healing individuals, families, and communities.

Helping and Healing from Generation to Generation

Unlike the exploration of social welfare histories of English- and French-speaking regions of Canada where a great deal of history has been written, exploring Indigenous helping and healing traditions centres on learning from oral histories passed down through the centuries. Ways of helping have been experienced with Indigenous Elders, traditional healers, and helpers who have shared their knowledge, abilities, spiritual paths, and experiences through role modeling, storytelling, ceremonies, and sharing circles (Reid, 2009; Hart, 2002). Today, there are serious concerns over the maintenance of cultural teachings and the ability for Elders to pass their historical knowledge on to those who may be the next generation of Elders, traditional healers, or helpers. These concerns are related to the loss of generations upon generations' knowledge due to the residential school system, where Indigenous children were systematically removed from their homes and denied their identities through assaults on their languages and spiritual beliefs (see Chapter 9 for a more detailed discussion of residential schools) as well as a diffusion of cultural characteristics in response to colonization. One Elder was particularly concerned about what he saw as the supplanting of his communities' Dene system with a system from the outside that was not teaching elements for seeking a healed, whole life.

I really believe that we have a system somehow to get across to our children. Our system, before the White man came, it was a storytelling system. This telling, the Elders have that, and all the parents attend that kind of gathering all day and the

Theory in Practice

THE MEDICINE WHEEL

THE MEDICINE WHEEL HAS MULTIPLE variations across peoples but shares concepts used by many Indigenous Peoples in the process of helping and healing (see Chapter 9 for a more detailed discussion of the Medicine Wheel and its role as a healing tool). With a proviso underscoring that there is no one Indigenous worldview in a region where there are more than 630 First Nation territories, more than 50 Indigenous languages, and hundreds of Inuit and Métis communities, Hart provides an overview of foundational principles grounded in the Medicine Wheel through which specific issues can be interpreted and addressed in practice, based on context. Contained within the Medicine Wheel, all principles are interconnected and reliant upon each other for seeking the good health of all. The following is a summary of the principles from Hart's (2002) book *Seeking Mino-Pimatisiwin*.

- *Wholeness*: This principle refers to understanding each aspect of the four cardinal directions of the Wheel (east, south, west, and north) and the directions' interconnections for holistic well-being.
- *Balance*: Related to wholeness, one should attend to each part of the whole—one part cannot eclipse others—and the ways in which they are connected. Balance is reflected in the harmony among the physical, emotional, mental, and spiritual elements of one's being. Imbalance is reflected in disease or ill health.
- *Connection*: This principle refers to the relationships among all the parts of the wheel. These connections consist of many different types of relationships, including relationships among people and with nature as well as with one's internal mental and emotional health.
- *Harmony*: Caring for these connections is central to the occurrence of harmony as seen broadly with regard to harmony within oneself, with others, with nature and non-humans, and in the world and universe. Hart notes that harmony "requires people to live within the natural cycles that move life and to find a fit between the components of life through collaboration, sharing of what is available, cooperation and respect for all elements of life" (p. 43).

Elders will tell the parents, "Teach your baby when your baby starts to talk. Teach him [*sic*] about [our Creator's] law, how to be good citizens. How you can love each other and work together. Good, no violence, no fighting, love each other . . . that way you will do good" (Blondin, 1999, p. 394).

Hart (2002) has described Elders, reflecting on their participation in sharing circles, as those who "spoke of their gratefulness that these ceremonies continue despite the historical oppression and persecution that Aboriginal people faced when utilizing them" (p. 63). Even in the face of battering, Indigenous cultural traditions are resilient, and some people feel that it is their obligation to never give up and to continue to pass along the sacred knowledge contained in the stories, ceremonies, healing practices, and sharing. For example, a Shayshas Elder called Elders' transmission of knowledge a duty:

I think in our line of duty as Elders and I call it a duty because it's something that the younger generation really needs to know some of the things, and I think today

- *Growth*: Growth is represented as the lifelong process of motion towards the centre of the Medicine Wheel, which contains wholeness, balance, connections, and harmony with oneself and all else in creation.
- *Healing*: Healing is important for an individual and for those around the individual given the teachings of interconnectedness. However, the starting point for healing is within the individual, as noted by Aiken (1990, p. 24, as cited in Hart): "The old Indian way of healing was first to know the illness and to know one's self. And because the individual participates in the healing process, it is essential that a person needed to know themselves, their innermost core, their innermost spirit and soul, their innermost strength" (p. 44). It is through taking personal responsibility for healing and growth that individuals, families, and communities can attain *mino-pimatisiwin*, a Cree word meaning "the good life." This journey can begin with sharing circles.

Hart describes one example of how putting these principles into practice relates directly to those who work in the helping professions such as social work. As helpers/social workers seek *mino-pimatisiwin*, they continually assess their own journey toward the centre of the Medicine Wheel, working through unhealthy behaviours. If these unhealthy behaviours are neglected, the helpers "will face difficulties in addressing the neglectful behaviours of the people they are helping" (p. 105). Following this approach means that helpers understand the importance of exploring their own health and wellness before and during work with others, and engage in ongoing work to maintain their own well-being as well as that of their families and communities.

Similar to Hart's notions of well-being, an Onondaga Elder described this rootedness of oneself within one's community, Nation, and universe this way:

> You pick the path that's yours and the Creator will show you your mission. Your mission is always for the good of the people. If it doesn't benefit human beings and the Creation, then it's not from the Creator. It's not your mission, and you'd better double-check your path. Your path is for your good, and your mission is for the welfare of others (Wall, 2001, p. 3).

it's much more. It should be taught much more because of the situation that young people are in today. They come into this White society with a different view of the things of life. Where we the Elders see different. Not because we are Natives, not because we are Indians, not because we are First Nations, but because of the things that were passed down for ages . . . We have no writings of any kind of our teachings. It's been passed down from generation to generation. It's up to each one of us to keep that going and that's why it's hard for this newer generation because they are much more into this White society . . . (Mason, 1999, p. 426).

Traditional healers are also integral to the health of Indigenous communities through assisting the body in healing not only by employing herbal medicines but also by practices such as "sleep therapy, walking therapy, running therapy, and rest therapy" (Nitsch, 1999, p. 85). Traditional healers "[do] not heal anyone . . . all they do is help the person who comes to them to help themselves by giving them what they need. [. . .] The process of healing [is] to become whole" (Nitsch, p. 86). Thus, a person in need of healing needs to be in a space where he or she is prepared for the interactions with a healer. As a Dene Elder described when seeking help from an Elder, "if a person approaches the Elders they are always ready to give good advice and the person is always ready to listen so that the individual will benefit from the advice from the Elders" (Rabesca, 1999, p. 367).

Traditional teachings are "given as a 'gift' by an Elder within a specific cultural context such as a ceremony, event, or time spent with an individual at a particular stage of his or her development" (Kulchyski, McCaskill, & Newhouse, 1999, p. xv). Elders are not simply those who have reached a particular age, but those who understand themselves in the context of all creation, maintain a centredness, and are able to pass on cultural teachings which they have received from their Elders. However, in order to transmit this knowledge, Indigenous Peoples need to be able to receive it and integrate it into their own lives in order to reach a place where they may share and pass on what they have learned and experienced, perhaps in the role of Elder, traditional healer, or helper. Thus, the transmission of oral histories takes on even greater importance given the attempt to eliminate Indigenous cultures in Canada through colonization processes. Indigenous cultures are seen as a critical element for healing (Hart, 2002), and Elders, given the responsibility by their communities, pass on knowledge at the same time as they incorporate their own experiences (Hart, 2009); therefore, Elders are critical knowledge links to the past, present, and future for Indigenous Peoples.

The idea of people living together and taking care of one another is also represented in the Inuit communal ethos which was woven into all aspects of daily life: hunters provided for the community; dwellings were commonly shared with extended family members; and Elders provided counselling and healing to those whom they identified as needing it, rather than waiting for the troubled or sick to seek help (Pauktuutit, 2006). A contemporary conceptualization of Inuit worldview from Nunavut is encapsulated in **Inuit Qaujimajatuqangit** (IQ). While this term, formally adopted by the Government of Nunavut, grew out of the wisdom of Nunavut Elders, "the descriptors used to capture the essence of Inuit Qaujimajatuqangit are recognized as being consistent with Inuit worldview as it is described in various Inuit circumpolar jurisdictions" (Tagalik, 2009, p.1).

Elders in Nunavut have conceptualized a foundation for IQ composed of four laws, or *maligait*, which contribute to "living a good life" (Tagalik, 2009, p. 1).

The four laws are

1. working for the common good;
2. respecting all living things;
3. maintaining harmony and balance; and
4. continually planning and preparing for the future.

There are six guiding principles that buttress traditional Inuit kinship, family, and community by supporting the practical application of IQ in Inuit communities (Arnakak, 2000):

1. service (*Pijitsirarniq*);
2. consensus decision-making (*Aajiiqatigiingniq*);
3. skills and knowledge acquisition (*Pilimmaksarniq*);
4. collaboration (*Piliriqatigiingniq*);
5. environmental stewardship (*Avatittinnik Kamattiarniq*); and
6. resourcefulness (*Qanuqtuurniq*).

While IQ incorporates present-day values of Inuit communities, it is grounded in the wisdom of past experience passed down through the generations by Elders who carry their communities' cultural values, knowledge, and skills (Arnakak, 2002). Contemporary Inuit social work practice integrates Inuit values and knowledge by, for example, placing a great

---

Inuit Qaujimajatuqangit
The Inuktitut (Inuit language) term for traditional or Indigenous knowledge of the Inuit or "that which has long been known by Inuit" (White, 2009, p. 75).

deal of emphasis on listening skills and on involving extended family in conflict resolution (Ives & Aitken, 2009). Traditional wisdom and learning is centred in practice, where ancestral values and practices have as much, if not more, answers to Inuit social needs. Safeguarding Inuit, First Nations, and Métis Elders' knowledge and wisdom is critical to preserving traditional approaches to problem solving and to informing contemporary healing and wholeness practices.

French Historical Foundations of Social Work

The history of Canadian social welfare cannot be fully understood without addressing its French historical foundations. Such traditions are of particular relevance to present-day innumerable French-speaking communities across Canada in addition to Quebec (see Table 1.1). This section presents a history of the provision of social welfare in early Quebec, key figures in the development of Quebec social services (see Table 1.2), the central role of the Catholic Church in the delivery of social work and social welfare, and how these historical factors have shaped social welfare legislation after the Great Depression.

Poverty Relief and the Involvement of the Roman Catholic Church

In the seventeenth century, French-speaking colonists in New France approached early poverty relief as did their ancestors in France. Welfare in Quebec was heavily influenced by

TABLE 1.1	Francophone and Acadian Communities of Canada (less QC)			
	Mother Tongue		First Official Language Spoken	
Province	Number Francophone	Percentage Francophone	Number Francophone	Percentage Francophone
Alberta	68,435	2.1	66,995	2.1
British Columbia	63,295	1.5	70,410	1.7
Manitoba	47,110	4.1	44,110	3.9
New Brunswick	237,575	32.8	236,100	32.7
Newfoundland and Labrador	2,225	0.4	2,030	0.4
Northwest Territories	1,025	4.0	1,060	2.6
Nova Scotia	34,920	3.9	32,940	3.6
Nunavut	455	1.4	465	1.6
Ontario	532,855	4.4	578,040	4.8
Prince Edward Island	5,875	4.4	5,180	3.9
Saskatchewan	17,575	1.8	15,225	1.6
Yukon	1,225	4.0	1,245	4.1
Canada (less QC)	1,012,530	4.3	1,053,800	4.4

Source: Statistics Canada, 2006 Census.

TABLE 1.2	Key Figures in Quebec Social Welfare History
Herbert Ames (1863–1954)	Ames was a businessman, politician, and philanthropist who focused on helping the poor. Ames authored *The City Below the Hill: A Sociological Study of a Portion of the City of Montréal* (1897), an analysis of conditions of Montreal's working-class communities. Ames' findings challenged conventional attitudes towards the poor, believing that poverty and its related social problems were less a consequence of laziness and intemperance than of sporadic and irregular employment with inadequate wages. His moral stance influenced his support for the development of Diamond Court, a 39-unit housing complex for Montreal's poor. In addition to advocating for the poor, Ames served as Montreal City Councillor from 1898 until 1906, focusing on health and education reform. From 1904–1920, Ames served in Parliament as a member of the Conservative party.
Marie Lacoste Gérin-Lajoie (1867–1945)	Influenced by the *résidence sociale* movement in France and the Settlement House Movement in North America, Gérin-Lajoie founded the Fédération nationale Saint-Jean-Baptiste in 1907, an organization that campaigned for social and political rights for women. In addition to its legal work, the Fédération nationale also championed social causes such as providing milk for children and mothers, fighting alcoholism and illness, raising awareness of infant mortality, and other issues that affected women's lives. In 1922, Gérin-Lajoie led a protest for women's suffrage in Quebec. (Quebec was the last Canadian province to grant the vote to women in 1940). In 1923, she founded L'institut Notre-Dame du Bon-Conseil and subsequently established social services at a parish level in Montreal (1938) and Saint Jerome (1939). Gérin-Lajoie also advocated for French-language university education for Quebec women. A professor at Université de Montréal, Gérin-Lajoie was also the author of *Traité de droit usuel* (1902) and *La femme et le code civil* (1929) where she argued against subordinate legal positions of married women in the Quebec Civil Code.
L'Abbé Charles-Edouard Bourgeois (1898–1990)	Bourgeois founded the first Francophone social service agency Sœurs Dominicaines du Rosaire in Trois-Rivières which focused on helping orphaned and neglected children. Public assistance from the government at the time was 24 cents per day, per orphan. In 1929, overwhelmed by need, religious institutions were unable to meet the demand for social services. Bourgeois organized community volunteers and raised funds from private donors and local parishes. When Bourgeois's friend Maurice Duplessis became Premier of Quebec in 1936, his diocese received substantial government subsidies for social services, effectively transitioning social services from church dominated to state controlled. In 1948, Bourgeois was appointed commissioner of an inquiry formed by the Quebec government to study juvenile delinquency. This led to the development of social welfare courses for educators and supervisors working with children in 1951 and the founding of the *l'École supérieure d'assistance sociale* in 1958.

France's emphasis on the family as the primary institution given responsibility by society for providing aid to its impoverished members. When families failed in their obligations to family members, the provision of relief depended on the charity of local parishes of the Roman Catholic Church and Christian-based charity. Rather than a coordinated system of relief however, relief was provided by multiple entities using their own evaluation criteria to address the needs of the poor of Quebec's cities and towns. For example, in 1688, *bureaux des pauvres* were established and operated in cities of Quebec, Montreal, and Trois-Rivières. These "offices of the poor," under the supervision of a priest, relied on funds through collections taken periodically by the parishes and then distributed to the poor (Lessard, 1987).

Providers of relief believed two major tenets regarding poverty, which also guided relief across Canadian territories. First, poverty was individually driven due to a perceived inability to live within the current economic and social system in combination with unfavourable character traits. Second, the poor were either "**deserving**" or "**undeserving**." The receipt of charity was not considered a right; thus, it was only conferred upon the "deserving." The "deserving" category included widows, orphans, the chronically ill, and the elderly who did not engage in what were perceived by providers of relief as immoral activities such as alcoholism (Fingard, 1974; Linteau, Durocher, & Robert, 1983). Those who were able to work though unemployed were seen as "undeserving" and were sent to workhouses. Examples included unemployed men, unmarried women, and migrants from other regions who were unemployed. If they refused to enter the workhouse, they could be denied aid. A *Maison d'industrie* (workhouse with poor conditions) was established in Montreal, combining relief with moral rehabilitation through labor and thus reaffirming the perspective that unemployment for those able to work was a result of immorality.

As in other provinces and territories across Canada, industrialization in Quebec brought huge benefits for technological progress, but at the same time, created deplorable conditions for working people in urban areas. In their historical account of working conditions in Quebec in the 1800s, Linteau, Durocher, and Robert (1983) described industrialization's effects on jobs: Factories employed more people than independent artisans and craftsmen, their conditions were minimally monitored, wages were low, and work hours were long. In Quebec, the workweek was 72 hours—12 hours per day. Those employed in domestic service (the majority of whom were women) worked even longer hours, with time off limited to half a day weekly. The depression of wages across many sectors prevented employed male heads of households from buffering their families from poverty. Thus, other family members were required to work, though the labour of women and children was valued less than that of men (Linteau, Durocher, & Robert, 1983).

Various services were provided to help find work for those who wanted it. As Linteau and colleagues (1983) note, this individualized conceptualization of poverty helps to explain why there was no public intervention except in cases of public health emergencies when small grants were given to entities providing assistance. Poor relief was primarily the domain of the Catholic Church, as described by Minville in *The Church and Social Welfare in Quebec* (1939):

> For a protracted period of Canadian history the Church was the only organization, at a time when the state acknowledged no responsibility in the matter, in possession of the staff requisite for the care of the poor. When Canada was founded, the Catholic Church, with many more than a thousand years of existence behind her, had a wealth of tradition, of discipline, and was possessed of a powerful material organization. All these she implanted here.

Quebec's churches played a foundational role in the development of private charity organizations. Quebec was predominantly Roman Catholic, with the 1871 census recording 85 per cent of the population adhering to Catholicism; Protestant denominations comprised over 14 per cent while only 0.2 per cent did not report any religion (Linteau, Durocher, & Robert, 1983). In the nineteenth century, most charitable activities were carried out under the supervision of or directly by churches. For example, based on the charity work of sixteenth-century priest St. Vincent De Paul, St. Vincent De Paul Societies, originally founded in France in 1833, were introduced in Quebec City in 1846. The Societies' model consisted of a local priest who participated in the program implementation of each society; programs focused on aiding the poor, migrants, the elderly, and orphans (Linteau, Durocher, & Robert, 1983; St. Vincent de Paul Society, n.d.). Assistance focused on home

deserving poor Those in poverty through no fault of their own.

undeserving poor Those considered physically capable of work in some form or another but are unemployed.

visits by Society members. The St. Vincent De Paul Societies are still active today across Canada; in 2008, Society councils were active in British Columbia, the Atlantic provinces, Ontario, Quebec, and Yukon.

Benevolent Societies and Other Ways of Helping

Benevolent societies in Quebec were a preliminary model for charity organization societies, supported by private donors and public and private fundraising activities. Benevolent societies were formed by the initiative of middle-class or wealthy women or based on recommendations by particular church denominations to serve the poor of their ethnic or religious group. Examples of early benevolent societies were the Female Benevolent Society of Montreal (1815), the Association des Dames de Charité (1827), the Congregation of the *Sisters of Providence* (1843) also founded in Montreal, and the Grey Nuns of Saint Hyacinthe, Quebec (1840) (Bradbury, 2007; Linteau, Durocher, & Robert, 1983). These societies typically operated in cities, as relief in the rural areas was the domain of local parishes. To coordinate English-speaking charity organization work, the Montreal Charity Organization Society was formed in 1900. In 1919, in order to coordinate the work of nonsectarian and Protestant charities, the Montreal Council of Social Agencies was formed.

Hospitals and hospices were also providers of care for the poor, organized along religious lines (Catholic and Protestant). Montreal did not have municipally nor provincially financed hospitals. Thus, those who were unable to work and/or to be supported by family, such as orphaned infants and children, the chronically ill, the elderly, and the mentally ill, were often sent to institutions such as the Hôtel-Dieu Hospital (Catholic) and the Montreal General Hospital (Protestant) which cared for them (Linteau, Durocher, & Robert, 1983). Those with mental illnesses were the only group whose care was funded by government entities.

Given the lack of any provincial- or federal-level programs to provide for those who became sick or for families of workers who died, mutual benefit societies were created, founded not by churches or middle-class patrons but by groups of workers themselves. These mutual benefit societies combined the advantages of mutual aid associations, insurance companies, and cooperatives to provide for workers and their families in case of sickness or death (Linteau, Durocher, & Robert, 1983). One example was the Union Saint-Joseph founded in the mid-1800s, where "each member paid a subscription [and] from the proceeds, members were paid a small pension if they were sick and their widows received an indemnity when they died" (Linteau, Durocher, & Robert, 1983, p. 176).

Charity work in Quebec was primarily the domain of English-speaking (Anglophone), middle-class, and wealthy women. For French-speaking (Francophone) women, employment in hospices, day-care centres ("with walls" crèches), hospitals, and orphanages was accomplished through entering a religious community, which meant becoming a nun (Linteau, Durocher, & Robert, 1983). In 1866, the Civil Code of Lower Canada sought to codify all aspects of civil relations, primarily persons, property, succession, and marriage (Young, 1994). Women were heavily affected in that this codification of legal and political rights served to compromise women's legal status. Under the Civil Code, which "reinforce[d] traditional social relations through the bias of the family" (Young, 1994, p. 121), married women, regardless of level of household income or societal position, held the same legal status as minors and those whose civil rights were taken away on the grounds of mental disability (Linteau, Durocher, & Robert, 1983). This entrenched women's dependence on men in Quebec and funneled them into positions traditionally conceptualized as women's work as opposed to independent entrepreneurs. A woman's role in Quebec was defined by her ability to be a wife and mother or as a nun—the only permissible option considered for unmarried women.

Myriad Approaches to Poverty Relief

In the early 1900s, municipal relief existed in the form of grants to charities, direct aid, or various services. However, social assistance programs were still not highly evolved. Montreal had four charitable financial federations that coordinated services to those in need: the Federation of Jewish Philanthropies (1916), the Financial Federation for Protestant and Non-sectarian Groups (1922), the Federation of Catholic Charities for English-speaking Catholics (1929), and the Fédération des oeuvres de charité canadiennes-françaises (French Canadian Federation of Welfare Services, 1933; Jennissen & Lundy, 2011). It was not until 1921 that the Public Charities Act of Quebec became the first social assistance legislation enacted, mandating that the government was required to intervene to help those in need. Economic hardships brought on by recessions (especially the Great Depression of the 1930s) forced government to step in. There followed a growing centralization of income protection functions, marking a shift in responsibility away from the municipalities to the provinces, and from there onto the federal government. As a result of the immense need generated by the Great Depression, the federal government was forced to take social policy action: social assistance became institutionalized in the form of categorical programs.

As noted above, in Quebec prior to the 1960s, hospitals, social service agencies, and community services were generally owned and governed by religious orders or structures, especially by the Roman Catholic Church. The Quiet Revolution in Quebec (beginning to mid-1960s), however, brought about significant changes in perspectives on religious institutions' involvement in social services through a rejection of conservative values: Quebec society quickly became secular and embraced progressive religious ideas, such as ecumenism and liberation theology, and effectively transformed them into social activism and community development. This may explain why faith-based development as articulated today is generally not widespread in Quebec (Mooney, 2009).

English Historical Foundations of Social Work

The origins of the present-day profession of social work in Canada can be seen in the early responses to addressing the needs of the vulnerable through community or Church-led initiatives. In the nineteenth century in English-speaking Canada, addressing the ramifications of poverty included poorhouses (also known as almshouses), provision of assistance to families in their own homes, and the removal of children to orphanages or apprenticeships. Increased organization of assistance in the late nineteenth century led to the development of Charity Organization Societies and the Settlement House Movement, foundational in the development of the social work profession. Significant upheavals in the early twentieth century, including increased migration, world wars, and the Great Depression, saw the development of the Social Gospel Movement, the formalization of social work education, and the broadening of municipal, provincial, and federal responsibility for public welfare.

Early Approaches to Addressing the Needs of Vulnerable Populations

Early features of Canadian social welfare reflected developments in Britain. Drawing heavily on its British roots, early poverty relief in English-speaking Canadian settlements was influenced by the Elizabethan Poor Laws of 1601 and focused on local poor relief. It was accepted that poverty existed and that it was the obligation of the family and the community to alleviate distress caused by poverty. Central to addressing the needs of the poor were oversight and the belief that poverty was a result of a flaw in one's character. Addressing that personal flaw was seen as the change that was necessary as opposed to analyzing the structures in society that created conditions of poverty. Public relief was supervised by "overseers of the poor" who were responsible for local poor relief options. Assistance was mainly provided by private charity organizations or religious entities. If families of the poor were not able to care for their own, care was provided through a combination of institutional options (**indoor relief**) and material provision of food, clothing, or fuel to people allowed to remain in their own homes (**outdoor relief**).

indoor relief Assistance provided in an institutional setting, such as a poorhouse, almshouse, or workhouse.

outdoor relief Material assistance given to individuals and families in their own homes.

A poorhouse or almshouse was typically used for older adults or individuals with physical or mental illnesses living in poverty while a workhouse housed those considered able to work but unemployed. Poorhouses were the preferred social response to extreme poverty in an ideological and political sense (Katz, 1996). Reformers predicted that the replacement of outdoor relief with poorhouses would curb the demand for relief, avoid interference with labor demands, and instil a strong work ethic.

The Elizabethan Poor Law of 1601 had informally influenced relief wherever colonists settled. In 1860 as Canada was consolidating its territories into provinces, some regions officially adopted the Poor Law and its subsequent amendment in 1834 while others adopted English Civil Law. One of the principles contained in the 1834 amendment to the Poor Law can still be seen in contemporary social welfare policy: the principle of "**less eligibility**." This principle addressed the fears of relief providers and others who feared that giving relief would create a permanent class of need recipients who would no longer have the motivation to seek work.

less eligibility Principle requiring that the standard of living of an individual receiving public assistance or the conditions of work (e.g., workhouse conditions) had to be less favorable than what a labourer would receive who worked the lowest-paying labour market job.

Upper Canada (present-day Ontario) adopted English Civil Law, which "meant that the responsibility for the poor rested with the individual, family, or the community, and when this failed, the poor relied on voluntary associations or fraternal organizations and agencies" (Jennissen & Lundy, 2011, p. 3). Outdoor relief was the primary method of assistance in smaller regions in Ontario in the late 1800s (Marks, 1995). Nova Scotia and New Brunswick adopted the Poor Law which meant that local municipalities oversaw assistance to the poor. Western provinces focused on the provision of assistance through municipal programs when they joined the Confederation (Osbourne, 1985).

Whether the assistance was coming from private philanthropies or from local authorities, central to the provision of that assistance, as in Quebec, was determining whether the applicant was "worthy" or "deserving" versus "unworthy" or "undeserving." This determination was subjectively based on whether the evaluator felt the reasons the applicant was not working were due to individual characteristics or through circumstances not of their own making; there were no processes of appeal if they were deemed "undeserving" (Marks, 1995). Moreover, charity providers expected recipients to be humble, grateful, and compliant.

The need for poor relief rose during the period of industrialization with the accompanying changes in social and economic structures and the increase of migratory wage laborers who were often working in hazardous, unhealthy conditions (Katz, 1996). Moreover, the harsh winters in Canada exacerbated the precariousness that all poor families faced. Many industrial sectors were dependent on the weather and thus many workers relied on seasonal employment (Fingard, 1974). There was little to no protection against bitterly cold winter weather conditions. As a result, religious entities and greater numbers of private charities became involved in responding to the needs of those living in poverty. For example, in St. John's, Newfoundland, a member of the St. Vincent de Paul Society reported that those they helped were in particular need in the winter months: "Imagine for a moment the condition of a poor widow, with a large family, young and helpless, cold and famishing, without fuel or food—without any employment whatever, during the dreary and bitter days of a protracted winter" (*St. John's Newfoundlander*, 11 December, 1856, as cited in Fingard, 1974, p. 68).

RULES AND REGULATIONS
OF THE
COUNTY POOR HOUSE.

RULE I.---Every person admitted must be thoroughly cleaned by a bath, his hair cut short, and clothes changed.

RULE II.---No obscene or profane language, or disorderly conduct allowed on any part of the premises.

RULE III.---The Keeper must be obeyed in all just demands, and any complaint against him must be made to the Inspector, at his visits; any inmate disobeying the rules of the Institution, must be reported to the Inspector, who will inflict such punishment as he deems proper.

RULE IV.---Every inmate, unless sick, shall rise at 7½ o'clock, and retire at 8 o'clock, in winter; and rise at 5½ o'clock, and retire at 9 o'clock, in summer. And all that are able to work must be kept employed.

RULE V.---No inmate is allowed to leave the premises without a pass from the Inspector. If any one wishes to visit friends, or go away on business, he, or she, must apply to the Inspector, at his usual visits, for a written pass, which pass must be presented to the Keeper before he or she will be allowed to leave the premises.

RULE VI.---If any one is sick, he or she must report to the Keeper, who will notify the Medical Superintendent.

RULE VII.---It is the duty of the Keeper to preserve order and see that the above rules are enforced, and to report any infringement of the same to the Inspector.

RULE VIII.---Any one infringing any of the above rules will be placed in solitary confinement, with bread and water diet, for such period as the Inspector shall direct, subject to the approval of the Medical Superintendent.

DANIEL MATTHEWS, Chairman,
THOS. W. CLARK,
JOHN WILSON,
JACOB SOVEREEN,
Committee of Management of the Poor House.

SIMCOE, COUNTY OF NORFOLK, ONTARIO

June 16, 1871.

Library and Archives Canada, Acc. No. 1984-4-901 Committee of Management of the Poor House

Although poorhouses provided shelter and food to the poor, the "inmates" had to follow strict rules and regulations to avoid more dire consequences.

Social Reform Post-Confederation

Charity Organization Societies

A widely held belief in Britain, based on the secularization of the Puritan doctrine of vocation, saw relief receipt leading to increased dependence which in turn caused character breakdown and the loss of a desire to work. To address the broad, unsystematic provision of aid believed to worsen poverty, England attempted to formalize and organize its charities through the Charity Organization of London in 1869, emphasizing the value of a methodical investigation system that could be taught over arbitrary, unsystematic charity giving. J.S. Woodsworth (1911) described this growing concern regarding "indiscriminate and harmful almsgiving," calling for a new method of relief than what was typically given in small communities:

> In a small community it is easy to give relief to the small occasional family. There exists a personal relationship which largely precludes imposition, and which goes far in encouraging thrift. But in the city, the situation is quite changed. The well-to-do neighbors are separated from their less fortunate neighbors by distance and by social cleavages of many kinds. The very numbers make personal knowledge and sympathy almost an impossibility. How to get the man who needs help into touch with the man who can help is the problem. With no system there has been on the one hand much indiscriminate and harmful almsgiving, and on the other hand, much needless misery, and, worse than all, no earnest attempt to cope with underlying evils (p. 280).

The growing movement of applying a "scientific approach" to alleviate poverty came to Canada and the USA in the late 1880s with the establishment of their own organized charity movements. The most famous and influential Charity Organization Society (COS) was founded in Baltimore, Maryland, where Mary Richmond began her standardization of provision of care for the poor. Richmond (1917) characterized this process as a casework approach, "for the betterment of individuals and families, one by one, as distinguished from their betterment in the mass" (p. 25). She promoted the approach of a "case-by-case response to the rehabilitation of the poor" (also referred to as the **social casework** method of investigation) through a method of "friendly visiting" (Jennissen & Lundy, 2011, p. 9).

social casework Addressing an issue by systematically gathering detailed data regarding an individual's environment and analyzing the data, followed by making a data-based diagnosis and treatment plan.

In a social casework approach, one addresses an issue by systematically collecting detailed data regarding an individual's environment, including family and other factors outside the family (termed "social evidence"), making inferences through the comparison of various data sources, and making a diagnosis through analysis of the data, leading to the creation of a treatment plan. Although Richmond's focus was on developing social casework to identify, diagnose, and treat individual-level problems, she never intended social casework to eclipse societal reforms, believing that "mass betterment and individual betterment are interdependent . . . social reform and social case work of necessity progressing together" (Richmond, 1917, p. 25).

COS proponents held the belief that training visitors and applying a rigorous, scientifically based welfare delivery system would provide "objective" evaluations of poverty's causes and encourage the poor's independence. The general assumption of the friendly visitors was that the corrosion of character was a leading cause of poverty; the visitors' own middle- or upper-income status was assumed to be an indicator of a higher moral nature. These "friendly visitors" would visit the poor in their homes, and, through teaching and modelling, believed that their role was "to make our fellow-creatures better through our charity, to touch the nature and make it respond to our own, till there shall be more of mutual faith and comprehension, as well as a more diffused sympathy through the different orders of society" (Jameson, 1859, p. 62).

Visitors would evaluate eligibility for relief and rehabilitate what was assumed to be weak in the moral character of those in need of relief. Thus, an individual's character, instead of the individual's social, economic, and political environments, was considered to be at the core of his or her poverty. Influenced by **Social Darwinism**, many COS-affiliated reformers also believed that only by separating poor children from their parents could they prevent the transmission of dependence from one generation to another. Social Darwinism was the application of Charles Darwin's theories of evolution to social theory, led by philosopher Herbert Spencer, which in turn influenced perspectives on the provision of relief to the poor.

While scientific charity was an attempted departure from the subjective, moral judgments of the causes of social problems, biases were still widespread, particularly with regard to socio-economic status and ethnic origin. Trained social workers who replaced charity volunteers were primarily White, middle- to upper-income educated women. For example, Charlotte Whitton (1896–1975) played an influential role in promoting social casework in Canada. Educated at Queen's University, she began her career in social work with the Social Service Council of Canada. In 1922, she became director of the Canadian Welfare Council and a staunch promoter of child welfare.

The largest Canadian Charity Organisation Societies were the Associated Charities of Toronto established in 1888, the Montreal Charity Organization Society established in 1900, and the Associated Charities Bureau in Winnipeg established in 1908. In 1912, these cities' charity organizations formed Associated Charities, which joined the US National Association of Societies for Organizing Charity (Jennissen & Lundy, 2011). By the 1920s, the longing for validation as a profession along with the desire to connect to the authority held by the science disciplines shaped the adoption of the medical model as a fundamental paradigm for social work practice (Irving, 1992).

Settlement House Movement

The Settlement House Movement was the second major development in the provision of social welfare by the voluntary sector. Industrialization, urbanization, and increased immigration contributed to the creation of unsafe, unsanitary living conditions within areas of major urban centres. These areas contained high concentrations of families living in substandard housing. As a response, educated volunteers, typically university students, moved into impoverished neighbourhoods in "settlement houses" alongside those living in poverty. It was believed that by living in poor communities, these volunteers would be better able to understand community members' lives and, using relationships with community members as a tool for social change, improve conditions through the social, economic, and political reconstruction of urban neighbourhoods. The houses emphasized social action through the provision of neighbourhood services and community development initiatives. One key difference between the Settlement House Movement (SHM) and the Charity Organization Societies (COS) lay in how they saw families and conceptualized the causes of poverty. Charity Organization Societies saw dysfunctional families as the root cause of poverty within a well-functioning society while Settlement Houses believed in the sufficient functioning of families who lived within a society in need of reform (Axinn & Levin, 1992).

Again Britain led the way, where the first settlement houses, typically funded through the charity of wealthy donors, were established in poor neighbourhoods in London in the mid-1880s (Axinn & Levin, 1992). These settlement houses, the first of which was Toynbee Hall established in 1884, offered food, lodging, and other basic provisions. A similarity between the SHM and the COS was the approach of addressing poverty through social relationships in order to "gain the confidence of the people of the district and seek to secure for them what they most value in their own lives" (Woodsworth, 1911, p. 297). However, proponents of the SHM, a precursor to community organizing in Canada, put greater emphasis on social reform than those of the COS. The most famous settlement

Social Darwinism As related to poverty, the belief that indiscriminate relief would weaken a person's moral character, leading to the weakening of society; those who were poor were "unfit" while those who were wealthy were not only "fit" but possessed higher moral character.

Case STUDY

J.S. Woodsworth, the City, and Social Reform

JAMES SHAVER WOODSWORTH (1874–1942), LABOUR activist, Methodist Church minister, Social Gospeller, and social worker, worked in Winnipeg's North End starting in 1904. He later became a Member of Parliament (Labour Party) who continually campaigned for labour rights, improved social welfare measures, and democratic socialism. In 1926–1927, he persuaded Prime Minister Mackenzie King to introduce Canada's first social welfare legislation: an old-age pension plan. A staunch supporter of the organized labour movement, he became the leader of the Co-operative Commonwealth Federation in 1933 (predecessor of the contemporary New Democratic Party).

Propelled by rapid population increases in urban areas and the accompanying social challenges, Woodsworth conducted a study in 1911, *My neighbour: A study of city conditions, a plea for social service*, to discover how "to be neighbourly not only in the wilderness, or in the comparatively simple life of a country community, but in the crowded city with its many and complicated interests" (p. 21).

Drawing from reports from mission visitors in Winnipeg, Woodsworth described the abysmal conditions of the time.

In a home of three young girls living in a tenement

"A small room at the back, very crowded, with double bed and table. The air was very, very bad and both door and window were kept tightly closed. Father was out looking for work. The mother was out washing. The stove was dirty and piled up with dirty pots and kettles. . . . The bed was all the beds in this class of home—mattress covered by an old gray blanket, two big, dirty-looking pillows and some old clothes. This was the children's playground, for there was no floor space uncovered" (p. 108).

In an immigrant home

"Shack—one room and a lean-to. Furniture—two beds, a bunk, stove, bench, two chairs, table, barrel of sauerkraut. Everything was dirty. Two families lived there. Women were dirty, unkempt, bare-footed, half-clothed. Children wore only print slips" (p. 108).

house was Hull House, founded in Chicago by Jane Addams in 1889. In her book, *Twenty Years at Hull House*, describing settlements, Addams wrote

> The Settlement, then, is an experimental effort to aid in the solution of the social and industrial problems which are engendered by the modern conditions of life in the great city . . . It is an attempt to relieve at the same time the over-accumulation at one end of society and the destitution at the other; but it assumes that this over-accumulation and destitution is most sorely felt in the things that pertain to the social and educational advantages (Addams, cited in Woodsworth, 1911, p. 302).

Toronto, the largest metropolitan centre of Canada, saw the birth of multiple settlement houses: the Young Women's Settlement in 1899 (renamed Evangelia in 1902), University

This entry, provided by one of the Mission visitors, a church Deaconess, included her intervention as well as a subjective assessment of the work ethic of the parents. In an immigrant home

"Shack. Family consisted of father, mother, eight children. Deaconess was in a [public] car one day in December when two half-clad, dirty children got in. They had no tickets and when the conductor proceeded to put them off, she paid the fares and took the children to the Mission supply room and sent them home clean and warmly clad. Two days later she went to the address given by the children and found the children dressed as before starting for town. The parents have a strong disinclination to work and send the children out with a well-worded story to appeal to the tender-hearted of Winnipeg. The home was very dirty, the children badly trained and not sufficiently nourished. Work was procured for both father and mother and when pressure was brought to bear upon them to make them provide for the needs of their family and educate their children, they hurriedly left town" (p.109).

Woodsworth saw city life as a "spider's web, pull one thread and you pull every thread" (p. 26). Thus, his suggestions for reforms touched on multiple spheres: labour conditions and wages, housing conditions, sanitation, family well-being, and child welfare, including children's nutrition, education, material needs, elimination of child labour, and the creation of dedicated play space. Based on his findings, Woodsworth advocated for greater involvement in social issues, particularly by the churches, asserting that "many of our profound thinkers believe that the real difficulty is a moral one, that so long as men [sic] are essentially selfish, no scheme, however attractive, can accomplish much. Men must be educated to altruism, or their hearts changed, before our social evils will disappear" (p. 87). Social reform, he reasoned, would only occur through the combined efforts of "social service," which he defined as consisting of charity organization societies, settlement houses, social work of churches, and city missions.

Settlement in 1910, Central Neighbourhood House in 1911, and St. Christopher's House in 1912. The first settlement house in Montreal was University Settlement House, established in 1910. Early social work schools in Canada were influenced by and/or associated with settlement houses. St. Christopher House in Toronto became a field placement site for social work students at the University of Toronto's School of Social Work (Keller & Ruether, 2006).

In 1894, the Association of Neighbourhood Houses of British Columbia was incorporated, bringing together the province's vast network of neighbourhood (settlement) houses. Settlement workers were politically active, advocating for better housing, improved child welfare, and child care opportunities. Unfortunately, however, settlement houses were influenced by the racism of the era. Settlement houses for Black and Jewish Canadian populations did not open until the mid-1920s. For Black Canadians in Montreal, the

Negro Community Centre was established in 1925 to provide educational, recreational, and social opportunities (Jennisen & Lundy, 2011). Also in Montreal, Settlement House, a settlement for Jewish children, opened in 1927 (Keller & Ruether, 2006).

Religion and the Provision of Relief

Organized religion and spirituality have had a profound impact on the development of social work in Canada (Graham, Coholic, & Coates, 2007). Social work's roots lie in religious congregation members' participation in poverty relief provision, particularly through the Charity Organization Societies and Settlement House Movement. Religious congregations have historically been involved in the provision of social services in communities either on their own, in partnership with other congregations, or working with secular agencies in the provision of social services (Axinn & Stern, 2007; Hiemstra, 2002; Salamon, 1995). The **Social Gospel Movement** was a theological and social movement devoted to social development and change, and played a key role in the development of the profession and the understanding and tackling of social issues.

Social Gospel Movement
An integrated theological and social movement centred on social development and change.

The central belief of the Social Gospel Movement was that "God was at work in social change, creating moral order and social justice" (Allen, 2007, p. 65). Adherents sought to address social and economic problems through Christ's teachings; members primarily belonged to Protestant-affiliated denominations: Methodists, Presbyterians, and Anglicans (Guest, 1997). The movement held an optimistic view of human nature and spoke of traditional Christian doctrine such as sin, atonement, salvation, and the Kingdom of God in social and collective terms (Allen, 2007). During this time, churches increasingly became places that offered social services through their social welfare and social reform activities (Guest, 1997). Women associated with Christian organizations founded the majority of settlement/neighbourhood houses across the country (Keller & Ruether, 2006). Some began as missions, such as the Methodist Sunday School in Winnipeg in 1899, later renamed All Peoples' Mission. Social Gospeller J.S. Woodsworth (see "Case Study" box above) led All People's Mission from 1907 to 1913, working with poor and immigrant families in Winnipeg's North End. In 1907, major Protestant and Methodist churches joined together to form the Moral and Social Reform Council of Canada. In an attempt to adopt a more scientific perspective and create distance from its founding religious base, the Reform Council became the Social Service Council of Canada in 1914.

In Black Canadian communities, congregations have long served as providers of services as well as facilitators of access to community programs and resources (Billingsley, 1995; Chaves & Higgins, 1992; Ward, Billingsley, Simon, & Burris, 1994; Williams, 1997). Social welfare provision to its members, such as giving food, clothing, and housing to newly arrived immigrants or refugees, was also part of that desire to build a sense of belonging and community among Black citizens (Este, 2007). Indeed, despite their efforts to integrate into Canadian society, Black Canadians experienced subtle and explicit forms of racism and discrimination by White Canadians (Este, 2004, 2007). These experiences served as a catalyst for members of Black communities to develop their own institutions, one of which was the Black Church (Este, 2007). Churches with predominantly Black congregations and communities have continued the tradition of addressing social, economic, and cultural needs of community members (Barnes, 2005).

Examining the role of the church in Black Canadian history, Este (2007) found two distinct interpretations. One view was that the church had a negative influence by acting as a barrier to integration and furthered Black Canadians' segregation from White society by promoting attitudes of patience, subservience, and resignation of their status as second-class citizens and increased the distance between Blacks and Whites in Canadian society (Henry, 1973; Winks, 1971). In contrast, another view saw the role of the church in Black communities more positively, seeing the reactions of Black churches as constructive and

In Their Own Words

THE BLACK CHURCH IN CANADA: PILLARS OF STRENGTH

A THIRD-GENERATION AFRICAN CANADIAN, I was born in Montreal and lived there for at least 13 years. One of the places I went to on Sundays was Union United Church (UUC), Montreal's oldest Black church, which was founded in 1907 by a group of African American railroad porters and their partners who decided to make the city their permanent home. My great-uncle, Reverend (Doctor) Charles Este, was the minister of UUC from 1923–1968. I recall meeting with my great-uncle on numerous occasions in his large office following the service.

It was not until I began my Master's Degree in history (Black Canadian), however, that I came to the realization of the role Black churches, such as UUC, played in the development of African-Canadian communities throughout the country. Whether it be in Halifax with the Cornwallis Street Baptist Church, the Shiloh Baptist Church in Edmonton, the African Methodist Church (AME) in Amherstburg, or the First Baptist Church in Toronto, these became the focal point in their communities.

Visits nearly a decade apart to two Black churches reinforced my belief in the continued importance of this institution in African-Canadian communities. In 1999, I spent two months in Halifax as part of my sabbatical. I attended the East Preston United Baptist Church with my colleague and friend, Dr Wanda Thomas Bernard. On this particular Sunday, the church was full to the rafters. For the first time in its history, women were being ordained as officers of the church. Family members gave testimonials about these women who were being honored. The pride and joy of this accomplishment was evident in every speech. The event, which lasted over three hours, attracted the media.

I also had the opportunity to attend the Cornwallis Street Baptist Church and Victoria Road United Baptist in the Halifax-Dartmouth area. True to custom, we were invited to dinner by a member of each congregation. It was readily apparent that the churches continued to serve as a vehicle to bring together the members of the African-Nova Scotian community, both spiritually and socially.

During the fall of 2008, I was a visiting professor at the School of Social Work at McGill University. I attended Union United Church several times. On my first visit, the church was celebrating the publication of a book by Maranda Moses entitled *Proud Past: Bright Future*. The book launch was well attended and received press coverage. I attended a bazaar in early December held in the basement of the church. The event served as a meeting place where members of the community, especially those who were advanced in age, came together to share their stories and experiences about the involvement with UUC. These visits provided me the opportunity to reconnect with members of the Montreal English Black community who were members of my great uncle's congregation. In February 2013, I attended a Black History event in Edmonton. As part of the celebration, Reverend Fraser, Minister of the Shiloh Baptist Church, gave an account of the role his church continues to play in the lives of African Canadians residing in Edmonton.

The opportunity to conduct research on some of the Black churches in Canada, to witness these institutions in action, and to hear a cross-section of African Canadians from different parts of Canada speak to the value of the presence of Black churches signifies to me that they are indeed still the "pillars of strength" within African-Canadian communities.

Dr David Este is a professor at the Faculty of Social Work, University of Calgary.

responsive to the racist and exploitative nature of Canadian society at the time by providing Black communities with a space for community members to experience feelings of belonging and develop their own identity and sense of self-worth (Hill, 1981; Walker, 1995).

Black churches' concerns with the social welfare of their members and the need to create a sense of belonging and community among Black citizens were evident in Nova Scotia in the late 1700s and in Ontario and Montreal in the 1800s (Este, 2007). One of the oldest, largest Black churches in Canada is the Union Congregational Church of Montreal (later known as Union United Church). The Church was founded in 1907 by a group of Black railroad porters who no longer felt welcome in White churches and wanted to control their own institution (Este, 2004; Walker, 1995). They approached the Congregational Home Mission who assisted them by providing funding for the building of their new church (Este, 2004). Besides building a place of worship, the founders recognized the need for the church to be a social welfare institution within the community: it served as a welcoming house for new residents in the community and provided winter clothing and food to those in need (Este, 2004). In the 1920s and 1930s, Union United Church and its pastor, Reverend Dr Charles Este, became active in housing and labour rights for members of Montreal's Black community as well as a strong advocate for Black women to gain equal access to higher education in fields such as nursing and education (Este, 2004).

Women and Poverty

At the heart of the social order in colonial society was the family, with men as the head of the household. Referred to as a patriarchal family, this family structure was supported by norms and laws necessary for survival, socialization, and social stability (Abramovitz, 1996). Whereas social rights for men were grounded in their participation in the market economy, social rights for women were based on their status as mothers and caregivers. Women's duties revolved around the maintenance of the household and care for family members. Deviations (e.g., unmarried mothers) were seen as a threat to social order.

In a historical review of the roots of the feminization of poverty and links to the contemporary welfare of women, Abramovitz (1996) discussed how mechanisms built into the structure of social welfare policies were designed to treat women differently based on how their lives related to the **family ethic**. Since colonial times, a woman's relationship to the family ethic determined the type of treatment she would receive under social welfare policies. A woman's adherence to the family ethic was grounded in obedience to her husband "and established a woman's femininity, her womanhood and her social respectability" (Abramovitz, 1996, p. 52). Thus, married women, widowed women, or those whose male breadwinners were able to support them (primarily White, middle-class women) were treated more favorably under social welfare policies then unmarried women, unmarried mothers, and women whose breadwinners were not able to sufficiently provide for their families.

In critiquing the family ethic, it is important to note that Abramovitz did not mean "to devalue the experience of sharing one's life with a partner or that of bearing, raising, and loving children . . . [but] rather . . . suggests that institutionally enforced rules of family organization do not necessarily enhance family life and they frequently disadvantage women" (p. 9). There are direct links to the poverty of women in Canada today. For example, in 2007, the prevalence of poverty among women either unmarried or not in common-law relationships was 27.5 per cent compared to 6.5 per cent among women in families (Collin & Jensen, 2009). A contemporary version of the family ethic requires women who work full-time outside the home to also be primarily responsible for caring for the family and running the household (Abramovitz, 1996).

family ethic A perspective that began in the colonial era defining a woman's role solely as a wife and mother.

Major Social Legislation from the Depression Onwards

The stock market crash in 1929 and agricultural failures in Western Canada brought on massive unemployment and poverty, deeply and widely felt across the country (Jennissen & Lundy, 2011). The enormity of need brought on by the Depression overwhelmed provincial, territorial, and federal governments. Social workers continued to serve those in need according to religious affiliation, with a few exceptions. One such exception was Montreal's University Settlement House, which provided relief-in-kind to all who lived in its surrounding neighbourhood, including newly arrived immigrants (Mortin, 1953).

In Saskatchewan, crop failures (even kitchen gardens) and plummeting wheat prices reduced total provincial income by 90 per cent; in some rural areas, 95 per cent of the population received relief (Berton, 2001). The city of Winnipeg had the highest percentage of relief recipients across cities in Canada and in 1933 in Quebec almost 33 per cent of the entire provincial population were receiving relief (Jennissen & Lundy, 2011). Going against Quebec's aversion to public welfare and in response to overwhelming need not able to be met by churches and charities, the Montreal Unemployment Relief Commission was created, the first instance of direct government responsibility for the welfare of the people in its province in Quebec history (Jennissen & Lundy). During this time, because of high percentages of people out of work and living in highly precarious conditions, governments were forced to depart from their previous approaches to relief

Library and Archives Canada / PA-168131

As a result of the Depression, the government of Quebec took direct responsibility for the welfare of the poor, offering relief services to anyone that was in need.

through churches and charities. Poverty was no longer confined to those without work or who had always lived in poverty; the Depression affected, albeit to different degrees, all strata of Canadian society.

Social workers across Canada were directly involved in the provision of relief at this time, and by necessity, focused greater attention on helping individuals and families survive than on individual case work. Significant social welfare legislation grew out of the Depression. Creating the context for the Canadian **welfare state**, these pieces of legislation were greatly propelled by the overwhelming number of people affected, the duration of profound need, and the realization that external forces could be a significant contributor to one's physical, economic, and social well-being (see Table 1.3).

welfare state A country in which the government assumes responsibility for ensuring that its citizens' basic needs are met.

TABLE 1.3	Timeline of Major Social Welfare Legislation in the Twentieth Century		
Events in Canada			**Events in Quebec**
1929–1939: The Great Depression Marked by mass unemployment; gave rise to support for federal aid and central planning; and fueled growth of social service sector.	1920s	**1921: Public Charities Act Adopted** Mandated government to intervene in helping the needy, an area restricted to the church and benevolent groups.	
1932: Co-operative Commonwealth Federation Founded Social-democratic political party that later became the New Democratic Party (NDP) in 1961. **1939–1945: World War II**	1930s	**1933: Fédération des Œuvres de Charité Founded** Lay philanthropic association with a focus on the family maintained ideas of deserving and undeserving poor. **1937: Assistance for Needy Mothers Enacted** Provided assistance for mothers with targeted assistance for children.	
1943: Marsh Report on Social Security Published Detailed the need for comprehensive and universal social programs to protect disadvantaged. **1945–1960: Baby Boom** Period of increased birth rates.	1940s	**1944: Labour Relations Act Enacted** Became cornerstone of private labour relations by protecting and favouring the rights of workers to collective bargaining.	
1952: Old Age Security Act Enacted Cornerstone of Canada's retirement income system. **1956: Unemployment Insurance Act Enacted** Provides federal assistance to the unemployed.	1950s		
1966: White Paper Published Recognized immigration as a major contributor to the national goals of population and economic growth. **1966: Canadian Assistance Plan Enacted** Transformed social assistance into a publicly funded and administered program.	1960s	**1960–1966: The Quiet Revolution** Represented period of rapid change characterized by secularization of society, creation of welfare state, and realignment of politics into federalist and separatist factions. **1963: The Boucher Report Published** Ended era requiring that a needy person have "good morals" as eligibility for assistance.	

	1970s	
1978: Immigration Act Amended Recognized refugees as a legitimate class of immigrants to Canada.		**1970: October Crisis** Triggered by kidnapping of government officials by members of radical political group and culminated in the peacetime use of War Measures Act.
1984: Canada Health Act Adopted Specified conditions and criteria with which health insurance programs must conform in order to receive federal assistance.	1980s	**1980: First Sovereignty Referendum** **1988: Act Respecting Income Security** Included work and employment incentives for those able to work; financial support for those unable to work; and parental wage assistance for those with children.
1992: Meech Lake Accord Rejected Proposed amendments to Canadian Constitution intended to give more power to provinces and declare Quebec "a distinct society" as compromise to keep Quebec part of Canada. **1999: Social Union Framework Agreement Enacted** Aimed to improve social policies and programs in Canada.	1990s	**1990: Oka Crisis** First well-publicized violent land dispute between First Nations and Canadian government in late twentieth century. **1991: Civil Code of Quebec Revised** As Quebec's "social constitution," addressed private laws. **1995: Second Sovereignty Referendum**
2005: Civil Marriage Act Adopted Legalized same-sex marriage across Canada. **2007: Veterans' Bill of Rights Adopted** Guaranteed benefits for veterans as "special citizens."	2000s	

In addition to ensuring that basic needs are met, Hoefer (1996) asserted that the fundamental idea of any welfare system through which policies are implemented is to increase equality. However, welfare states differ based on ideology as to whether they are committed to equality of opportunity or equality of outcome. Titmuss (1958) categorized welfare states on a continuum ranging from residual to institutional. In residual welfare states, the state provides limited support as a last resort—only in cases where the family or the market fails. Institutional welfare provides support to the entire population in the form of universal programs, committing to areas critical for societal well-being. Canada could be considered a hybrid—not operating primarily from a residual model (e.g., as in the United States) although at times providing social assistance begrudgingly, with restrictive conditions, and to populations through means-testing. On the other hand, the Canadian welfare state offers universal programs such as Medicare, Old Age Security, and Employment Insurance for all citizens.

The Development of Social Work as a Profession

Early responses to poverty relief, including the works of Charity Organization Societies and Benevolent Societies, the Settlement House Movement, and the Social Gospel Movement, created the foundational context for social work. The political, economic, and social upheavals in the first half of the twentieth century called for social work's

TABLE 1.4	Founding Dates of Early Canadian Schools of Social Work
School	**Date Founded**
University of Toronto	1914
McGill	1918–1932
	1945*
University of British Columbia	1930
University of Manitoba	1943
St Patrick's	1949
Maritime School	1941
Laval University	1943
Université de Montréal	1943

*McGill's School of Social Work closed in 1932. For 12 years, it was Montreal School of Social Work. The school returned to McGill University in 1945.

Source: Adapted from Jennissen & Lundy, 2011, p. 215.

professionalization. During this period, schools of social work were being founded across the country (see Table 1.4).

The development of Indigenous social work education in Canada began in the early 1970s. In 1974, Maskwachees Cultural College was formally established by the Four Bands of Hobbema (Alberta). The College created an Aboriginal Social Work Diploma program. Saskatchewan Indian Federated College (SIFC), established in 1976, offered Social Work as one of six programs (in 2003, SIFC changed its name to the First Nations University of Canada School of Indian Social Work). Today, there are myriad configurations of programs focused on Indigenous social work. Faculties, Schools, or Departments of Social Work offer Bachelor of Aboriginal or Indigenous Social Work degrees (BASWs or BISWs), Masters of Aboriginal or Indigenous Social Work degrees (MASWs or MISWs), and Indigenous-centred BSWs and MSWs. Such programs are found across the country, including at First Nations University of Canada, Nicola Valley Institute of Technology in association with Thomson Rivers University, St. Thomas University, University of Manitoba, University of Northern British Columbia, University of Regina, and Wilfred Laurier University.

From All Our Histories to Today: A Vision of Contemporary Canadian Social Work

The social work profession is exceptionally versatile, working at multiple levels. While social workers may share the pursuit of individual and collective well-being and social justice, their paths to those goals differ. Social workers work in a variety of settings, as clinical social workers, case managers, group workers, community practitioners, researchers, educators, advocates, and/or policy analysts. Regardless of social work role, however, all social workers should be aware of how shifting historical, political, and institutional conditions shape the nature and content of practice (Mosley, 2013). Major social issues facing individuals, families, groups, and communities "do not stand a chance of being justly resolved unless they are addressed at both micro (individual) and macro (policy) levels—unless social and economic development issues are considered as crucial as human and individual development issues" (Breton, 2002, p. 25). Social workers are as integral to social service provision as they are to designing social programs and policies. Schneider (2002) reminds us that "if social workers do not exert policy leadership, they allow other people with less commitment to the well-being of vulnerable and oppressed people to shape the human services delivery systems" (p. 115).

Our multiple histories—Indigenous, French, and English—have contributed to the development, composition, and definitions of social work in Canada. These three traditions have merged together in multiple ways as well as clashed with each other. Contemporary Canadian social work must draw on these foundational sources of knowledge composed of myriad histories, theoretical frameworks, and research-based practices to understand human behaviour in countless social, cultural, political, and economic contexts. Knowledge from these sources shapes how social workers conceptualize issues needing intervention, where they locate the "problem," and how they approach their practice with individuals, families, groups, and/or communities.

The foundation of social work in Canada can be represented as interwoven braids, each braid representing Indigenous, French, and English histories and contemporary approaches to social work practice and policy. Each braid is composed of countless strands, or stories, which reflect Canada's diverse history and relationships among its peoples. In addition to the existence of the Indigenous, French, and English traditions, most recent Canadian census data (2006) demonstrate that Canada's demographic landscape has been and continues to be shaped by and transformed through international migration, taking on other strands from numerous cultural communities in Canada. In this sense, as the landscape changes, diverse perspectives and approaches form new braids that continue to be woven into the Canadian landscape. In order to be effective with the populations with whom we work, Canadian social work should embrace the creation of space for contributions from multiple communities, whether they are newly arrived in Canada or have been up-to-now un- or underrepresented populations in social work approaches to practice.

One example of blending is from the Indigenous tradition of exploring one's own health and wellness before and during work with others and maintaining one's own well-being as well as that of one's families and communities. This caring can also be understood as self-care, or the act of taking responsibility for one's own personal well-being through activities that promote constructive energy, harmony, and health (Bickley, 1998; Spitzer, Bar-Tal, & Ziv, 1996). The French and English traditions of helping, rooted in caring as an expression of religious faith, have historically focused on the well-being of the client, the care recipient. However, working in tense, demanding settings has important implications, and social workers themselves can be especially vulnerable. Occupational exposure to stress can lead to burnout (Urdang, 2010), "compassion fatigue" (Radey & Figley, 2007), and/or vicarious traumatization (Dane, 2002), which may reduce one's practice effectiveness, hinder one's ability to concentrate, and impair decision-making. Self-care can be "an integral part of multiple aspects of a person's life, including health and wellness" (Collins, 2005, p. 264). Thus, Indigenous traditions teach that it is critical to conceptualize one's health from a holistic perspective, including the mental, physical, emotional, and spiritual, and pay attention to and acknowledge the value of multiple facets of one's own well-being. To ignore any element of health is to ignore an important source of strength for individuals and communities.

Conclusion

Although Canada first adopted multiculturalism as official policy in 1971, its historically diverse ethnocultural and religious populations are centuries old, and in the case of

Indigenous Peoples of Canada, the history is measured in millennia. This chapter has reviewed the foundations of working with vulnerable individuals and families from three different traditions: Indigenous, French, and English. These three groupings of traditions evolved alongside or oftentimes in conflict with one another. Contemporary social work should be considered an integration of multiple histories—Indigenous, French, and English—that have contributed to the development of social work in Canada. This integration reflects a plurality that includes the political, social, or cultural realities of all who live in Canada.

QUESTIONS FOR CRITICAL THOUGHT

1. To what extent are the principles of early social welfare from the English and French traditions reflected in contemporary social policy and social work practice?
2. In what ways can non-Indigenous social workers integrate foundational principles of healing and helping of Indigenous Peoples into their own practice? What are key considerations to take into account when exploring Indigenous approaches?
3. One's beliefs and values shape how an issue is perceived, and whether it is seen as a social problem, or, for example, a personal failing. Therefore, what is a social problem? How would you define it? What role does public opinion play in its definition?
4. What are the implications of a growing "scientific emphasis" in and professionalization of social work for the role of the social worker in society? Do these changes push social work in the direction of a particular approach to practice (e.g., locating problems in the individual or social structure)?

RECOMMENDED READINGS

Baskin, C. (2011). *Strong helpers' teachings: The value of Indigenous knowledges in the helping professions*. Toronto: Canadian Scholars' Press. This book covers topics related to social work with Aboriginal Peoples such as child welfare, justice, and holistic healing with examples of successful programs in these areas.

Hart, M.A. (2002). *Seeking Mino-Pimatisiwin: An Aboriginal approach to helping*. Halifax, NS: Fernwood. Michael Hart presents one approach to Aboriginal helping and healing through his interpretation of the Medicine Wheel. He shares his personal and professional experiences working with Elders, traditional healers, and helpers as well as the role an Aboriginal approach plays in resistance and decolonization.

Jennissen, T., & Lundy, C. (2011). *One hundred years of social work: A history of the profession in English Canada 1900–2000*. Waterloo, ON: Wilfred Laurier Press. This text chronicles the beginnings of social work post-Confederation through World War I, the Depression, and World War II through the latter half of the twentieth century. The authors describe the development of the social work profession through a discussion of the evolution of the Canadian Association of Social Workers (CASW).

Linteau, P.-A., Durocher, R., & Robert, J.-C. (1983). *Quebec: A History, 1867–1929*. Translated by Robert Chodos. Originally published as *Histoire du Québec Contemporain: De la Confédération à la crise*. Toronto: James Lorimer. Although mainly a history text, this historical account of Quebec from Confederation up to 1929 has numerous chapters relevant to the development of social work and social welfare policy in Quebec, including those focused on Quebec society and the evolving responses to need.

RECOMMENDED WEBSITES

The Canadian Association of Social Workers/Association canadienne des travailleuses sociaux
http://www.casw-acts.ca/
The Canadian Association of Social Workers/Association canadienne des travailleuses sociaux (CASW/ACTS) is active both nationally and internationally, providing leadership in the International Federation of Social Workers (IFSW) and Canada. On an international level, CASW's focus is on social policy, social justice, and social advocacy. In Canada, CASW works proactively on issues relevant to social policy/social work through the production and distribution of resources for members and through the initiation and sponsorship of special projects. The website offers information about upcoming events and conferences, social work publications and other resources, and links to provincial and territorial social work websites.

The Canadian Centre for Policy Alternatives
http://www.policyalternatives.ca/
The Canadian Centre for Policy Alternatives (CCPA), an independent, non-partisan research institute, is one of the leading progressive voices in public policy debates. The CCPA focuses on local, national, and international issues of social and economic justice and offers analysis and policy ideas to the media, general public, social justice and labour organizations, academia, and government through research studies, policy briefs, books, editorials, commentary, and other publications. Special projects include the Alternative Budget Project, the Climate Justice Project, Social Watch, and Transforming Inner-City and Aboriginal Communities.

The Canadian Council on Social Development
www.ccsd.ca
The mission of the Canadian Council on Social Development (CCSD), a non-profit, non-governmental organization, is to develop and promote social policies inspired by social justice and equality. CCSD accomplishes this through research, consultation, public education, and advocacy. Issues of focus include poverty, social inclusion, disability, cultural diversity, child well-being, employment, and housing.

Social Work Theories

LEARNING OBJECTIVES

- To examine the role of theory in social work practice.

- To explore the process and implications of selecting a particular theoretical perspective.

- To introduce the major theoretical perspectives in social work.

- To highlight the practical application of each theoretical perspective.

- To identify the strengths and limitations of each theoretical perspective.

- To underscore the vital interconnection between theory and practice and the role of critical reflexive practice in assuring this ongoing interconnection.

Chapter Outline

This chapter examines the key theoretical perspectives that have informed social work thinking and practice over time. The chapter begins with a discussion of the role of theory in social work. It explores theory's multiple meanings and definitions, addresses why theories are useful, their limitations, and the process of selecting theories to guide our practice. We then discuss the issues of power and politics within the development of theory in social work. The chapter then summarizes key theoretical perspectives in social work. The first theoretical perspective examined is ecosystem theories. This is followed by a discussion of four theoretical perspectives that are grouped metaphorically into "onion-peeling theories"; "faulty-engine theories"; "story-telling theories"; and "mountain-moving theories." These four metaphorical distinctions are intended to capture the essential character of each cluster of theoretical ideas, and are inspired by the work of Connolly and Harms (2012). The chapter concludes by addressing the key interconnections between theory and practice and the role of critical reflexive practice in helping to ensure this interconnection.

Theory and Social Work: An Awkward and Unwanted Partnership?

> Many social workers either turn cold or rebel at the mere mention of theory. Theory is often viewed as esoteric, abstract and something people discuss in universities. Practice, on the other hand, is seen as common sense, concrete, and occurring in the real world (Mullaly, 2007, p. 204).

Theoretical discussions and direct social work practice have frequently been perceived as being at direct odds—as opposite sides of the social work spectrum. Practicing social workers and social work students may view theory as largely abstract principles that have little bearing or relevance on their everyday practice and, thus, may actually obscure the "true" practical nature of social work. There may be a perceived or real tension between the classroom and the field setting—one context where theory is taught, and the other where social work is actually practiced. In addition, social work students may enter field settings where practicing social workers are skeptical of the theories being taught in the classroom and who may, instead, emphasize the importance of experience. In some cases, an aversion to theory may lead to its formal rejection. As Mullaly (2007, p. 205) notes, "many social workers elevate theoretical ignorance to a level of professional virtue."

Perhaps part of the problem is that the intrinsic relationship between theory and practice has not been emphasized enough, both inside and outside the classroom. In reality, theory is part of everyday life—we all use theory. In fact, Sheldon (1995, p. 8) suggests that humans are unable to avoid theorizing: "it is psychologically impossible not to have theories about things. It is impossible at the basic perceptual level, at a cognitive and emotional level. The search for meaning, as a basis of predicting behavioural success and avoiding danger, appears to have been 'wired' in our brains." As social workers, we use professional theories in our everyday professional lives even often without realizing it. Mullaly (2007, p. 205) provides the following example:

> When we see dark clouds in the sky and tell ourselves that it is going to rain, we have expressed a theory about the relationship between dark clouds and water falling from the sky. Imagine if we could not make generalizations about things and every time we saw a dark cloud we had to get wet in order to conclude that it was going to rain.

Howe (1987) argues that all practice is theory-based, as we are constantly perceiving, assessing, and making decisions. These activities are never theory-free because they are based on certain fundamental assumptions about the nature of people, society, and the relationships between the two. These assumptions enable social workers to make sense of any situation, and making sense is what Howe (1987) refers to as a "theory-saturated activity."

What Is Theory?

A theory represents an explanatory framework that aims to help us make sense of the complexity of human lives and behaviour. In aiming to help us "make sense" theories help us structure and organize our thinking, and enable us to establish what we think is going on. As Howe (2009) explains, "if you can make sense of what is going on, then you are halfway towards knowing what to do." Indeed, the more that the world makes sense or feels meaningful, the easier it is to negotiate our way around it. A theory thus provides us with a way of organizing our practice and aims to understand people and their experiences. Theories can act like a blueprint to guide practice: A theory can provide relatively clear direction and structure for intervention and action.

A theory can be considered a "way of seeing." The analogy of putting on a pair of glasses and viewing the world in a particular way can be useful when trying to understand the essence of theory. If we consider a theory as a lens through which we see the world, each pair of glasses/theory has a unique way of seeing and understanding individuals, institutions, society, the social world, the ways in which they interact, as well as subsequent social work interventions.

Below are some selected definitions of social work theory by various authors, all of which can help to better frame and understand the place of theory within the practice:

- Theories represent a "systematic ordering of ideas, drawn from a range of sources that help us to understand a person's circumstances and how we might helpfully intervene" (Connolly & Harms, 2012, p. 12).
- A theory "refers to the range of knowledge, or ideas, skills and beliefs we draw upon to help us make sense of 'what social work is,' which in turn influences our view of 'how to do social work' "(Oko, 2011, p. 5).
- Theories are instruments, providing us with tools for critical thinking, and methods for carrying out our work. Borden (2010) argues that theories enlarge our way of seeing, understanding, and acting over the course of psychosocial intervention.
- A theory is a "system of interconnected abstractions or ideas that condenses and organizes knowledge about the social world. It is a compact way to think about the social world" (Kreuger & Newman, 2006, p. 44).
- Theories "are sets of languages and discourses that allow us to communicate more easily with other people. They also provide a beginning frame of reference, from within which to make sense of new situations" (Fook, 2002, p. 69).

While theories hold particular worldviews and assumptions, the changing nature of knowledge development means that theories change and alter as new information influences the way we understand things or disproves our ideas altogether. Theoretical explanations should therefore be seen as fluid, changing and shifting as new knowledge emerges. In this sense, theory should be regarded as growing, open, unfolding and expanding (Kreuger & Newman, 2006).

Concepts are building blocks of theory and tend to have two parts, a symbol (representing a word or term) and a definition. Concepts also contain built-in assumptions of the nature of human beings, social reality, or a particular phenomenon. Concepts often form

concepts Building blocks of theory and tend to have two parts, a symbol (representing a word or term) and a definition.

a specialized language or jargon. Jargon can be an efficient way to communicate; however, it can also be used to confuse, exclude, or denigrate others (Kreuger & Newman, 2006).

Can One Theory Do It All?

Given the complexity of human experiences, contexts, situations, and the multiple layers and issues that clients may bring to the table, can one theoretical perspective or lens really suffice? Social workers are often drawn to theoretical approaches that are consistent with their overall view of the world and their practice orientation. If a social worker develops expertise in a particular theoretical approach and applies it consistently to her or his client population, this is known as a **purist approach** to theory application (Connolly & Healy, 2009).

In this case, a particular theory is drawn upon regardless of the nature of a client's presenting issues. A strength of the purist approach is that the theoretical blueprint provides relatively clear direction and structure for a social worker's intervention. Moreover, workers can clearly articulate the rationale for their practice approach, can articulate this rationale to a client—evoking greater clarity and transparency—and follow an established path for intervention and action. However, a key challenge is whether or not one theoretical perspective is relevant, useful, and appropriate for all clients and contexts. While one

purist approach When a particular theory or theoretical perspective is regularly drawn upon regardless of the nature of a client's presenting issues.

Practical TIP

How Does One Choose a Theory?

CHOOSING A PERTINENT THEORY INVOLVES much critical thinking and reflection which may include the following:

- the aims of practice and the practice context (e.g., one might not want to apply lengthy psychodynamic approaches and interventions with someone in immediate crisis);
- one's own intellectual and theoretical inclinations, political views, beliefs, and convictions;
- the perceived merits and conceptual rigour of a particular theory;
- the availability of research and evidence demonstrating a theory's effectiveness;
- current modes of thinking about practice and theories that reflect the socio-historical and political context.

It is useful to determine one's intellectual and theoretical inclinations as well as which theory or set of theories are best suited to our practice realities. Schriver (1998) suggests that social workers engage in a process of theory "analysis":

> . . . a helpful process for becoming more aware, constructively critical, and analytical in our interactions inside and outside the formal context of our education . . . Put simply, [theory] analysis is learning to "think [theory]." It is a process of continually asking questions about what the information, both spoken and unspoken, that we send and receive reflects about our own and others' views of the world and its people, especially people different from ourselves. It is a process of continually "thinking and thinking." [Theory] analysis requires us to continually and critically evaluate the many perspectives we explore for their consistency with the core concerns of social work (Schriver, 1998, pp. 9–10).

particular theory may fit well with a worker's worldview, it may not resonate with a client, may be at odds with a client's goals and desires for change, and may be inappropriate to a particular culture or context. For example, a theory developed for populations living in the context of urban North America, may be highly inappropriate to use with populations living in rural Africa.

In response to this challenge, some social workers opt for an **eclectic approach** to practice. When using an eclectic approach, a social worker does not specifically favour one theory but uses theory flexibly, which ensures that no approach is systematically excluded.

Here, workers are able to draw upon a range of lenses and techniques from different theoretical perspectives that may be considered helpful. While this approach ensures that the social worker's theoretical agenda is not predetermined, it raises other challenges. First, a lack of in-depth knowledge of a numerous theories may lead to a superficial and even inappropriate use of a variety of theories and their application. Second, amalgamating theories can be problematic if the fundamental assumptions of the theories are inconsistent. For example, if one theory focuses on working through the past, while another focuses on the present, this could not only lead to confusion for both the worker and the client, but also could affect successful intervention outcomes. Ultimately, a social worker may adhere to more than one theoretical perspective at a time. However, what is most important is to be aware and transparent about the type of worldviews and theories that one adheres to and the rationale behind choosing a particular theory or set of theories.

Ultimately, before employing any theory, social workers have a responsibility to acquire an in-depth knowledge of the theories upon which they are drawing. As Mullaly (2007) writes, "theoretical ignorance is not a professional virtue, but an excuse for sloppy and dishonest practice" (p. 205). Moreover, given its importance and impact on clients, choosing and employing a particular theoretical perspective or amalgamation of perspectives must be accompanied by a process of reflection and critical thinking on the part of the social worker. Preliminary questions that one must ask include the following:

- Why have I chosen this/these particular theoretical perspective(s)?
- How will it/they benefit the client(s)/case in question?
- What are some limitations of drawing upon the theory/theories into my daily practice?
- How can these limitations be addressed?
- What are some potential alternatives?

eclectic approach When using this approach, a social worker draws upon a range of theories and techniques from different theoretical perspectives.

Practical TIP

The Process of Theory Analysis

AN ANALYSIS OF THEORY INVOLVES asking basic questions about each theory to determine its compatibility with core concerns and values of social work:

- Does the theory contribute to preserving and restoring human dignity?
- Does the theory recognize the benefits of, and does it celebrate, human diversity?
- Does the theory assist us in transforming ourselves and our society so that we welcome the voices, the strengths, the ways of knowing, and the energies of us all?
- Does the theory help us (social workers and clients) to reach our fullest potential?
- Does the theory reflect the participation and experiences of diverse groups and multiple populations and voices?

Source: Adapted from Schriver, 1998, p. 10.

In Their Own Words

WALKING ON EGGSHELLS?

I MOVED TO THE YUKON IN 2006. Since 2007, my work has primarily involved providing consultation, staff training, and more recently, therapeutic services to the owner/operator of a specialized, long-stay, residential treatment program. As I've gotten to know my colleagues in the north, I have become aware that a few of our local non-Aboriginal social workers experience additional anxiety, and what looks to me like contrived tentativeness, when working with Aboriginal People. "Walking on eggshells" and side-stepping of difficult issues is sometimes acknowledged as a means to avoid an "angry outburst" or being "blamed" for the continued suffering that is a consequence of acculturation policies, including the legacy of residential schools. I find myself wondering if there isn't also a quality of unconscious racism at play beyond the seemingly self-protective function. Is it possible that we social workers might get caught (even unconsciously) in a cultural bias—presuming some unwillingness, or an inherent lack of capacity that would preclude exploring or confronting the difficulty at hand? Or is it simply a matter of "white guilt"? That is, is it possible that positioning oneself exclusively in the role of the always solicitous, unfailingly effusive with positive regard "helper" might be driven by a desire to be a "Good" White Social Worker and not that "Bad" White Social Worker (i.e., one who unwittingly perpetuates the aims of colonization)?

I believe social work as a profession has yet to engage in the kind of "Truth and Reconciliation" process that many of us feel is necessary if helping relationships with Aboriginal citizens and communities are to significantly improve. Whatever flavour of truth is currently privileged in the theoretical critique of social work, this need for reconciliation remains largely unmet in practice. True reconciliation calls for consistency between the articulated values of the profession with the attitudes *and by the actions* of its practitioners. In my experience as a master's-level student, there is ambivalence if not outright hostility brewing in the House where the Master keeps the Tools (Lorde, 2007); one room is being refurbished with Evidence-Based Practice wallpaper whilst the post-modernists are driving a Cat® [bulldozer] through the front parlour. I don't think this is helping matters. Nor do I believe that Anti-Oppressive approaches to practice will suffice. I do not, for instance, accept that reflexivity is a viable antidote against our human vulnerability to constructions of race, class, gender, and so

Ways of Seeing and Ways of Knowing: Power and Politics in Social Work Theory

Theorizing is not a neutral process. Theories vary according to time, social conditions, cultures, and contexts. Theories and the development of theories typically express and reflect the social, historical, geographic, cultural, political, and economic contexts in which they have emerged. Theories may even represent extensions of the theorists themselves, as theorists' concerns, values, and overall worldview are often reflected in the theories that they construct. In this sense, the socio-political climate and theorists' worldview will inevitably shape and influence the content, direction, and development of theory. For example, during the Enlightenment era where science and reason was perceived to provide all the answers to the universe, it makes sense that theorists during this period would turn to purely scientific explanations to explain social and individual problems.

on. Such constructions may well remain out of reflexive reach if professional "values" render them so shameful as to banish them from conscious awareness. Rejection of unsightly attitudes does not mean they simply melt away in the rays of enlightened practice theory. Nor are we immune to the impact of our own personal wounds—for these also impact on our strengths and vulnerabilities in the work that we do.

So how can social workers in the north practise in ways that are respectful of Aboriginal culture, supportive of social justice, and also consistent with ethical standards of the profession? Bruyere (2010) proposes that non-Aboriginal helpers who want to work in solidarity with Aboriginal Peoples may need to "step back from being part of the change process," and simply stand in solidarity through "consistent, respectful attempts to ask questions" regarding culturally appropriate actions, despite the likelihood of mistrust, anger, or frustration . . . that has emerged from the "emotional legacy of our shared history" (p. 9). Baskin (2011) advises that social workers look to Indigenous ways of helping—that we be guided by the principles and values of holism, and the ethics provided within the Indigenous worldview; in essence, social workers who are willing to loosen their grip on dominant-culture thinking can readily adapt their practice framework to one that is more consistent with a First Nations culture, and thus better able to engage with First Nations communities that are striving to heal from the multiple impacts of colonization.

Drawing in the sand the image of a circle as he speaks, elder Phil Lane Sr explains it this way, "this is the hoop of the people . . . the hurt of one is the hurt of all. The honour of one is the honour of all" (Bopp & Bopp, 2001, p. 23). For those of us who subscribe to a worldview in which healing work is both an individual as well as a collective responsibility, there is a root system at work that presumes we are all connected. Indigenous worldviews have much to contribute to social workers and other helpers in both their personal and professional development. Social work, as a profession, offers a broad set of skills, coupled with an orientation to social justice. At this point, some people within Aboriginal communities carry justifiable wariness of the social workers in their midst. Ultimately, it is up to them to decide if our offer will be accepted, as part of the collective effort to repair the circle. From my perspective, the social work profession has barely stepped up to the perimeter.

Yvette Lepage is a social worker in the Yukon.

Indeed, the social context plays a critical role in nourishing certain ways of theorizing about practice. If the prevailing social context changes and people begin to experience life differently, there may be a corresponding shift in the way people see their world and the people in it. Previous social work theories may thus lose their appeal, and other perspectives will increasingly make sense to larger numbers of people. In essence, it is critical to keep in mind that social work theories reveal as much or more about those who invent them and the social context, as they do about the profession of social work itself.

It is also important to consider why, with the multitude of available and potential theories, some theories predominate and endure, while others fall to the wayside or remain on the margins. Why does one theory "become mainstream" or take precedence over others within a discipline or a profession? One cannot ignore the role of power and privilege when considering the development of theories in social work. It is interesting to note that until relatively recently, the vast majority of well-known authors of social theories, upon which social work has drawn, have been White males who have developed theories and theoretical ideas in the context of the Global North (Marx, Weber, Mills, Berger and Luckmann, Freud, Bowlby to name but a few). Historically speaking, Indigenous Peoples, women, racialized groups, and scholars and practitioners from the Global South have been largely invisible as authors and creators within mainstream theoretical discussions. This has only recently been rectified with the establishment of feminist, Indigenous, critical, and post-colonial theories.

Such realities highlight not only that social context and power relations are key to understanding the development, content, and context of social work theory, but also that social work theories may wittingly or unwittingly generate "blind spots" that may obscure critical realities. Continuing with the analogy that each theoretical perspective represents a unique pair of glasses or lenses from which to see the world, each pair of glasses—or theoretical position that we take on—illuminates unique key elements and realities. And yet this same pair of glasses may simultaneously obscure or entirely conceal other vital and/or multiple realities. Bruyere (1998) poignantly describes the ways in which social work education has embraced scientific theories, scientific knowledge, and scientific ways of knowing at the expense of other forms of knowledge and theories, namely, Indigenous ones:

> What really bothered me about the process of fulfilling the academic requirements was that there was an expectation to follow a certain framework outlining rationale for the project, the methodology, the explication of data gathering and a summation of my findings or conclusions. What seemed truly difficult in approaching the subject of an Aboriginal way of knowing in this manner was that it could become a self-conscious process, envisioned, organized, and written in consideration of and potentially in deference to another way of knowing. It did seem to me that there are different ways of knowing, and that there could be a distinctly Aboriginal way of knowing (p. 171).

With an established and "agreed upon" body of knowledge and established theories in social work, as students, researchers, and practitioners, we are often expected to follow particular "recipes." Bruyere notes that this "recipe" was ultimately incongruent with Indigenous culture and values, and ultimately drew him away from Indigenous ways of knowing:

> I felt pressured to conform to a manner of conduct that was understandable and acceptable to non-Aboriginal people. I wanted to conduct my learning within what I understood to be an Anishnabe way of knowing and being, knowing to my core that it was equal to, not greater or less than, another way of knowing . . . The implication of these acts of omission is that a potentially liberating experience, education, simply continues to be indoctrination into and perpetuation of a colonial relationship between indigenous peoples and the newcomers (Bruyere, 1998, p. 173, 175).

Bruyere's thoughtful analysis illustrates the value-laden nature of theory in social work. It also highlights its Eurocentric focus, alongside existing theoretical blind spots and the silencing of multiple voices. The question of social work's ability to capture multiple realities and multiple ways of knowing and seeing has long been an area of contention. As Martinez-Brawley (1999, p. 334) notes:

> Discussion in social work centers on the question of whether social work proposes one single truth or many truths; whether a single worldview, language, form of

discourse or paradigm will dominate social work knowledge or whether there are many ways of knowing and practicing. Social work has always had moralizing undertones; this was understood and appropriate in a profession based on overtly stated values. It often prescribed best ways of or orthodoxies of helping based not only on the prevailing values but also on dominant, often Eurocentric, theoretical assumptions and methods (as cited in Drucker, 2003, p. 64).

Given the politics of theory and theory development in social work, it is critical that in analyzing existing theories, we do so with a critical eye, highlighting a theory's strengths and limitations and that we attempt to illuminate any potential blind spots. When examining the theoretical perspectives in the following section, it is vital to ask ourselves the following questions: Are these theories "created" with multiple contexts and cultures in mind? In each theoretical perspective, who is speaking? Who is silent? What are the implications for practice?

Theoretical Perspectives

The next section addresses five key theoretical perspectives that have influenced and shaped social work practice over time. We begin our exploration of theoretical perspectives with **ecosystem theories**, arguably one of the most influential sets of ideas to shape social work practice. We explore ways in which ecosystem theories help us to think about interactions between people and their social and physical environments. Following this, we address four theoretical perspectives using metaphorical language— language that attempts to capture each theoretical perspective's fundamental essence (see Connolly & Harms, 2012). **Onion-peeling theories** describe theories like psychodynamic theories and person-centred practices that seek to "peel back the layers of experience so that people can gain insight into what prevents them from moving forward in their lives" (Connolly & Harms, 2012, p. xiii). The **faulty-engine theories** describe theories like behaviourism and cognitive-behaviourism that shift the focus of practice attention not to the past, but to the here and now. These sets of theories aim to alter faulty or distorted thinking that are said to be impeding optimal functioning. **Story-telling theories** explore **narrative** and are fundamentally interested in the ways that stories can be reinterpreted to enable more positive and rewarding life-outcomes. Building on notions of strengths-based practice, story-telling theories focus on externalizing problems and finding narrative solutions that lead to a greater sense of well-being. **Mountain-moving theories** seek to eliminate disadvantage and empower people to realize their hopes for themselves, their families, and their communities. These theories, which include feminist, anti-oppressive, Indigenous, structural social work, and critical social work, connect the personal with the political and shift the focus from individual blame to collective solutions across social, economic, and political domains.

Ecosystem Theories

Ecosystem theories force us to look beyond individual malfunction when understanding human distress. This set of theories focuses on individuals as part of and incorporating other systems, thereby integrating social and psychological elements of practice (Payne, 2005). Ecosystem theories study the reciprocal relationships among individuals, groups, organizations, and communities; examine mutually influencing factors in the environment; and seek holistic change by examining the interacting components. Assessment and intervention focus on improving the relationship between people and their social environments.

ecosystem theories Focus on the fundamental interactions between people and their social and physical environments.

onion-peeling theories Focus on peeling back the layers of past experiences in order for people to gain insight and awareness into what prevents them from moving forward in their lives.

faulty-engine theories Shift the focus of practice attention not to the past, but to the here and now.

story-telling theories Focus on the ways that stories can be reinterpreted to enable more positive and rewarding life-outcomes.

narrative "A story which performs social functions" (Fook, 2002:132). Narratives are said to have particular structures that serve to provide some kind of meaning for the teller. Most narratives contain a temporal ordering of events, or an incident and a consequence that follows.

mountain-moving theories Focus on eliminating disadvantage and empowering people to realize their hopes for themselves, their families, and their communities.

To work with people without consideration of their environments or vice versa, would be losing the distinguishing strength and complexity of social work practice. This set of theories contribute to understanding the dynamic web of interconnections among networks and recognize the interplay of various external factors on human functioning. Ecosystem theories offer hope that changes can occur at various points in a system and may serve as a catalyst for subsequent changes in other areas. As ecosystem theories see social work as concerned with improving the fit between the individual and his or her social environment, it thus requires us to think about the social and personal elements in any social situation and how those elements interact with each other to integrate into a whole.

Mary Richmond's early text *Social Diagnosis* provided one of the first analyses of social work practice that is now recognized as a systems approach. Working with the poor and marginalized in the United States in the early 1900s, Richmond identified the interdependence of people and context and challenged the notion that there was a single cause of family difficulty. Richmond's approach was novel, as she was writing at a time when psychodynamic theories—which focused solely on the individual—dominated social work thinking and practice. She writes: "The common inclination is to seek for one cause. Social workers, however, need to bear in mind that where cause must be sought in human motives, as is apt to be the case in their work, they must expect to find not that it is a single, simple cause, but that it is complex and multiple" (Richmond, 1917, p. 92). Richmond identified the systems and forces in which poverty was occurring for families. These systems included personal forces, family forces, neighbourhood forces, alongside civic and public relief forces and institutions. For Richmond, these interconnected institutional systems created interdependencies and a conceptual framework that could be used to support people in their difficulties and to find viable solutions within the broader context. While Richmond's approach was novel and identified many of the aspects of an individual's social environment that were relevant to their particular concerns, her approach did not provide a way of theorizing these interactions.

It was the development of General Systems Theory that increased our depth of thinking and theorizing. In the 1920s, Austrian biologist Ludwig von Bertalanffy developed General Systems Theory—a theory of interactions in the biological world. This biological theory sees all organisms as systems, composed of subsystems, and in turn part of supersystems. Von Bertalanffy argued that a system, whether an atom, a cell, or an integrated universe of symbolism, has holistic properties that are not found separately within the parts. Instead, these properties arise from the relation taken on by the parts forming the whole. This approach was seen to be generalizable not just to the natural world, but also to social systems such as groups, families, and societies. General Systems Theory was regarded as a way of understanding human adaptation and interactions with one another and with their environment. Andreae (2011) notes that General Systems Theory is "a conceptual orientation that attempts to emphasize holistically the behavior of people and societies by identifying the interacting components of the system and the controls that keep these components (subsystems) stable and in a state of equilibrium. It is concerned with the boundaries, roles, relationships and flow of information between people" (p. 243).

Healthy systems are not static but dynamic and in a constant state of flux. Not only are systems in constant movement, but also the interfaces between systems are constantly in the process of change (Andreae, 2011). Individuals both affect and are affected by the systems in which they operate including family, neighbourhood, school, community, social agency, and society. Problems are said to arise when there is a lack of fit between the needs/expectations of an individual and his/her social environment. The interdependent nature of individuals and social systems means that change in one will result in changes in others.

In his landmark work, Uri Bronfenbrenner (1979), a developmental psychologist, argued that human development cannot be understood without attention to the social

JSMimages / Alamy

Is it fair to assume that this woman is responsible for living in poverty, or is the surrounding environment playing a critical role in the state she lives in?

context in which it occurs. According to Bronfenbrenner, four layers of social systems must be considered:

1. *The microsystem*: A pattern of activities, roles, physical and mental abilities, and interpersonal relations experienced by the developing person.
2. *The mesosystem*: The interrelations among the systems in which the developing person actively participates, such as school, work, family, or neighbourhood.
3. *The exosystem*: One or more systems that do not involve the developing person directly as an active participant but in which events occur that can affect or are affected by the person, such as a parent's workplace or the working conditions of a nurse providing care to the individual.
4. *The macrosystem*: Systems that exert influence on all other systems, such as social policies, societal norms and values, and economic systems.

Bronfenbrenner placed these layers or systems within a *chronosystem*—or time context (historical, biographical, chronological, cyclical, and future time dimension). He saw each layer as reciprocal and mutually influential in understanding individual experience and development.

Since the 1990s systems theories have continued to evolve into complex systems theories to encapsulate the increased complexity of contemporary life and the influences of chaos theory, which highlights the importance of non-linearity and the "non-proportional relation between cause and effect" (Hudson, 2000, p. 220). This theorizing explains why someone dealing with multiple stressors can be overwhelmed by a seemingly minor stressful event occurring simultaneously or why someone living in a highly disorganized context can suddenly engage in positive change and recovery. The concept of resilience (whether retaining, building and/or losing) within people, communities, and environments are of interest to complex system theorists.

From Mapping to Crisis Intervention

Ecosystem theories lead to a practice approach that focuses on identifying the interface between people and their environments and the ways in which challenges are perpetuated or improved. Social work assessments informed by this approach call on social workers to explore how presenting problems expressed by clients are a result of incompatibilities between clients' needs and their environment's ability to respond to those needs. When examining clients' needs/issues social workers explore how presenting issues are exacerbated or minimized by social resources. In 1975 Ann Hartman developed the **eco-map,** a pictorial representation of a person's connection to other persons or systems in his or her social environment. Eco-maps can be used to highlight how social environments may be supporting or draining clients and what connections warrant improvement.

Ecosystem approaches can also be applied to crisis situations, as it is during these times an individual's family or community systems of coping, interaction, and support are

eco-map A pictorial representation of a person's connections to other persons or systems in his or her environment.

Practical TIP

How to Make an Eco-Map

To CREATE A BASIC ECO-MAP, ask a client to place him- or herself within a circle at the centre of the page. Ask the client to identify important relationships or organizations, and represent each by a circle. Draw lines between circles where relationships exist. The lines can either be solid representing a strong relationship, jagged representing a tense relationship, or dotted representing a weak relationship. Finally draw arrows towards, away, or in both directions from the client to indicate if the person or organization is a source of energy or a strain on the energy of the individual. Figure 2.1 provides an example of an eco-map.

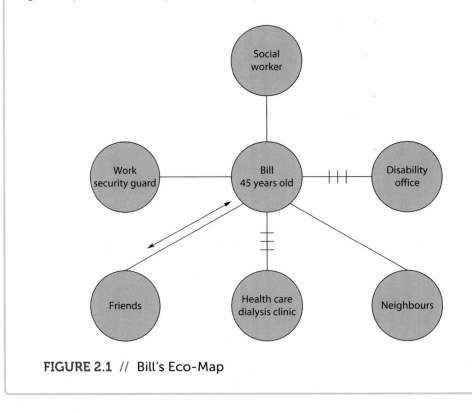

FIGURE 2.1 // Bill's Eco-Map

often disrupted. Familiar ways of adapting are not possible and achieving a sense of balance may be compromised. In such situations, social workers can help to introduce new forms of support, thinking, and coping, as well as develop innovative supports through a variety of systems and networks. Some key elements involved in crisis intervention include

- undertaking a rapid psychosocial assessment;
- drawing upon clients' strengths, whether psychological or social networks;
- providing resources to help people build a new language and understanding of their experiences; and
- creating a strong rapport with clients.

The strengths inherent to ecosystem theories are many. Ecosystem theories provide a "map" of social work territory and a language for thinking about the interactions between people and their environments. The theories also help to identify interacting risk and protective factors. They also encourage simultaneous thinking and intervening at micro-through-macro levels shifting the focus beyond an individual analysis. At the same time, however, critics suggest that earlier theories drawn from biology result in a reductionist approach to human experience. Moreover, the theories are more descriptive than prescriptive for interventions. Finally, the assumption that change in one part of a system results in changes to other parts overlooks the notion of power. Simply put, some systems (macro-systems) exert more power over other systems (microsystems) than vice versa.

Onion-Peeling Theories

From the perspective of onion-peeling theories, human behaviour is a consequence of complex relationships, drives, personality development, and the conscious and unconscious mind. Using the metaphor of an onion, this theoretical perspective views the human condition as a complex layering of experiences that fundamentally influences our lives, often in intricate and repetitive ways. While these layers have the capacity to protect us, they can also act as barriers to the realization of our needs and desires. Onion-peeling theories, which include psychodynamic theories and person-centred approaches, concentrate upon peeling back these layers in a way that enables us to see how they shape and influence our current lives. With greater understanding of the influential layers and their origins, this theoretical perspective asserts that conscious change, greater emotional maturity, and optimal functioning become increasingly possible. Onion-peeling theories provide a rich source of complex ideas for exploring clients' inner lives, emphasizing insight and change. While a prevalent approach among social workers during the 1950s, there was a visible "retreat from psychodynamic theory" during the 1960s and 1970s when social workers focused more upon social concerns (Healy, 2005, p. 51).

Psychodynamic theory, which represents the core foundation of onion-peeling theories, reflects a literature of vast scope that has spanned more than 100 years originally introduced by Sigmund Freud in the 1920s. Psychodynamic theorists hold the belief that our inner world—namely our dreams, fantasies, and unconscious experiences—profoundly influence who we are, how we feel, and what we do. Key themes attached to psychodynamic theories are the key role the past plays in our present lives, the importance of inner drives and motivations, the organization of our inner selves, stages of psychosocial development, and attachment, all of which are addressed in greater detail below.

The Role of the Past in the Present

From the perspective of psychodynamic theory, our past is critical to understanding our present—whether current behaviours, realities, and/or problems. It argues that unresolved

Childhood traumas, such as bullying, can create health and social obstacles into adulthood. Onion-peeling theories focus on the past to understand an individual's present reality.

© mactrunk/iStockphoto

past conflicts that can be traced back to particular events, such as childhood traumas or developmental challenges, bring forth responses that inhibit optimal functioning in the present.

Inner Drives and Motivations

Our inner lives—our unconscious drives and motivations—are in constant interaction with the external world. Freud devoted his life to the study of inner drives and motivation, and psychodynamic theory was intended as a science of discovery—a tool by which to rediscover unconscious thoughts, feelings, and drives. While psychosexual drives were seen as core elements in early Freudian thinking, more contemporary understandings focus on safety and security as primary drives.

Organization of the Inner Self

Freud began to think of the mind as an organization of hierarchical mental systems in which higher systems regulate the activity of lower systems, which are more primitive. The **id** is entirely unconscious and is composed of powerful forces of drives, instincts, and desires. The **superego** acts as "the conscience" and develops during one's childhood through socialization. The superego represents the internalization of the values and norms of society, taught by parents and caregivers. The superego is meant to control the drives and desires of the id. Between the id and the superego is the **ego** or the reality principle. The ego works to balance and mediate the desires of the id and the external demands of the superego. From a psychodynamic perspective, major causes of client difficulties are a malfunctioning ego or superego, such as an overly developed id (giving in to your instinctual desires) or an under-developed superego. In both cases, the ego is weak and unable to mediate between drives and restraints. In the case of the over-developed id, individual desires take precedence over societal responsibility.

id Refers to one's unconscious, composed of powerful forces of drives, instincts, and desires.

superego Acts as "the conscience" and develops during one's childhood through socialization. It is the internalization of the values and norms of society, taught by parents and caregivers. The superego is meant to control the drives and desires of the id.

ego Balances and mediates the desires of the id and the external demands of the superego.

Developmental Stages

Freud identified key stages (oral, anal, phallic, latency, genital stages) through which humans move as they age. In each of these stages, an individual experiences particular challenges, which are normally resolved, and then moves on toward the next stage of development. However, any childhood trauma that takes place during a particular stage may lead to the individual becoming "stuck" at that stage, potentially leading to future difficulties in adulthood.

Attachment

Theories of attachment focus on emotions and early childhood development as the basis for later relationships and emotional problems. A key interest is on the ways in which early experiences of attachment are an important foundation for later social competence. John Bowlby (1984) developed a theory of how seeking attachment to others is a basic drive. Bowlby focused on how children separated from their mothers in early life later experienced anxiety, feelings of loss, and eventually disturbances in behaviour. In contrast, if the important attachment relationships are coherent and consistent, children learn the skill of relating to others and experience themselves as "potent"—that they are able to have an impact on the situations they are in.

Person-Centred Approaches

Person-centred approaches, which also fall within the realm of onion-peeling theories, emerged from the work of Carl Rogers, who provided important building blocks for thinking about intersubjectivity and the co-creation of the meaning and experience that occurs within the context of the therapeutic relationship. Similar to psychodynamic approaches, person-centred approaches are concerned with "changing dynamics of what comes to awareness, the changes in the processes of the mind, and the dynamics of human relations (Owen, 1999, p. 166). However, in contrast to psychodynamic approaches, person-centred approaches put the client at the centre of the practice and focus on client self-determination. From a person-centred perspective, the therapeutic relationship is conceptualized as a co-created space where change can occur. Whereas traditional psychodynamic approaches tend to focus on the practitioner taking on the role of the parental figure to help resolve past conflicts, Rogers believed in developing genuine relationships with clients where they together could examine the client's past. Notions of dignity and respect are at the heart of person-centred approaches and represent an attempt to redress the demeaning experiences that many social work clients have experienced in their daily lives. In contrast to the more traditional psychodynamic theories that prioritized listening followed by the directive interpretations of the social worker, person-centred approaches focus on the client sharing his or her inner world experiences in a non-directive, safe, and empathic relationship.

The Therapeutic Relationship: Fostering Acceptance, Insight, and Awareness

What do onion-peeling theories look like in actual practice? This approach typically uses insight as the primary means of working through conscious and unconscious processes that appear to be preventing a person from optimal functioning. Practice techniques focus upon developing a strong therapeutic alliance and encouraging deep conversations concerning a client's past conflicts, past experiences, and inner world—all of which aim to foster meaning, interpretation, insight, and understanding. The role of intervention is to work through conscious and unconscious processes, which are at the foundation of clients' difficulties. Psychosexual and relationship factors are explored in an in-depth fashion, as would how past patterns may be mirrored in the therapeutic relationship through **transference** and **counter-transference**.

Goals of psychodynamic practice include working towards changing unhelpful patterns of relating, finding a balance between autonomy and mutuality, developing impulse control, and developing an integrated self-identity. The following represent key elements of practice:

1. *Establishing a trusting relationship and fostering a corrective emotional experience.* The therapeutic relationship is regarded as providing a corrective emotional experience and, in fact, is perceived as vital to positive outcomes. Ideally, the therapeutic relationship is an opportunity for clients to experience a positive adult relationship that mirrors a protective parental relationship. Change and healing can occur through the pivotal relationship with a social worker.

2. *Providing a safe space to talk.* Giving voice to inner experiences, making links between the past and present are key to onion-peeling theories. As such, through talking and verbal expression, it is believed that people can be released from emotions, thoughts, and behaviours that have been keeping them in problematic ways of being. Clients are encouraged to "free associate" (say whatever comes to mind), which fosters awareness and insight—the key drivers for change.

3. *Enabling interpretive exploration.* Non-directive exploration techniques are used to uncover clients' histories, thoughts, feelings, relationships, and perceptions as they

transference Refers to the translocation of past experiences to the present without conscious awareness. Transference reactions involve attitudes, fantasies, desires, and conflicts from historically significant object relationships to the therapist.

counter-transference Refers to therapists' emotional reaction to a client, whether conscious or unconscious. Examples during practice include unusual interest, admiration, boredom, anger, hatred, anxiety, or dread in relation to a client that become an obstacle to effective clinical work.

apply to both the past and present. Social workers using this approach make observations, inquire "why," and summarize clients' feelings, which are essential parts of the interpretive process.

4. *Containment.* Clients may experience varying degrees of anxiety and discomfort in discussing difficult past and present events. The need for safety and security is thus deemed paramount, and this is normally accomplished through the establishment of boundaries, expectations, and "an exquisite empathy and thoughtfulness with which the [worker] responds to the client throughout the session" (Gibney, 2003, p. 46). Strategies of containment include establishing clear boundaries around meeting times and setting, affirming a client's inner world experiences and enabling them to share their feelings regardless of their nature, and (with regard to psychodynamic practice) providing clients with direction in decision-making to ensure their safety in relation to potential external threats. These strategies are said to provide the client with the opportunity to experience safety and boundary in their inner worlds.

5. *Humanistic values in practice.* The goals of person-centred approaches include building insight, awareness, and self-actualization. From a person-centred theoretical approach, which is insight-focused and where worker congruence and the therapeutic relationship are central, practice techniques are client-centred, and as noted above, in contrast to psychodynamic approaches, are non-directive, ultimately working towards the client developing an honest, self-affirming sense of self. Reflecting humanistic principles, social workers aim to exude warmth, acceptance, express genuine concern, empathy, and accept clients as valued human beings. These humanistic values in practice are adopted to encourage self-actualization and the expression of feelings. The recognition of the client's reality, conditions for safety, and full-identity expression form the basis of practice.

The strengths of the onion-peeling theories are numerous. Psychodynamic theories have been absorbed and popularized, and continue to pervade our intellectual life and our common culture. Concepts such as "Freudian slips," "Oedipus complex," and "separation anxiety" have continued to be used in contemporary times, demonstrating this perspective's powerful and long-standing influence and impact over time. Moreover, subjective reports of client satisfaction are typically high in psychodynamic and person-centred therapy: deep listening and interpretation, and experiencing positive relationships appear to have healing outcomes. Onion-peeling theories also bring rich insights into the relational aspects of practice and the dynamics of the therapeutic alliance. Proponents of the theories also maintain that they help to uncover the complexity and depth of our minds and experiences.

Critics of the onion-peeling perspective argue, however, that the focus on the past as the core influence in our formation is reductionist and deterministic. For example, it infers that childhood trauma and/or abuse invariably leads to irreparable damage. If this is the case, how can the theory explain the many individuals that undergo significant trauma and yet go on to lead healthy, fulfilling lives? Many also highlight that onion-peeling theories fail to consider the ways in which multiple systems of oppression, such as racism, homophobia or the broader social, economic, and political context may play a role in client concerns and challenges. Others argue that psychodynamic theories are rooted in middle-class, western, individualistic approaches that focus on clear developmental trajectories, the nuclear family, and what represents "normal" and "abnormal" behaviour, making the approach largely inappropriate for cross-cultural practice. There is also a lack of strong evidence base to support the effectiveness of psychodynamic interventions. Finally, psychodynamic and person-centred approaches typically require long-term interventions. Given that social workers tend to be employed in settings that expect short turn-around times, the long-term interventions required for successful outcomes may be unrealistic and unfeasible.

Faulty-Engine Theories

Faulty-engine theories shift the attention from the past to the present and emphasize concrete evidence of change. These sets of theories tend to be more structured and directive than other theories and they aim to actively alter faulty thinking and behaviours in the here and now. In general, these sets of theories, namely behavioural approaches and cognitive-behavioural approaches, focus on changing problem behaviours by using well-defined techniques combined with careful assessment and monitoring, typically done with behavioral measurements.

Behavioural Approaches

B.F. Skinner, who was a key figure in leading behavioural approaches, believed that behaviour could be directly observed and measured. Skinner argued that science needed to concentrate on the positive and negative reinforcers of behaviour in order to predict how people will behave. Behavioural approaches, which were strong in social work during the 1960s and 1970s, assert that behaviour is acquired through learning. Moreover, a faulty learning environment can create unhelpful and problematic behavioural responses. Just as behaviour is learned, however, it can also be unlearned. Practice approaches thus focus upon creating a learning environment in which unhelpful behaviour can be reduced or extinguished. A key focus is on understanding the behaviour, and practice techniques are specific and measurable. For example, a natural outgrowth of Skinner's work in behaviorism is **behaviour therapy**, a technique that aims to alter an individual's maladaptive reactions to particular stimuli.

behaviour therapy
Techniques that alter an individual's maladaptive reactions to particular stimuli.

It involves the most basic methods of altering human behaviour, such as rewards and punishments, reinforcement, and even biofeedback, using conditioning techniques, with an emphasis on life skills. In social work, behavioural approaches tend to be used with autistic youth, in work with clients with chronic mental illness, as well as in substance abuse.

"Faulty" Thinking and Cognitive-Behavioural Theories

Cognitive-behavioural theories developed out of a growing dissatisfaction with behavioural approaches and their unilateral focus on behaviour. Emphasizing the importance of the way people think as well as feel, cognitive-behavioural theories view behaviour as learned and shaped by our interpretations of the world (cognitions). When flawed or inaccurate, these interpretations can lead to irrational or maladaptive behaviours. Interventions aim to correct the misunderstanding or "flawed" thinking so that our behaviour reacts appropriately to the environment. As noted by Teater (2010), three fundamental assumptions are linked to cognitive-behavioural theories. First, thinking mediates emotions and behaviour. Second, "faulty" thinking leads to psychological distress and dysfunction; and third, altering distorted thinking and behaviour can reduce stress and dysfunction.

The following are a few examples of "faulty" or distorted thinking patterns:

- absolutist thinking ("I am a total failure");
- overgeneralizations ("My mother is on my back all the time");
- selective abstraction ("My book report [which received a good mark, but with critical comments] was a disaster");
- arbitrary inference ("I'll never find a good friend");
- magnification and minimization ("It wasn't very significant" [when in fact it was] . . .or "catastrophizing" a situation: "This is going to ruin the entire project").
- personalization ("If only I had done things differently, it would never have happened").

In these situations, emotions and behaviour are influenced by faulty thought patterns and beliefs. For the most part, these are caused by irrational, unrealistic, or negative beliefs that individuals may hold about themselves. Nonetheless, these patterns are likely to undermine an individual's sense of well-being. A key practice approach, to be explored further in the next section, is to challenge the irrational thoughts and change the ways in which people think about their lives, their relationships, and themselves.

Challenging Cognition and Reframing

From a cognitive-behavioural framework, clients are viewed as proactive, autonomous agents who are able to influence their lives and situations. As such, in the therapeutic relationship, the social worker may be directive, yet there is a goal of collaboration, openness, and transparency in practice.

Social workers help to identify and assess cognitions that may be contributing to undesirable behaviours or a lack of well-being. Social workers using this approach work with clients to understand the thought patterns that bring about certain behaviours, as well as what sustains these patterns. In order to make this happen, social workers work to challenge negative cognitions and faulty thinking by contradicting the faulty-thinking patterns. Through practice, social workers develop and reinforce alternative positive cognitions.

As an example, "reframing" is an important social work practice skill that aims to change both thought and behaviour. Reframing works to "change the conceptual and/or emotional setting or viewpoint in relation to which a situation is experienced and to place it in another frame which fits the 'facts' of the same concrete situation equally well or even better, and thereby change its entire meaning" (Watzlawick et al., 1974, p. 95). By reframing a situation, a social worker creates the potential for an alternative reality, and can bring forth in a client greater compassion for themselves and less attribution of blame.

From a cognitive-behavioural approach, social work interventions are structured, problem-oriented, goal-oriented, brief, and time limited. Moreover, treatment is specific and concrete, and the use of homework assignments and practice skills is common. There is also an emphasis on the ability to problem-solve. Cognitive-behavioural practice has been used in response to conditions such as phobias, panic disorders, anorexia, and bulimia where distorted thinking prevents optimal functioning.

Cognitive-behavioural theory has a strong evidence base to support its overall effectiveness, which has led Howe (2009, p. 73) to refer to it as "a top-rank social work theory." Both behavioural and cognitive-behavioural approaches provide key insights into the here and now and address clients' immediate and pressing concerns. For example, implementing a behavioural approach and working with parents to manage a constantly screaming child is highly practical and useful. Faculty-engine theories can bring forth a sense of hope, as the theory underscores human capacity to learn and unlearn behaviours, providing hope for change and recovery.

At the same time, critics argue that some thinking processes are deeply entrenched and not easily amenable to quick change. Moreover, it has been suggested that some belief systems or cognitions may not be irrational, but instead a natural and appropriate response to difficult life events (such as victimization, bereavement, and/or discrimination). Following this, a danger of faulty-engine theories is that appropriate human reactions may be pathologized. Another critique of faulty-engine theories is that they are highly individualistic in focus with less attention paid to broader structural considerations, family, and community realities, cultural beliefs, and the ways in which such factors may influence cognition. There has also been concern about potential ethical problems with implementing faulty-engine approaches with populations in Global South, alongside

In Their Own Words

ASYLUM SEEKERS

I HAVE BEEN WORKING AS A social worker and advocate for refugee and asylum-seeking populations since 2003. I typically provide direct assistance to asylum-seekers in detention during regular visits to an immigration holding centre. In my work, I tend to draw upon two main theoretical perspectives: ecosystem theories and critical social work theory. Working with detained asylum seekers requires an approach that draws many elements from ecosystem theories. Detention practices in particular, and immigration laws in general, tend to create categories and sub-categories around people's lived experience. To even begin to work with clients in detention, it is necessary to ascertain where they "fit" into a complex web of immigration policies, procedures, and legal definitions. By exploring how a person "fits" within this system, it becomes possible to then examine how they interact with their environment through a set of rules, requirements, rights, and responsibilities. Once emerging challenges and difficulties within this interaction are uncovered and understood, a social worker is able to work towards providing clients with an appropriate combination of legal information, relevant referrals to a lawyer or other resources and services, psychosocial support, as well as concrete assistance (such as a phone card to call home). These varied forms of advocacy and assistance can enable asylum seekers to more easily interact with their environment and mitigate the multiple forms of adversity they face.

However, it is not enough to simply look at how detained asylum seekers "fit" into a system and attempt to reduce adversity and challenges by easing their interactions with that system. Further analysis is required. I believe that drawing upon critical social work theory is necessary for two key reasons. First, this perspective works to ensure that the focus is not solely on improving an individual's ability to interact with their environment, but is also on identifying injustices and areas for advocacy. Second, critical social work theory places power dynamics at the centre of clients' lived experiences. Asylum seekers are confronted by a foreign government, represented by individual decision-makers, who have tremendous power over their lives and futures: they hold the ultimate power to deprive liberty or to grant freedom; to accord status or to deport. In this context, every interaction is shaped by power relations, even a "helping" relationship, and thus must be examined accordingly.

Jenny Jeanes, MSW, is a social worker with detained asylum seekers, Action Réfugiés Montréal.

their universal applicability. Finally, it has been noted that faulty-engine theories fail to adequately address the importance of the therapeutic relationship that is a vital component to positive outcomes.

Story-Telling Theories

Storytelling is said to be an integral part of the way we communicate with others and make sense of our experiences—it is a fundamental human activity. People tell stories and construct narratives to make meaning of incidents, their lives, and/or situations. Long before we recorded situations or events in written form, powerful narratives have been passed down within families and communities from generation to generation. There may be family, organizational, or broader national narratives or cultural narratives. These narratives shape and influence one's identity and sense of well-being. Narratives are said to have particular structures, which serve to provide some kind of meaning for the teller. Most narratives contain a temporal ordering of events, or an incident and a consequence that follows. Fook (2002) maintains that there is some sense of a "cause and effect of events that happened which in turn caused others. This appears to be a central concern of most narratives" (p. 67).

strength-based social work
An approach asserting that people have inherent strengths and are motivated towards well-being and optimal functioning.

The origins of story-telling theories lie in several important influences. One is **strength-based social work**—an approach asserting that people have inherent strengths and are motivated towards well-being and optimal functioning. Strength-based social work is optimistic about people's capacity for change and their ability to find innovative solutions without having to go into lengthy therapy to explore past problems. People are seen as holding the key to their own solutions and social workers are the guides of that process.

Cultural influences have also been important to the development of story-telling theories. "Storying," rich oral traditions, and narration have been fundamental to Indigenous cultures for centuries, and are ways in which culture and history have been preserved over generations. Social constructionist theories have also been influential to the development of story-telling theories. Social constructionism proposes that as humans, we construct shared meanings that help us create coherence and ways of understanding the world around us. From this perspective, we live in the context of constructed dominant stories that have the potential to influence the direction of our lives. Finally, the work of Michel Foucault has been influential to the development of story-telling theories. Foucault argued that language and discourses are not neutral, but instead reflect and normalize certain "truths" while silencing others. These "truths" tend to be internalized leading to individuals being subjected to the power of dominant stories.

Story-telling theories in social work, like narrative therapy, focus on the stories we live by, and the ways in which stories and narratives influence and shape individuals, families, and communities. This theoretical approach maintains that stories, particularly stories featuring strength and resilience, can positively influence how we think, feel, and act. By making efforts to listen to our own stories, we can begin to understand their meaning and their impact on the ways in which people live their lives. Story-telling theories focus on the ways stories can be "re-authored" to enable more positive and rewarding life outcomes. Thus, an understanding and analysis of narratives and the role they play in the politics of people's lives, at macro and micro levels, can be used effectively in changing the politics of situations. Story-telling theoretical approaches maintain that the way people tell stories reveals how they understand the world, their relationship with it, and provide insight into their core values and beliefs. In the context of practice, narrative therapies focus on examining and changing narratives that are harmful to clients.

Highlighting Strengths and Narrative Ways of Working

Story-telling approaches maintain that in the context of practice, strengths and resources are what need to be amplified, rather than the overwhelming nature of a particular problem. As such, the aim is to facilitate a context within which a client can discover or rediscover a sense of self, purpose, and power. Interviewing for strengths—a client's skills and competencies—is key. Moreover, reconstructing a personal identity along more powerful and valued lines can be an important aspect of healing and assistance. In essence, the focus of narrative therapy is on these preferred stories and how they can become the new dominant stories in a person's life. The emphasis is less on insight into current behaviour and more on foresight and the capacity to shape a better future.

There is a common set of processes involved in reconstructing narratives. The process moves from uncovering or deconstructing an existing narrative to creating an alternative narrative. Fook (2002) summarizes the process as follows:

1. uncover with the client the narratives involved, taking care to identify those that are dominant;
2. identify the functions of different narratives, including those that are empowering and disempowering;
3. validate the narratives that are performing an empowering role and those that are being marginalized by dominant narratives;
4. externalize the narratives that are disempowering;
5. build alternative narratives and "re-story" them with narratives of strength, transformation, and empowerment;
6. create further validation by creating an audience for the new narratives.

The social worker using narrative approaches is there to stimulate new ways of thinking through questions and enquiry of the story. Focusing on a relationship of co-creation and collaboration, the client-worker relationship provides a safe, supportive context in which a person's story can be heard, witnessed, and validated. A strong emphasis is placed on client expertise and empowerment in finding the solutions they need.

Story-telling approaches are not only applicable at an individual level. At the group level, a story-telling approach can assist groups previously without voice to articulate their experiences. The process of expressing, legitimating, and creating a social identity for marginalized groups using a narrative approach is widely recognized as an important step in addressing unequal power relations and has been noted with regard to social movements such as feminism, disability, and gay rights.

At an organizational level, a story-telling approach that involves organizational identity reconstruction allows for the multiple voices of all members to be expressed and valued and has the potential to construct a more inclusive organizational identity. It also has the capacity for individual members to reconstruct their identities in relation to their employing organization.

The strengths of story-telling theories lie in the fact that they are client-centred and solution-focused. They are also optimistic in their orientation and build upon the client's strength and resilience. At the same time, many argue that story-telling theories emphasize the positive at the expense of understanding the depth of despair and distress in clients. Also, while these theories aim to be client-centred, it has been suggested that it is in fact the social worker that drives the intervention and directs the "re-storying" process, throwing into question notions of client empowerment. Finally, some argue that given the focus on the intricacies of language, story-telling theories are inherently geared towards a middle-class, educated clientele, who may have greater experience and privilege in exploring the subtleties of language and meaning.

Mountain-Moving Theories

This set of theories share a common aim to connect the personal with the political and in doing so, shift the focus from individual blame to collective solutions across social, economic, and political domains. These theories can be seen as transformational, as they propose that social work should seek to change the way societies create and respond to social problems. Theories that fall within the realm of mountain-moving theories include feminist theories, anti-oppressive practice, Indigenous approaches to social work practice, structural social work, and critical social work. These perspectives have in common the desire to eliminate disadvantage and empower people to realize their hopes and aspirations.

The perspectives apply a "mountain-moving" effort to create a more equal society. They are emancipatory in nature as they are concerned with freeing people from the restrictions imposed by the existing social order. Intervention may involve advocacy, helping clients find, recognize, and utilize their own power bases. Practice focuses on participatory and/ or revolutionary consciousness-raising and political action.

Feminist Theories

There are multiple conceptualizations and definitions of feminism and numerous formulations and debates within feminist theories. While there is a multiplicity of feminist voices and theoretical perspectives, a common core assumption is that sex-role stereotypes and certain social structures perpetuate women's subordination. From a feminist perspective, a unilateral focus on class and economic inequality neglects the essential dynamics and realities of gender oppression (Connolly & Harms, 2012). Feminist social work applied feminist theory in a powerful way to influence thinking and assumptions about women across social structures.

Liberal feminists reinforced the importance of equality and laid the groundwork for equal opportunity for women at all levels of society. Liberal feminists seek equality between men and women, particularly in the workplace and child-care and family responsibilities in the household. This view focuses on how sex differences between women and men are, through cultural assumptions, translated into gender relations, which then affect broad social relations. Key concepts put forth focused upon citizenship, democracy, and rights, as well as reducing inequality through legislation, and altering socialization processes so that children do not grow up accepting gender inequalities. **Marxist feminists** brought forth a class analysis and highlighted the unequal distribution of power as critical components of women's oppression. It elevated women's oppression from an individual to a collective level. **Socialist feminists** emphasized the interpersonal and relationship aspects of women's oppression as created by patriarchy. It also broadened the analysis of feminist theory to include questions of sexuality and identity. **Radical feminists** were more controversial in their response to gender inequality and were early users of the term "**patriarchy**"—an all-encompassing term to denote women's oppression, and the urgent need to dismantle it. Patriarchy is a social system characterized by men's power and privilege. From a radical perspective, women's freedom depended upon the elimination of patriarchy. This view seeks to promote separate women's structures within existing organizations and women's own social structures. **Black feminism** points to the diversity of women and the different forms of oppression by which they are affected. Given that Black women are oppressed in many areas of social and domestic life, their experience of oppression is heightened as compared to White women. Important connections are made to family experience in slavery and historic family and social patterns derived from African and other originating countries. **Post-modern feminism** challenged the very core of feminist theory itself. As Orme (2009) writes: "feminists embraced postmodernism to disturb the roots of patriarchy and modernism, but also disturbed feminism. Black women, women with disabilities, and older women questioned postmodern feminism defined by white, able-bodied, young, middle-class, educated women who had divested of its political force. This has led to exploitation of diversity and difference" (p. 58). Post-modern feminism highlights the complexity of social relations that involve women by focusing on how discourse shapes how women are and should be treated. This perspective seeks to interrogate and throw into question discourses and categories, rather than accepting them.

Feminist ideologies have been influential both with respect to strengthening the critical edge of social work practice and in inspiring empowerment practices with women. Feminist social work emerged from activism by women working with women in their

liberal feminism Seeks equality between men and women, particularly in the workplace and in the home.

Marxist feminism Highlights the unequal distribution of power as the critical component of women's oppression, elevating women's oppression from an individual to a collective level.

socialist feminism Emphasizes interpersonal and relationship aspects of women's oppression as created by patriarchy.

radical feminism Asserts that women's freedom depends upon the elimination of patriarchy.

patriarchy A social system characterized by men's power and privilege.

Black feminism Points to the diversity of women and the different forms of oppression by which they are affected.

post-modern feminism Highlights the complexity of social relations that involve women by focusing on how discourse shapes how women are and should be treated.

communities, linking the personal and local predicaments with public issues. Dominelli (2002) defines feminist social work as practice that starts from an analysis of women's experience of the world and focuses upon the links between women's position in society and their individual predicaments to create egalitarian client-worker relationships and address structural inequalities. Orme (2002) identifies four main areas of feminist social work:

1. women's conditions—women sharing their experiences of oppression and discrimination; professionals being disadvantaged in pursuing professional advancement;
2. women's centred practice—the focus is on identifying women's needs and responding to them;
3. women's different voice—women experience the work differently than men, particularly in matters of social and moral concern. This "different voice" should be acknowledged and valued;
4. women with diversity—as a result of their shared experience of oppression, women are able to identify, value, and respond to social diversity.

Dominelli (2002) highlights the following important steps in engaging in feminist social work practice:

* combat "women-blaming" exaggeration of feminist gains;
* commit to avoiding gender stereotypes;
* engage men in caring, affirm alternative child-care practices;
* debate the role of men where women and children have been oppressed;
* identify and analyze privileging of men;
* avoid gender dichotomies;
* avoid seeing alternative family structures as inadequate;
* work in partnership with women to achieve their aims; and
* challenge assumptions of men's violent nature.

Anti-oppressive Practice

This theoretical approach recognizes multiple forms of oppression that exist in everyday experiences and the ways in which oppression can be harmful. Oppression emerges from unequal power differentials and social workers can reduce the negative impact by adopting a critically reflective approach and response that avoids client disempowerment. The goal of anti-oppressive practice is to acknowledge the existence of oppression in all forms and the complex nature of identities. This approach to practice can be adopted within statutory and interpersonal practice contexts. Anti-oppressive practice (AOP) aims to provide a pathway for critical theorizing about the lived experiences of clients that is historicized and contextualized and can be used to overcome oppressive relationships at the individual, institutional, or societal level, and broadly contribute to social justice.

Anti-oppressive social workers try to provide services to those seeking it, but they also try to help clients, communities, and themselves to understand that their problems are linked to social inequality—to understand why they are oppressed and how to fight for change. AOP is thus a set of politicized practices that continually evolve to analyze and address constantly changing social conditions and challenges. These practices fall under the following 10 core themes drawn from Baines (2011):

First, macro and micro social relations generate oppression. However, as these macro and micro relations are organized and operated by people, they can be halted or reorganized by them as well. Second, everyday experience is shaped by multiple oppressions. Gender, class, disability, sexual orientation, and race overlap, contest, undermine, and/ or reinforce one another in ways that depend on a variety of factors in the immediate and global environment. Third, social work is a highly contested and highly politicized practice. Everyday struggles are political despite the relatively widespread sentiment that most of everyday life is completely apolitical. Fourth, social work is not a neutral caring profession, but an active political process. Every action that we undertake as social workers is a political one and ultimately related to power and resources. Fifth, social justice-oriented social work assists individuals while simultaneously seeking to transform society. Rather than an exclusive focus on individuals, attention must be turned to challenging and transforming forces in society that perpetuate inequity and oppression. Sixth, social work needs to build allies with social causes and movements. Social work must join with other groups to organize and mobilize to ensure large-scale, lasting transformative change. Seventh, social work's theoretical and practical development must be based on the struggles and needs of those who are oppressed and marginalized. Social work knowledge needs to be grounded in the lives of those we serve, ensuring that we are not unintentionally reproducing forms of oppression. Eighth, participatory approaches are necessary between practitioners and "clients." Clients are perceived as active in their own liberation and as such, their voices and knowledge must be a part of every program, policy, planning effort, and evaluation. Ninth, self-reflexive practice and ongoing justice analysis are essential components of AOP. Social workers should be aware of their own participation and link in social processes. Tenth, a multi-faceted approach to social justice provides the best potential for politicized, transformative social work practice. Incorporating the strengths of various critical approaches provides the greatest potential to deliver emancipatory theory and practice. AOP highlights clients' strengths while being keenly aware of the ways in which their experiences and life chances have been limited and shaped by larger, inequitable social forces.

An important question that is often asked is, how does AOP differ from "good" practice that may include respectful and consultative approaches with clients, advocacy, and policy critique? First, Baines (2011) argues that mainstream social work draws upon a number of theories that see social and economic systems as politically neutral and that fail to recognize the serious inequities in our society or the way these injustices are embedded in the profit-model of patriarchal, racialized, homophobic, colonial capitalism. Second, AOP attempts to see the bigger picture of the impact of oppressive policies, practice, and social relations, as workers address immediate crises and emotional pain, instead of individually focused interventions (Mullaly, 2010). For example, "clinical depression" cannot be addressed in isolation from the poverty, sexism, racism, social alienation, and other oppressive forces that people who experience depression may endure. Third, social problems are often individualized and depoliticized by giving them medical or psychiatric diagnoses or criminal labels that are often used unquestioned. From an AOP perspective, labelling is seen as destructive, perpetuating oppressive power relations.

Indigenous Approaches to Social Work Practice

As will be addressed in greater depth in Chapter 9, traditional and carefully balanced Indigenous systems of knowing and helping were disrupted by European political, economic, and social welfare forces and colonial practices. The creation of the "Indian social welfare system" not only displaced traditional helpers, but also created the Indigenous social service worker who became a legitimized "holder, applier, and generator of social helping" (Baikie, 2009, p. 54). A manifestation of colonial authority, these Indigenous paraprofessionals, who held vital cultural knowledge and practice were, however, deemed subordinate to "real" social workers—the young and inexperienced university graduates who were the products of Euro-western professional socialization (Baikie, 2009). The consequences of the highly oppressive and colonial practices by the social work profession in

Indigenous communities, in the form of residential schools, the Sixties Scoop, and the continued overrepresentation of Indigenous children in both the child welfare and justice systems, have been devastating (Sinclair, 2009; Trocmé, Knoke, & Blackstock, 2004). As Sinclair has written:

> Our Elders remind us that in order to know where we are going, we have to know where we have been. In the Canadian social work context that implies that as Indigenous social work educators and practitioners, we need to understand our personal histories and cultures and how the colonization of our lands has affected us as individuals, families and communities. It also requires us to have an understanding of the historical impact of colonialism in the contemporary social, political and economic contexts and to assess how these dynamics have influenced and are currently manifesting in the social work milieu (2009, p. 19).

Yellow Bird and Gray (2010) argue that a major shortcoming of social work is that in neither the profession's mission statement nor *Code of Ethics*, which are central to the profession, was fully or partially conceived of by Indigenous Peoples and the hidden world of colonialism has continued to be embedded in social work practice.

The responsibility of helping is being reclaimed by Indigenous social helpers, including the more formalized social work professional. A growth of writings and teachings on Indigenous approaches to social work practice has since followed (e.g., Briskman, 2007, Gray, Yellow Bird, & Coates, 2008; Sinclair, Hart, & Bruyere, 2009). Indigenous approaches to social work practice are grounded in Indigenous epistemologies, or ways of knowing, and incorporate several key principles:

1. the recognition of distinct Indigenous worldviews with the understanding that there is diversity of perspectives and beliefs across Indigenous communities;
2. the development of Indigenous consciousness regarding the impact of colonialism;
3. an emphasis on the importance of cultural knowledge and traditions, particularly valuing Indigenous connections to the land and the linkages between the natural environment and spirituality; and
4. the use of the concept of Indigenous empowerment and self-determination.

As was mentioned earlier in this chapter, a person-in-environment framework is concerned with the individual (physical, psychological, including affective and cognitive) and their environments (whether social, economic, political, and cultural) and the complex dynamic interactions within and between these elements. In contrast, Indigenous perspectives understand the person in their totality—physical, spiritual, mental, and emotional—and do not separate the "inner space" from the "outer space." An Indigenous approach requires a broad, grounded, contextual understanding of Indigenous Peoples: their histories and cultures interwoven with the political, economic, social, legal, and health systems in which they live (Ives & Loft, 2013). Indigenous-centred social work does not preclude Euro-western ideas, but instead "foregrounds local and global Indigenous knowledge, identities, ways of knowing, values, attitudes, practices, protocols and concerns" (Baikie, 2009, p. 48). An Indigenous-centred social work moves Indigenous practices "out of the localized and disconnected while still accounting for both the global diversity of Indigenous Peoples and their distinct ways of social helping . . . it means establishing places and spaces where Indigenous ways of knowing, doing and being are reclaimed, redefined and represented" (Baikie, 2009, pp. 50, 56). Incorporating these key principles into social service delivery ensures that services are delivered "in a manner that is effective and consistent with local cultures and contexts—local knowledge, local traditions and local practices" (Gray et al., 2008, p. 6).

Borg et al. (1995) call upon social workers to adopt a perspective that criticizes systems of power and inequality as an avenue for genuine empowerment where allies support, but not lead, Indigenous People. As they assert that "the ideal outcome . . . would be Aboriginal people as a unified people advocating for themselves . . . co-constructing their presents and/or futures with the assistance of the social work profession" (p. 130).

Structural Social Work

This theoretical approach originated with the work of Canadian social work professor Maurice Moreau. Structural social work focuses on the impact of wider social structures such as racism, homophobia, and patriarchy on personal problems. It also considers secondary structures such as family, community, and bureaucracy. A starting point for structural social work is that it sees society as a struggle between social groups with competing interests, rather than society being ordered and stable. It focuses upon economic and political institutions that influence and are influenced by welfare institutions. These, alongside other social institutions, are sites of social relations, which are supported by the dominant ideology. This theoretical perspective argues that there is a consistent and systematic bias in social relations towards the interest of the dominant and privileged groups. Bob Mullaly (2007) has written extensively on structural social work and further developing its

© Paul McKinnon / Alamy

An anti-gay rights protestor preaches to a participant at the 2013 Gay Pride Parade in Ottawa. In such cases, a social worker may consider structural social work to work with an individual's struggles with societal structures.

core assumptions and ideas. In his book entitled *The New Structural Social Work*, Mullaly (2007) identifies the major elements of structural social work. The theory's core assumptions can be merged into the following key themes: the role of state, the relationship between the individual and structure, and the nature and role of social work.

The Role of the State

From a structural social work perspective, social problems, including discrimination on the basis of class, gender, race, and so on, are built into the structures of society. Moreover, the welfare state in a capitalist society upholds capitalism and operates in a way to reproduce all oppressive social relations. Structural social workers also believe that the state's institutions, for example the law and the education system, function as instruments of oppression and benefit the privileged groups.

The Relationship Between the Individual and Structures

With the importance and emphasis given to structures, structural social workers believe focusing on the individual as the cause of social problems blames the victim. In order for social problems to be resolved, it is the social structures that must change. Importantly, social structures, ideology, and personal consciousness are interrelated—each element or component of society affects the others. In keeping with this perspective, Mullaly also argues that the traditional dichotomy between the individual and society needs to be challenged—individual problems cannot be divorced from the social context.

The Nature and Role of Social Work

Another core assumption of structural social work is that conventional social work perpetuates social problems by focusing on personal change rather than fundamental social change. For Mullaly, an anti-oppressive approach to social work should be adopted. Moreover, when considering and understanding oppression, all sources and forms of oppression are to be rejected and no hierarchy of oppression should be developed. In this sense, no single source of oppression can claim primacy. The dominant order must be challenged or resisted by developing counter discourses to victim-blaming and welfare-dependency.

Structural social work focuses upon several important practice strategies including empowerment, consciousness-raising, normalization, and dialogical relations. Empowerment focuses on increasing the service user's control of personal and physical resources. It also focuses on ensuring that organizational policies support clients rather than control or seek conformity. Through consciousness-raising, social workers can promote an understanding of the dehumanizing structures and how to overcome their effects. Through normalization, social workers help clients to see that their problems are not unique, especially by linking them with others who share similar problems. Drawing upon dialogical relations means maintaining a dialogue of equals with clients and demystifying activities as a social worker.

Critical Social Work

This perspective focuses on the impact of wider social structures on personal problems and is concerned with notions of inequality and oppression. Critical social work seeks to contribute to a transformation of everyday lives, working towards changes in economic, social, and political structures, relations, and organizations: "Critical theorists examine the socially constructed character of society. They show how ruling and powerful social groups are able to justify injustice and inequality by their control of the language, media education, political agenda and terms of debate" (Howe, 2009, p. 130). Allan (2009) argues that critical social work favours multiple ways of working as opposed to focusing within a particular method, for example, working with individuals, families, groups, or communities. Critical social work is practised across methods integrating key concepts such as the interconnection of the person and the political and the importance of consciousness raising. These ideas have emerged in social work writing internationally, but have been particularly predominant in Australia. The work of Jan Fook (2002) has been at the forefront of these developments where the merging of post-modernism and critical social work is evident:

> A postmodern and critical social work practice is primarily concerned with practicing in ways which further a society without domination, exploitation and oppression. It will focus both on how structures dominate, but also how people construct and are constructed by changing social structures and relations, recognizing that there may be multiple and diverse constructions of ostensibly similar situations. Such an understanding of social relations and structures can be used to disrupt dominant understandings and structures, and a basis for changing these so that they are more inclusive of different interest groups (p. 18).

Critical theory in social work is viewed as transformational, proposing that social work should seek to change the way societies create social problems. It is also emancipatory as it is concerned with freeing people from the restrictions imposed by the existing social order. Some have argued however, that the mix of theoretical perspectives (post-modern, radical ideals, and critical theory) has weakened critical social work and its potential to achieve the necessary intellectual rigour of theorizing (Gray & Webb, 2009).

The above intellectual movements have provided social work with a critical edge that contrasted sharply with individualized treatment approaches that tended to focus on individual deficits and moral or personal failure. Mountain-moving theories have evolved and developed in response to contemporary issues and concerns. The overall contribution of mountain-moving theories led to changing some of the often apolitical and oppressive practices of social work and underscored the value of collective action to tackle structural problems. They emphasize social reform, acknowledging that social work is not a neutral profession, but an active political process. These theories advocate for the search for social justice and have provided social work with a much-needed critical edge.

Partnership, Empowerment, and Participation

Theorists identify a number of practice principles that address unequal power relations and forms of oppression and exclusion. Social workers need to be critically self-reflective and cognizant of the way in which their own **social location** shapes their practice and relationships with clients, recognizing the role of power in shaping both what clients experience and what the social worker does (Mullaly, 2009).

social location An individual's affiliation as a member of a group based on race, ethnicity, gender, ability, class, religion, citizenship status, and sexual/gender identity, and so forth.

In addition, social workers need to critically assess a client's experiences of inequality and oppression, linking individual realities to larger social forces impinging on the choices and lived realities of clients. Ultimately, it is imperative that workers remain aware of the part that power plays at the personal and professional level (Howe, 2009). As Healy (2005) notes, "the processes of critical reflection extend also to reflection on how the language one uses in assessment is shaped by dominant ideologies that convey and sustain oppressive power relations" (p. 184).

Empowering clients to overcome structural and personal disadvantage using the least intrusive intervention is key. These theoretical approaches seek to empower clients (individuals and/or groups) by supporting and encouraging them to realize their own power and take action for themselves. In this context, empowerment draws upon the development of personal, interpersonal, and political power to enable individuals and groups to improve their circumstances. Parrott (2010) emphasizes two elements of empowerment: (1) control—people defining their own situations and needs, and (2) self-actualization—enabling clients to take power for themselves by developing their confidence, skills, and knowledge.

Partnership, or working collaboratively with clients, is strongly advocated and comprises engaging and involving them throughout the assessment process, ensuring transparency, seeking out their views, involving them in decision-making, and valuing their contribution as equal participants in the process. Social workers must also build partnerships and allies with broader social causes and movements. While partnership is an important principle, it is nonetheless important to consider the complex nature of developing partnerships with clients in contexts that reflect inherently unequal and hierarchical relationships.

Participatory practices are also encouraged whereby clients—represented by all user groups and reflecting the diversity of users—are engaged and involved in the design and delivery of services and are also involved in developing services in partnership with relevant organizations. This approach challenges the traditional view of social worker as "expert" and promotes more inclusive workplaces and practices. Participatory approaches inherently work to ensure services are reflective of clients' needs and are non-stigmatizing. However, participatory processes and approaches take time and resources. Clients and practitioners need to discuss timetables and ways of working that provide meaningful and realistic opportunities for clients to join and contribute. Organizational commitment to a participatory process is key and social workers need support to enable them to reflect upon clients' concerns and participation.

Mountain-moving theories have many strengths. They offer a distinct analysis of social issues that helps social workers think critically about their practice and respond to concerns about oppressive practice. The multiple theories summarized above individually and collectively highlight the important role and impact of power relations, oppression, and exclusion in people's daily lives and the ways in which the personal is very much political. These sets of theories look toward establishing fundamental structural changes to improve and promote empowerment in the lives of the marginalized. On the negative side, a focus on collective action and structures may neglect the immediate personal needs of clients and may ignore clients' personal and emotional challenges. Moreover, mountain-moving theories often work from their own set of assumptions, instead of directly from the voices and needs of people served. Finally, mountain-moving theories do not offer explanations that can be tested or assessed empirically.

Conclusion

As highlighted at the beginning of the chapter, theories provide us with a way of organizing and guiding our practice. Acting as a powerful blueprint, theories can provide much needed direction and structure for intervention and action. Yet, as we have also illustrated, theories may hold blind spots, illuminating some realities, while concealing others. In some cases, theories, on their own, may be inadequate to address the profound complexities of everyday practice and work with diverse populations. Annette Riley (1996) makes this point clearly when she describes her involvement with a case of a mother whose child dies. Riley explains how she found formal theory largely futile when confronted with the possibility that the mother may have murdered her child. Riley's anguish and confusion in dealing with the mother's changed identity (from client to murderer) highlighted her realization that there was no existing theory that could guide her thinking or practice in this situation. Fook (2002) asserts in such situations, one's response and interpretation will likely reflect an amalgamation of the formal theories one subscribes to, but also to one's own subjective position, personal history, and practice wisdom and experience. Connolly and Harms (2012) refer to this as the practitioner relying upon "professional artistry" to help them respond to unique and challenging practice situations. In the context of practice, this "artistry" mirrors a process of action and reflection—one reflects upon their work, possible outcomes, and once a course of action has been taken, a worker reflects upon what could have been done differently, potentially leading to a changed future response. However, pushing this process even further, Connolly and Harms (2012) argue that **reflexivity** and not mere reflection is required. Reflexive practice adopts a critical stance, compelling the practitioner to reflect on the ways in which power relations and social location embody and shape our interactions with clients. When applying the concept of reflexivity to the theoretical realm, engaging in reflexive practice can also help to assure that workers are consistently and critically engaging in the theory/practice dialectic, ensuring that one builds upon and is never without the other.

reflexivity A process by which the worker's thinking influences the action—ensuring a more sophisticated analysis of practice.

The separate worlds of theory and practice appear to reflect and mirror the hierarchical split between social workers and clients, and researchers and practitioners. Constructing theory and practice as separate entities by privileging one over the other serves to perpetuate a dominance of researcher over practitioners and professional over client perspectives. Ultimately, the relationship between theory and practice is an interconnected one. Engaging in critical reflexivity is one way to ensure that theory and practice remain intertwined, whereby one is never entirely divorced from the other.

QUESTIONS FOR CRITICAL THOUGHT

1. What has been your relationship with theory up until this point? How has theory influenced (or not) your social work practice?
2. Which theoretical perspective(s) do you most closely identify with or believe that you will draw upon in your everyday practice? Why?
3. Reflect on each of the cluster of theoretical perspectives addressed in the chapter. What element(s) of practice do you feel is/are neglected or overlooked by some or all of the clusters/theories? As a result of your answer, what direction should theoretical social work take in the future?
4. Draw up a case study involving a client facing multiple family problems. Take the time to explore and analyze the case study using a theoretical perspective from each metaphorical grouping. How would each theory understand and respond to the issue(s) at play?

RECOMMENDED READINGS

Affilia: Journal of Women and Social Work. This is the only scholarly social work journal to address the concerns of social workers and their clients from a feminist point of view, offering a unique mix of research reports, new theory and creative approaches to the challenges confronting women.

Allan, J., Briskman, L., & Pease, B. (2009). *Critical social work: Theories and practice for a socially just world*. Sydney: Allen & Unwin. *Critical Social Work* is a resource to inform progressive social work practice. It includes case study chapters on disability, older people, children, rurality, and violence and abuse.

Fonagy, P. (2001). *Attachment: Theory and psychoanalysis*. New York: Other Press. This book shows scientifically how our earliest relationships influence our later relationships in life. This book offers an introduction to the findings of attachment theory and the major schools of psychoanalytic thought.

Freeman, A. (2006). *Cognitive behavioral therapy in clinical social work practice*. New York: Springer Publishing. From traditional techniques to new techniques such as mindfulness meditation, the contributors provide an up-to-date presentation of CBT. Covered are the most common disorders encountered when working with adults, children, families, and couples.

Gray, M., Coates, J., Yellow Bird, M., & Hetherington, T. (2013). (Eds.). *Decolonising social work*. London: Ashgate. This edited volume furthers scholarship on the analytical and activist paradigm of decolonization. Indigenous, and non-Indigenous social work scholars examine local cultures, beliefs, values, and practices as central to decolonization. Included are trends, issues, and debates in Indigenous social work theory, practice methods, and education and research models.

Sinclair, R., Hart, M.A., & Bruyere, G. (2009). *Wícihitowin: Aboriginal social work in Canada*. Halifax: Fernwood Publishing. *Wícihitowin* is the first Canadian social work book written by First Nations, Inuit, and Métis authors who are educators at schools of social work across Canada.

RECOMMENDED WEBSITES

The Association of Community Organizations for Reform Now
http://www.acorncanada.org
The Association of Community Organizations for Reform Now (ACORN) Canada is a community organization of low-and moderate-income families working together for social justice and stronger communities.

The Canadian Association of Cognitive and Behavioral Therapies
www.cacbt.ca
The Canadian Association of Cognitive and Behavioral Therapies represents the multidisciplinary association working to advance the science and practice of CBT in Canada.

The Canadian Counselling and Psychotherapy Association
www.ccpa-accp.ca
The Canadian Counselling and Psychotherapy Association is a national and bilingual organization dedicated to the enhancement of the counseling profession in Canada. They offer a student membership program.

Narrative Approaches
www.narrativeapproaches.com
Narrative Approaches provides resources on narrative therapy, including academic resources.

Ethics in Social Work Practice and Research

LEARNING OBJECTIVES

- To review the historical development of ethical guidelines in practice and research.

- To introduce the CASW *Code of Ethics* and its contemporary applications.

- To highlight the interconnectedness of social work practice and research.

- To address current ethical issues in the context of historical ethical misconduct.

- To review approaches to social work research and related ethical considerations when conducting research.

- To contextualize ethical social work practice and research through a reflexive lens.

Chapter Outline

This chapter introduces students to the guidelines for ethical behaviour in social work practice and research and the development of contemporary ethical standards. Particular areas of focus include approaches to ethical decision-making and essential ethical considerations in research studies, including ethical frameworks for working with Indigenous Peoples.

Why Are Ethics Important in Social Work?

Social work is often thought of as a profession where social workers "do good" or "help people." However, in some contexts, social workers can be seen as the enemy; when one of the authors asked a high school class what the first thing was that came to their minds when they heard the words "social work," one student raised her hand and said, "Run for your life!" (Ives & Loft, 2013). Social work is a profession with a distinct value base grounded in the pursuit of social justice and the elimination of oppression. Social workers' personal, professional, and organizational commitments to social justice are shaped by adherence to core values and principles which promote ethical behaviour and guide work with clients. However, social workers often feel pulled in multiple directions, faced with multiple paths to choose, where no simple path is apparent or where different paths supported by different parties are in conflict with one another. A social worker may find him- or herself positioned between protecting clients' interests and addressing "societal demands for efficiency and utility" (IFSW, 2012, Preface) and may also have to navigate multiple roles that may include advocate at times and controller at others. Ethical challenges arise in abundance in social work practice and research contexts, requiring social workers to exercise a great deal of judgment. Decisions requiring the exercise of judgment are made by social workers on a daily basis, and they are rarely straightforward. More often than not, a social worker is faced with situations where "it is not merely about taking the least risky option and following pre-established procedures, but often requires grappling with hairy demons that would have us toe the party line when our compassionate self cries out to respond to the call of the suffering other" (Gray & Gibbons, 2007, p. 235). There are, although few and far between, cases where social workers have committed ethical misconduct. Reamer (2012) notes that the reasons for ethical misconduct by social workers who exhibit personally and professionally destructive behaviour are varied, and could include financial worries, greed, and personal impairments such as addictions or professional burnout.

Social work ethics encompasses work with individuals, groups, and communities, and should be woven into the interactions with those with whom we work whether in a practice or research setting. Research and practice are interdependent and the ethics to which a social worker adheres spans work across spheres. It is integral to our commitment to providing clients with competent services that social workers are aware of contemporary, progressive discourse in their issue area, are able to critically analyze study findings that relate to their client population, and reflect on the utilization of those findings for clients. Moreover, it is an ethical imperative that social workers "learn as much as possible about the historical and current experiences and analyses of groups who are oppressed. For social workers who want to practice in solidarity with their clients, this is essential learning" (Baines, 2011, p. 72).

A Brief History of Ethics in Social Work

Social workers' concern and engagement with ethical issues has evolved considerably over time. Reamer (1998) has suggested that the profession's concern with ethics reflects four, often overlapping, periods: the "morality period," the "values period," the "ethical theory and decision-making period," and the "ethical standards and risk management period." When examining the evolution of ethics in social work, it becomes evident that what began as a fairly superficial concern about ethics in the late nineteenth and the early twentieth century has more recently transformed into in-depth attempts to explore, analyze, and resolve complex ethical issues and dilemmas faced by social workers in their daily practice and research.

The Morality Period

In the early twentieth century, when social work was establishing itself as a profession, a common assumption made by social workers was that the problems and challenges that people encountered were a result of their individual moral failures. As such, at that time, the role of the social worker was believed to be to lead clients to a "better" life by influencing their individual values and behaviours and "strengthening their morality." Social problems such as poverty and unemployment were understood to be a direct result of the so-called "wayward" lives and habits of the poor and the marginalized. Reflecting this highly paternalistic view, social workers were less concerned with the morality, obligations, or ethics of the profession, or their own ethical practice or professional conduct, and were instead more focused on the ethics and morality of clients themselves.

Values Period

Over time, concerns about clients' morality were overshadowed by debates about the profession's future and the necessity of developing a consensus around the profession's core values. In the early 1950s, social workers in North America began to place an increasing focus on the morality, values, and ethics of the profession and its practitioners. Reamer (1998) notes that a large portion of scholarship and literature during this period focused on the need for social workers to examine their own personal values and the impact of these values on the profession as well as on their clients. Discussions and debates in the literature tended to centre on the profession's mission, establishing a set of agreed upon core professional values and the realities of competing values (particularly between the groups served by social workers and social workers themselves). Furthermore, during this period, social work associations in North America began to collectively develop and publicize ethical standards and guidelines.

Emergence of Ethical Theories and Decision-Making

The 1970s saw a surge of interest in the subject of applied and professional ethics. Professions including medicine, law, business, journalism, nursing, social work, and criminal justice began to devote significant attention to the subject. The growth of interest in professional ethics was due to a number of factors. Controversial technological developments in health care, such as the termination of life support, organ transplantation, genetic engineering, and test-tube babies, sparked increased ethical debate. Alongside this, through highly publicized events like Watergate in the USA in the early 1970s, the public became increasingly aware of professional misconduct, triggering considerable interest in professional ethics. Terminology was introduced in society regarding patient's rights, women's rights, prisoner's rights, and welfare rights, all of which helped to shape professional thinking about the need to address ethical concepts and considerations.

Professionals from a variety of disciplines also had an increased appreciation of the limits of science and its ability to respond to complex questions professionals face. Science had, in the past, been placed on a pedestal and regarded by many as the key to many of life's mysteries. However, professionals working in diverse contexts and disciplines began to acknowledge that science could not answer a variety of questions that are fundamentally ethical in nature.

In the 1960s and 1970s, social workers began to direct considerable attention to matters of social justice, social reform, and civil rights. The social turbulence of this era had enormous influence on the profession, primarily because of social work's concern about human rights, welfare rights, equality, discrimination, and oppression. Values such as dignity, self-determination, autonomy, client empowerment, commitment to social change, respect, justice equality, professional competence, respect for diversity, and service to others came to the forefront of social work's discussions and debates. In addition, the broader realities of war, genocide, unethical scientific experiments on human subjects, awareness of generalized structural inequalities, and exploitation all worked to challenge the profession to devote greater concern and focus on ethical considerations. Moreover, the increase in litigation and malpractice along with publicity of unethical professionals forced the profession to take a closer look at ethical traditions and training.

The result of these developments was an emergence of a critical mass of literature on social work ethics and theories of ethics, drawing upon moral philosophy, ethical concepts, and ethical principles in analyzing and attempting to resolve complex ethical dilemmas in social work. In addition, ethical theories, which aimed to integrate bodies of principles and rules, began to be drawn upon to provide a framework for ethical decision-making. The two types of ethical theories frequently discussed in the social work literature are utilitarian/consequentialist or deontological/duty-based. **Utilitarian theories** suggest that actions are right and wrong according to their outcomes rather than their intrinsic features.

For example, when deciding whether to tell the truth, one opts for telling the truth because of the possible consequences of not telling the truth. **Deontological theories** maintain that certain acts are intrinsically good or bad in and of themselves, irrespective of their consequences. For example, when deciding whether or not to tell the truth, one opts to tell the truth because truth telling is good in itself and a rule that one ought to obey regardless of the circumstances.

utilitarian theories Theories that suggest actions are right and wrong according to their outcomes rather than their intrinsic features.

deontological theories Theories that maintain certain acts are intrinsically good or bad in and of themselves, irrespective of their consequences.

The Ethical Standards and Risk Management Period

The most recent stage in the development of social work ethics in North America (from the early 1990s to the present) reflects the significant expansion of ethical standards to guide practitioners' conduct and the increased knowledge concerning professional negligence and liability. This period includes the creation and formalization of a comprehensive code of ethics for the profession and the emergence of literature focusing on malpractice, liability, and risk-management strategies. Ethical code development along with various strategies for managing risk is designed primarily to protect clients and prevent ethics complaints and ethics-related lawsuits.

Reamer (1998) argues that as a result of increased litigation against social workers—a significant portion of which alleges some kind of ethical violation—social work education programs, agencies, licensing boards, and professional orders have increasingly included training on professional ethics. Greater attention has been focused on issues of confidentiality, conflicts of interests, boundary issues, ethics in social work research and evaluation, professional malpractice, termination of service, and documentation. As the nature of the profession alters and evolves, and as globalization and technological developments continue to affect society, the profession will need to evolve alongside it in order to meet the growing complexities of contemporary caseloads and their ethical implications.

The Canadian Association of Social Workers' *Code of Ethics*

Nearly all professions have developed Codes of Ethics to assist practitioners who face ethical dilemmas—most of which were developed during the twentieth century. In 2005, the Canadian Association of Social Workers adopted the current iteration of the Canadian *Code of Ethics for Social Work* (hereafter referred to as the "*Code*"; see Appendix) that is consistent with the International Federation of Social Workers (IFSW) and the *International Declaration of Ethical Principles of Social Work* (2004). The *Code* requires that social workers have "a responsibility to maintain professional proficiency, to continually strive to increase their professional knowledge and skills, and to apply new knowledge in practice commensurate with their level of professional education, skill and competency, seeking consultation and supervision as appropriate" (CASW, 2005a, p. 8). Social workers rely on the values and principles of the *Code* and the *Guidelines for Ethical Practice* (2005b) to guide social workers' professional conduct by outlining ethical responsibilities to clients, in professional relationships, to colleagues, in the workplace, in private practice, in research, to the profession, and to society. Although the work with which social workers engage and the areas in which social workers work are diverse, the responsibility to adhere to the *Code* is shared by all as a professional obligation. In Canada, each province and territory is responsible for regulating the professional conduct of social workers to ensure the protection of the public. (See "Practical Tip" box below for contact information on regulatory bodies across Canada.)

Practical TIP

Contact Information on Regulatory Bodies across Canada

British Columbia Association of Social Workers
Suite 402, 1755 West Broadway
Vancouver, BC V6J 4S5
Tel: 604.730.9111/1.800.665.4747 (BC residents only)
Fax: 604.730.9112
Email: bcasw@bcasw.org
Website: www.bcasw.org

Saskatchewan Association of Social Workers
2110 Lorne St.
Regina, SK S4P 2M5
Tel: 306.545.1922
Fax: 306.545.1895
Email: sasw@accesscomm.ca
Website: www.sasw.ca

Manitoba Institute of Registered Social Workers
Unit 101–2033 Portage Ave.
Winnipeg, Manitoba R3J 0K8
Tel: 204.888.9477
Fax: 204.831.6359
Email: admin@mirsw.mb.ca
Website: www.mirsw.mb.ca

(Continued)

New Brunswick Association of Social Workers
P.O. Box 1533, Postal Station A,
Fredericton, NB E3B 5G2
Tel: 506.459.5595/1.877.495.5595 (NB residents only)
Fax: 506.457.1421
Email: nbasw@nbasw-atsnb.ca
Website: www.nbasw-atsnb.ca

Nova Scotia Association of Social Workers
1891 Brunswick St., Suite 106
Halifax, NS B3J 2G8
Tel: 902.429.7799
Fax: 902.429.7650
Email: nsasw@nsasw.org
Website: www.nsasw.org

Newfoundland and Labrador Association of Social Workers
P.O. Box 39039
St. John's, NL A1E 5Y7
Tel: 709.753.0200
Fax: 709.753.0120
Email: info@nlasw.ca
Website: www.nlasw.ca

Prince Edward Island Association of Social Workers
81 Prince Street
Charlottetown, PE C1A 4R3
Tel: 902.368.7337
Fax: 902.368.7080
Email: vrc@eastlink.ca
Website: www.peiasw.ca

The Association of Social Workers in Northern Canada (ASWNC)
c/o Geri Elkin
Box 2963
Yellowknife, NT X1A 2R2
Tel: 867.920.4479
Fax: 867.669.7964
Email: ed@socialworknorth.com
Website: www.socialworknorth.com

Code of Ethics Core Values

1. *Respect for inherent dignity and worth of persons*: Social workers must uphold clients' human rights and their right to self-determination, respect diversity among clients, and ensure client choices are made based on voluntary, informed consent, paying particular attention to issues where clients are children.
2. *The pursuit of social justice*: Social workers must provide services, resources, and opportunities that work to benefit humanity and protect individuals from harm. It is the role of social workers to advocate for social fairness and equal access to resources, services, and benefits. Social workers must uphold a commitment to reducing barriers

and increasing choices among all people, but particularly to vulnerable, marginalized, or disadvantaged populations. The pursuit of social justice includes countering prejudice, discrimination, and oppression, and addressing and challenging the stereotypes of individuals or groups within society.

3. *Service to humanity*: Social workers must aim to promote the personal development of individuals and groups as outlined in the *Code*. In addition, the power they are given is to be used responsibly and in ways that meet the needs of clients and promote social justice. The knowledge and skills they possess are to be used to resolve conflict and address the wide range of consequences resulting from conflict.

4. *Integrity of professional practice*: Social workers respect and promote the values, purpose, and ethical principles of their profession and their field of practice. They strive for impartiality and refrain from imposing their personal values, views, and preferences on clients and maintain a high level of professional practice. They develop and maintain appropriate professional boundaries and do not negatively affect the reputation of the profession.

5. *Confidentiality in professional practice*: Social workers respect their clients' right to privacy and the importance of the trust their clients have placed in them. This entails keeping client information confidential unless consent has been given by the client or a legal representative of the client to disclose certain information. However, confidentiality can be broken if disclosure is necessary to prevent serious and imminent harm to a client or others or if a court order requires the social worker to disclose specific information received from a client. Social workers must therefore inform their clients about the limitations of the confidentiality agreement before any information is shared.

6. *Competence in professional practice*: Social workers respect their clients' right to be offered the highest quality of service possible. Thus, social workers limit their professional practice to areas where they are most competent. If a social worker is unable to meet the needs of a client, the client must be referred to another social worker or agency. Social workers must continuously focus on professional development as it relates to skills, research, and knowledge relevant to the profession and contributing to the development of the profession as a whole.

In addition to the six core values, the CASW published the *Guidelines for Ethical Practice* (2005b). The *Guidelines* serve as a companion document to the *Code* and provide guidance on ethical practice by applying values and principles in the *Code* to common areas of social work practice. The *Guidelines* outline the responsibilities that social workers hold to clients, professional relationships, colleagues, the workplace, research activities, the profession, and society.

Strengths and Limitations of the CASW *Code of Ethics*

The *Code* provides general principles and a framework to help guide the conduct of social workers and thus holds many important strengths. First, it provides direction and guidelines when ethical dilemmas arise. Second, the *Code* assists in creating and maintaining a professional identity. The presence of the *Code* and its content affirms that social workers, as members of a single profession, share and are publicly committed to the stated values and principles. Third, the *Code* establishes norms related to the profession's mission and methods. Fourth, the *Code* provides standards that can help adjudicate allegations of misconduct, ensure public accountability, and protect clients from malpractice or abuse. Finally, the *Code* provides a public declaration that members of a certain profession should ensure that they have relevant and up-to-date skills, and that they will not discriminate against clients.

Case STUDY

Ethics and Dual Relationships

SOME SOCIAL WORK APPROACHES GROUNDED in the experiences and world-views of Canada's southern regions may be incompatible with the approaches needed for effective practice in Canada's north (Delaney & Brownlee, 2009). Social service delivery differs markedly between Canada's southern and northern regions, shaped by climate, geography, and educational and economic opportunities. Small rural and remote communities have unique features that shape social work practice; thus, approaches to practice in these areas should be contextualized by region-specific realities. One key issue is ethical considerations faced by social workers living and providing services in the same community.

In a qualitative study published in *International Social Work*, Halverson and Brownlee explored perspectives from Canadian social workers living and working in remote communities who must address dual relationships in their practice. Dual relationships were defined as a context where "in addition to the professional relationship between worker and client another meaningful relationship exists" (Halverson & Brownlee, 2010, p. 248). The reality of these types of relationships in rural and remote Canadian communities, particularly in Canada's northern regions, can put social workers in direct conflict with the suggestion by the *Code of Ethics* (CASW, 2005a) that dual relationships be avoided if possible. Researchers interviewed 10 Aboriginal, Francophone, and Anglophone social workers or social service workers in the northern region of Ontario. Participants represented communities numbering 200–300 to 15,000. Key findings were as follows:

Pervasiveness of dual relationships: Rather than the exception in small communities, dual relationships are more of a rule. In these communities where there was only one social worker for a particular service or the social worker was the only worker for all social services in the community, avoiding dual relationships was not feasible. Participants described negotiating dual relationships in a small community context as "inevitable" and a "fact of practice" (p. 252).

While the importance and utility of the *Code* cannot be understated, there are nonetheless limitations that should be acknowledged. There have been increasing critiques of codes and their purpose in social work education and practice (Briskman, 2001). First, the presence of the *Code* may, in some cases, lead social workers to adopt a cautious, formal relational style with some clients. Although a formal relationship style may protect social workers from unwarranted ethical accusations, it may also diminish the quality of client relationships. This same cautiousness may also discourage social workers from considering alternative ethical perspectives. Second, the formal authority of written codes of ethics and their universal approach may overlook or neglect alternative ethical systems, such as those emphasizing collective rather than individual responsibilities. This will be addressed further in Chapter 13 when discussing ethics in a cross-cultural context. Third, some argue that codes of ethics are reflective of dominant discourses and hierarchical power relations and function in ways that preserve the status quo and social order. Codes of ethics are informed by and place high value on individualism, independence, and homogeneity of the client characterized by a liberal democratic philosophy (Noble & Briskman, 1996). In this sense, codes and rules, although necessary and well-intentioned, may favour people

Issues to consider in dual relationships: Ethical decision-making models can be used for social workers faced with potential dual relationships to provide guidance as to whether they should transfer the case to another worker. However, for social workers in small communities with no option to transfer the case to another worker, they used decision-making models and their own intuition and personal and practice experience to assess "the effectiveness of a dual relationship made 'inevitable' by the absence of other alternatives" (p. 253). Some participants also noted that dual relationships were not inherently negative; the effectiveness of the service provided in the context of a dual relationship was affected by the type of "information exposure or power dynamic inherent in the practice area" (p. 254). Thus, while services around education or employment were relatively conflict-free, child welfare, mental health, or abuse areas of practice were the most problematic.

Education and training in dual relationships: All but one participant felt that the social work education curriculum lacked the information and training they felt they needed to successfully negotiate dual relationships. Thus, participants felt that navigating dual relationships was "something you sort of have to learn on your feet" (p. 256). Participants would have also appreciated having self-care strategies offered in the social work curriculum. Social workers who had previous urban experience had the most difficulties with dual relationships, and were only able to continue in this role by creating a buffer zone from community members, isolating themselves. This survival strategy served to increase workers' personal tension, decreasing its effectiveness as a long-term strategy. Others described providing social work services to family or close friends as "draining" (p. 256). Without context-based support strategies and corresponding ethical decision-making models grounded in the realities of social work in small or remote communities, social workers can experience marginalization when receiving training and ethical guidelines that conflict with their everyday realities. Participants recommended that the social work curriculum "equip students with the right tools so they don't have to create their own solutions on the spot" (p. 257).

in certain positions over others. Taking this position even further, some have argued that ethical prescriptions may represent instruments of control rather than moral guides. Fourth, in many situations, the *Code* appears deliberately ambiguous, and the interplay of professional standards, laws, and personal ethical standards can be a challenging part of the social worker's decision-making process. Finally, many have argued that the realms of morality and ethics are inherently socially constructed. In this sense, the moral authority of any group or speaker is historical, rather than timeless, and subject to revision.

Addressing Ethical Dilemmas: The Process of Reflexive Decision-Making

Major ethical issues are inherent in the work of any profession. Yet social workers often confront complex problems, situations, and realities. For example, a social worker may be confronted with a situation where he or she is faced with client behaviours that may be in conflict with his or her personal belief system as well as professional mandate. In this case, a social worker must consider weighing whether "a group has cultural practices that fall outside those of mainstream society but are not hurtful to anyone . . . [or when] cultural practices result in physical or emotional injury" (Mullaly, 2010, p. 243). Or, in practice contexts in small communities, social workers may have to address ethical considerations raised when they live and provide services in the same community.

Each area of social work may have its own unique set of ethical issues. Social workers in daily practice and research make a continuous series of decisions, weighing the relative advantages and disadvantages of various strategies. The work is especially difficult because it has a strong impact on the everyday aspect of the lives of those served. There are multiple, often competing obligations—to clients, clients' families, communities, and the broader society. The work places social workers on the front lines of very real struggles: a struggle for rights, justice, survival, dignity, respect, recognition, peace, and the possibility of a good life. Through university course work and field placements, social workers are now given ethical training and guidelines. Social workers may be provided with guidance, supervision, and formal organizational policies to help frame their work and decisions. However, in the end, social workers must sometimes make ethical decisions on their own. In many situations, social workers may have only a few days or even a few hours to consider what should be done, all the while knowing that the effect of these decisions are likely to have a critical impact on the lives of multiple individuals, families, and communities. Moreover, while the professional *Code* provides a helpful framework and guidelines, it does not offer prescriptive directions, such as "in situation A, you should do B," nor does it establish which values are most important in a given context. In fact, the *Code* states that

> [t]he CASW *Code of Ethics* does not provide a set of rules that prescribe how social workers should act in all situations. Further, the *Code of Ethics* does not specify which values and principles are most important and which outweigh others in instances of conflict. Reasonable differences of opinion exist among social workers with respect to which values and principles should be given priority in a particular situation (p. 2).

As a result, social workers must deal with multiple "grey zones," where competing values are at play. Take the following case example: The client is a 14-year-old adolescent who discloses that she is pregnant. She asks the social worker not to disclose the pregnancy to her parents. Whose interests should the social worker consider foremost? Should it be the client and her right to self-determination? What about the client's parents and their right to know that their child is pregnant? What about the safety and needs of the unborn child? What about the social worker's duty to maintain client confidentiality?

While the *Code* provides guidelines for ethical behaviour, it does not answer questions of individual outcomes in particularly challenging contexts, nor does following the *Code's* guidelines guarantee ethical behaviour. Social workers are confronted with different types of ethical dilemmas all the time on a daily basis whether in research or in practice. The social work literature has increasingly provided frameworks designed to guide practitioners' ethical decision-making to unravel the complexities and address dilemmas that social workers face. While they do not guarantee easy solutions to difficult ethical choices, they provide guidance to assist professionals facing daunting ethical situations. Although these frameworks vary, they tend to share common elements. These include defining the particular case and context, defining the ethical problem, exploring values and biases, gathering relevant information, and considering the multitude of available options.

Before examining the elements included in most ethical decision-making frameworks, it is important to keep in mind that they must not be followed simply and solely in a linear

© Angela Hampton Picture Library / Alamy

A spouse with failing health is having difficulty meeting her husband's caring needs. The social worker has tried to link her with services that would provide her with a restful break and her husband with quality care. The woman has refused everything. The social worker is facing an ethical dilemma as to whether to respect her wishes or step in.

progression. Indeed, a danger in portraying decision-making in a linear way is that the social worker may be perceived as a detached observer to the process. Importantly, social workers are not detached, but are inextricably part of the process. Betan (1997) maintains that this is vital because

> ethics is rooted in regards to human life, and when confronting an ethical circumstance, one calls into service a personal sense of what it is to be human. Thus one cannot intervene in human affairs without being an active participant in defining dimensions of human conduct and human worth (p. 353).

Similarly, Mattison (2000) argues that while logic and rationality are key aspects of decision-making, social workers must also employ reflexivity into their decision-making or what she refers to as "ethical self-reflection." Such self-reflection entails learning more about oneself as a decision-maker, and to better understand the lens one uses to make decisions, as it is impossible to remove personal values, attitudes, and biases from the decision-making process. Therefore, social workers must engage in an active process by considering how their prior socialization, social location, cultural values and orientations, personal values, worldview, the client's values, worldviews, and beliefs, the organizational context, culture and policies, professional context (i.e., values of the social work profession), and societal context (i.e., societal norms) all play a role in influencing moral decision-making. While the elements addressed below may assist social workers in methodically working through ethical dilemmas, the rational aspects of decision-making must not eclipse creativity, multiple ways of knowing and understanding, and reflexivity.

Describe the Case and Context

Because social work ethical issues are usually embedded in complex personal or social issues, one of the most difficult tasks in ethical decision-making is focusing on the problem that must be addressed. In order to do that, social workers begin with a brief description of the setting and a presentation of the case, alongside the contextual (individual, family, community, structural) factors that are key to understanding the case (Loewenberg & Dolgoff, 1996).

Define the Ethical Problem

There is often a large amount of information that has been gathered about the client(s), practice setting(s), and relevant policy. An important task is thus to sort through all the material, until the "bare bones" of the ethical issue can be viewed clearly. This is often challenging as social workers are typically trained to focus upon the interrelationship between elements, but also there may be more than one ethical issue at play in each case. Nonetheless, Loewenberg and Dolgoff (1996) suggest that each ethical issue must be separated out individually as attempting to address more than one issue at a time may confuse the process and issues at play. In complex cases, they argue that it is best to determine the central issue and begin there. In that process, the other issues may resolve themselves. If they continue as problems, after the central issue has been resolved, they can be addressed separately.

When identifying the ethical issue, it is imperative to reflect upon the social work values and duties that may be conflicting. One must also reflect upon and identify the individuals, groups, and organizations that are likely to be affected by the ethical decision. Once an issue has been clearly identified, it may be phrased as an ethical dilemma. For purposes of clarity, dilemmas often take the form of _____ versus _____ (confidentiality vs. duty to warn; or agency policy vs. primacy of the client).

Explore Values and Biases

Throughout the process of decision-making, it is imperative to examine relevant personal, agency, professional, and societal values and biases. Social work professionals should identify all the different values that impinge on their worldviews—their own personal values, unique life experiences, social location, training, and belief systems. Personal values affect the way in which a dilemma is interpreted, and the theories and principles used to arrive at a resolution. It is important to recognize any personal biases that are likely to have an impact on decision-making.

The agency in which a social worker operates and the ethical position of supervisors, colleagues, and directors can strongly affect decision-making. Workers must understand that sharing an ethical dilemma with a colleague or supervisor can lead to his or her values becoming a factor in the equation, which also must be considered.

The resolution of an ethical dilemma should be compatible with the client's values, social location, worldview, religious beliefs, and other factors relevant to the client. It is the responsibility of each worker to examine and understand client values, so that these can be integrated into the decision-making process. This approach is supported by the core values of dignity and worth of the person.

Gather Information: Research, Theory, and the _Code of Ethics_

To make competent and informed ethical decisions, social workers must conduct thorough research about the issue and case at hand. As an example, for an elderly client who

In Their Own Words

INDIGENOUS ETHICS

ETHICS STEM FROM OUR WORLDVIEWS and our cultural ways of knowing. In Indigenous contexts, ethics are derived from Indigenous ontologies (the nature of existence) and epistemologies (science of knowledge). Denzin (2008) described Indigenous epistemology as

> a sacred, existential epistemology [that] places humans in a non-competitive, non-hierarchical relationship to the earth, to nature and to the larger world. This sacred epistemology stresses the values of empowerment, shared governance, care, solidarity, love, community, covenant, morally involved observers, and civic transformation. This sacred epistemology recovers the moral values that were excluded by the rational, Enlightenment science project (p. 117–118).

The sacral and spiritual preeminence hints at the nature of Indigenous ethics and how these might shape social activities such as social work and research practices. There are many fundamental ethical tenets common to Indigenous nations globally, but here just three will be articulated: the ethics of interrelatedness, community, and reciprocity. These ethics stem from natural law as learned by Indigenous ancestors and encompass codes of conduct entailing moral and social imperatives. They highlight concomitant values, beliefs, protocols, practices, and responsibilities to self, family, and community. Within the ethic of interrelatedness is a communitarian ethic that frames individuals as one part of a larger connected whole. This ethic is captured in the universal Indigenous concept of "All My Relations" (King, 1990). We conduct ourselves not only as a member of a family, community, and nation; the responsibilities span time in the sense that our actions require us to be accountable to our ancestors who prayed for us and to the future generations to whom we leave mother earth. Humans are bound by a web of kinship to all human beings, animals, and to all of nature. The ethic of reciprocity is one way that we honour interrelatedness because it specifically acknowledges the ebb and flow, give and take of life. For example, time and knowledge are gifts that humans give each other all the time and so the tobacco offering, *Pakitinâsowin* in Cree (Michell, 1999), is a protocol that honours the ethic of reciprocity. This is why Indigenous cultures give gifts and medicines. The acts of both giving and receiving honour the ethic of reciprocity, which in turn honours the ethic of interrelatedness. Indigenous ethics hold human beings to certain protocols and conduct and the accrued responsibilities span spiritual, cultural, and social realms. In social work, Indigenous ethics stemming from Indigenous sciences of knowledge and understandings of nature and the cosmos are the foundations from which we develop, frame, and structure our work and the processes and protocols that we undertake in daily practice. All My Relations!

Dr Raven Sinclair is an associate professor at the Faculty of Social Work, University of Regina.

is refusing to enter into long-term care, information gathering may include research about clients who remain at home in precarious conditions, statistics on injuries to elderly clients who live alone, laws about personal rights and freedoms, research on adjustment of patients to long-term care settings, exploration of available resources or services in the home for older adults, studies about life satisfaction at home and in institutional settings, information about the client's medical conditions, an examination of the client's family and support network, and so forth. In addition, it is also helpful to explore the broader principles, rights, and obligations that define the dilemma. For example, using this example, it would mean examining the concept of self-determination—what it means and the conditions under which it may be limited—will help the worker gain a deeper level of understanding. Helpful information is often available within the agency itself and information gathering should occur by consulting with colleagues, supervisors, and program directors who are likely to have insight to offer regarding the resolution of ethical dilemmas.

To assist in resolving an ethical dilemma, workers can gather information on available ethical theories and principles to guide their thinking. Ethical theories can help to provide a framework that can be used to determine the principles that aid in ethical decision-making and provide general strategies for defining the ethical actions to be taken in any given situation.

When resolving an ethical dilemma, information and guidance should be sought from the *Code*. The *Code* should be reviewed carefully and sections that are applicable to one's dilemma should be considered. The *Code* can assist social workers as it clearly defines professional behaviour and expectations in many areas. Social workers can also draw upon relevant laws and case decisions.

Explore Options

Using all available information, the social worker can begin to explore several possible options for action. All possible courses of action should be considered alongside the participants involved and the possible benefits and risks. The social worker must thoroughly examine the reasons in favour of and opposed to each possible course of action and the options must be feasible and realistic. The worker can list all of the potential benefits and harms or costs of a particular course of action. In some cases, the costs are so high that options are likely to be eliminated completely. In considering various options, social workers should hypothesize about the possible consequences of different decisions, identifying who will benefit and who will be harmed. In addition, it is important to also address and assess alternative courses of action and their potential harms and benefits. In the course of defining and considering all available options, social workers should continue to consult with colleagues both within and outside of the profession. This can include agency staff, supervisors, the clients and their support networks, agency administrators, attorneys, and ethics scholars.

As options are gradually and carefully discarded, the worker may determine the best course of action and implement it. If unforeseen issues arise that render the option unfeasible, unrealistic, or problematic, the social worker may resort to another option or begin the process again. From the several possibilities that have been considered in depth, the option that is selected should be one that maximizes benefits to all involved. Once an option has been selected, an implementation plan needs to be developed. Moreover, the social worker should keep track of the immediate and long-term consequences of the process and the decision(s) made through careful monitoring and evaluation.

As noted earlier, following ethical guidelines does not guarantee ethical social work practice (Gray & Gibbons, 2007). Moreover, linear guidelines can often create the false notion that risk and consequences can be predicted, and that ethical issues can be easily resolved with rational and logical thinking. As such, while social workers may draw upon ethical guidelines to assist in the decision-making process, it is imperative that they accept the uncertainty and ambiguity inherent in ethical dilemmas, and engage in a reflexive process integrating social work knowledge, skills, theory, experience, and values into their practice. As Gray and Gibbons (2007) write:

> It is necessary for [social work students] to be able to accept and deal with uncertainty and ambiguity and the absence of cookbook solutions, and to learn that when moral conflicts or ethical dilemmas arise, they can only be resolved through dialogue and a process of moral reasoning, where existing knowledge, theory, skills, values and ethical guidelines are brought together to inform the decision-making process (p. 224).

Social Work Ethics in Research

How Is Research Connected to Social Work?

Before beginning a discussion of ethical issues in research, it is important to emphasize the mutually dependent relationship between social work practice and research. In order to best fulfill their responsibilities to clients, social workers must strive to provide the most effective services available as well as increase their practice effectiveness. If you are a social worker meeting for the first time with a client who has come for help in addressing a particular issue, where do you start? Do you look at how other practitioners have worked with clients with the same or a similar issue? Do you review current research that has been conducted on that issue? Social workers need to feel comfortable utilizing research generated by others and be able to critically evaluate research. Research studies are not equal in terms of quality nor are their findings relevant for all clients. You might read about an intervention's impressive outcomes, but how do you know if it will be effective with your client? Who comprised the study sample? Were research participants similar to your client in terms of socio-economic status, ethnocultural background, years of education, level of literacy, or proficiency in English or French? Research is context-bound—findings relevant for an intervention for one particular client at one particular time may not be applicable for another client facing the same issue or for same client at a different point in time. All social workers—not only those focused on research or policy analysis—should have a fundamental understanding of social work research with regard to what constitutes evidence for "best" practices and how multifaceted economic, political, ethical, and cultural contexts shape all aspects of the research process.

Research in the Social Work Education Curriculum

Research courses are included in the social work curriculum for multiple reasons. Reasons include

- introducing **quantitative** and **qualitative approaches** in social work research;
- increasing familiarity with research methods used to evaluate research in order to apply findings to practice;
- gaining an understanding and appreciation of an analytic approach to building knowledge for practice;
- applying social work ethics and values to the research process;
- growing an awareness of gender, sexual orientation, and culturally related research issues;
- cultivating an ability to critically review published research; and
- applying lessons learned to social work practice.

quantitative approach
Focuses on the production of numerical findings that can be statistically interpreted in order to generalize them to populations beyond the study sample. Ways of collecting data typically include questionnaires, experiments, and using data collected previously (called secondary data).

qualitative approach
A way to "study things in their natural settings, attempting to make sense of, or interpret, phenomena in terms of the meanings that people bring to them" (Denzin & Lincoln, 2005, p. 3). Ways of collecting data typically include in-depth interviews, field observations, and reviews of written documents and data are expressed as words, images, objects, or sounds (Neuman & Robson, 2012).

Studies have found that although research is an important part of practice—integrating practice experience into research and utilizing research evidence to inform practice—there remains reticence, and in some cases antagonism, regarding the incorporation of research into the social work curriculum at both the master's and bachelor's level. Epstein (1987) found that "no other part of the social work curriculum has been so consistently received by students with as much groaning, moaning, eyerolling, bad-mouthing, hyperventilation and waiver-strategizing as the research courses . . ." (p. 71). Secret, Ford and Rompf (2003) found that women social work students or those less familiar with statistics were fearful of taking required research courses. In a qualitative study of social work students' perceptions of the research process, Maschi, Probst and Bradley (2009) reported that nearly two thirds of respondents (n=70) used such descriptors of their experiences of their research course as "stressed," "overwhelmed," "petrified," and "drained" (p. 69). Maschi and colleagues traced the tensions of social workers to research in the early years of organized social work at the turn of the twentieth century when Mary Richmond called for the adoption of the scientific approach in order to systematize and professionalize social work practice. As part of Value 6 of the *Code*, Competence in Professional Practice, there is clear promotion for social workers to dedicate themselves to upholding and enhancing their professional knowledge and skill by contributing "to the ongoing development of the profession and its ability to serve humanity, where possible, by participating in the development of current and future social workers and the development of new professional knowledge" (2005, p. 8). So although social work research and practice are mutually reinforcing, there remains some resistance to reinforcing these linkages in the social work curriculum. It is in the context of social work education that these linkages should be made so as to reduce tendencies to reinforce divisions between research and practice that maintain unhelpful within-discipline silos.

Evidence-Based Practice

Social work has a tradition of developing, expanding, and continually revising practice models in order to address the needs of diverse populations of clients. However, the effectiveness of social work interventions is rarely studied with regard to client outcomes (Proctor & Rosen, 2008). Increasingly, social work students and practitioners are being trained to systematically and critically review the published literature to identify models of practice for which there is some evidence of effectiveness (Gambrill, 2006) and to appraise the relevance of these models for the clients they serve and issues they are hoping to address. This **evidence-based practice** approach aims to help practitioners use research findings to guide clinical decision-making.

evidence-based practice
An approach that "bring[s] practice and research together so as to strengthen the scientific knowledge base supporting social work intervention" (Mullen, Bledsoe, & Bellamy, 2008, p. 326).

Advocates of the approach suggest that evidence-informed practice maximizes ethical standards by ensuring a rational approach to service delivery that is just, equitable, and effective (McCracken & Marsh, 2008; Mullen, Bledsoe, & Bellamy, 2008). The approach is guided by a series of steps designed to help practitioners (1) convert their need for information into an answerable question; (2) locate the best evidence to answer the question; (3) critically appraise the evidence for validity and usefulness; (4) integrate research knowledge, clinical expertise, and client preferences into a practice decision; and (5) evaluate the outcomes of their actions (Sackett, Straus, Richardson, Rosenberg, & Haynes, 2000).

practice-based evidence
Calls upon practitioners to think about the outcome they and their clients hope to achieve and represent the outcome in a measurable way.

Connected to the evidence-based approach is **practice-based evidence**, which calls upon practitioners to think about the outcome they and their clients hope to achieve during the course of their interactions, and implement a means of representing the outcome in a measurable way.

This process of generating research from practice asks practitioners to become more aware of what they are trying to accomplish by incorporating research-based concepts, theories, and data-gathering techniques to structure daily practice. Thus, outcomes tailored to the goals of a specific case can be more easily evaluated. Carried out by practitioners in the context of their work, this approach helps formalize the process of evaluation that occurs naturally when practitioners reflect on a case, consult with a colleague, or prepare a report to justify a treatment plan (Wade & Neuman, 2007).

Overview of Social Work Research

Social work research is as diverse as the field of social work itself. Social work researchers may employ quantitative or qualitative approaches or a mixture of the two in order to explore new areas of study, describe interventions or social phenomena, explain why something happens the way it does, evaluate the effectiveness of an intervention or program, create social change in a particular area and/or for a population facing a particular issue, or utilize research as advocacy. What we seek to know shapes our approach to knowing and that approach must be infused with ethical considerations from the beginning of the research process. Not only are study findings important for social work practice, but also the ways in which research is conducted has critical implications for research participants and their communities as well as the trust relationships that are made between researcher and participant. This is particularly true for communities that have been historically marginalized. Social work research must be conscious of the tendency to perpetuate

> research through 'imperial eyes' [that] describes an approach which assumes that Western ideas about the most fundamental things are the only ideas possible to hold, certainly the only rational ideas, and the only ideas which can make sense of the world, of reality, of social life and of human beings (Tuhiwai Smith, 1999, p. 56).

There are ethical considerations in every research study regardless of approach, sample size, purposes, and degrees of engagement with individuals who provide the data.

Exploratory research typically focuses on a "new" topic about which the researcher wants to learn more and seeks to build a foundation of general knowledge about a topic and provide support to initial theory making. Exploratory designs assess the study outcomes without attempting to prove a link between those outcomes and activities believed to have caused them. An exploratory approach is useful in showing whether a participant's objective is changing in a desired direction but is limited in that one cannot draw conclusions that the intervention is causing the perceived change. **Descriptive studies** use systematic, intentional data collection in order to describe a population, organization, and so forth, such as the Canadian Census or the Longitudinal Survey of Immigrants to Canada (LSIC), to provide an accurate portrait of various characteristics of populations. Such quantitative studies are based on quantitative data obtained from a sample of people thought to be representative of that population. Descriptive studies may show that two variables are related (correlation) but they cannot establish causality between variables. Building on exploratory and descriptive studies, **explanatory studies** seek to answer the "why" question by testing hypotheses, expanding a theory's explanation for a particular phenomenon, or assessing which explanation, such as an intervention, is most effective for particular populations. These studies are designed to establish causality: they seek to show that an intervention (independent variable) caused change in the behaviour/condition being measured (dependent variable). There is typically random assignment to treatment groups. An explanatory design would be used to understand and predict outcomes. They are often called experimental designs. **Evaluation studies** might use any or all three of the previous approaches to assess a program, an intervention, or a service. For example, if one is exploring the service needs of a community, one might first have exploratory interviews with community members. Then one might construct a descriptive community survey based on the interview findings to

exploratory research Focuses on a "new" topic about which the researcher wants to learn more.

descriptive studies The use of systematic, intentional data collection in order to describe a population, organization, and so forth to provide an accurate portrait of various characteristics of populations.

explanatory studies Focuses on seeking to answer the "why" question by testing hypotheses, expanding a theoretical explanation, or assessing which explanation is most effective for particular populations.

evaluation studies The use of any of the approaches from exploratory, descriptive, and explanatory research to assess a program, an intervention, or a service.

In Their Own Words

ETHICS AND COMMUNITY-BASED RESEARCH

AS A COMMUNITY-BASED RESEARCHER, ETHICS are something I consider and struggle with throughout every step of a research project. From how the research is framed to how findings are disseminated, community-based research has the potential not only to increase our understanding of a particular social issue, but also to have direct impacts, be they positive or negative, on those involved with the research. In my experience, using participatory approaches can increase the potential of the research to act as an empowering process for community participants.

While the agency I work with occasionally conducts research in partnership with a university, which requires a formal ethics review process through the institution's research ethics board, the majority of our research is conducted independently, or in partnership with other community agencies. In such cases, there is no formal review process. Ethical considerations are critically discussed amongst colleagues taking participant and community interests, agency and professional guidelines, and previous learnings into account.

One area frequently discussed during such formal and informal review processes relates to how research participants can and should be compensated for contributing their expert knowledge. I see the use of honorariums as a way to recognize these contributions and reduce potential barriers to participation for those with lower incomes. However, such compensation must be balanced with the possibility of overly incenting participation and potentially jeopardizing its voluntary nature. We also work to make

see the proportion of community residents who have a particular problem and need corresponding services. After the descriptive study, one might employ an explanatory design to ascertain whether certain factors explain why some groups have higher utilization rates than others. Clear expectations and guidelines are essential when conducting evaluations at the request of an agency. What if the study findings reflect poorly on the agency? When working within a single site, how does the researcher ensure that a participant's responses remain confidential?

While research findings from exploratory, descriptive, explanatory, or evaluation studies can be used for the purposes of creating social change, social work researchers also utilize the research process itself as a vehicle for social change. This action-oriented approach to research seeks to promote self-discovery of individuals, build communities, and serve as a catalyst for the promotion of social justice. For action research projects, participants are actively involved, often in the design, implementation, analysis, and dissemination stages of the research. Action research projects typically challenge the traditional hierarchy of researcher and participant and are often conducted with individuals and groups who have traditionally been marginalized. Often, action research projects include training components to promote skill building and increase capacity in the communities with which researchers are working.

Conducting Ethical Research

As was noted earlier in the chapter, while the *Code* (2005) provides guidelines for ethical behaviour, it does not answer questions of individual outcomes in particularly challenging contexts and does not guarantee ethical behaviour in practice or research. Social workers also have an obligation to learn about ethical issues in the context of social work research sure project logistics support our ethical considerations, including the use of safe and accessible locations and spaces for focus group discussions, for example, and ensuring access to other types of support, such as free counselling services, when needed.

By involving community members throughout the process, I see the potential to mitigate some of the power imbalances related to voice and representation, which are often evident in the researcher-participant relationship. While working on a digital storytelling project with youth, for example, participants narrated a story or experience of importance to them and chose related images, photographs, and other visual tools to create a short video. The participants were active agents in the research given their role as the storytellers and their ability to directly frame and give voice to their experience. They were also the ultimate owners of the videos they created: each time there was an opportunity to show the videos publicly, the storytellers were able to decide if they wanted to share their video at that forum with that audience. Storytellers also had the ability to share their videos in their own, independent ways, and they could decide if they wanted their story used for academic research purposes or not.

I think a goal to always strive toward with community research is that participants truly own the project, the research findings, and the actions the process inspires. Through my work with community, I see research as an exciting and powerful tool for not only deepening our understanding of social issues but for meaningful social change.

Alison Kent is a community-based researcher in Alberta.

and consider the ways in which who we are—our social locations, values, beliefs, and traditions, our theoretical practice and/or research paradigms—shape how research is utilized and conducted. The *Code* cites that "both the spirit and the letter of this *Code* will guide social workers as they act in good faith and with a genuine desire to make sound judgements" (p. 2). Social workers cannot be separated from their social location, which unavoidably influences what is considered acting in good faith as well as making sound judgments. Thus, it is essential to incorporate and reflect upon the *Code* in social work decision-making.

Origins of Contemporary Ethical Guidelines in Research

While the importance of including ethical guidelines in research would seem to be a foundational piece in the history of research, the codification of ethical conduct in research is a relatively recent phenomenon. It was only after World War II and the revelations of the atrocities committed by Nazi doctors that the international research community moved for universal principles of research to which researchers should be held accountable. Based on the trials in Nuremberg, Germany, of Nazi doctors accused of committing heinous, tortuous experiments on human beings imprisoned in concentration camps during the war, ten principles were developed to protect human research participants (Shuster, 1997). These ten principles, referred to as the Nuremberg Code, were specifically designed for medical research but also have served as the foundation for research ethics guidelines across disciplines. Key elements included voluntary consent to participate in research, conducting research beneficial to participants as well as society at large, avoiding unnecessary physical and psychological harm to participants, and participants' rights including the right to withdraw from a research study.

Jadwiga Dzido, victim of medical experiments while held captive in a concentration camp, testifies at the Nuremberg Trials in 1942.

In 1964, the World Medical Assembly adopted the Declaration of Helsinki to provide greater protection to research participants across disciplines. Key areas of the Declaration of Helsinki included the importance of participant well-being over scientific and societal interests, the need to respect participants and protect their health and rights, the recognition of specific populations that require additional protections (such as children and individuals with disabilities that could influence their ability to provide informed consent to research participation), and the requirement that researchers have a research ethics board review potential research (Perlman, 2004). Today, researchers are required to submit an ethics application to the university body, research institute or other entity to which the researcher is affiliated. The purpose of the review is to determine the ethical administration of research involving human participants in order to protect their rights and welfare. In universities, these bodies (often titled Research Ethics Boards or Institutional Review Boards) have the power to approve, disapprove, or require modifications in order to approve studies being conducted by university faculty, staff, or students.

Even with entities committed to reviewing research proposals to ensure ethical acceptability, research has had a tumultuous relationship with Indigenous communities in Canada, which has left behind a legacy of mistrust due to unethical research practices by some non-Indigenous researchers (Brant Castellano, 2004; Brown, 2005). Past research in Indigenous communities has been assailed for being "conducted in ways that excluded the people it aimed to understand" and contributing to the continuation of negative stereotypes of Indigenous Peoples (First Nations Centre, 2007, p. 3). Schnarch (2004) provides a comprehensive list of ways in which "research has gone wrong" (p. 81), including entities collecting data on Indigenous Peoples without their knowledge or consent and using data for purposes other than what Indigenous Peoples consented to without permission. For example, from 1982 to 1985, a medical genetics researcher from the University of British Columbia (UBC), Dr Richard Ward, collected blood samples from the Nuu-chah-nulth people in Vancouver (Wiwchar, 2005). Eight hundred and eighty-three members of the Nuu-chah-nulth community consented to participate in a study exploring genetic pre-disposition to rheumatic diseases in First Nations communities and thus provided blood samples. The study was completed, and the findings did not reveal genetic markers in the DNA of study participants. However, the findings were not communicated to participants, and the lead researcher left UBC for another institution and subsequently used the blood samples for a biological anthropology research project unrelated to the study to which participants had consented. One outcome of this unethical conduct was the development of the Nuu-chah-nulth Research Ethics Committee. Other Indigenous communities have also created committees to control access to their communities for research purposes as well as developed codes of research ethics (See "Theory in Practice" box for a description of the Kahnawá:ke Schools Diabetes Prevention Project). Although research and practice are intertwined, history is filled with examples of research that has been misused with various populations, which although not necessarily contributing to a fear of research, certainly contributed to an animosity towards it.

Ethical Considerations for Social Workers in Research

Central to the social work profession is the protection of clients. Therefore, what are social workers' ethical responsibilities regarding research? For social workers committed to social justice, it is imperative to understand the myriad ethical issues that can occur in any research study, identify our dual roles as researcher and social worker, and position ourselves in relation to these issues (Padgett, 2008).

Ownership, Control, Access, and Possession (OCAP)

Given the negative history of research with Indigenous Peoples in Canada, there are particular guidelines one must follow that go above and beyond what is provided in policies guiding Canada's main research-funding institutions (Canadian Institutes of Health Research, Natural Sciences and Engineering Research Council of Canada, and Social Sciences and Humanities Research Council of Canada, also known as the Tri-Council). The OCAP principles grew out of the context of an overabundance of past research that had seen First Nations Peoples only as research subjects and that had been used against and/or had perpetuated harmful stereotypes of First Nations Peoples (First Nations Centre, 2007). While the OCAP principles can be pertinent and applicable to Inuit and Métis populations as well as Indigenous Peoples internationally, the OCAP principles were developed in a First Nations context, informed by their aspirations for self-determination and sovereignty and their historical connections to the research process in Canada (Schnarch, 2004). Guidelines for ethical research practice are centred around the OCAP principles, which stand for Ownership, Control, Access, and Possession. Ownership refers to "the relationship of a First Nations community to its cultural knowledge/data/information. The principle states that a community or group owns information collectively in the same way that an individual owns their personal information" (First Nations Centre, 2007, p. 4). Control refers more broadly to the rights of First Nations to control all aspects of their lives, and more specifically, all research and the information and data generated which affect them. This includes control of review processes, theoretical and conceptual development, and ways in which to manage data. Access highlights First Nations Peoples' rights to be able to access data about them and their communities regardless of the location

Theory in Practice

KAHNAWÁ:KE SCHOOLS DIABETES PREVENTION PROJECT

THE KAHNAWÁ:KE SCHOOLS DIABETES PREVENTION Project (KSDPP) Center for Research and Training in Diabetes Prevention is a community-based participatory research project developed in response to a high rate of Type II diabetes in the community (Horn, Jacobs-Whyte, Ing, Bruegl, Paradis, & Macaulay, 2007; Montour & Macaulay, 1985). In 1994, KSDPP was created as a partnership between the Kanien'kehá:ka (Mohawk) community of Kahnawá:ke and researchers affiliated with KSDPP from the community as well as McGill University, Université de Montréal, and Queen's University. The project's main goal is to mobilize the community to promote healthy lifestyles with the long-term goal of preventing diabetes, thus contributing to positive health outcomes for present and future generations of Kanien'kehá:ka (Macaulay, Cargo, Bisset, Delormier, Lévesque, Potvin, & McComber, 2006). The community of Kahnawá:ke directs the project, ensuring that Kanien'kehá:ka traditions are infused into decision-making at all levels.

A key outcome of the project has been the development of KSDPP's own *Code of Research Ethics*, a result of negotiations between Kahnawá:ke community members and academic researchers (Brown, 2005). The *Code*'s purpose is "to establish a set of principles and procedures that will guide the partners to achieve the goals and objectives of the KSDPP" (KSDPP, 2007, p. 3) and is designed to guide the partnership throughout all stages of research. The *Code* explicitly integrates decolonizing methodologies and Haudenosaunee (Iroquois Peoples) philosophy:

> Solving issues of ethically responsible research requires an understanding of what it means to be Onkwehón:we [the Original People]. The development of distinctly Indigenous research practices facilitates culturally appropriate solutions to various research concerns. In this way, not only are Onkwehón:we peoples contributing to developing respectful research protocols in their own communities, they are also using the knowledge they have inherited to understand themselves better (KSDPP, 2007, p. 3).

> Principles in the *Code*, relevant for all community-based research, include

- the Kanien'kehá:ka and the philosophy of the Kanien'kehá:ka must be respected;
- academic researchers and the professional responsibilities of academic researchers must be respected;

of the data. Possession literally refers to stewardship of the data and ensuring a respectful relationship between ownership and possession.

Do No Harm—Physical, Psychological, or Otherwise

Social work research should not cause injury to participants who are involved in a study. Precautions must be in place to eliminate or greatly reduce any potential physical or psychological harm or emotional distress for participants. Researchers must consider whether the possible cost to participants outweighs the benefit for the social work knowledge base or more directly for others with similar experiences to participants. For example, in planning a study of torture survivors, a researcher must consider the possibility

- research must respect and include Indigenous methodologies, incorporating the strengths, knowledge, experiences, and culture of the community;
- the community is an equal partner in all aspects of the research. Continuous consultation and collaboration must characterize the partnership;
- research must be relevant and beneficial to the community;
- research must provide opportunities for involvement of community researchers and utilize community resources;
- meaningful community capacity-building must be incorporated into all aspects of the research process;
- all research must undergo the Review and Approval Process for Ethically Responsible Research;
- ethical approval must be granted from all partners before research begins;
- active, free, and informed consent must be obtained from all participants;
- research must ensure confidentiality and anonymity of individuals, organizations, and communities unless these parties choose to be named when the results are reported;
- research analyses, interpretations, and results must be presented to and discussed by all partners to ensure accuracy and avoid misunderstanding;
- reports and summaries must be returned in a language and format that is comprehensible to the community;
- research results must be presented to the community before being disseminated in the public domain;
- all partners must be involved in making decisions about the publication and dissemination of the research;
- a partner has the right to dissent concerning interpretation of research results. A differing interpretation of results must be fully explained and agreed upon through the consensual decision-making process. The community retains ownership, control, access, and possession of all data collected. As guardian of the data, the community must continue to ensure confidentiality and anonymity of individuals, organizations, and communities;
- academic researchers must keep a copy of data to meet their institutional responsibilities. (All future use of data must comply with all the above-mentioned principles).

For more information, visit http://www.ksdpp.org/elder/code_ethics.php.

of retraumatization when asking participants to recount their experiences. Or in another study, participants may be asked to reveal behaviours that could be considered atypical or even illegal, attitudes they feel are uncomfortable, or personal characteristics they may find demeaning (Rubin & Babbie, 2005). Revealing this type of information could make the participant feel uncomfortable. Social work research projects may also force participants to face aspects of themselves that they may not have faced before or which they see as problematic. Any research has the potential of causing harm to people. Researchers must be sensitive to the issue of focus and be highly aware of possible implications of the findings, first and foremost for the community from which data were gathered. For example, while Kovach (2009) is referring to work in Indigenous communities, her discussion of the

OCAP principles is applicable to the interests of any individual or group that is the focus of research. She asserted that OCAP "provides researchers with explicit guidelines for assessing whether said research is exploitative or beneficial to Indigenous interests" (p. 145).

Research Participation Should Be Voluntary and Informed

Social work research follows a major principle of medical research ethics: participation must be voluntary. All volunteers must be aware that they are participating in a study, be informed of the consequences of the study, and consent to participate. Researchers must be aware of the potential for coercion. For example, one must consider carefully how much to provide when offering cash remuneration for study participation as an amount too small might not be an incentive or could be insulting whereas an amount too large risks coercion (Padgett, 2008). One must also examine the relationship between the researcher and potential participants and consider the power dynamics. Individuals may feel pressured to participate in a study if asked by a professor who is currently teaching them or supervising them. Involuntary clients, such as those who are incarcerated, may feel that

Practical TIP

Key Elements of a Consent Form

- explicit statement that the study involves research;
- clearly described research purposes;
- expected duration of the participant's participation;
- what study participation will entail;
- clear identification of any experimental procedures;
- explanation of possible risks or discomforts the participant may experience as a result of participating in the study;
- description of any benefits to the participant or to others which may reasonably be expected from the research;
- disclosure of an alternative procedure or intervention, if any, that might be beneficial and available to the participant;
- description of measures taken by the researcher to protect the participant's privacy (a clear statement regarding confidentiality or anonymity of the participant's information and identity);
- clear statement regarding any compensation provided for study participation;
- explanation as to whether any medical treatments are available if injury occurs and, if so, what they consist of or where further information may be obtained;
- explanation of whom to contact for answers to questions about research and research participants' rights (sometimes the Ethics Officer at a university or research institute), and whom to contact in the event of a research-related injury to the participant;
- statement that participation is voluntary, refusal to participate will involve no penalty or loss of benefits for which the participant is eligible, and the participant may withdraw from the study at any time without penalty.

These are fundamental elements—each consent form should be specifically tailored to the research context, shaped by the specific type of study, the research approach, and the participant sample.

although not stated, their "cooperation" could influence treatment or services they receive. In these cases, participation is not voluntary but is spurred by other reasons apart from an interest in the study.

A consent form should be provided to all research participants. Always bring two copies for each participant so that the participant can have a copy and the researcher will have the original in case it is difficult to locate participants later on (Padgett, 2008). In most cases, researchers should obtain signatures from participants, except in cases where the process of signing could jeopardize the participant's welfare (for example, participants may not want to sign consent forms if they are in Canada without legal status).

It is important to adapt the consent form (or assent form if the participant is a minor) to the perceived literacy levels of participants as well as translate them into participants' language of origin if possible. As the goal is informed consent, the researcher should make every effort to ensure that the participant is fully informed regarding what he or she is signing.

Disclosure and Deception

The need to conceal the nature of the study from those who are being observed is another ethical issue that involves the principle of voluntary participation and informed consent. How much should a researcher disclose to participants or to those in the research setting? This need stems from the concern that participants' knowledge of the focus of the study might significantly influence the processes being studied among those participants. Padgett (2008) outlined a range of concealment situations that researchers face: (a) Disclosure, where a researcher is transparent about the nature of the study and the researcher's role in it; (b) Neglect, where the researcher does not inform people that they are being observed; and (c) Full Deceit, where the researcher hides both the study and his or her role in it. Where a study might fall on the continuum depends on the research purposes and the approach being used. For example, it would be highly unlikely for a researcher who is using an action research approach to conceal his or her identity from study participants. It is important to note in some qualitative research studies that involve observation, it may not be required that to notify "every person within eyesight of the researcher" (Padgett, 2008, p. 65). However, given the substantial harm that deception has caused to those unknowingly involved in research studies in the past (see Questions for Critical Thought, Question #3 below), in order to justify using deception to a Research Ethics Board to obtain approval for the study, one would need to demonstrate that the study could not be conducted unless deception is used, debriefing sessions with participants had been arranged after completion of the study, and most important, the benefit of the study (and thus the deception) vastly outweighed the risk to participants (Padgett, 2008).

Protect Participants' Privacy by Keeping Their Information Anonymous or Confidential

It is the researcher's responsibility to protect the identity of study participants. It is important to clarify for participants if their data will be anonymous or confidential. **Anonymous data** mean that no one, including the researcher, can trace the data provided by a participant back to the participant who provided it. **Confidential data** are data that could be linked with a particular participant; however, it is the researcher's responsibility to ensure that these connections are not made public (Rubin & Babbie, 2005).

Therefore, it is a critical component of research studies to be explicit as to how one will maintain confidentiality and thus protect a participant's privacy. For example, any interview transcript or questionnaire should not contain any link to the participant's identity. This means that the participant's name, initials, or date of birth should not linked to the data in any way. Rather, a unique identifier should be used in organizing the data

anonymous data
Information that no one, including the researcher, can trace back to the participant who provided it.

confidential data
Information that could be linked with a particular participant but those connections are not made public.

(e.g., Participant 1 or a pseudonym) and any master list connecting participants to identifiers should be kept securely. An important exception to the maintenance of participant confidentiality is in cases of child abuse. Researchers (as well as social work practitioners) are legally mandated to report child abuse.

Dissemination of Findings

Dissemination of research findings is a key piece to ethical research. It is the researcher's responsibility to ensure that the research is available and accessible to the community (whether it is a community connected by ethnicity, culture, history, geography, etc.) from whom it was gathered, in addition to other entities such as academic journals and government reports. The researcher should be accountable to the relationship that was built with the community and ask how he or she as the researcher can give back to the community in a way that is available and accessible (Kovach, 2009). While the findings might be geared toward the research or practice communities, part of the "trust obligation" that the researcher has with the study participants "requires . . . that the products that came from the work of people are attributed rightfully back to the people, in a manner that is recognizable and attached to its initial formulation" (First Nations Centre, 2007, p. 1). For example, the researcher could provide a summary of the findings suitable for a community newsletter, reducing social work and research jargon to strive for accessibility for those who read it.

Conclusion

It is essential to incorporate and reflect upon the ethical standards provided in the *Code* and the *Guidelines for Ethical Practice* in social work decision-making in both practice and research. How does one decide which path to take? What approach is relevant for this particular context? What must one consider in the decision-making process? What are the ethical implications of the choices one makes? This chapter reviewed ethical considerations in social work practice and research. Special attention was paid to the history of ethics in social work, the CASW *Code of Ethics*, ethical decision-making, ethical research with Indigenous Peoples, and ensuring ethical behaviour when conducting research.

QUESTIONS FOR CRITICAL THOUGHT

1. The CASW *Code of Ethics* was published in 2005. Based on your knowledge of the *Code* and your practice and research experience, if the *Code* is revised in the future, what aspects of the *Code* should be included, revised, or further developed?
2. Reflect upon a recent ethical dilemma that you experienced in your work. Drawing on your knowledge of the *Code* and *Guidelines*, alongside the ethical decision-making tools noted above and "ethical self-reflection," how might you resolve the dilemma?
3. What are some of the challenges to obtaining informed consent in research? Discuss how you might go about obtaining informed consent from (a) youth, (b) participants whose first language is not English or French, and (c) participants who are not literate in their language of origin.
4. Look up the "Tuskegee Study of Untreated Syphilis" conducted by the US Public Health Service from 1932 to 1972 on African-American men and the study by Laud Humphries chronicled in his book, *Tearoom Trade: Impersonal Sex in Public Places* (1970) on gay men. How would informing the people who were the focus of the study change the study outcomes? Can you think of a contemporary situation where deception in a research study would be harmful to the researcher and to the research participant?

RECOMMENDED READINGS

Canadian Association of Social Workers (CASW). (2005). *Code of Ethics*. Author. The *Code* sets forth the six values and principles to guide social workers' professional conduct. These include respect for inherent dignity and worth of persons, the pursuit of social justice, service to humanity, integrity of professional practice, confidentiality in professional practice, and competence in professional practice.

Canadian Association of Social Workers (CASW). (2005). *Guidelines for Ethical Practice*. Author. The *Guidelines* outline the responsibilities that social workers hold to clients, professional relationships, colleagues, workplace, research activities, the profession, and to society.

Kovach, M. (2009). *Indigenous methodologies: Characteristics, conversations, and contexts*. Toronto: University of Toronto Press. This text discusses what Indigenous research methodologies are and ways in which they differ from mainstream Western approaches. One chapter focuses specifically on ethical practice of Indigenous research.

Reamer, F.G. (2006). *Social work values and ethics* (3rd ed.). New York: Columbia University Press. This classic text offers an in-depth introduction to the discussion of ethics and values in social work practice. Chapters focus on social work values, ethical dilemmas and decision-making, ethical dilemmas in direct and indirect social work practice, and ethical misconduct.

RECOMMENDED WEBSITES

The Canadian Association of Social Workers Code of Ethics
http://www.casw-acts.ca/en/what-social-work/casw-code-ethics
The Canadian Association of Social Workers Code of Ethics site provides a link to the current *Code of Ethics* and *Guidelines for Ethical Practice*. It also outlines the historical development of the *Code of Ethics*.

First Nations Centre of the National Aboriginal Health Organization
http://www.rhs-ers.ca/node/2
The First Nations Centre of the National Aboriginal Health Organization seeks to advance First Nations health knowledge by working with First Nations to create, promote, and share health information and research. The Centre also develops tools and processes that assist in building capacity and transferring knowledge. Links are available for resources that guide ethical research practices with First Nations communities.

The Journal of Social Work Values and Ethics
http://www.socialworker.com/jswve/content/view/1/1/
The Journal of Social Work Values and Ethics examines the ethical and values issues that affect and are interwoven with social work practice, research, and theory development. Students can browse the Journal for articles on an array of ethical issues related to social work.

Panel on Research Ethics
http://www.pre.ethics.gc.ca/eng/policy-politique/initiatives/tcps2-eptc2/Default/
The Panel on Research Ethics website provides a comprehensive resource: the *Tri-Council Policy Statement: Ethical Conduct for Research Involving Humans*. The site also has a tutorial on research ethics under "Education" which provides interactive exercises and multidisciplinary examples covering the Core Principles of the Tri-Council Policy Statement and key components for a research ethics board review.

PART II

Foundational Skills for Social Workers

Social Work with Individuals and Families

LEARNING OBJECTIVES

- To outline different aspects of social work practice with individuals and families.

- To understand the critical role of relationship-building and maintenance in practice with individuals and families.

- To identify the different phases of practice with individuals and families.

- To learn about the skills and tasks associated with direct practice.

- To appreciate the importance of assessment as both a process and a product.

- To identify techniques and tools specific to working with families.

Chapter Outline

This chapter introduces foundational principles of social work practice with individuals and families. The first section provides an overview of the different roles social workers play when practising with individuals and families in a variety of contexts and settings. The components of relationship-building and maintenance and the critical role they play in practice with individuals and families are also introduced. The second section reviews the stages or phases of the helping process including exploration/assessment, contracting/planning, implementation/intervention, and ending/evaluation and their application to different social work settings. Particular emphasis is placed on the importance of assessment both as a process (i.e., developing rapport, asking critical questions) and as a product (i.e., the written record). This section also highlights skills and techniques specific to direct practice with families.

Historical Contexts of Social Work with Individuals and Families

Social work with individuals and families in Canada and the USA finds its origins in friendly visiting where volunteers from charity organizations provided one-on-one support to those living in poverty. The process of friendly visiting—which became known as social casework—aimed to systemically gather information on an individual and a family's situation, formulate inferences of the source of their issues, and develop a treatment to help improve their circumstances (see Chapter 1 for a more detailed discussion). Mary Richmond, best known for developing this approach in North America, further believed that good information gathering was only possible when caseworkers communicated care and concern for each person's and family's circumstances. Felix Biestek (1957) in his influential text *The Casework Relationship* concurred with Richmond and listed the principles of non-judgment and acceptance among those factors critical to the approach. Still evident in today's understanding of direct practice with individuals and families are remnants of the casework approach with the attempt to resolve issues on a one-to-one or case-by-case basis and the acknowledgement of the importance the pivotal role relationship-building plays in work with individuals and families. Some differences in today's formulation of direct practice with individuals and families include the focus on collaboration (joint identification of issues between client and worker) rather than diagnosis (expert driven identification of issues) and the identification of strengths alongside challenges (Bogo, 2006; Hepworth, Rooney, Rooney, Strom-Gottfried & Larsen, 2010; Miley, O'Melia & DuBois, 2011; Seabury, Seabury & Garvin, 2011).

Practice with Individuals and Families

Social work with individuals and families is practised across the life span (from new-borns, children, adolescents, young adults, to older adults), in a variety of settings (schools, hospitals, community-based organizations, etc.), addressing myriad issues (child welfare, immigrant and refugee issues, health and mental health, housing/financial issues). Social workers work with individuals and families who have initiated their own request for services, those who have been referred for services by a third party (such as a teacher, physician, friend, or neighbour), and those who have been legally required to seek services.

Regardless of the life stage, setting, issue, or referral type, social work with individuals and families involves both **clinical work**—focused on helping individuals and families

clinical work Focuses on working with thoughts, interactions, behaviours, and emotions of an individual or family.

manage feelings, transform patterns of communication, adopt behaviours that support well-being, and identify areas of strength—and **case management**—focused on helping people locate and access needed resources by providing information about the health and social service system, initiating referrals to needed services, and advocating for access when services have been difficult to attain (Ungar, 2011). Some organizational settings may lend themselves to a primary focus on clinical work, for example, a short-term counselling department in a health clinic for individuals and families managing difficult life events. Others may position the social worker role as that of a case manager; such as a community-based mental health team that focuses on helping people with severe and persistent mental health challenges remain in the community. However, what distinguishes social work from other helping-professions is its focus on both functions despite the organizational setting or presenting issue. An emergency room hospital social worker who meets with a woman survivor of domestic violence, for example, will offer both: short-term emotional support and safety-planning (clinical work), and information about resources available to women living with domestic violence (case management). If desired, the social worker may also coordinate a short-term stay in a women's shelter (case management).

> **case management** Focuses on helping individuals and families navigate their way to resources.

The Social Work Relationship

The clinical component of social work practice with individuals and families can be informed by multiple theoretical perspectives (described in more detail in Chapter 2) and the case management function can range from brokering or connecting people with resources to advocating for access to services and overseeing their delivery. However, all forms of direct practice with individuals and families depend on the formation of a relational base between worker and client(s). Research evidence supports the conclusion that relationship is the most crucial determinant of success for work with individuals and families (Duncan, Miller & Sparks, 2004; Horvath & Bedi, 2002). For this reason helping-professionals refer to the elements of relationship-building as **common factors** present in all orientations to practice with individuals and families. One cannot foster change and insight in an individual or family without also establishing a level of connection and trust that encourages them to share important aspects of their lives. Similarly one cannot successfully link individuals and families to services without expressing the care and concern necessary for them to identify their struggles and needs so that appropriate services can be sought.

> **common factors** A term used to emphasize the common relational elements in all approaches and techniques informing direct practice with individuals and families.

The important characteristics of social work relationships are presented in almost all current texts on social work practice with individuals and families. While terms used vary, the components of relationship valued by social work practitioners and clients across settings tend to cluster around four related aspects:

1. care and concern;
2. genuineness;
3. empathy; and
4. collaboration.

(Bogo, 2006; Hepworth, Rooney, Rooney, Strom-Gottfried & Larsen, 2010; Miley, O'Melia & DuBois, 2011; Seabury, Seabury & Garvin, 2011).

Care and Concern

Care and concern emanate out of the social work value of dignity and respect. When social workers believe that all individuals and families, even those they have trouble connecting with and "liking," are people worthy of respect and improved circumstances, then they commit themselves to caring or being concerned about individuals and families

> **care and concern** Expressed when the social worker seeks to understand an individual and family out of a genuine desire to help.

experiencing distress. When a worker sincerely cares about what happens to an individual or family, difficult emotions or issues can be disclosed and addressed. Caring and concerned workers are also motivated to persistently search for resources and advocate for the interests of individuals and families. For example, research in child-protective services has identified care and concern to be highly valued by parents. Care and concern are apparent when workers are flexible and make special efforts to help parents feel supported, such as availing themselves during times of crisis and helping them access needed resources (Maiter, Palmer, & Manji, 2006). Care and concern can also be communicated by asking about and recognizing how experiences of marginalization and discrimination affect individuals and families. Listening for and validating these experiences can help to develop a trusting relationship.

Genuineness

genuineness Being open, real, and sincere with individuals and families.

Genuineness, also referred to as authenticity or congruence, requires that social workers working with individuals and families truly believe what they say and are truthful and honest about their capacity to help, the power and authority they hold, and their perceptions of how individuals and families are doing. If a worker verbalizes that he or she is concerned but does not demonstrate this in his or her tone, body language, or actions, the client will undoubtedly question how committed the worker truly is to helping. Being genuine can be communicated by keeping individuals and families well informed about policies, processes, and decisions that affect them, being truthful about the extent of power and authority held in a given situation, and being personable. For example, it is not uncommon for older adults with chronic care needs whose families have insisted on a social work assessment to fear being told they must relocate. A genuine social worker will offer information on the placement process, render a professional judgment on safety, and inform older adults of their rights which may include declining the suggestion to relocate despite the risk, or challenging a judgment that questions their capacity to make informed decisions.

Empathy

empathy The capacity to understand and respond to another person's subjective experience.

Empathy is often described as an ability to put oneself in another's shoes. To communicate empathy, social workers must first develop an understanding of how an individual or family is feeling or experiencing an issue or event. Empathy can be communicated by asking about clients' feelings and reactions to a situation, by using empathic statements such as "that must have been devastating for you," or by offering insights of how the social worker may have felt or reacted in a similar situation, such as "If I had to face what you did I would have been extremely angry." Empathy is also communicated when the social worker acknowledges and recognizes how the social location of an individual and family intersect with their experiences. For example, a social worker working with a gay-identifying older adult who has not disclosed his sexual orientation to the day-program workers for fear of discrimination may express empathy by not only validating the fear and but also recognizing how difficult it must be to be exposed on a daily basis to heteronormative values, beliefs, and assumptions.

Collaboration

collaboration The development of mutually agreed on goals and tasks between a social worker and individuals and families.

Collaboration is an important element of relationship-building in social work. Whether an individual or family seeks assistance or is required by law to accept social work services, some level of agreement between the social worker and client on the nature of the issues to be worked on and how those issues should be addressed is considered necessary. Social workers who do not establish a compatible understanding with their clients on the nature

The Canadian Press/Chris Young

To develop a strong and effective relationship, a social worker must be able to understand and empathize with an individual's struggles.

of the work to be achieved may refer clients to resources they do not feel they need or focus on emotions, thoughts, behaviours, and areas of a client's life considered by the client to be irrelevant to his or her issues or concerns.

Bogo (2006) highlights three processes that underlie the components of the social work relationship outlined above. First, social work with individuals and families is **client-centred** in that it focuses on helping individuals and families tell their stories, identify their needs, and consider what can be done to alleviate their concerns. By focusing on the needs and concerns of individuals and families, social workers set the stage for communicating genuine care and concern for their perspective and empathy for their situation. They also set the stage for establishing goals and tasks that are collaborative rather than social-worker driven. Second, social work with individuals and families is dependent on worker **self-awareness** as the social worker must be acutely aware of his or her own reactions, beliefs, and experiences (see Chapter 9 under integrating culture into practice approaches for a discussion on the importance of cultural awareness—an extension of self-awareness). Social workers who are experiencing negative emotional reactions towards individuals or families will have difficulty developing care and concern for them. Recognizing and understanding the internal processes that may be interfering with this connection is paramount in these circumstances. Self-awareness includes recognizing personal places of privilege and engaging with one's own experiences of marginalization. Only through this recognition can social workers work through the feelings of guilt, shame, anger, or deep sadness that may emerge when working across difference (Pace & Pizana, 2004). Third, social work with individuals and families requires **attunement** to how each individual is experiencing the relationship and the focus of the interactions. It is not enough for a social worker to feel caring, genuine, and empathic; he or she must be experienced as such by individuals and families. Seeking feedback on the helping process and recognizing and addressing when individuals and families feel misunderstood, alienated, and mistrustful helps social workers to develop and maintain the helping relationship. Being attuned requires social workers to invite and tolerate challenges and expressions of suspicion from clients. It also requires social workers to recognize the impact of their actions despite what they see as their best intentions.

Client-centred An approach that places individuals and families at the centre of the helping relationship honouring their perceptions and experiences and supporting their active involvement in solutions.

self-awareness Refers to a social worker's insight into how he/she affects and/or is affected by others.

attunement The worker's attention to how the individuals and families are reacting to him/her and the work being done together.

Practical TIP

The Helping Relationship Inventory

POULIN AND YOUNG (1997) DEVELOPED the Helping Relationship Inventory which is a tool that can be used to help social workers become attuned to how well they are communicating important aspects of the helping relationship. You can use the following sample of questions to determine how your clients view the level of collaboration you have established. Once completed, you can discuss the results with your client and work towards improving your level of collaboration. If you do not want to be so formal you can use the questions as a guide and verbally ask some of the questions below the next time you wonder about your client's perceptions of the collaboration you have established.

The questions below are about the extent to which you feel involved and included in the direction of the work we are doing together. There are no right and wrong answers. Please answer the following questions as honestly as you can.

How much input do you feel you have had in determining the goals we are working on?

    (1) none   (2) a little bit   (3) a lot.

To what extent do you feel we have discussed the specific actions you will take to address your difficulties?

    (1) none   (2) a little bit   (3) a lot.

How much input do you feel you have had in determining how your progress will be assessed?

    (1) none   (2) a little bit   (3) a lot.

How much have we discussed the specific issues you want help with?

    (1) none   (2) a little bit   (3) a lot.

Source: Adapted from Poulin, J., & Young, T. (1997). Development of a helping relationship inventory for social work practice. *Research on Social Work Practice, 7*, 463–489.

Self-disclosure: A Contested Issue in Supporting the Development of Common Factors

self-disclosure Typically described as an intentional attempt at revealing something about the self of the worker.

Self-disclosure is a widely debated topic in the helping literature with conflicting views on what, when, and how often self-disclosure by a worker is legitimate (Farber, 2006; Zur, 2007). In general terms self-disclosure can be considered appropriate if consciously used by a worker to convey empathy, strengthen the relational bond, or help a client gain insight into a particular situation. Despite these guidelines, what one self-discloses is still a contested issue. Gibson (2012), for example, in her writings on self-disclosure in a therapeutic context, shares a decision to disclose her identity as a lesbian woman to an adolescent boy she was working with in the context of a mental health clinic when he started speaking about gay bashing. Her decision was motivated by an interest in helping her young client critically reflect on his possible actions. While her disclosure stimulated his reflections on his planned behaviour and created what she believed to be a stronger bond with the young boy, it resulted in compromising her relationship with his parents. Following this disclosure the parents complained to the mental health organization who asked that she no longer discuss personal matters with the boy.

Reactions about when and what self-disclosure is appropriate must be understood within the context of divergent theoretical orientations (see Chapter 8, "In Their Own Words" box by Cree Elder Joanne Dallaire for a discussion of self-disclosure from an Indigenous perspective). In traditional analytic definitions of self-disclosure, the worker is viewed as somewhat "neutral" with the role of reflecting back only what the client brings to the encounter. From this perspective self-disclosure can and should be controlled and used sparingly as the risk of revealing a worldview or perspective may outweigh the benefit of communicating empathy, offering insight, or strengthening the bond. This view on self-disclosure has continued to exercise a strong influence in most public organizations employing social workers and likely played a role in both the parents' and the organization's response to Gibson's self-disclosure. Critical theories, by contrast, assert that the "neutral" worker is one that is blind to the impact of social location on the helping process. Aiming for neutrality a worker may fail to recognize how her or his physical appearance, language, or comments reveal something about her or his worldview, which if unacknowledged can create a harmful distance between a worker and a client. From this perspective self-disclosure is inevitable and should become an explicit component of the therapeutic process. Social workers working in organizations who have adopted critical perspectives may be encouraged to disclose their social locations as this form of disclosure may be viewed as an important vehicle towards change. Gibson (2012), cited above, also worked in a drug treatment program for LGBT-identifying adults, where she was expected to disclose her sexual orientation as a matter of policy. Informed by a feminist and anti-oppressive perspective, the organization viewed such disclosure as supporting positive change by providing a sense of community to clients.

Hope: A Neglected Common Factor

Alongside the development of a positive helping relationship, hope has been found to be a critical ingredient in successfully working with individuals and families across settings, issues, and approaches (Duncan, Miller & Sparks, 2004; Horvath & Bedi, 2002). Despite the vital importance of fostering hope with individuals and families, scant attention has been given towards how social workers can both impart hope and remain hopeful amidst adversity (Flaskas, 2007). The little that does exist suggests that individuals and families benefit when social workers and other helping-professionals appear hopeful that their situations will improve by seeing and pointing out signs of strength and resilience and offering relevant support and information (Lemma, 2010). How social workers remain hopeful working with individuals and families in seemingly hopeless situations of personal trauma and oppressive structures is rarely explored or addressed.

Official Language Legislation and Social Services in Canada

Canada proclaims itself to be a bilingual country with two official languages, English and French. However, a closer examination of federal and provincial legislation reveals that many Canadians, including those who speak French in a predominantly English-speaking province or English in a predominantly French-speaking province may have difficulty accessing health and social services due to linguistic barriers. The Canadian Official Languages Act (adopted in 1985 and amended in 1988), for example, only guarantees access to either English or French for services or written information provided directly by the Federal government. Furthermore, most provincial governments have adopted a unilingual stance guaranteeing service delivery at the provincial level in English only. French-speaking Canadians residing in these provinces (e.g., Ontario) are not guaranteed access to any health and social service

In Their Own Words

REMAINING HOPEFUL WHILE WORKING WITH IMMIGRANTS AND REFUGEES

AS A FORMER SETTLEMENT WORKER (SW) in Halifax, Nova Scotia it was my job to co-facilitate participants' settlement and integration into their new host community, Halifax. This work included collaborating with participants to develop personalized goals that they felt would help them become familiar with and grounded in their new community and cultivate a sense of belonging, acceptance, and citizenship while maintaining (or preserving) a past identity and important cultural worldviews.

Fostering belonging and citizenship was extremely challenging given the structural barriers imposed on new immigrants to Canada including the difficulty sponsoring family members in need of protection, changes to the Interim Federal Health Program, changes in the English Benchmark levels in order to obtain citizenship, unrecognized employment and education credentials, and many more discriminatory policies. It often felt as if the participants and I were "swimming upstream" with little hope of ever arriving at our desired destination. Despite the many challenges in this role, however, my work was quite fulfilling; one of the many reasons for fulfilment in my work as a SW is the notion of *hope*.

I believe what allowed me to retain and impart hope to participants included the resilience I continued to see within them, the commitment and opportunities I found from other colleagues, and the efforts I saw within the broader community of Halifax to advocate for change. While listening to my participants' stories of trauma, I was continuously perplexed, amazed, and inspired. Through such stories of adversity and atrocity, there were generally threads of hope, resiliency, and growth woven together. I always found it remarkable to hear about, observe, and be invited into participants' vibrant and thriving families, faith groups, and ethnic/cultural communities, which all served as circles of vital support for my participants. Many of these "circles of care" supported their identities and fostered a sense of cultural preservation. I also found hope seeing participants' resourcefulness and innovation, especially when some of them would come to Canada with so little or nothing at all.

As a social worker in direct practice I found it important to continue participating in interprofessional learning, support, and group-care (as opposed to "self-care"), which included critical reflexivity (i.e., reflecting and debriefing challenging situations), professional development opportunities, teamwork initiatives, establishing a network of allies (i.e., fighting against inequalities and taking social action), attending and presenting at conferences, developing educational resources, and simply getting to know one another via social events. Such interprofessional learning, support, and care equipped me to continue practising with passion, hope, and compassion.

In my eight years as a settlement worker I found hope and inspiration through my greater community, Halifax, which is rich in partnerships that address key social issues with an anti-oppressive stance (challenging power and oppression) or collaborations amongst community members to challenge the status quo. I find it remarkable how a community comes together to work towards real change, which inspires social movements from the grassroots. As social workers, it is essential to remember the strengths that feed our souls, as we embrace this profession. For me, some of these strengths are the hopeful encounters I have found and continue to find along the way.

Emma Larson-Ure is a Social Worker in Nova Scotia.

French-speaking citizens at this Service Ontario location may face linguistic barriers if provincial services are not accessible in their native language.

provided outside of the mandate of the federal government (e.g., social assistance agencies) in their mother tongue. Northwest Territories, in an effort to highlight the rights of Canadians who speak an Indigenous language, adopted legislation guaranteeing access to government reports in French, English, and nine Indigenous languages. More limited than the federal policy, government services were not included in their legislation, suggesting that Indigenous communities cannot be guaranteed access to social services in their mother tongue in any social service agency across Canada. The two provinces that have adopted policies around access to both English and French (New Brunswick and Manitoba) have included a guarantee of bilingual service in government agencies and health services. Despite these efforts, minority-speaking French persons in these provinces report implicit pressures to speak English and the unavailability of workers proficient in French when accessing social services (Turner, 2005). One solution to addressing this barrier is to actively engage third-party translators into direct practice with individuals and families. The art of integrating translators into the helping relationship has, however, received limited attention to date (Tribe & Thompson, 2009). Given social work's commitment to service access this is an area of direct practice worthy of further exploration.

Phases of the Helping Process

Social work with individuals and families has been described as evolving over a series of stages or phases that proceed successively and represent distinctions in the frequency and intensity with which social work activities and skills are employed (Bogo, 2006; Hepworth et al., 2010; Ungar, 2011). These phases may be employed in the one and only encounter a social worker has with an individual or family or may evolve more slowly when ongoing support or case management is part of the social worker's mandate. A typical hospital-based referral to social services is initiated one day before discharge. In this context, a social worker cycles through the phases of the helping process in one face-to-face meeting with a client and a number of follow-up interactions within a 24-hour period. By contrast, a social worker working with adults experiencing mental health challenges in the community may work with a client on a monthly basis for years.

Phase I: Exploration and Assessment

The initial collection and analysis of information is central to the first phase of the helping encounter as it forms the template that guides the work the social worker and individual and family will do together. In some contexts, assessments are guided by standardized forms aimed at developing a comprehensive understanding of a client's issues and the fit between his or her concerns and the mandate of the organization. Standardized forms are typical in organizations where the social work role is viewed primarily as one of case management. In other contexts, assessments are relatively unstructured and social workers are given more freedom to explore the nature of the presenting issues and possible courses of action. Even in the context of heavily prescribed assessments, following the client's lead, timing questions well, and eliciting information in an empathic caring manner are critical aspects of the assessment process. Hence, while the **product** or written assessment may be highly structured and standardized in a particular organization, the **process** or act of gathering the information should still follow the lead of the client.

The focus of social work assessments can vary depending on the context in which a social worker is practising, the primary role the social worker is playing, and the theoretical orientation informing the process. For example, a social worker in a community organization offering emotional support to people who have been diagnosed with cancer may explore how a client understands and is reacting to his or her medical condition. A social worker functioning as an addiction counsellor in a mental health setting may explore a client's motivation to address his or her addictions. Finally, a social worker functioning as a case manager for a public home-care program will typically focus on an individual's abilities to perform tasks within his or her home environment, and engage in an in-depth exploration of supports or services already in place. Despite these variances in information gathering and analysis, all social work assessments elicit how individuals and families understand their issues, what they hope to be different as a consequence of the social work encounter, and the strengths and limitations that may help or hinder their capacity to address the issues that have been identified. In keeping with the value base of the profession, strengths and limitations are typically understood broadly to include individual, environmental, cultural, and societal constraints and resources. This broad understanding requires social workers to move beyond the initial reason behind the request for service. A mother may come into a community health clinic requesting to see a social worker to get formula for her infant. In addition to reviewing the process of receiving formula the social worker will engage with the mother and explore other potential avenues for assistance. How is the mother coping with motherhood? Who can she rely on for support? Are there other stressors associated with this new life change? How do societal beliefs and expectations about mothering affect how this mother views herself?

The process of exploring and assessing clients' issues and concerns is guided by the nature in which an individual and family came to the attention of a social worker or social service agency. A client who sought social work services himself or herself can be asked questions such as "What brings you here today?" or "Tell me a bit about what led you to call our agency." A client who has been pressured or mandated to seek services by a third party may require a brief statement of the concerns expressed by the third party before being invited to share his or her own perceptions of the situation. A teenager who has been told by his parents that he must seek help or face being kicked out of his home may be told, "I understand that your parents are concerned about your behaviour these days. What do you think about that?" Whether the initial request for services was **voluntary** or **involuntary**, a central task associated with the first phase of work with individuals and families is to invite an individual or family to explore the issues concerning them.

Most social work assessments are informed by verbal reports and observations made during client interviews. However other forms of information may also be used to develop

product Refers to the written assessment.

process Refers to the manner in which a social worker gathers information.

voluntary Requests for services wherein clients have self-referred or agree with those referring them that social work services are warranted.

involuntary Requests for services wherein clients have been pressured to seek the services of a social worker either by a court mandate or by facing a sanction for not seeking service.

an understanding of the nature of client issues, including interviews with other informants affected by the presenting situation (with the client's permission) and other professional reports. Identifying who else, if anyone, to engage in this phase of information gathering is an important aspect of the assessment process. Although the collection and analysis of information continues throughout the helping process (ongoing assessment), the initial collection, analysis, and recording of data is central to the first phase of the helping process, as it forms the crucial foundation for case planning and intervention.

Practical TIP

Questions to Reflect on During the Exploration and Assessment Phase of the Helping Process

- What are the issues identified by the client?
- Why is the client experiencing this (these) issue(s) at this time (consider developmental stages and life events)?
- How do others' interpretations of the presenting issues resemble or differ from that of the client?
- What individual and environmental strengths and resources exist that can positively affect the issues identified by the client?
- What individual and environmental obstacles and constraints need to be addressed?
- What experiences of discrimination and marginalization exist that may affect the client and the situation?
- Are there other issues noted by the social worker not expressed by the client? What might be behind these discrepant views?

Source: Adapted from Bogo, M. (2006). *Social work practice. Concepts, processes & interviewing* (page 161). New York Columbia University Press.

Theory in Practice

WRITING PSYCHOSOCIAL ASSESSMENTS

THE WRITTEN PSYCHOSOCIAL ASSESSMENT CAN provide social workers with the opportunity to engage in the reflection and analysis necessary to form a conceptualization that integrates professional knowledge with the priorities and perspectives of individuals and families (Howe, 2009). Despite the clinical importance of the written record, many social workers view the records they are expected to produce for their organizations as time consuming and administratively driven rather than relevant and meaningful for their practice (Dias & Paré, 2000). This is especially the case for social workers who integrate clinical work within their case management function as the assessments required of them by their organization are typically standardized and can focus predominantly on identifying required resources. As a consequence many complete the task long after the social work activity is finished.

In an effort to address the gap between process and product, Keefler (2006) developed a template for writing psychosocial assessments that can be applied

(Continued)

to any social work setting. It is currently being used to train social work students in two Montreal-based universities. It has also informed the assessment guidelines developed by a Montreal-based university hospital network. The problem-solving perspective is evident in the model as the template guides social workers to succinctly record all relevant problems or issues identified by individuals and families and offer an analysis of the factors thought to contribute or perpetuate identified problems (Epstein & Brown, 2002; Perlman, 1957). A strengths perspective is also incorporated as social workers are asked to record the capacities individuals and families have brought to the social work encounter and the solutions or efforts they have already made to address their issues (Salabeey, 2009). Finally, the ecosystems framework is evident as the model guides social workers to record how interactions within family units or between individuals, families, and other social systems may be affecting presenting issues (Germain & Gitterman, 1996; Mattaini & Meyer, 2002). Importantly the guidelines are general enough that an open application of other theoretical perspectives is also possible (Keefler, Bond, & Sussman, 2013). For example, precipitating factors could include rules or regulations that may be marginalizing an individual or family.

The model, presented below, directs social workers to organize and classify information in a way that distinguishes facts, client inferences, and professional conclusions or implications. This forces the worker to make explicit the links between information they have acquired and the theoretical and empirical knowledge they have used to interpret the meaning of this information, such as its relevance to the presenting issues (Keefler, Bond, & Sussman, 2013). Even social workers in settings that require minimal recording can elect to enhance their agency-driven recording with a template such as this.

ELEMENTS OF A COMPREHENSIVE PSYCHOSOCIAL ASSESSMENT

Client Identification

This identification section should be based on your consideration of information *that seems pertinent* to the presenting issues. Information under client information is generally factual (rather than inferential) and is typically based on information from the client but may also be attained from colleagues or case notes.

Demographics: Client age, gender, marital/parental status, ethnicity, language, and family composition can be noted in this description section.

Employment/Education: Type and status of the client's employment or education if the client is a child or adolescent.

Income and Source: Actual income of the client and/or its source if applicable to the presenting problem.

Living Environment: Type of housing, description of neighbourhood, transportation, and work environment *if applicable to the presenting problem*.

Reason for Referral

This section should identify the referral source and summarize his/her reasons for making the request for services. Sometimes this section is completed by the referral source himself or herself.

Sources of Information

List all sources of information informing this assessment and the context in which that information was gathered. The number of contacts that informed this assessment may also be included.

Problem Definition

This section should include a brief description of the problem and/or needs *as described by the client*. It may include the *history/antecedents* of the problem/issues such as precipitating events, *frequency of problem*, and the *contributing factors* that the client thinks perpetuates the problems/issues including personal factors and environmental factors.

Past Solutions

This section lists the solutions the client may have already tried to resolve the problems/issues outlined above including past help sought from other agencies/professionals.

The Client System

This section includes the combination of information *reported by the client* and *observed by the worker*.

Functioning: This section includes the client's physical and mental health, intellectual/cognitive (including problem solving) abilities, behavioural responses, emotional functioning, performance in social roles, and activities of daily living. As in the client identification section, list those elements of functioning that seem pertinent to the presenting issues.

Relationships and Social Support: This section provides a description of the quality of the client's current interpersonal relationships including those with the worker and the agency. Also included are any significant others in the extended family or community who are the source of affective or instrumental support for the client or who are a source of distress. Concrete resources and information needed to resolve the issues and obstacles to their access can be noted here as well.

Strengths/Coping Skills: The client's strengths and positive coping skills as reported by the client or perceived by the worker is included in this section. Strategies the client has already tried to address the issue and qualities the client has that may be helpful in the current situation can all be highlighted here.

Professional Opinion

In this section the worker offers an analysis and synthesis of the information gathered that reflects a comprehensive understanding of the problem(s) based on the combination of client perceptions, agency/legal requirements, and social work knowledge. The formulation can include hypotheses related to the severity of the problem (degree of distress the problem is causing), the context/location of the problem (e.g., is the problem exacerbated in a particular setting or location?), the priority given to the solution of the problem, and the client's motivation to solve the problem(s). Any other hypotheses related to understanding the causes/consequences of the problem should also be included in this section. Including the *criteria* on which all hypotheses

(Continued)

are based is an important component of this formulation. In this section the worker may offer discrepancies between his or her observations of the presenting issues and those reported by the client.

Plan

This section outlines the planned intervention activities, the goals or desired outcomes, and the details of the working contract with the client. The degree of collaboration between the worker and client in formulating this plan can be communicated in this section if there are discrepancies between the two.

Source: Adapted from Keefler, J., Bond, S., & Sussman, T. (2013). L'évaluation psychosociale (translation : Psychosocial assessment). In E. Harper and H. Dorvil (Eds.), *Le travail social: théories, méthodologies et pratiques (translation: Social Work: Theories, Methodologies and Practices)* (pp. 267–290). Montreal: Les presses de l'Université du Québec à Montreal, Québec.

Phase II: Contracting/Planning

During the process of eliciting information that provides both the social worker and client with an understanding of the issues or challenges being faced, a social worker also helps to develop a focus for the work that is agreeable to the client and that falls within the mandate of the social worker's organization. This process of developing a shared understanding of the issues to be addressed within the social work encounter is referred to as contracting or planning. Seabury, Seabury, and Garvin (2011) identify five components to planning or contracting: First, the social worker works with individuals and families to elicit a clear sense of **purpose.** By eliciting what an individual or family needs and offering information about what falls within and outside the mandate of the social worker in a given context, the social worker and client identify the reasons they are engaging in an encounter together. Typical purposes include facilitating access to services that have been difficult to attain, providing information about a particular issue or service system, encouraging opportunities for reflection and processing of troubling issues, offering opportunities for observing and commenting on family interactions, and facilitating and mediating meetings with other professionals or key members of a community network. If social workers and clients are confused about why they are meeting or working together in the first place, one or both can experience anxiety and confusion about the work being carried out.

purpose The rationale for service.

Second, alongside establishing a purpose for the work together, social workers and clients begin to identify **target problems** that will be addressed. The issues described by clients at this stage may include frustrations with a particular service or team of professionals, unwelcome or unanticipated life events, challenges with interpersonal relationships, or a lack of basic resources such as financial security, food, and/or shelter. If it appears to the workers that an individual or family is facing a series of interrelated issues, questions can be asked to help identify the most pressing issues from the client's perspective. Summarizing key issues and asking for client feedback on priority areas can also help worker and client to focus on issues warranting more immediate attention.

target problems Issues or challenges clients face that they wish to change.

Third, once the worker and client feel they have identified key issues or concerns, work focuses on identifying **goals** or solutions that may help to alleviate or minimize the issues clients are facing. Clients often present goals in general terms such as "get the services I need," "have a better relationship," or "get out more." It is incumbent on social workers to work with clients to explore what will be different for them when goals are achieved as this exploration provides benchmarks for both workers and clients to evaluate if they have

goals Future, desired end states for the client.

succeeded in their work together. Questions that can achieve this level of reflection include "What will be different when you are happier?"; "What would having a better relationship look like to you?"; and "How would getting out more make a difference in your life?"

Fourth, where possible, **time limits** for the work should be specified including the overall length of services (e.g., one meeting, three months), the length of meetings, the frequency of contact within a given period (daily, weekly, monthly), or the anticipated length of time it may take to access a needed service. Decisions related to time limits may be theoretically or empirically driven but are also often agency driven. For example, in public home-care agencies social workers may be expected to re-evaluate client needs every six months despite the worker's or client's assessment of need for review.

Fifth, **actions, activities, and responsibilities** expected of each party should be specified. This may include referrals a social worker agrees to follow up with or issues clients and social workers both agree to explore together. It is important to be open to reviewing and revising agreed-on actions as the work unfolds. Activities not followed through by clients may be a result of changed priorities or changed circumstances. Furthermore, social workers who initially agree to offer information about a service or program may take on a more active role such as contacting the organization with the client if a client experienced frustration and discouragement.

In most social work contexts, contracting is a verbal process negotiated and renegotiated over time. Some contexts encourage written contracts perceiving them to provide explicitness and accountability to both parties. Having a written contract, however, does not ensure that it is understood by both parties. Moreover, a signed contract is not necessarily indicative of true agreement and may instead reinforce power differentials between social workers and clients.

Phase III: Implementation/Intervention

At some point during the helping process, the focus of interactions between social workers and individuals and families shifts from exploring needs and issues and developing collaborative goals and plans to actively working towards change within the individual or family, the environment, or both. When lack of resources or services have been identified as part of problem, the social worker directs his or her attention to helping the client access those services either through referral, supporting a client's efforts to obtain services, or advocating on the client's behalf. Once services are attained, a period of monitoring is required to ensure the services requested and attained match client needs and preferences. When supporting a client through a difficult life event is a goal, the social worker will elicit the client's expression of emotion, normalizing his or her feelings and reactions, and will offer information that may help the client to understand and accept his or her responses. If the problem is perceived to be one of interaction between family members, the social worker will turn the attention to patterns of communication and decision-making by observing and offering insights into when and how family members relate to one another and the impact this may be having on individuals within the family.

As the worker proceeds to introduce interventions—such as questions that challenge client's perceptions, statements that offer alternate ways of reacting, information that elicits new insight, observations of interactive patterns, mediation between a client and members of a service system, or accompaniment to a new program—the worker and client remain attuned to what is working and what is not. Only by working towards initially identified goals can the worker and the client test out if the target problems and causes they identified in their initial assessment were useful. For example, a social worker working with a middle-aged adult with developmental disabilities may determine that it would be useful for the client to participate in parenting classes if he wants to continue parenting his child. The client agrees that this would be useful and accepts to call a program recommended

time limits The time parameters social workers and clients establish for the work they will do together.

actions, activities, and responsibilities The negotiated expectations workers and clients establish for the work they will do together.

Case STUDY

Electronic Communication and Social Work

TODAY'S GENERATION OF YOUTH, ADULTS, and older adults increasingly rely on digital communication for information and social exchanges such as planning, personal discussions, and advice. The cultural trend towards "letting our fingers do the talking" has implications for social workers and other practitioners faced with questions about when, what, and how much email exchange is appropriate between clients, what personal information is posted on social networking sites, and how, if at all, to use digital exchanges to support engagement and intervention with individuals and families (Fantus & Mishna, 2013; Mattison, 2012; Reamer, 2013). Integrating electronic exchanges such as texting and emailing into face-to-face practice has been shown to enhance the practitioner-client relationship and improve clinical outcomes. Electronic communication between meetings, for example, is often viewed by clients as indicative of social workers' care and concern for their well-being (Murdoch & Connor-Greene, 2000). Such communication has also been found to support and encourage clients between meetings, increasing follow-through on tasks, and homework assignments (Whitlock, Lader & Conterio, 2007). E-communication, however, is not without its challenges. Expectations around worker availability, potential misinterpretations, and threats to client confidentiality have lead many social workers to limit electronic communication to practical and administrative purposes only (Finn, 2006; Mattison, 2012).

To better understand the nature and scope of electronic communication between social workers and clients engaged in traditional face-to-face practice, Mishna and colleagues conducted a qualitative study in a large metropolitan city in Canada (Mishna, Bogo, Root, Sawyer, & Khoury-Kassabri, 2012). A total of 13 social workers participated in one focus group and two additional social workers participated in individual interviews.

Social workers suggested it was unrealistic and counter-indicative for practitioners or their agencies to refuse to communicate electronically, especially for administrative and practical purposes such as re-scheduling meetings or providing information. Many reported that clients expected and often initiated this form of electronic communication and it felt rigid and unresponsive to deny this level of electronic engagement, even if agency policies advised against it.

Nonetheless, in some instances, cyber-communication elicited a slippery slope that they had not anticipated. In some cases, for example, emailing about resources and meetings gradually shifted to personal disclosures made by clients. These more personalized interactions were not always anticipated and left social workers feeling uncomfortable and confused about the renewed boundaries between themselves and their clients.

In some cases, social workers' electronic communication became part of the clinical work. Clients who sat silently in much of a face-to-face encounter were able to email post-meeting thoughts and feelings that could be used in subsequent face-to-face encounters. Allowing for this electronic interaction was seen as productive because it moved the work along. Importantly, as in the previous situations, these exchanges were rarely invited by practitioners but became a pattern of interaction through client initiation.

Findings from this research remind us that e-communication is often client initiated and can be expected to "creep into" social work practice. Organizations, professional bodies, and social workers themselves must learn to anticipate these communications and reflect on how to use them to enhance rather than hinder their relational base with clients.

by the worker. The following week the client discloses that he did not contact the group because he worries about being judged by other group members. This results in an exploration of his feelings of self and the impact this is having on his belief in his parenting abilities. Like other phases of the helping process the work or intervention stage is guided by the combination of research, theory, client preference, organizational constraints, and professional judgment.

Phase IV: Ending/Evaluation

The ending phase of a social work encounter may be activated by a number of circumstances. In the best scenarios, endings are negotiated and anticipated by workers and clients when the goals identified during planning or contracting appear to be achieved. In other circumstances, endings are forced because clients elect not to continue engaging with the social worker or because workers leave an organization. When endings are forced by circumstance, they can be more challenging and emotionally charged. Worker-imposed endings are those most commonly faced by social work students who end professional relationships with clients at the cessation of their field placements (Gelman, 2009). Leaving when in the midst of work can elicit strong feelings of guilt on the part of students. It can also exacerbate emotional reactions such as feelings of loss, anger, and abandonment from clients. When these endings are anticipated, much time and effort should be put into discussing emotional reactions and planning for case transfers. Similarly, endings initiated by clients who stop attending or returning calls can leave unresolved emotions for both workers and client. Social workers in these cases should reach out to clients and invite some form of reflection on the helping process including what worked, what did not work, and what comes next for the individual and/or family.

The intensity of the helping relationship also affects how an ending is processed and negotiated. A social worker called in to initiate a discharge plan for an individual and family at the end of their hospitalization may place little emphasis on the ending of the social worker-client relationship per se, and focus more appropriately on the individual and family's feelings about leaving the hospital and facilitate a referral for post-hospital support. Conversely, a social worker working in child-protective services who has worked with a family for many years may spend months preparing for, anticipating, and exploring clients' feelings related to the ending of both the relationship and the services.

Despite the different circumstances precipitating endings, Bogo (2006) identifies four interrelated processes that can facilitate "good" endings; social workers are encouraged to facilitate these processes wherever possible.

1. **Reviewing progress** and change, includes noting differences in client functioning, networks, or resources from initial meetings to present day. It also involves anticipating future obstacles and reflecting on internal and external resources that may help to overcome challenges.

2. **Consolidating gains** involves helping clients to take ownership for what they did to encourage the change that occurred. It can also include soliciting feedback from clients about helpful and less helpful aspects of the process.

3. **Planning next steps** includes reviewing and reflecting on other resources an individual or family can draw on if and when facing future difficulties. This may include offering referrals and facilitating linkages to other organizations.

4. **Processing the emotional bond** is particularly applicable when social workers and individuals and families have worked together over an extended period of time. It is normal for both workers and clients to experience feelings about endings including pleasure, relief, anger, and sadness. As stated above, these feelings can be amplified when endings are forced. Clients may at times express these emotions indirectly by

reviewing progress Facilitated by the worker to help clients reflect back on their initial concerns to elicit insights about progress made.

consolidating gains Involves reinforcing the capacities within clients that led to positive change.

planning next steps A process of exploring and anticipating future needs and potential resources to address them.

processing the emotional bond Refers to facilitating the expression of emotion associated with ending the work between worker and client.

ending early, missing meetings, or appearing indifferent to meetings. In these cases, social workers can offer their observations and invite a discussion of feelings and emotions associated with endings. It is useful for social workers to express their own feelings of sadness around ending. Also helpful is sharing what they have gained and learned from the client.

The Helping Process with Families

All social workers engaged in direct practice consider families when exploring and assessing client concerns. A social worker helping a woman new to Canada with her adjustment process will inevitably ask family-related questions such as how other members of her family are reacting to the relocation. Although a family perspective informs all direct social work practice, when multiple members of a family are involved in the social work encounter, some family-specific skills and techniques are utilized.

Social workers who meet with multiple members of a family must connect and establish rapport with everyone. Part of this process involves eliciting each member's understanding of how he or she came to engage with the social worker. It is not uncommon to learn that some family members have entered the social work encounter involuntarily under the pressure of others. Also commonly expressed are statements describing issues or concerns with one family member, such as "We are here because of my son's problems at school" or "The doctor asked you to see us because of our mother's depression." Working to engage each family member involves inviting all members to express their feelings, apprehensions, and perceptions about their engagement with the social worker, and helping the family consider presenting issues in relational terms. The mother who describes her encounter with social work as a consequence of her son's behaviour can be asked how his behaviour is affecting other members of the family. The adult daughter expressing her understanding of seeking a social worker's assistance because of her mother's depression can be asked "When your mother's mood is better what is different about your family?"

Eliciting each member's concerns typically involves managing inter-member dynamics. Stopping others from interjecting, encouraging members to listen, and asking family members to repeat and react to what has been said about them are all techniques that can be used to ensure each member's concerns are expressed and heard. As a social worker asks a young adult why he thinks his parents want him to speak to a social worker, his father may interject and state "because he isn't taking his medications." The social worker can gently inform the father she is interested in his perspective but wonders if she can hear from his son first.

As the social worker attends to the content being presented by each member she is also **tracking** patterns of interaction between members. Some observations that help to elicit important information about the family include how members negotiate disagreements, who speaks for whom, who protects whom, and what does and does not get discussed (Seabury, Seabury, & Garvin, 2011). Observing the process of interaction provides the worker with valuable information about how, if at all, **family structure** may be connected to the presenting issues (Kilpatrick & Holland, 2006; Nichols, 2011). The social worker, in the case described above, may observe many instances where the father concerned with his son's medication non-compliance speaks for him. She may suspect that the son's refusal to take medication is related to an attempt at asserting his voice and being heard within the family. With this observation the social worker begins to focus her work on helping the father and son change their pattern of interaction. Techniques may include raising all family members' awareness, asking the father to listen to the son for 10 minutes a day without interruption, or inviting another family member to point out the pattern when it happens at home. The social worker will invite family members to report back on their progress.

tracking Involves observing patterns of interaction between family members while listening to the issues they are discussing.

family structure Refers to the way the family is organized including roles family members hold and closeness and distance between members.

The **genogram** has been designed specifically to assess and work with family patterns. The tool is particularly useful for eliciting intergenerational patterns of interaction and legacies passed down from previous generations (Iverson, Gergen & Fairbanks, 2005; McGoldrick, Gerson & Shellenberger, 1999). A genogram uses symbols to represent key events, roles, rules, and relational dynamics within a family. The genogram originated out of the work of Murray Bowen (1961) who believed that multigenerational patterns were important to review in work with families. This schematic diagram of family relations is now used widely with slight adaptations to fit differing theoretical orientations. The diagram can be done with the family during one or a series of meetings or alone by the social worker interested in reflecting on patterns of interaction that she can share with the family. The genogram typically includes information about members of the current family and two generations previous. Information captured includes dates for significant life events within the family such as births, deaths, relational unions, separations, and illnesses. Also depicted is sibling position, race/ethnicity, religion, or other pertinent indications

genogram A visual representation of family that illustrates a family's history, structure, demographics, functioning, and patterns of relating to one another.

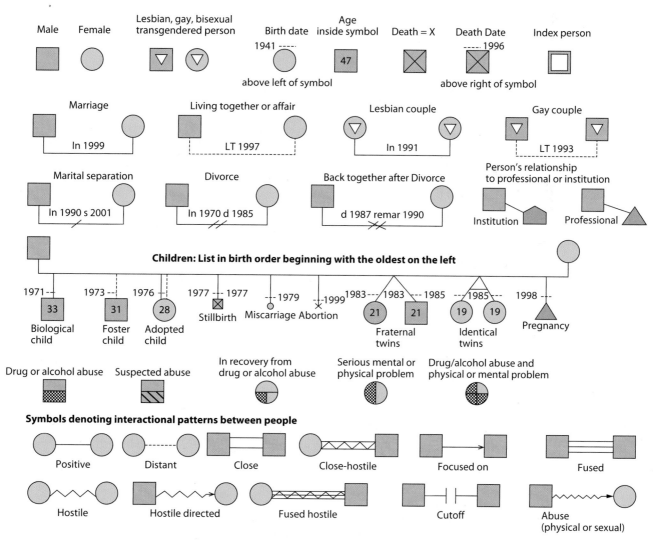

FIGURE 4.1 // Standard Symbols for Genograms

Source: Adapted from http://courses.wcupa.edu/ttreadwe/courses/02courses/standardsymbols.htm. Used with the permission of Tom Treadwell.

of social location for each family member. When critical life events have been noted the worker asks and records how different family members reacted to the event. In designing a genogram, the worker also asks relational questions to explore patterns of interaction, legacies, and roles passed down from preceding generations. Questions to elicit relational patterns include: "Are there any family members who do not speak to one another?" and "Who would you describe as particularly close with whom?" Asking about nicknames or labels ascribed to different family members also elicits important information about roles and patterns in the family structure. Tension, closeness, and stress among relationships are recorded using symbols (see Figure 4.1 for an example). Tailoring questions to particular practice issues may also be helpful in eliciting pertinent information to inform the family structure. When working with an interracial or interfaith family, the worker might ask "Are there people in your family who have difficulty with your relationship?" Working with a family with one or a number of Indigenous family members, a worker may ask "Has anyone in your family lived through the residential school system?" Recent genogram iterations have included adaptations (new symbols and suggested questions) for exploring family structure in the context of more specific issues such as culture/ethincity, sexual orientation, and sprituality (Hodge & Limb, 2011; Ward, 2012). If done together with the family, the tool functions as a form of intervention, helping families see family patterns and their potential relationship to current issues or concerns.

Conclusion

This chapter reviewed the common elements associated with direct practice with individuals and families. Particular focus was given to the factors associated with establishing and maintaining positive working relationships with clients across settings. The chapter also outlined the stages of the helping process and offered tasks, skills, and functions associated with each stage or phase. Particular emphasis was placed on assessment as the cornerstone of clinical and case management practice. Tools to support relationship-building and assessment practices were introduced. Specific skills and techniques for social work with families were also offered.

QUESTIONS FOR CRITICAL THOUGHT

1. Can you identify a time you wanted to disclose something about yourself to a client but decided not to? Based on the discussion of self-disclosure above, what do you think of your decision now?
2. How do the phases/stages of social work practice apply to your current context?
3. How do you currently use electronic communication in your practice? Is there anything you might think about or do differently after reading the case study on electronic communication?
4. What type of reactions do you anticipate from your clients when you end your field placement? How and when might you start addressing these issues?
5. Can you identify patterns of interacting in your own family that tell you something about your family structure?

RECOMMENDED READINGS

Bogo, M. (2006). *Social work practice concepts, processes & interviewing*. New York: Columbia University Press. This book illustrates how conceptual frameworks and models, helping processes, and practice skills interweave together to guide social work assessment and intervention with individuals and families. The book includes a chapter that offers field instructors and social work students a model for teaching and learning how to integrate theory, evidence, and case-based material in the real world of practice.

Hepworth, D.H., Rooney, R.H., Rooney, G.D., Strom-Gottfried, K., & Larsen, J (2010). *Direct social work practice: Theory & skills* (8th ed.). Belmont, CA: Brooks/Cole. This book provides an overview of social work practice with individuals and families across settings. It describes the skills, knowledge, and values required of social workers engaged in direct practice during each phase of the helping process. Particular attention is devoted to the skills required of social workers across contexts.

Kilpatrick, A.C., & Holland, T.P. (2006). *Working with families: An integrative model by level of need.* Boston: Pearson Allyn & Bacon. This book provides a comprehensive overview of social work approaches to working with families. By using an innovative framework for assessing family level of need, the book provides beginning practitioners with welcome direction on how to match family intervention with the concerns and issues most pressing for families.

Nichols, M.P. (2011). *The essentials of family therapy* (5th ed.) Boston: Pearson Allyn & Bacon. This book provides a solid foundation of the rich history, classic schools of thought, and the latest developments in family therapy. Key concepts from each perspective are clearly presented and well linked to practice material.

Ungar, M. (2011). *Counselling in challenging contexts: Working with individuals and families across clinical and community settings.* Belmont, CA: Brooks/Cole. This book illustrates how a social ecological model, which combines an ecosystems framework with strength-based perspectives and structural issues, can be used to inform both the clinical and case management aspects of social work practice across settings. The detailed case illustrations help to highlight how the complex circumstances and issues social workers encounter in their work with individuals and families can be negotiated and navigated.

RECOMMENDED WEBSITES

The Canadian Association of Social Workers
http://www.casw-acts.ca/
The Canadian Association of Social Workers is a national association that monitors employment conditions and establishes standards of practice within the profession. The website provides links that offer detailed information on direct social work practice in over 13 specific settings. Go to "Practicing Social Work in Canada" and click on "What Social Workers Do" to read about the specific tasks and skills involved in direct practice in a variety of social service setting across Canada.

Genograms
http://www.genograms.org/about.html
This website provides a comprehensive overview of what, when, and how to use genograms in direct practice. Key concepts and components of genograms are explained and linked to case material. The site also includes detailed descriptions on interpreting genograms, cautions, and caveats as well as a list of key readings.

The National Case Management Network
http://www.ncmn.ca/
The National Case Management Network (NCMN) is a Canadian, non-profit organization created to connect, support, and sustain those who provide case management services. The website provides an overview of the skills and competencies involved in delivering case management services to clients across health and social service networks.

Social Work with Groups and Communities

LEARNING OBJECTIVES

- To outline different types of social work with groups and communities.

- To identify how process and structure affect social work with groups and communities.

- To understand the theoretical models underlying group and community practice.

- To examine factors that shape group leadership and facilitation.

- To appreciate how purpose guides group membership, interactions, and dynamics in group and community work.

Chapter Outline

This chapter introduces foundational principles of social work practice with groups and communities. In social work practice, groups fall primarily into two categories: treatment groups and task groups. The first section of this chapter provides an overview of different types of groups (e.g., therapeutic groups, task groups), different group structures (e.g., open ended, time limited), and different models of facilitation (e.g., self-help, professionally led). The stages of group development and how to apply these principles to different group types are also introduced. The second section provides an overview of different approaches to working with communities and introduces the principles and practices informing community development from multiple perspectives. Particular emphasis is placed on the importance of community histories in the formation of partnerships, identification and mobilization of community capacity, and sustainability in community work. Woven throughout the chapter are demonstrations of the ways personal and professional values shape work with groups and communities.

Historical Contexts of Social Work with Groups and Communities

Social work with groups and communities finds its origins in early social work and other community-organizing movements. Group and community work was informed by social reform-oriented settlement houses, developed in the late 1800s/early 1900s (see Chapter 1 for a more detailed discussion), as well as by the more contemporary civil rights movements of the 1970s. Adherents to the settlement house movement were volunteers who believed that moving into poor neighbourhoods alongside those living in poverty would improve conditions through the social, economic, and political reconstruction of urban neighbourhoods. Thus, group and community work grew out of a settlement house focus on education, recreation, socialization, and community involvement with new immigrants. Community work emphasized mutual support and promoted democratic participation. Initial writings emphasized helping processes that occurred during group interactions (e.g., Coyle, 1930).

Social work practice with groups and communities contains its own theoretical bases, key values, and skills. Group- and community-based social work practice utilizes individuals' strengths, skills, talents, commitment to a common purpose or goal(s), connections through mutual aid, and other resources to either address members' individual needs (**treatment groups**) or accomplish specific tasks not exclusively related to members (**task groups**).

treatment group A group that focuses primarily on socio-emotive or behavioural needs of participants.

task group A group that focuses on completing a specific assignment or goal for a clientele, organization, or community.

Different Forms of Social Work Groups

One group can look very different from the next, depending on the purpose of the group and its composition. For example, treatment groups range from a therapy group whose purpose is corrective led by a professional with expertise in an issue or approach, such as a behaviourally oriented eating disorder group, to a more egalitarian self-help group where the group worker is a peer who shares the same issue as the group, such as Alcoholics Anonymous. Task groups can range from a committee made up of employees of the same organization whose purpose is to make recommendations to an organization to a social action group made up of people with different relationships to

TABLE 5.1	How Theoretical Perspectives Apply to Group Work*
Faulty engine theories	Cognitive-behavioural theories emphasize the importance of the way people think, feel, and perceive behaviour as learned and shaped by our interpretations of the world (cognitions). These cognitions play a critical role in shaping one's psychological reactions to issues, events, and experiences. "Faulty" interpretations can lead to irrational or maladaptive behaviours. Teater (2010) noted three fundamental assumptions linked to cognitive-behavioural theories: (1) Thinking mediates emotions and behaviour; (2) "faulty" thinking leads to psychological distress and dysfunction; and (3) altering distorted thinking and behaviour can reduce stress and dysfunction. Group interventions engage members' feedback on other members' interpretations in order to challenge and correct the faulty thinking so that one's behaviour more closely matches the social situation. Different from individual work, the group format allows participants to practise other ways of interacting in social situations. It also allows participants to give rather than only receive feedback, which has been found to be a valued and important factor in group work (Lindsay et al., 2008; Shechtman & Perl-Dekle, 2008).
Ecosystem theories	Ecosystem theories emphasize the importance of examining interactions between members of a system. All social-work group workers use elements of ecosystems thinking in their work with groups by paying close attention to how the group as a system is supporting or hindering individual members. Problems of "fit" between group interactions and individual needs are named and used to enhance group cohesion and support individual growth. For example, a group worker focused on interactions may observe a group's tendency to avoid difficult issues by changing the subject or making a joke when members begin to discuss their sadness or anger. If one of the goals of the group is to facilitate the safe expression of emotion, this group tendency may be named by the worker so that interactions around difficult subjects can change and the group as a system can accommodate its members' needs for expression (Connors & Caple, 2005).
Story-telling theories	Narrative theories in social work focus on our personal stories and how stories and narratives shape individuals, families, and communities. Social constructionist theories also influence the development of using a storytelling approach in social work. From a social constructionist perspective, we construct shared meanings that frame the creation of how we understand the world around us. These theoretical approaches maintain that stories, particularly stories featuring strength and resilience, can positively influence how we think, feel, and act. Problematic constructions or stories can be harmful. In a social work group, members listen to their own stories as well as the stories of others. This provides members with the opportunity to address negative or damaging life stories and collaborate in the stories' reconstructions. The reconstructed stories should bring out members' strengths, highlight their abilities to empower each other, and contribute to each other's healing (Hall, 2011; Poole, Gardner, Flower, & Cooper, 2009).
Onion-peeling theories	Many forms of psychotherapy assume that problems and stress experienced by individuals are often expressions of unresolved interpersonal conflicts and issues. The group format allows these conflicts to resurface as the members are helped to recognize how deep-seated beliefs from their families of origin affect their reactions to other group members and the group leader (transference and counter-transference) and the subsequent relationships they form with group members (transference). The group also allows members to gain insight into these tendencies, act out their conflicts in a safe and supportive environment, and experience what it is like to engage in more positive interactions with others (Yalom & Leszcz, 2005).

*See Chapter 2 for an in-depth discussion of theories in social work generally; these categories correspond to the categories in Chapter 2; Connolly & Harms, 2012.

an issue (personal experiences, professional expertise) who come together to pressure a decision-making body to change a policy. While most groups discussed in this chapter are created or formed by social workers for a particular purpose, some groups come together spontaneously. These naturally formed groups are often pivotal to identify and engage when trying to work with a community around a specific issue. Identifying and reflecting on the function of the social worker in natural groups can also help to gain awareness regarding the roles typically played in groups and the learned reactions and sensitivities to group dynamics.

Group social work has been defined as a "goal directed activity with small treatment or task groups aimed at meeting socioemotional needs and accomplishing tasks. This activity is directed to individual members of a group and to the group as a whole within a system of service delivery" (Toseland & Rivas, 2012, p. 11). While treatment groups focus primarily on individual change and task groups focus primarily on accomplishing a task for an organization, community, or to advance a social issue, in reality these "types" are not always mutually exclusive. One could, for example, have a group of older women in a community convened because they are identified as socially isolated for the purpose of enhancing their connections to one another and the work around them. The primary purpose is therefore to change their individual circumstance of isolation (treatment). However, the group by working together may note that social isolation is a common issue for older adults in part because of how society views older adults as dependent and/or non-productive. The group may decide to engage in some action within its community to propose a different view of older adults (transforming it into a task group). Conversely one may bring a group of neighborhood residents together to talk about how to make their neighbourhood safer (task group). In the process of advocating for programs and services, members of the community who were disempowered may feel more empowered (individual change). Another example of a group's evolution from a treatment group to a task group would be when a group helping adolescents address their eating disorders (treatment) decides, as an outcome of their treatment, to create a public awareness campaign focused on adolescent body image and the influence of the media (task).

Across all groups, social-work group practitioners share several key values. These values include respecting and viewing all group members as equal participants capable of helping one another, encouraging solidarity and mutual aid among group members, empowering group members to access their own capacity to make change within themselves and their communities, recognizing how diversity in groups according to ethnic origin, age, religious affiliation, and other aspects of social location shapes group processes, ensuring that power structures inherent in members' social location are acknowledged so that collaboration and shared decision-making can be achieved, and honouring each members' right to express issues of concern and share ideas. Integrated with these values is a group worker's social location, which shapes the expression of these values as well as his or her interactions with the group, including facilitation and leadership. It is critical to ensure that external power structures are not replicated in groups by paying attention to diversity and ensuring that power and privilege are recognized and discussed so that each member can contribute equally, and shared decision-making and collaboration can be achieved (Marbley, 2004).

Groups come in all shapes and sizes as well as all lengths and formats. A therapeutic treatment group aimed at insight building among members may comprise only 6–8 members so that all have ample opportunities to share their personal stories and experiences. An educational group aimed at imparting knowledge may have 20–25 participants as exchange between members is expected to be low. A group can be **open** or **closed** depending on the purpose of the group and the mandate of the organization that houses the group

open group A group where members can come or go at any time so group membership changes throughout the life of the group. It is often open ended, meaning that there is no specified ending to the group. Members leave when they feel ready and return when needed.

closed group A group with a fixed or closed membership, where membership does not change during the life of the group.

(Toseland & Rivas, 2012). Open groups allow new members to join or leave the group at any time. Because membership changes between sessions it is important to make sure every group has a beginning (introduction of purpose, topic, and membership), middle (where the majority of the work occurs), and an end (summary in recognition that any meeting could be a first or last one for any member). Turner (2011) noted that in open groups where membership fluctuates, group cohesion and mutual support may be promoted by the facilitator through **linking**. By linking issues and remarks raised by present group members to experiences made by members who attended previous group sessions, facilitators are able to use previous members' insights to help current participants. This also allows facilitators to keep members connected to the group should they elect to return at another time. A group can also be closed, which describes a group with a fixed membership from the beginning of the group. This means that individuals cannot join the group in the middle of its life. There are advantages and disadvantages to both types of groups, although it is critical to match the purpose of the group with an open or closed structure. For example, an open membership group might not be appropriate with a group that is helping members discuss experiences of child sexual abuse for the first time because members may be more likely to discuss their intimate feelings and reactions with group members they come to know well over time. An open group might be a good match for individuals struggling with addictions because members more advanced in their healing can provide hope and direction to those who are recognizing their issues for a first time. Groups with open membership are often open ended, meaning that there is no specified ending to the group. Instead members leave when they feel ready and return when needed. Groups with closed membership are most typically close ended or time limited.

> **linking** Defined as "the practitioner's conscious attempt to make connections between similarities in feelings or experiences that exist among members" (Kosoff, 2003, p. 35).

Treatment Groups

Treatment groups are designed to meet members' individual needs including emotional support, skill development, growth, and change. A group worker has a dual responsibility: he or she is responsible to attend to the goals of the individuals in the group and to the functioning and goals of the group itself. Possible benefits of group treatment include empathy from multiple sources (feeling that one is not alone with an issue), feedback from multiple perspectives, mutual aid, normalization, broader pool of resources within capacities of the group, social support, and validation (Toseland & Rivas, 2012). Negative outcomes could occur when the group is ineffectively facilitated or managed, when members breach confidentiality, when more vocal members dominate the group, when members do not express their own perspectives but conform to what they see as the group norm, or when societal structures of power and privilege are replicated within the group (Toseland & Rivas, 2012). Examples of treatment groups include support groups, self-help groups, talking/sharing circles, psychoeducational groups, therapy groups, and socialization groups. Key characteristics consist of purpose, leadership, focus, bond, composition, and communication. It is important to keep in mind that some issues can be addressed in multiple formats, while others are more effectively and appropriately addressed in particular formats.

Support Groups and Self-Help Groups

In support groups, group leaders facilitate the group and foster the creation of group norms that encourage sharing. Primary goals of support groups are: "(a) fostering mutual aid, (b) helping members cope with stressful life events, and (c) revitalizing and enhancing members' coping abilities so they can effectively adapt to and cope with

By disclosing personal experiences with members facing similar obstacles, the group works together to foster change.

future stressful life events" (Toseland & Rivas, 2012, p. 10). A leader in a support group facilitates empathic understanding and fosters mutual aid by offering connections between different members' experiences and encouraging members to talk directly to one another. Both functions support the development of cohesion and universality among group members, which promotes members' abilities to share information, experiences, and coping strategies (Lindsay, Roy, Montminy, Turcotte, & Genest-Dufault, 2008). Depending on the issue being discussed, leaders of support groups may also provide members with educational material and information aimed at normalizing their reactions and enhancing their coping abilities. Because members share a particular issue for which they are seeking support (e.g., coping with caregiving or coping with an illness), group membership may be diverse. Self-disclosure is typically limited to emotions related to the issue for which members are seeking support. In this way discussions typically focus on the present.

The main characteristic distinguishing support groups from self-help groups is leadership. Support groups are professionally led while self-help groups are peer led or led by someone with professional training who shares the issue the group shares. Many models have both types of leaders. Both support groups and self-help groups can effectively accommodate up to 12 members, depending on the issues being discussed. The purpose of a self-help group is to help members solve their own problems. Hence leadership is taken on by a member of the group. The defining characteristic of self-help groups is that the group workers/leaders share the same issue as the group members and infuses their own experiences into group discussions. Disclosure is expected from group members and the leader. Like support groups, self-help groups encourage exchange between members founded on the assumption that peers sharing a similar issue or concern are well positioned to help one another and benefit from the reciprocity offered by a group format.

The following are examples of issues commonly and effectively managed in support and/or self-help groups:

- an online group (e-community) for parents whose children have committed suicide;
- a group of older adults transitioning into an assisted living home;
- a group of refugees coping with barriers to family reunification;
- a group for individuals struggling with addictions, such as Alcoholics Anonymous (AA);
- a group for families of individuals struggling with addictions, such as Al-Anon;
- an online group for individuals with social phobias.

Talking/Sharing Circles

Talking/sharing circles have been a First Nations traditional gathering model for millennia. Council meetings, ceremonies, and social gatherings were traditionally conducted in a circle (Hart, 2002). The main purpose of talking or sharing circles is to provide a place of safety where people can share experiences and perspectives on issues brought to the circle in order to help and/or heal each other (Hart, 2002). The goals of circles, reflected in a First Nations approach to social work, are the "initiation of the healing process, promotion of understanding, joining with others, and growth" (Hart, 2002, p. 61). A circle may be open or closed ended, and the membership composition varies depending on the purpose of circle. If a circle is intended to "address more serious issues, for example sexual or substance abuse . . . a screening process [would] assess suitability for participation" (Dylan, 2003, p. 122). The formal leadership of the group is typically the responsibility of an elder, who opens the group with a prayer or ceremony. Norms are fairly unchanging, thus anyone who participates understands that when the elder is finished speaking, the sacred object he or she is holding is passed around so that others may take turns speaking. Those not speaking are actively engaged in respectful listening. The person holding the object may choose to speak and does so without interruption, although "silence is [also] a respected and valid option in the circle" (Dylan, p. 128). Dylan describes talking circles as most similar to self-help groups (described above) where "the group-as-a-whole (including the elder) makes use of the unmistakable bond of commonality, a bond that is assumed a priori, experienced existentially within the group, and reinforced culturally and structurally via the [talking circle] model" (p. 125). Unlike support or self-help groups where patterns of sharing are relatively random, talking circles tend to follow the contours of the circle when sharing. Examples of issues that have been addressed in talking/sharing circles:

- a circle for women survivors of sexual abuse;
- a circle for adults processing the pain of attending residential schools;
- a circle for students attending university;
- a circle for community members addressing a proposal to institute a decolonizing approach in a local social service agency.

See Chapter 9 for a discussion of restorative justice or sentencing circles.

Psychoeducational Groups

Psychoeducational groups combine the goal of an educational group (to impart knowledge) and support. Typically these groups have a rather structured format where information is delivered in the first phase of the group and then a skill is practised in the second phase to help members cope or respond better to this issue. This can be accomplished through presentations, discussions, and experiential exercises. The group leader acts as a teacher and provider of structure for group discussion. The linkages among members are common interests in learning and developing skills. Group members typically have similar educational backgrounds or skill levels. Research has shown that education alone is typically not enough to change behaviour and that the experiential component appears to make a difference in individual change (Cooke, McNally, Mulligan, Harrison, & Newman, 2001; Hales & Cowels, 2009). Depending on the balance between education and support, the group size may be large (e.g., up to 50 members). Given that group dynamics are important, facilitators need to pay particular attention to members' verbal and non-verbal responses to the material and to one another. Examples of issues that can be addressed in psychoeducational groups include the following:

- a group offering support for first-time caregivers;
- a health education group for families with children with asthma;
- a group for couples transitioning to parenthood;
- a group for school faculty and administrators focused on the psychosocial needs of two-spirited, lesbian, gay, bisexual, trans and queer teens.

Therapy Groups

Therapy groups come together to address issues, led by the group worker who is seen as the expert and/or authority figure. While members are connected by the common goal of personal growth, their specific issues or concerns may be more diverse than members of support or self-help groups. These groups are typically highly interactive where members often take responsibility for communicating their insights and observations of one another in the group. The focus of therapy groups is on individual members' issues, concerns, or goals, and the leader may work with individuals within the group, as the "etiology and development of each member's problem is unique" (Toseland & Rivas, 2012, p. 25). An ideal size of a therapy group is eight members. Members' self-reflection, interpersonal learning capabilities, and ability to reach **catharsis** are critical contributors to the group's ability to achieve its goals for its members (Yalom, 1995). Groups that are designed for members' healing and growth provide leader-supported spaces for members to utilize self-reflection and the group members' perceptions to modify the ways in which they think, feel, and behave.

> **catharsis** Release of emotional tension through an activity or experience.

Connections are based on sharing a common purpose with separate member goals. Relationships are shared among group members, such as leader-member or member-member, or member-group. Leader-member or member-member communication is typical, and self-disclosure is moderate to high. Examples of therapy groups include the following:

- a counselling group for couples experiencing marital difficulties;
- a cognitive-therapy group for young women with anxiety disorders;
- a mindfulness-based group for adults with depression;
- an emotion-focused group for women with metastatic breast cancer.

Socialization Groups

Socialization groups can focus on learning social skills or can be recreational. These groups typically employ program activities such as games, role plays, and outings to help members accomplish individual goals. The purpose of socialization groups is to learn through modelling in order to improve communication, social skills, and interpersonal relationships through activities, structured exercises, role plays, and so forth. The group worker leads as a director of the group's activities or programs. The group is a medium for activity, participation, and involvement. Members are connected through participation in a common activity, enterprise, or situation. The composition of the group depends on its

Case STUDY

Arts-Based Group Work

LEARNING ABOUT ONESELF THROUGH OTHER'S reactions and reflections is critical for personal growth. Utilizing arts-based approaches is an innovative method for facilitating inner reflection, particularly with children for whom it may be more natural than using words. Coholic, Lougheed, and Lebreton (2009) used a holistic group work approach with children living in foster care to develop their self-esteem and self-awareness through the engagement of other members' reactions and reflections. They found that using a holistic art-based approach with foster children was effective in assisting with specific problems, facilitating expression, and helping to address trauma-related crises. These methods used in a group format can "create novel experiences and an environment within which group participants are encouraged to explore their viewpoints, feelings, and behaviours to develop their self-awareness and improve their self-esteem" (p. 34).

This qualitative, collaborative research project was conducted in partnership with the local child protection agency for the districts of Sudbury and Manitoulin, Ontario. Data were gathered from 15 six-week groups composed of children and youth ranging in age from 8 to 15. A total of 35 children and youth participated, some attending multiple groups. Initial groups contained only teenage girls, while the remaining 12 groups were composed of boys and girls, aged 8 to 12.

The group work was focused on using art-based methods to assist children in locating their imaginative selves; exploring their own feelings, thoughts, and behaviours; paying attention for periods of time; and recognizing and developing their strengths. For many of the group participants, this was the first time they were given space to learn to "notice, identify, and reflect on their feelings as a new skill and practice" (p. 37). Group facilitators sought to avoid children's associating this group with more traditional therapy groups that brought up feelings of vulnerability via sharing experiences that could be painful. Thus, they conceptualized the group as one focused on promoting self-esteem and self-awareness. Some participants who required further assistance may have felt more comfortable expressing feelings after participation in the arts-based group and therefore felt better prepared for a more traditional counselling group. Findings suggested that overall, children connected with knowledge about themselves while some "learned and applied new skills, were coping in a more positive manner, connected with feelings, and felt more positive about themselves" (p. 41).

Key findings included the following:

Children deriving enjoyment from group participation and desiring a continuation beyond the initial six weeks: Children identified the group activities as "fun," enjoying the opportunities to play games and engage in creative activities, sharing and discussing thoughts and dreams, and, at times, reimagining them with other group members, meeting new people, and engaging in quiet meditation.

Positive outcomes of participation via reports from children's child care workers, foster parents, and children: Child care workers, foster parents, and child participants were all able to provide examples that illustrated the ways in which group participation fostered the children's self-esteem and self-awareness. These examples included being able to see positive differences in behaviour after participation compared to before participation, children feeling confident in standing up for themselves, improved familial relationships, and feeling more in control of life situations. Some children reported using the techniques and experiencing a heightened awareness of feelings outside of the group.

location and purpose, and can be homogeneous or heterogeneous. Self-disclosure is relatively limited. Social skills are typically smaller than recreational groups with the former compromising no more than eight members and the latter over ten. Examples of a socialization group include the following:

- a settlement organization orientation group for newly arrived refugees;
- a summer camp for children run by a local agricultural organization;
- a social group for individuals with severe disabilities living in the community;
- a Game On! group (Big Brothers, Big Sisters Canada) for boys and young men, which works through current lifestyle issues through non-traditional physical activities.

Task Groups

Task groups are oriented toward the completion of a mission: finding solutions to a problem, developing new ideas and/or making decisions, and focusing on addressing the needs of clients, an organization, or a community. The purpose of a task group is to accomplish a goal that is neither intrinsically nor immediately linked to the needs of the group members; the goal will affect a broader constituency, not just group members. Task groups should represent people from different backgrounds, typically have an agenda, focus on consensus building and decision-making, and can be advisory or charged with making a decision. Addressing the needs of clients, organizations, and communities through a task group can be accomplished through teams, treatment conferences, staff development groups, committees, cabinets, boards of directors, coalitions, and social action groups.

Teams

A team is a collection of "individual staff members, each of whom possesses particular knowledge and skills, who come together to share their expertise with one another for a particular purpose" (Toseland, Palmer-Ganeles, & Chapman, 1986, p. 46). Team members are a group of people who work together on behalf of a particular client group (Toseland & Rivas, 2012). Rather than individuals simply reporting to one another what they individually plan to do for a given client, teams that function as a group collaborate with one another to plan for client care (Parker-Oliver, Bronstein, & Kurzekeski, 2005). Social workers' skills are particularly valuable to the creation and maintenance of multidisciplinary teams because they are trained not only to focus on outcome but also process, which may be interfering with collective problem-solving and decision-making. Additionally, role clarification is critical in a team. Within a team environment, roles can overlap, as members are required to go beyond their position to meet clients' needs. Essentially, team members may need to become knowledgeable in other backgrounds in addition to their own, such as a social worker finding out about new medications or a physician searching out available community services.

Staff Development Groups

The goal of staff development groups is the improvement of service provision by developing and updating workers' skills. Development groups provide workers with opportunities to learn about new treatment approaches, resources, and community services as well as practise new skills and review and learn from their previous work with clients. For example, a staff development group could be a group of social workers who attend a series of seminars highlighting new approaches to mental health treatment. Although personal

Theory in Practice

MULTIDISCIPLINARY TEAMS

TO ADDRESS LIVING WITH HIV/AIDS, an individual's needs must be met on multiple levels: psychological, emotional, social, and spiritual in addition to physical (Mah & Ives, 2011). This involves focusing more on the person than on the virus, which can often occur in a hospital and medical setting with health professionals (Gebbie, 1995). One profession or area of expertise alone cannot address all the needs an HIV infection demands. Multidisciplinary teams are by their very nature bio-psychosocially oriented with appropriate membership (medical doctors, nurses, and physiotherapists for the bio arena; psychologists or social workers for the psychological arena; and social workers and occupational therapists for the social arena). By bringing in professionals trained predominantly in one aspect, collective problem-solving and expertise can be holistic. A team composed of members from different disciplines combines knowledge from diverse disciplines and can also widen one's own skill set and gain an appreciation of other disciplines' perspectives (Korazim-Kőrösy Mizrahi, Katz, Karmon, Garcia, & Bayne Smith, 2007). Working in collaboration amongst professions also challenges the long tradition of specialization and subsequent fragmentation of services in the health-care field (Bronstein, 2003: Lasker & Weiss, 2003). HIV treatment originated within a medical model; however, a holistic model is more inclusive of the social, psychosocial, and psychological needs of patients.

A multidisciplinary team approach requires many considerations, including: within-team communication (regular, periodic meetings), community collaboration, role clarification, protection of client confidentiality, and a client-centered approach. Key components to multidisciplinary collaboration include understanding the multiple perspectives involved, willingness to share one's expertise, flexibility, acknowledging work of support staff, involvement of financial, managerial, and administrative staff, implementation of staff support systems such as counselling, and knowing one's role within the team as well as understanding the roles of team members (Hinshaw & DeLeon, 1995: Lifshitz, 1996; Pinching, 1989). With true respect among members, case discussions and planning can be comprehensive. Professionals on an HIV multidisciplinary team are required to combine knowledge from their own discipline with an expertise on HIV/AIDS as well as be in regular, direct communication to prevent fragmentation and duplication of services. It is also important when meeting to share experiences to gain meaning from their work in a compassionate, trusting environment which can help to mitigate the effects of job-related stress (Dando & Finlon, 2003). This is essential when working with vulnerable populations who have had traumatic life experiences, in addition to the inevitable loss of patients from AIDS. These teams also sometimes bring the client and family in to discuss and plan for their situation, which honours the clients' personal values and preferences and allows clients to be treated holistically (rather than to reserve certain questions for certain team members).

disclosure is expected to be low, disclosure about difficulties with particular clients and issues may be an expectation to enable participants to fully engage and apply the ideas presented in workshops to their practice situations. Hence, these groups often require an established level of trust so that workers can share their critical client moments and learn from the trainers and one another how to apply the concepts being presented to the real world of social work (Barlow, Rogers & Coleman, 2004).

Committees

A committee is a group of people appointed or elected with a particular charge. Personal disclosure in committees is typically low; discussions usually revolve around an agenda. Decision-making can be by consensus (i.e., talking together to collectively make a decision) or democratic. Some committees also use parliamentary procedures. They are typically advisory to a higher body such as a director. For example, a committee in a health and social services agency might be charged with reviewing their policies regarding how members receive services. One specific type of committee is a coalition, which is a group of stakeholders from different organizations who join together in order to advocate for a particular issue. A challenge to decision-making in coalitions can be tensions stemming from representing the interests of the coalition when they may conflict with interests of one's organization.

Social Action Groups

The pursuit of social justice is inextricably linked to community organizing and group work, as "the vast majority of community-organizing work is conducted through task-oriented groups" (Staples, 2012, p. 288). Social action groups consist of community members who get together or are brought together to advocate for a particular social issue that affects individuals but also has applicability in the broader community. Social action groups can also be called grassroots groups as they grow from concerns from community members who occupy marginalized positions. Goals of social action groups could be

The Canadian Press/Ryan Remiorz

In September 2013, a social action group protests against Quebec's proposed Values Charter that would disallow the display of religious symbols for public employees in the workplace.

"making fundamental changes in the community, such as the redistribution of resources and gaining access to decision-making for marginal groups, and changing legislative mandates, policies, and practices of institutions (Ohmer & DeMasi, 2009, p. 8). A social worker working with social action groups may have multiple roles such as an enabler role, where the social worker educates the group as to various resources and different types of advocating strategies, or a directive role, where the social worker, based on his or her expertise, may be asked to be the spokesperson for the group, advise as to the most effective techniques considering the context of the issue of focus, or outline relevant opportunities for potential advocacy initiatives (Toseland & Rivas, 2012). It is important to highlight, however, that a key element in social action groups is the encouragement of leadership from within the community and broad participation from those involved directly and indirectly with the issue of focus. Community participation is a critical element for collective action and sustainable change. Engaging community members "provides access points for new emerging community leaders to develop their experience, confidence and skills, thereby building community capacity, which increases voluntary action through 'people power' and insures greater sustainability and staying power due to the increased commitment and follow through of community members" (Staples, 2012, p. 288). Broad participation by community members facilitates the use of **social capital**. Social capital theory suggests that community organizations are a source of bonding, bridging, and linking capital.

Bonding capital is characterized by interactions or relationships that reinforce a common identity and exclude outsiders and is likely to be found within families or within members of an immigrant group; bridging capital extends across more diverse and more weakly connected social spheres, such as business associates or friends from different ethnic groups (Putnam, 2000). Bridging capital is necessary for moving beyond one's immediate ethnic or familiar networks. For example, if a religious congregation-based group offered sponsorship to a refugee living abroad, it could hypothetically offer (a) greater support from relationships within the congregation, (b) greater access to community-based networking with local resources, and (c) wider opportunities for language acquisition or increased language proficiency through the recruitment of congregational volunteers than a resettlement agency could offer. Linking social capital plays a similar role as bridging social capital, but bases its connections on relationships between persons outside the local social networks in various hierarchies and places of power (Szreter & Woolcock, 2004). Thus, from the example above, the religious congregation-based group could also partner with other local groups and provincial- and national-level organizations supporting refugees to advocate for the repeal of stringent family reunification laws for refugees living in Canada to enable them to reunite with their families.

Other examples of a social action group include the following:

- a group of migrant women workers lobbying for changes in policy practices that discriminate against women;
- a group of university students seeking support for increased tuition assistance for students from families with low incomes;
- a group of social workers advocating for increased social and health services for youth transitioning out of institutional care;
- an association or organization focused on preserving and celebrating culture as well as advocating for the rights of its members. For example, the Vancouver Métis Community Association advocates for members of the Métis community through public education, communication with all levels of government and the promotion of harmony between the Métis people and all groups of society.

social capital Refers to "features of social organizations such as networks, norms, and social trust that facilitate coordination and cooperation for mutual benefit" (Putnam, 1995, p. 67).

In Their Own Words

WORKING WITH ABORIGINAL PEOPLES IN SMALL COMMUNITIES

AS A STUDENT I STUDIED group work as part of my program, and this knowledge has proven invaluable, particularly in working with Aboriginal Peoples and in small communities where resources are limited and the needs are great. My experience includes work in small communities in Northern Quebec, rural Ontario, the Northwest Territories, and Yukon as well as working with Aboriginal Peoples in an urban environment.

In urban centres Aboriginal Peoples often gravitate together for mutual support and may not be comfortable seeking help from non-Aboriginal agencies. While working for Inuit Patient Services in Montreal I used social work students and volunteers to bring people together to ease homesickness and loneliness. I also linked with external groups for specialized support. Alcoholics Anonymous tirelessly provided individual mentoring and on-site meetings. Hope and Cope, a Cancer support network was another agency that was happy to provide outreach services. These linkages enabled me to offer many more services to clients than I could have managed alone.

Family and community are everything in Aboriginal communities. Joining together to deal with crises and address social issues is part of their cultures and traditions. Small communities have traditions of mutual assistance. Social workers can use group work knowledge to support and enhance these networks. With the technological advances of the Internet and video conferencing we can also help communities to access additional resources such as educational programming and support services. For example, Alcoholics Anonymous offers meetings by video conferencing in communities where there is no local group. Group work knowledge can build community capacity.

As a social worker in a small community, I have found that being involved in professional networks is essential for support and professional growth. Local interagency groups can coordinate services and share the load of high-need clients. Many communities also have social action groups such as the Yukon Anti-Poverty Coalition, joining professionals and community members in work for community change.

Wider professional networks can link social workers within their region and nationally. In Yukon I was part of the Council of Yukon First Nations Health and Social Development Commission, a body that included the Health and Social Services from all Yukon First Nations. As a group we were able to access funding and develop projects that benefited everyone, with the workload being shared. In the Northwest Territories and Yukon, I have been an active member of the Association of Social Workers in Northern Canada and the Canadian Association of Social Workers. Being part of a national voice for social work in Canada and being connected across the country helps keep me current with best practices and other important developments.

If you stop to think about it, you will find many ways to use your group work skills to enhance your practice and develop capacity in your community. You can only do so much on your own, so reach out, connect, and make the best use of the resources available.

Lynn Sparks, MSW, is a sessional instructor at Yukon College.

Stages of Group Development

What happens in the life of a group? How do the relationships among the group members come together and evolve in order to address the purpose of the group and achieve its goals? The **stages** of group development have been conceptualized in various ways.

Broadly, most groups whether they are task oriented or treatment oriented go through the broad stages that have a beginning, middle, and end. What occurs in a group's stages of development and the length and breadth of those stages are shaped by group purpose, member goals, time availability, and the context in which the group is situated.

Tuckman's (1965) conceptualization of group development stages was foundational in group theory and is widely accepted and understood in the field of group work (Fall & Wejnert, 2005). Tuckman's stage model provided a framework for understanding how group dynamics within a closed group change over time, suggesting that a group's development moves through a series of defined activities and behaviours over its lifetime. There have been subsequent models that illustrate group development processes as significantly more complex and differ in the content and emphasis in the beginning and middle stages (e.g., Garland, Jones, & Kolodny, 1976; Hartford, 1971; Klein, 1972; Runkel, Lawrence, Oldfield, Rider & Clark, 1971). However, a framework based on Tuckman's stages can be helpful in thinking about the life stages of a group, and can be applied generally to fit various group settings. His model for the stages through which a group progresses consists of

1. testing and dependence;
2. intragroup conflict;
3. development of group cohesion; and
4. functional role-relatedness.

These stages of group structure are also known as forming, storming, norming, and performing. Tuckman and Jensen (1977) added a fifth stage of adjourning to acknowledge the evaluation and termination that occurs in a group.

In the forming stage, members "discover, define, evaluate, and test the behaviors that group members will find acceptable and functional" (Runkel, Lawrence, Oldfield, Rider & Clark, 1971, p. 181). This first stage is characterized by context setting, which includes a discussion and clarification of group purpose, relationship-building, and boundary setting. Members may feel anxiety and apprehension regarding their participation. The group's purpose should dictate the logistical questions that go into planning the group. How long should the group run? How many members should the group have? Should it be open or closed?

It is also in this stage that the group begins to develop cohesion. Cohesion, introduced by psychologist Kurt Lewin in the 1940s, is a central concept in understanding group dynamics. Cohesion generally refers to a sense of belonging shared by a group of people who feel accepted by each other (Lindsay, Roy, Montminy, Turcotte, & Genest-Dufault, 2008). Without cohesion, the group may disband, without achieving its goals. A group leader can facilitate cohesion by helping a group of strangers evolve into a group bound together by a sense of unity around a common focus on a particular issue (Forsyth, 2010). Lewin defined cohesion as "the forces that keep groups intact by pushing members together as well as the countering forces that push them apart" (Forsyth, 2010, p. 119). Cohesion must be present in a group in order to engage other therapeutic factors, such as creating a trusting environment in order for members to share freely and give each other constructive feedback (Brabender, Smolar, & Fallon, 2004).

stage A distinct period in a process of a group's growth and development.

After the group is formed, members also begin the initial development of group norms. Adherence to group norms is greater when members contribute to their development. While norms vary according to the group context, some examples include the following:

- actively listening to members' ideas;
- acknowledging that each member's perspectives and opinions are valuable;
- refraining from interrupting while someone is talking;
- agreeing to be open, yet honoring privacy;
- agreeing to the confidentiality of all that is discussed within the group;
- respecting each member's personal context;
- being supportive rather than judgmental;
- all members offering their ideas and resources;
- encouraging each member to take responsibility for the work of the group;
- agreeing that when there is a difference of opinion, group members will discuss the differences without individualizing.

The next stage is referred to as storming, which is characterized by conflict among the members as well as with the group leader. This is a natural stage in a group's life where "facades and personas give way to more honest views of others, and group members begin to take intra- and interpersonal risks in the form of feedback and deeper sharing of self" (Fall & Wejnert, 2005, p. 317). However, there may be differing levels of comfort in addressing conflict. Conflict may come when members experience "a discrepancy between their initial hopes for the [group] and the realities of working together" (Bens, 2012, p. 68) or simply from members not liking each other. A group leader needs to feel comfortable in addressing conflict(s) within the group directly, rather than seeing if it will resolve itself. Conflict is a natural, expected part of group work. In addition to occurring among members, conflict may also occur directly with the group leader. Members may challenge or reject the leader and/or his or her ability to adequately facilitate the group. If the group leader is unable to manage the group effectively, members may try to compensate, which could lead to power struggles and, in turn, could derail the group in its pursuit of its goals.

Having survived storming by addressing conflict and issues that may have been on the surface or underneath, the group members and leader come to the norming stage. At this stage, the group has developed greater cohesion as well as optimism that members will be able to accomplish their goal(s). In addition to discussing their issues and working through them, the group has re-established or revised norms developed earlier, clarified roles, accepted feedback, and come up with new ways of working together, planning, and accomplishing goals. Group members have come to a place of acceptance of the group and the unique contexts of other members and are encouraged to begin the work of the group in the next stage.

Moving through norming means that the group is ready for the next stage, performing, where the group members focus on the work that brought them to the group. At this point, the group leader may be able to pull back from his or her leadership position, with more members taking responsibility for facilitation and the work that is occurring in the group. Communication is more effective, bonds among members are stronger, and responsibilities and planning are democratically distributed (Bens, 2012), thus allowing an environment conducive to high productivity.

The last stage of evolution of a group is its adjourning phase, also called termination or ending. Although endings are a foreseeable outcome in a group—whether the group ends or the member leaves—endings should include the processing of the socio-emotional life of the group and feelings of attachment that members may have to other group members, the group leader, and the group itself. Thus, as in social work focused on working with individuals, social work with groups also needs to address separation and moving on after the group, for both members and the leader. Endings are addressed when members are able to reflect on successes achieved within the group, identify challenges that were presented and perhaps overcome in the group, speak to the group about personal experiences within the group including the extent to which their goals were achieved, express their appreciation for group members and celebrate successes with the group. The group leader's primary role at this stage is to provide process tools that allow the group to reflect on past experiences and direct attention toward wrapping up activities.

As research and practice with groups has developed, more refined theoretical frameworks have emerged that provide structure for groups depending upon their particular purpose. For example, Schiller (2007) described a relational model of development particularly for groups affected by trauma, oppression, and loss. In this model, the group leader works to establish a relational base for a time-limited group, "which includes heightened attention to the safety of group members" (p. 62). The second stage is focused on relationship-building, finding commonalities, and creating or restoring a sense of community. After a "felt sense" of safety has been established, the group worker encourages direct expression of differences and makes room for conflict to be processed by members. This model differs from Tuckman's model in that the hypothesis is that true conflict in a group setting may only emerge after (and not before) a relational base has been established among its members; in other words, norming precedes storming. In the third stage, the worker works to engage mutuality and interpersonal empathy, which combines elements of connecting through and in spite of differences that can help members to expand their worldview of self and others that may have contracted in the face of trauma, loss, or oppression. In the fourth stage, group members are ready to navigate the challenges of conflict and change. In this stage, members' work fosters their ability to find and use one's voice, increase a sense of personal and social empowerment, and move out of a victim mentality to one that re-embraces self-efficacy, hopefulness, and improved functioning. The final stage is the termination stage where the group leader assesses the extent to which each member has had his or her "turn" at being challenged in order to grow before the end of the life of the group. While stages are expected in all groups, far less is known about how open groups pass through these developmental stages as membership changes and the group never adjourns.

Group Leadership and Facilitation

Social-work group workers play a central role in the process of a group's development and its ability to achieve its goals. Early perspectives on styles of leadership ranged from authoritarian to democratic to laissez-faire but were critiqued based on their exclusion of key situational factors, such as individual, group, and broader environmental contexts (Toseland & Rivas, 2012). Later approaches incorporated context as well as the importance of leaders who empower members and affirm their individuality as they pursue personal and group goals (Toseland & Rivas, 2012). Current thinking regarding leadership in a social work context is shaped by ecological theory and an **interactional model** (see Figure 5.1).

A group leader holds considerable power, particularly in the formation and initial meetings of a group as well as facilitating a group's cohesion. How leaders navigate their leadership roles shapes the extent to which they can work with the group "to achieve goals

interactional model
A model where leadership is not the exclusive domain of the leader but is shared among the members as an empowering function (Toseland & Rivas, 2012).

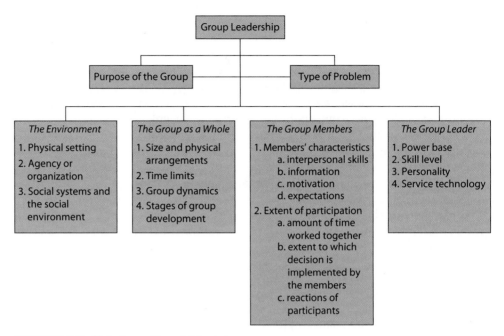

FIGURE 5.1 // Interactional Model

Source: Toseland & Rivas, 2012, p. 105. © 2012. Printed and Electronically reproduced by permission of Pearson Education, Inc., Upper Saddle River, New Jersey.

that are consistent with the value base of social work practice and meet the socio-emotional needs of members" (Toseland & Rivas, 2012, p. 98). Being the leader of a social work group can be intimidating for a beginning social worker with limited experience facilitating groups. Kurland (2006) cautioned that social workers new to group practice "may, at first, believe that they have to take responsibility on their shoulders alone for all that takes place in the group" which she describes as "a heavy burden" (p. 14). She advised reflecting questions, comments, and issues back to the group and providing feedback to the group through observations regarding what one is seeing occurring rather than trying to jump in and solve the group's problems. Group practice is not social casework conducted in a group format; a group is centered on its ability to stimulate and engage mutual aid and empathy while promoting members' strengths in order to address issues. Thus, the responsibility rests on the active participation of all members, including the leader.

Social location also has a considerable impact on group processes. Yu and Gregg (1993) highlighted this, noting that "the presence of a culturally different person in a counselling group has more implications than a mere difference in birthplace or ethnic origin" (p. 87). Marbley (2004) identified the need to examine the impact of diverse social locations of leaders as well as group members within a group's interrelationships. She highlighted the challenges of a facilitator from a traditionally marginalized group facilitating a primarily White group as well as group members of colour being members of a predominantly White group. Her recommendations included ensuring that "group facilitators of color and group members of colour [be protected] from group experiences that may result in further exposure to racism and cultural bias, thus thwarting the therapeutic effectiveness of the group experience" (p. 253). Additionally, Greeley, Garcia, Kessler & Gilchrest (1992) noted that it is critical that facilitators are self-reflective and aware of their own biases. This will reduce the potential that behaviours considered culturally based are misrepresented as problematic.

Practical TIP

Tips for Facilitating and Leading Groups

- Give yourself adequate time for preparation and planning the group.
- Help members create norms for giving and receiving feedback to ensure group members feel comfortable and safe.
- Offer feedback and invite input.
- Encourage group members to contribute to problem identification and problem-solving.
- Make time for self-reflection regarding how the group is proceeding and what issues have been raised for you personally.
- Pay attention to group dynamics, particularly issues, biases, or agendas hidden below the group's surface.
- Probe offensive behaviour by group members; consider whether to explore possible underlying issues that behavior may express or confront directly.
- Assist members in navigating interpersonal conflicts.
- Encourage others to take on leadership roles.
- Support members while they make improvements.
- Address taboo topics directly.

Sources: Bens, 2012; Rubin, 2011; Wayne & Gitterman, 2004.

Community-Based Social Work Practice

As noted earlier in the chapter, group work and community work are not mutually exclusive; in fact, they are overlapping and closely interconnected. For example, some community groups rely heavily on the work of small groups which may be the impetus for social action on the community level. In turn, community advocacy may also lead to the development of a small group focused on a particular topic of concern to the community. The main goal of community-practice focused social workers is to assist individuals in creating groups designed to address social problems facing communities (Weil & Ohmer, 2013).

What or who is a community? Fellin (1995) conceptualized community as (a) communities of locality or place, (b) communities of interest and identity, or (c) an integration of the two. Thus, communities could be physically constructed as members of a neighbourhood, municipality, or other geographic region as well as a collection of people connected through shared identities, interests and/or experiences (e.g., ethnicity, religion, ideology, gender, sexual orientation, educational or professional background, common experiences of particular events, etc.). Recent conceptualizations of community include those that build community in virtual settings or "e-communities" such as for online learning (e.g., Palloff & Pratt, 2001) or support (e.g., Jones & Meier, 2011).

Community practitioners' work typically reflects the following assumptions (DiNitto & McNeece, 2008):

- economic and social injustice stems from the failure of the larger society to assist all individuals in meeting their potential;
- all members of a community have the right to participate directly in decisions that affect them;
- when provided with information, citizens will participate in the decision-making process;

- failure of members of a community to participate in the democratic process may be due to their lack of knowledge about the process, injustices that disenfranchise them, or discomfort with participating due to histories of exclusion.

Given these assumptions, social workers from outside communities may find it necessary to intervene in order to galvanize participation to bring about social justice.

In Their Own Words

THE "OUTSIDERS"

I ALWAYS KNEW THAT ONE DAY I wanted to tell my mother's story. Back in the '60s and '70s, she was a single mom on welfare raising my five sisters and me in Point St. Charles, a slum of Montréal.

When the "Outsiders" invaded the Point—social work and medical school students from McGill who wanted to raise awareness and politicize the residents—everything changed. My mother became involved with grassroots organizations that fought for equality in education and health care, which often involved protests that ended with face-offs against the Montreal riot squad on the six o'clock news.

My father didn't welcome the Outsiders like my mother did. He thought these students believed that if they "played" at being poor by doing things like renting an apartment in the Point and hanging around with welfare "bums," they'd somehow share a common understanding of what it felt like to be powerless and poor. But my father always saw it as a costume they could simply pull off at the end of the day. They were mimicking the symptoms without the disease. The one thing they couldn't play at—the one thing they couldn't replicate—is that sense of powerlessness and shame that the culture of poverty often includes.

Sometimes it seemed like a social worker's job was to help dismantle the very survival skills one needed to live in a tough neighbourhood, or with an abuser, or without a voice or any real power. When a social worker's ideas seemed like they set you up for failure, making you even more vulnerable and weak, it was hard not to see them as the enemy. Or at the very least, completely clueless and therefore not to be taken seriously, and certainly not someone to allow "in."

But as we quickly learned, these Outsiders were trying to help us form a common language, so that what they said would be what we heard. And what we said is what they would hear. But mostly, they taught us, or at least me and my sisters, so much simply by their example. They didn't *tell* us what to do. They showed us.

I was just a kid when those social work students arrived filled with all kinds of ambitious ideas of how to make some real changes in the community. Before they came, we had no health, dental, or eye care available in the Point. Some of our schools lacked the most basic necessities. We were invisible in every way. Outside of the Point we simply did not exist. Until these students arrived, I'm not sure if it had even occurred to most of us to even expect more. To ask for more. To demand more.

I watched and learned as the students helped to transform my mother from a defeated welfare recipient, to an angry, but very well-organized, community activist. They not only helped to politicize her, they also helped her find her voice.

Their confidence in the mothers of Point St. Charles made all the difference.

Kathy Dobson has a BA from the University of Waterloo and two certificates in social work, and is a journalist, with her work appearing in the Globe and Mail, National Post, Ottawa Citizen, *and the* Montreal Gazette.

Community-Practice Frameworks

Community-practice frameworks assist social workers in structuring appropriate intervention strategies. Various approaches exist that are shaped by community context, goals of the community work, the degree to which community members are involved in the stages of addressing community needs, and the change strategies and techniques adopted. In considering frameworks, it is important to reflect on what assumptions one has about the community, one's ideological perspectives on working with marginalized communities and others in need, whether the emphasis is on process (goals focused on building a community's capacity and ability to function over time) or task (goals focused on ameliorating/addressing particular problematic issues), and what skills, roles, and areas of expertise would be most beneficial for this work. Thus, an important role for the practitioner is "facilitation to assist individuals, small groups, and organizations through processes of analysis, action, and reflection (Freire's *praxis*) in ways that encourage emancipatory and transformative learning" (Weil & Ohmer, 2013, p. 148) in order to collaboratively create positive community change.

Rothman's Modes of Community Intervention

A foundational community-practice framework was conceptualized by Rothman (1968, 1995) who identified three modes of community social work practice: locality development, social planning, and social action. Although the modes are presented as distinct approaches to community practice and have differing goals, areas of emphasis, social worker roles, and intervention strategies, they can overlap in order to develop inclusive intervention strategies or organizing plans. In practice, community workers employ a range of techniques and approaches from locality development, social planning, and social action models in their work with communities.

The locality development mode of community practice is a participatory approach which "presupposes that community change should be pursued through broad participation by a wide spectrum of people at the local community level in determining goals and taking civic action" (Rothman, 1995, p. 28). The focus of the approach is to engage a wide variety of community members in order to plan, employ, and evaluate an intervention, which contributes to sustainable change. Central themes of this approach include following democratic procedures, recruiting community-based volunteers, supporting the development of leadership from the community, and advancing educational objectives in the community (City of Calgary, n.d.). Thus, building community capacity is a central feature of this approach through the process of bringing community members together to discuss common issues of concerns and of constructing plans for addressing these issues. In fact, in some contexts, the process through which the community comes to consensus regarding its problems and how it develops strategies to address them can be more important than the resolution of the issue. A historical link is seen between a locality development approach and the early work of settlement houses. Today, a locality approach is behind work of organizations such as Jewish Immigrant Aid Services of Canada in communities across the country and the Canadian International Development Agency (CIDA) on the international level.

The social planning mode of community practice focuses on the technical aspects of problem-solving. This approach relies on the analysis of statistical data, needs assessments, and other community-based evaluations in order to determine community needs. Goals of social planning are task-oriented, "conceptualizing, selecting, establishing, arranging, and delivering goods and services to people who need them . . . [as well as] fostering collaboration among agencies, avoiding duplication and filling in gaps in services" (Rothman, 1995, p. 30). Organizations adopting a social planning approach are focused on addressing specific community needs via programs, which may, at times, preclude broader discussion of the issue of focus within a larger context. Community-member participation varies, as there is a heavy reliance on technical analytical skills, although some organizations strive to include community members in the identification of community strengths. Data are analyzed and then a committee, which may or may not include community members, comes together to make decisions on how to direct practice. For example, United Way Centraide Canada endeavors to connect with and empower community members to capitalize on community engagement. Through partnerships with communities, United Way Centraide uses programs and services to mobilize communities to improve access to and availability of resources, which in the long term can contribute to revitalized neighbourhoods. Of the three modes of community practice, this approach is the most limited in building community capacity. The degree to which social planning can increase community capacity is dependent upon the ways in which organizations integrate and leverage community members' knowledge, skills, expertise, and experience.

The social action mode of practice assumes the presence of a marginalized group that could be organized to bring about change in the broader community to increase resources and/or demand equal treatment (Rothman, 2001). Social action's focus is on organizing community members to mobilize and defend their rights through fundamental social change (See "Social Action Groups" above regarding skills facilitators can use and issues commonly addressed by these groups). Targeted areas of change are social practices, decision-making processes, and legislative mandates, policies, and practices of major institutions as well as a redistribution of power and resources (Ohmer & DeMasi, 2009). Unlike the other two modes, the social action mode's explicit goal is to challenge the community's status quo through conflict, confrontation, direct action, and negotiation. This mode of practice has roots in the conflict organizing model developed by Saul Alinsky (1941, 1971) as well as Paulo Friere's (1970) approach to social change through reflection and action. This mode seeks to bring recognition and discussion of oppression, marginalization, and inequality into community discourse. Smock (2004) further refined social action into "power-based" social action and "transformative" social action. "Power-based" social action refers to a focus on power imbalances; thus, the solution lies in restoring balance through shifting to or building up in areas where power is low.

The Occupy Movement, a worldwide effort, is an example of organized groups demanding equal treatment in the broader community.

Fred Lum/The Globe and Mail/CP

Theory in Practice

PROJECT GENESIS

IN PRACTICE, SOCIAL WORKERS CAN utilize a range of approaches and techniques from all three modes of practice in their work with communities. For example, Project Genesis, founded in 1977 by social worker Dr Jim Torczyner in the Côte-des-Neiges section of Montreal, connects individual service provision with community organizing to tangibly improve the lives of community members through social and economic rights advocacy. Project Genesis was designed to reconcile individual-service provision and organizing by responding to a central question: What types of individual services fit with what types of organizing? Out of this grew a multifaceted organization with a storefront that addresses individual issues through local volunteers who work with community members to (a) access rights, (b) organize, which takes the form of creating alternative services (i.e., Multicaf—Community Cafeteria and Food Bank as well as a community council), (c) engage in social action around changing policy (welfare for the homeless, welfare investigation of those living in poverty), and (d) practise legal advocacy. The organization is volunteer-driven, professionally managed, and academically linked as a field placement site for schools of social work. Additionally, given the multicultural community of Côte-des-Neiges, Project Genesis has worked on developing a common agenda among myriad ethnic groups and organizing from a perspective of building commonalities, thus seeing sources of oppression and how divisions among groups reinforce inequality.

The goal of "transformative" social action is a restructuring of systems of power as the belief is that these systems are fundamentally flawed (Ohmer & DeMasi, 2009).

Alternative Community-Practice Frameworks

Other community-practice frameworks can also be applicable given the community context. The main goal of consensus organizing is "the development of deep, authentic relationships and partnerships among and between community residents and stakeholders, and members of the external power structure to facilitate positive and tangible community change" through discussion and collaboration (Ohmer & DeMasi, 2009, p. 13). A key feature of the model is the development of social capital and networks among these various groups to facilitate the creation of opportunities for positive community change. Consensus organizing shares some similarities of the approaches described above. For example, as with locality development, consensus organizing focuses on the community's assets or resources, and engages a broad range of stakeholders and businesses, schools, and other organizations. It differs in that consensus organizers identify and engage a core group of members of the external power structures, such as social, political, cultural, or economic structures, who could help and support the community.

Boehm and Cnaan (2012) developed a practice-based approach for community work, critiquing approaches that adopt a model before entering a community. The authors were concerned that using existing community practice models, even those that centre on community engagement and participation, serves to reduce community members' possible contributions and ignore communities' unique realities. Believing that community practice models tend to be "less-community-oriented" and "more conceptually top-down," Boehm and Cnaan developed a "road map" model where "each set of users can choose the roads to take based on the vehicle they drive (resources), the specific terrain they will be traveling (obstacles and problems), and their desired destination (end goal)" (p. 144).

They proposed an approach that (a) guides processes of change but can be integrated into a community's unique reality, (b) draws on key features of the community practice knowledge and research base, (c) could be generated through a discursive process that involves all possible stakeholders and is grounded in local knowledge and practice experience, (d) is flexible to allow for change, (e) could be used with or without an outside expert, and (f) includes issues central for social change, supporting feasibility. The approach is a scaffold, composed of issues represented by two opposing positions (see Table 5.2).

TABLE 5.2   Model for Community Practice

Geographic community: Defined by interests and identities of people based on their geographic location. Developing responsibility and spirit of a local community.	Community of interest: Defined by interests and identities of groups and populations that cross geographic boundaries. Developing inter-local networks.
Enhancing community integration: Focus on mixing groups that are distinct in terms of culture, identity, and interests.	Maintaining group identity: Preserving and fostering the unique identity and character of each group.
Focusing primarily on activists: Informing and explaining tactics.	Appealing to indifferent community members: Persuasion tactics.
Integral/comprehensive change: Attempting to tackle a host of problems at the same time as a means to eradicate the root problem.	Targeted focused intervention: Attempting to tackle one, most often pressing, problem.
Intra-community-focused change: Focusing on change within the community. Cultivating self-help, building strengths, and assets within.	External change: Focusing on change outside the community, such as legislation, and importing outside resources.
Collaboration with government: Change and programs are based on government support.	Collaboration with non-profit organizations: Including informal, non-profit, and private organizations.
Technical-rational approach: Change managed by means of systematic planning and activities. Each phase is based on the previous phase.	Organizational-political approach: Change is managed by negotiation with interest groups. Activities conducted to support social justice.
Incremental process: Change involves a constant, continuous process. The process of change occurs in phases over a long period of time.	Breakpoint change: Process of change dramatic and immediate. Shift is fundamental in nature.
Mass mobilization: Change achieved through mobilization of a mass of people who advocate a specific change, assuming the mass creates power.	Small action system: Change achieved through coordinated/joint activity of a relatively small, defined group of professionals as well as community leaders.
Collaborative strategy: Concern for all groups that may be of relevance. Change achieved through mutuality, understanding, and agreements.	Confrontational strategy: Concern only for the client's interests and/or action system; aspires to win.
Directive approach of professionals: Professionals are the focus of the action and decision-making process.	Non-directive approach of professionals: The clients are the focus of the action and decision-making process.
Routine activity: Focus on central services; linear planning; solutions for varied needs; long-term processes and treatments.	Activity in crisis: Focus on "reaching out"; immediacy, short-term thought and action; spontaneous and intuitive action; activity directed at meeting human needs; authoritative activity.

Source: Boehm & Cnaan, 2012, p. 155.

As a planning template, it can focus areas of discussion by helping practitioners think through issues with a community and discuss how they want to approach an issue based on the possibilities described.

The approach becomes a model tailored to the specific needs and contexts of the community as community members discuss their positions with regard to each issue anchored by polarities. The process is critical as "a key step in formulating the model is the actual debate, managed at the community level, or issues that are relevant to the specific community in question . . . [leading to] an integrative and unique model that includes a 'road map' of policy and action directions, tailored to the particular conditions and desires of that community" (p. 154).

Conclusion

This chapter highlighted critical modalities informing social work practice with groups and communities. Groups in social work practice are used in countless ways: group members come together or are brought together to address myriad issues for diverse purposes. Social workers are involved in all types of groups which run on a continuum from professionally led to group led by members. This chapter outlined different types of social work with groups and communities as well as contextual factors critical for the achievement of group goals. Attention was given to understanding various theoretical models underlying group and community practice as well as how purpose shapes group membership, interactions, and dynamics in group and community work. Real-world illustrations were provided demonstrating group and community practice in action.

QUESTIONS FOR CRITICAL THOUGHT

1. How do the different theories of stages of group development prepare facilitators for what they might anticipate in their groups?
2. What are the benefits and challenges of a self-help group versus a professionally led support group?
3. Discuss how the planning template in Table 5.2 could inform your discussions with a local neighbourhood community centre concerned about student retention.
4. Choose a social issue. Discuss how Rothman's modes of community intervention (locality development, social planning, and social action) would lead you to address this issue.

RECOMMENDED READINGS

Crass, C. (2013). *Towards collective liberation: Anti-racist organizing, feminist praxis, and movement building strategy.* Oakland, CA: PM Press. This book is a collection of essays focused on engaging with the dynamic questions of how to create and support effective movements for visionary systemic change. Included are discussions of the challenges and the opportunities of anti-racist work in White communities, feminist work with men, and integrating women of colour feminism into social movements.

Hardcastle, D.A., & Powers, P.R. with Wenocur, S. (2011). *Community practice: Theories and skills for social workers* (3rd ed.). Oxford: Oxford University Press. This text is a resource for social workers, community practitioners, and social work students who want to engage communities to change oppressive structures. Authors integrate theory and practice, with main sections focusing on understanding the social environment and social interaction and community practice skills for social workers using the social environment.

Parkins, J.R., & Reed, M.G. (Eds.). (2012). *Social transformation in rural Canada: Community, cultures, and collective action.* Vancouver: UBC Press. This text explores the nature of community practice in Canada's rural Aboriginal and non-Aboriginal communities. Writings draw on the work of researchers from diverse disciplines who explore social transformation in rural settlements and illustrate a portrait of local forms of action, adaptation, and identity.

Shragge, E. (2013). *Activism and social change: Lessons for community organizing* (2nd ed.). Toronto: University of Toronto Press. This book situates contemporary community organizing in a post-9/11 context with discussions of national and international organizing efforts. Also included is a case study of the Immigrant Workers Centre in Montreal, offering one of the few English-language discussions of community organizing in Quebec.

Toseland, R.W., & Rivas, R.F. (2012). *An Introduction to Group Work Practice* (7th ed.). Boston: Allyn & Bacon. This is a comprehensive, detailed introductory textbook for social work students interested in group work practice that aligns its content with the core competencies of the Council for Social Work Education.

Tully, G.J., Bacon, J., & Dolan-Reilly, G. (2013). *Group work: An international conversation highlighting diversity in practice.* London: Whiting & Birch. This book is a collection of case studies and practice accounts from many countries presented at the 2012 AASWG (renamed the International Association for Social Work with Groups) Symposium which illustrate applications of the social group work model in a range of settings.

RECOMMENDED WEBSITES

The Community Foundation of Newfoundland and Labrador
http://www.cfnl.ca/
The Community Foundation of Newfoundland and Labrador (CFNL) is an example of a community funding entity. The CFNL supports healthy communities across the province by providing grant funding to a wide range of community organizations, combining a broad, province-wide scope with a grassroots focus on small organizations in local communities to address community problems and enrich the lives of community members.

The International Association for Social Work with Groups
http://iaswg.org/
The International Association for Social Work with Groups is a not-for-profit organization of group workers, group-work educators, and group-work advocates who support its program of advocacy and action for professional practice, education, research, training, and writing about social work with groups. The website provides a wealth of resources related to social work with groups, including conference information, group practice standards, and literature for practitioners.

The Native Council of Nova Scotia
http://ncns.ca/about/our-destiny/
The Native Council of Nova Scotia (NCNS) is an example of an Aboriginal Peoples Representative Organization. The NCNS is directed by and accountable to the community members who live on the traditional homelands of Mi'kma'ki. The goal is to operate and

administer a strong and effective organization that serves, advocates for, and represents their community through programs and services such as the Native Social Counselling Agency and Welkaqnik Next Step Shelter.

The Tamarack Institute for Community Engagement
http://tamarackcommunity.ca/index.php

The Tamarack Institute for Community Engagement develops and supports learning communities that support collaboration and knowledge creation, and achieve collective impact on complex community issues. Its vision is to build a connected force for community change. One project is Vibrant Communities, which links communities from British Columbia to Newfoundland and Labrador in a collective effort to test the most effective ways to reduce poverty at the grassroots level.

PART III

Fields of Social Work Practice

Social Work and Health

LEARNING OBJECTIVES

- To review the historical conditions and events that shaped the development of the Canadian health-care system.

- To highlight key provisions of Canada's health-care delivery system.

- To identify health inequalities in the Canadian health-care system and social workers' roles in addressing these inequalities.

- To illustrate how forms of privatization have entered into Canada's universal health system.

- To outline various roles social workers fulfill in health- and social-care settings.

- To introduce the social determinants of health model to understand contributors to the physical and mental health of individuals and families.

Chapter Outline

This chapter describes the development and contemporary delivery of health care in Canada and discusses the assumptions and principles informing the social determinants of health by illustrating relationships between health and social factors through an overview of Canadian health profiles. Different types of health issues are discussed (chronic, acute, terminal) and their impact on individuals, families, groups and communities are explored. In addition, the roles and functions of social workers in the field of health are described.

Early Health-Care Provision

In the early colonial era, health-care services were provided on a casual basis, typically by in-home caregivers and barber/surgeons for the non-Indigenous populations and by healers and others providing traditional care and remedies for Indigenous communities. Indigenous practitioners were well equipped to care for their populace in pre-contact times, but with the advent of the Europeans and European diseases, traditional healers were overwhelmed and hundreds of thousands of Indigenous Peoples died as a result of exposure to the colonists.

By the second half of the nineteenth century, the individual provinces were responsible for crafting policy to oversee health care for their citizenry. In 1867, under Section 92(7) of the Constitution Act, Canadian provinces were officially mandated to create, maintain, and manage health facilities, such as hospitals and asylums (Forest, Marchildon, & McIntosh, 2004). Because health care was still considered within the purview of family responsibility, charitable institutions, or religious communities, access to such institutions was limited (Maioni, 2004). Government intervention and subsidies were available for health issues that posed a public health concern (Guest, 1997).

Prior to World War II, accessing health care was generally dependent on the ability to pay. However some provinces (Manitoba, Saskatchewan, and Alberta) established their own hospital plans to ensure access to the most urgent medical care for all citizens of the province. This was motivated in part by the profound impact of the Great Depression and severe droughts (Health Canada, 2012), mobilizing them to respond to calls for reform that would assist their residents with little to no income to access medical and hospital care (Marchildon, 2009). Saskatchewan took the lead by introducing a province-wide public hospital insurance in 1944. Its model was soon followed by others. In 1956, the federal government offered an open-ended, 50–50 cost-sharing arrangement with the provinces and by 1958 all provinces had introduced universal hospital coverage.

In the 1960s, only a few years following the establishment of hospital insurance in all provinces, debates began to expand coverage to medically necessary health care outside of the hospital setting. The need for universal coverage of non–hospital-based health care was reinforced in 1964 when the Royal Commission on Health Services published a report, also known as the Hall Report for its chairperson Supreme Court Justice Emmett Hall, which found that millions of Canadians did not have health-care coverage. This report garnered widespread support for its recommendations of comprehensive, publicly administered, universal health care. In a Canadian Broadcasting Company (CBC) radio interview, Justice Hall answered the question of why universal health care is important:

> From a humanitarian standpoint, there is, we believe, an obligation on society to be concerned with the health of its individuals. But on the economic side, investments in health are investments in human capital. Just as investments in engines

and railroads are investments in capital, so are investments in health, and they pay off in the economic field and they pay great dividends to a nation that looks after the health of its people. So what we say is that society has an obligation to assist the individual to accomplish that which he, by his own efforts, cannot attain.

Source: http://www.cbc.ca/archives/categories/health/health-care-system/the-birth-of-medicare/the-royal-commission-on-health-services.html

The federal government expanded their reach in health care beyond financing by establishing the Hospital Insurance and Diagnostics Services Act of 1957 and the Medical Care Insurance Act of 1966 which stipulated that provincial hospital-based and medically necessary programs would have to be comprehensive, universal, portable, and publicly administered in order to receive federal funding. By insisting on uniformity and portability of benefits for all Canadians, the federal government was attempting to avoid the development of a patchwork approach to health-care provision. It was recognized that there was diversity across provinces and thus differences in implementation, so the primary goal

was not to impose uniformity in the playing field, since provincial plans demonstrate[d] varying degrees of diversity, but rather to ensure that the provinces played by the same "rules of the game" and that Canadian taxpayers' money would be used to help finance publicly accountable health insurance systems that ensured some sort of "equality" of social rights among Canadian citizens, regardless of their province of residence (Maioni, 2004, p. 187).

Quebec in the 1960s was characterized by what came to be called "the Quiet Revolution," a period where the provincial government enacted a series of major reforms, primarily in health care and education. These reforms increased the role of the state, decreasing the role of the Roman Catholic Church in governance and provision of services.

By 1972, health care coverage was achieved, providing Canadians with guaranteed access to essential medical services, irrespective of income level or employment or health status (Burke & Silver, 2013). However, amid rising health-care costs, accompanied by low fees to doctors, under the legislation, physicians were allowed to opt out of the system and to practise extra billing for services. By the late 1970s and early 1980s, the practices of extra billing and user fees were pervasive, creating calls for reform.

Contemporary Approaches to Health-Care Provision

In Quebec in 1968, members of the Commission of Inquiry into Health and Welfare (Commission d'enquête sur la santé et le bien-être social–CESBES) visited Great Britain, France, Sweden, and Czechoslovakia to evaluate how different political regimes approached health-care provision (Gaumer & Desrosiers, 2004). The Commission tabled their report in 1970, which marked the creation of the Quebec health-care system, including the establishment of public primary health-care centres, which are today's local community service centres (Centres locaux de services communautaires [CLSCs]) (Gaumer & Fleury, 2008). The uniqueness of the CLSCs original mandate lay in its holistic approach to providing an array of basic health-care and social services in one setting, primarily delivered by multidisciplinary teams. Delivering both health- and social-care services under one administration was meant to prevent a silo approach to health. CLSCs were mandated to oversee the delivery of preventative, restorative, and ongoing health and social services at

TABLE 6.1	Canadian Health Provision Timeline	
Events in Canada		Other World Events
1867: Section 92(7) of Constitution Act Mandates provinces to create, maintain, and manage health facilities. **1867–1919:** Department of Agriculture responsible for health care.	pre-1900s	
1919: Department of Health created.	1910s	**1914–1918: World War I**
1920s: Municipal hospital plans established in Manitoba, Saskatchewan, and Alberta.	1920s	**1929–1939: The Great Depression**
	1930s	**1937:** Soviet Union implements universal health care. **1939–1945: World War II** **1939–1941:** New Zealand creates a universal health-care system.
1944: Saskatchewan introduces public hospital insurance.	1940s	**1945–1960: Baby Boom** **1945:** French national health insurance established. **1948:** National Health Service established in UK.
1956: Government offers cost-sharing agreement with provinces. **1957: Hospital Insurance and Diagnostics Services Act** **1958:** All provinces have universal hospital coverage.	1950s	**1955–1964:** Universal health insurance introduced to Nordic countries (Sweden, Iceland, Norway, Denmark, and Finland).
1960s: Quebec provincial government during the period known as the Quiet Revolution enacts series of major reforms, primarily in health care and education. **1960:** Northwest and Yukon Territories create hospital insurance plans **1964: Hall Report** Finds millions without health care. **1966: Medical Care Insurance Act** **1966: Castonguay Commission** Recommends free, accessible, and universal public health system.	1960s	**1961:** Japan implements universal health insurance.
1970: Report by Commission of Inquiry into Health and Welfare (Commission d'enquête sur la santé et le bien-être social—CESBES) Marks creation of Quebec health-care system, including establishment of public primary health-care centres (Gaumer & Fleury, 2008). **1972:** All Canadians guaranteed access to essential medical services.	1970s	**1974 and 1984:** Australia introduces universal health care. **1978:** Italy establishes universal national health services. **1979:** Portugal introduces universal national health services.

1984: Canada Health Act Adopted	1980s	1983: Greece implements universal national health insurance.
Specifies conditions and criteria with which health-insurance programs must conform in order to receive federal assistance.		1986: Spain implements universal national health insurance.
		1989: South Korea implements universal health insurance.
1996: Canada Health Act linked to Canada Health and Social Transfer (CHST).	1990s	1995: Taiwan and Israel introduce national health services.
2001: Romanow Report	2000s	2009: The US adopts the Affordable Health Care Act.
Calls for reform of health system based on Canadian values.		

home, school, work, or in a clinic to older adults with loss of autonomy, at-risk children and families, persons with physical disabilities, children with learning disabilities, persons living with mental health challenges, and persons in need of family physicians, and address issues of public health. Furthermore, these centres were "born in the creative enthusiasm of the local communities . . . deliberately aimed at mobilizing local communities and encouraging their empowerment in taking greater control over their own health and welfare" (Gaumer & Fleury, 2008, p. 102). Services were drawn from three main categories: (1) basic curative and preventive health care, (2) social services to meet individual needs, and (3) community action focused on encouraging community members to be involved in identifying and solving health and social problems through information and discussion (Gaumer & Fleury, 2008). Today, CLSCs are the point of entry to the Health and Social Service Networks (centres de santé et de services sociaux [CSSSs]) established in 2005 to combine the administration of CLSCs, acute and chronic facility-based care, and family medicine groups (http://www.santemontreal.qc.ca).

In 1984, the federal Canada Health Act combined the existing federal hospital and medical care insurance acts, introduced a mechanism through which the government could unilaterally impose financial penalties on the provinces, and restated the existing conditions into five principles: universality of coverage, comprehensiveness of services, portability of benefits, public administration, and uniform terms and conditions governing equal access to care (see Table 6.2). This last provision was designed to ban extra-billing and user fees by imposing deductions on cash **transfer payments** for provinces and territories that did not comply (Madore, 2005; Maioni, 2004).

Instead of having one national plan such as in the United Kingdom, Canadian health-care coverage is composed of 13 interconnected provincial and territorial health-insurance plans, which must meet the five Medicare principles (See Table 6.2). However, while the provinces were being legislated to offer more comprehensive services, the funding formula shifted to transfer payments from a 50–50 cost-sharing mechanism. This meant that the federal government provided provinces with a capped pool of funding, despite provincial health-care costs. Provincial/territorial reciprocal billing agreements were established for individuals undergoing outpatient hospital services outside of his or her home province/territory.

In 1996, the Canada Health Act was linked to the Canada Health and Social Transfer (CHST). The provinces had to meet all the criteria and conditions specified in the Act in order to be eligible for their full share of the federal cash contribution. The federal government directly funds health-care provision for members of First Nations and Inuit communities as well as for Canadian military personnel (Maioni, 2004).

transfer payments Refer to federal funds used to help cover a portion of the costs of a provincial program (Maioni, 2004).

TABLE 6.2	Five Medicare Principles
The Canada Health Act (1984) stipulates that health care must be publicly administered, universal, comprehensive, accessible, and portable.	
Public Administration	Provincial and territorial plans must be administered and operated on a non-profit basis by a public authority accountable to the provincial or territorial government.
Universality	The provincial and territorial plans must insure all medically necessary services provided by hospitals, medical practitioners, and dentists working within a hospital setting.
Comprehensiveness	The provincial and territorial plans must entitle all insured persons to health insurance coverage on uniform terms and conditions.
Accessibility	The provincial and territorial plans must provide all insured persons reasonable access to medically necessary hospital and physician services without financial or other barriers.
Portability	Provincial and territorial plans must cover all insured persons when they move to another province or territory within Canada and when they travel abroad. The provinces and territories have some limits on coverage for services provided outside Canada and may require prior approval for non-emergency services delivered outside their jurisdiction.

In 2002, Roy Romanow, chair of the Commission on the Future of Health Care in Canada, published *Building on Values: The Future of Health Care in Canada*. The comprehensive report comprised 47 recommendations to preserve as well as improve health care in Canada. Recommendations were around the following themes:

> implement series of measures to improve transparency across the system, make decision-making structures more inclusive, accelerate the integration of health informatics, provide for secure electronic health records for Canadians that respect their right to privacy and give Canadians greater say in shaping the system's future (Romanow, 2002, p. xix).

The Romanow Report called for a system based on Canadian values. Moving somewhat away from the Hall Report's focus on health's link to economic enterprise, Romanow wrote that "Canadians view Medicare as a moral enterprise, not a business venture" (Romanow, 2002, p. xx). The design of health care in Canada has reflected a commitment to collective responsibility and to the bonds of community in a diverse society. No other government program is as universal as provincial health-care systems; at least in theory, everyone has access, on equal terms and conditions, without taking into account gender, language, membership in a racialized or ethnic group, or income (Maioni, 2010). Since 1 April 2004, the Canada Health Act has been linked to the Canada Health Transfer (CHT), similar to its predecessor although dedicated to health care (Madore, 2005).

The Privatization of Health Services in Canada

Despite Canada's public universal health-care system, further analysis reveals that privatization is prevalent in the Canadian health system. The last two decades have seen a rise in for-profit providers, out-of-pocket payments, and demands on individuals and families to perform care work (Armstrong & Armstrong, 2010; Randall, 2008). While private providers have always played a role in health-care delivery, the number of private providers for such services as diagnostic testing, ancillary hospital services (i.e., cleaning, food services),

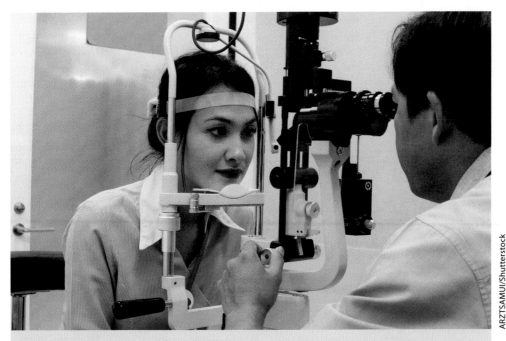

ARZTSAMUI/Shutterstock

In 2004, the Ontario Health Insurance Plan (OHIP) delisted eye examination coverage for adults aged 20–64.

and community-based health services such as nursing, has increased across the country. The expansion of private, for-profit providers in health care has been justified by suggestions that introducing market completion for some health-care services will lead to a more efficient and cost-effective system. Privatization critics point to inadequate evidence that market competition in health-care provision increases efficiency and express concerns that access, equity, and quality of care will become secondary to profitmaking (Armstrong & Armstrong, 2010; Randall, 2008).

Privatization has also been prevalent in increases in out-of-pocket expenses for health-related services. Many provinces have begun delisting services once covered by universal insurance such as vision care and medical forms, framing these services as "extended" rather than necessary. As a result, approximately 30 per cent of total health-care costs in Canada are now covered privately through out-of-pocket payments and private insurance plans, with the portion of private contributions increasing at a faster rate than public expenditures (Canadian Institute for Health Information, 2009; Ramji & Quiñonez, 2012).

Privatization in the form of out-of-pocket expenses and caring labour has also been a result of a shift in spending. Over the last two decades, all provinces and territories have expanded the delivery of home-based care for post-acute, rehabilitation, and palliative services, targeting much funding towards the development of health services outside institutional walls. Few would argue against the benefits of allowing individuals to receive health care in the comfort of their own home. However, the gradual shift in health delivery from hospital to home has taken a large portion of Canadian health services outside of the jurisdiction of the Canada Health Act. Within this context, six provinces have implemented means testing for the provision of some home-care services (contrary to the principle of universality) (Canadian Home Care Association, 2008) and most have placed stringent caps on the type of services provided and the number of hours available through public programming, leaving those unable to purchase additional services with many unmet needs.

While the delivery of comprehensive home-care services is motivated, in part, by a desire to improve the quality of health services, it is also motivated by cost containment. Seen as a cheaper way of delivering service, the drive towards community-based services has been accompanied by shortened hospital stays and more stringent admission criteria for facility-based palliative and rehabilitation services (Canadian Institute for Health Information, 2009). As a result, services previously funded or provided within the confines of a hospital such as personal-care support have been off-loaded to private households. This effectively amounts to public health-care savings falling on the backs of individuals with health issues and their family members. These in-kind contributions tip the private contributions to health spending well beyond the 30 per cent captured in direct monetary expenses.

Social Work Practice in Health Care

Hospital-Based Social Work

Social workers play a pivotal role in hospital settings across Canada. Tremendous stress often stems from hospitalizations that are sudden and, at times, related to catastrophic illness or injury. Stressors such as decreased personal control, information overload, and change in functional ability can lead to a range of emotional responses for both persons admitted to hospital and their families (Ontario Association of Social Workers, 2004). Social workers support individuals and families during their hospitalization by facilitating communication with staff about their preferences, needs, and concerns, offering opportunities for reflection and emotional expression, providing information about a complex array of services, and advocating for access to needed services both within the hospital and upon discharge to the community. These tasks are increasingly complex in the context of reduced hospital stays and limited community services (Craig & Muskat, 2013; Wilder Craig, 2007).

Social Work and Mental Health Care

Social workers are integrally involved in working with individuals, families, and groups in various mental health-care settings such as hospitals or community clinics. Social workers in mental health settings typically provide mental health services related to mental illness prevention, treatment, and rehabilitation. They can provide direct services and/or case management, work with communities to facilitate the identification of mental health needs from a community perspective, provide clinical supervision and quality management of other social workers in direct practice, teach in social work programs, and be involved in program, policy, and resource development in hospitals, clinics, and other care settings as well as mental health research and evaluation (CASW, n.d.).

Mental health is defined as

> the capacity of the individual, the group and the environment to interact with one another in ways that promote subjective well-being, the optimal development and use of mental abilities (cognitive, affective, and relational), the achievement of individual and collective goals consistent with justice and the attainment and preservation of conditions of fundamental equality (CASW, n.d.).

Mental illness is seen as "characterized by alterations in thinking, mood or behaviour associated with significant distress and impaired functioning . . . arising from a complex interaction of genetic, biological, personality and environmental factors"

(Government of Canada, 2006 p. 30). Major types of mental illness include anxiety disorders, such as generalized anxiety disorder, phobias and panic disorders, obsessive-compulsive disorders, traumatic stress disorders, co-occurring or dual diagnosis disorders where mental illness co-occurs with a substance abuse problem, dementia, eating disorders such as anorexia nervosa, bulimia and binge eating, mood disorders such as depression, bi-polar disorder, and seasonal affective disorder, and personality disorders such as schizophrenia (Government of Canada, 2006). The 2012 Canadian Community Health Survey found that 2.8 million Canadians aged 15 or older, or 10.1 per cent, reported symptoms consistent with at least one mental or substance-use disorder (Pearson, Janz, & Ali, 2013). Hospitalization was traditionally most commonly used for individuals with mental illness; today it is only one of many approaches to mental health care, typically limited to acute cases. The availability of multiple approaches is due in large part to advances in the development of a range of community-based mental health services, technological innovations (see "Case Study" box below), high costs of hospitalization, and advances in psychiatric medications (Government of Canada, 2006).

Mental health has also been conceptualized as a balance or harmony among the various aspects of one's physical, mental, emotional, and spiritual being, which includes the individual and community (i.e., the physical and social environment) (Smye & Mussell, 2001). A community mental health perspective sees mental health promotion and illness treatment as a public health issue, connected to issues of social justice. This approach promotes mental health by

- addressing health from a population perspective;
- seeing clients in a socio-economic context;
- generating information on primary prevention;
- focusing on individual as well as population-based prevention;
- having a systematic view of service provision;
- advocating for open access to services;
- emphasizing the importance of team-based services;
- seeing mental health from a long-term, longitudinal, life-course perspective; and
- exploring cost effectiveness in population terms.

(Drake, Szmukler, Mueser & Thornicroft, 2011).

Social Work and End-of-Life Care

Palliative care services aim to deliver comfort-oriented holistic care that supports quality of life rather than cure. This form of end-of-life care can be provided in hospital, long-term care, hospice, and home settings (DeMiglio & Williams, 2012; Williams et al., 2010). The profession of social work shares much compatibility with principles of palliative care as both consider individuals in the full context of their lives and both regard families as part of the care process. In the Canadian context, social workers have been implicated in palliative care since its earliest history (Cadell et al., 2010). Social workers in palliative care work as members of multidisciplinary teams to provide emotional, psychological, and spiritual support to individuals and families, advocate for access to needed services, facilitate open discussions with individuals and families on issues related to death and dying such as advanced care planning, and provide bereavement support to surviving families. With as little as 15 per cent of Canadians able to access particular forms of palliative care including hospice services and specialized care units, social workers also have a role to play in systemically advocating for recognition of end-of-life services as a human right that should be accessible to all Canadians in the location of their choosing (Freeman et al., 2013).

Case STUDY

Telehealth and Mental Health Training

ACCESS TO MENTAL HEALTH SERVICES in rural Canadian communities can be limited. Barriers to access include (a) difficulties in creating trusting relationships with staff due to high staff turnover and burnout rates, (b) long distances to facilities, and (c) limited opportunities for training and support. Community members and health-care professionals often feel under-prepared to manage the complex social, psychological, and psychiatric needs of their rural communities. A study by Cornish and colleagues (2003) reported the results of a demonstration project that examined the potential role of Telehealth in offering mental health training and support for health professionals in the rural Central-East region of Newfoundland and Labrador. Telehealth technology has been explored as a method to provide mental health training and consultation via satellite to physicians and mental health workers based in rural areas. The study, as well as the training component, was conducted by an "urban team" consisting of two psychologists, one psychiatrist, and two family physicians based in Memorial University of Newfoundland in St. John's, Newfoundland.

The "rural team" consisted of 34 professionals representing clergy, family medicine, nursing, nurse practitioners, physiotherapy, police, psychology, school guidance counselling, social work, community youth leadership, and teaching who participated in satellite video conferences over a 14-month period. Social workers, school guidance counsellors, and nurses attended the video conferences most frequently. Video conferences, based on a community needs assessment, covered such topics as relationships, grief and bereavement, stress and burnout, anxiety and panic disorder, stress management and cognitive behavioral therapy, sexual abuse, depression in families, adolescent depression, and using the Internet. Qualitative interviews were conducted with rural team members after video conference training.

A recurring theme after the training was the gradual development of comfort with the method of training delivered via the video-satellite as well as trust in other participants (members of both rural and urban teams). Also contributing to developing trust and comfort was attention paid to group process and community context.

Social Determinants of Health in Canada

In Canada, even with universal health-care coverage, there are significant differences in health outcomes. These differences have contributed to an increasing interest in the ways in which the social environment affects the health of individuals, families, and communities. For example, examining levels of socio-economic status, those who have low incomes have substantially shorter life expectancies, higher mortality rates, and more illnesses than those who are wealthy (Galea & Vlahov, 2002; Mikkonen & Raphael, 2010). Adopting a holistic perspective where health is not only confined to individual physical or mental illness is known as the **social determinants of health** model.

There are several variations of this model that support the shift of focus from a provision of medical care on an individual level to addressing the social and economic conditions associated with poor health outcomes more broadly, that is, in the population. Although social determinants of health models suggest diverse ways through which social determinants shape health, there is general consensus that social factors, either directly or indirectly, are intricately linked to health outcomes (e.g., Galea & Vlahov, 2002;

social determinants of health A model that incorporates economic and social conditions which shape the health of individuals, communities, and jurisdictions (Raphael, 2009).

Several rural participants identified the sessions on grief and bereavement as pivotal as the first training session was conducted shortly after several community members died in an accident.

Key findings included the following:

Expanded knowledge and skills: All rural participants reported enhanced knowledge and skills related to addressing mental health issues after the 14 weeks.

Heightened sensitivity to mental health: Rural participants who were less directly focused on mental health (i.e., physicians, nurses, clergy, and police) reported an increased awareness of mental health issues.

Enhanced knowledge of roles: Most rural respondents commented that their knowledge of the roles and expertise of other disciplines had increased. One nurse practitioner noted that through participation in this project he learned that social workers are qualified to provide counselling for sexually abused clients.

Increased cross-disciplinary connections: Several rural participants reported increased cross-disciplinary connections and referrals. The involvement of clergy, police, and community youth leaders broadened the range of support services available beyond those provided by typical mental health professionals.

Greater cohesion and collegial support: Cross-disciplinary connections led many rural participants to feel closer and more supported by others. A physician noted that "previously, we probably spent less time connecting with other people who were involved in mental health issues. . . . We've become closer knit and sort of share ideas and provide more support. I think it's just opened a lot of doors that way" (p. 68).

This project relied on Telehealth technology, which can be used to facilitate mental health training and promote interdisciplinary collaboration in a rural setting. Authors of the study noted, however, that greater technological refinement was needed so as not to be affected by weather conditions. Future plans included moving to a case presentation format to replace the original "expert talking heads" format to increase greater responsibility and ownership by community participants and expand the program to additional sites in Newfoundland and Labrador.

Link & Phelan, 1996; Raphael, 2009; Wilkinson & Marmot, 2003). Across these models, social determinants of health encompass the

- economic and social conditions that shape individuals, communities, and jurisdictions' health overall;
- primary determinants of whether an individual stays healthy or becomes ill;
- extent to which a person has the physical, social, and personal resources to identify and achieve personal aspirations, meet needs, and cope with his or her environment; and
- quantity and quality of resources that a society makes available and accessible to its members (Raphael, 2009, p. 2).

Adopting a social determinants of health approach means focusing health policy and programming around how a society organizes and distributes its resources and how that organization and distribution affect health outcomes in multiple contexts and over the life course. Integrating a life-course perspective allows for a "focus on exposure to a variety of health determinants through different life stages, from gestation, through childhood and early adulthood, to midlife" (Waldram, Herring, & Young, 2006, p. 122). These determinants are not mutually exclusive; as illustrated in the sections below, they are interdependent, overlapping and influencing each other. Thus, the state of one's health over the life course can be thought of as an intricate web whose durability is regulated by multiple determinants.

The origins of health inequalities in Canada are numerous and interdependent. While health inequalities have been connected to differences in genetic composition and biology, social factors have been identified as important sources of health inequalities. Numerous studies have examined social determinants of health and have included different elements in their models. Income is consistently included as a primary determinant in multiple models (Benzeval, Judge, & Shuls, 2001; Kosteniuk & Dickinson, 2003; Mikkonen & Raphael, 2010; Raphael, 2009). Overshadowing all social determinants of health with regard to its comprehensive effects is income. Research has documented a relationship between health inequalities and socio-economic status, particularly the variables of income, education, occupational status, and employment status (Denton, Prus & Walters, 2004; Wilkinson & Marmot, 2003). This section will explore this determinant in various contexts and with different populations to illustrate how income shapes experiences with regard to other social determinants of health. Although income is a determinant of health in itself, it also determines the quality of early life, education, employment, unemployment and working conditions, food security, housing quality, and the quality of life experiences for Indigenous Peoples in Canada, members of racialized groups, people with disabilities, and women (Raphael, 2009). Health outcomes are also shaped by the level of access one has to health-care services, whether one struggles with addictions or one's level of educational achievement.

Canada does not have a government-mandated poverty line as in the USA. To estimate poverty, the most commonly used measure, since 1967, is the low-income cut-off (LICO). **LICOs** are income thresholds below which a family will likely dedicate a larger share of its income on the necessities of food, shelter, and clothing than the average family. A family is considered to be living in poverty if the income that it spends on food, clothing, and shelter is 20 per cent greater than what is spent by the average equivalent household. Statistics Canada calculates 35 different LICOs, covering five different community sizes, and seven different family sizes. However, these estimates are based on residents of provinces only; residents of the Yukon, the Northwest Territories, and Nunavut, residents of institutions, and persons living on First Nations territories are not included. The reference year which was used in the calculations for overall household spending on food, shelter, and clothing is 1992; Statistics Canada no longer collects data necessary to update spending reference points (Citizens for Public Justice, 2012).

The length of time that Canadians can expect to live and whether or not they will experience illness is very much influenced by their quality of life, which is directly shaped by income (Mikkonen & Raphael, 2010). The same pattern exists with regard to their children's health, where events such as surviving beyond children's first year of life, experiencing childhood illnesses and injuries, and falling behind in school are strongly related to the social determinants of health they experience. Poverty has been associated with an increased risk of chronic disease, injury, compromised infant and child development, mental health issues, and premature death (Lawlor, Davey Smith, Patel, & Ebrahim, 2005; Mikkonen & Raphael, 2010; Phipps, 2003; Raphael, 2011).

LICOs An estimate of poverty; income thresholds below which a family will likely devote a larger portion of its income on the necessities of food, shelter, and clothing than the average family.

Early Childhood and Adolescence

The foundations of adult health are laid before birth and in early childhood. Prenatal care is critical for healthy fetal development, which in turn influences infant development. **Latency effects** refer to how early childhood experiences predispose children to either

latency effects Effects of early childhood experiences that predispose children to either good or poor health regardless of their experiences in later life.

good or poor health regardless of later life circumstances (Mikkonen & Raphael, 2010). **Pathway effects** are those that are generated by a child's exposures to risk factors at one point in time but that do not have immediate health effects. Rather, these effects lead to future health scenarios that do have consequences. For example, a lack of school readiness may not be an immediate health issue for a child, but his or her limited learning abilities can lead to experiences that are harmful to one's health later in life such as lower educational attainment (Mikkonen & Raphael, 2010). When infants and children experience multiple disadvantages over time, they can be predisposed for illness. These **cumulative effects** describe a situation where the longer a child lives with material and social deprivation, the more likely he or she is to show adverse health and developmental outcomes (Mikkonen & Raphael, 2010).

pathway effects Refer to a situation when children's exposures to risk factors at one point do not have immediate health effects but later lead to situations that do have health consequences.

cumulative effects Long-term effects of material and social deprivation which make children more likely to experience adverse health and developmental outcomes.

Family income during early childhood and adolescence is a strong predictor of who develops and dies from illness. Fifteen per cent of Canadian children live in poverty, ranking Canada 20th out of 30 wealthy countries (OECD, 2008). Typically, when a child lives in a family with a low income, he or she lives in a lone-parent, female-headed household: 80 per cent of all lone-parent families are headed by women (Canadian Teachers' Federation, 2009). Single mother households are more likely to have low incomes than single father households. In 2007, 23.6 per cent of female lone-parent families had a low income compared to 10.8 per cent of male lone-parent families (Collin & Jensen, 2009).

In 2010, one in five or 21.8 per cent of children in lone-parent families were living in poverty, compared to 5.7 per cent of children living in two-parent families (CPJ, 2012). Children born into poor families are more likely to be born underweight, which is a predictor for future health problems (CTF, 2009). Children and youth who live in poverty suffer from higher rates of asthma, diabetes, and mental health issues (Canadian Women's Foundation, n.d.). Moreover, children living in poverty have more speech and hearing problems and score lower on cognitive tests. They are also more likely to struggle in school. Research has shown that poor children have "a reduced motivation to learn, delayed cognitive development, lower achievement, less participation in extra-curricular activities, lower career aspirations, interrupted school attendance, lower university attendance, an increased risk of illiteracy, and higher drop-out rates" (CTF, 2009, p. 3). Children who are racialized, immigrant, and/or Indigenous, and children with disabilities are at greater risk of living in poverty and thus have a greater likelihood of poor health outcomes (CPJ, 2012). Families with low incomes also show an increased risk of having their children placed in out-of-home care (Esposito, Trocmé, Chabot, Shlonsky, Collin-Vézina, & Sinha, 2013).

Children and youth need a safe educational environment in order to thrive. Victimization and harassment inside and outside of school prevent a safe environment, harming the health of children and youth. Bullying, a component of victimization, is pervasive in Canadian schools. A report on bullying (Canadian Council on Learning, 2008) found that 38 per cent of adult males and 30 per cent of adult females reported having experienced occasional or frequent bullying during their school years; 47 per cent of parents reported that they had a child who had been bullied; and 16 per cent indicated that their child being bullied was a frequent occurrence. It is important to note that the health and well-being of both those who have been bullied as well as those who have bullied is compromised. Those who bully in childhood have been found to exhibit antisocial behaviour in adulthood and experience limited opportunities to achieve socially desired and/or acceptable objectives (Hurrelmann & Richter, 2006).

Unemployment and Working Conditions

Being employed and monetarily caring for one's family are associated with better physical and self-reported health status (Kosteniuk & Dickinson, 2003). This is due both to the

Case STUDY

Victimization and Harassment in Childhood and Adolescence

THERE IS AMPLE EVIDENCE THAT supports the public health concerns regarding victimization and harassment. Those who are bullied are more likely to experience headaches, stomach aches, backaches or dizziness, as their non-bullied peers and more likely to experience symptoms related to depression such as difficulty sleeping, tiredness, and helplessness (Due et al., 2005). The experiences of victimization and harassment in one's childhood and/or youth have lasting effects on one's mental and physical health (Abada, Hou, & Ram, 2008).

In order to assess the effects of victimization and harassment inside and outside of school among Canadian adolescents, Abada, Hou, and Ram (2008) analyzed data from 1996/1997 to 2000/2001 from the National Longitudinal Survey of Children and Youth (NLSCY), developed collaboratively by Human Resources and Skills Development Canada and Statistics Canada. The NLSCY followed the development of children in Canada and collected information on various aspects of children and their parents. The focus of the Abada, Hou, and Ram study was to assess the longitudinal effects of harassment and victimization 2–3 years later on perceived health status and mental health status among Canadian adolescents.

Key findings included the following:

Prevalence of harassment: Approximately 46 per cent of 14- to 15-year-old Canadian youth reported having experienced some kind of harassment at school in the last 12 months and 40 per cent having experienced harassment outside of school. The most frequent type of harassment was verbal aggression, with 41 per cent and 35 per cent reporting this form of victimization at school (or on the school bus) and outside of school, respectively. The prevalence of experiencing a threat was also pervasive, with 24 per cent at school and 19 per cent outside of school. About one-tenth of participants reported having physically attacked or assaulted at school or outside of school.

Effects on health status: The study's central finding was that the greater the frequency of victimization within the school environment, the greater the likelihood of youth reporting overall poor health and depression. Measures of depression and self-rated health status were positively associated with victimization, meaning that as victimization increased, so did rates of depression and self-rated health status among participants. Protective factors such as neighborhood cohesion, parental nurturance, peer support, and school attachment were negatively associated with victimization at school and outside of school, meaning that as those protective factors increased, the likelihood of victimization decreased. Participants who lived in a single-parent family were more likely to be victimized outside of school. The relationship between harassment and mental health was particularly pronounced among girls, immigrant children, and those living in single-parent households.

Findings suggest that schools must reinforce the need for strict anti-harassment and -victimization programs. Programs must emphasize the role of parents, teachers, and community leaders not only to address the problems of bullying but also to provide support for those who were victims of bullying. In promoting a safer school environment, it should be noted that certain subgroups are more vulnerable to victimization; in particular, immigrant youth may be more prone to bullying. It is imperative that anti-victimization measures recognize racialized identity and ethnicity as possible bases for harassment.

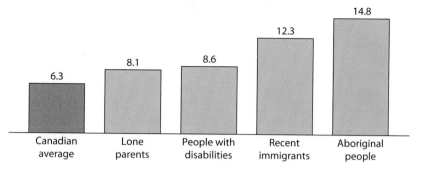

FIGURE 6.1 // Unemployment Rate, Selected Groups, 2006
(per cent of labour force)

Source: Data for lone parents, people with disabilities, recent immigrants, and Aboriginal people, HRSDC calculations based on Statistics Canada. *Census 2006 data* (not published). HRSDC, n.d.; and for people with disabilities, Statistics Canada. *Education, Employment and Income of Adults with and Without Disabilities–Tables*. Ottawa: Statistics Canada, 2009 (Cat No. 89–587-XIE).

straightforward rewards of employment in the form of income and work-related benefits as well as symbolic rewards that are associated with paid work such as a sense of identity and a structure for daily living (Mikkonen & Raphael, 2010). The link between unemployment and income is clear—lacking an adequate income makes it difficult to pay for basic needs such as food and shelter. The relationship between health and employment/unemployment is also relatively direct, with demonstrated effects on physical and mental health. Health effects start before unemployment, when those who are working feel insecure about their position (Wilkinson & Marmot, 2003). Job insecurity has been shown to increase effects on mental health (particularly anxiety, depression), self-reported ill health, heart disease, and risk factors for heart disease (Wilkinson & Marmot, 2003). Those who are employed report higher levels of physical health and lower levels of mental distress than those non-employed. Unemployment frequently leads to both social and material deprivation. Unemployment is also associated with depression, anxiety, and the adoption of unhealthy coping behaviours (Mikkonen & Raphael, 2010). Recent data from Human Resources and Skills Development Canada (HRSDC) showed that the unemployment rate in Canada was 7.2 per cent in 2012, a reduction from 8.3 per cent in 2008. The 2012 rate varied, however, across the country and across population groups. Geographically, the unemployment rate was lowest in Alberta (4.6 per cent) while highest in Newfoundland and Labrador (12.5 per cent; HRSDC, n.d.). Data from 2006 show the differential rate across groups (See Figure 6.1), with the unemployment rate for Indigenous Peoples highest at 14.8 per cent, for recent immigrants at 12.3 per cent, for people with disabilities at 8.6 per cent, and for lone parents at 8.1 per cent (HRSDC, n.d.).

Unemployment has also been linked with stress. In 2010, 24 per cent of Canadians aged 15 and older reported that most of their days were very or extremely stressful (Statistics Canada, 2012). Social, economic, and psychological circumstances can cause stress. A classic definition of stress is a "nonspecific response of the body to any demand made upon it" (Selye, 1973, p. 692). Another conceptualization of stress is "life events or sudden changes that require major behavioural adjustment in a relatively short period of time (e.g., marital breakdown, death, financial loss, and residential moves)" (McDonough, Walters, & Strohschein, 2002, p. 769). Stress sends the body into a "fight or flight response," a normal reaction to an alarming situation mediated by context, such as the nature of one's work. Thus, stress in and of itself is not necessarily harmful, and in some cases may be not only beneficial but necessary when working toward deadlines or when facing physical dangers. However, stress becomes detrimental to one's health when the exposure is prolonged. Prolonged exposure to stress weakens the neuroendocrine, autonomic, metabolic, and immune systems, increasing vulnerability to health problems such as heart disease, rheumatoid arthritis, diabetes, and increased risks of infection (Brunner & Marmot, 2005). Stress in the workplace increases the risk of disease. People who have more control over their work have better health. Work-related stress has been linked to differences in health, sickness, absence, and premature death (Wilkinson & Marmot, 2003).

While those who are employed may be better off financially than those who are unemployed, working conditions are an important social determinant of health because of the great amount of time spent in workplaces (Mikkonen & Raphael, 2010). Highly unsatisfactory or insecure jobs can be as harmful as unemployment; having a job will not always protect physical and mental health. People who are already at greater risk for poor health outcomes due to their socio-economic status and level of education are also the ones most likely to experience adverse working conditions. Moreover, high-stress jobs predispose individuals to high-blood pressure, cardiovascular diseases, and development of physical and psychological difficulties such as depression and anxiety (Mikkonen & Raphael, 2010).

Food Insecurity

Despite Canada's wealth, approximately 1.6 million Canadian households faced food insecurity in 2011, which amounts to nearly 1 in 8 Canadian families (Community Foundations of Canada, 2013). Food insecurity is characterized by a lack of access to sufficient, safe, quality, nutritious food in order to meet the requirements of an active and healthy life. This includes consuming fewer servings of fruits and vegetables, milk products, and vitamins than those in food-secure households (Mikkonen & Raphael, 2010). At the household level, a family's nutritional status depends on sufficient food availability, equitable distribution of food within the household, and sufficient variety, quality, and safety of food (Wilkinson & Marmot, 2003). Most recent data indicate that food insecurity in Canada is increasing, with 450,000 more Canadians living in households affected by food insecurity in 2011 than in 2008, and rates of food insecurity in Alberta, New Brunswick, Nova Scotia, Quebec, and Saskatchewan reporting the highest observed rates yet (CFC, 2013). In one winter month in 2012, 882,188 people received food from a food bank in Canada (CFC, 2013). Nunavut, Prince Edward Island, and New Brunswick had the highest prevalence of children living in food-insecure households at 57 per cent, 27 per cent, and 25 per cent respectively (CFC, 2013). More than 1.1 million Canadian children or 1 in 6 were living in a home where people reported struggling to put food on the table in 2011 (CFC, 2013).

An adequate supply of safe, nutritious food is a key component of physical and mental health. Lacking this supply not only leads to malnutrition, but has also been linked to deficiencies in dietary intake (Wilkinson & Marmot, 2003). These deficiencies have been found to be more common among food-insecure households and are associated with an increased likelihood of developing and having difficulties managing chronic diseases (Mikkonen & Raphael, 2010). Food-insecure households are 80 per cent more likely to report having diabetes, 70 per cent more likely to report food allergies, and 60 per cent more likely to report high blood pressure than food-secure households (Mikkonen & Raphael, 2010). Overconsumption of foods low in nutrients, also a form of malnutrition, is problematic in that it contributes to cardiovascular diseases, diabetes, cancer, degenerative eye diseases, obesity, and poor dental health (Wilkinson & Marmot, 2003). Malnutrition during childhood has long-term effects on a child's physiological and psychological development.

Residents in rural Canadian regions face high costs in transporting food to their areas. For example, Nunavut residents spend an average of $14,815 per year on food, or 25 per cent of their total expenditures compared to an average of $7,262, or 11 per cent of total expenditures in Canada overall (CFC, 2013). Traditional methods of obtaining food are becoming increasingly difficult. Food imported from southern Canadian regions can be expensive and may not entirely satisfy community nutritional needs. In Inuit communities, "country food" (seals, walruses, whales, fish, muskox, caribou) used to be the central food staples; hunting and fishing not only provided food for families but also contributed to household livelihoods. Today, while Inuit can hunt and fish for themselves and their families, they cannot sell most of their country foods in local stores because of the licenses needed and the provincial and federal requirements that must be met (Ives et al., 2012). The changing Inuit diet over time that has incorporated larger proportions of southern, imported food and less country food in addition to a more sedentary lifestyle has contributed to an increased risk of diabetes, high-blood pressure, and heart problems (Marchildon & Torgerson, 2013).

People on social assistance, single-parent families, immigrant families, and those who identify as First Nations, Métis, and Inuit are all at higher risk of needing nutritional assistance (CFC, 2013). For example, Winnipeg has high rates of child poverty and a large urban First Nations population with social and economic challenges. Growing diet-related health problems have been seen in First Nations as well as in immigrant populations after coming to Winnipeg. In response, a community foundation has worked to build the capacity of charitable organizations with nutrition programs. Working in collaboration with the Child Nutrition Council of Manitoba, Food Matters Manitoba, and the Manitoba Food Security Network, the community foundation created the Nourishing Potential Fund for afterschool nutrition, recognizing that "hungry children can't learn" (CFC, 2013, p. 6).

Families who experience poverty contend with many issues, including food insecurity. For example, in Guelph, Ontario, neighbourhood assessments found that food insecurity and hunger were key issues in particular neighbourhoods with families with low incomes. As a response, funding to Family and Children Services of Guelph & Wellington County provided support for part-time coordinators to work with these neighbourhoods where hunger and food security were acute issues (CFC, 2013).

Housing

Safe, affordable, environmentally appropriate housing is critical for health and well-being. Without it, individuals and families are at greater risk for health challenges (Mikkonen & Raphael, 2010). Recent media coverage of communities such as Attawapiskat First Nation at the mouth of the Attawapiskat River at James Bay has highlighted the fact that homes in some Indigenous communities across the country lack clean water, basic sanitation, and adequate ventilation. Moreover, these homes are **crowded** and inappropriate for environmental conditions, making their inhabitants at risk of homelessness.

Poor quality housing can be characterized by the presence of lead and mold, poor heating and insulation, inadequate ventilation, vermin infestation, and overcrowding, which contribute to poor health outcomes (Mikkonen & Raphael, 2010), particularly among children who suffer in childhood and then later in adulthood. Health experts maintain that inadequate housing can be associated with a host of health problems. Crowded living conditions can lead to the fast spread of infectious diseases such as tuberculosis and hepatitis A as well as elevated risks for injuries, mental health problems, family conflict, and violence (Statistics Canada, 2006).

Housing and shelter circumstances can be categorized into the following typology (Gaetz, Donaldson, Richter, & Gulliver, 2013, p. 4):

* Unsheltered, where one is living on the streets or in places not intended for human habitation;

crowding Defined as more than one person per room (bathrooms, halls, vestibules and rooms used solely for business purposes are not counted as rooms) (Statistics Canada, 2006).

The Canadian Press/Adrian Wyld

Donald and Jessica Jacasum eat and sleep in this tiny one-room shelter in Attawapiskat, Ontario. Lack of adequate living conditions can have severe consequences on their overall health.

homelessness Refers to a situation of an individual or family without stable, permanent, appropriate housing, or the immediate prospect, means, and ability of acquiring it (CHRN, 2012, p. 1).

- Emergency Sheltered, where one is staying in overnight emergency shelters designed for people who are **homeless**;
- Provisionally Accommodated, for people who are homeless whose accommodation is temporary or insecure, including interim (or transitional) housing, people living temporarily with others (couch surfing), or living in institutional contexts (hospital, prison) without permanent housing arrangements;
- At Risk of Homelessness, where people are not homeless, but whose current economic and/or housing situation is precarious or does not meet public health and safety standards.

On any given night in Canada, 30,000 are homeless, 2,880 are unsheltered, 14,400 are staying in emergency homelessness shelters, 7,350 are staying in violence-against-women shelters, and 4,464 are provisionally accommodated (Gaetz, Donaldson, Richter & Gulliver, 2013).

A decline in the availability of quality rental housing combined with flat or decreasing incomes, benefit reductions, and economic fluctuations since the 1980s has translated into greater numbers of Canadians spending a larger proportion of their income on housing; nearly 381,000 households live in severe housing need, defined as living in poverty and spending more than 50 per cent of their income on rental housing (Gaetz, Donaldson, Richter & Gulliver, 2013). Table 6.3 illustrates that over 27 per cent of Canadian households live in core housing need, with approximately 10 per cent living in situations of severe housing need (CMHC, 2010). Over 30 per cent of Canadians live in rental housing. High average rents can make housing unaffordable in many communities across the country and low vacancy rates in larger Canadian cities of between 1 per cent and 1.7 per cent put further pressure on housing costs (Gaetz, Donaldson, Richter & Gulliver, 2013).

Risk of homelessness increases when it intersects with populations living in vulnerable contexts. Interpersonal violence is one of the leading contributors to the housing

| TABLE 6.3 | Affordable Housing in Canada |

Census Metropolitan Areas	Population	Homeownership Rate (%)	Vacancy Rate (%)	Average Rents (Bachelor/ 1 Bed)	Core Housing Needs (# of households/ incidence)	Severe Housing Needs; Renters (% of households)
Canada	33,476,688	68.4	2.8	$655 $855	981,750 27.2%	10.5
Victoria	344,615	64.7	2.7	$695 $828	12,480 26.5%	10.9
Vancouver	2,313,238	65.1	1.8	$864 $982	79,365 31.2%	12.3
Calgary	1,214,839	74.1	1.3	$776 $958	22,515 22.4%	8.6
Edmonton	1,159,869	69.2	1.7	$743 $882	28,750 24.6%	9.4
Saskatoon	260,600	66.8	2.6	$655 $815	6,525 22.2%	10.7
Regina	210,556	70.1	1.0	$633 $831	5,535 24.3%	8.9
Winnipeg	730,018	67.2	1.7	$527 $704	20,915 23.9%	7.6
Hamilton	721,053	71.6	3.5	$569 $735	22,105 31.4%	12.4
Toronto	5,583,064	67.6	1.7	$837 $1,007	198,295 37.4%	13.2
Ottawa	921,823	66.7	2.5	$754 $916	29,560 28.9%	10.4
Moncton	138,644	70.1	6.7	$485 $619	3,850 26.7%	10.9
Halifax	390,328	64.0	3.0	$690 $773	14,700 28.4%	12.8

Source: Gaetz, Donaldson, Richter & Gulliver, 2013.

insecurity of women and children (Baker, Billhardt, Warren, Rollins, & Glass, 2010). Emergency shelters serve women and children forced to leave their homes in the face or under threat of violence. Across Canada, provinces and territories operate nearly 400 emergency shelters with more than 15,000 permanent beds, from Ontario with 132 shelters and 6,806 permanent beds to Nunavut with 1 shelter and 20 permanent beds (HRSDC, 2012). Shelters can offer safety from violence as well as linkages to support services such as legal aid, health and community resources, medical interventions, housing, and employment counseling. Members of racialized communities and LGBTQ youth are at greater risk for homelessness (Abramovich, 2012; Kidd, 2007; Lenon, 2000).

Homelessness in Indigenous communities is extremely high, particularly in urban areas (Gaetz, Donaldson, Richter, & Gulliver, 2013). While the focus on Indigenous homelessness is primarily seen as an urban issue, the poor conditions of housing on reserves as well as high unemployment contribute to migration to urban areas. First Nations, Métis and Inuit were almost four times as likely as non-Indigenous people to live in a crowded dwelling. They were three times as likely to live in a home in need of major repairs (Statistics Canada, 2006).

Indigenous Status

The health of Indigenous Peoples of Canada is inextricably bound with their history of colonization (Mikkonen & Raphael, 2010). This has taken the form of legislation such as the Indian Act of 1876, disregard for land claims, forced relocation, and the establishment of and forced attendance at residential schools. The result has been adverse health outcomes. Indigenous Peoples in Canada suffer from a poorer quality of life when measured only by mortality and morbidity as compared to their non-Indigenous counterparts (Waldram, Herring, & Young, 2006; Wilson & Rosenberg, 2002). Even within the Indigenous populations of Canada, there is a gradient grounded in the Indian Act's

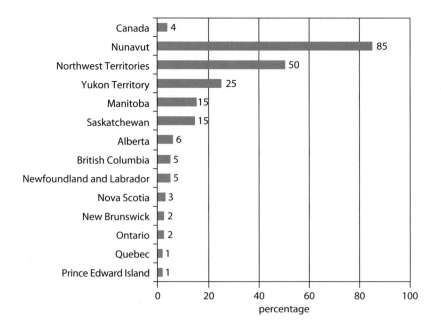

FIGURE 6.2 // Percentage of Aboriginal People in the Population, Canada, Provinces and Territories, 2006.

Source: Statistics Canada, *Census of Population*, 2006.

discriminatory definitions. Health promotion and treatment programs, such as health centres, federal substance abuse programs, and pre- and post-natal programs, are available to First Nations and Inuit Peoples but not to non-status First Nations Peoples or Métis despite similar social and health challenges (Kirmayer, Tait, & Simpson, 2009).

Income again is a key determinant in the well-being of Indigenous families. Indigenous Peoples in Canada have much higher poverty rates than non-Indigenous Canadians. The origins of this lie in the lower **labour force participation rates** and higher unemployment of Indigenous Peoples (OECD, 2002). Some groups have appallingly high rates of poverty, such as in Manitoba and Saskatchewan where 62 per cent and 64 per cent of Aboriginal children are poor, respectively, (Macdonald & Wilson, 2013). The non-Indigenous child poverty rate is 15 per cent for Manitoba and 16 per cent for Saskatchewan (Macdonald & Wilson, 2013).

> **labour force participation rate** The percentage of the population identified as either employed or unemployed and seeking employment relative to the entire population (HRSDC, 2011).

In 2006, the median income for Indigenous Peoples was $18,962 while the median income for the non-Indigenous population was $27,097 (Wilson & Macdonald, 2010). Income is firmly bound to the determinants described in this section. Lower wage rates play a part: in most provinces the incidence of low income is between two and three times greater in Indigenous families. Additional contributing factors are the relative lack of economic development in communities in which Indigenous Peoples live, lower education levels of the Indigenous population, poorer health of Indigenous Peoples, and ongoing discrimination in the labour market. In 2005, according to the Census, it was estimated the poverty rate for the entire Indigenous population (i.e., both on and off-reserve) was 18.7 per cent among Indigenous families and 42.8 per cent among unattached individuals.

In Canada, Indigenous Peoples are disproportionately affected by determinants which affect physical and mental health across the board. Indigenous Peoples experience lower graduation rates from high school and lower rates of higher education, lower life expectancy, higher morbidity and mortality rates, and a higher incidence of family abuse, alcoholism, living in substandard housing, and unemployment (OECD, 2002, Plourde, 2007). Life expectancy and infant mortality illustrate significant disparities. In 2001 for Indigenous Peoples overall, the life expectancy was 71 years for Indigenous men and 77 years for Indigenous women (Statistics Canada, 2006). The estimated life expectancy specifically for Inuit was lower, with 63 years for men and 72 years for women. For the total Canadian population, life expectancy for men was 77 years and 82 years for women (Statistics Canada, 2006). Nunavut's infant mortality rate is three times the Canadian average (Marchildon & Torgerson, 2013). Indigenous Peoples are also more likely to die from injuries or poison, have three times the rate of diabetes than non-Indigenous peoples in Canada (OECD, 2002) and twice the incidence of disability (Veenstra, 2009) than other members of the Canadian population. The rate of incarceration of Indigenous Peoples is 8.5 times higher than that of non-Indigenous Peoples in Canada (OECD, 2002) and the suicide rate is much higher for Indigenous youth than for any other group of Canadian youth (Tester & McNicoll, 2004). Indigenous elders have poorer health outcomes and do not receive the same level of health-care services as non-Indigenous older adults (Health Council of Canada, 2013).

Access to quality, safe, affordable housing provides a clear illustration of the intersection of income, health, and Indigenous status. The proportion of Indigenous people living in crowded dwellings or in dwellings in need of major repair was substantial in western urban centres. In particular, Indigenous Peoples living in Prince Albert, Regina, Saskatoon, and Edmonton were 4 to 11 times more likely to live in crowded conditions than their non-Indigenous counterparts. In contrast, Indigenous people living in Montreal, Ottawa–Gatineau, Vancouver, and Toronto were less likely than non-Indigenous people to live in crowded homes. Across all major census metropolitan areas however, Indigenous Peoples are two to three times more likely than the non-Indigenous population to live in dwellings needing major repairs (Statistics Canada, 2006).

TABLE 6.4	Average Employment Income, Canada, 2005	
	Racialized	Non-racialized
Women	$25,204	$28,584
Men	$35,329	$45,327
Total	$30,385	$37,332

Source: Block & Galabuzi, 2011 from Statistics Canada–2006 Census, Catalogue Number 97-563-XCB2006060.

Crowded living conditions in Inuit communities are some of the worst in Canada. In 2006, about 15,600, or 31 per cent of all Inuit lived in crowded homes. In contrast, 3 per cent of the non-Indigenous population in Canada lived in crowded conditions in 2006. First Nations Peoples were five times more likely than non-Indigenous people to live in crowded living conditions; this phenomenon is more common on reserves, where just over one-quarter (26 per cent) live in crowded conditions (Statistics Canada, 2006).

Racialized Identity

Being a member of a racialized group affects health outcomes. Again, level of income makes a difference; historically, racialized Canadians earned less than non-racialized Canadians (See Table 6.4; Block & Galabuzi, 2011).

Using data from the Canadian Health Survey, studies have also found disparities in service utilization as well as health outcomes depending on one's background (Quan et al., 2006; Veenstra, 2009). In Veenstra's (2009) study, respondents identifying as Aboriginal, Aboriginal/White, Black, Chinese, or South Asian had significant relative risks for poor health and those who identified as Aboriginal or Aboriginal/White reported some of the highest risks for diabetes and fair/poor self-rated health in a large, diverse sample. Given the political nature of using racialized/ethnic categories in a government-sponsored census as well as the fluid nature of identity, "identification of a contemporary suite of salient racialized identities in multicultural nations like … Canada [is] an inherently problematic endeavor" (Veenstra, 2009, p. 539). However, there is a reality for Canadians of colour that is shaped by their self-identification, visible or not. Veenstra highlighted how institutional racism shapes experience, such as limiting opportunities for higher education that could lead to prestigious jobs with high salaries (or any jobs at all) as well as jobs with quality supplemental health insurance coverage. Institutional racism can also lead to "groups of people in economically impoverished regions possessing relatively few health and social services or [to living] in segregated urban residential areas that suffer inordinately from a lack of amenities or the presence of environmental toxins" (p. 539). Quan and colleagues used categories of "visible minorities" in their study, and found that members of visible minority groups were less likely than White respondents to have been in contact with specialist physicians, admitted to hospital, or to have had a Prostate-Specific Antigen test, mammogram, or Pap test (Quan et al., 2006).

Racialized immigrant groups are increasingly vulnerable, as they have higher rates of poverty (Galabuzi, 2006), are more likely to have precarious employment (Vosko, 2006), and, largely as a result of low income, are more likely than the Canadian-born population to spend more than half of their total household incomes on housing (Hiebert et al., 2006; Rose, 2001), much of which is inadequate (Leloup & Zhu, 2006) and situated in declining neighbourhoods (Carter & Osborne, 2009). Housing insecurity for immigrants has also been linked to pressure on social networks, limited social capital (D'Addario et al., 2007), and isolation and social exclusion (Danso, 2002; Ray & Preston, 2009).

Social exclusion refers to the lack of or denial of resources, rights or goods, and services to marginalized groups and involves limitations on the ability to participate in the normal relationships and activities—in economic, social, cultural or political arenas—that are engaged in by the majority of people in society (Wilkinson & Marmot, 2003).

Disability

According to the 2006 Participation and Activity Limitation Survey, 4.4 million Canadians (or 14.3 per cent) reported experiencing an activity limitation due to a physical, mental, or other health-related condition (see Chapter 12, Table 12.2, Prevalence of Disability by Age in Canada). Rates vary across the country, with Nova Scotia having the highest rates in all age categories.

Income intersects with disability with regard to employment and subsequent benefits and unemployment, thus shaping health outcomes. The gap in the unemployment rates between people with and without disabilities was relatively consistent across gender and age yet there were some notable differences across the provinces and territories. Quebec has the largest gap in unemployment, with the unemployment rate for people with limitations nearly double that of people without limitations (14.7 per cent versus 7.9 per cent). Similarly, Quebec's labour force participation rate for people with limitations (52.0 per cent) was below the national average (59.6 per cent). Alberta has the smallest gap in the unemployment rate between people with and without disabilities (5.5 per cent versus 3.5 per cent) and the gap for Yukon Territory was also relatively small (11.8 per cent versus 9.2 per cent). Labour force participation in Alberta (70.8 per cent) and the Yukon Territory (75.4 per cent) was also above the national average (Disabled Persons Commission, 2009).

In prime income-earning years, younger working-age adults with disabilities are far less likely to work or be looking for work than younger working-age adults without disabilities, with the labour force participation rate for adults with disabilities aged 25 to 54 at 66.0 per cent, compared to 88.2 per cent for same-aged adults without disabilities. Gender also intersects, with younger working-age women with disabilities less likely to participate in the labour force (63.0 per cent) than younger working-age men with disabilities (69.6 per cent) (HRSDC, 2011).

Studies have shown that as the degree of disability becomes more severe, labour force participation rates decrease and unemployment rates increase (HRSDC, 2011; Williams, 2006). Many employment issues are related to the workplace being either unable or unwilling to accommodate the needs of persons with disabilities (Mikkonen & Raphael, 2010). For example, in 2006, for those with a mild disability, the unemployment rate was about 7.2 per cent (about the same as the non-disabled population), compared with 16.8 per cent for those with a severe or very severe disability (Williams, 2006). Canada's levels of benefits to persons with disabilities are very low; they do not help individuals with disabilities out of poverty in most cities. Support for integration of persons with disabilities into Canadian society is below the Organisation for Economic Co-operation and Development (OECD) average (OECD, 2003). OECD (2003) reports show that Canada spends 1.28 per cent of GDP on all disability programs: contributory (earnings related) and non-contributory disability benefits, sickness cash benefits, and work injury benefits and employment-related programs for individuals with disabilities. This percentage of spending on disability-related benefits and programs ranks Canada 18th out of the 20 member countries of the OECD.

Gender

Gender plays a key role in shaping health outcomes. Health and health outcomes are inseparable from how people experience the health-care delivery system. Women have lower

© SCPhotos / Alamy

Because she is a woman, a mother, a person of colour, and single, this woman faces greater risk of financial and health challenges.

rates of mortality but, paradoxically, report higher levels of depression, psychiatric disorders, distress, and a variety of chronic illnesses than men (Baum & Grunberg, 1991; McDonough & Walters, 2001; Verbrugge, 1985). Women with little education and low household income have poor health outcomes (Denton, Prus, & Walters, 2004).

Due to gender inequality, women experience more adverse social determinants of health than men. A primary determinant for women is economic well-being. The likelihood of women being poor increases if they are single mothers, single senior women, alone, with a disability, Indigenous, of colour, of immigrant origin, lesbians, or migrants. In addition, women carry more responsibilities for raising children and taking care of house work. Women are disproportionately represented in part-time employment (70 per cent) (Williams, 2010) and multiple job holding and are less likely to be eligible for unemployment benefits due to length of time attached to the labour market. Moreover, women are employed in lower paying occupations and experience more discrimination in the workplace than men (Mikkonen & Raphael, 2010). While women have greater life expectancies, they endure more disabilities and chronic diseases and greater depression rates than men (Kosteniuk & Dickinson, 2003). A recent study found that the proportion of women experiencing economic hardships was 17 per cent compared to 12 per cent for men (Ahnquist, Wamala, & Lindstrom, 2012).

Women experience poverty at far higher rates than men. High poverty rates are concentrated in three family types: unattached women under 65 (40.3 per cent women vs 29.8 per cent men), unattached women 65 and older (45.6 per cent women vs 32.8 per cent men) and single mothers with children under 18 (45.4 per cent women vs 10.8 per cent men). In 2011, women's average annual earnings ($32,100) were only 66.5 per cent of their male counterparts' earnings ($48,100) (Statistics Canada, 2013). Geography is also a factor in **income inequality** (See Table 6.5).

income inequality The extent to which income is unequally distributed in a population (Raphael, 2009).

In Alberta, women's total incomes were 55 per cent of men's in 2008 ($34,000 for women and $61,700 for men); in Newfoundland and Labrador, women's incomes were 57 per cent of men's. The gap was smallest in Prince Edward Island and Quebec. In Prince Edward Island, women's incomes were 78 per cent of men's; in Quebec they were 72 per cent of men's. The health of Canadian women will become worse as income inequality continues.

Women with children are likely to earn less money than women without children (Zhang, 2009). Women's disadvantage is seen clearly when looking at poverty statistics. This phenomenon is grounded in the fact that "priority is given to paid work over unpaid work, while the work for caring for others, overwhelmingly the work of women, is typically regarded as a private responsibility" (Evans, 1997, p. 91). Years of unpaid work translate into fewer years of employment and subsequently lower contributions into retirement programs. Evans attributed this to the early notion of the "family wage" which assumed that male wages should be sufficient to support several dependents and thus served as a justification for the exclusion of women from paid industrial work. Similarly, assumptions of dependency are built into a social insurance system in which women traditionally have been more likely to benefit indirectly, as wives of unemployed or retired men, rather than as direct claimants on the basis of their own work record.

TABLE 6.5	Average Total Income of Women and Men, by Province, 2008	
Province	Women ($)	Men ($)
Canada	30,100	47,000
Newfoundland and Labrador	24,000	41,900
Prince Edward Island	27,900	36,000
Nova Scotia	25,200	41,000
New Brunswick	24,600	37,900
Quebec	28,500	39,600
Ontario	31,600	48,600
Manitoba	27,900	45,400
Saskatchewan	29,800	47,900
Alberta	34,000	61,700
British Columbia	29,100	47,600

Source: Statistics Canada, CANSIM table 202—0407 (Williams, 2010).

A two-track system exists where women are overrepresented in the social assistance track and underrepresented in the social insurance track. This means that women are more likely to benefit from the inferior tier of income security (social assistance where claims are made based on need, are more stigmatized and scrutinized, and benefits are low) than men who are more likely to claim benefits based on their participation in the labour market (social insurance where benefits are typically more generous, less stigmatized, and the process of claiming is less onerous) (Evans, 1997).

Employment insurance was expanded in 2000, allowing parents to receive benefits for up to one year while caring for a child, but many women find that they are still not eligible. Single mothers are especially at risk of entering poverty because of the lack of affordable child care and women's generally lower wages (Mikkonen & Raphael, 2010). While Quebec has $7-a-day child care, it is challenging to actually find a space, which poses a significant barrier to working mothers. Employment as noted below is also an important health determinant for women. Paid work enhances women's health, despite certain "costs" that it entails in terms of additional stress (Denton, Walters, & Strohschein, 2004).

There are certain areas where men are at greater risk than women for experiencing negative health outcomes. For example, men face more extreme forms of social exclusion manifested in homelessness and severe substance abuse (Mikkonen & Raphael, 2010). Men's suicide rates are four times higher than those for women and men are more likely to be perpetrators and victims of robbery and physical assault. Moreover, men are disproportionately represented in the prison population, where approximately 95 per cent of Canada's prison population is male (Mikkonen & Raphael, 2010).

Access to Health Services

Unlike in the United States where access to health care is typically equated with access to health insurance coverage, access to health care in Canada is interpreted differently due to a universal health-care system. The main purpose of the system is to protect the health of citizens and permanent residents and share health-care costs across the population. According to the Canada Health Act discussed earlier in this chapter, all provinces and territories must meet all "medically necessary" services on a universal basis (comprehensiveness). The principle of universality of the Canada Health Act requires that all residents of a province or territory be entitled, on the same terms and conditions, to the publicly funded health services covered by provincial/territorial plans. Universality is often considered by Canadians as a fundamental value that ensures national health-care insurance for everyone wherever they live in the country and that has removed obstacles to receiving appropriate, high-quality care (Parliament of Canada, n.d.; Sibley & Weiner, 2011). However, because the provinces and territories determine their own funding sources within the guidelines of health-care law, the range of services varies. Moreover, coverage of home care and nursing services varies across provinces and territories as well, and Medicare does not provide coverage for prescription drug costs.

Access has been defined as the ability for an individual to have a health-care need met if he or she has a need for a health-care service in the past year (Lasser, Himmelstein, & Woolhandler, 2006). Another definition of access is actual use of health-care services, taking into consideration facilitators and impediments to use (Andersen, Rice, & Kominski, 2011). Therefore, a lack of access is illustrated by a person who has had an unmet health-care need for which he or she felt he or she had needed, but had not received, a health-care service in the past year.

While Canadians have access to health-care coverage through the Canada Health Act, research has found other barriers to accessing health-care services. A significant factor is income. Canadians with low incomes are three times less likely to fill a prescription because of the cost and dental plans are available only to 26 per cent of workers with low incomes (Mikkonen & Raphael, 2010). Children in families with low incomes are less likely to have preventive and primary care visits (Guttman, Shipman, Lam, Goodman, & Stukel, 2010).

Geography is also associated with health status, health behaviours, and access and utilization of health-care services (Sibley & Weiner, 2011; Timony, Gauthier, Hogenbirk, Wenghofer, & Wenghofer, 2013). Residents living in very rural or remote areas are least likely to have had a flu shot, use specialist physicians, or have a regular medical doctor (Sibley & Weiner, 2011). For example, Inuit, especially those living in Inuit Nunangat, may face challenges in accessing the health-care system (Romanow, 2002). None of the 52 Inuit communities have year-round road access and only a few have hospitals. The other communities are serviced by health centres staffed by nurses. Inuit must be flown out of their communities for treatment requiring physicians or for appointments with medical specialists, and the ability to fly depends on weather conditions (Tait, 2008).

Language also shapes health-care access and utilization. Health practitioners may not speak the first language of clients, jeopardizing the opportunity for effective communication. This could be the case for immigrant-born clients, as well as for clients from Indigenous communities across Canada, where more than 50 Indigenous languages are spoken. Access may even be impeded for clients for whom one of Canada's official languages is their mother tongue. According to the 2006 Census, more than 1,000,000 Canadians outside Quebec claim French as their mother tongue, with the majority in Ontario (see Table 1.1). Research has found that Francophone communities have experienced challenges accessing linguistically appropriate services (Bouchard, Batal, Imbeault, Gagnon-Arpin, Makvandi, & Sedigh, 2012). Racialized Francophones are multiply challenged, facing access issues either within Quebec as a racialized community or outside Quebec as a racialized community and linguistic minority. One study of health care in Ontario found that 52 per cent of Francophone clients spoke French with their family doctor while nearly 100 per cent of Anglophone clients spoke English with their family doctor (Bouchard, Batal, Imbeault, Gagnon-Arpin, Makvandi, & Sedigh, 2012). Another Ontario study found that more than half of Ontario's French-speaking family physicians and general practitioners had located their practices in communities virtually uninhabited by Francophones, creating a situation where communities that are least likely to need French-language medical services have more French-speaking family physicians and general practitioners, and communities with the greatest need may be underserved (Timony, Gauthier, Hogenbirk, Wenghofer, & Wenghofer, 2013).

In addition to whether the services are physically accessible, there is a concern regarding services' cultural relevance. A lack of comfort or familiarity with the health-care system and/or experiences of discrimination can affect one's willingness to access services and thus can be a significant barrier (Sharif, Dar, & Amaratunga, 2000). Not only should services be culturally relevant and safe for service users but health-care providers who provide those services must be aware of cultural context as well, regardless of the country of origin of the service user.

Substance Use and Abuse

Substance use and abuse can be seen as both a response to challenging life circumstances as well as a contributing factor in worsening health inequalities (Wilkinson & Marmot, 2003). One's income level may play a role in determining high-risk behaviors that are directly linked to poor health outcomes and can affect health-care access, quality of health care received, and preventive behaviours of substance users (Galea & Vlahov, 2002). Legal and illicit substance use and abuse have been found to have strong relationships with indicators of social and economic disadvantage (Wilkinson & Marmot, 2003). Any type of social deprivation, whether measured by poor housing, low income, single parenthood, unemployment, or homelessness, is associated with high rates of smoking and very low rates of quitting, which consumes a significant portion of poor people's incomes in addition to causing serious illnesses and premature death (Wilkinson & Marmot, 2003). Alcohol abuse can compromise educational achievement due to missing classes and getting behind in school work as well as risk behaviours such as unprotected sexual activities and exposure to dangerous environments (Hurrelmann & Richter, 2006). For young people, adverse health outcomes from alcohol use are common and many alcohol-related causes of death occur relatively early in life (Schmid & Nic Gabhain, 2004). Regarding illicit drug use, Patton and colleagues (2002) found that frequent cannabis use in teenage girls predicted depression and anxiety later in life, with daily users carrying the highest risk and Meshesha and colleagues (2013) found that daily heroin use was associated with poorer perceived health.

Substance abuse is also closely linked to mental health. Individuals dealing with substance abuse problems often have mental health-care needs as well. **Co-occurring disorders** describes this situation, that is, when an individual has co-existing mental health and substance use disorders. As noted above, social determinants of health overlap and influence each other. Studies have found that individuals with co-occurring disorders have greater rates of unemployment and homelessness, and poorer physical health (Johnson, Brems & Burke, 2002; Watkins et al., 2004).

co-occurring disorders
Refers to an individual having co-existing mental health and substance abuse issues. Dual diagnosis is another term used to describe this same situation.

Education

Education is an important contributor to health (Marmot, 2005; Marmot & Wilkinson, 2005). Those with higher education levels are more likely to be healthier than those with lower education levels (Mikkonen & Raphael, 2010). Education contributes a unique

Theory in **Practice**

COUNCIL OF YUKON FIRST NATIONS CULTURAL ORIENTATION AND PROTOCOLS TOOLKIT

IN 2009, MEMBERS OF ORGANIZATIONS WORKING in health and social services in Yukon First Nations (YFN) communities identified a need for cultural competency training in order to support resource workers working in YFN communities. For remote communities that may rely on the services of people outside the community, effective preparation and orientation is a critical contribution to successful service outcomes, including retention of qualified staff. Developed collaboratively by the Council of Yukon First Nations, the Yukon First Nation Health and Social Development Commission, and the Yukon Territory Government Health and Social Department, the result was the Yukon First Nations Cultural Orientation and Protocols Toolkit. The Toolkit's purpose is to provide information and learning experiences for health and social resource workers who are working for Yukon First Nation people and for individuals who are supervising and supporting these service providers. This is accomplished by providing a self-administered toolkit of basic information about YFN people common for all communities, including YFN/community-specific information for participating YFN, using written and visual materials with curriculum elements to promote engagement, and supporting the toolkit with a brief community profile and recommendations for further learning.

The learning objectives of the toolkit are as follows:

- to learn about pre-contact lifestyles of Yukon First Nations people;
- to understand the multigenerational trauma caused by the experiences of residential schools and how those experiences have shaped and continue to shape the lives of Yukon First Nations individuals, families, and communities;
- to develop an informed picture of current community realities/dynamics related to governance, programs, and services;
- to begin learning and developing an understanding of YFN cultural values, protocols, and practices;
- to improve relationships between resource workers and First Nations and support the development of relationships built on mutual understanding and respect.

The kit is divided into eight self-administered modules consisting of written and DVD-based materials. Engagement is developed through questions and exercises, and space is created for participants to reflect on their learning through journaling. Each toolkit has a Yukon-specific section that is the same in all toolkits as well as a community-specific version of the toolkit that reflects the uniqueness of each First Nation in Yukon. Included in the Yukon-specific section is (1) information about cultural

element to one's social status trajectory with aspects that make it critical to health. It interacts with other social determinants to influence health in all stages of the life course, beginning in childhood. The relationship between children's educational performance with their parents' education levels would be reduced if affordable and high quality early learning programs were available in Canada (Mikkonen & Raphael, 2010). Lacking these programs has a major influence on many children's intellectual and emotional development.

awareness, (2) knowledge and understanding for service providers, (3) an introduction to relational cultural competence and reflective practice, (4) the Canadian context and Yukon agreements, (5) First Nation linguistic groups, (6) traditional territories and pre-contact life ways, (7) the impacts of contact and colonization, (8) Yukon First Nations cultures and values, and (9) examples of applying this learning in palliative care and institutional and community mental health settings. This section provides information that can orient service providers to Yukon communities such as Champagne and Aishihik First Nations (Haines Junction) in the south to Vuntut Gwitchin First Nation (Old Crow) in the north. It is important to highlight that the community-specific versions do not contain traditional knowledge, but do share information about community history, current status in land claims/self-government, communication and relationships, specific cultural values and beliefs, traditions related to birth and death, potlatch traditions, marriage, traditional laws, traditional health and healing practices, community-specific protocols, and community-specific details about people and their health and social well-being.

There has been significant interest in the Toolkit throughout Yukon and Canada, from provincial and territorial governments to Yukon College, the RCMP, other provincial health systems (in Manitoba and British Columbia), and the Canadian Executive Services Organization. Approaching health and social services from a context-specific framework is time and resource intensive; thus, implementation has been challenging. Ongoing evaluation and discussion assist in ways to better share the importance of this information for health and social service providers and how to track and update the toolkit when needed. Further information regarding the Toolkit is available from the Council of Yukon First Nations, www.cyfn.ca.

Council of Yukon First Nations. Used with permission

High-quality early childhood education programs for children from families with low incomes can mitigate some of the harmful effects of living in poverty. Research has found that when young children participate in high-quality early education programs, they make cognitive and social emotional advances associated with improved adult health (Friedman-Krauss & Barnett, 2013). Program participation positively influences later educational attainment, income, family stability, and job quality (Muennig, Schweinhart,

In Their Own Words

INDIVIDUALS WITH CO-OCCURRING DISORDERS

I HAVE BEEN PRIVILEGED OVER THE last 12 years to be working within the field of addictions—substance use and abuse with many different clientele types, their families, friends, and community supports. Social determinants of health often inform my evaluation as well as my treatment plan, which is developed collaboratively with the clients I have worked with. There is no specific social determinant of health that I believe is a defining factor in who will be faced with an addiction issue but more so how the social determinants of health influence the level of risk for substance use and abuse.

One of my areas of interest and where I work presently is with individuals with co-occurring disorders. The clients primarily are diagnosed with a severe mental health issue such as schizophrenia and a substance use or abuse issue. I have always been humbled and cognizant of the internal and external struggles this particular clientele face as they are often at greater risk due to their vulnerability and lack of social support in society. Often my work is framed through a recovery model where I accompany clients in achieving their true potential.

I feel honoured with the responsibility of voicing the needs of and advocating alongside this clientele due to the accumulated risks they have acquired over time. Often they have been hospitalized numerous times over long periods. They have taken medications that have adverse secondary effects that limit certain capacities. There are fewer housing resources that can accommodate their needs. They are limited financially and often their personal relations with social supports and their families are strained, leaving them in isolation.

My role among other things has been to break this isolation and assist wherever I can to help clients access the needed services and resources by physically accompanying them through their journey in whatever this may be. If the clients want to maintain their consumption I will work with this, and assure that it is done safely and that the individual's basic needs are met. If a client desires to reduce the harmful effects of his or her consumption or abstain then that will be incorporated into the goals of the work needed to be accomplished either through finding appropriate treatment centres or through education. Furthermore, an important aspect is assisting clients in maintaining their acquired successes through active participation such as employment, volunteerism, or even social activities.

I am always appreciative that clients have allowed me into their lives. I take this responsibility very seriously as their level of vulnerability dictates the need for constant advocacy as well as a deep understanding of the elements that they have been faced with over time.

Mark Demaine, MSW.

Montie, & Neidell, 2009). These positive influences are in turn associated with improved health status through decreases in behavioral risk factors, enhanced job safety, safer neighborhoods of residence, reduced psychological stress, and better access to healthy foods (Muennig, Schweinhart, Montie, & Neidell, 2009). Additionally, due to pre-enrollment health requirements and periodic assessments, the likelihood that they will interact with the health system in some way and thus receive immunizations and dental care increases, critical for a healthy foundation. Moreover, preschoolers and their parents often learn about nutrition and health, which can result in lifestyle changes that address issues such as obesity and malnutrition (Friedman-Krauss & Barnett, 2013).

Educational achievement sets the scaffolding for building social status at the start of adulthood, functioning as the main bridge between the generations and also as the main path of upward mobility (Mirowsky & Ross, 2003). Education accomplishes this through its influence on occupation and occupational status, wages, personal and household income and wealth, promotion of healthy behaviours, increasing options and awareness of options for addressing ill health and stress, and either freedom from economic hardship or creating a buffer in difficult economic times (Marmot & Wilkinson, 2005). One's income potential is directly related to one's accumulation of abilities, skills, and educational experiences in childhood, which is directly related to one's ability as an adult to find employment. Thus, education is considered a key mediator in this association, being firmly shaped by family context in childhood and a key determinant of one's income in adulthood (Benzeval, Judge, & Shuls, 2001).

During economic crises, having an education can facilitate one's ability to negotiate with one's employer, make one more resourceful, and improve one's chances of obtaining whatever one might need and/or improvising with what one has (Mirowsky & Ross, 2003). Education has also been found to make one more adept at societal and economic resource substitution, which is defined as using one thing in place of another. Those with more education have an increased capacity for resource substitution, which makes the absence of any one resource less harmful, while those with lower education levels are less skilled at obtaining and creating resources, increasing one's dependence on each standard resource (Mirowsky & Ross, 2003).

Conclusion

Despite Canada's wealth, on particular indicators for certain populations, its standing is unacceptably low. For example, a UNICEF survey ranked Canada 17th out of 29 wealthy countries according to the well-being of their children across five dimensions: material well-being, health and safety, education, behaviours and risks, and housing and environment (UNICEF, 2013). While Canada ranks 11th on the United Nations Human Development Index (HDI), when the HDI is calculated for Indigenous and non-Indigenous Peoples in Canada as well as Indigenous Peoples in Australia, the United States and New Zealand, there is a consistent gap of 6–18 per cent (UNDP, 2010). Across the board in these countries, Indigenous Peoples have lower life expectancy, poorer education outcomes, and smaller incomes. While universal health-care coverage is a critical step to addressing the health needs of Canadians, this chapter has demonstrated that one's social location and social and economic environment require greater examination in order to develop a clearer understanding of the associations between social determinants and health outcomes. Carefully examining the relationship between income and health is central as "income is one of the most malleable policy instruments" (Benzeval, Judge & Shouls, 2001, p. 377). Social workers are involved directly and indirectly in all areas that touch human health. Social workers are especially equipped to work within a social determinants of health framework, employing knowledge of the ways in which various social locations can interact on multiple levels. Social work theories help us understand that changes in health cannot happen in isolation but must be addressed from a systems perspective. If we are to improve health in Canada and reduce health inequities, we must consider a broad conceptualization of health.

QUESTIONS FOR CRITICAL THOUGHT

1. Look at a recent health-related article in your local newspaper. How has the media presented the issue? Is there a discussion of related social determinants of health? Identify contributing social determinants of health in the context of this health issue.

2. Identify a source of stress in your life. Is this stress short term or long term? Connect it to the social determinants of health discussed in this chapter. Which social determinants are connected to this stress? Within each connected determinant, write down one concrete suggestion for addressing the stress that has manifested itself in that particular determinant.

3. Discuss the impact of income and social determinants of health. Why is level of income implicated so strongly in each determinant? What are some historical barriers to income equality? What are some barriers grounded in social location?

4. With food bank use in Canada rising, what do you think might be the criteria used to evaluate users' eligibility? In what ways might this intersect with historical evaluations of those in need?

5. Discuss how changes in health-care delivery in Canada may be affecting access. What groups are most vulnerable?

RECOMMENDED READINGS

Armstrong, P., & Armstrong, H. (2010). *The wasting away of care: The undermining of Canadian health care* (2nd ed.). Oxford: Oxford University Press. This text provides a clear and comprehensive examination of how changes in who provides care, who funds care, and who decides on care have resulted in a retrenchment of accessible health services for many Canadians.

Bryant, T., Raphael, D., & Rioux, M. (Eds.). (2010). *Staying alive: Critical perspectives on health, illness, and health care* (2nd ed.). Toronto: Canadian Scholars' Press. This edited volume provides perspectives on health and health care as well as human rights and political economy perspectives on health, focusing on Canada and the United States within an international context. Chapters focus on pharmaceutical policy, social class, race, gender and care, the social construction of illness and disability, approaches to promoting population health, discussions of inequality, women's health, public health and public policy, First Nations health, and discussion of the historical development of the Canadian Medicare system.

McGibbon, E.A. (2012). *Oppression: A social determinant of health*. Winnipeg, MB: Fernwood. Oppression and health are intricately connected. Chapters include an overview of oppression as a social determinant of health, how oppression operates to produce health inequities and a discussion of health as a human right as well as special attention to the intersections of health and oppression with different groups such as older women, racialized groups, Indigenous Peoples, immigrants, and those struggling with mental health issues.

Raphael, D. (Ed.). (2008). *Social determinants of health: Canadian perspectives* (2nd ed.). Toronto: Canadian Scholars Press. This edited volume reviews social determinants of health for Canadians, which establish the extent to which Canadians possess the resources to identify and achieve personal aspirations, satisfy needs, and cope with the environment. The revised volume is divided into sections focusing on a review of the concept of social determinants of health, income security and unemployment, education, food and shelter, social exclusion, and public policy. As discussed in this chapter, a social determinants of health approach is critical to understanding patterns of health and illness in Canada today.

RECOMMENDED WEBSITES

Canadian Mental Health Association
http://www.cmha.ca/
The Canadian Mental Health Association, established in 1918, is one of Canada's oldest voluntary organizations. Each year, the CMHA provides direct service to more than 100,000 Canadians through the combined efforts of more than 10,000 volunteers and staff across Canada in over 120 communities. The Association promotes mental health and supports the resilience and recovery of people experiencing mental illness through advocacy, education, research, and service.

The Canadian Public Health Association
www.cpha.ca
The Canadian Public Health Association (CPHA), founded in 1910, is the only Canadian non-governmental organization focused exclusively on public health with links to the international community. CPHA is composed of a diverse membership that represents more than 25 professions. Frontline Health: Beyond Health Care is one of the programs specifically dedicated to exploring the impacts of social determinants of health in Canada.

Health Council of Canada
http://www.healthcouncilcanada.ca/index.php
The Health Council of Canada, established in 2003, informs Canadians and their governments regarding progress towards a health-care system that better serves the Canadian public. The Council publishes periodic reports on health-care reform, Aboriginal health, health-care innovation, and themes related to primary care provision.

Social Determinants of Health
www.thecanadianfacts.org
Social Determinants of Health: The Canadian Facts website provides information and resources on the social determinants of health, which explain how environmental and systemic living conditions shape the health of Canadians.

World Health Organization Commission on the Social Determinants of Health (CSDH)
www.who.int/social_determinants/en
This site provides a wealth of multimedia resources focused on social determinants of health around the world. Country reports highlight emerging trends in approaching health policy from a social determinants of health perspective as well as lessons learned in various contexts.

7

Social Work Practice with Children

LEARNING OBJECTIVES

- To highlight key issues affecting Canadian children.

- To review the historical conditions, events, and realities that have shaped and informed the development of child welfare and youth justice systems in Canada.

- To identify the varied models and approaches used to explain why families may come into contact with the child welfare system.

- To explore contemporary child welfare practice and the roles and duties of social workers.

- To trace the changing approaches to youth justice, the laws that have accompanied these approaches, and the role of social workers working in the realm of youth justice.

- To highlight the role of prevention in social work practice with children.

- To address the inherent tensions experienced by social workers when working in child welfare and youth justice.

Chapter Outline

This chapter explores social work practice with children and its surrounding complexities. Social work with children in Canada can be divided into three distinct, but often overlapping areas of practice: child welfare, youth justice, and prevention. As each Canadian province and territory has authority over social planning in the realms of health, education, and welfare, there is provincial variation in terms of the legislation, programs, and practices that govern social work with children. And yet, there are numerous similarities and parallels. The first section addresses issues and realities affecting Canadian children. It then traces the changing conceptions of childhood and the history of child welfare in Canada. It also explores social work practice in the context of child welfare. The chapter then provides an overview of Canada's youth justice system, both its history and contemporary issues, as well as the role of the social worker in the realm of youth justice. Preventive social work with children is then discussed, alongside the dilemmas and tension of practice in relation to child welfare and youth justice.

Canada's Children: Issues, Facts, and Figures

Child Poverty

The UNICEF *Innocenti Report Card 7* provides a picture of international child poverty in the world's wealthier countries in 2007. This report card ranks six dimensions of child well-being including material well-being, health and safety, educational well-being, family and peer relationships, behaviours and risks, and subjective well-being. Importantly, the children in the world's wealthiest countries are not necessarily the bestoff. While Canada does well with respect to education and material well-being (based on family income and employment), it does poorly with regard to preventing injurious behaviours including violence and substance abuse, and in regard to maintaining children's health and personal satisfaction with their lives. In an overall assessment of child well-being, Canada ranks 12th out of 21 nations, behind many European countries. A more recent report by UNICEF (2012) ranked Canada 18th out of 35 industrialized countries when child-poverty rates are compared with overall poverty rates. In addition, Canada is in the bottom third—at 13.3 per cent—when it comes to the percentage of children in poverty.

Substantial disparities in poverty rates exist across provinces. Those typically considered "wealthy provinces" do not have the lowest rates of child poverty. As an example, British Columbia, historically considered a wealthy province, has the highest provincial rate of child poverty followed by Manitoba, Saskatchewan, and New Brunswick. Prince Edward Island and Newfoundland/Labrador, historically "have not" provinces, have the lowest rates of child poverty, alongside resource rich Alberta (Schissel, 2011).

Poverty intersects with and is shaped by factors such as immigrant/refugee status, race, and cultural background and heritage. According to the National Council of Welfare (2007), in provinces across Canada, the highest rates of poverty occur for children who are recent immigrants (33 per cent), Indigenous children (28 per cent) and visible minority children (26 per cent). In comparison, the poverty rate for non-visible minority children is 12 per cent, while the overall rate is 18 per cent.

Children living in conditions of poverty are at a considerable disadvantage relative to their wealthier counterparts with respect to physical, emotional, and cognitive health and are at a higher risk of poor health, low success in education, victimization, greater contact with the legal system, and greater behavioural problems in their formative years (Schissel, 2011). Research on children and poverty shows that raising the incomes of poor families, even just barely above the poverty line, will improve the learning ability and performance of young children (Smith et al., 1999).

Family Violence

Family violence continues to have a profound effect on Canadian children and families. In 2010, 18,710 children and youth aged 17 and under were the victims of police-reported family violence. This represents about one-quarter of all violent offences committed against children and youth. Police-reported rates of family violence were generally higher among older children and youth, though this was not the case for homicides. Between 2000 and 2010, the rate of family homicide was highest among infants under one. Over this same 10-year period, the vast majority of homicides of infants and toddlers were committed by parents (98 per cent of family homicides against infants under one, and 90 per cent of family homicides of children aged 1 to 3 years). Girls were more than

Case STUDY

Child Maltreatment in Canada: The Canadian Incidence Study of Reported Child Abuse and Neglect

THE CANADIAN INCIDENCE STUDY (CIS) is conducted every five years and describes the characteristics of children reported to child welfare authorities across Canada. Two national cycles of the CIS were completed in 1998 and 2003, in addition to the first province-wide incidence study completed in Ontario in 1993. A key finding from the comparative analysis of data in the 1998 and 2003 versions of the CIS is the growth in the estimated number of children investigated in these two different years. Although incomplete data from Quebec prevented detailed comparisons on some variables, the incidence of investigation per 1000 children increased by 86 per cent in the rest of Canada and substantiation rates increased by 125 per cent. Statistics from the CIS-2008 indicate that the number of maltreatment investigations in 2008 were quite similar to 2003 (235,842 and 235, 315 respectively) (Public Health Agency of Canada, 2010). Below are statistics emerging from CIS-2003:

Physical Abuse: Cases involving physical abuse constituted 24 per cent of all substantiated investigations in 2003. This represents a 107 per cent increase from 1998.

Neglect: The incidence of substantiated neglect between 1998 and 2003 increased by 78 per cent. In the CIS-2003, neglect was the primary form of maltreatment in 29 per cent of substantiated investigations.

Sexual abuse: The CIS-2003 noted a decline in the incidence of substantiated sexual abuse investigations. In 2003, sexual abuse cases made up only 3 per cent of substantiated investigations, compared to 9 per cent in 1998.

Emotional maltreatment and exposure to domestic violence: The incidence rate of emotional maltreatment increased from 0.86 in 1998 to 3.23 per 1000 children in 2003. In relation to exposure to domestic violence, the incidence rates increased from 1.72 in 1998 to 6.17 in 2003. In 2003, emotional maltreatment comprised 15 per cent of substantiated investigations and exposure to domestic violence accounted for 28 per cent of substantiated investigations.

The changes noted between 1998 and 2003 have important implications for social workers as they have placed increasing pressures on resources within the child welfare field, including staff time to respond appropriately to these demands.

four times likely than boys to be victims of sexual offences committed by a family member (134 victims per 100,000 population versus 30 per 100,000) (Sinha, 2012). Between 2004 and 2009, there was an increase in the proportion of spousal violence victims reporting that children heard or saw assaults on them (from 43 per cent to 52 per cent of spousal victims with children).

Child Maltreatment

The number of children needing care and protection increased quite dramatically between 1998 and 2003. According to the Canadian Incidence Study of Reported Child Abuse and Neglect 2008, there were an estimated 85,440 substantiated child maltreatment investigations in Canada in 2008 (14.19 investigations per 1,000 children). The two most frequently occurring categories of substantiated maltreatment were exposure to intimate partner violence and neglect. Thirty-four per cent of all substantiated investigations identified exposure to intimate partner violence as the primary category of maltreatment (an estimated 29,259 cases or 4.86 investigations per 1,000 children). In another 34 per cent of substantiated investigations, neglect was identified as the overriding concern (an estimated 28,939 investigations or 4.81 investigations per 1,000 children). Twenty-two per cent of substantiated cases (an estimated 18,510 investigations) involved children of Indigenous heritage. Parental neglect in Indigenous communities is intimately tied to structural factors such as inadequate housing, unemployment, and social exclusion, as well as the devastating impact of colonization and cultural genocide.

Changing Conceptions of Children in Canada: A History of Child Welfare

Child welfare is a term used to describe a set of government and private services designed to protect children and encourage family stability and is considered a special area of practice within the profession of social work (CASW, 2012). According to the Canadian Association of Social Workers (CASW), the mandate of child welfare agencies is to

> work with the community to identify children who are in need of protection and to decide how to best help and protect those children. A fundamental belief is that government interference in family life should be as minimal as possible, except when parental care is below the community standard and places children at risk of harm. The major guiding principle is always to act in the **best interest of the child** (CASW, 2012).

best interest of the child Refers to the principle that the best interests of the child must be the primary consideration in all actions concerning children.

Child welfare is typically organized into five key activities:

- *family support*: child welfare agencies provide services aimed to support families who need assistance in the protection and care of their children;
- *child protection*: child welfare agencies receive and investigate reports of possible child abuse and neglect;
- *child placement*: child welfare agencies arrange for children to live with kin, foster families, or licensed group-home facilities when they are not safe at home;
- *adoption*: child welfare agencies arrange permanent adoptive homes for children;

- *foster care*: child welfare agencies arrange and support the placement of children in alternative care arrangements. Foster parents provide the day-to-day care for a child on behalf of a provincial children's aid society. Child welfare agencies also provide independent living services for youth leaving foster care.

There are between 75,000 and 80,000 children under the care of provincial children and family services agencies across Canada. Since ten provinces and three territories (not the federal government) have legal jurisdiction over child welfare, when we speak of "child welfare," it cannot be described as a single, unified system. As reflected in Canada's three main cultural traditions, alongside unique provincial variations, child and family welfare practices mirror the cultural, linguistic, religious, historical, geographic, and institutional contexts in which they have evolved (Cameron et al., 2007, p. 2). For the most part, in drafting their child welfare legislation, provinces have drawn upon provisions and principles already established by other provinces, while still maintaining specific forms and concepts that reflect their province's unique contexts and histories (Swift & Callahan, 2006).

While not identical, child welfare legislation across the country follows similar principles and often uses the same language and concepts. Common features include the following:

- the best interests of the child, which must be considered when a child is found to be in need of protection;
- respect for the parent's primary responsibility for child rearing;
- continuity of care and stability as important for children;
- views of children as important to take into consideration when decisions are being made that affect their futures;
- respect for cultural heritage, particularly for Indigenous children.

Some key provincial differences lie in the definition of a "child" for the purposes of protection. As indicated in Table 7.1 each province and territory has a distinct age range for protective services.

Indeed, the concepts of "child" and "childhood" are contested ones and embody social constructions that varies in form and content across contexts, cultures, social groups, and as defined by localized understandings and values (Kemper, 2005). Defining "children" solely by age may also be problematic as it not only reflects a bias towards western notions of childhood that are rooted in biomedical theory, but it also downplays the importance of other cultural, social, and economic factors that are used to define childhood. In Canada, perceptions of children have changed and evolved according to three unique stages (Covell & Howe, 2001). During the first stage, children were viewed as possessions and objects of parental authority. In the second stage, children were perceived to be vulnerable individuals in need of protection. More recently, children have been regarded as subjects with inherent rights of their own. These changing perceptions of children are important as they are intricately related to the changing responses to children generally, to child welfare more specifically, as well as the role of social workers called upon to work with children.

Stage One: Children as Objects: The Absence of Legal Rights and Protections

Early perceptions of children from colonial times to the nineteenth century reflected a social laissez-faire philosophy where children were viewed largely as possessions or objects of

TABLE 7.1	Child Welfare Legislation by Province or Territory				
Province	Agency Responsible for Child Welfare[1]	Definition of Child for Purposes of Protection[2]	Title of Child Protection Legislation	Year Legislation Established	Location on the Internet
Alberta	Ministry of Children and Youth Services	under 18 years old	Child, Youth and Family Enhancement Act	2004	www.qp.alberta.ca/documents/Acts/c12.pdf
British Columbia	Ministry of Children and Families, Child Protection Division	under 19 years old	Child, Family and Community Service Act	1996	http://www.bclaws.ca/EPLibraries/bclaws_new/document/ID/freeside/00_96046_01
Manitoba	Ministry of Family Services and Housing, Department of Child and Family Services	under 18 years old (can be extended to 21 in special circumstances)	The Child and Family Services Act	1985	http://web2.gov.mb.ca/laws/statutes/ccsm/c080e.php
New Brunswick	Department of Health and Community Services, Family and Community Services Division	under 16 years old (or under 19 if a child with a disability)	Family Services Act	1983	http://www.gnb.ca/0062/pdf-acts/f-02—2.pdf
Newfoundland and Labrador	Department of Health and Community Services, Children's Services Division	under 16 years old	Children and Youth Care and Protection Act	1998	http://www.assembly.nl.ca/Legislation/sr/statutes/c12-2.htm
Northwest Territories	Ministry of Health and Social Services, Department of Child and Family Services	under 16 years old (or 18 if already in care)	Child and Family Services Act	1997	http://www.canlii.org/en/nt/laws/stat/snwt-1997-c-13/latest/snwt-1997-c-13.html
Nova Scotia	Ministry of Community Services, Department of Community Services (as well as independent Children's Aid Societies)	under 16 years old	Children and Family Services Act	1990 (amended 2008)	http://nslegislature.ca/legc/statutes/childfam.htm
Nunavut	Ministry of Health and Social Services, Department of Child and Family Services	under 16 years old (or 18 if already in care)	Child and Family Services Act	1998	http://www.canlii.org/en/nu/laws/stat/snwt-nu-1997-c-13/latest/part-1/snwt-nu-1997-c-13-part-1.pdf

Ontario	Ministry of Community and Social Services (which authorizes services by independent Children's Aid Societies)	under 16 years old, or 18 if already in care	The Child and Family Services Act	1990	http://www.e-laws .gov.on.ca/html/ statutes/english/ elaws_statutes_ 90c11_e.htm
Prince Edward Island	Ministry of Health and Social Services, Department of Social Services and Seniors, Child and Family Services Division	under 18 years old (21 for adoption)	Child Protection Act	2003	www.gov.pe.ca/ law/statutes/ pdf/c-05_1.pdf
Quebec	Ministère de la santé et des services sociaux (Department of Health and Social Services)	under 18 years old	Loi sur la protection de la jeunesse (Youth Protection Act)	2002	http://www.canlii .org/en/qc/laws/ stat/rsq-c-p-34.1/ latest/rsq-c-p-34.1 .html
Saskatchewan	Department of Social Services	under 16 years old (18 for adoption, for those in "dangerous situations" or who are being encouraged to engage in prostitution)	Child and Family Services Act	1989–90	http://www.qp.gov .sk.ca/documents/ english/statutes/ statutes/C7-2.pdf
Yukon	Department of Health and Social Services	under 19 years old	Child and Family Services Act	2008	www.gov.yk.ca/ legislation/acts/ chfase.pdf

[1]Because child welfare services fall under the jurisdiction of provincial and territorial authorities, it is difficult to compile statistics at the national level. The most notable variations between provinces include mandate variation by jurisdiction with respect to the age at which children are eligible for services, differences in the length of time a child can receive out-of-home care, and the definition of out-of-home care.

[2]Children with disabilities are eligible for protective services until age 19.

parental authority (Covell & Howe, 2001) and as economically valuable. In rural Canadian settings, there was little separation between work and family domains. In urban contexts, children were frequently engaged in wage labour and were forced to "earn their keep" (Brade, 2007). Although parents were required by common law to provide their children with the necessities of life, they were given free rein in child rearing. Therefore, parents had the parental right of "reasonable chastisement" leaving them with considerable freedom in discipline. Reflecting the view of children as objects rather than individuals with fundamental rights, there were no protective laws or legislation against child abuse or neglect.

© Bettmann/Corbis

Can you imagine young children of today's society working long hours each and every day to contribute to their household? Without rights, these conditions were a reality for many children in the early nineteenth century.

Stage Two: Children as Vulnerable Individuals in Need of Protection

From the time of Confederation to the mid-twentieth century, views and perceptions of children changed significantly. Influenced by an increased recognition of children's developmental stages, and a newfound sentimentality towards children, children began to be considered not as parental property or as possessions, but as a separate and special class of immature persons. The overarching theme that reflected this second stage was the perceived vulnerability of children and their need for protection. It was argued that the state had a duty to prevent child cruelty and maltreatment and if parents failed in the protection and welfare of their children, the state must intervene (Covell & Howe, 2001). While clearly progressive in some respects, children continued to be viewed as objects in need of care either by their parents or by the paternalistic state.

These sets of assumptions were influential in the development of new protective laws and legal principles. For example, in 1888, the *Act For the Protection and Reformation of Neglected Children* formally established state responsibility for children. In 1891, the first Children's Aid Society was established in Toronto by J.J. Kelso, with the objective of helping orphaned, abandoned, and neglected children. Kelso also played a role in the development of similar societies across Ontario and in other English-speaking provinces. In 1893, the *Act for the Prevention of Cruelty to and Better Protection of Children* was established in Ontario. The Act made child abuse an indictable offence, promoted foster care, and supported Children's Aid Societies. Reformers like Kelso persuaded the Ontario legislature to grant Children's Aid Societies broad legal powers, including the right to remove neglected or abused children from their homes and to become legal guardians for such children. By the early twentieth century, many other Canadian provinces followed suit, developing similar child welfare legislation. In Quebec, during this time period, it was the Catholic

Church that held primary responsibility for child welfare, offering charitable assistance and support for children and families in need. It was not until 1977 that formal child welfare legislation was passed in the form of the Youth Protection Act. Newfoundland, which did not become a province until 1949, also has a long tradition of religious influence over child protection matters. The Territory of Nunavut, formed in 1997, has (comparatively) only recently developed its child welfare system.

Early child welfare agencies of the late 1800s focused primarily on issues of neglect, behaviour management, the most obvious cases of abuse, and juvenile delinquency. The agencies also had responsibility for the placement and adoption of children orphaned or born to single mothers (Bala, 2011). State intervention in cases of child maltreatment occurred not because children were perceived to hold inherent rights, but because their parents had failed. Therefore, the focus of child welfare was on individual families and separating children from the perceived "immorality" found in their homes and communities. While the courts exercised a supervisory function over cases involving the removal of children from their homes, in practice, the system was largely informal. Bala (2011) notes that most judges working in family courts at this time lacked legal training and lawyers rarely appeared in proceedings. Most of those parents whose children were removed from their care were poor and socially marginalized.

Many refer to this period of child welfare as the "child saving era." Originating in England and making its way to Canada, the **child savers** movement was made up of middle-class philanthropists who were not concerned about the individual feelings, emotional world, or perspectives of the child, nor did they seek to "rescue" children from suffering or hardship. Instead, for child savers, to "save" was to train, discipline, and render children obedient so that they would transform into future contributors of society. "Saving" was steeped in religious conviction. As Cameron et al. (2007) note: "To save was a high calling: it was a demonstration of Christian faith and the antidote to society's moral downturn" (p. 5).

> **child savers** Middle-class philanthropists who saw the state, society's moral decline, deficient parenting, and the hazards of urban life as "evils" from which children required saving.

In the wake of World War I and the Great Depression, where hundreds of thousands were without jobs and poverty prevailed, came a shift in social philosophy regarding the role of the government in intervening in the economic and social lives of Canadians. As the social welfare state grew, there was an increasing demand for social work as a profession to help manage these new activities. However, between 1920 and 1950, the issue of child welfare received minimal government attention and commitment, particularly given the Depression and two world wars that absorbed much of the government's attention (Cameron et al., 2007). Archival documents nonetheless show that the everyday responsibility for the protection of children was carried out mainly by women, some trained as social workers. Gradually, these workers became more professionalized with the creation of Schools of Social Work and formalized training. Historical records indicate that much of the direction of child welfare work held "a strong leaning towards British moral traditions of individual responsibility, the nuclear family, and at least the appearance of 'proper' morality" (Swift & Callahan, 2006, p. 120).

Stage Three: Children as Subjects

Following World War II, state paternalism gradually gave rise to a third and new perception of children. This shift grew out of many historic realities and events, including the treatment of children during World War II, where millions of children had been killed or subjected to Nazi persecution or medical experimentation. In particular, the Polish delegation to the UN pressed the Commission on Human Rights to deal with the numerous child-related problems that had arisen out of the war. In 1959, the United Nations (UN) officially recognized the human rights of children by adopting the United Nations

Declaration of the Rights of the Child. The essential theme underlying this non-binding declaration was that children are entitled to special protections and that "the best interests of the child shall be considered paramount" (Todres, 1998). With this gradual change in perspective, children began to no longer be viewed as objects in need of state protection, but as subjects—existing persons with dignity and basic rights of their own (Freeman, 1997). Given that children held inherent rights, both parents and the state had obligations to provide for these rights.

Enormous changes occurred with the realm of Canadian child welfare in the mid-twentieth century. Among the first of these changes, echoing the UN Declaration of the Rights of the Child, "the best interest of the child" emerged as a key guiding principle of child-protection decisions. Another impetus for change was the "discovery" of the **Battered Child Syndrome** by an American physician, Dr C. Henry Kempe, in the early 1960s. Kempe urged physicians to report to authorities any evidence of broken bones in infants and children and raised new concerns about the extent to which parental psychopathology could place children at risk. New child welfare legislation in most jurisdictions mandated professionals to report suspected cases of child abuse or neglect.

While the best interest of the child principle gained international prominence in child welfare, its "application" to Indigenous children (or lack thereof) brought with it a legacy of colonial policies and longstanding forms of abuse and trauma. From 1950–1980 the child welfare system oversaw the removal of thousands of children from their homes and communities. In 1951, a revision to the Indian Act meant that child welfare became a provincial responsibility, enabling child welfare agencies to extend their reach into Indigenous communities. At the outset of the change, most on-reserve child welfare services were provided only in emergencies, as funding to create on-reserve services was not included in the revision to the Indian Act. However, by the mid-1950s Indian and Northern Affairs Canada began to provide funds for on-reserve services. In 1975, a Supreme Court decision cemented provincial responsibility for providing child welfare services for Indigenous families living on-reserve. The extension of provincial services to reserves led to an enormous growth in the number of Indigenous children in care. This period is often referred to as the "**Sixties Scoop**," drawn from the words of a remorseful social worker from British Columbia who conveyed the manner in which social workers "would, quite literally, scoop children from reserves on the slightest pretext" (Johnston, 1983, p. 23). By 1980, Indigenous children, who made up 2 per cent of Canada's child population, represented more than 10 per cent of children in care (Johnston, 1983). Reports suggest that children were removed from their communities in large numbers, sometimes with little or no justification other than poverty or cultural differences in parenting (Sinha et al., 2011).

Many of the children apprehended during this period were permanently removed from their homes and communities. Significantly, over 11,000 Indigenous children—as much as one third of the child population in some Indigenous communities—were adopted between 1960 and 1990 (Royal Commission on Aboriginal Peoples, 1996). Moreover, between 70 per cent and 85 per cent of all Indigenous children adopted between 1971 and 1980, were adopted by non-Indigenous families, including many in the United States, leading to a further loss of language, culture, tradition, and identity (Johnston, 1983). Such child welfare policies were key to colonial aims of the assimilation of Indigenous Peoples, wreaked havoc on the lives of children and families, and left a legacy of disenfranchisement, disrupting traditional patterns of care. As will be discussed in Chapter 9, the problem of overrepresentation of Indigenous children in care has not been resolved by the passage of time.

In response and resistance to the apprehension of Indigenous children, a growing activism within Indigenous communities emerged in the 1970s and 1980s and alongside

Battered Child Syndrome
A term coined by C. Henry Kempe that refers to injuries sustained by a child as a result of physical abuse, usually inflicted by an adult caregiver.

Sixties Scoop Refers to the practice that occurred from the 1960s to the1980s of apprehending unusually high numbers of Indigenous children and fostering or adopting them, largely to non-Indigenous families. This removal led to further loss of cultural identity, contact with their families and communities of origin, and, in some cases, loss of their status under the Indian Act.

it came an increased number and scope of Aboriginal Child Welfare Agencies, with four agencies in 1981 and 30 in 1986. Agencies focused upon culturally appropriate and preventive services including services off-reserve.

In the wake of the Sixties Scoop, the 1980s saw changing ideas about child protection relating to notions of risk and harm as criteria for involvement by authorities. There were concerns raised regarding the broad discretionary power of social workers and the potential violation of the rights of parents and children. In 1984, the notion of **least intrusive measures** of intervention was encoded in the protection legislation of the Child and Family Services Act. This legislation promoted family preservation as much as possible and worked to ensure that child welfare interventions are at the least intrusive level, while nonetheless protecting children from harm.

least intrusive measures Meant to ensure that child welfare interventions are at the least intrusive level while nonetheless protecting children from abuse and neglect.

Another significant event in Canada was the release of the **Badgley Report** in 1984 that reported that one in two Canadian females and one in three Canadian males have experienced unwanted sexual acts, and that four in five of these occurred in childhood. Moreover, the report uncovered that most perpetrators were known to the child, and were often family members. Sexual abuse rose to the forefront of attention in child protection. Law reform followed in the form of Bill C-15 (1988), which amended the sexual assault provisions of the *Criminal Code of Canada* and also changed the Canada Evidence Act in order to facilitate the pressing of charges and giving evidence by children.

Badgley Report Published in 1984, it shed light on the prevalence of sexual abuse of children across Canada.

The introduction of the **Canadian Charter of Rights and Freedoms** in 1982 also had an impact on child welfare legislation and practice, albeit not until more recently. In the 1999 Supreme Court Decision *New Brunswick (Minister of Health and Community Services) v. G.(J.)*, [1999] 3 S.C.R. 46, a strong message was sent that parents have a vital interest in their relationship with their children, an interest that is entitled to protection under section 7 of the Charter as an aspect of the "security of the person." In his ruling, Chief Justice Lamer noted: that the state may only remove custody from a parent when it is necessary to protect the best interests of the child; that both the parents and the child's right to security of the person, as outlined in the Charter, are at stake in such proceedings; and that because of the need for a fair process in determining custody, an indigent parent is entitled to legal aid counsel in such proceedings. Bala (2011) notes that the courts continue to struggle to balance the concerns of protecting the rights of parents and children with the need to ensure that children are not put at risk by the recognition of these legal rights. Such complexities have ultimately led to a much more legally oriented child protection process, including an expanded legal aid system, ensuring representation for parents, and in some jurisdictions, children. Moreover, child protection proceedings have become more complex and hence, more costly, not only for legal aid plans, but also for child protection agencies and for the court system. There is also an important human cost: due process takes time. Delays because of lengthy court processes are very stressful to children and families. And while an emphasis on due process may ensure fairness in decision-making, it can make the job of the social worker seem more difficult, and adversarial with social workers having their opinions and decisions challenged in the sometimes hostile environment of the courtroom by lawyers (Bala, 2011).

Canadian Charter of Rights and Freedoms A bill of rights entrenched in the Canadian constitution that guarantees certain political rights to Canadian citizens and civil rights to everyone in Canada. It is designed to unify Canadians around a set of principles that embody those rights.

Other significant changes in child welfare have come as a result of changing demographics. Throughout the 1960s, those who migrated to Canada were primarily White Europeans. Migration patterns have since altered significantly with immigrants and refugees coming to Canada from dozens of countries in Asia, Africa, South America, and the Caribbean. Such changes, representing new populations, cultures, and languages, have precipitated the need for new, expanded, and culturally relevant services for children and their families. At the same time, however, given that language and linguistic differences in Canada are intimately tied to youth identity and well-being (Pilote & Magnan, 2012), programs and services must also continue to serve the unique needs of Francophone-minority youth across the country.

Theory in Practice

WHY DO FAMILIES EXPERIENCE DIFFICULTIES?

AT THE ROOT OF EVERY child welfare system are central ideas about the nature and causes of child maltreatment and the reasons why families experience challenges in providing adequate care for their children. Cameron et al. (2007) draw attention to the various models and approaches that have been put forward in an attempt to explain why children are maltreated. Some of these perspectives have heavily influenced the policies and practices of existing child welfare systems, while others have garnered only minimal recognition. By examining the various ways in which families in difficulty are conceptualized, we can see the vast range of perspectives and viewpoints.

Parental Deficiency

Within this perspective, parents who abuse their children are often described as having personality characteristics that prevent them from adequately providing and caring for their children. Interventions focus on producing change in individual parents (frequently the mother) as opposed to the environment and context in which they live.

Family Breakdown

Here child maltreatment is viewed as a symptom of family dysfunction or breakdown. The central concern from this perspective is the health of the family as the basic unit of socialization and child development. This perspective advocates supporting families and maintaining child-family connections.

Societal Breakdown

This perspective views child development as a shared responsibility of society. Child abuse and maltreatment and family breakdown are considered as much a failure of society as individual families. In fact, child maltreatment is considered to be a product of inadequate support and resources. This viewpoint tends to emphasize social provisions to support families and children. Moreover, there is a greater involvement of the community in family functioning.

United Nations Convention on the Rights of the Child (CRC) Applies to "every human being below the age of eighteen years" and integrates broad categories of rights, including civil and political rights and economic, social, and cultural rights.

The late 1980s saw the entrenchment of children's rights, particularly through the creation of the **United Nations Convention on the Rights of the Child** (CRC), adopted in 1989 and ratified by 192 states. The CRC, applicable to "every human being below the age of eighteen years," firmly established the separate and distinct rights of children, emphasizing children's empowerment and participation in decisions that affect them. As a signatory of the CRC in 1991, the Canadian government pledged its commitment to meeting the needs and assigning and respecting the rights of Canadian children. However, the CRC does not have the legal status of a statute and cannot therefore be imposed to override national laws of signatory nation-states. In Canada the CRC is recognized as an "interpretive guide" for situations where legislation is ambiguous or silent (Denov, 2005). Where Canadian laws are found not be in accord with the standards

Continuum of Normal Behaviour

This approach considers child maltreatment to be a continuation or exaggeration of patterns found in most families and in society as a whole. In fact, it is assumed that at some point in their lives, most families will receive social welfare assistance. Here, child abuse is not identified as a specific problem and is not a necessary or even typical precursor for families' involvement with authorities. Instead, emphasis is placed on high levels of support and social provision for families, as well as maintaining the parent-child bond.

Risk and Protective Factors

Proponents of this perspective argue that there are risk and protective factors that contribute to the likelihood that families will experience difficulties. In keeping with this, families with several risk factors are likely to experience more problems than others. To address child maltreatment and family breakdown, treatment and prevention programs, which need to be intensive and long-term, should address these risk and protective factors in ways that cross jurisdictional boundaries.

Economic Distress and Community Disintegration

This perspective views family difficulties as a result of economic distress and community disintegration. Advocates of this approach highlight that the strongest statistical predictors of having to open child protection cases are living in extreme conditions of poverty and deteriorating neighbourhoods. As a response, the focus here is on placing child and family healing within the context of the healing process for the entire community. Emphasis is also placed on high levels of support and social provisions for families.

Systems of Oppression

This perspective views child maltreatment as rooted primarily in economic, class, gender, and racial oppression. Child welfare and protection agencies are believed to reinforce oppressive relationships and be destructive toward people and traditional ways of living. This approach prescribes a radical shift in existing relations between agencies and oppressed groups. Proponents not only favour more generous social provisions, but also emphasize the critical importance of collective and participatory responses that respect and empower families and communities.

Source: Adapted from Cameron et al., 2007

of the CRC, Canada has agreed to amend its laws over time and harmonize them with the CRC. An example of this will be highlighted below with the creation of the Youth Criminal Justice Act.

When ratifying the CRC, Canada made reservations to Article 37, which means that Canada chose not to be bound by these provisions. Under Article 37, children held in custody must be held separately from adults unless this is not in their best interests. Canada has reserved the right not to be bound by this provision, thus enabling children to be held in adult remand or correctional facilities. Article 21 addresses the adoption system and aims to ensure that the best interests of the child remain paramount during the adoption process. Canada declared that out of respect for Indigenous cultural traditions and practices, it could not apply a section that called for state regulation of adoption. Instead, it intended to leave room for Indigenous control over the adoption process given the many historical abuses involving the removal of Indigenous children from their homes.

Contemporary Child Welfare Practice

Social workers in child welfare agencies are involved with the planning and delivery of a variety of services for children and families, such as family support, advocacy, adoption and foster care programs, and child protection. The social worker's task is to "understand a variety of factors related to the child, the family and the community, and to balance the child's safety and well-being with the rights and needs of a family that may be in need of help" (CASW, 2012).

Canada has legislation around mandatory child abuse reporting. While every member of society has a responsibility to report suspected child abuse or neglect when there are reasonable grounds for believing a child may be in need of protection, service professionals have a particular responsibility to ensure the safety and security of children. In the course of their duties, professionals, including social workers, are mandated to report any suspicions of child maltreatment. This is referred to as a **duty to report**. If professionals fail to report suspicions of **child abuse** and **neglect**, they can be convicted and fined up to $1,000.

When a case is reported, a child welfare worker must assess whether the child has been harmed or is at risk of being harmed due to abuse or neglect. Child abuse is the physical or psychological mistreatment of a child by an adult (biological or adoptive parents, step-parents, guardians, or other adults). This includes physical abuse, sexual abuse, emotional maltreatment, and exposure to domestic violence. Neglect refers to situations in which a child's caregiver fails to provide adequate clothing, food, or shelter, deliberately or otherwise. The term "neglect" can also apply to the abandonment of a child or the omission of basic care such as medical or dental care. A required first response to each abuse report received is a formal investigation to determine its validity and seriousness. A social worker will determine whether the child has been abused and or neglected, and assess the immediate safety needs of the child, the capacity of the family to protect the child, and the required services for the child and family. Typically, a **risk assessment** is conducted to determine the likelihood of future abuse or neglect, so that action can be taken to prevent it. Although utilization of a structured risk assessment has been promoted to improve accuracy and consistency in identifying children at high risk for severe future maltreatment, risk assessment instruments are not a panacea for decision-making. As Cash (2001) notes, "decisions should be optimally made through a combination of both empirical evidence (science) and practice wisdom (art), as one without the other is incomplete. The synergy created by the art and science of risk assessment provides for a more holistic and effective assessment" (p. 825). Importantly, one's social and cultural context and biases play a significant role in the "art" of risk assessment, which needs to be kept in mind.

Only families that fall below the prescribed minimal child-care standards enter into the formal child protection system. If, based on an initial assessment, parents do not fall below this minimal level of care, their investigation is closed, and they usually do not receive any services or assistance from the agency. If, following an investigation, a child protection case is opened, responses include referrals to other programs to assist the family with their difficulties, supervision orders (voluntary and involuntary) to ensure that parents are complying with agency expectations, and out-of-home placement of children (usually involuntary). Removal from parental care is only justified if it can be demonstrated that remaining in parental care poses significant risk to the child. In the vast majority of cases, investigations do not result in the child being removed from the family.

Social workers working in child welfare can provide **in-home services** that aim to assist and support families to live together harmoniously in a safe and secure environment.

duty to report Refers to a professional's obligation, in the course of her or his duties, to report any suspected child abuse or neglect when there are reasonable grounds for believing a child may be in need of protection.

child abuse The physical or psychological mistreatment of a child by an adult (biological or adoptive parents, step-parents, guardians, or other adults), including physical abuse, sexual abuse, emotional maltreatment, and exposure to domestic violence.

neglect Refers to situations in which a child's caregiver fails to provide adequate clothing, food, or shelter, deliberately or otherwise. "Neglect" can also apply to the abandonment of a child or the omission of basic care such as medical or dental care.

risk assessment An activity designed to determine the likelihood of future abuse or neglect so that action can be taken to prevent it.

in-home services Aim to assist and support families to live together harmoniously in a safe and secure environment.

A social worker conducts a risk assessment at a family's home to determine whether the child is living in a safe and healthy environment.

Services include family counselling, parental support, in-home child care, homemaker services and educational services for parents and families. **Out-of-home services** are services such as family foster care, kinship care, group residential care, institutional care, and adoption for children who have been placed in the custody of the state and who require living arrangements away from their parents.

Importantly, the realities of child abuse and neglect are not restricted to a particular region, economic or cultural group, or race. However, child welfare agencies are more likely to be involved with families from disadvantaged social, economic, and cultural groups. Indigenous children, in particular, continue to be overrepresented among children in care across the country (Kufeldt & McKenzie, 2011, p. 354).

Many argue that the child welfare systems in Canada require a major overhaul. Swift and Callahan (2006) outline the many challenges at play:

The system has been widely and publicly criticized. Its processes have become highly litigious, and in many communities, rigidly managed. For many front-line workers, time spent on paperwork outstrips, by far, time spent working directly with families and children. Perhaps as a result, recruitment and retention of staff have become critical problems across the country. At the same time, caseload numbers are climbing steeply, while more children are being brought into already burdened alternative care arrangements. When things go wrong, individual parents and workers are blamed, while systemic problems are patched up or glossed over (p. 118).

Cameron et al. (2007) maintain that "child saving" continues to direct the Canadian child welfare system, obscuring the real picture of child abuse, neglect, and maltreatment.

out-of-home services Implemented when the home situation is deemed unsuitable for the child. Such services include placement in day-care centres, foster care, group homes, institutional care, family housing assistance, and adoption.

In Their Own Words

CHILD WELFARE WORKERS

THROUGH MY WORK IN CHILD welfare over 13 years in two Canadian provinces (Manitoba and Quebec), I have been struck by the variations in how each system functions. The different provincial legislation governing child welfare inevitably leads to the availability of different programs to assist families experiencing challenges, and due to varying socio-economic and demographic characteristics, there is a great deal of provincial variation in terms of the families who come to the attention of child welfare agencies. But one thing remained constant: the tension my colleagues and I experienced between our roles as "helpers" and as "agents of the state." We continually struggled to reconcile our advocacy efforts to help children and families, with the legal mandate that required, at the very extreme, the removal of children from the care of their parents (which, incidentally, happens much less frequently than is generally thought).

Child welfare workers have a unique and challenging role in advocating on behalf of children and families, connecting them to needed services, while ensuring the safety and protection of children. This often leads to tensions that can create distrust between families and child welfare workers. Ultimately, this has the potential to impede positive outcomes. However, I found that openly acknowledging this tension with families was important in laying the foundation for future collaborative work. Exploring and critically reflecting upon the values held by families, as well as the values we hold as workers, can facilitate thoughtful decision-making. Our role as practitioners in influencing outcomes cannot be underestimated. By taking into account these values alongside the codes of ethics and legal principles that guide child welfare practice, we can learn to become more reflective in our practice and ultimately contribute to better decision-making that truly benefits children and families.

Despite these tensions, my decision to work in the multidisciplinary field of child welfare has been one of the best I have ever made. While child welfare work can be very challenging at times, and as we know is often underappreciated, it allows us to connect with children and families in ways that remind us of their individuality and importance.

Lise Milne, MSW, is a child welfare worker, supervisor, and trainer in Winnipeg and Montreal.

They argue that despite the passage of time, current systems continue to focus upon individual deficiencies, such as psychological issues or the "immorality" of parents, erroneously emphasize the importance of the nuclear family, and overlook broader social and structural conditions affecting families including poverty, inequality, and racism.

Youth Justice in Canada

In many ways, the evolution of Canada's youth justice system parallels the evolution of the child welfare system in that it echoes the key societal values associated with each of the three stages of "childhood" highlighted earlier. This section outlines the history and transformation of Canada's youth justice system.

Children as Objects: The Absence of Legal Protections

During the nineteenth century, when children were viewed as largely objects and the possessions of adults, for children who committed crimes, there was no separate system of juvenile justice. Legal doctrine held that all suspected criminals were acting rationally when they committed their crimes and should therefore be held accountable. Therefore, children over the age of 13 who came into conflict with the law were governed in much the same way as adults: they came before the same judges, they were sentenced to the same prisons, and they received the same punishments as did adults (Hogeveen, 2005). Under English common law, the special **doli incapax** (literally meaning "incapable of wrong") defence was developed for children under the age of 13. A child under age 7 was deemed incapable of committing a criminal act. For children between 7 and 13 years, this could be rebutted if there was evidence to establish that the child had sufficient intelligence and experience to know the nature and consequences of the conduct and to appreciate that it was wrong.

However, if the court could demonstrate that the accused possessed the ability to determine right from wrong, was able to understand the consequences of his or her conduct, and could appreciate the nature of his or her wrongdoing, the presumption of doli incapax was overturned and the accused was ordered to stand trial. If convicted, the young person was subjected to the same punishment as adults, including hanging and imprisonment (with adults).

doli incapax A defense developed under English common law whereby children under the age of 7 were deemed incapable of committing a criminal act. For children between 7 and 13 years, this defense could be rebutted if there was evidence to establish that the child had sufficient intelligence and experience to know the nature and consequences of the conduct and to appreciate that it was wrong.

The Vulnerable Child and "Parens Patriae": The Introduction of the Juvenile Delinquents Act

During the early twentieth century, reflecting a welfare-oriented approach and premised on the concept of *parens patriae* (literally "parent of the country"), the role of the state was to protect children from cruelty and abuse. Therefore, if parents failed to adequately protect and provide for their children, the state had a duty to intervene on the child's behalf. This changing philosophy and welfare-oriented approach paved the way for a separate youth justice system. Contrary to viewing children in conflict with the law as having the same level of intent as adults, during this era delinquent children were perceived as being in need of aid and assistance as they were regarded as "misdirected and misguided." With the formal establishment of the Juvenile Delinquents Act (JDA) in 1908, children were no longer governed and judged according to adult legal principles. During this period, legislation and carceral institutions not only recognized childhood as a unique stage of life, but also located the causes of child delinquency in a child's immediate environment including difficult life circumstances and "corrupting" role models. Moreover, there was an overarching assumption that children were malleable and amenable to rehabilitation (Hogeveen, 2005). The social protection of youth was said to be best achieved by concentrating resources on their rehabilitation and by protecting them from the full glare of public accountability (Bala, 2005). Under the JDA, little emphasis was placed on due process, such as the right to legal representation. Moreover, there was enormous discretion given to youth courts in terms of the process followed in court and the resulting sentences for young people (Green & Healy, 2003). The philosophy of this period also supported the use of indeterminate sentences for young offenders, which was premised on providing involuntary treatment as long as this was in accordance with the best interest of the young offender. The welfare-oriented JDA remained in force with little dissent until the 1960s.

Children as Subjects? The Creation of the Young Offender's Act, and the Youth Criminal Justice Act: The Clash Between "Rights" and "Accountability"

Within the context of a heightened awareness of human rights, growing social and civil rights movements of the 1960s and 1970s, and the constitutional entrenchment of the Canadian Charter of Rights and Freedoms in 1982, the lack of legal rights for youth in conflict with the law, the use of indeterminate sentences, and the abuse of their due process rights—all inherent to the JDA—became increasingly difficult to justify. Moreover, the notion of the "reformable young offender" was increasingly being called into question. This changing political and social context led to the eventual demise of the JDA and its replacement by the Young Offender's Act (YOA) in 1984.

The establishment of the YOA marked an important turning point in Canadian youth justice. Unlike the JDA which focused heavily on rehabilitation, the YOA placed an increasing emphasis on the philosophy of punishment and shifted to a "law and order" approach whereby youth and other marginalized groups tended to be singled out as a risky population in need of control (Alvi, 2002). Moving away from the child-welfare philosophy of the JDA, the YOA emphasized due process and advocated that young offenders be held accountable for their actions, albeit not as accountable as adults (Bala, 2005). The YOA held seemingly contradictory principles in that it referred to young people as in a "state of dependency" who have "special needs and require guidance and assistance" as well as "supervision, discipline and control" (YOA, Section 3). On the one hand, the YOA provided for the special needs of children in conflict with the law, advocated for the implementation of alternative measures to youth imprisonment, and promoted children's legal rights and freedoms. On the other hand, it called for increased youth accountability, responsibility, and emphasized the need to protect victims and society (Denov, 2005). However, many have suggested that the latter principles were given greater authority and credence: "the [YOA] favours a strategy that pays lip service to the possibilities inherent in alternative measures, overemphasizes individual responsibilities and traits and, in the end, witnesses a steady entrenchment of punishment and incarceration" (Alvi, 2002).

With the establishment of the CRC in 1989, the broader international discourse on children's rights gained momentum and prominence, and emphasized the importance of rehabilitative and reintegrative strategies for children in conflict with the law. This was, however, in stark contrast to the principles reflected in the YOA, as well as the voices of the Canadian public who clamoured for harsher punishments for young offenders. There was, therefore, a growing conflict and disjuncture between the rehabilitative and rights-based principles within the CRC and the seemingly punitive philosophy of the YOA. This clash between the tenets of the CRC in regard to youth justice and the YOA became even more apparent upon Canada's ratification of the CRC in 1991.

Demands for politicians to "get tough" on youth crime grew particularly loud in the late 1990s: a nationwide petition circulated in 2000 generated almost one million signatures of individuals demanding harsher sentencing for youth (Tufts & Roberts, 2002). Nearly two thirds of the Canadian public supported lowering the age of criminal responsibility from 12 to 10 years (Angus Reid Group, 1998). Approximately two thirds of the public opposed the existence of a separate youth justice system, and 93 per cent thought that youth court sentences were too lenient (Sprott, 1998). This concern about rising youth crime has not always coincided with actual trends. Although 60 per cent of the public polled in 2000 believed that youth crime has been rising recently, these rates had been in decline for almost a decade (Roberts, 2003). The Canadian public's views on youth crime appear to be shaped by high profile cases of homicide involving young offenders both in Canada and abroad. Perhaps the most well-known examples are the murders of Jamie Bulger in the UK, Reena Virk in Canada, and the murders committed at Columbine High School in the US.

The punitive reaction to youth crime had a predictable effect on politicians. In the 2000 federal election, all opposition parties, except for the Bloc Québecois, promised if elected to introduce reforms that would make the youth justice system tougher. This highlights some provincial variations in policy responses to youth crime whereby the Quebec government has typically embraced more rehabilitative and preventive approaches to youth crime, seemingly at odds with other provinces. Following increased public and political pressure to get tough on youth crime, the government responded with youth justice reforms that were intended to respond to the "disturbing decline in public confidence in the youth justice system" (McLellan, 1999). In April 2003 the YOA was replaced by the Youth Criminal Justice Act (YCJA).

With the introduction of the YCJA, the Canadian government sought to appease two diverse groups. First were the vocal law and order critics of the youth justice system who emphasized the need for greater accountability, especially for serious violent offenders. Second were the child advocacy groups who clamoured for a more supportive and preventive approach to youth justice (Bala, 2005).

A key factor was the reality that Canada was known internationally for having one of the harshest regimes for young offenders in the western world (Mallea, 1999). In 1997, the federal Standing Committee on Justice and Legal Affairs reported that Canada's rate of youth incarceration was more than twice that of the United States, and 10 to 15 times higher (per one thousand youth population) than New Zealand, Australia, and many European countries (Parliament of Canada, 1997). During the era of the YOA, Canada jailed nearly four times as many youth as adults, despite ongoing evidence demonstrating that punishment is generally not effective and may actually increase crime rates (Green & Healy, 2003). At the time, the federal government recognized that Canada relied too heavily on expensive and often ineffective court-based responses and custody for the majority of young offenders who have not committed serious offences (Bala, 2005).

Ultimately, the YCJA, introduced in 2003, brought forth the following changes:

- It increased the number of extrajudicial measures available (such as police warnings, referral to restorative justice agencies, and deferred custody orders, whereby a young person can avoid incarceration by showing good behaviour).
- It reintroduced the concept of Youth Justice Committees, last used under the JDA. Composed of groups of citizens, a committee's purpose is to develop community-based solutions to youth offences. These can include extrajudicial measures such as restitution, arranging community support for the youth, or arranging a meeting between the victim and the young offender.
- It established that the court process is reserved for more serious offences. Police must consider all other options, such as a warning or making restitution, before laying charges.
- It made provisions for reintegrating youth in custody back into society. The YCJA introduced a graduated sentence, where youth spend two thirds of their time in custody, and one third in the community under supervision.
- It made substantive changes to the current system for sentencing youth as adults. First, youth would no longer be transferred to adult court. Instead, youth court judges have the authority to impose adult sentences. Second, the legislation lowered the age for sentencing youth as adults. Under the amended YOA, there was a presumption that cases involving youth aged 16 or over charged with murder, attempted murder, manslaughter, or aggravated sexual assault would be transferred to adult court. The

YCJA lowered the age of presumption to 14. However, individual provinces can raise the age to 15 or 16. Furthermore, judges are able to hand out adult sentences to repeat serious offenders.

Since its inception, the YCJA has been successful in significantly reducing the use of courts and the rates of incarceration among youth, particularly for those who have committed less serious offences (Statistics Canada, 2007). There has been an increase in the number of youth being sentenced to supervision in the community, as well as deferred custody orders. Moreover, there has been a greater emphasis placed on extrajudicial measures, such as referral to restorative justice agencies.

Youth Crime in Canada

The following provides some key statistics in relation to youth crime in Canada.

* Both the rate and severity of youth crime decreased in 2010, down 7 per cent and 6 per cent respectively. The severity of violent crime committed by youth also decreased, down 4 per cent from 2009.
* In 2010, 42 per cent of youth accused were formally charged by police while the remaining 58 per cent were diverted by other means. This change corresponds with the implementation of the YCJA and its clear objectives for the use of extrajudicial measures (i.e., informal sanctions) for youth.
* Similar to the trend in overall crime, the rate of crime committed by youth has been generally declining over the past decade. The 2010 youth crime rate fell 7 per cent from the year before and was 11 per cent lower than a decade ago.
* Decreases in the severity of youth crime in 2010 were reported in every province and territory without exception. The youth Crime Severity Index was lowest in Québec, followed by Prince Edward Island and British Columbia. The rate of youth crime also declined across the country with the exception of the Northwest Territories and Nunavut, which each reported small increases.
* In 2010/2011, the number of cases completed in Canada's youth courts declined for the second year in a row, down 7 per cent from the previous year. The decline in youth court cases occurred in every province, with the exception of Manitoba. Nova Scotia and Prince Edward Island reported the largest declines, down 15 per cent and 13 per cent respectively. Youth court cases were also more likely to involve males (77 per cent) than females (23 per cent).
* The use of custodial sentences for youth has decreased over the past 10 years, falling from 29 per cent in 2000/2001 to 16 per cent in 2010/2011. However, there has been a slight increase in the proportion of cases being sentenced to deferred custody and supervision since it became a sentencing option under the YCJA. Source: Brennan, 2012 (Statistics Canada).

Recent Reforms: Bill C-25 and Bill C-10

Youth justice issues remain an ongoing point of contention in Canada. The Conservative government's "get tough on crime" agenda has remained intact and has influenced the introduction of two new Bills, both of which emphasize the protection of society as a primary goal of the YCJA. In 2007, the government introduced Bill C-25 which included provisions to amend the YCJA by adding "denunciation" and "deterrence" as principles of youth sentencing. Both these principles are reflective of a crime control model rather than a rehabilitative one.

Case STUDY

Indigenous Youth and the Criminal Justice System

INDIGENOUS YOUTH ARE OVERREPRESENTED AT every stage of the criminal justice process including arrests, convictions, and populations in youth detention facilities. While youth 12–17 years old who self-identified as Indigenous represent 6 per cent of the Canadian population, in 2008/9 they made up about 36 per cent of youth admitted to custody, and 24 per cent of youth who received probation (Calverley et al., 2010, p. 12). Moreover, female Indigenous youth are also overrepresented in the youth justice system compared to non-Indigenous female youth and they experience greater overrepresentation than their male counterparts (Calverley et al., 2010, p. 13). The overrepresentation is most pronounced in the Prairies, British Columbia, and Ontario. Not only is the Indigenous population overrepresented in terms of offenders, it is overrepresented in terms of victims of crime (Statistics Canada, 2001). Colonization, assimilation policies, social and cultural upheaval, poverty, residential schools, the sixties scoop, and their links with involvement with the criminal justice system have been well documented. As Chartrand (2005) notes, these deprivations have an important effect on a child's development and in many cases may manifest in violence and aggression toward the self and/or others. Chartrand and McKay (2006) assert that "while Aboriginal youth often become engaged in criminality, their involvement is often a component of their continued victimization" (p. 32).

In 2002, during readings of the YCJA, the Canadian Senate objected to the law's lack of attention to the special needs of Indigenous youth. In response, the law was changed to include a sentencing principle, similar to section 718.2(e) of the *Criminal Code of Canada*. This section of the Criminal Code, requires judges to consider alternatives to incarceration for Indigenous adult offenders at the time of sentencing. Not only has this sentencing principle been incorporated into the YCJA for consideration when sentencing Indigenous young offenders (sec. 50.1), but section 38(2) (d) also directs judges when sentencing young offenders to consider: "(d) all available sanctions other than custody that are reasonable in the circumstances . . . *with particular attention to the circumstances of aboriginal young persons*" (emphasis added).

In March 2010, the Conservative government reintroduced amendments to the YCJA in Bill C-4 and in September 2011, it incorporated these amendments into its post-election victory omnibus crime bill (Bill C-10). Bill C-10, approved by Parliament in 2012, adds denunciation and specific deterrence as principles of youth sentencing. It requires courts to consider adult sentences for youth convicted of serious crimes, and will allow the publication of the names of youth who have committed violent offences. Children's rights advocates have vehemently and publicly rejected the Bills, arguing that they counter some of the most fundamental provisions of the CRC. The provinces of Newfoundland, Quebec, and Ontario have all spoken out against the Bill. The Quebec government has been particularly vocal, arguing that the Bill fails to adequately embrace the principle of rehabilitation, will cost the province $500 million to implement its provisions, and will require new prisons and additional costs for longer sentences. The province of New Brunswick, which supported the Bill, has indicated that it cannot afford to pay the costs associated with the changes (Galloway & Séguin, 2012).

The Role of Social Workers in Youth Justice

A social worker's role within youth justice may involve providing an assessment of a young offender. Baker et al. (2011) define an assessment done in the realm of youth justice as "a dynamic, multi-faceted process of information gathering and analysis that leads to in-depth understanding of a young person's offending behaviour. It provides the basis for the planning of interventions in order to help a young person avoid reoffending, assist a young person to achieve their potential, [and] help to protect victims and communities" (p. 12).

Social workers may also provide support to young people on a one-to-one basis, or within the context of group work, or **restorative justice**, which involves victim–offender mediation. Direct practice with youth in conflict with the law is complex and there is limited knowledge to inform why some interventions work better than others. Restorative justice is a process whereby the parties with a stake in a particular offence come together to resolve collectively how to deal with the aftermath of the offence and its implications for the future. Within Indigenous communities, restorative justice practices aim to restore the balance after harm has been committed. Some of these methods are, for example, sentencing circles which involve the person who has done the harm, the victim, and community members such as Elders and family members. Drawing from the findings of a large number of studies through meta-analysis, examples of programs with positive outcomes for youth in conflict with the law include social skills training, cognitive-behavioural programs, parent training programs, and multi-modal interventions such as multi-systemic therapy (Pickford & Dugmore, 2012).

In addition to working directly with young people, social workers may also work directly with families, providing support and assistance. Family intervention treatment has been found to reduce significantly the recidivism of young offenders compared to traditional non-familial responses to youth crime (Latimer, 2001). Social workers may also provide outreach and referral services.

Social workers in youth justice may work in multi-agency teams, working closely with a range of other professionals including lawyers, police officers, judges, as well as other agencies including courts, and the correctional system. In order to be an effective practitioner in youth justice, developing key skills in multi-agency and inter-professional workings and having a greater understanding of the complex system is likely to result in improved practice.

Social workers often provide the court with valuable information concerning the young person, including an analysis of the young person's contextual realities such as family situation, peer relationships, and school performance. Social workers may also direct court officials to a variety of social services programs.

Social workers may testify as witnesses in court hearings and may inform a judge regarding the youth, his or her family, mitigating or aggravating circumstances, and the availability and advisability of particular social services for the youth in question.

Social workers may act as key advocates at an individual, family, community, and societal level, encouraging and advocating for more reflective policies and practices with regards to provincial and national responses to youth in conflict with the law.

Preventive Social Work with Children

Early forms of social work practice with children focused upon addressing and correcting the "deficiencies" of the individual child and/or parents. Today, social work with children encompasses far more than the child welfare system and youth justice. It involves a range of activities based within communities and in schools that aim to reduce the risk of negative behaviours and outcomes and promote protective factors that allow children to grow and develop. Prevention has thus increasingly become a key component of social work

restorative justice A process whereby the parties with a stake in a particular offence come together to resolve collectively how to deal with the aftermath of the offence and its implications for the future. Within Indigenous communities, restorative justice practices aim to restore the balance after harm has been committed.

Theory in Practice

YOUNG OFFENDERS AND COGNITIVE-BEHAVIOURAL THERAPY

COGNITIVE-BEHAVIOURAL THERAPY (CBT) IS PREMISED on the notion that problematic behaviour and stressful states such as anxiety, depression, and anger are often maintained or exacerbated by biased or irrational thinking (Leahy, 2003). It is a therapeutic approach that has been advocated as particularly effective in supporting the reintegration of offenders (White & Graham, 2010). Cognitive-behavioural therapy used with youth in conflict with the law focuses on changing problem behaviours by using well-defined techniques combined with careful assessment and monitoring, typically done with behavioral measurements. Social workers using this approach work with young offenders to understand the faulty thought patterns that typically bring about offending behaviours, as well as what sustains offending patterns. Cognitive-behavioural techniques used with young offenders include:

- *Pro-social modelling*: This is where the practitioner strategically models positive behaviour and rewards and reinforces pro-social behaviour in young people. Empirical studies have found that the use of pro-social modeling, as defined by the quality of the interpersonal therapeutic relationship, the effective use of authority, anti-criminal modelling and reinforcement, and accessing community resources, consistently correlated with lower re-offending and tends to be most effective with young, high-risk, violent, and drug-using offenders (White and Graham, 2010).
- *Motivational interviewing*: Aims to encourage youth to be motivated to make changes in their lives. Skills consistent with a motivational interviewing approach include the use of open-ended questions, affirming, simple reflections, complex reflections, summaries, emphasizing control, and evocative questioning. These skills facilitate clients towards resolving ambivalence, building motivation, fostering commitment to change and progressing towards behaviour change.
- *Problem solving*: Offending is said to be reduced by enhancing problem-solving skills, often using scenarios and requiring youth to identify problems and solutions and developing consequential thinking skills. Youth are encouraged to define a problem, generate solutions to it, choose the best ways of acting on it, and review progress.
- *Social skills training*: Improving young people's skills in social situations that may include role-play and assertiveness training.
- *Moral reasoning*: Providing young people with a range of moral dilemmas to discuss and make informed decisions.

Despite the promising features of this approach, social workers must nonetheless be cognizant of the limitations of relying upon a single theory or approach. As Goldson (2001) notes, "the lives of young offenders are complex and reliance on a single theory of 'reasoning and rehabilitation' or a discrete form of cognitive intervention is unlikely to produce good results. We cannot expect, nor should we expect, to discover law-like universals" (cited in Pickford and Dugmore, 2012, p. 177). The need to view young people in the context of their wider circumstances and involving families is vital and should be attempted as much as possible.

in Canada. Most prevention programs target so-called "at-risk" youth, whose social and economic conditions have made them statistically more likely to experience homelessness, drug abuse, criminal activity, and early pregnancy.

Preventive activities encompass a variety of approaches, including the use of arts, media, and other forms of expression designed to engage children and youth and promote positive self-expression. The emphasis of interventions tends to be on empowering young people and fostering resilience, as the examples below highlight.

- *Leave Out ViolencE* (LOVE) (Montreal, Toronto, Vancouver, Halifax, New York City, Eilat, Israel, and Uganda): LOVE's mission is to reduce violence in the lives of youth and in communities by building a team of youth who communicate a message of non-violence. Through school and community violence prevention outreach programs, youth leadership training, and a media arts program, youth who have been witnesses, victims, and/or perpetrators of violence learn how to identify, analyze, and document the issues surrounding the violence in their lives and develop reality-based solutions to end violence.
- *Take-a-Hike-Program* (Vancouver, BC): The Take-a-Hike Program focuses on at-risk youth aged 15–19, grades 10–12, who are at risk of dropping out of school or who

CJ Cromwell/LOVE

An activity by the Ontario Leave Out ViolencE encourages members to healthily deal with anger and stress.

have already dropped out. The purpose of the three-year program is to assist students who have been unable to achieve success in mainstream classes to develop the positive behaviours they need to become healthy, productive citizens. It balances academic requirements and adventure-based activities.

Preventive social work also happens directly within the school setting. School-based initiatives include programs that address violence prevention, suicide prevention, teen pregnancy, bullying, and substance abuse prevention. Social workers can be found working as staff members in schools, acting as a resource and support for students in need. Regardless of the types of prevention programs, interventions at all levels of a child's life, whether individual, family, school, and/or community, are essential towards providing protection and promoting overall health and well-being.

Key Challenges in Child Welfare and Youth Justice: Implications for Social Workers

Several key areas of tension are evident when engaging in social work practice within child welfare and youth justice. The following issues represent but a few of the significant dilemmas for social workers, which they must constantly reflect upon in their everyday practice.

In child welfare, a social worker may struggle between balancing parental rights and child-protection concerns. In youth justice, a social worker may struggle between balancing the rights of youth in conflict with the law, the rights of victims, and the protection of society.

In child welfare, a social worker must constantly manage the complexities involved with "care" and "control" aspects of state intervention into family life: parents are keenly aware of the enormous legal and social power of the worker who has the ability to remove children from their care and to put their lives under the scrutiny of the court. Moreover, children, despite being victims of abuse or neglect, may fear the intrusion of the social worker in their lives.

In the realm of youth justice, social workers must deal with the tension between regarding children as "in need" or as individuals who are expected to take full responsibility for their actions.

Conclusion

Social work practice with children represents a number of critical activities that fall within the realms of child welfare, youth justice, and prevention. However, it is important to realize that these areas of practice should not be seen as mutually exclusive. Increasingly, practitioners and policy-makers are recognizing the overlap of the child welfare and youth justice systems, as well as the importance of prevention (Wiig & Tuell, 2008). This overlap is evidenced by maltreated children who come into conflict with the law, young offenders who have histories of maltreatment, and families who have intergenerational histories with both systems. It is also evidenced by some administrative and operational realities, in that agencies face duplication of services, competition for scarce program dollars, unmet service needs, and a dearth of prevention activity to help stem the tide of children coming into the two systems. Social workers need to be aware of these overlapping realities and their role in ensuring collaboration and inter-agency cooperation and understanding. Moreover, greater emphasis needs to be placed on prevention and education.

QUESTIONS FOR CRITICAL THOUGHT

1. Explore the range of explanations as to why families experience difficulties. Which approach(es) do you feel is/are most relevant and why?
2. How would you rate the "effectiveness" of current child welfare practices? Recommend changes that would make the system more "effective" in achieving its stated goals.
3. What lessons are to be learned from the oppressive and damaging social work practices of non-Indigenous social workers during the Sixties Scoop? How do oppressive practices from that era shape practice today?
4. Given historical and cultural realities, what strategies should be used to address the overrepresentation of Indigenous children and youth in the child welfare and criminal justice systems?
5. What types of policies and practices do you think would effectively prevent youth crime? What role can social workers play within such prevention policies and practices?
6. Obtaining resources and funding for the creation and maintenance of prevention programs for children and youth is often challenging. What arguments would you raise in support of increased funding for social work prevention programs aimed at children and youth?

RECOMMENDED READINGS

Cameron, G., & Adams, G. (Eds.). *Moving toward positive systems of child and family welfare: Current issues and future directions.* Waterloo: Wilfrid Laurier University Press. This book draws inspiration from experiences with three broad, international child welfare paradigms—child protection, family service, and community healing/caring (First Nations)—to look at how specific practices in other countries, as well as alternative experiments in Canada, might foster positive innovations in the Canadian child welfare approach.

Freymond, N., & Cameron, G. (Eds.). *Towards positive systems of child and family welfare.* Toronto: University of Toronto Press. The volume examines child protection and family service approaches within Western nations—including Canada, the United States, England, the Netherlands, France, and Sweden. It is also the first comparative study to give equal attention to Aboriginal community caring models in Canada and New Zealand.

Wien, F., Blackstock, C., Loxley, J., & Trocmé, N. (2007). Keeping First Nations children at home: A few federal policy changes could make a big difference. *First Peoples Child & Family Review, 3,* 1, 10–14. Drawing upon a case study, this article addresses several areas where the formulation of better federal child and family service funding policy for First Nations children and young people, could go a long way toward improving the lives of First Nation children on-reserve.

Winterdyk, J., & Smandych, R. (2012). *Youth at risk and youth justice: A Canadian overview.* Oxford: Oxford University Press. This contributed text offers an introduction to juvenile delinquency in Canada. Offering students a solid foundation to the fundamentals of the field, the book explores topics such as restorative justice, the sexual exploitation of adolescent men, and Quebec's approach to youth justice.

RECOMMENDED WEBSITES

Canadian Child Welfare Research Portal
http://www.cecw-cepb.ca/
The Canadian Child Welfare Research Portal provides access to up-to-date research on Canadian child welfare programs and policies.

The Child Welfare League of Canada
www.cwlc.ca
The Child Welfare League of Canada (CWLC) is the voice for child welfare issues across Canada. CWLC plays a significant role in promoting best practices among those in the field of child welfare, child rights, children and youth mental health, and youth justice.

Native Child and Family Services of Toronto
http://www.nativechild.org/
Native Child and Family Services of Toronto is an organization that serves Native families and children in the Toronto area including First Nations, Métis, Inuit, and all those with Indigenous heritage who choose to be served by the agency.

The Department of Justice: Youth Justice
http://www.justice.gc.ca/eng/pi/yj-jj/
The Department of Justice: Youth Justice is a government website that provides information on aspects of the youth justice system including the YCJA, youth justice initiatives, educational tools, funding, and research and analysis.

National Alliance of Children and Youth
http://www.nationalchildrensalliance.com/nca/index.htm
The purpose of the National Alliance of Children and Youth is to promote the health and well-being of children and youth in Canada in ways that are beneficial to the community. The organization brings diverse not-for-profit organizations together in a collaborative network dedicated to enhancing the well-being of children and youth in Canada.

8

The Role of Social Work in the Lives of Aboriginal Peoples

Cyndy Baskin, Ryerson University

LEARNING OBJECTIVES

- To acquire basic knowledge of Canadian history from an Aboriginal perspective.

- To appreciate current social challenges of Aboriginal Peoples as the impacts of colonization.

- To understand Aboriginal worldviews as theories for helping/ social work.

- To apply appropriate terminology to diverse populations of Aboriginal Peoples.

- To appreciate the strengths, resistance, and resiliency of Aboriginal Peoples.

- To come to view oneself as a helper and/or ally.

- To identify how Aboriginal values can be applied to all areas of social work.

Chapter Outline

This chapter provides an overview of the most significant aspects of what social work is to **Aboriginal Peoples** in Canada. There has always been a troubled relationship between the social work profession and this population as social work has mostly served as an element of social control and an arm of **colonization** throughout history to the present day. The chapter begins with Aboriginal ways of helping and caring for families and communities prior to contact with European settlers and then explores social work's role in the **cultural genocide** of Aboriginal Peoples primarily through the **residential school** and child welfare systems. The current challenges that Aboriginal Peoples face are discussed in the context of the impacts of colonization and the often ongoing role of social work as an agent of social control. The chapter then presents the ways in which Aboriginal Peoples are recreating their original ways of helping within their communities and their successes in doing so.

The chapter explores how Aboriginal **worldviews**, in the context of helping and healing, can, in part, work together with promising social work theories such as **structural** and **anti-oppressive social work**. Specific examples connect theories to practice; case studies will provide concrete examples; and the voices of several Aboriginal Peoples will be included to bring the examples to life. The chapter concludes with a discussion of the value of Aboriginal ways of helping to *all* people and the role of non-Aboriginal social work allies in working with Aboriginal Peoples.

Aboriginal Peoples The original people of Canada, encompassing First Nations, Métis, and Inuit.

colonization Invasion or taking over sovereignty of another nation.

cultural genocide Processes that destroy the cultures of a group of people.

residential schools A program that forcibly removed Aboriginal children from their families and communities to eradicate their cultures.

worldview The lens through which a group of people sees the world, their values, and their relationships.

structural social work Focuses on social problems in structural rather than personal terms by analyzing the impacts that structures in society have on people.

anti-oppression social work Acknowledges oppression in societies, economies, cultures, and groups and attempts to remove or negate it.

Haudenosaunee The people whose traditional territory is now southern Quebec and Ontario.

Turtle Island Haudenosaunee term for North America.

Indians A Canadian government term applied to Aboriginal people with legal status under the Indian Act.

Métis People of mixed First Nations and European ancestry who do not have status under the Indian Act.

Inuit People who traditionally occupied the four northern regions of Canada that comprise Inuit Nunangat (homeland): Inuvialuit, Nunatsiavut, Nunavik, and Nunavut.

Who Are Aboriginal Peoples?

Aboriginal Peoples are the original inhabitants of what the **Haudenosaunee** Nation calls **Turtle Island** or what is referred to as the continent of North America. According to the Canadian Constitution, there are three groups of Aboriginal Peoples: **Indians**, **Métis**, and **Inuit**.

Despite the diversity among these groups, evident in the differences in geographical territories, languages, cultures, political systems, and spirituality, there is a foundation of worldviews, values, and beliefs that are common to all. This foundation and a history of colonization ties Aboriginal Peoples together. In the 2006 Census, 1,172,790 people in Canada reported some Aboriginal heritage, which makes up about 4 per cent of the total population (Statistics Canada, 2008). In this same census, 54 per cent of Aboriginal Peoples reported that they live in urban areas and over 50 per cent are under the age of 25. Although recognized under the Canadian Constitution, Métis are not recognized under the Indian Act, which means they face ongoing constitutional battles. In January 2013, the Supreme Court of Canada agreed that both Métis and non-status Indians should be considered "Indians" under a section of the Constitution Act.

Since the Beginning of Time: Aboriginal Ways of Helping

Aboriginal worldviews, or the lens through which Aboriginal Peoples see the world around them, consist of a foundation which guides how one sees the environment/land, people, communities, challenges, causes of problems, and possible solutions to such problems. A worldview provides principles, values, and ethics for learning, living, and behaving. It offers direction on how we relate to people and how we treat them. Aboriginal Peoples

In Their Own Words

BEING MÉTIS

BEING MÉTIS MEANS BEING CONNECTED with your history and community, knowing the stories that go along with your specific community, as they will differ from community to community. We have a strong affinity for the stories of our own local communities and families, as well as the stories of the Métis Nation as a whole. Historically, Métis people came from two very different cultures (e.g., First Nations and European) and we have reconciled such differences to make it our own thing—a distinct Aboriginal group in Canada.

We share a lot with our First Nations brothers and sisters, but we have distinct traditions and specific stories. We have more in common with First Nations than we are led to believe by the Canadian government. The government has placed Métis and First Nations people into different silos and has put us in the position to need to compete with one another for resources from the government. Due to my geographic location, I don't see many similarities with the Inuit, but I am sure that there are many between those Métis who live further north, as there will be greater connectedness between northern Métis and Inuit. However, there are similarities among all three Aboriginal groups in Canada regarding their relationship with the land and co-existing with it without environmental impact, and a common history of oppression.

Regarding the recent Supreme Court decision on the Daniels case, it was decided that Métis people and non-status Indians would now be recognized as "Indians" within the meaning of the expression "Indians and land reserved for Indians" in s. 91(24) of the Constitution Act. From this decision, the federal government would recognize Métis and non-status Indians. Right now, however, it is unclear how things will proceed. Métis people have proven to the federal government that there are Métis communities, which this government did not deny during the court proceedings. At this point, the government has appealed the decision, but regardless of what does or does not happen, the decision does not change our identity as Métis people. It does not change who Métis people are or tell us anything that we did not already know about ourselves. The only thing that may change, if the decision remains, is that the government will be forced to recognize Métis people.

Mitch Case is the president of the Métis Nation of Ontario (MNO) Youth Council and the Youth Representative of the Provisional Council of the MNO and a fourth year history and Indigenous Studies student at Agloma and Shingwauk Kinomaage Gamig Universities in Ontario.

view all life from a **holistic approach**, including one's connection to the land, the family, and the community. The emphasis is on the collective, rather than the individual, with teachings that stress how all life is connected. Therefore, what one person does to another human being, or the earth herself, has an impact on everyone else. Rather than biological parents being solely responsible for raising children, each person is viewed as carrying this responsibility. Rather than adult children taking care of the elderly, all people in the community do so. Sharing is highly valued and **egalitarianism** is practised.

A holistic approach also emphasizes how each person is made up of four aspects—spiritual, physical, emotional, and psychological—and these are all interconnected, thereby

holistic approach
Recognition of the whole person including spiritual, physical, emotional, and psychological elements.

egalitarianism A belief that all people should share equal social, political, and economic rights and opportunities.

influencing one another. For example, if a person were to have an accident and be left with two broken legs, not only the body would be affected but so would that person's spirit, feelings, and mind. Perhaps such a person might become depressed because he or she no longer is able to enjoy physical activities or join in spiritual ceremonies. Thus, a holistic approach focuses on the healing of all of these aspects, rather than only the physical, with medicines and ceremonies taking this into account.

Healing also comes into play in terms of dealing with people who have harmed others through, for example, physical hurt or stealing from someone. Instead of punishment, people are brought together, including the person who did the harm, the person who was harmed, and the families and friends of both, to hear what happened, how it affected everyone concerned, and what can be done to compensate for the harm. In this way, the person who did the harm must take responsibility for his or her actions and offer apologies, payment of some kind, or do work that will benefit the family. This is an example of a holistic approach since it is believed that many people, rather than only the person who was harmed, are affected and need to take part in restoring balance within the individuals, families, and community.

Another major component of Aboriginal worldviews is spirituality, which can be defined as "a set of personal beliefs derived from an individual's perception of self and his or her relationship to both the natural world and some metaphysical realm" (Canda, 1989, p. 37). Traditionally, Aboriginal Peoples do not have religions. The significant difference between religion and spirituality is that religion is a structured form of spirituality that usually has a group following, whereas spirituality can include individual experiences with or without a structured belief system (Baskin, 2002; 2011). Spirituality embodies interconnectedness with all life. Everyone and everything is seen as being equal and interdependent, part of the great whole, and as having a spirit. This view underscores an Aboriginal vision of life, land, and the universe. For example, Inuit see an individual as constantly interacting with the physical environment, which occurs through hunting, fishing, and taking in the essence of animals and fish into their bodies through eating them (Kirmayer, Fletcher, & Watt, 2009). In this way, the land has a central focus in Inuit cultures and spirituality. For most Inuit, the land is a healthy entity that brings insight and peace to those who are struggling, as well as strength and resilience to survive in the present day (Kirmayer, Fletcher, & Watt, 2009).

All worldviews include values. It is important to have an understanding of the original values within Aboriginal worldviews. The following general values within Aboriginal worldviews may be of significance to the field of social work:

- permissiveness
- extended Family
- interdependence
- cooperation
- humility
- respect for Elders
- non-interference
- children are gifts
- communal living
- emphasis on group/clan
- emphasis on sharing
- harmony with nature

The following are a few examples of how some of these values express themselves in attitudes and behaviours. Permissiveness can be applied to the raising of children.

Within Aboriginal worldviews, children learn from observing what parents, older siblings, and other adults, such as Elders, do. Adults are the role models for children showing them, rather than telling them, how to behave. Children are taught in non-directive ways through, for example, the telling of stories that contain moral teachings. They are allowed some freedom to make choices for themselves, with natural consequences, both positive and negative.

Non-interference is an Aboriginal value that refers to not getting in the way of another person's journey or preventing someone from doing something simply because we do not agree with it. It means not giving advice, not being directive, and not participating in another person's process unless invited to do so. Many aspects of Aboriginal worldviews in Canada are universal for many **Indigenous Peoples** of the world, from Australia to Africa to South America, such as the emphasis on family and community, spirituality, and holistic approaches. Such aspects are expressed very differently through many cultures, but the foundation remains the same.

Indigenous Peoples The people who are native to the area in which they live. This term usually refers to these people internationally and is a term used by the United Nations. In Canada, the term Indigenous also refers to First Nations, Métis, and Inuit Peoples.

Colonization: The Time of the Great Struggle

To understand the present struggles of Aboriginal Peoples today, one needs to understand their histories and treatment since the time of colonization by those who came from the European countries of England and France. Colonization can be defined as

> cultural dimensions which involve efforts to achieve normative control over a minority group or culture. [With Aboriginal Peoples] these efforts included: displacement of traditional forms of governance with representative democracy and an authoritarian model of leadership; the devaluation of traditional spirituality, knowledge, and practices through the actions of missionaries, the residential school system, the health system, and the child welfare system; and the imposition of artificial legal distinctions among Aboriginal peoples (Morrissette, McKenzie, & Morrissette, 1993, p. 94).

The **Indian Act of 1876** was the vehicle used to destroy much of the way of life of Aboriginal Peoples. It came to control every part of Aboriginal Peoples' lives. This Act imposed a White, capitalist, patriarchal governance structure on Aboriginal Peoples and attempted to eradicate Aboriginal values through education and religion. A colonizing government nearly destroyed traditional tribal structures that were **clan** oriented**, matriarchal**, and communal.

This Act, which is the only legislation in the world designed for a particular "race" of people, continues to control the lives of Aboriginal Peoples today and ignores Aboriginal Peoples' inherent right to **self-determination** (Thunderbird, 2012). The Indian Act was also used to assign Aboriginal Peoples to the categories of **status** or **non-status**. Those who were simply not present when government officials showed up to count heads in the late nineteenth century were simply not recognized as status "Indians." This meant that they were not registered as an "Indian," which in turn prevented them from entitlement to certain rights and benefits as outlined by the federal government (Thunderbird, 2012). Additionally, the Act also contained a section referred to as **enfranchisement** which was a process whereby "Indians" could become Canadian citizens and have the right to vote by relinquishing their ties to their communities, which included any rights to land (Thunderbird, 2012). Canadian government officials believed that this would also mean that Indians would give up their cultures and traditions which, of course, did not happen entirely. Of historical interest, the Indian Act formed much of the basis for the

Indian Act The Indian Act was created by the Parliament of Canada to define "Indian" status and outline the administration of "Indian" rights although it does not grant Indian rights.

clan Groups of families that have the same inherited social and political roles.

matriarchal A system of social and political inheritance through female lineage.

self-determination The ability to make decisions and choices for oneself.

status First Nations Peoples who are registered under the Indian Act based on blood quantum and historical policy.

non-status The opposite of having "status." Non-status Aboriginal Peoples are not registered under the Indian Act and, therefore, cannot access any of their rights under this Act.

enfranchisement A process whereby "Indians" could become Canadian citizens, gaining the right to vote but only by relinquishing their ties to their communities, which included any land rights.

reserve The reserve system was set up to restrict Aboriginal Peoples registered under the Indian Act to particular areas of Canada that were considered unattractive to settlers.

Indian agent White government officials who displaced traditional Aboriginal leadership and held the power to enforce the Indian Act, including deciding who would have status and acting as arresting officers, prosecutors, and judges all in one.

assimilation A process by which individuals' cultural identities are minimized or eliminated, and replaced by the cultural identities of the larger society.

introduction of oppressive apartheid policies against Black people in South Africa which continued for decades (Thunderbird, 2012).

Although **reserves** were created for status "Indians," they did not own this land; it belonged to the British Crown. Implications are that, to this day, without ownership of land, Aboriginal Peoples in First Nations communities cannot develop the land because they are unable, for example, to obtain bank loans as they have no collateral (Thunderbird, 2012). In addition, until well into the 1940s, "Indians" living on reserves were not allowed to leave the reserve unless they obtained written permission from government officials, known as **Indian agents**. This meant that they could not take care of their own basic needs to eat through hunting, fishing, and gathering plants, which had been the basis of their economies since the beginning of time. Furthermore, in 1927, "Indians" were banned from raising money for legal purposes, such as hiring lawyers, to assist them in fighting against such racist oppression (Thunderbird, 2012). Policies such as these have resulted in high rates of poverty and hopelessness in many First Nations communities today.

The Indian Act further created serious social upheaval within Aboriginal communities by attacking women and children in particular. For example, the Act stripped Aboriginal women who married non-Aboriginal or non-status Aboriginal men of their status and did not allow them to pass it on to their children; it banned them of their political leadership, made them the property of men, and forced them to undergo sterilizations (Anderson, 2011; Annett & Lawless, 2007; Milloy, 1999; Truth and Reconciliation Commission, 2012). Some people regained their status through changes in the Indian Act with the introduction of Bill C-31 in 1985 and Bill C-3 in 2011. Throughout colonial history, policies also removed status for veterans, people who attained a university degree, and for those who were employed off of their reserve.

"Kill the Indian in the Child"

One of the most harmful attacks on Aboriginal Peoples' ways of life was the residential school system which began in the 1870s. Those who ran the residential schools attempted to eliminate Aboriginal cultures by indoctrinating children into the Christian churches that ran the schools. Children were forced to practise a religion that had nothing to do with their own spirituality (Indian and Northern Affairs Canada, 2004). When the Canadian government decided that physical genocide was no longer an option for addressing the "Indian problem," they turned to the **assimilation** of Aboriginal Peoples into mainstream society, focusing on the young. The belief was that there would be a better chance at moulding Aboriginal children, rather than adults, into mainstream society. In the beginning of the 1920s, the Canadian government made it illegal for Aboriginal parents to keep their children out of residential schools (Jacobs & Williams, 2008). In most cases, if parents objected, they were jailed and the children were taken.

The residential school system is an example of Canada's shameful "Indian policies" (Dion Stout & Kipling, 2003; Fontaine, 2010; Fournier & Crey, 1997), which involved removing children as young as three years old from their homes and communities and forcing them to reside within institutions where languages and cultures were forbidden. Seven generations of Aboriginal children attended residential schools (CBC Learning, 2012a). In recent years, many Aboriginal Peoples have disclosed their experiences in these schools, which include painful stories of sexual and physical abuse, experimentations, and the death of many children at the hands of authorities (Annett & Lawless, 2007; Dion Stout & Kipling 2003; Fontaine, 2010; Indian and Northern Affairs Canada, 2004). Horrific stories such as children's tongues being pierced through with needles, starvation, and impregnation of girls by those who ran the institutions followed by the murder of the infants who were born, are not uncommon (Annett & Lawless, 2007). In fact, half of the

The General Synod Archives, Anglican Church of Canada

Aboriginal children were forced out of their homes and placed in residential schools in an attempt to remove their Aboriginal culture by denying them the ability to speak their own languages and practise their cultural traditions.

children who went to residential schools never returned to their communities. Some died of diseases such as tuberculosis and accidents such as falling under the wheels of farm machinery (CBC Learning, 2012a). Others went missing; their bodies have never been found (CBC Learning, 2012). In addition, residential schooling led to the decline of traditional parenting as children were denied their appropriate parental role models. If one wishes to eradicate a people, the best group to target is the children because it is children who carry cultures into the future.

There are no longer residential schools for Aboriginal children in Canada, although the last one closed in Punnichy, Saskatchewan, only in 1996 (CBC Learning, 2012a; General Synod Archives, 2008; Milloy, 1999). However, even today, education for Aboriginal children is not what it is for non-Aboriginal children. Schools in First Nations communities continue to be funded 30 per cent less than schools everywhere else in the country (CBC Learning, 2012b). Some First Nations communities in the north, such as Attawapiskat on James Bay in northern Ontario, as of 2012 have no schools (CBC Learning, 2012b).

When most of the residential schools were phased out in the 1960s (Aboriginal Healing Foundation, 2008; Royal Commission on Aboriginal Peoples [RCAP], 2004), the "**Sixties Scoop**" followed. This term is used to describe the practice that emerged in the 1960s whereby large numbers of Aboriginal children were removed from their families by social workers in child welfare and placed in White homes not only in Canada, but in the United States and as far away as Germany, where many were treated in the same way as those who attended the residential schools (Baskin, 2011; Blackstock, 2012; Gosek & Bennett, 2012; Sinclair, 2009). Of major interest is Blackstock's (2008) observation that in 2008,

Sixties Scoop A term used to describe the removal of high numbers of Aboriginal children from their families in the 1960s and their placement in non-Aboriginal homes for adoption or foster care.

there were three times the number of Aboriginal children placed in the care of the child welfare system than were placed in residential schools at the height of their operation. In fact, Aboriginal children are placed in the care of child welfare at a rate six to eight times higher than non-Aboriginal children (Blackstock, 2008, 2012).

Contemporary Challenges in Aboriginal Communities

Colonization, including Canada's government acts and policies, has contributed to the multitude of social problems facing Aboriginal Peoples today. The research on this topic is well established (Aboriginal Healing Foundation, 2008; Baskin, 2011; Hart, 2002; RCAP, 1996). The survivors of residential schools and the child welfare system continue to have poor overall health status, commonly referred to as intergenerational effects or historical trauma. These impacts of colonization include poverty, high unemployment rates, lack of education, inadequate or lack of affordable housing, and dependency on social services due to policies of the Indian Act (Aboriginal Healing Foundation, 2008; Baskin, 2011).

intergenerational trauma
Refers to trauma passed down from generation to generation in Aboriginal communities, resulting in unhealthy family relationships such as violence, mental health challenges such as depression, and internalized oppression sometimes manifested as substance misuse.

The term **intergenerational trauma** is often used by Aboriginal and non-Aboriginal writers to describe social problems in Aboriginal communities. This term is interpreted to mean that the trauma suffered by Aboriginal parents, grandparents, and great-grandparents has serious impacts on Aboriginal Peoples' lives today. It often manifests itself as unhealthy family relationships such as violence, mental health challenges such as depression, and internalized oppression sometimes manifested as substance misuse (Baskin, 2011; Gray, 2011; RCAP, 1996; Truth and Reconciliation Commission, 2012).

A widespread example of this has occurred as a result of the treatment of Aboriginal children in the residential schools. Sometimes colonized and traumatized people turn to alcohol and drugs to deal with the depression and grief they are experiencing, which may lead to self-destruction. Other times, survivors turn all of the oppression they have experienced inward on themselves and come to believe the negative stories that the oppressors have created about them. Pain and rage are also internalized and tends to be taken out on those who are close to us because we are not able to direct it at those who are responsible for it.

Furthermore, many of the residential school survivors who had children experienced a great deal of difficulty parenting them. Some treated their children the same way they were treated—with harsh discipline, coldness, and even abuse. Others were emotionally unavailable to their children, afraid to touch them, express love, or teach them through appropriate discipline. These were the forms of parenting that they inherited from their developmental years in the schools. It is extremely difficult to parent in healthy ways when one has never experienced it.

Intergenerational trauma is a term that focuses on individual families whereas historical trauma describes what Aboriginal Peoples have inherited as an entire group. It means that *all* Aboriginal Peoples have been victims of genocide and affected by colonization and all its tools, even though they may not have been to a residential school, been taken away from their families by child welfare authorities, or live in poverty. It means that every Aboriginal person lives with loss: loss of culture, land, identity, and what should have been.

The collective trauma experienced by Aboriginal Peoples includes collective images of traumatic events that have become implanted in the social memory of Aboriginal Peoples. Although those born in the twentieth century will not fully consciously remember the suffering of their ancestors, they nevertheless carry images and feelings that are shaped by memories that are passed on by many people they have never known (Neal, 1998). On top of these collective memories from the past are traumatic events happening to Aboriginal

In Their **Own Words**

THE SIXTIES SCOOP

OF THE CHILDREN WHO WERE adopted between the years of 1960 and 1990, 70 per cent were adopted into non-Aboriginal homes. The breakdown rate for these trans-racial adoptions is also 70 per cent by the time children reached their mid-teen years. Although a halt on trans-racial adoption took place in Manitoba in 1985 and other provinces followed suit, Aboriginal children are still being removed from families and regularly placed into permanent care, mostly in non-Aboriginal homes, via the child welfare system. Legal cases now provide the precedents for courts to give more weight to attachment to foster families over Aboriginal cultures in determining the best interests of Aboriginal children. However, research tells us exactly the opposite. Attachment depends solely upon the strength of the familial context and, over time, culture becomes more significant for Aboriginal youth-in-care and young adults.

Some adoptees have positive adoption experiences, which is one of the most significant predictive factors for adult well-being. That is, for adoptees that had at least one parent or family figure who expressed unconditional love and support, the outcome for emotional and psychological well-being has been good. For other adoptees, finding that supportive person among friends and spouses in later years has been significant in helping them to find a sense of self as Aboriginal Peoples. Many adoptees, now adults, have reunited with birth families and communities. However, a substantial number of these adoptees face cultural and identity challenges as the result of having been socialized and assimilated into a Euro-Canadian middle-class society. For trans-racial adoptees, questions about cultural identity and family roots may be worsened by other problems arising during the search and reunion experience. The identity concerns of adoptees may be intensified by being reacquainted with one of the most marginalized and oppressed groups in North American society.

As a survivor of the Sixties Scoop, I would describe my years growing up as a mix of negative and positive experiences. I faced a lot of racism as the only Aboriginal child in my family and social environment. My parents were not able to recognize the racism in our social contexts because they believed the mythology that Canada is a place where racism and inequity do not exist. Although there are some situations where trans-racial adoption can be a strong and positive thing, generally adoptive and foster families, like mine, do not subscribe to the notion that adoption creates a bi-racial family unit. However, taking this approach can help the child to not be alone in dealing with the challenges of being a minority in a Euro-Canadian context. Where children are isolated and lacking in cultural mirrors, the turmoil of trans-racial adoption leads to problematic mental health and well-being. The research shows that adoptive/foster youth and adults will inevitably **repatriate** to their birth families and cultures because a natural human tendency is to want to know where we belong and who our people are.

Investing in strategies that enhance cultural continuity and maintain ties of families and communities of origin during the adoptive years will go a long way in supporting Aboriginal children and their bi-racial families towards positive adoption outcomes.

Raven Sinclair, Cree/Assiniboine/Saulteaux Nations from Saskatchewan, is an associate professor at the Faculty of Social Work, University of Regina and a founding editorial member of Indigenous Voices in Social Work, as well as regional editor for AlterNative: An International Journal of Indigenous Peoples, and the creator of Iportal: Indigenous Studies Portal Research Tool website.

repatriation The process of locating an Aboriginal person's First Nation community and reuniting with the birth family as well as registering him or her as a status Indian under the Indian Act.

Peoples in the present since the impacts of colonization continue. Thus, the past is real today even though the times have changed.

Furthermore, there is genetic research that suggests that traumatization may be passed on in the same way as some hereditary diseases are (Wesley-Esquimaux & Smolewski, 2004). In this way, the sense of loss and grief experienced by Aboriginal Peoples in the present may be directly linked to the genetically coded trauma they have inherited (Wesley-Esquimaux & Smolewski, 2004). Every present trauma experienced then builds on and triggers what is already stored in the collective memory (Brave Heart, 2004, 2000; Duran, 2006; Duran & Duran, 1995). For example, for Aboriginal youth who live in an isolated and impoverished community, the social context in which they are living is a trigger for memories of suffering experienced by their parents, grandparents, and so forth. Thus, accumulating many positive memories to combat the negative ones can be a challenge for Aboriginal Peoples because each trauma and loss has been quickly followed by another. There has never been enough time in between various traumas to heal and so one unresolved trauma snowballs into another in the lives of each generation.

Steps toward Healing

Aboriginal Peoples show tremendous strength and resilience in overcoming the challenges they have inherited from colonization. We are breaking the silence about our experiences, reclaiming traditional values and teachings, speaking for ourselves, and creating our own images of ourselves. A strong example of this is the truth telling and healing processes that have happened through the Truth and Reconciliation Commission (TRC). The TRC (2012) was established in 2008 with the mission statement to "reveal the complete story of Canada's residential school system, and lead the way to respect through reconciliation . . . for the child taken, for the parent left behind" (p. 1). The vision statement further states that the TRC will help to establish a renewed sense of Canada that is inclusive, respectful, and enables reconciliation. The truth telling and reconciliation process is an acknowledgement of the injustices and harms experienced by Aboriginal Peoples in Canada and the need for continued healing. As this chapter was being written, the TRC hired archeologists to find the graves of the hundreds of children who went missing at residential schools across Canada (CBC Learning, 2012b; Truth and Reconciliation Commission, 2012).

Established in 1998, the Aboriginal Healing Foundation (AHF) was another national healing initiative to support the development of sustainable healing programming for the survivors of residential schools and their descendants. Part of this organization's mandate was to conduct research and evaluation on healing-focused programming. A significant finding from their evaluations was that "research on promising healing practices points to evidence that cultural activities are legitimate and successful healing interventions" (Castellano, 2006, p. 148). Several programs funded by the AHF supported this finding, including the Qul-Aun Trauma Program at the Tsow-Tun Le Lum (Moving Beyond the Traumas of Our Past) in Lantzville, British Columbia, Building a Nation in Saskatoon, Saskatchewan, the Pisimweyapiy Counselling Centre in Nelson House, Manitoba, and the Mi'kmaw Family Healing Program in Truro, Nova Scotia. Aboriginal Peoples who have participated in these programs cite the following as effective healing principles:

- cultural coherence that underlies the development of a strong identity as First Nations, Métis, and Inuit Peoples
- importance of a helper's personal experiences;
- traditional ceremonies and teachings help families heal;

Residential school survivors walk in unison at the opening ceremonies of the 2013 Truth and Reconciliation Commission of Canada event in Vancouver.

- no fixed timetable for making changes as this is a personal journey;
- regaining of collective strength as Aboriginal peoples;
- flexible and diverse healing modalities;
- restoration of Aboriginal values (AHF, 2006, 2008; Andersen, 2011; Archibald et al., 2012; Fiske, 2008; Fletcher & Denham, 2008; Gone, 2008; Pannekoek, 2001; Reimer & Chartrand, 2004; Wahbung Abinoonjiiag Inc., 2011; Waldram et al., 2008; Warriors Against Violence, 2010)

The Medicine Wheel as a Healing Tool

Many Aboriginal social work programs implement variations of the Medicine Wheel (see Chapter 1) as a holistic method of addressing individual, family, and community healing, positive change, and social justice. According to the teachings of the Cree Nation, the Medicine Wheel also promotes balance and harmony within people and communities (Mawhiney & Nabigon, 2011; Nabigon & Wenger-Nabigon, 2012). The Medicine Wheel offers a guide to understanding problems and finding solutions that take into account "emotional, cognitive, social, and physical functioning [of a person, family or community] in a spiritual context" (Nabigon & Wenger-Nabigon, 2012, p. 48).

The following is a brief explanation of how the Medicine Wheel can be used in healing, helping, and social work practice (Baskin, 2012). The teachings of the Medicine Wheel direct us to begin with the self, which is depicted in the centre of the Wheel, which means that we need to take care of ourselves before we are able to help others. We must walk what we talk, address our own challenges as they arise, and constantly be in a place of healing and learning. Each of the directions and their accompanying colours represent the four directions of the world. Four of the sacred medicines and four of the clan animals are also represented in the Wheel and are used for cleansing, clarity, focusing, and guidance.

Theory in Practice

THE ABORIGINAL HEALING AND WELLNESS STRATEGY (AHWS)

IN ONTARIO, THE ABORIGINAL HEALING and Wellness Strategy (AHWS) funds both on- and off-reserve communities in their promotion of healthy individuals and families. Many of the funded programs combine traditional helping methods of Aboriginal Peoples with mainstream social work techniques in the areas of reducing family violence and improving the overall health of communities. Since it was launched in 1994, the AHWS has had many successes both on- and off-reserve in building the capacity of First Nations, Métis, and Inuit communities to implement community controlled, holistic, and culture-based frameworks. Since its creation, the AHWS has funded health access centres, healing lodges, family shelters, and crisis-intervention teams across the province. It has supported nearly 500 community-based health and healing programs and close to 700 jobs in health and social services (Aboriginal Healing and Wellness Strategy, 2012).

Initiatives such as the AHWS support Aboriginal communities by helping members take care of their own healing, which leads to regaining control over their own lives. Such healing and control is spreading across the country in areas such as youth suicide prevention. Examples of this are occurring in some Nunavut communities, such as Qikiqtarjuaq, where people of all ages in the community have been coming together since 1993 to talk about suicide and how they want to make it stop (Kral & Idlout, 2009). People are identifying shared feelings and concerns about suicide as well as ideas to prevent it. One important prevention method was encouraging people to talk with anyone they came into contact who seemed to be worried, sad, depressed, or withdrawn. Another was to remove the closet rods—which had been the primary method of suicide through hanging—in all of the community's housing, which could be done as all of the housing is publicly funded rather than owned privately (Kral & Idlout, 2009). Typically, when a chosen method of suicide is removed, people do not usually change the method to another one (Kral, 1998, 1994; Kral & Idlout, 2009). These two related methods have significantly reduced youth suicide in this community.

Beverly Doxtator

Healing lodges such as this one—Kiikeewanniikaan, Southwest Regional Healing Lodge and Learning Centre, located on Munsee–Delaware Nation, near London, Ontario—offer traditional and contemporary approaches to treating adddiction, domestic and sexual abuse, and family discord.

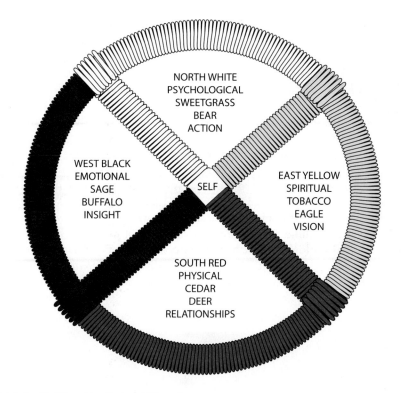

FIGURE 8.1 // The Medicine Wheel

Source: Baskin, 2012

Each direction also holds a gift that guides us in the work that we do. We begin in the east with the gift of vision, meaning that first we dream, imagine, and look forward into the future to see what it is we wish to accomplish. Next, we move into the southern direction where we begin the important task of developing relationships with those with whom we are going to work. This is critical to working with people as we need to get to know them, share stories, and begin to feel comfortable with one another before we can assist them in what they are struggling with. Insight is the gift of the western direction where we begin to explore what may be underneath the behaviours of people and the root causes of their situation, such as poverty or depression. Lastly, we move into the northern direction which is the place of action or movement. We take all that we have learned, thus far, from the other three directions and put this into practice.

Aboriginal Worldviews as Theories in Social Work

The recent literature on Aboriginal worldviews as theories for helping in social work reveals some common themes. A prevalent theme emphasizes a return to Aboriginal traditional teachings as a guideline for social work practice. As discussed earlier, Aboriginal Peoples had their own governmental systems, values, and ways of helping each other prior to contact with Europeans. With assimilation came a suppression of Aboriginal ways of life and a movement towards taking up many Western ways for survival.

Anishinaabe The people who originally lived in central and northern Ontario and Manitoba.

All Aboriginal populations have their own unique healing methods and ways of achieving social justice. For example, the **Anishinaabe** have medicines, ceremonies such as the sweat lodge, songs, and dances.

The Haudenosaunee have longhouses, medicine societies, and prayers that help their people with any social problem they encounter. The Métis have their own styles of prayer, music, and dance as artistic forms of ensuring health and well-being. For Inuit, the eating of country foods such as raw seal and fish as well as camping on the land are what keeps them well in a holistic way.

For more than 30 years, Aboriginal worldviews have been affecting how Canada views criminal justice. This began with concerns about the overrepresentation of Aboriginal Peoples in the criminal justice and correctional systems and has since influenced most of the mainstream reforms in this area (Baskin, 2011; Laprairie, 2005). What stands out is how it is the activism of Aboriginal political organizations, social services agencies, and communities that are behind these significant changes. Of most significance is the influence that Aboriginal worldviews have had on the emergence of alternative forms of justice.

It needs to be recognized that First Nations are diverse; different Nations have different needs and histories. In particular, Métis people have been disadvantaged over the years

restorative justice Methods of restoring the balance within an Aboriginal community after harm has been committed. Some of these methods are, for example, sentencing circles which involve the person who has done the harm, the victim, and community members such as Elders and family members.

Family Group Conferences Processes involving extended family in decisions regarding the protection and care of children while strengthening and supporting families.

Case STUDY

Restorative Justice

ALTHOUGH **RESTORATIVE JUSTICE** IS STILL seen as relatively new in mainstream systems, it has been a traditional part of Aboriginal societies. It is viewed as a community-based initiative and an important component of Aboriginal self-governance; it is the accepted approach in several provinces, including Saskatchewan, British Columbia, Alberta, Nova Scotia, and New Brunswick (Laprairie, 2005). A widely used form of restorative justice is **Family Group Conferences,** which began in New Zealand with the Maori people and now form the basis of programs such as the Family Group Decision-Making Project in Newfoundland and Labrador, which deals with cases of family violence (Laprairie, 2005) and several child welfare agencies across the country. Preliminary research on the experiences of caregivers, child welfare workers, and children in both the Children's Aid Society and the Catholic Children's Aid Society in Toronto as well as rural areas in Ontario, such as Algoma, identifies how families may feel more empowered and, thus, more likely to follow long-term plans for the care of children after participating in family group conferencing (C. Usher, personal communication, March 10, 2009; Ontario Association of Children's Aid Societies, 2011; Sherwin, 2010).

Other forms of restorative justice that are being taken up by mainstream systems are diversion, alternative measures, mediation, and dispute resolution, all of which hold community control and involvement as the key to their success (Baskin, 2011; Laprairie, 2005). Such community-based initiatives take place in First Nations communities across the country, but are also present in large urban centres including Toronto, Winnipeg, Regina, and Vancouver where diverse communities are identifying their own concerns, determining strategies to deal with them, and offering programs to assist those involved (Laprairie, 2005). Thus far, it is clear that the most effective community initiatives involve the participation of local people and link participants to community services, which indicates a strong need for the role of social work in the area of restorative justice.

as they are denied access to programs and services that are available to First Nations and Inuit. For example, the Medical Services Branch of Health Canada delivers programs and services to status First Nations and Inuit (e.g., alcohol and drug abuse programs, short-term counselling, and initiatives for at-risk children), but none of these programs benefit the Métis, even though they often face identical social and health difficulties. Métis needs in the area of social and health programming have been identified as a gap. The Aboriginal Healing Foundation (2006) put forth recommendations regarding planning for successful programs for Métis people such as

- the individuality of Métis communities and community members must be recognized;
- Métis people have methods to address community and individual healing needs, but they are unique to the regions and communities in which they live;
- Métis people look to their Elders, Senators, and community members for healing needs;
- healing programs for Métis people should be designed according to regional and community-specific needs, as they vary in size, history, and location;
- programming should include traditional and contemporary beliefs of the particular Métis community. Many Aboriginal social workers combine a mixture of Aboriginal and Western healing methods and theories to assist them in their work. Values such as those in the Anishinaabe's Seven Sacred Teachings like wisdom and humility (Baskin, Strike & McPherson, in press; Baskin, Strike & McPherson, 2012) can be equated to social work values and standards of practice such as self-determination and dignity of the person (CASW, 2005).

Some social work theories, such as anti-oppression, structural, **postmodern**, and **anti-colonial**, fit with Aboriginal worldviews because they recognize how certain populations, including Aboriginal Peoples, are marginalized in society and that there are many ways of seeing the world and assisting marginalized groups.

An anti-oppressive perspective, which includes structural social work theory, asserts that it is oppression rather than "individual deficiency or social disorganization" that "is the major cause of and explanation for social problems" (Mullaly, 2002, p. 15). This perspective can be linked to anti-racism and anti-colonialism because it "can be used to understand better the nature and extent of racism in our society and how it contributes to the oppression of visible minority groups. It can be used to understand better the nature of colonialism and how it contributes to the oppression of Indigenous persons in our society" (Mullaly, 2002, p. 180).

Postmodern theories within the profession of social work take the position that reality is socially constructed through language, maintained through narratives, and carries no essential truths (Baskin, 2011). Thus, reality is made up of multiple stories, is fluid, and is historically specific. These theories centre on asking critical questions such as whose languages, knowledges, and voices are privileged in society because they are heard and whose are not?

Post-colonial or anti-colonial theory comes from the people who have been colonized and so emphasizes how Indigenous Peoples around the world have been affected by colonization as well as addressing the relationships between the colonized and the colonizers (Baskin, 2011). Rather than Indigenous Peoples being written about, anti-colonial theory ensures that they are the ones doing the writing while bringing Indigenous worldviews into the centre of the discussions. Importantly, anti-colonial theory stresses strategies of resistance and **decolonization** led by Indigenous Peoples in various forms across the planet today.

It is important to keep in mind that Aboriginal worldviews as a social work theory stands on its own. However, these worldviews can be linked to transformative theories that are being put into practice at the present time.

postmodern An understanding that reality only comes into being through how one interprets the world around him or herself. Thus, there is no one truth, but rather, there are many truths.

anti-colonial Theories that examine colonial literature and history through the eyes of those who have been colonized which debunks the notion of European racial superiority and works towards decolonization.

decolonization Aboriginal and non-Aboriginal Peoples working together to dismantle the attitudes, powers, and institutions that keep practices of colonization alive.

In Their **Own Words**

BRIDGING THE GAP

WHEN I WAS WORKING AT AN Aboriginal health centre, myself and a colleague were asked to attend "grand rounds" with the psychiatry, psychology, and social work departments of two major urban hospitals and assist in their efforts of service delivery to Aboriginal clients. My colleague presented background information on the effects of residential schools and how colonization establishes the "why" many Aboriginal Peoples may have issues with helpers who are non-Aboriginal and operating within large institutions. My role was to offer a bridge. I started with something like, "All that you were taught in school about not sharing any personal information about your life experiences, you must throw out the window. Instead, you need to share your story with the Aboriginal clients you come into contact with." There was a noticeable collective gasp in the room. I continued to explain that in Aboriginal communities, we seek guidance and help from others who have already walked through the issues we seek guidance for. When an Aboriginal person goes to an Elder or a traditional counsellor, it is expected that these helpers will share their story as it relates to the help that is sought.

I explained that we can educate ourselves through reading and studying, but that does not give us first-hand experience. Knowledge and practical application are two different entities. I further explained that it is paramount to establish trust and this is most effectively done by the offering of personal information. This ensures that the helper knows what the person is dealing with. For example, if I were to work with Aboriginal Peoples who had been sexually abused, I would first share my own experience of this and how I recovered. You see, Aboriginal Peoples believe that a helper cannot take a person where they have not already gone. This would likely be discouraged in mainstream social work, but without sharing the knowledge that you have some understanding of what the client is going through, they will not open up to you.

These beliefs come from a long history of our teachings taught through storytelling, hands-on work, and from our willingness to be vulnerable and open with others. In the past, we were first encouraged to go into the woods and be with self to discover our own answers and, if we required more than this, we would seek out others who had walked the same path or understood what we were feeling.

Even though non-Aboriginal helpers haven't experienced life as an Aboriginal person obviously, they can demonstrate that they can relate to the emotional impact of someone. Everyone understands what it is like to be betrayed, lied to, hurt, or abused by another, which can assist them in emotionally relating to their clients. Aboriginal Peoples need to know you can hear them emotionally.

Cree Elder Joanne Dallaire is a helper/healer/social worker who has been working in the fields of counselling, staff training, and educating on Aboriginal concerns for over 30 years.

Being an Ally

Non-Aboriginal social workers, academics, and other allies are beginning to have discussions and write about their role in the past and present social problems of Aboriginal Peoples in Canada and how they can participate in processes of decolonization (Baskin, 2011;

Bishop, 2005, 1994; Carniol, 2005; Mullaly, 2010, 2002, 1997). They are forging strong relationships with Aboriginal Peoples. For example, Regan (2010) states that she now understands that the dysfunction, violence, and poverty that exists for Aboriginal Peoples is part of the intergenerational legacy of the residential schools and that she now sees Aboriginal Peoples through new eyes. She also tells allies of Aboriginal Peoples to re-story dominant society's version of history and create decolonizing spaces where this can occur. Also of great significance is how these allies are beginning to understand that many aspects of Aboriginal worldviews are applicable to *all* people.

What does it mean to be an ally to Aboriginal Peoples? It involves bringing to light all the stories of the people who have been harmed by colonization as every single Canadian needs to hear about them. It means ending denial and use of master narratives of "discovery" and "**manifest destiny**." This must happen before reconciliation can begin. Allies closely examine their taken-for-granted privileges and come to understand that they have these at the expense of Aboriginal Peoples. Allies listen even when they do not want to. They reject constructions of "**otherness**," examine how they exclude certain groups, and question what is presented as "**universal truths**." Allies also refuse to participate in "new age" appropriations of Aboriginal traditions, spirituality, and markers of identity, such as the current fashion of wearing factory-made "moccasins" and "mukluks," as they know that this also is an assault on Aboriginal Peoples.

It is true that non-Aboriginal Peoples are not accountable for what happened over the past few centuries nor is feeling guilt over what happened of any use. However, if we do not participate in reconciliation now, then we should feel guilty in the future. Solutions to the current stress between Aboriginal and non-Aboriginal Peoples in Canada is based, in large part, on seeing the strengths, resiliency, survival, and resistance of Aboriginal Peoples today and joining with them for a just country.

manifest destiny A force that predetermines an inevitable series of events for the future.

otherness The condition of being viewed as strange or different.

universal truths Beliefs that are accepted by the entire world.

Steve Russell/GetStock.com

The Idle No More movement strives to bring public awareness of Native issues in Canada.

In Their Own Words

BEING AN ALLY TO ABORIGINAL PEOPLES

MY TRIP TO THE NORTH will be one I will never forget. Whether the area is called Yellowknife or Tso' Tine, Northwest Territories, Land of the Midnight Sun, or Denendeh—the Land of the People in the Dene language, I am forever thankful for what I learned from the people and the land there. I spent two weeks living at Camp Connections, an Aboriginal youth camp just off the Cameron River with nine others, both Aboriginal and non-Aboriginal. It was a course on social work with Aboriginal Peoples that started me on my journey of being an ally to Aboriginal Peoples and sparked me to go on this exchange.

Working alongside communities can be an extremely enriching experience; however, when working with communities you are not a part of, there are a number of barriers and struggles. One needs to be cautious of becoming overbearing and encroaching on the community and their goals. Through listening and taking part in discussions with a number of inspiring people in Yellowknife and the surrounding area, I now have a better understanding of how to be an ally whilst feeling out of place amongst an extremely welcoming community.

This is what I have learned about being an ally to Aboriginal Peoples thus far: First, it is okay to feel like an outsider. Time after time, we are taught that we can never fully understand a group that we are not a part of, but that this is okay. This means one needs to learn how to be comfortable with discomfort, feeling out of place, and helpless at times. Second, listen and learn. When you want to be supportive of a group because you believe in their goals, then you need to learn about them from the people themselves. This means dedicating some time to slowing down and listening to or reading stories from community members directly about their lived experiences. To move forward with action means you need to be informed, so learning about the historical and social context of a present concern is vital. Third, in addition to beginning to know the group you are working with, you need to understand yourself. Acknowledge and own the privileges you hold, so you can work with them, instead of being hindered by remaining ignorant. Lastly, being an ally is not about standing up for a community; it is about standing alongside them. You need to learn that you cannot always be on the front lines participating in every aspect. It is more about taking a step back and listening to how you can help, which resources you can offer, or just how you can be supportive. It may be difficult, as at times you may feel that you could be doing more, but this is a task of patience well worth the wait.

Christine Anthony is a non-Aboriginal third-year Bachelor of Social Work student at Ryerson University in Toronto who recently participated in the Canadian Roots Exchange.

Aboriginal Peoples have resisted colonization in various ways over the years. From going underground with their ceremonies during the nineteenth century when they were outlawed and retaining some of the languages, to publishing their versions of colonization and its impacts and joining educational institutions as professors and researchers, to road blocks and protesting, Aboriginal Peoples have expressed great strength and commitment to make the world a better place for the next seven generations. At the time of writing this chapter, a powerful resistance movement took over the front pages of Canadian newspapers and the nightly news on television. What is particularly fascinating about the Idle No More movement is that much of its message is being spread through social media, including Facebook and Twitter, and it is made up of a diversity of Aboriginal Peoples including youth, activists, and academics. The founders of Idle No More are three Cree women and a non-Aboriginal woman from Saskatchewan. They began this grassroots movement in October 2012 and it spread rapidly not only across Canada and the United States, but as far away as Bolivia in South America (Gordon, 2013).

Bill C-45 lit the fire that has spread across the country as it brings forward changes to the Indian Act that lessens community consent in the buying and selling of reserve lands by resource companies such as mining and oil, further violates treaties, and aims to continue attempts at assimilating Aboriginal Peoples. Moreover, it is critical that Canadians also realize that Bill C-45 is a clear attack on the bodies of water that all Canadians share as it aims to make serious changes to environmental legislation, such as to the Canadian Environmental Assessment Act, which will take away the protection of the majority of our lakes (Gordon, 2013). The Bill will exempt companies, such as those who create major pipeline and interprovincial power line projects, from having to prove they will not damage or destroy waterways while doing so (McFarlane, 2013).

The Idle No More movement is demanding sustainable development on reserve lands, believes in healthy, just, equitable, and sustainable communities, and has a vision and plan of how to build them. This is not new information, but it seems that the voices of those who support Idle No More are louder than ever before. This is a movement about everyone in Canada coming together and standing united on important concerns that will affect all of us now and in the future.

Some Aboriginal Peoples today are talking about the **eighth fire**, which is a time when Aboriginal and non-Aboriginal Peoples will come together to develop new relationships. It is true that Aboriginal and non-Aboriginal Peoples live somewhat in two different worlds, but we can build bridges between these worlds. We can create closer links, learn from each other, ensure that the rights of Aboriginal Peoples are upheld, and take care of the earth. We are heading in the same direction, but in different canoes.

eighth fire According to the prophesies of the Anishinaabe, this is a time in the future when non-Aboriginal Peoples will turn to Aboriginal Peoples for help.

An example of an initiative that aims to bring young Aboriginal and non-Aboriginal Peoples together to learn from each other is the Canadian Roots Exchange (CRE), a federal not-for-profit initiative. The CRE believes that in order to bridge the gap between these two groups, everyone needs to become educated and aware of the daily realities within Aboriginal communities. Groups travel to cities, towns, and traditional territories across the country in an effort to break down stereotypes, open a dialogue, build relationships, and begin processes of reconciliation.

One of CRE's pivotal activities is organizing experiential educational programs in Aboriginal host communities across Canada where participants have the opportunity to learn in both formal and informal settings. These programs emphasize personal growth, leadership development through individual and group learning, and personal reflection facilitated by project coordinators and educators from each community. Thus far, CRE has served over 300 youth through 15 trips to communities such as Eskasoni, Nova Scotia, Moosonee, Ontario, and Tso'Tine, Northwest Territories (Canadian Roots Exchange, 2012).

Conclusion

All Aboriginal Peoples have been victims of genocide, colonization, and their current impacts which are mostly silenced by Canadian governments. However, we are breaking that silence by speaking for ourselves and creating our own images of ourselves. We have resisted colonization in various ways over the years. In the past and often still today, the profession of social work carries negative connotations for many Aboriginal Peoples. The paradigm through which social work is typically taught and practised is Eurocentric and, therefore, how to teach social work students to understand Aboriginal worldviews as well as ways of interacting and helping must actively be incorporated into education. Promotion of empowerment, positive self-esteem, and a strengthening of both individual and collective identities as Aboriginal Peoples leading to the promotion of self-determination among us can be done through social work practitioners if they are willing to learn from us.

Healing is happening on a large scale today with Aboriginal Peoples everywhere and some of this is happening through social work initiatives in areas such as family violence prevention, working with youth, and restorative justice, which incorporate Aboriginal worldviews. Some social work educators are also incorporating Aboriginal worldviews into teaching. In fact, recently the Canadian Association of Social Work Education and the Canadian Association of Social Workers (2013) put out a press release stating the following:

> We are aware of the colonial legacy that impacts the physical, emotional and spiritual wellbeing of Indigenous Peoples and of the historical contribution of social work to this legacy. We call upon all Canadian citizens to join with Indigenous Peoples in advocating for laws, policies and practices that end colonialism and restore right relationships among all Canadians.

Let us begin.

QUESTIONS FOR CRITICAL THOUGHT

1. How has the profession of social work been an arm of the colonization of Aboriginal Peoples in Canada?
2. What are the major principles of Aboriginal ways of helping and how are these being applied in social work today?
3. How might Aboriginal worldviews inform social work theories, policies, practices, and research?
4. How can non-Aboriginal social workers be allies of Aboriginal Peoples and communities?

RECOMMENDED READINGS

Andersen, C. (2011). Moya 'Tipimsook ("The People Who Aren't Their Own Bosses"): Racialization and the misrecognition of "Métis" in Upper Great Lakes. *Ethnohistory*, 58, 1, 37–63. doi: 10.1215/00141801–2010-063. Anderson notes the central place of racialization in the last five centuries of colonial rule and the cross-racial colonial encounters, which are rarely discussed. This article explores how, in the absence of much documentation on historical self-identification, Métis settlements came to be. It appeals for a Métis "counter-ethno history" anchored in an analysis of peoplehood.

Baskin, C. (2011). *Strong helpers' teachings: The value of Indigenous knowledges in the helping professions*. Toronto: Canadian Scholars' Press Inc. This book covers topics related to social work with Aboriginal Peoples such as child welfare, justice, and holistic healing with examples of successful programs in these areas.

Blackstock, C. (2011). Wanted: Moral courage in Canadian child welfare. *First Peoples Child & Family Review* 6, 35–46. Written by a prominent advocate in the area of child welfare and Aboriginal Peoples, Blackstock outlines the problems inherent in this area while asking social workers to make positive changes.

Kirmayer, L.J., Fletcher, C. & Watt, R. (2009). Locating the ecocentric self: Inuit concepts of mental health and illness. In Kirmayer, L. & Valaskakis, G. (Eds.). *Healing traditions: The mental health of Aboriginal peoples in Canada* (pp. 289–314). Vancouver: University of British Columbia Press. These authors discuss how Inuit articulate what it means to face mental health challenges as stemming from changes in their environment and the importance of the environment to healing processes.

Nabigon, H.C., & Wenger-Nabigon, A. (2012). *"Wise practices"*: Integrating traditional teachings with mainstream treatment approaches. *Native Social Work Journal 8*, 43–55. Nabigon and Wenger-Nabigon, two social work academics, highlight the Medicine Wheel as an important tool of helping and healing and how it can be implemented alongside mainstream forms of social work practice.

RECOMMENDED WEBSITES

The Aboriginal Healing Foundation
www.ahf.ca

The Aboriginal Healing Foundation was created to manage and implement healing strategies for First Nations, Inuit, and Métis people who were affected by the legacy of abuse in residential schools throughout Canada.

First Nations Caring Society
www.fncaringsociety.com

First Nations Caring Society was developed at a national meeting of First Nations Child & Family Services Agencies (FNCFSA) in 1998. The purpose of the organization is to provide research, policy recommendations, and professional development and networking to support First Nations children, youth, and families, particularly in the area of child welfare. This organization also publishes the *First Peoples Child and Family Review*.

Idle No More
www.idlenomore.ca

This website aims to educate all Canadians about the current impacts of colonization and the attacks on Aboriginal sovereignty in Canada and how to build alliances particularly regarding the care of the land and waters.

The Métis Nation of Canada
http://www.metisnationofcanada.org/

The Métis Nation of Canada's website contains information about the Métis specific governance structure and other useful information on Métis resources.

National Aboriginal Health Organization
www.naho.ca

Arising from community-based interests, the National Aboriginal Health Organization works to improve Aboriginal health through Aboriginal worldviews.

Social Work with Immigrants and Refugees

LEARNING OBJECTIVES

- To appreciate the international, social, political, and economic factors that lead people to leave their countries of origin.

- To identify similarities and differences among various migrant groups.

- To recognize how Canadian immigration policies shape settlement.

- To have an increased sensitivity to the experiences of social injustice, prejudice, racism, and discrimination encountered by members of certain migrant groups.

- To identify groups within the foreign-born populations that have particular needs.

- To appreciate the ways in which practitioners' cultural values, beliefs, and attitudes influence their work with immigrant and refugee clients.

- To develop a culturally and linguistically appropriate social work practice working with immigrant and refugee clients.

- To identify and access community, provincial, and national resources including periodicals, databases, websites, and other resources designed to help professionals working with immigrants and refugees.

Chapter Outline

This chapter introduces students to the needs and issues facing refugee and immigrant clients and explores theoretical approaches and ecological contexts in which social workers work with these populations. Particular groups requiring distinct supports are identified within the foreign-born populations. The chapter also includes information about periodicals, databases, websites, and other resources to help social workers working with immigrants and refugees.

Overview of the Contemporary Canadian Migration Landscape

With increasing global interconnections, economic immigration has become vital for immigration-destination countries as well as immigration-source countries. Economic immigration provides benefits to immigrants as well as the communities in which they reside. Canada's population growth relies on immigration, as the fertility rate is only 1.68 children per female (Citizenship and Immigration Canada, 2011a). From 2002 through 2011, on average, 246,000 immigrants and refugees settled in Canada each year for a total of close to 2.5 million (CIC, 2011b). In 2006, the proportion of foreign-born Canadians was 19.8 per cent. In Toronto, more than half (54 per cent) of women are immigrants (Chui, 2011). Nearly one quarter of Canada's population speaks languages other than English and French. Accurate figures for the undocumented population in Canada are non-existent; estimates vary widely, from anywhere between 20,000–500,000 (Boyd, 2006; Magalhaes, Carrasco, & Gastaldo, 2011). These changing demographics across the country have created unique challenges for social workers. Barriers to economic, social, cultural, legal, and political integration faced by migrant groups require social workers to adapt their practice in order to provide services that are culturally safe, relevant, and effective.

The nature of armed conflict has changed over the last century. According to United Nations estimates, 10 per cent of casualties in World War I were civilians. In World War II, this percentage rose to 45 per cent. Today, civilians have been brought into the centre of armed conflicts; UNICEF estimates 90 per cent of casualties are civilians. Wars and armed conflicts around the world have forced more than 15 million people from their countries of origin (UNHCR, 2012). Wealthy countries have responded to the world's refugees by instituting diverse **resettlement** policies and programs to provide protection, economic support, and integration into the settlement country.

Refugees who are permanently resettled are accorded the major benefits and entitlements possessed by settlement country citizens, cannot be forced to return to their country of origin even post-conflict, and have the right to apply for citizenship after a period of time. Resettlement policies and programs reflect the ideologies of settlement countries and their perspectives on the needs of refugee populations. Resettlement is used when there are grave threats to a refugee's life, liberty, safety, health, or other fundamental human rights.

In the face of increased immigration, there has been a recent cooling trend towards migrants in Canada. The last decade has seen a pronounced increase in border security in Canada (Hugman, 2010; Weber, 2006), making it more difficult for migrants to reach Canadian territory. This has especially affected the number of refugee claimants in Canada, which has decreased drastically since 2009. This practice violates international law, which obligates states to respect the right to flee persecution and seek refuge. Some Canadian politicians and media carry simplistic messages that can dangerously represent one group of immigrants or refugees as more deserving than another. Refugees living in

resettlement The process by which refugees are given permanent legal residency in a settlement country.

Practical TIP

Ethics and Immigrants and Refugees

AS SOCIAL WORKERS, WE HAVE a responsibility written into our *Code of Ethics* to serve immigrant and refugee clients. For example, Value 2 of the *Code of Ethics* mandates that we pursue social justice, calling on us to reduce barriers for clients who face marginalization, disadvantage, and vulnerability, to oppose prejudice and discrimination against any person for any reason, and to challenge perspectives that perpetuate the stereotyping of particular persons or groups. Value 3 highlights social workers' service to humanity, emphasizing that we are to promote individual development and pursuit of individual goals as well as the development of a just society.

camps who are chosen through Canada's Resettlement Program are often presented as "good" refugees who wait patiently overseas while refugee claimants who come to Canada on their own to claim refugee status are presented as "queue jumpers." For example, in a press conference in August, 2012, discussing Bill C-49, the Preventing Human Smuggling Act, federal Immigration Minister Jason Kenney noted that "while Canada is maintaining its humanitarian tradition of providing a safe haven for legitimate refugees, we will not stand by while our immigration system is being abused by queue jumpers and human smugglers" (Posadzki, 2012).

Who Are Today's Migrants?

Establishing definitions of populations can be divisive, and can limit individuals' and groups' abilities to find common ground. An encompassing term that highlights the commonality of movement from one country to another is **migrant**, which is the term used in this chapter.

> **migrant** A person who has moved from one country to another either temporarily or permanently.

It is important to understand, however, that there are differences in the experiences of migrants based on their legal status. It is critical for social workers to understand the implications of migrant status as that status will shape the intervention for the client. For example, a social worker may structure an intervention for a refugee who has landed immigrant status differently from an intervention for a refugee claimant, who may have his or her asylum claim rejected and face deportation. Below is a list of definitions based on Canadian immigration policy that provide guidance for working with migrant populations. There are many areas that significantly overlap with regard to experiences of and challenges faced by migrant groups. However, an immigration reality is that policy-based definitions and subsequent legal statuses dictate eligibility for services and ultimately the legal right to reside in Canada.

An **immigrant** is a person admitted to Canada as a lawful permanent resident. Immigrants are those persons lawfully accorded the privilege of residing permanently in Canada. There are three basic categories of permanent residents: economic immigrants, family class, and refugees. The family class consists of foreign nationals sponsored by close relatives or family members in Canada and includes spouses and partners, dependent children, parents, and grandparents. The largest category of permanent residents in Canada is economic immigrants. In 2008, nearly 150,000 economic immigrants and their dependents came to Canada as skilled workers, business immigrants, and live-in caregivers.

> **immigrant** A person admitted to Canada as a lawful permanent resident.

refugee A person who is outside his or her country of nationality who is unable or unwilling to return to that country because of persecution or a well-founded fear of persecution based on race, religion, nationality, political opinion, and/or social affiliation.

refugee claimant A temporary resident in the humanitarian population category who requests refugee protection upon or after arrival in Canada but whose claim has not yet been decided.

temporary foreign worker A person hired by a Canadian employer to fill temporary labour or skill shortages.

undocumented migrant A person who has come to Canada as a visitor, student, or temporary worker, or refugee claimant and then has continued residence in Canada after either visa expiration or denial of refugee claim.

Canada's refugee definition is based on the definition in the Convention Relating to the Status of Refugees (1951). A **refugee** is any person who is outside his or her country of nationality who is unable or unwilling to return to that country because of persecution or a well-founded fear of persecution. Persecution or fear of persecution may be based on a person's race, religion, nationality, political opinion, and/or social affiliation. Refugees are eligible to apply for permanent lawful residence after one year of continuous presence in Canada. Permanent residents in the refugee category include government-assisted refugees, privately sponsored refugees, refugees landed in Canada (also referred to as refugee claimants or asylum seekers whose applications have been accepted) and refugee dependents (i.e., dependents of refugees landed in Canada, including spouses and partners living abroad or in Canada). In 2011, Canada resettled nearly 28,000 refugees, including their dependents (CIC, 2011b).

A **refugee claimant** is a temporary resident in the humanitarian population category who requests refugee protection upon or after arrival in Canada but whose claim has not yet been decided. A refugee claimant receives Canada's protection when he or she is found to be a Convention refugee (as defined by the United Nations 1951 Geneva Convention Relating to the Status of Refugees and its 1967 Protocol), or when found to be a person needing protection based on risk to life, risk of cruel and unusual treatment or punishment, or danger of torture as defined in the Convention against Torture. A refugee claimant whose claim is accepted may make an application in Canada for permanent residence. The applicant may include family members in Canada and abroad.

A **temporary foreign worker** is someone who has been hired by a Canadian employer to fill temporary labour or skill shortages. The two main programs that utilize temporary foreign workers are the Live-In Caregiver Program and the Seasonal Agricultural Worker Program. In general, temporary foreign workers do not have the automatic right of permanent residency, freedom of movement between employers and jobs, and access to rights and entitlements of social citizenship.

An **undocumented migrant** refers to someone who has come to Canada as a visitor, student, or temporary worker and then continued residence in Canada after his or her visa has expired or a refugee claimant whose claims for asylum are denied but who remains in Canada (Elrick, 2007).

Who Is Where? Migrant Countries of Origin and Settlement Across Canada

Before 1961, more than 90 per cent of immigrants to Canada were from the USA, the United Kingdom, and other European countries; from 1991–2001, American and European immigration had decreased to 22 per cent while immigration from Asia increased to 50 per cent (see Figure 9.1) (Boyd, 2011). Today, top immigration-source countries include China, Philippines, and India.

In 2006, the top three source countries for refugees selected under Canada's resettlement program were Afghanistan, Colombia, and Ethiopia. Every year, refugee claims are made, rejected, abandoned, withdrawn, and/or finalized, with a large number pending from one year to the next. When claims are finalized, they are then reviewed by the Immigration and Refugee Board of Canada for acceptance or refusal. In 2011, there were 24,981 refugee claims filed; that same year, 34,257 claims were finalized, with 12,983 refugee claims accepted (38 per cent approval rate; University of Ottawa Human Rights Research and Education Centre, 2012). For that year, Hungary, China, and Colombia had the highest number of applicants for refugee status. However, looking at acceptance rates of refugee claims, the three countries with the highest rates of refugee claims accepted (per number of applicants) were Pakistan (67 per cent), Nigeria (63 per cent), and Sri Lanka (57 per cent). Hungary had the lowest acceptance rate of 8 per cent.

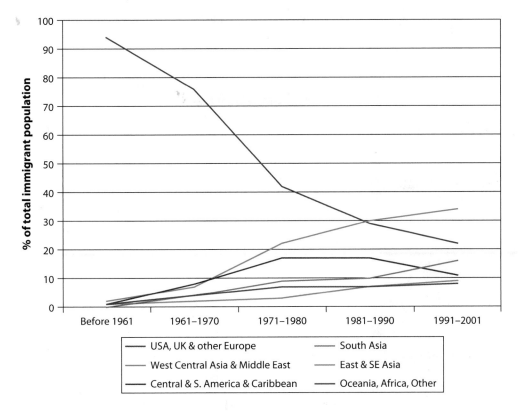

FIGURE 9.1 // Canadian Immigration Trends

Source: Based on Boyd, 2011

Most immigrants live in large Canadian cities, and their concentration in the large centres has been increasing. More than 60 per cent of immigrants and 70 per cent of recent immigrants (since 1986) live in Canada's three largest cities—Toronto, Montreal, and Vancouver; each city has over 250,000 recent immigrants. The five second-tier immigrant destinations of Edmonton, Calgary, Winnipeg, Hamilton, and Ottawa each have between 40,000 to 100,000 recent immigrants. Between 5,000–15,000 recent immigrants live in the third-tier immigrant destination cities of Victoria, Saskatoon, Regina, Québec, and Halifax (CIC, 2005).

Migration Policy Overview

Policy contexts shape government approaches to settlement. Canada's migration policy has been shaped by its ideological traditions as discussed in Chapter 1, as well as economic concerns, humanitarian crises, foreign policy, and general public opinion (Ighodaro, 2006). Migration policies shape social work practice with migrant populations as national laws determine eligibility for entrance as well as for services and benefits after arrival.

International-Level Policies

International humanitarian, human rights, and refugee laws provide guidelines regarding how countries manage and respond to citizens and documented and undocumented residents. For example, the guiding legislation for Canada's treatment of refugees is

© Christian Kober 1 / Alamy

This Chinatown in Vancouver, British Columbia, acts as a familiar enclave to many migrating individuals from various Asian countries.

nonrefoulement (literally meaning "no return") Prohibits the return of persons—no matter what their crime or suspected activity—to a place where they would be at risk of torture and other ill-treatment.

the UN Convention Relating to the Status of Refugees (1951) drafted after World War II to help countries address massive population displacements. The Convention provided signatory countries with the first universal refugee definition, recognized the right to remain and right to return, the principle of **nonrefoulement**, and the right of first asylum, defined minimum standards of treatment for refugees, and outlined determination procedures and eligibility criteria for refugee status, although the Convention provisions were linked firmly to "events occurring in Europe or elsewhere before 1 January 1951."

In 1967, the Optional Protocol relating to the Status of Refugees removed the temporal and geographic restrictions of the 1951 Convention; in 1969, Canada acceded to the Convention and Optional Protocol. This definition of refugee still applies today. States interpret it to include—or restrict—certain categories of people. For example, Canada recognizes that women who are fleeing gender-related persecution fall under "member of a particular social group" as do members of LGBTQ communities who are persecuted based on sexual orientation.

National-Level Policies

Canada has always been considered an immigrant-receiving country, similar to Australia and the USA. Before Confederation, as a British colony, Canadian immigration centred on recruiting citizens of the British Commonwealth to Canada as well as persons from the USA and other European countries. From 1869 to the end of WWII, Canadian legislation focused on recruiting foreign-born, non-British to fill service and unskilled undesirable labour categories and excluding people based on country of origin. Those foreign-born, non-British who were recruited for dangerous, poorly paid manual labour were considered "disposable" labourers. While they were not denied permanency outright, they faced obstacles that, in effect, often blocked permanent settlement, such as the Head Tax on Chinese immigrants (initially $50 in 1885 rising to $500 in 1903 for each Chinese immigrant) which discouraged them from bringing their families to Canada.

In Canada, there have been seven major acts focused on immigration: 1869, 1919, 1952, 1976, 2002, 2010, and 2012. The Cabinet can adjust elements of legislative acts without major legislative revisions by issuing Orders-in-Council (Simmons, 2010). In the twentieth century, the federal immigration department used its power to implement an Order-in-Council to prohibit landing of immigrants "belonging to any race deemed unsuited to the climate or requirements of Canada, or of immigrants of any specified class, occupation, or character." Between 1896 and 1911, immigration by African Americans, particularly farmers, at the turn of the twentieth century was discouraged by agents hired by the Canadian government (Canadian Council for Refugees, n.d.). In 1911, an Order-in-Council was drafted that would have explicitly excluded African Americans on the basis that they would be considered in the category of "any immigrant belonging to the Negro race, which race is deemed unsuitable to the climate and requirements of Canada" (CCR, n.d., p. 4). Although the Order was not made into law, decades of discriminatory practices were apparent as fewer than 1,000 of the 1 million Americans who immigrated to Canada were African Americans (CCR). In the 1930s and 1940s, discriminatory policy continued, denying protection to thousands of European Jews as they tried to flee Nazi Germany. The Canadian government rejected the lobbying efforts of its own citizens to change the restrictionist immigration policy (Abella & Troper, 2010).

The Immigration Act of 1952 maintained "preferred classes" categories for British and French citizens while setting quotas for immigrants from India, Pakistan, and Ceylon (now Sri Lanka). Generally, the Act did not explicitly discriminate against specific groups of immigrants but the Cabinet was allowed to deny people entry on the basis of nationality, customs, or other criteria thought to be unsuitable to Canadian climate or culture. In 1955, the Domestic Scheme created a special category of immigrants that enabled women from the British West Indies to immigrate as domestic servants. These women had to be single, aged 25–40 with at least a Grade 8 education, be in good health, and promise to work as a domestic for one year. The Canadian government had the right to expel workers at any time if they were deemed "not suitable," even though they had immigrant status. Women enrolled in the program were thus highly vulnerable to employer exploitation. Contemporary targeted immigration for domestic labour is outlined in the Live-In Caregiver Program (see "Theory in Practice" box) and the Seasonal Agricultural Worker Program, which provide conditional access to citizenship.

Prior to 1967, Canadian immigration policy was structured around encouraging permanent immigration from white Northern and Western European countries. This contributed to the myth of Canada as a "White nation state," ignoring its colonist roots and the heritages of the Indigenous Peoples within its borders. However, in an effort to increase the national population and support economic growth, a point system was introduced that opened pathways for people of colour to enter Canada. There were no longer "ethnic factors" in immigration but "points" allotted based on nine areas, including education (Grade 12), occupation, and financial resources. A high total point score strengthened a potential applicant's immigration application. The point system was an effort to remove all discrimination and prejudice from immigration policy, although it still privileged those with at least a Grade 12 education, French or English language proficiency, and access to financial resources. With the removal of ethnic factors, the pattern of immigration began to shift from European to Asian migrants.

The Immigration Act of 1976 outlined permanent refugee policy, instituting designated categories of Geneva Convention refugees, government-sponsored and privately sponsored refugees. Previously "prohibited" categories were replaced by "inadmissible" categories for those who could become a "burden" on social welfare or health services. Thus, people could be refused not based on country of origin but by having serious medical problems or a disability. The Act also established the *Private Sponsorship of Refugees Program*, which allowed Canadians to be involved directly in refugee resettlement. While many resettlement countries have a formal public-private partnership between the government and voluntary agencies to provide basic, short-term necessities of resettlement, only two resettlement countries, Australia and Canada, currently have categories that support direct participation by citizens in the resettlement process. In 1986, the United Nations awarded the Nansen Medal to the Canadian people "in recognition of their major and sustained contribution to the cause of refugees" for assistance provided to Vietnamese refugees through the Private Sponsorship of Refugees Program.

Under the Immigration and Refugee Protection Act (IRPA, 2001), while some protections were expanded, such as the expansion of refugee claims to include gender persecution and sexual orientation, others were curtailed. In 2004, the Canadian government

Safe Third Country
A provision of IRPA that designates the USA a "safe third country," forcing most refugee claimants who have transited through the USA to seek asylum there.

implemented the **Safe Third Country** provision of IRPA, designating the USA as a "safe third country," which effectively closed the land border to most refugee claimants.

Thus, refugee claimants cannot make an asylum claim in Canada if they have transited through the USA (unless one is an unaccompanied minor or has nuclear family members with status in Canada). Recent, significant amendments to IRPA have been in the form of the Balanced Refugee Reform Act (2010) and the Protecting Canada's Immigration System Act (2012). One important change was the implementation of a Refugee Appeal Division at the Immigration and Refugee Board of Canada (IRB). Previously, although included in IRPA, an appeals process was never implemented. While instituting an appeals process is a positive step, the amendments also require mandatory detention for those aged 16 and older who are considered irregular arrivals as well as those coming from "designated countries of origin," countries described by Citizenship and Immigration Canada (CIC) as places "where it is less likely for a person to be persecuted compared to other areas." Canada operates three detention facilities, in Vancouver, BC, Mississauga, ON, and Laval, QC.

Another sign that Canada's doors are closing is that recent immigration policy has made it more difficult for refugee claimants to reach Canada to apply for asylum. For example, after the Canadian government instituted visa requirements for entry in Canada for residents of Mexico and the Czech Republic, asylum claims dropped dramatically, from 7,606 in 2009 to 1,221 in 2010 to 677 in 2011 from Mexico and 2,101 in 2009 to 32 in 2010 to 27 in 2011 from the Czech Republic (CIC, 2011c). There are still long delays in the processing of applications for sponsored refugees as well as for family reunification applications for refugees' spouses and children.

Theoretical Approaches to Working with Migrant Populations

Theoretical approaches widely used in general social work practice are relevant and applicable when working with migrant populations. Settlement work with immigrants and refugees requires a holistic approach where the social worker addresses the person in his or her context as well as the strengths and stressors in the migration experience, ways in which cultural context shapes settlement, and the roles that power plays in the negotiation of life in a settlement country. (See Chapter 2 for more detailed information on theories used in social work practice).

Ecological Systems Theory

Because of its comprehensive examination of the ways in which the relationship between an individual and his or her immediate environment is mediated by forces originating from greater physical and social surroundings, ecological systems theory (Bronfenbrenner, 1979) has been traditionally adopted by social workers as an effective approach to practise. For migrants specifically, an ecological approach is particularly pertinent given its explorations of an individual's present as well as past contexts. Adopting an ecological approach requires the social worker to look at influential members in the migrant's environment as well as systemic factors that shape settlement. Adapted from science to human behaviour, Bronfenbrenner's ecological systems theory examines the fit between an individual and his or her myriad environments, or systems, as well as interactions that take place within and across systems (Furuto, 2004).

Strengths and Empowerment Approaches

The strengths and empowerment approaches enable social workers to access and utilize migrants' and their own knowledge, capabilities, and belief systems to work together toward mutually agreed-upon goals (Furuto, 2004). Coming to a country of settlement underscores the incredible strengths that migrants possess. Exploring these strengths and integrating them into practice with migrant clients mobilizes their strengths, rather than focusing on problems, and draws on the human capital they have brought with them from their country of origin (see "Theory in Practice" box on page 238). Working from a strengths perspective requires that social workers consider clients' talents, knowledge, capacities, capabilities, skills, aspirations, and family and community alongside their problems and challenges. Adopting a strengths approach in social work practice "highlights clients' strengths while being keenly aware of the ways that their experiences and life changes have been limited and shaped by larger, inequitable social forces" (Baines, 2007, p. 11).

Traditionally, an empowerment approach focuses on the process of increasing personal, interpersonal, or political power of people belonging to marginalized groups so that individuals can take action to improve their life conditions and to see themselves as competent. Social workers help individuals and groups become aware of their power status and foster awareness of how political structures affect individual and group experiences. They also focus their and clients' energies on the causes of powerlessness in order to eradicate them.

Integrating Culture into Practice Approaches

At the core of social work with migrants should be an approach that incorporates an immigrant or refugee's cultural context—that is, the ways in which a client's set of norms, values, attitudes, beliefs, and knowledge are taken into account in practice with attention to how the client's background intersects with the cultural context of the social worker. Attention should also be paid to the "skills that a social worker must possess in order to work effectively with clients who are from a different cultural background than the worker" (Potocky-Tripodi, 2002, p. 123). Lum (2007) outlines four key components of a framework that incorporates culture in order to guide practice and interventions: cultural awareness, knowledge acquisition, skill development, and inductive learning. The first component, cultural awareness, centres on the necessity of understanding ourselves before working with clients who have different cultural backgrounds. Social workers must be aware of their own life experiences, consciously asking what has informed their own life perspectives including personal biases. Self-reflection should be continual, underscoring the idea that integrating culture into practice is an ongoing process—each new client has his or her own unique context which can become the space for cultural dialogue (Mah & Ives, 2010).

Practical TIP

Learning about Other Cultures

TO LEARN ABOUT OTHER CULTURES, look for resources from government agencies and NGOs working with migrant populations. Other sources include discussions with members of the client's cultural group, volunteering at an ethnic community-based organization that represents the client's culture of origin, reading narratives written by immigrants and refugees, and watching documentaries by and/or about members of the cultural group.

Theory in Practice

EMPOWERMENT

EMPOWERMENT ON A MACRO LEVEL seeks to increase a sense of control over social and political structures. Historically, exploitation has been experienced primarily by people with low- and mid-level incomes, women, and people of colour. Canadian immigration history has demonstrated a reliance on gendered and racialized labour importation to meet labour needs (Choudry, Hanley, Jordan, Shragge, & Stiegman, 2009). Introduced in 1992, the Live-In Caregiver Program (LCP) brought in thousands of workers to meet Canada's labour shortages of affordable live-in child and older adult care. Given stringent education and financial resource requirements of current immigration policy, women rarely have the opportunity "to enter Canada as independent immigrants—the LCP is one of only a few options legally available to women without capital or skills recognized as economically beneficial to Canada" (Choudry, Hanley, Jordan, Shragge, & Stiegman, 2009, p. 76). Around 80 per cent of LCP workers are from the Philippines (Torres et al., 2012). From 2001 to 2010, approximately 82,000 live-in caregivers came to work in Canada.

Since 1991, PINAY (Filipino Women's Organization) has been organizing Filipino women caregivers at the grassroots level to reduce powerlessness and support immigrant workers' calls for social justice in the workplace and beyond. PINAY provides direct services to live-in caregivers from the Philippines living and working in Quebec who are experiencing issues with employers. In order to eventually obtain permanent residency and be able to reunite with their families in Canada, workers in the LCP need the equivalent of 24 out of 48 months of live-in employment; thus, they are in a difficult position to negotiate work-related issues, particularly with regard to salary, work hours, and vacation time. If they must change employer, it is the worker's responsibility to find another employer and apply for a new employer-specific visa. A delay can cost the worker his or her permanent residency. Attempting to exercise their full rights can place LCP workers' immigration possibilities in jeopardy, which has consequences for remittances to the country of origin and family reunification in Canada. PINAY puts empowerment-focused strategies into practice that address workers' feelings of powerlessness. Their strategies include (a) reducing workers' isolation through social events, strengthening connections among Filipinos and with broader Quebec communities; (b) educating LCP workers about their labour and immigration rights;

The second component is acquiring knowledge of the client's culture of origin and his or her migration trajectory. This includes learning about why the client left his or her country of origin; demographic characteristics, including characteristics of the diaspora, cultural traditions, norms and values; experiences of oppression; and particular strengths; and critically evaluating that knowledge. For example, a social worker can use the **culturagram** in an assessment to understand multiple facets of a client's migration experience (Congress, 2004). Other tools include a cultural genogram (see Chapter 4) (Warde, 2012) and Intercultural Assessment Guidelines (Roy & Montgomery, 2003).

The third component is skill development, where the social worker must adapt social work interventions with an appreciation of the complexity of issues of social justice within and between particular cultures. Particular attention should be paid to the intersection

culturagram Tools used for assessment with migrant clients (Congress, 2004), which can also be used by social workers themselves, to help uncover and understand cultural contexts and how those contexts shape world views and thus interactions between social workers and clients.

(c) doing rights advocacy with workers whose rights have been violated; (d) developing leadership among caregivers to represent their interests to the public and to the government; and (e) creating alliances with other organizations to support organizing efforts targeting equal rights for domestic workers. PINAY collaborates with numerous community organizations, including the Immigrant Workers' Centre (IWC) in Montreal, a community-based migrant labour rights organization that offers PINAY technical assistance on labour rights. In Quebec, domestic work is explicitly excluded from compensation in the case of work-related accidents or illness. Currently, workers in the LCP in Quebec have no support if faced with medical expenses, loss of income, and possibly loss of capacity to work if they are injured on the job. In collaboration with community partners, PINAY has enacted targeted campaigns to bring public awareness to the oppression and exploitation of LCP workers.

PINAY. Used with permission.

of social locations within cultural groups and the occurrences of oppression that may exist through social divisions such as gender, ethnicity, or educational status (Parrott, 2009). Social workers are frequently required to be skilled in both direct intervention with clients as well as intervening in systems that perpetuate discrimination and inequality (Russell & White, 2001). Social workers can draw on anti-oppression practice approaches to understand the social inequalities that are embedded within Canadian social structures, practices, and processes as well as those that exist in the client's country of origin. The fourth component is inductive learning which underscores the importance of reflecting on the knowledge and experiences gained through this process and weaving that back into practice learning. The social worker works back and forth between experiences with migrant clients and theoretical and practice models.

In Their Own Words

THE THREE "SPHERES"

MY SOCIAL WORK PRACTICE WITH refugees is shaped by three spheres: immigration and refugee policies, culturally oriented interventions, and social context. In practice, these spheres are intertwined. As social workers, we deal with immigration and refugee policies on the international and national levels. For the last three decades, Western countries including Canada have been implementing restrictive immigration measures towards refugee claimants, also called asylum seekers, either by blocking them before arrival to our borders or by making in-land life conditions very tough. I have seen how deeply these measures affect refugees, their life conditions, and their physical and psychological well-being. Many of my clients are refused medical care or employment opportunities because of their status as refugee claimants. The second sphere where I work revolves around culturally oriented interventions. For the last 10 years, I have been a social worker working with different cultural groups and diverse populations who require culturally and linguistically adapted practices. We all—social workers, our clients, our institutional settings—have cultural values, customs, and beliefs. Social work practice is challenged by these differences and constructed on the juxtaposition of at least two culturally different actors and their willingness to find common ground. When I work with my clients, I am always highly aware that my own understandings of issues such as child-rearing practices or marital roles, expectations, and responsibilities may be vastly different from theirs. This means developing enough of an understanding of one another's worldviews to be able to co-create a space in which work can happen. The third sphere is social context. A refugee, like any individual, may face different social problems, such as conjugal violence, mental health issues, financial difficulties, lack of adequate resources, and struggles with addiction. In addition to these challenges, and due to the precariousness of the immigration status, a refugee may also face social exclusion, racism, discrimination, and status-related problems.

Every intervention I co-formulate with my clients takes into consideration these three spheres, at the same time with the same importance. Interventions have to be constructed by exploring and analyzing how these spheres are intertwined with regard to a specific client/situation. From my perspective, this is the way to ensure a deep contextual understanding and thus help find an effective, culturally relevant solution. One of my clients is a victim of conjugal violence. She is also facing deportation. Her cultural and religious background is totally different from mine. The intervention with this client can only be constructed taking into consideration the intertwining of her immigration status and its critical consequences, our different cultural and religious backgrounds, and how they shape our professional relationship, the conjugal violence, and the suffering she is experiencing.

Grace Chammas is a social worker in Quebec.

Stages of Migration Framework

Settlement work with migrants requires understanding their experiences prior to arrival in Canada. One traditional approach to exploring these experiences is by examining significant issues and events that occur prior to leaving one's country of origin, during transit or flight from the country of origin, during "temporary" settlement, and in resettlement (Drachman, 1992).

Prior to Leaving One's Country of Origin

Understanding why migrants have left their countries of origin helps to direct and shape practice approaches as well as policies and services provided. Numerous theories have been developed to provide frameworks for understanding why people migrate. For example, push/pull theory describes migration as a product of the two interrelated processes: factors "pushing" one away from his or her country of origin include poor economic or educational prospects, high population density, an environmental crisis, or persecution (Folson, 2004). Pull factors to a country of settlement include increased demand for unskilled and skilled labour, presence of family members in the settlement country due to earlier migration, or a sense that the person would be safe and protected in that settlement country. Criticism of push/pull theory centres on its individual focus and failure to consider circumstances where migrants may have little choice. Other theoretical frameworks consider the imbalances of economic and political power in the world economy, and how these imbalances tend to exploit inequalities that exist between countries as well as issues surrounding migrants' decision-making processes in the context of previous colonial relationships (Folson, 2004). Other systemic factors shape international migration, such as the increased number of global conflicts or natural disasters (the latter, usually compounded by political and economic problems; McGregor, 1993), an increase in open borders (as within the European Union), and greater physical border controls (such as between the USA and Mexico). Regardless of the perspective drawn upon, it is important to remember that each person's migration trajectory is unique.

Refugees may not realize their precarious status until they are in the process of flight from their homeland. For some, it is not a sudden occurrence but the gradual erosion of civil and political rights where people are slowly denied access to jobs and services and cannot exercise basic rights, resulting in their need to leave their country of origin. Displacement can be precipitated by a loss of ownership of land, loss of income, food shortages, and other sanctions. Others may have more direct experiences, such as being subjected to or witnessing physical violence and/or prison detention. Immigrants may have the opportunity to apply for permanent residency as a skilled worker in Canada and so may have the opportunity to psychologically, emotionally, and economically prepare for leaving. Skilled workers are selected by the Canadian government or Quebec (depending on where one has applied) based on multiple criteria, including education history, work experience, and fluency in English and/or French. Leaving one's country of origin represents an event which, even if accomplished with planning and in safety, can affect one's emotional and cognitive well-being. Migrants are often faced with leaving family behind, and, for some, it is the first time that they are leaving their homeland.

Transit or Flight from the Country of Origin and Temporary Settlement

Transit or flight to the settlement country may or may not be of short duration. For refugees, this stage can range anywhere from weeks to years. The length of flight is shaped by whether there has been international recognition of the crisis in the refugee's country of origin, the level of armed conflict, geographical location of the country of origin, and presence of political unrest and/or armed conflict in neighbouring countries. For example, the period of flight for thousands of refugee boys and girls from Sudan lasted

Although conditions may be better than the war-zone country from which this woman fled, conditions of this Syrian refugee camp in Iraq are still a far cry from ideal.

nearly five years. Aged 8 to 18, they were separated from their families and fled southern Sudan, covering 1,000 miles on a journey from Sudan to Ethiopia, back to Sudan, and finally to Kakuma Refugee Camp in Kenya.

For some refugees, the length of time from leaving one's country of origin to arriving in a refugee camp may be short, but the length of time living in a refugee camp is long and may last decades or generations, as in the case of Palestinian refugees. Refugee camps may afford protection to those who have sought refuge there, but refugee camp conditions can also be dangerous and highly insecure. Moreover, there are specific concerns for women and children. Women refugees' risks include sexual violence, being forced to engage in sex work or "survival sex," and reduced access to training, literacy, or other development programs. Children may not have access to consistent educational programs. For a majority of the world's nearly 15 million refugees who cross only one border, the physical conditions from which they have fled are at times not much better than those to which they flee.

Settlement in a New Country

Settlement is often the final stage in the migration experience, although return to the country of origin is possible, either permanently (as in the case of repatriation for refugees) or temporarily, if, for example, the migration is cyclical. For refugees, resettlement is a formal process and requires the collaboration of multiple entities in local, provincial, national, and international spheres. The primary international organization that is mandated to protect refugees is the Office of the United Nations High Commissioner for Refugees (UNHCR). The UNHCR is tasked with protecting the rights of refugees, including ensuring that refugees are treated in accordance with recognized international standards of law, are able to apply for asylum, and are not forcibly returned to the countries from which they have fled. In settlement, while migrants no longer directly experience the issues that precipitated their departure from their homeland, they may be facing the stress that results from these experiences. For example, a risk factor such as trauma-related stress could hinder a refugee's integration into the settlement society, resulting in his or her isolation and detachment from broader societal connections outside one's cultural and linguistic community. **Integration**, the outcome of settlement regarded by settlement programs as the optimal mode for refugee well-being, is defined as participation in economic, social, cultural, and political areas of life of a settlement country while retaining connections to one's country of origin (Berry, 2002; Valtonen, 1999). **Acculturation** is the process of adaptation between two cultures—the ways in which traditions, values, language, and beliefs change as they come into contact with a new (usually dominant) culture.

Acculturation challenges in settlement stem from being faced with a different cultural environment, loss of relationships and property from the country of origin, and longing for home. Although acculturation does not have to be stressful, efforts to meet the challenges of this process can lead to emotional distress. Information and programming for migrants may not adequately reflect an understanding of their realities and, at times, can even serve to make acculturation in the settlement country more difficult if the assistance is neither useful nor appropriate (Fadiman, 1997).

Historical approaches to adapting to a new country focus on assimilation of the newcomer. Assimilation is defined as a process by which individuals' cultural identities are greatly minimized or eliminated, replaced by the cultural identities of the larger society.

Current trends, however, highlight the acceptance of involuntary or voluntary migrants rejecting assimilation and creating and promoting a neo-ethnic space instead (Lehrer & Sloan, 2003). Increased attachment to one's ethnicity from the country of origin has been found to be a protective factor in settlement, particularly buffering stresses on migrants' mental health (Beiser & Hou, 2006). The **Canadian Multiculturalism Act** (1988) provided recognition of Canada's diversity with regard to "race, national or ethnic origin, colour and religion [noting they are] a fundamental characteristic of Canadian society" and committed "to a policy of multiculturalism designed to preserve and enhance the multicultural heritage of Canadians" (http://laws-lois.justice.gc.ca/PDF/C-18.7.pdf). New conceptualizations of identity challenge the classic melting pot conceptualization by advancing the integration of identities (e.g., some could be Argentinean-Canadian or identify as a Canadian with "roots from Argentina"). This challenges what it means to be a Canadian, changing the definition of Canadian to allow for multiple interpretations where each is given significance, and reshaping the discourse on Canadian culture. However, even in the context of growing space for ethnic identity development, migrants still face discrimination. Discrimination can be based on country of origin, religious affiliation, and/or skin color, and can be found in multiple spheres, from employment to housing, from education to sports, creating barriers to integration. For example, migrants may be denied access to employment based on their ethnic background (Canadian Human Rights Commission, 2001). Migrants who are unemployed may see aspects of their cultural context blamed for their job status, rather than the social, political, and economic structures in which they live in Canada. As with all clients regardless of country of origin, social workers can advocate to contest the normalization of discrimination (Mullaly, 2010) by uncovering the origins of contemporary racism, xenophobia, and other mechanisms of exclusion.

integration Participation in economic, social, cultural, and political areas of life of a settlement country while retaining connections to one's country of origin.

acculturation A process of adaptation between two cultures, particularly how traditions, values, language, and beliefs change as they come into contact with a new (usually dominant) culture.

Canadian Multiculturalism Act Enacted in 1988, this act recognized Canada's diversity with regard to "race, national or ethnic origin, colour and religion [as] a fundamental characteristic of Canadian society" and committed "to a policy of multiculturalism designed to preserve and enhance the multicultural heritage of Canadians."

Settlement Issues Facing Migrants in Canada

Migration research has uncovered myriad factors that shape migrants' experiences in settlement and, thus, their integration. When migrants face the challenges brought on by these factors during settlement, their lives can evolve in one direction or another according to situational and human agency factors. These challenges could hinder or facilitate migrants' participation in economic, social, cultural, and political domains, that is, integration. Factors that challenge migrants during settlement and shape integration include (a) own goals and expectations, (b) language proficiency, (c) education/employment issues, (d) housing issues, (e) health issues, and (f) availability of social support.

Goals and Expectations

Effective social work practice with migrants addresses migrants' own short- and long-term goals and expectations of life in a settlement country and incorporates them into settlement programming. Migrants' self-reported goals should serve as foundational information for creating specific supports to assist in the process of reconciling goals of both settlement country governments and migrants. For example, self-reported goals of Vietnamese re-settled in Canada included stable employment, sustaining ties to family, cultural preservation, and educational opportunities for the second generation (Valtonen, 1999).

Those involved in policy-making and program implementation need to understand and acknowledge the weight that goals carry within cultures. This is particularly relevant for some populations regarding higher education and thus has significant implications for refugee resettlement policies that emphasize immediate employment. A "work first" policy implicitly promotes the notion among those working in settlement countries that higher education is a luxury for refugees as opposed to a viable opportunity to improve their personal resources thereby helping them find higher paying employment and upgrading from minimum-wage, no-, or low-skilled jobs. While optimism can be effective in helping migrants build their lives in a new country, unrealistic expectations can lead to dissatisfaction with life in the settlement country and, subsequently, a marginalized or isolated existence as well as to a sense that migrants have been cheated or misled.

Employment and Education

Finding work shortly after arrival is imperative and thus there is substantial pressure to accept any type of employment. However, there can be a fragile connection between a migrant's educational history and his or her labour market participation; disregarding the validity of foreign qualifications is a common grievance of migrants (Krahn, Derwing, Mulder, & Wilkinson, 2000). For some, the process of obtaining required documentation such as transcripts or diplomas from the country of origin can be time-consuming and difficult. For many refugees, it can be practically impossible to access the necessary documentation and apply for and receive reaccreditation considering the one-year timeline in which economic self-sufficiency is expected. Migrants with university and professional education or vocational accreditation must undergo evaluation and subsequent recertification, and/or formal recognition of their credentials in order to practise their professions or continue their studies. For example, completing Canadian accreditation requirements, such as those for medical doctors, could mean several years' additional work, a great underutilization of human capital.

Case STUDY

Refugee Youth and Education

EDUCATION IS A CHILD'S FUNDAMENTAL right. Typically, refugee children and youth have had their studies interrupted by the armed conflict in their country of origin. CIC data (2009) show that in 2009, a majority of refugees (approximately 65 per cent) 15 years and older had 12 years of schooling or less. Little is known about the educational outcomes of refugee youth once in Canada as their outcomes are typically hidden within "foreign-born" statistics. This hinders the creation and implementation of specific supports for refugee students that incorporate their educational disruptions and possible traumatic experiences before arrival in Canada.

A collaborative, community-based research project in Toronto (Shakya et al., 2010) gathered perspectives of refugee youth, ages 16–24, from three groups: Afghan, Karen, and Sudanese to illuminate post-migration educational gaps and challenges that refugee youth encounter. A key element was the intention to engage refugee youth in an authentic partnership to create solutions to challenges they face. Researchers collaborated with 8 refugee youth peer researchers and conducted 10 focus groups and 13 interviews with refugee youth. Key findings included:

Educational aspirations of refugee youth: Afghan, Karen, and Sudanese youth respondents highlighted the centrality of education to their well-being as well as that of their families. Respondents contrasted their opportunities in Canada with the restricted educational opportunities in their countries of origin or refugee camps due to war. Unlike situations in their countries of origin or refugee camps where they faced discrimination regardless of educational attainment, respondents saw a strong connection between being educated and increased job opportunities and thus quality of life in Canada.

Challenges and barriers to education in Canada for refugee youth: Refugee youth described the tensions in balancing their own educational goals with family responsibilities, particularly with regard to relationships with parents and grandparents who had lower literacy levels and little proficiency in English or French. Participants' parents had limited capacity to support their children academically and provide them with effective educational guidance regarding courses of study. Respondents also relayed that they felt as if they were funnelled into particular educational "streams" or areas of study not based on their educational goals or academic ability but on their refugee status as well as bias against their educational attainment in their countries of origin. They also struggled with English proficiency and did not feel they received effective linguistic support.

Strategies refugee youth utilized to help attain their educational goals included seeking support from siblings or peers to bridge the information and guidance gap, searching for services focused on education for refugees, and resolutely claiming their right to advocate for themselves and others with regard to their educational goals. The advocacy piece can be a challenge for refugees in a resettlement system guided by policies that seem to "serve to entrench rather than overcome the vulnerabilities that refugees face" (Shakya et al., 2010, p. 74).

Language

Proficiency in English and/or French is essential to integration in Canada, particularly as it relates to employment, education focused on improving job marketability, training opportunities, and social involvement outside the migrant's linguistic community. In 2009, 44.4 per cent of refugees had no English or French proficiency upon arrival in Canada; this percentage was 21.1 per cent for economic immigrants in the same year (Shakya et al., 2010). Lacking English or French proficiency means that most jobs that will be available to migrants will be low paid and/or provide little opportunity for growth and skill development (Boyd & Cao, 2009). These jobs can mire them in low-wage sectors of the labour market from which upward mobility is difficult (Korac, 2001). Since 1992, the Language Instruction for Newcomers to Canada (LINC) program has provided funding to service provider organizations that offer English or French language instruction to immigrant adults for up to three years from the time they begin the training. One criticism of LINC is that the training is primarily basic-level English or French, and most immigrants need advanced or employment-specific language training in order to access employment. A lack of strong English or French fluency can prevent migrants from obtaining apprenticeships and entering the mainstream job market as well as limiting options to those solely within their linguistic community.

Learning English or French can be a major challenge to refugees who have experienced traumatic events. Trauma experiences during the process of fleeing the country of origin have been found to affect memory and concentration (Miller et al., 2002). Memory difficulties greatly impair one's ability to learn a new language. Language instruction is designed to give migrants a working knowledge of the language and seldom incorporates elements that would address problems related to impaired memory and diminished concentration (Miller et al.). An inability to communicate in English or French can also create a mental health burden and contribute to refugees' feelings of social isolation.

Health

Social workers need to have an understanding of health implications of voluntary and involuntary migration (Montgomery, 2008) as well as coping and adjustment processes associated with migration. Practitioners working with migrant populations require specialized training that highlights migrants' unique needs (Potocky-Tripodi, 2002) and provides them with skills and strategies that sensitize them to discrimination and cultural context (Lyons & Stathopoulos, 2001) to better enable them to provide effective practice with migrant clients. Limited English or French affects migrants' access to and understanding of health care and social services. In some cases, migrants may not even be literate in the language of their country of origin. Cultural differences and misunderstandings created by language barriers could be problematic when communicating information regarding prevention, diagnosis, treatment, or other service aspects. One's cultural beliefs shape health perceptions, including how one handles a diagnosis and approaches to treatment.

Settlement programs are traditionally focused on meeting subsistence needs; physical and mental health needs considered "nonemergency" are often neglected due to a lack of available financial and technical resources as well as language and cultural barriers. However, migrants, particularly refugees, may have experienced traumatic events. Witnessing, experiencing, and/or confronting violence can create extreme stress that is often translated into debilitating symptoms that can occur around the time of the traumatic event(s) or years afterwards. For example, one study found that Bosnian refugees who had resettled in Canada suffered from sleep difficulties, eating and digestive disorders, increased smoking, anxiety, depression, and anger (Kopinak, 1999). Social workers should keep in mind the possibility of traumatic experiences of a refugee client and the ways in which those experiences could lead to compromised mental and physical health. Compromised physical and mental health particularly affects economic participation where migrants must find employment in a short timeframe and become economically self-sufficient.

Housing

Housing can be a significant stressor in settlement. Oftentimes there are problems of affordability, availability (in general or of appropriately sized housing), and safety. Migrants may face obstacles to emergency or temporary shelters due to language barriers and lack of culturally appropriate services, and may have significantly fewer resources to address housing challenges. Traumatic stress, racism, language difficulties, unemployment or underemployment and subsequent poverty, lack of recognition for qualifications, experience, or skills acquired in the country of origin, and the absence of support networks are significant factors in contributing to migrants' precarious housing and homelessness. A recent study in Montreal on homelessness among migrant women found that financial insecurity, immigration status, exploitation, and physical illness were central reasons for ongoing housing insecurity (Walsh, Hanley, Ives, Hordyk, & Mahano, 2011).

Housing can also be problematic if a migrant is an adult with no dependents (if they are permanent residents) as migrants with families are given priority for public housing and other government subsidies. Finding appropriate housing for large families seeking to rent usually results in accommodation shared with other people (not necessarily from the same region) in single-family houses or in inappropriately sized housing for families with several children. Even when suitably sized housing is available, the suitability of the location may be questionable in terms of access to one's employment, language instruction, or physical safety.

Social Support

Social networks, key to the process of adaptation of migrants in a settlement society, are understood as sets of interpersonal links created by kinship, friendship, and shared national, ethnic, and cultural origin that connect migrants and non-migrants in destination areas (Korac, 2001). Social support can be the informal assistance, compassion, and information that are available and accessible from family, friends, community, and ethnic groups. Informal support from relatives, friends, and the local community can provide opportunities for assistance in addressing various settlement issues and relieving social isolation. Some migrants rely on ethnic social networks for employment opportunities. For example, in Montreal, Lam (1996) found that ethnic small businesses were one of the few ways a refugee could achieve economic and occupational mobility, a strategy used by Vietnamese refugees to address the problem of restricted access to economic opportunities on the part of the cultural majority. Social support can also be provided by institutional entities such as ethnic community organizations, resettlement and public welfare agencies, and religious congregations.

Whereas some migrants settle with nuclear and/or extended families relatively intact, other migrants' social networks have been left behind in the home country. Migrants who lack social support may struggle with loneliness, isolation, and, as a result, marginalization. Those who were used to many supportive social interactions and relationships on a daily basis grapple with their networks' disintegration. Having access to the practical and psychological support of family, community members, and other informal ethnic networks in Canada can decrease mental health issues and decrease stress levels, which in turn can reduce the intensity and likelihood of mental illness.

Settlement Services for Refugees and Immigrants

Settlement services are federally funded but delivered at the local level by community-based service providers. Organizational settings that provide formal settlement assistance and resources include settlement organizations, public welfare agencies, ethnic community-based organizations, and religious congregations. These entities work with migrants by making available and/or providing access to resources, services, and programs for settlement as well as helping migrants maintain their own culture and navigate the multiple cultural contexts of Canada. For example, the federally funded Immigrant Settlement and Adaptation Program (ISAP) supports organizations across Canada that provide services to migrant communities and facilitate community integration.

Settlement organizations and public welfare agencies have the opportunity to make significant contributions to the well-being of migrants. All provinces and territories have some type of settlement service for migrants, although eligibility for these services depends on the category to which a migrant belongs (See Recommended Websites for CIC links). Settlement programs direct their energies toward economic and social integration, such as assistance in finding employment and job training. For example, in Ontario, immigrants are helped by OCASI, the Ontario Council of Agencies Serving Immigrants. OCASI provides assistance with interpreting and translating documents, completing forms and applications, and providing information about community resources. In the Toronto and Ottawa areas, ISAP-funded Newcomer Information Centres (NICs) assist migrants upon arrival with the provision of information and referrals and access to a resource library (Biles, Burstein, & Frideres, 2008).

There are numerous ways social workers can utilize community-based resources to address challenges within the settlement process. Support organizations such as ethnic community-based organizations (ECBOs; also called ethno-specific organizations) are entities operated by migrant communities. ECBOs, widely used in Canada and in other settlement countries, are supported by public funding to provide social services directed toward settlement policy goals and have been found to be a valuable component in migrant communities by providing human services and strengthening ethnic support systems (Ahearn, 2000).

Vulnerable Groups

Particular groups within the migrant population require distinct supports based on migration trajectory, experiences in the country of origin, social location, and legal status in Canada. Some of these groups are described below. These groups are not mutually exclusive; members of any of these groups could also be members of other groups. The complex intersectionality of migrants' lives underscores the important role social workers play in weaving together multiple sources of knowledge and multiple levels of intervention needed in working with migrant clients.

Gender and Migration

Male and female migrants experience settlement differently due to their gender-shaped experiences of life before leaving their countries of origin, experiences in transit, and settlement. For example, although all refugees face the threat of torture and/or death, women and girl refugees face the additional risks of sexual violence, engaging in sex work and

survival sex, and having limited access to training, literacy, or other development programs in refugee camps. In any refugee population, approximately 50 per cent of the
uprooted people are women and girls. In 2011, approximately 25,000 asylum seekers were
in Canada, of which nearly half (11,495) were women (CIC, 2011d). Women and girls
may experience the trauma of harassment and physical punishment and be prime targets
for rape and sexual assault, compounding their traumatic experiences. Women and girls
who experience sexual violence during war may not receive psychosocial support or any
type of medical care.

Female migrants can face great difficulty during settlement when entering the
labour market in settlement countries. Ingrained gender stratification in countries of
origin translates into fewer opportunities for women for education and work experience, saddling them with lower levels of education than those of men and limited
labour market skills and experiences. Migrant women in Canada experience barriers
to health and social services, particularly those who have low-income jobs with limited flexibility and heavy caregiving demands (Stewart et al., 2006). These additional
responsibilities of child care and care for other dependents add to their challenges
(Bloch, Galvin, & Harrell-Bond, 2000). These challenges can also be shaped by religious and traditional roles in the family.

Social workers should be aware of the condition of migrant women and girls' support
networks. Women migrants may have difficulty establishing networks, as often they follow
partners, having to work harder than their spouses to re-establish social and/or professional networks (Salaff & Greve, 2004). Without a support network, migrant women are also
vulnerable to domestic violence. A coalition advocating for immigrant and refugee rights
and services found that 25 per cent of Filipinas and 35 per cent of Latinas are victims of
spousal abuse (Cho, 1996). A Quebec Parliamentary commission found that migrant
women were overrepresented in cases of conjugal violence appearing before the courts,
attributing this to family stress during the settlement process (CEFJI, 2004) and to women
whose legal status is dependent upon their husband's sponsorship (Smith, 2003). Social
workers can counter discriminatory practices against women migrants by promoting equal
opportunity in employment, education, and health, recognizing that these opportunities
exist within a framework of intersecting diversities of race, gender, sexual orientation,
socio-economic status, religion, and other social locations.

Migrants and Trafficking

Canada is a source, transit, and destination country for trafficking. The RCMP estimates
that 800 persons are trafficked into Canada annually, but estimates by NGOs are in the
thousands. The range of estimates stems from disagreement over the definition of trafficking. Article 3 of the Protocol to Prevent, Suppress and Punish Trafficking in Persons,
Especially Women and Children, which supplements the United Nations Convention
Against Transnational Organized Crime, defines trafficking in persons as

> [t]he recruitment, transportation, transfer, harbouring or receipt of persons, by
> means of the threat or use of force or other forms of coercion, of abduction, of
> fraud, of deception, of the abuse of power or of a position of vulnerability or of
> the giving or receiving of payments or benefits to achieve the consent of a person
> having control over another person, for the purpose of exploitation.

The disagreement centres around what elements must be present to classify a particular situation as trafficking in persons. How should people who have been smuggled into

Timea Nagy immigrated to Toronto, Canada from Budapest, Hungary in hopes of earning extra income, but instead, she was victim to human trafficking. As a strong survivor, Timea founded Walk With Me, an organization supporting human-trafficking victims in Canada.

Canada and then coerced into forced labour be categorized? Without in-depth knowledge of the context in the country of origin, it is unclear as to whether a migrant's arrival in Canada was voluntary or forced. Definitions dictate eligibility—what legal status a person holds and for which services a person is eligible. However, the bottom line is that trafficking in persons is a human rights violation, and those affected by trafficking may need legal assistance, physical and mental health resources, housing, and other supports.

Section 118 of the Immigration and Refugee Protection Act (2002) prohibits transnational human trafficking and imposes a maximum penalty of life imprisonment and a fine of up to $1 million. On a federal level, Citizenship and Immigration Canada (CIC) can provide trafficked persons with a special temporary resident permit (TRP) which gives them legal immigration status in Canada and provides eligibility for health benefits and counselling under the Interim Federal Health Program as well as applying for a work permit (CIC, n.d.). While the majority of trafficked persons are foreign-born, it is critical to highlight that Canadian-born women and girls are trafficked for commercial sexual exploitation across the country as well as into the USA, with Indigenous women and girls being especially vulnerable (US Dept. of State, 2012). Primary responsibility for direct service provision for trafficked persons lies with provincial and territorial governments. Services, which include access to shelters, short-term counselling, and legal assistance, are provided through general crime victim services, for which trafficked persons are eligible. Highlighting the complex service needs of trafficked clients, provincial and territorial governments often collaborate with law enforcement and community-based organizations. For example, the non-profit Action Coalition on Human Trafficking (ACT Alberta) brings together law enforcement, government agencies, NGOs, and volunteers to identify and respond to human trafficking.

Practical TIP

Trafficking

SOCIAL WORK PRACTICE WITH TRAFFICKED persons can include

- establishing a dependable safety network for trafficked persons to utilize and en-suring all their basic needs are met;
- ensuring privacy and confidentiality to protect trafficked persons and their fam-ilies and friends;
- soliciting support of other social workers, medical experts, and psychologists who are trained in human trafficking and can provide trauma-specific therapy;
- attending to trafficked persons' physical well-being;
- providing collaborative, culturally integrated therapies;
- fostering an empowering environment in which trafficked persons actively par-ticipate as consumers of therapeutic and other services;
- assessing trafficked persons for self-injurious and suicidal behaviour;
- screening for traumatic stress, substance abuse/dependence, depression, and anxiety that can develop as a result of being trafficked;
- providing unconditional support, especially amidst trafficked persons' potential denial, distrust, reticence, shame, or anger;
- working towards social and familial reintegration;
- rebuilding identity;
- re-establishing skill-sets, self-esteem, and personal interests.

Source: US Dept. of State, Trafficking in Persons, 2012.

Unaccompanied Minors

Of the 33.9 million people of concern to UNHCR, almost half are children. These include children who are refugees, asylum seekers, and stateless persons, returnees, and internally displaced children. **Unaccompanied minors**, under 18 years of age, arrive in a potential settlement country without the presence of an adult. **Separated minors** may be with an adult who is not a parent or previous primary caregiver. Even though in the presence of an adult, a separated minor can still be considered a "person of concern" as the accompanying adult may not be able to adequately provide for the child or might be a trafficker. From 2000–2004, 1,087 unaccompanied minors and 1,683 separated children arrived in Canada, accounting for 1.61 per cent of the total refugee claimant population (Wouk, Yu, Roach, Thomson, & Harris, 2006). The mean age of new arrivals was 15 and the top countries of origin were Sri Lanka, China, Burundi, Somalia, and Colombia.

Canada was the first country to develop guidelines for dealing with unaccompan-ied minors (Ali, 2006). A designated representative (DR) must represent any minor ap-pearing in proceedings before the Immigration and Refugee Board (IRB) (Dauvergne, 2012). Often, social workers fill this role. The three provinces that receive the great-est number of separated children (Quebec, British Columbia, and Ontario) provide a combination of legal and social services to unaccompanied minors. In Quebec, the *Programme régional d'accueil et d'intégration des demandeurs d'asile* (PRAIDA), a regional program specializing in the reception and integration of asylum seekers, is

unaccompanied minors Children under 18 years of age who arrive in a potential settlement country without the presence of an adult.

separated minors Children who may be with an adult who is not a parent or previous primary caregiver.

notified by CIC when an unaccompanied minor arrives. Each minor is assigned two case workers: one for the IRB and one for settlement services. In British Columbia, the Ministry of Children and Family Development has a Migrant Services team that provides representation at IRB hearings as well as reception, screening, and placement services. In Ontario, a panel composed primarily of immigration lawyers acts as the DR for unaccompanied minors before the IRB (Elgersma, 2007) and the Children's Aid Society and the Catholic Children's Aid Society provide child protection services for minors up to age 16. Minors may be housed in group homes, foster homes, apartments, or in detention (if deemed necessary as a last resort by the IRB). Such differences occur because unaccompanied minors fall under the realm of child welfare, a provincial jurisdiction. A national policy on unaccompanied minors and separated children has yet to be established in Canada.

Unaccompanied and separated children have a right to attend school, although this is not always recognized and respected by school administrations (Elgersma, 2007). It can be difficult for unaccompanied and separated minors to comply with routine school requirements (e.g., accessing immunization records, obtaining parental signatures) and they can have difficulty in obtaining some community services, such as library cards or bank accounts (Montgomery, 2002). Social workers can actively work with school administrators and educators to bridge services for unaccompanied and separated minors, assisting in referrals to and collaboration across agencies.

Lesbian, Gay, Bisexual, Transgender, and Queer (LGBTQ) Immigrants and Refugees

Presently, LGBTQ individuals can potentially gain residency and eventually citizenship in Canada through all categories identified within the Immigration and Refugee Protection Act (2002). LGBTQ individuals can enter Canada under the family class, same-sex partner sponsorship, or economic class, or as a skilled worker, temporary worker, and/or refugee claimant. Although Canada eliminated openly discriminating against LGBTQ individuals within immigration policies in 1977, there still remain areas of immigration and refugee policy where LGBTQ individuals encounter particular challenges, both in gaining status and in their settlement experience. This is especially the case for LGBTQ refugees.

Soon after the first gay refugee was accepted under grounds of persecution based on sexual orientation in 1991, the Supreme Court of Canada ruled in 1993 that sexual orientation was valid grounds to claim refugee status (LaViolette, 2009). However, LGBTQ refugee claimants have to "prove" their sexual and/or gender identity, with IRB members often determining refugee claims based on rigid stereotypes related to appearance and behavior (Lee & Brotman, 2011). For example, stereotypically masculine-looking men were not believed to be gay and stereotypically feminine-looking women have not been believed to be lesbian. Bisexual refugee claimants have been found to be especially unsuccessful in gaining status, as IRB decision-makers either did not believe in the claimant's bisexuality, held negative views about bisexuality, or believed that a claimant's bisexuality could remain invisible (Rehaag, 2009). More recently, Canadian refugee law appears to have shifted, with the Federal Court having made several decisions which have acknowledged the contextual and fluid nature of sexuality (Berg & Millbank, 2009). In addition, many refugees' claims have failed not because of an inability to prove their sexual orientation or gender identity, but because of lack of country conditions documentation (related to LGBTQ human rights violations), suggested availability of state protection and internal flight alternatives, and identifying some forms of violence as discrimination and not persecution (LaViolette, 2009).

Working with LGBTQ clients who have migrated to Canada requires the social worker to understand how their sexual and/or gender identity has shaped their perceptions of self and their experiences of migration. Did they enter Canada as children, youth, or adults? To what extent were they able to be open about their sexuality and/or gender identity in their country of origin? Are they in Canada because they had been persecuted for their sexual orientation and/or gender identity? If a client immigrated to Canada with their heterosexual parents or hid their sexual and/or gender identity when living in their country of origin, there may be a number of reasons for why they may be reticent to seek out health and/or social services that would respond to their multiple identities (for example, as immigrant and LGBTQ). In Ontario, the Positive Spaces program recommends creating a recognizably welcoming environment, using inclusive language, reporting incidences of homophobic or transphobic violence, gathering and sharing information about homophobia and transphobia, and seeking training opportunities to counter discriminatory attitudes and actions.

Refugee and Immigrant Older Adults

Migrant older adults make significant social and economic contributions to their families and communities, apart from age, health status, or ability to work. They are often responsible for family caregiving activities, enabling other family members to join the paid workforce. Yet there are few migrant older adult-focused, culturally integrated services beyond housing, income support, and health-care services that are given to the family (Chenoweth & Burdick, 2001). The confluence of biological and contextual factors can accelerate the aging process for migrants. The World Health Organization defines refugee older adults as persons 60 years or older. CIC provides a more detailed breakdown that better highlights the distinct challenges migrant elders face along the life cycle. Migrant older adults are categorized long term (landed in Canada aged 40–49 years), short term (landed in Canada aged 50–59 years), and immediate (landed in Canada aged 60+ years) (Dempsey, 2005). Those who have arrived in Canada through the Family Class have access to almost all programs and benefits, including health benefits, with the exception of pension benefits (Old Age Pension, Guaranteed Income Supplement, CPP/RRQ) for the first 10 years in Canada. After 10 years, they are eligible for the Universal Pension. Older adults' sponsors are financially responsible for them for 10 years; during that period, any social welfare benefits must be reimbursed by the sponsor. Migrant older adults have no access to low-cost housing, and long-term care costs must be paid by the older adult or sponsor.

While migrant older adults share concerns that older adults in Canada might have, migrant older adults also face challenges related to service utilization, seeking employment in a labour market that may not recognize their work experience in the country of origin, family expectations, loss or reduction of social support networks, and language barriers. Settlement situations can be complicated to manage without external help from settlement workers. While services to assist migrant older adults in the settlement process might be available and needed, they might be reluctant to utilize these services. Limited English or French proficiency will limit older adults' access to employment and broader social networks, and in many cases, limit those networks to the ethnic community to which the family belongs. While ethnic networks are socially dynamic and can provide social support and referrals to services and employment perhaps in the migrant older adult's language of origin, these networks can also be exploitative, depending on the relationships and characteristics of the individuals or groups involved. For example, migrant older adults who are sponsored and are not proficient in English or French are highly dependent on their families and can be vulnerable to mistreatment or abuse. Social workers working with migrant older adults need to consider the family context holistically and the types and levels of supports the older adult is able to access. Multiple resources from service organizations across sectors, ECBOs, and faith-based organizations should be accessed to support their complex needs, thereby working to reduce isolation, decrease the likelihood of elder abuse, and strengthen older adults in their traditional position in families.

Migrants with Disabilities

The World Health Organization estimates that 15.6 per cent of any population is composed of persons with disabilities, with statistics ranging from 11.8 per cent in countries with higher average incomes to 18 per cent in countries with lower incomes (WHO, 2011). Forced migration is challenging for migrants with disabilities as they may face barriers to access and participation in humanitarian and other relevant programs due to physical, social, economic, cultural, and political discrimination (UNHCR, 2011). Moreover, they are often overlooked during needs assessments, which can translate into decreased access to health and support services (Women's Refugee Commission, n.d.).

Immigration legislation has created multiple barriers for people with disabilities who want to immigrate to Canada. Early legislation explicitly excluded immigration by those who were categorized as belonging to so-called "Prohibited Classes," based on ableist notions of potential social dependence that ignored contributions that people with disabilities make (Hanes, 2011). Although language changed from "Prohibited" to "Inadmissible," in the Immigration Act of 1976, persons with disabilities were still excluded under Section 19(1). This exclusion centred around whether the potential immigrant "might be reasonably expected to cause excessive demands on health or social services . . ." Article 38 of the Immigration and Refugee Protection Act (2002) made this excessive demand clause even more explicit, outlining that application for permanent residence would not be accepted if a person's health were a danger to public health or safety or would cause excessive demand on health or social services in Canada. This article has been used to deny permanent residence to migrant applicants. However, individuals who have applied for a permanent resident visa as a Convention refugee or a person in similar circumstances are exempt from the excessive demand clause. The Council of Canadians with Disabilities continues to advocate for Canada to make a commitment to the UNHCR to accept at least 50 refugees with disabilities each year out of the more than 12,000 resettled annually.

Survivors of Torture

For refugees who have experienced physical and psychological torture, settlement acculturation challenges are compounded by the need to address short- and long-term physical and psychological sequelae from torture. Moreover, experiences of torture may make it more difficult to trust those who are trying to provide help. Torture is defined by the UN Convention Against Torture and Other Cruel, Inhuman or Degrading Treatment or Punishment (entered into force and ratified by Canada in 1987) as

> . . . any act by which severe pain or suffering, whether physical or mental, is intentionally inflicted on a person for such purposes as obtaining from him or a third person information or a confession, punishing him for an act he or a third person has committed or is suspected of having committed, or intimidating or coercing him or a third person, or for any reason based on discrimination of any kind, when such pain or suffering is inflicted by or at the instigation of or with the consent or acquiescence of a public official or other person acting in an official capacity.

There are never circumstances in which torture is justified. The UN Convention Against Torture clearly states that, "No exceptional circumstances whatsoever, [. . .] may be invoked as a justification of torture" (Article 2, 2). Both physical and psychological torture can have long-lasting health consequences and negatively affect settlement (Lie, 2002). Social work practice with refugees should include a screening for torture in order to provide targeted assistance for torture's short- and long-term physical and psychological consequences. Consequences may include nightmares, chronic pain, anxiety, irritability, flashbacks, depression, impaired memory or memory loss, sexual dysfunction, and lack of self-esteem. There are specialized agencies across Canada that work with survivors of torture. For example, funded by federal, provincial, and municipal government agencies, the Canadian Centre for Victims of Torture (CCVT; www.ccvt.org) in Toronto has worked with over 14,000 torture survivors from 136 countries since 1977.

Social workers may bear witness, sometimes repeatedly, to people's stories of torture, which may invoke detachment from the client, colleagues, and/or supervisors (Profitt, 2008). There should be recognition for work-related stress reactions that social workers might have as a result of working with people who have been affected by extreme hardships, and strategies for self-care should be in place to reduce incidence of burnout (Urdang, 2010), compassion fatigue (Radey & Figley, 2007), and/or vicarious traumatization (Dane, 2002).

Conclusion

Immigrants and refugees settling in Canada share challenging experiences of relocation, separation, and adjustment in a different cultural context. This chapter has reviewed approaches to working with refugee and immigrant clients, areas where migrants need support, and groups within the migrant populations that call for particular knowledge and expertise. Also presented was the rationale for social workers working with migrant populations to learn about the specific cultures their clients represent as well as explore their own cultural contexts and the ways in which their contexts intersect with those of their clients.

QUESTIONS FOR CRITICAL THOUGHT

1. What are some differences between immigrants and refugees? In what ways are their experiences similar? In what ways can differences in status influence public perceptions of migrants?
2. What biases might you have about a client's country of origin/religious faith/cultural traditions? How might you misinterpret interactions with or behaviours of a client based on your own cultural norms?
3. How would you describe a "typical Canadian" to a migrant who has just arrived in Canada? Discuss with a classmate how your description intersects with your own cultural context and social location.
4. Describe the ways in which economic concerns, humanitarian issues, foreign policy, and general public opinion shape Canadian migration policy.
5. Describe a cultural barrier and a structural barrier migrants might face in the utilization of health and/or social services.
6. The chapter reviewed several groups within the migrant population that require particular supports. What are some other migrant groups that would benefit from services targeted to their distinct experiences?

RECOMMENDED READINGS

Biles, J., Burstein, M. & Frideres, J. (2008). *Immigration and integration in Canada in the twenty-first century.* Montreal: McGill-Queen's University Press. This collection of research-based essays focuses on the multiple conceptualizations of immigrant integration across Canada.

Showler, P. (2006). *Refugee sandwich: Stories of exile and asylum.* Montreal: McGill-Queen's University Press. Written by a former chairperson of the IRB of Canada, these fictional vignettes give insight into the Canadian refugee determination system from the perspectives of claimants and adjudicators.

Simmons, A.B. (2010). *Immigration and Canada: Global and transnational perspectives.* Toronto: Canadian Scholars' Press. This book offers contextualized discussions of contemporary immigration in Canada through an overview of the evolution of Canadian immigration and covers key debates around immigration policy, immigrant employment, and issues affecting different migrant populations.

Valtonen, K. (2008). *Social work and migration: Immigrant and refugee settlement and integration.* Surrey, England: Ashgate. The author focuses on social work practice with migrants in settlement countries through the presentation of theoretical frameworks and discussion of practice modalities, intergenerational issues, policy development, and subsequent settlement programming.

RECOMMENDED WEBSITES

The Canadian Council for Refugees
www.ccrweb.ca
The Canadian Council for Refugees is a non-profit umbrella organization focused on the rights and protection of refugees in Canada and globally and to refugee and immigrant settlement in Canada.

Citizenship and Immigration Canada
www.cic.gc.ca and **www.cic.gc.ca/english/refugees/outside/resettle-providers.asp**
The Citizenship and Immigration Canada homepage provides resources, statistics, and detailed information regarding the application processes for immigrants and refugees. Also available is a list of Resettlement Assistance Program Service Provider Organizations across Canada with their contact information.

Division of Social and Transcultural Psychiatry, McGill University
http://www.mcgill.ca/tcpsych/
The Division of Social and Transcultural Psychiatry, McGill University, is a network of scholars and clinicians devoted to promoting research, training, and consultation in social and cultural psychiatry. Broad themes of research and training include (a) social causes and consequences of psychiatric disorders, (b) mental health of immigrants and refugees, Indigenous Peoples, and ethnocultural minorities, and (c) cultural critiques of Western psychiatric theory and practice.

Migration Policy Institute
www.migrationinformation.org
This website collects data from numerous global organizations and governments, offering global analysis of international migration and refugee trends, specific country descriptions of their migration programs, and information from the Migration Policy Institute Data Hub. A free, online newsletter is available which provides links to research papers and just-released statistical data.

The United Nations High Commissioner for Refugees
www.unhcr.org
The United Nations High Commissioner for Refugees (UNHCR) website provides detailed information on UNHCR programs around the world, targeted work with specific populations and a wealth of online resources, including global statistics and operational data.

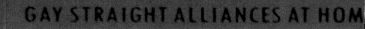

Social Work and Sexual and Gender Diversity

Edward Ou Jin Lee, McGill University
Shari Brotman, McGill University

LEARNING OBJECTIVES

- To understand the historical, social, structural, and political dimensions of sexual and gender identity and expression in Canada and around the world.

- To identify and explore the terms used to label sexual and gender identity.

- To explore the diverse identities and expressions of sexuality and gender within the Canadian context.

- To increase understanding of the experiences of social injustice, exclusion and discrimination experienced by two-spirited, lesbian, gay, bisexual, trans, and queer (TSLGBTQ) individuals.

- To describe and apply intersectionality as a central theoretical framework for understanding TSLGBTQ individuals and their realities.

- To explore the barriers facing TSLGBTQ individuals across health-care and social service settings.

- To identify the relationship between institutional power and social location when engaging in social work practice with TSLGBTQ individuals.

- To identify and explore the ways in which TSLGBTQ individuals and communities engage in individual and social advocacy to resist oppression.

- To identify community, provincial, and national resources that may assist social workers who work with TSLGBTQ individuals.

Chapter Outline

This chapter introduces the everyday realities of two-spirited, lesbian, gay, bisexual, trans-gendered, and queer (TSLGBTQ) individuals, and the theoretical and practice approaches used by social workers working with these communities. By engaging with the theoretical framework of **intersectionality**, we recognize and affirm the diversity of queer and trans people and communities. Intersecting systems of oppression reinforce, multiply, or complicate each other, in context and site-specific ways. Intersectionality reveals the ways in which new forms of exclusion and marginalization are created from mutually reinforcing systems of oppression, complicating one's social location and multiple identity formation.

In addition, this chapter explores key policy and practice concerns when working with TSLGBTQ individuals across multiple health-care and social service settings. Case studies and vignettes are used throughout in order to highlight key aspects of working with TSLGBTQ individuals. The chapter concludes with information about resources to assist practitioners working with TSLGBTQ individuals.

intersectionality Systems of oppression based on race, class, gender, ability, religion, citizenship status, and sexual/gender identity that intersect with each other.

Taking Up Sexual and Gender Identity Terms

This chapter uses the terms TSLGBTQ due to their common social usage. Queer, trans, and sexual minority are also used as umbrella terms. We shift between these terms in order to call attention to the limitations of any one term in capturing the complex ways in which people self-identify and express sexual and gender diversity.

With so many terms related to sexual and gender identity and debate about terminology, which terms should social workers use in practice? The easiest and most effective approach is to respect the ways that people self-identify. The process of self-identification is complex, and in fact, the terms that people use to identify their sexual and/or gender identity can shift and change over time. It is important to pay attention to the particular historical, social, cultural, and geographic contexts that may shape which terms individuals take up. Making space for people to self-identify ensures that we are not making assumptions about the terms and/or labels with which people feel comfortable.

TABLE 10.1	Sexual and Gender Identity Terms
Commonly Used Terms Related to Gender and Sexual Identity	
gender identity	An individual's subjective sense of self as male, female, or in-between.
sexual identity	Pattern of romantic and/or sexual attraction to men and/or women, which reflects an individual's sense of personal and social identity, often (but not always) aligned with a person's sexual behaviour and membership within communities who share their social identity.
two-spirited	Emerged from interpretations of Indigenous languages used during the pre-colonial era for people who were considered to have both male and female spirits (Meyer Cook, 2008). Being reclaimed by Indigenous People today to acknowledge the effects of colonialism and the social roles of two-spirited people within First Nations (Meyer Cook, 2008).

Commonly Used Terms Related to Gender Identity	
gender expression	How an individual expresses his or her gender identity.
gender non-conforming	Gender non-conforming includes individuals whose physical sex/gender assigned at birth does not align with their gender expression.
transsexual/transgender	When an individual's physical sex/gender assigned at birth differs from their gender identity. Oftentimes people who identify as a transsexual woman or man undergo hormone-replacement therapy or sex reassignment surgery. Debate and differences of opinion related to ways that both terms are utilized. Transgender is commonly referred to as an umbrella term.
cissexual/cisgender	Refers to individuals who understand their gender identity and physical sex as aligned and therefore do not identify as trans or gender non-conforming (Serano, 2007). Term "cis" is used to identify someone who is not trans or gender non-conforming.
intersex	An individual whose biological body has both male and female characteristics as understood by conventional medical standards.
Commonly Used Terms Related to Sexual Identity	
heterosexual	When one is romantically and/or sexually attracted to members of the opposite gender.
lesbian	Trans, gender non-conforming or cis women who are romantically and/or sexually attracted to other women.
gay	Trans, gender non-conforming or cis men who are romantically and/or sexually attracted to other men; sometimes used as an umbrella term.
bisexual	Trans, gender non-conforming or cis women or men who are romantically and/or sexually attracted to both men and women.
asexual	People who do not experience sexual attraction.
homosexual	Originated as a medical term to describe same-sex sexuality as a social identity. Historically used as term to pathologize TSLGBTQ individuals. Still commonly used to describe TSLGBTQ individuals in Francophone regions.
Commonly Used Umbrella Terms	
trans	Used as umbrella term to describe individuals who identify and/or express their gender as different from the sex they are assigned at birth. Often understood as short hand for transgender and transsexual.
queer	Historically used within Anglo European and North American contexts as a derogatory term towards non-heterosexual and non-cissexual people. More recently, it has been re-appropriated by some people as an umbrella term for TSLGBTQ individuals. Understands sexual and gender identity as fluid and/or ambiguous. Genderqueer is also used for people who may specifically experience their gender identity as fluid and/or ambiguous. Within an academic context, queer theory engages with term queer as an analytical tool.
sexual minority	Umbrella term used for people who are part of the group whose sexual and gender identity or expression differ from majority of surrounding society.

In addition, a single term can have different meanings, depending upon the person and context. This is especially the case for historically derogatory terms that have recently been taken up by some queer and trans people as affirming identity markers. For example, a group of urban TSLGBTQ youth who belong to an advocacy organization may describe themselves as queer as a means of expressing their sense of political and social power. However, if they are in a restaurant and hear a group of people calling them queer in a derogatory or threatening manner, they know that the term is being used as a homophobic threat designed to make them feel afraid and ashamed.

Overview of the TSLGBTQ Human Rights Global and Canadian Landscape

This section maps out the legislative frameworks and social contexts that either promote TSLGBTQ human rights or foster violence against queer and trans people in Canada and around the world. Exploring the history of TSLGBTQ human rights enables social workers to better understand what queer and trans communities have faced and continue to face in their fight for recognition.

Global Context

There are differing levels of acceptance towards queer and trans people across continents and countries. State legislative frameworks range from the death penalty and criminalization of same-sex sexual activity to TSLGBTQ human rights and anti-discrimination legislation. Conducting a TSLGBTQ human rights global overview of UN member states, a report published by the International Lesbian, Gay, Bisexual, Trans and Intersex Association (ILGA) in 2012 found that

- the death penalty still applied to consensual sexual acts between adults of the same sex in 7 countries;
- 78 out of 193 UN-member countries have laws that criminalize same-sex sexual activity;
- 15 out of the 113 countries where same-sex sexual activity is legal have unequal age of consent for same-sex and heterosexual sexual acts, including Canada;
- 19 countries prohibit employment discrimination based on gender identity and 52 countries prohibit employment discrimination based on sexual orientation;
- Canada and 9 other countries have same-sex marriage, 8 countries offer partial marriage rights, and another 14 countries allow for same-sex civil partnerships and unions.

A state's legislative framework related to sexual and gender identity influences the overall level of violence, persecution, and discrimination within each country. This is especially the case for countries that criminalize or impose the death penalty for same-sex sexual activity. Many TSLGBTQ individuals continue to experience intense forms of violence and persecution, including torture, arrest, imprisonment, extortion, rape, and death threats due to their sexual and/or gender identity. However, it is important to note that the well-being and safety of queer and trans people cannot entirely be measured by a state's legislation related to sexual and gender identity. There are still various levels of violence, persecution, and discrimination against queer and trans people in countries that have legalized same-sex sexual activity, human rights legislation, and same-sex marriage. In addition, not all queer and trans people are affected by legislation related to sexual and

© Stephanie Bosset / Alamy

Protestors worldwide show their support to the TSLGBTQ community in Russia during the 2014 Sochi Olympics.

gender identity in the same ways. There are systemic differences in the ways in which TSLGBTQ human rights and anti-discrimination legislation affects TSLGBTQ individuals based on class, race/ethnicity, gender, ability, and citizenship status.

It is becoming increasingly common to blame immigrant communities for the homophobia that exists in Canada as coming from "homophobic cultures." Rather than identify homophobia (or transphobia) as simply a cultural practice, we encourage social workers to examine the historical, social, economic, and political contexts that result in differing levels of violence against sexual minorities globally (Jenicek, Lee, & Wong, 2009). In Canada, homophobia operates differently in different regions and communities, depending on particular historical, geographic, and social contexts. Even in countries where same-sex sexual activity is criminalized and/or have high levels of violence and persecution against sexual minorities, there is a diversity of opinion among individuals and communities related to their acceptance of sexual and gender diversity. Many of the laws against same-sex sexual activity in various African and Asian countries originated from British (and other European) colonial rules in the early twentieth century (Gupta, 2008). Homophobia is a global phenomenon with site-specific historical and geo-political roots. Rather than identifying homophobia in Canada as cultural practices of immigrant communities, we can instead push for acceptance of sexual and gender diversity and TSLGBTQ human rights by developing advocacy and organizing strategies that attend to particular historical, economic, and social contexts.

Canadian Context

In this section, we explore Canadian history of queer and trans communities. Taking into consideration the particular historical and social dimensions of how sexual and gender diversity have been understood and expressed within the Canadian context reveals a rich and complex history of moments of both discrimination and affirmation of TSLGBTQ individuals. Exploring the historical dimension of sexual and gender diversity allows us to better understand the contemporary context.

First Nations Conceptualizations of Sexual and Gender Diversity

An important starting point in understanding the historical context of sexual and gender diversity in Canada is exploring the ways in which many First Nations, prior to colonial contact, understood and affirmed sexual and gender difference. In fact, the social organization of many Indigenous communities affirmed and honoured those who entered same-sex relationships and/or were gender non-comforming (Meyer Cook, 2008). Indigenous communities had terms in their own languages to identify sexual and gender diversity (Meyer Cook, 2008). Some Indigenous communities used a term that would be similar to two-spirited to identify people who had both male and female spirits (Meyer Cook, 2008).

However, two-spirited identity was not analogous to the term sexual minority, as it signified not only sexual and gender difference, but also a person's social role and status within Indigenous communities (Driskell, Finley, Gilley, & Morgensen, 2011). For example, being given the gift of two spirits meant that this individual had the ability to see the world from two perspectives at the same time (Meyer Cook, 2008). Two-spirited beings were revered as leaders, mediators, teachers, artists, seers, and spiritual guides (Meyer Cook, 2008). Many First Nations tribes were organized through communal societal arrangements, which included flexible marriage laws that included same-sex marriage (Carter, 2008).

The arrival of British and French (and other European) settlers was marked by the imposition of foreign views and values on Native spirituality, family life, and traditions (Anderson, 2003; Meyer Cook, 2008). During earlier phases of colonization, European settlers identified, at particular junctures, same-sex sexuality and gender variance within Indigenous communities as unnatural and pagan practices, in order to justify political and military intervention (Anderson, 2003; Bleys, 1995). During this time period, two-spirited people were often beaten, killed, or driven out of their homes and communities (Bleys, 1995; Meyer Cook, 2008).

In the late nineteenth century, British settlers began to transport strict Victorian and Christian notions of gender conformity and heterosexuality (Bleys, 1995; Kinsman, 1998). Although values of social and racial purity through strict marriage laws were being promoted, European settler colonies were also establishing urban centres of industrialization. A by-product of this system of colonial capitalism was the fact that individuals were able to survive outside the confines of the family (D'Emilio, 1998). As the power of the Church coalesced with scientific knowledge, the term homosexuality emerged to label sexual and gender difference as both sinful and deviant (Kinsman, 1998).

During this era when the emerging social work profession was promoting social and sexual purity by promoting moral and social reform (Valverde, 2008), homosexuality became classified as a mental disorder within psychiatry. Through policies such as the Indian residential school system, social workers were complicit in pathologizing same-sex sexuality and destroying the acceptance of two-spirited people within First Nations (Anderson, 2003; Meyer-Cook, 2008; Meyer-Cook & Labelle, 2004).

At the same time, the Canadian government had criminalized same-sex sexuality just as various British (and other European) colonial regimes did across the globe (Bleys, 1995). By the early twentieth century, the criminalization of consensual homosexuality served to target two-spirited people and racialized men from Asia for police surveillance and imprisonment in particular and site-specific ways (Ingram, 2003). For example, in British Columbia, the first legal hearings related to consensual homosexuality were mostly with Sikh men (Ingram, 2003). The medical classification and criminalization of homosexuality also extended into immigration policy, where in 1927, the Canadian Immigration Act explicitly included the exclusion of people who were identified as sexual deviants (White, 2010). Describing the emergence of homosexuality as a social identity in Canada demonstrates the ways in which the Church, medical establishment, and the Canadian state engaged in social and population control against those that were deemed as sexual deviants and degenerates (Kinsman, 1998).

From this historical context emerged contemporary queer and trans activism in Canada. As Canada moved through the First and Second World Wars, major urban centres became spaces for TSLGBTQ individuals to meet and socialize (D'Emilio, 1998; Warner, 2002). With the emergence of the black power and civil rights movement, the red power movement, the feminist movement, and anti-war movements in the 1960s, the gay liberation movement was born. Below is a brief TSLGBTQ human rights timeline in Canada.

TABLE 10.2	Timeline of TSLGBTQ Human Rights Movement in Canada
	Timeline
1960s	**1964:** Association for Social Knowledge (ASK)—first homophile (gay) organization in Canada formed in Vancouver. **1968:** First service conducted by a nondenominational gay-specific Christian church. **1969:** Stonewall Riots—In New York City, patrons at gay bar serving mostly poor/working-class drag queens, sex workers, street youth, and people of colour fought arrest and police repression. **1969:** Decriminalization of private same-sex sexual activity between consenting adults. Police surveillance and raids of gay and lesbian social spaces and gay bath houses continue.
1970s	**1971:** First francophone gay organization in Canada formed in Montréal—Front de liberation homosexuel. **1971:** First publicly organized gay rights-specific demonstration in Canada on Parliament Hill, in support of "We Demand" brief sponsored by Canadian gay rights groups. **1972:** Canada's first Gay Pride Week held in Toronto. **1973:** American Psychological Association (APA) removes homosexuality from the Diagnostic and Statistical Manual of Mental Disorders (DSM). **1973:** First national lesbian conference held in Toronto. **1976:** Prior to Olympic Games, Montreal police targeted and arrested sex workers, street people, and "homosexuals"—hundreds were arrested in gay bar raids. **1977:** After multiple public protests in response to police violence during Olympic Games, Quebec government becomes first province in Canada to introduce sexual orientation as prohibited grounds of discrimination. **1977:** All references to homosexuals and homosexualism removed from Canadian Immigration Act. **1977:** Toronto Rainbow Alliance of the Deaf formed.
1980s	**1980:** HIV/AIDS crisis emerges in Canada, with first known cases of gay men dying of AIDS. People mobilize and engage in activism to fight homophobia and serophobia. **1980:** Gay Asians of Toronto (GAT) formed. **1981:** Over 150 police officers raid four gay bath houses in Toronto, arresting over 300 men. Thousands of people protested in response. **1984:** Zami, group for Black and West Indian gays and lesbians formed. **1987:** The term "two-spirited" emerges out of third International Gathering of American Indian and First Nations Gays and Lesbians held in Winnipeg.

(Continued)

TABLE 10.2	(Continued)
1990s	**1990:** World Health Organization's (WHO) International Classification of Diseases code (ICD-9) removes homosexuality from list of mental disorders. **1991:** First gay refugee claimant in Canada is accepted based on persecution due to sexual orientation. **1991:** First LGBTQ Muslim organization, Salaam, holds its first meeting in Toronto. **1995:** Prohibition of discrimination based on sexual orientation read into section 15(1) of the Canadian Constitution. **1998:** Delwin Vriend fired from lab coordinator position at King's College in Edmonton due to sexual orientation and eventually wins Supreme Court case. **1998:** All provinces, territories, and the federal government have prohibited discrimination on the basis of sexual orientation. **1999:** APA decrees it to be unethical for any professional to treat homosexuality as pathology. **1999:** Supreme Court of Canada declares any provincial law recognizing common-law relationships that does not extend equality to same-sex couples is unconstitutional. **1999:** Northwest Territories is the first province to include protection of gender identity in human rights legislation.
2000s	**2002:** Calgary police raid gay bath house and arrest 19 men. **2004:** Alberta journalist discovers government records that reveal in Alberta between 1995 to 2004, doctors used the ICD-9 to treat homosexuality as mental disorder 1750 times. **2006:** Federal government passes same-sex marriage laws.
2010s	**2013:** Alberta journalist discovers doctors in Alberta treated homosexuality as mental disorder 5 times. **2013:** Gender identity (but not gender expression) included as prohibited ground of discrimination in Canadian Human Rights Act (CHRA) and as relevant factor in hate crimes sentencing under the Criminal Code.

Source: Adapted from Warner, 2002.

Violence, Discrimination, and Stigma

With the recent passing of same-sex marriage legislation in 2006, some people believe that TSLGBTQ individuals have achieved legal and social equality. Although Canada is returning to levels of acceptance of sexual and gender diversity that were present across most First Nations during the pre-colonial era, there still exists **homophobia** and **transphobia**. Despite Canada's legislative shifts over the past 50 years that are meant to promote the human rights of TSLGBTQ individuals, there remains varying levels of violence and discrimination against LGBTQ individuals across regions (Janoff, 2005).

homophobia The irrational fear, hatred, and intolerance of lesbian, gay, and bisexual people.

transphobia The irrational fear, hatred, and intolerance of trans people.

Out of 1401 police-reported hate crimes in 2010, 218 were motivated by sexual orientation (Statistics Canada, 2012). Two thirds of these reported hate crimes were identified as violent in nature (Statistics Canada, 2012). Between 1990 and 2004, 120 homicides and 350 acts of overt homophobic and transphobic violence were reported in Canada (Janoff, 2005). Even these numbers are questionable as homophobic and transphobic violence is underreported, with TSLGBTQ youth, prisoners, sex workers, trans people, and refugees being the most vulnerable (Janoff, 2005). Although overt homophobic and transphobic violence can be easily identified, there are also forms of violence and discrimination that are part of everyday life and are mostly hidden.

microaggressions Verbal, behavioural, or environmental indignities, intentional or unintentional, that communicate hostile, derogatory, or negative slights and insults.

Initially used to describe everyday experiences of racism, **microaggressions** is a useful conceptual tool for revealing everyday experiences of many forms of discrimination. The three main aspects of microaggressions are microassault, microinsult, and microinvalidation (Sue et al., 2007). Microaggressions are brief and constant verbal, behavioural, or environmental indignities, whether intentional or unintentional, that communicate hostile, derogatory, or negative slights and insults (Sue et al., 2007). Microassault can be demonstrated in derogatory name-calling and purposeful discriminatory actions (Sue et al., 2007). Microinsult can be verbal and non-verbal behaviours that demean or discredit people (Sue et al., 2007). Microinvalidation occurs when TSLGBTQ individuals' experiences are excluded or negated (Sue et al, 2007).

Another way in which society stigmatizes TSLGBTQ individuals is through media representations. The vast majority of mainstream media representations tend to be of heterosexual and gender normative people. When queer and trans people are represented, stereotypes are often reinforced. In addition, mainstream media representations are mostly of gay white men, while women, people of colour, and trans people are rarely visible (Munoz, 1999). However, recently, alternative media has made initiatives that centre TSLGBTQ life experience (Munoz, 1999). An important avenue for viewing media that centres queer and trans experiences are the various TSLGBTQ film festivals across Canada.

An important way in which queer and trans people experience violence and discrimination is through systemic or institutional practices. For example, **heterosexism** and **cissexism** can be experienced when attempting to obtain housing or employment. Heterosexism and cissexism occurs at the structural and cultural levels, but is also experienced at the personal level.

In addition, structural forms of discrimination can be found across health-care, social service, and educational institutions. Structural violence can be understood as complex and often hidden social processes, relations, and practices embedded within policies, institutions, and laws that favour some groups within society over others (Mullaly, 2010). These policies, institutions, and laws result in an unequal distribution of life chances and intergenerational social inequities such as poverty, unemployment and mental health consequences (Mullaly, 2010).

> **heterosexism** The assumption that heterosexuality is natural and the norm and that any other form of sexual identity or expression is inferior.
>
> **cissexism** The belief that cissexuality is natural and the norm and that any other forms of gender identity and expression are inferior.

Internalized Homophobia and Transphobia

One of the primary effects of heterosexist and cissexist stigma, violence, and discrimination is internalized homophobia or transphobia. Internalized oppression can be defined as

> the acceptance and internalisation by members of oppressed groups of negative stereotypes and images of their groups, beliefs in their own inferiority, and concomitant beliefs in the superiority of the dominant group. This could be internalised in hurt and anger at being treated badly by members of the dominant group if accompanied by a belief that one deserves such treatment (Smith, 1997, p. 289).

Social workers should be attentive to the ways in which TSLGBTQ individuals may internalize feelings of inferiority due to their sexual and/or gender identity.

Intersectionality as a Theoretical Framework

Emerging in the 1980s, double jeopardy theory took an additive approach to understanding oppression. For example, if you are a racialized older adult then you likely experience ageism plus racism. Rather than taking an additive approach, intersectionality suggests that people who are multiply oppressed experience entirely new and complex forms of marginalization. The lived experience of multiple marginalizations is based upon the whole of a person's identity and not just the sum of its parts. Intersectionality theory highlights the ways in which systems of oppression, based on such social locations such as race, class, gender, ability, religion, citizenship status, and sexual/gender identity, intersect with each other and are mutually reinforcing, resulting in a complex set of relations of power. These intersecting systems of oppression reinforce, multiply, or complicate each other, in context- and site-specific ways.

Two key facets of intersectionality are described below due to their implications for social work practice: structural and political intersectionality (Crenshaw, 1991).

- Structural intersectionality occurs when the burdens faced by a specific group of multiply marginalized people result in particular systemic discriminatory practices within the realms of housing, employment, immigration, and health care (Crenshaw, 1991). Intersectional marginalization does not necessarily result from intentional practices of institutions, but rather occur as the consequence of different forms of oppression interacting with each other, creating new dimensions of disempowerment (Crenshaw, 1991). For example, trans refugees as a group, cannot apply for a legal name and sex designation change until after they become permanent residents or citizens (depending on the province).
- Political intersectionality occurs when a specific group of people are situated within two subordinated groups that frequently pursue conflicting political agendas (Crenshaw, 1991). For example, women of colour have often had to choose between social movements, either anti-racist movements that were sexist or feminist movements that were racist. Choosing either meant setting aside efforts to address their particularized experience of racism and sexism and exposing themselves to discriminatory environments within political movements.

Theory in **Practice**

IDENTITY FORMATION

A STUDY ON IDENTITY FORMATION AMONG lesbians of ethnic ancestry in Canada provides an exploration of political intersectionality and its impact upon one woman, Paula, a lesbian of Greek ethnic origin living in Toronto (Brotman & Kraniou, 1999). Intersectionality theory was used as a framework to explore the processes of political and social exclusion that resulted as Paula attempted to find community belonging and solidarity as *both* Greek *and* lesbian. She was active in both her Greek community (through family and community) and in her lesbian community (through lesbian feminist groups) but was unable to find space that acknowledged and celebrated both of her identities simultaneously. By being defined as an outsider in multiple spaces, Paula faced exclusionary practices, all of which acted together to fragment and silence her. For example, her commitment to family and partnership were identified as "too ethnic" and as the internalization of patriarchal oppression by her lesbian community, while her desire to build a loving partnership with a woman was rejected as "unnatural" by her ethnic community. As a result, Paula often had to choose pieces of herself to present as wholeness, depending on in which community (ethnic or lesbian) she was involved. Her resistance to this fragmented shaping of herself as multiple "other" is a struggle that many ethnic minority lesbians face in Canada.

Intersectionality, Identity, and Social Location

Essential to intersectionality is the notion that oppression and subordination as they exist in the real lives and experiences of people cannot be separated and analyzed individually. Intersectionality requires critical analysis of how an individual's social location interacts with multiple systems of oppression. **Social location** refers to someone's affiliation as a member of a group based on race, ethnicity, gender, ability, class, religion, citizenship status, sexual/gender identity, and so forth. An individual's social location includes the particular geographic and socio-historical context into which one is born (Rich, 1984). A person's various group affiliations intersect and operate at the structural/institutional, cultural, and interpersonal levels, resulting in differential access to social power and privilege (or penalty), depending on group affiliation. Understanding social location in this way allows us to witness how these different positions intersect and operate at structural and institutional levels as well as how they are experienced by people in their daily lives (Grenier & Brotman, 2010).

This requires social location and identity to be constantly defined and re-defined in order to disrupt the dominant assumption that identity is somehow fixed and immutable. Instead, identity is fluid, flexible, and shifting according to situation and context, along with being shaped by many factors including age, racial/ethnic background, gender, language, ability, citizenship status, socio-economic status, educational background, and sexual and gender identity. In addition, social location and identity is not always self-defined or self-managed. There are social and structural forces that shape the complex ways in which individuals understand their social location. However, although people are influenced by social forces and their various group affiliations, they are not fully determined by them (Baines, 2011).

The concept of intersectionality is important for social work practice with TSLGBTQ individuals as it helps to reframe how multiple forms of oppression result in different marginalizations that shape how people come to understand their intersecting identities. The shifting territory of identity and social location is not easily captured through basic categorical definitions so prominent in health-care and social services. These constructions are not only inadequate but serve to limit the potential for agency within and among communities. Instead, intersectionality provides an opportunity to challenge oppressive practices affecting those whose identities and social locations emerge in the intersection of class, race, sexual/gender identity, gender, ability, and citizenship status. Social workers interested in understanding the connections between identity, discrimination, and lived experience can use intersectionality as a base to understand and work with queer and trans communities.

social location Refers to the personal, cultural, and social context of one's structured position within society.

Disclosure of Sexual and Gender Identity: Coming Out

The phrase "coming out of the closet" or "coming out" refers to when a TSLGBTQ individual discloses his or her sexual and/or gender identity. Earlier research in the fields of psychology and social work described coming out as central to positive health and well-being for lesbian and gay people. The mental stress, lowered self-esteem, and social isolation that resulted from hiding one's sexual orientation often led to increased risks for substance abuse, addictions, suicide, increase in high-risk behaviours, and even physical health deterioration (Brotman, Ryan, Jalbert & Rowe, 2002).

In Their Own Words

WORKING WITH TWO-SPIRITED PEOPLE

AS A TWO-SPIRITED ANISHINAABE-KWE (OJIBWE) and mixed descent person, it has been painful to learn about the brutality of colonization and Euro-Western racism. I don't like the term post-colonial because I don't think we are there yet. We still have the Indian Act, which is a racist piece of legislation and it's not hard to see the ways in which it attempts to destroy Traditional Indigenous gender, family, and community systems in the past and continues to operate in peoples' lives today.

Aboriginal Peoples as a whole experience multiple forms of discrimination from inequities in education, housing, health, and access to clean drinking water and are at higher risk of experiencing severe violence as well as removal to institutionalized settings (e.g., child welfare services, youth custody, and incarceration) in their lives. With the last residential school only closing in 1996 in Canada, intergenerational legacies persist. While there are some Aboriginal communities where abuse, addictions, and suicide rates are much lower than the national average, recurrent traumas, multiple grief, and loss continue in others. As two-spirited people struggle with "coming out" and deal with feelings of rejection, isolation, or partner loss, they may be doing so in a context made more difficult by structural factors such as poverty, poor housing, lack of safety, violence, lack of mobility, or by unhealed and ongoing trauma legacies.

Indigenous Peoples have also had to struggle with a long period of cultural imperialism and attempts at erasure. Dominant hetero-normative European religious views harm those questioning their sexual orientation or gender identity and make it difficult to be "out" in communities. Being a scapegoat in a community dealing with unhealed legacies and high levels of lateral violence is highly stress-inducing and can lead to tragic results. The urban scene, while more anonymous, is not necessarily a panacea for two-spirited people where racism, exoticization, and multiple systemic barriers exist.

As social workers we can use our skills in counselling and social justice, and our knowledge of social welfare to ensure the material needs of two-spirited people are met and that they are supported in working through the challenges they identify in their lives. Good relationships are at the heart of what we do. We help people strengthen relationships in their own lives and in turn we need to mirror that. We get better at that as we take care of our own selves spiritually and pay attention to our wellness issues. A helping relationship based on respect, non-coercion, and mutuality is a good place to begin as an antidote to the history of coercion and erasure.

When working with two-spirited people, knowing what not to do is also important. Letting two-spirited people we work with know about two-spirited gatherings and local cultural circles can be really helpful. These have helped a lot of people keep connected to cultural traditions and bring the worlds of one's culture and gender and sexual identity all together in one place in fun, healthy, humane, and informal ways.

Fiona Meyer Cook is Anishinaabe (Ojibwe) and mixed descent with ancestry from Little Current, Manitoulin and the Sheguiandah First Nation and is presently a PhD Candidate at the School of Social Work at Carleton University.

Causal theories between coming out and well-being have been challenged by scholars and activists applying intersectionality to their analysis (Ryan, Brotman, Baradaran, & Lee, 2008). Identifying coming out as the final stage to healthy and positive well-being is being challenged as reinforcing racist, sexist, and ageist notions of what "counts" as queer and trans identity (Lee & Brotman, 2011). Not all people aspire to come out as a sign of healthy identity formation and the decision to not come out is not always related to fears of violence or rejection (Ryan et al., 2008). For example, some queer people of colour understand coming out to prioritize white and western conceptualizations of sexual and gender identity (Ryan et al., 2008). For many queer people of colour, positive well-being is not linked to coming out but to affirming all aspects of their identity with respect to race/ethnicity, class, gender, ability, citizenship status, and so forth (Ryan et al., 2008).

Rather than viewing coming out as the last stage to healthy well-being for TSLGBTQ individuals, it is more useful for social workers to critically reflect on the different ways that coming out and disclosure of sexual and/or gender identity shape their interactions with health-care and social services. Understood in this way, coming out should be understood as a process which is fluid, flexible, and context specific. One can come out in one way at a specific time and place and in another way at another time or place. Coming out is not a one-time event but changes across the life cycle.

One can come out to oneself, one's family, one's friends, one's co-workers, one's community all at once, one at a time, or in one environment and not another. Some of today's older adults have married and had children in the context of heterosexual marriage, come out to friends and family in middle age, and then choose not to come out when moving into a residence in old age. As this example suggests, the reasons for personally or publically coming out at different times and different contexts are varied and diverse but safety is a central feature of a person's decision to come out publically as TSLGBTQ in specific environments. Rejection, exclusion, loss of resources, or security and violence are all reasons for deciding on whether or not to come out. In the following sections of this chapter, the issue of coming out and disclosure will constantly resurface as a major theme in queer and trans people's lives.

Families and Communities

This section aims to explore the important role of families and communities in the lives of queer and trans people. This includes exploring the diverse ways in which sexual minorities negotiate their families of origin while at the same time forming alternative family structures. In addition, it is important for social workers to be aware of the complexities for queer and trans people in navigating multiple communities. Being aware of the diversity of TSLGBTQ family and community formation will assist practitioners in various social work settings.

Families

Previous research in the 1980s about TSLGBTQ individuals within the context of families focused upon the relationship between heterosexual and cissexual parents and their lesbian or gay children (Tremble et al., 1989). The role of supportive parents within a nuclear family structure was identified as an important element to determining positive well-being for lesbian and gay youth (Tremble et al., 1989). Negative responses contributed to myriad health and mental health issues such as depression, suicidal ideation, addiction, and homelessness (Tremble et al., 1989). Certainly, the relationship between parents and their lesbian or gay children within a nuclear family structure influences the degree to which some lesbian and gay children affirm or devalue their sexual identity.

Creatas/Thinkstock

Research has shown that a child's health, well-being, and happiness have nothing to do with the sexual orientation or gender identity of the parent.

However, there are multiple ways that TSLGBTQ individuals are situated within nuclear and diverse family structures. Queer and trans people are not only children of heterosexual and cissexual parents, but they are also uncles and aunts, brothers and sisters, nieces and nephews, parents and grandparents. Queer and trans people who become parents challenge the myths that TSLGBTQ individuals are at worst dangerous to children and at best cause children to be maladjusted. Research affirms that there are no negative consequences from having same-sex parents (Goldberg, 2010). Instead, children of same-sex parents are vulnerable when exposed to social discrimination from family members, peers or persons in authority, such as teachers and service providers (Goldberg, 2010). There is an emerging awareness about the importance of attending to the experiences of both trans parents and of gender non-conforming and trans children (Pyne, 2012).

It is also important to consider the different ways that TSLGBTQ individuals are situated within diverse family structures. For example, within many Indigenous and racialized communities, the extended family plays a larger role in the raising of children (Kundouqk & Qwul'sih'yah'maht, 2009). For Indigenous and racialized TSLGBTQ individuals, their extended family networks are crucial pathways to support in their lives. However, TSLGBTQ individuals may experience homophobia or transphobia from various family members. In addition, families of origin may also encounter barriers in accessing information and resources about sexual and gender diversity related to language, class, race/ethnicity, gender, ability, and so forth.

Queer and trans people do not always define a sense of community from within these families. TSLGBTQ individuals can experience isolation within their families of origin, even in contexts where the individual is supported and accepted by some or all of their family members. Seeking out friendship and a sense of community from others who are TSLGBTQ is particularly important among queer and trans youth but is part of the process of identity and belonging for most (but not all) TSLGBTQ individuals of any age. Building a support network made up of people who are not part of your family of origin is often described as the creation of chosen families (Weston, 1991).

Chosen family members oftentimes provide life-saving and affirming emotional and material support in times of needs, yet they are not always recognized. For example, TSLGBTQ older adults often describe the role of chosen families in providing care in times of health crisis that is not always recognized by health-care and social care institutions. This is particularly important when the TSLGBTQ person is unable to tell service providers who they want included in their care plan. Without a "chosen family" policy, queer and trans people are vulnerable to the decisions of health-care providers as to whether or not non-biological family is included as a part of the individual's support team. Families of choice for queer and trans people can be made up of TSLGBTQ and heterosexual/cissexual people.

An important aspect of a queer and trans person's family structure is intimate partner relationships. Same-sex couples and couples where one or both people identify as trans can encounter similar issues facing heterosexual and cissexual couples. However, same-sex and trans couples will often also face the complex issue of social discrimination, as individuals and as couples. Couples often self-identify using different terms and choose to come out differently within multiple contexts. For example, one member of a couple may be out at his or her workplace while the other is not. In addition, the stress associated with experiences of discrimination can sometimes cause difficulties within couples. This stress becomes more complex when one or both people face multiple forms of marginalization.

Communities

Within larger urban settings, a key geographic space for queer and trans community formation is what is commonly known as the "gay village." The gay village is usually a geographic area where there is a high concentration of TSLGBTQ individuals who go to stores, bars, cafes, and restaurants that are tailored to their interests. The gay villages that are situated in major cities across Canada have their own particular histories and have served as crucial geographic spaces for queer and trans people to socialize and build community. They have served to help propel the TSLGBTQ human rights movement, as demonstrated by the riots that occurred in Montreal after the bath house raids in the early 1970s.

The "gay village" is an important resource for queer and trans people who want to link up with other TSLGBTQ individuals and be a part of the community. At the same time, it is not always the safest place for all queer and trans people. Although the gay village is an important space for socialization for many TSLGBTQ individuals, it is also oftentimes a cis-, white-, and male-dominated space. This means that women, people of colour, trans people, and older adults risk facing intersecting experiences of racism, sexism, cissexism, and ageism within these spaces. In addition, gay villages have become highly commercialized spaces, and so poor and working class queer and trans people, especially those experiencing homelessness, may feel excluded.

In any geographic area, but especially within larger urban settings, there are usually a diverse set of TSLGBTQ communities, rather than just one "gay community." It is important to be aware of the many avenues for queer and trans people to be a part of multiple TSLGBTQ communities. For example, there are often alternative spaces or geographic areas in which there is a high concentration of specific communities (such as queer women, queer people of colour and/or trans people). In more rural areas, there may be a smaller version of the gay village or simply a geographic area, community organization, special event, or local bar or restaurant where people gather.

Another key space of socialization for queer and trans people is through the Internet. Certainly, the Internet allows all people avenues for connection and socialization. The Internet serves as an important way for queer and trans people to meet each other. This is especially the case within smaller urban or rural areas where there may be limited spaces where people can meet in person. There are queer- and trans-oriented arts or social events that are mostly organized and promoted through social media sites. The anonymity through which queer and trans people can find other TSLGBTQ individuals can open space for important exploration. However, as with the gay village, virtual spaces for socialization can reproduce larger societal patterns of social exclusion such as racism, sexism, ageism, and cissexism. The Internet can also be a space where TSLGBTQ individuals can end up being vulnerable to overt and covert experiences of homophobia and transphobia.

Another avenue for queer- and trans-community building is through activist groups and community organizations that serve as crucial spaces for socialization and activism. There is a huge amount of diversity when it comes to the vision, goals, and priorities for TSLGBTQ activist groups and community organizations. Many serve the needs of particular groups within queer and trans communities, such as LBQ cis women, trans people, LGBTQ newcomers, queer and trans youth, and so forth. Some community organizations are funded by the government to provide specific services, while others are organized entirely by volunteers.

Sometimes, queer and trans people's affiliations with diverse communities can also cause complications and tensions. For example, queer people of colour often experience conflict in their relationship with their varying communities: on one hand, queer people of colour may encounter overt and covert experiences of racism within white-dominant LGBTQ communities. On the other hand, they may experience homophobia or transphobia within their racialized community. As a result, queer people of colour can internalize both racism and homophobia or transphobia.

Social Work Practice with TSLGBTQ People across Health-Care and Social Service Settings

Attention is now shifted to the ways in which social workers can use this knowledge base in order to address the particular experiences and barriers that queer and trans people encounter across health-care and social service settings. Fostering an anti-oppressive and social-justice–oriented social work approach includes engaging in critical analysis and reflexivity. Engaging in reflexivity provides space for social workers to consider the relationship between the institutional power they hold and their particular social location and how this shapes their social work practice with TSLGBTQ populations.

Historical Dimensions

Until recently, little documentation existed on the health and social service needs and experiences of TSLGBTQ individuals outside the realm of HIV prevention and treatment for gay and bisexual cis men. As a result, health-care and social service providers and policy-makers knew very little about the global health and well-being of queer and trans people. This absence of knowledge about the global health and social service needs of queer and trans people can be traced to historical and contemporary forms of exclusion encountered by TSLGBTQ individuals within society generally and within health and social service institutions specifically.

Because sexual and gender diversity has historically been socially defined within medical terms as a mental disorder, the health-care system has been one of the primary arenas through which control over TSLGBTQ lives was exerted. Health-care and social service providers were often charged with the task of "healing" queer and trans people from their so-called unhealthy same-sex attractions or gender expressions through such means as electroshock therapy or aversion therapy (Kinsman, 1998). Although homosexuality was removed from its classification as a mental disorder in the Diagnostic and Statistical Manual of Mental Disorders (DSM) in 1973, some health-care and social service providers continue to harbour heterosexist bias. Government records revealed that in Alberta, from 1995–2004, doctors used the International Classification of Diseases (ICD-9) to "treat" lesbian and gay people more than 1750 times (Kleiss, 2012).

In addition, gender dysphoria and Gender Identity Disorder (GID) are still classifications within the DSM as a psychiatric disorder. The describing of trans identity and expression as a disorder, and thus abnormal, clearly reveals the ways in which cissexism is embedded within health-care and social services. However, the inclusion of gender identity within the DSM as a psychiatric disorder has also served as a pathway for trans people to obtain health-care insurance for hormone-replacement therapy and sex-reassignment surgery.

Given this history, queer and trans people often have an uneasy relationship with and lack of trust of the health and social service system. Continued pressure from queer and trans communities and their allies on health-care and social service providers and policy-makers has resulted in some improvements to varying degrees across Canada. TSLGBTQ individuals (as both service users and workers) as well as allies, continue to resist heterosexist and cissexist practices by documenting historical and current injustices, advocating for changes in policy and best practices, and sharing expertise in queer and trans issues. Both HIV/AIDS activist and women's health movements have also helped to channel energies on the health and social service needs of diverse TSLGBTQ populations.

Social Dimensions

An important consideration when working with queer and trans people is understanding the ways in which social determinants of health shape queer and trans people's access to health-care and social services. Understanding larger social dimensions that determine health allows us to more clearly understand structural barriers that TSLGBTQ individuals have in accessing equitable health-care and social services. Previously identified social determinants of health within the Canadian context include education, employment security and working conditions, housing, food security, income distribution, and social exclusion (Mullaly, 2010).

Critical to understanding the realities of multiply marginalized queer and trans people is that there are specific groups who are especially vulnerable to these social determinants of health, including First Nations, trans people, people of colour, older adults, immigrants/refugees, and people with disabilities (Ezra, 2013; Mullaly, 2010). By using an intersectional lens, the specific ways in which poor/working-class queer and trans people, especially those who are racialized and/or living with a disability, are made particularly vulnerable to social determinants of health is brought to light. Within and across these particular groups are two-spirited, queer and trans people of colour, LGBTQ immigrants and refugees, and TSLGBTQ youth and seniors. The following section explores the complex ways in which class, gender, race/ethnicity, ability, citizenship status, and First Nations status shape how queer and trans people access health-care and social services. This kind of intersectional analysis makes concrete the ways in which political and structural forms of intersectionality result in unequal distribution of life opportunities, health, and well-being.

Case STUDY

Disconnection and Community Belonging

BASED OUT OF WINNIPEG, RISTOCK and colleagues' (2010) community-based research project focusing on the health and migration of Aboriginal TSLGBTQ individuals infused feminist and Indigenous approaches into their research process (Kovach, 2005; Ristock & Pennell, 1996). This project situated the contemporary migration and health of Aboriginal TSLGBTQ individuals within the context of historical trauma, through colonial policies such as Indian Residential Schools and the Sixties Scoop (as explored in Chapter 8). One of the legacies of these colonial practices was the introduction of shame towards same-sex attraction and gender-variant behaviour (Anderson, 2003). What emerged from the findings of the project were two interrelated themes of disconnection and community belonging.

Within the broader context of historical and intergenerational trauma, Indigenous TSLGBTQ individuals experienced disconnections from their Indigenous languages, culture, and positive histories. One of the reasons for leaving their Indigenous community and moving to an urban area was due to experiences of homophobia and transphobia within their Indigenous communities, which ironically stem from colonial policies. In addition, they experienced loss and grief due to leaving their home and community. On the other hand, Indigenous TSLGBTQ individuals also described the vital importance of creating a sense of belonging within the urban setting through creating chosen families and practising Indigenous ceremonies. However, they also encountered cultural and structural forms of racism, resulting in barriers in securing stable housing and employment. Disconnection and community belonging have major implications for the health and well-being of Aboriginal TSLGBTQ individuals.

Concrete recommendations to improve health outcomes from Aboriginal TSLGBTQ individuals both in reserve communities and within urban settings included the need for transition services to assist people who are moving to the city, education and awareness training about Aboriginal TSLGBTQ-related concerns across health-care, social services, and educational settings and promoting awareness of already existing community resources for Aboriginal TSLGBTQ individuals.

Access to Health Care for Specific TSLGBTQ Groups

Trans and Gender Non-conforming People

Notwithstanding the recent inclusion of gender identity (but not gender expression) as a prohibited grounds of discrimination in the Canadian Human Rights Act (CHRA), trans and gender non-comforming people continue to face significant levels of stigma, violence, and discrimination within society. It should not be a surprise that trans and gender non-conforming people encounter multiple layers of cissexism across health-care and social service settings. The process of **transitioning** results in specific concerns for trans people, particularly with respect to access to health care. The experience of a trans person that transitions may (or may not) involve a new name, new pronoun, new clothes, hormone-replacement therapy, and/or surgery (Ezra, 2013).

One barrier for trans people is changing their legal name and sex designation. The process for trans people to obtain a legal name and sex designation varies across provinces, but in many cases, it can be a long and arduous process (Ezra, 2013). Trans migrants and refugee claimants have an even longer wait time since they can only apply for a legal name

transitioning Refers to the process through which trans people start to move away from their gender assigned at birth to their preferred gender expression and identity (Ezra, 2013).

and sex designation change after they have been accepted as a refugee and gained permanent residency status or, in some provinces, Canadian citizenship. In most cases, trans people have to "prove" their gender identity before being allowed a change in sex designation, meaning trans people often enter health-care settings where their gender identity and expression do not match their legal name and sex designation.

Most hospitals and clinics have policies and procedures around legal name and sex designation that assume that everyone is cissexual. The cissexism embedded within health-care settings results in trans people being routinely and systematically exposed to transphobia. For example, in a hospital or clinic waiting room, if a health-care provider calls out someone's legal name or uses a gender identifying term that does not correspond to their gender expression, it publicly outs this person as trans and/or gender non-conforming. This practice of outing occurs throughout the health-care intervention—from speaking to the intake worker, the waiting room, speaking to each health-care provider and even post-visit when picking up prescriptions at the pharmacy.

Another barrier for trans people is trans specific health care, which includes cross-gender hormone-replacement therapy and trans-specific surgery. Hormone-replacement therapy can be prescribed by a general practitioner (or family doctor), a specialist (such as an endocrinologist or gynecologist), or through a gender clinic (Ezra, 2013). The degree to which hormone treatment (and/or therapy that is attached to hormone treatment) is covered by health-care insurance varies across provinces and there could be out-of-pocket costs, which are costly for many trans people with low incomes (Ezra, 2013).

While trans activists are against defining their trans identity as a disorder, many provincial governments require this unnecessary labelling to benefit from health-care insurance coverage for hormone therapy and sex-reassignment surgery.

Criteria, requirements, and health-care coverage for sex-reassignment surgery also vary across provinces. In order for trans people to access either hormone-replacement therapy or sex-reassignment surgery, they must be diagnosed as having **gender dysphoria** by a medical professional.

The inclusion of gender identity within the DSM as a psychiatric disorder clearly has implications for the ways in which trans and gender non-conforming people negotiate health-care institutions. The describing of trans identity as a disorder, and thus abnormal, clearly reveals the ways in which cissexism is embedded within health institutions. Many trans activists have denounced labelling trans identities and expressions as a form of disorder (Ezra, 2013). At the same time, this diagnosis is directly linked to health-care insurance coverage.

gender dysphoria
Identified within the DSM as a psychiatric disorder for those whose gender assigned at birth differs from their gender identity (Ezra, 2013).

TSLGBTQ *People Living with HIV*

Health-care and social services for queer and trans people emerged from the mobilizing of HIV and queer rights activists in the 1980s during a time when hundreds of gay men were dying of AIDS both in Canada and the US (Warner, 2002). Although HIV has historically been viewed as a "gay man's disease," this perception is slowly shifting. Even though anyone can contract HIV, recent research indicates that gay men, trans people, racialized people, and Indigenous People are disproportionately at risk of contracting HIV (Harper, Jernewall, & Zez, 2004). Rates of HIV among older people are also on the rise (Wallach & Brotman, 2012).

There still clearly exists social stigma and common misconceptions around HIV. HIV is a retrovirus that infects t-cells that are a part of a person's immune system and necessary for the body to fight off infections. The final stage of HIV infection is called AIDS (Auto Immune Deficiency Syndrome), as the body's immune system starts to break down. In order for an individual to die of AIDS, their HIV needs to continue to break down the body's immune system to the point where a person will be more likely to catch other diseases, such as Kaposi's sarcoma, cancer, and/or pneumonia. Although there is not yet a cure or vaccine for HIV, there have been medical advancements that have allowed people to live much longer lives.

The stigma and discrimination against those living with HIV result in various psychological, social, and economic consequences. Due to the fear of loss of their social support network, many people living with HIV have difficulties in disclosing their HIV status. The challenges of disclosing HIV status can be akin to the issues of disclosing one's sexual and/or gender identity. This difficulty of coming out related to HIV status can result in challenges in accessing adequate and equitable health care. Within major urban settings, there are usually health-care or social service settings that are specifically targeted towards facilitating HIV treatment for gay cis men. There are services that are starting to emerge to address the particular issues of queer people of colour, trans people, and Indigenous TSLGBTQ Peoples; however, in smaller urban and rural areas, it can be more difficult for TSLGBTQ individuals living with HIV to get services tailored to their needs.

TSLGBTQ Older Adults

Although older TSLGBTQ adults have lived through the queer rights movement of the 1960s and 1970s, many have not fully reaped its benefits. The necessary strategies for survival over the life course among today's older members of TSLGBTQ communities often require sexual and/or gender identity to be hidden, with social engagement limited to the private sphere (Cronin et al., 2011). Among older TSLGBTQ adults who were born prior to the development of the queer rights movement or who lived in regions with little opportunity to develop a sense of collective queer community, remaining discrete about their sexual and/or gender identity is still a common survival strategy. In fact, queer and trans older adults may neither self-identify as TSLGBTQ nor feel a sense of belonging within the queer community.

Certainly, there are many TSLGBTQ older adults that exhibit positive mental and physical health and general life satisfaction. In fact, older TSLGBTQ adults have been identified as being resilient and resourceful in part due to managing stigma over the life course, which has helped them face ageist stigma successfully. However, research also suggests that there is a disproportionate number of TSLGBTQ older adults with difficulties managing stigma related to heterosexism and cissexism, in addition to dealing with mental health challenges (such as depression, suicidal ideation, suicide, etc.). Given this context, it is clear that TSLGBTQ older adults face particular structural barriers in accessing equitable health care.

Although older adults expect their health to worsen as they age, there is consistent distrust of health-care providers and fear of age-related bias and heterosexist/homophobic/transphobic discrimination, based on past experiences or perceived prejudice (River, 2006). Older adults often arrive in the health-care system only after their condition has significantly worsened (Brotman, Ryan & Cormier, 2003). While most older adults prefer home-care provision, rather than residing in a long-term care facility, TSLGBTQ older adults preferences are complicated by heterosexist/homophobic/transphobic environments that currently exist in these settings (Sussman et al., 2013).

Because of discomfort with or ignorance of TSLGBTQ issues, health-care settings often perpetuate heterosexist and cissexist practices by assuming that TSLGBTQ older adults either do not exist or have the exact same needs as their heterosexual and cissexual peers (Brotman et al., 2003). In addition, TSLGBTQ older adults are forced to make decisions about whether or not to disclose their sexual and/or gender identity to either their home-care provider or both providers and co-residents in a residential-care setting. This is especially challenging for TSLGBTQ older adults who are also low income as this often reduces the kinds of home-care and/or residential-care options that are available to them. Finally, lack of recognition of chosen families renders older adults more vulnerable to exclusionary practices. An example is the all too common story of Marie and Joanne who lived together for 30 years. Marie broke her hip and was rushed to the hospital. When her partner Joanne tried to access information about the discharge plan for Marie, the social worker asked if she were a family member. Joanne expressed her identity as "Marie's friend" to which the social worker replied that only family were allowed to be involved in the care planning.

Access to Social Services for TSLGBTQ People

Queer and Trans Youth in Care

Historically in Canada, children and youth placed in out-of-home and residential care were often from historically marginalized groups, especially from low-income and immigrant backgrounds. First Nations children were especially targeted (Finney, Dean, Loiselle & Saraceno, 2011; Strong-Boag, 2007). Today, overrepresentation of these groups within youth-care systems remains a concern (Lavergne, Dufour, Trocmé & Larrivee, 2008). There are presently no statistics available that track the number of queer and gender non-conforming youth in out-of-home and residential care. Surveys completed in the US context suggest that queer and gender non-conforming children and youth, especially those that are Indigenous and racialized, along with being from low-income backgrounds, are most likely overrepresented within out-of-home and residential-care systems (Finney et al., 2011).

Questioning and exploring one's subjective understanding of sexual and/or gender identity can be a lifelong process that shifts and changes over time. Although questioning one's sexual and/or gender identity can begin in childhood, adolescence is a time period where some youth begin to self-identify as TSLGBTQ. Queer and trans youth in care may have a difficult time finding space to safely explore their sexual and/or gender identity. One of the main challenges for queer and trans youth in care is social isolation. There is often no one to speak to about the issues that they are facing and no structured opportunities to safely explore sexual and gender identity.

Due to the overrepresentation of a variety of marginalized groups within out-of-home and residential-care settings, social workers will most likely be working with multiply marginalized youth, including those who are Indigenous or racialized and from low-income backgrounds. As a result of the multiple and intersecting forms of violence, discrimination, and stigma they face on a daily basis, the majority of these youth often face negative mental health outcomes, including issues of depression, anxiety, suicide, and so forth.

Within many out-of-home and residential-care settings, varying degrees of heterosexism and cissexism are embedded within institutional and organizational practices. In many cases, these settings do not have any policies or practices that address sexual and/or gender identity, resulting in the assumption that all youth and workers in that setting are heterosexual and cissexual. This could mean issues of sexual and gender diversity are never talked about or youth workers and fellow youth could feel free to make stereotypical or homophobic/transphobic comments. This can be especially difficult for gender non-conforming youth, who may or may not want to explore their sexual and/or gender identity, but whose gender-variant behaviours often result in transphobic comments by staff members and transphobic verbal and physical violence by fellow youth. TSLGBTQ and allied workers within these settings should foster dialogue and awareness about issues of sexual and gender diversity, allowing an open space for some youth to break social isolation and safely explore their sexual and/or gender identity. In these cases, it becomes up to individual workers, many of whom self-identify as TSLGBTQ, to create these spaces. This means

In Their Own Words

AT HOME

WITHIN THE FIRST HOUR OF meeting her, attempting to get to know who she was, and how I might help her feel "at home" in the group home, she looked me square in the eyes and stated, "Just so you know, I like girls." She goes on with even more conviction, "and, no, I am not struggling with my sexuality. There's no struggle!" I sat, unsure how to respond. I wasn't unsure because I was uncomfortable. In fact, it was a great invitation into this young person's world. I simply did not want to close this door that had been opened and I was intrigued. I wondered how she had developed this confidence in herself and in her expression of her sexuality. I wondered what prompted her to need to disclose her sexual orientation. As we talked more, it seemed that she had identified me as someone who could not understand her. She, like many youth in the group home, was Indigenous and had grown up on reserve. She had taken one look at me and decided that I was as different from her as she could imagine. Her sexuality was simply another way in which she saw our dissimilarity.

This interaction served as an important reminder for me. Having worked with youth in care for many years, I was confident in my ability to discuss sexuality openly. I knew that adolescence is a time in which many youth develop a sense of themselves as sexual beings and that it was imperative that I take responsibility, as a trusting adult, to discuss relationships and sexuality as well as sexual orientation and gender identity. To be fearful of discussing this facet of life could leave these young people vulnerable in many ways, ranging from misinformation, to shame, or even abuse. The reminders for me were twofold. Firstly, experiencing one's sexuality as anything other than heterosexual is not, in and of itself a problem. Queer youth do not, simply by nature of being queer, need support with their sexuality. Secondly, this exchange reminded me that my own position as a married lesbian woman is valuable in role modelling the wellness and belonging of TSLGBTQ people in our society. In her simple statement, this young person had expressed that she had already learned that others saw her sexuality as a problem or "struggle." She had expressed that she experienced herself as "other." To put too much emphasis on her sexual and gender orientation and expression would distract me from supporting other areas of this child's identity and needs. Yet, neglecting my own could diminish what I can offer.

Vanessa Scrivens is a social worker in Manitoba.

that education and awareness about sexual and gender diversity becomes dependent on individual worker initiative, and there is potential for backlash from supervisors, fellow workers, youth, or even family members of youth.

Intimate Partner Violence

Just as it occurs within heterosexual and cissexual-only couples, intimate partner violence may occur within same-sex couples and trans-inclusive intimate partnerships. Although there are many feminist scholars and activists that have identified the consequences of violence against women in intimate relationships, more recently attention has been placed upon the realities of queer and trans people experiencing violence within intimate relationships (Ristock, 2008).

Although there are social services across Canada geared specifically for cis women experiencing intimate partner violence, there are oftentimes very few policies and procedures that meet the particular needs of queer and trans people.

Queer and trans people who are accessing services due to intimate partner violence face particular barriers. They are most likely to encounter heterosexist and cissexist practices where there is an implicit assumption at initial contact that the person asking for services is heterosexual and/or cissexual. In addition, very few social services attend to the complex intersectional and systemic barriers that TSLGBTQ individuals who are survivors of intimate partner violence encounter.

There are very few, if any, social services that have policies or programs that respond to the specific needs of gay and bisexual men facing same-sex partner violence. Lesbian and bisexual women risk encountering homophobia by service providers if they try to access a women's shelter. There may be challenges with the issue of disclosure, especially if the service users do not want their sexual identity to be known. Thus, disclosure of sexual identity may result in exposure to discrimination while not disclosing may compromise the services they should have the right to access. Trans women risk not being allowed into women's shelters or experiencing transphobia by service providers and fellow users if allowed entry. Queer and trans migrants whose status is linked to a Canadian citizen who is sponsoring them will be particularly vulnerable to intimate partner violence.

Barriers to Access for TSLGBTQ Individuals across Health-Care and Social Service Settings

In the previous section, we explored barriers to health-care and social services for specific TSLGBTQ groups including Indigenous two-spirited and LGBTQ Peoples, queer and trans people living with HIV, TSLGBTQ older adults and youth in care, queer and trans people experiencing intimate partner violence, and LGBTQ refugees. It is important to note that these groups are not exhaustive and they are all interrelated. Although there were important specificities in the kinds of intersectional barriers that each group encountered, there were also key barriers that cut across all groups.

One key barrier experienced by each group is related to disclosure of sexual and/or gender identity. At the same time, particularities in the specific ways that barriers related to disclosure occurred. For trans people, the barriers related to disclosure of gender identity focused upon the transition process and legal name/sex designation change. For youth in care, the barrier was related to social isolation and lack of safer spaces to explore identity. LGBTQ refugees and victims of intimate partner violence were compelled to come out by various legal systems. Across contexts, many TSLGBTQ individuals have difficulties in coming out in health-care and social service institutions because of embedded heterosexist and cissexist practices.

Another key barrier for queer and trans people across health-care and social service settings is the issue of invisibility. In many cases, service providers underestimate the proportion of queer and trans people because individuals are often reluctant to disclose their sexual and/or gender identity. It is evident that most health-care and social service policies are developed with the assumption that the service user is heterosexual and/or cissexual. Another way that TSLGBTQ people experience invisibility is when all promotional and information materials display only heterosexual and cissexual images. For example, promotional materials for long-term care facilities do not often represent TSLGBTQ individuals.

Health-care and social service settings often operate from an "indifference model," whereby queer and trans people are seen as just the same as everyone else. This has resulted in a lack of attention to the unique experiences of TSLGBTQ individuals and the impact of heterosexism/cissexism on their lives and access to/use of services. Since TSLGBTQ identity is fluid and labels are complex, people may be hesitant or have a difficult time articulating how they self-identify. They may also be fearful of being labelled by a health-care provider. Over their life span, queer and trans people often have had to face negative experiences with service providers who make assumptions about their sexual and/or gender identity or who are openly homophobic and/or transphobic. Due to these experiences, TSLGBTQ individuals often choose not disclose their sexual and/or gender identity and/or delay accessing health-care and/or social services.

The Continuum of Attitudes towards Sexual and Gender Difference in Health/Social Services

Attitudes towards sexual and gender diversity range on a scale from the most overt forms of hatred to alliances based upon respect and mutual solidarity. The continuum presented here (adapted from Ryan, 1999 in Brotman & Ryan, 2001) addresses this range of attitudes, which are made manifest in individual beliefs, institutional practices, and government policies. Oftentimes, the task of dismantling the multiple and intersecting forms of social and institutional discrimination falls upon TSLGBTQ individuals and activists. Social workers should engage in critical self-reflection to identify where they and their workplaces stand on the treatment of TSLGBTQ individuals, in order to engage in processes of change to move towards an environment of solidarity.

Homo/bi/transphobia   Hetero/Cissexism   Indifference   Tolerance   Solidarity

FIGURE 10.1 // A Continuum of Attitudes Towards Sexual and Gender Difference in Health/Social Services

Source: Adapted from Ryan, 1999

Guidelines for Social Workers to Foster Safe and Affirming Space for TSLGBTQ People

Depending on the region or province, health-care and social service settings may or may not have policies meant to guide practitioners in how to address sexual and gender diversity. Some institutions in major urban settings will also have TSLGBTQ-specific initiatives and programs. Some institutions will have policies or best practices for how to work with TSLGBTQ individuals. In many cases, there is often a lack of specialized training to work with TSLGBTQ populations or mainstream services adapted to meet their particular needs.

Social workers need to examine agency policies in order to determine the degree to which agencies incorporate policies related to sexual and gender diversity. For example, in order to better serve trans and gender non-conforming people, social workers should familiarize themselves with the laws that regulate legal name and sex designation changes in their province, in addition to agency policies around the use of preferred names. Social workers can then tailor their practice based on the specific ways in which health-care and social service policies address (or do not address) issues related to sexual and gender diversity within their particular workplace.

Within their particular work context, practitioners can work towards creating spaces that are open, affirming, and safe for TSLGBTQ service users. Using an intersectional approach allows social workers to better understand the impact of multiple forms of oppression on everyday realities of specific groups of queer and trans people. This also allows social workers to develop concrete strategies that recognize and affirm people's multiple and intersecting identities. For example, practitioners can be aware of the various ways in which age, racial/ethnic background, class, ability, gender, and citizenship status all play a role in how queer and trans people address issues of disclosure. Taking intersectionality into consideration will assist practitioners in developing context-specific strategies to ensure respect, trust, or a therapeutic alliance with queer and trans people.

Practical TIP

Creating Safer Spaces for TSLGBTQ People

- Post signs that openly state that their office is a safe space for TSLGBTQ people.
- Have posters or visual materials that include same-sex couples and trans people.
- Be aware of language and terms you use related to sexual and/or gender identity and affirm the ways in which people self-identify, understanding this may shift and change over time.
- Do not assume one's sexual and/or gender identity. If you are asking about an intimate relationship, ask about a partner, rather asking about a husband/wife or boyfriend/girlfriend.
- Do not assume that one's sexual behaviour always needs to "match" self-identification of sexual identity.
- Do not assume that one's gender expression will always "match" self-identification of gender identity.
- Validate TSLGBTQ individuals' experiences of heterosexism and/or cissexism.
- Do not assume what a person's biological or chosen family structures may be and understand that family formations may change over time.
- Learn more about the degree to which someone participates within TSLGBTQ and other communities.

Social Location and Institutional Power

In order for social workers to develop an anti-oppressive and social justice-oriented practice, it is crucial to engage in critical analysis and reflexivity in order to situate themselves in relation to the kinds of institutional power they hold as a social worker. This requires

Theory in Practice

AGIR (ACTION LGBTQ WITH IMMIGRANTS AND REFUGEES)

ONE EXAMPLE OF ENGAGING IN collective empowerment can be drawn from the initiatives of AGIR. AGIR is a non-profit organization in Montreal whose mandate is to engage in support work and community organizing with queer and trans migrants. Open to all LGBTQ migrants, AGIR has developed programs and community organizing initiatives specifically for queer and trans refugees. AGIR is a multilingual organization and functions in both French and English and thus, operates within Francophone, Anglophone, and Allophone milieus. A key challenge that LGBTQ refugees encounter is related to disclosure of sexual and/or gender identity throughout the refugee process. For example, IRB officials required LGBTQ refugee claimants to "prove" their sexual orientation, asking for details not required by claimants seeking refuge on other grounds (Lee & Brotman, 2011).

LGBTQ refugees not only have to repeatedly retell their stories of persecution, but they are also repeatedly compelled to come out. Many queer and trans refugees survived in their country of origin by hiding their sexual or gender identity in order to prevent being persecuted. Ironically, sexual minority refugees who have been profoundly traumatized must come out repeatedly and in a systematic way in order to be deemed a credible refugee. This repeated coming out occurs the moment individuals apply for refugee status, for example, when speaking to border officials and airport authorities or when meeting lawyers, doctors, psychologists, social workers or employers. Along with this outing comes increased exposure to homophobia or transphobia in their interactions with almost any institution, service provider, or employer.

In June 2010, AGIR and the Mapping Memories project came together in order to produce *Entry Point: Queer Refugees in Montreal*, a collaborative media project by and about 13 queer and trans people with refugee experiences. Project participants included those who were Francophone, Anglophone, Spanish speaking, and multilingual. Goals for this digital storytelling media project included using workshops as a space to bring community members together and tell their own stories, offering an introduction to various media skills, and providing opportunities for community members to share their stories to a wider audience. This collective media project allowed LGBTQ refugees to develop their own narratives of migration, share their experiences with the public through media, and engage in collective empowerment in a number of ways. First, it broke social isolation.

As all the participants shared their stories with each other, they engaged in critical consciousness-raising and started to identify the ways in which refugee policy and law shaped their everyday lives. In this process of collective empowerment, the participants were able to push back against the forms of structural violence that is embedded within Canadian refugee policies and practices. Canadian refugee policies do not reflect how the coming out process is not one definable moment but rather an activity that is repeated continuously over multiple contexts, with varying results and consequences (Berg & Millbank, 2009), nor do they take into consideration the many reasons for why sexual minority refugees may choose to conceal their sexuality.

Also, by having space to create their own story and media project, each participant was able to take control over how they wanted to construct their own narrative and how they wanted to present it within public spheres. Their taking control challenges and complicates the prevailing public narrative of LGBTQ refugees as simply fleeing homophobic countries to migrating and finding liberation by coming out in Canada.

identifying the concrete forms of **institutional power** held within particular work contexts. Institutional power could be related to having decision-making power, the power to distribute resources, the power to accept or deny access to specific programs or services, the power to include or exclude information in a client's file, and so forth. In addition, the kinds of institutional power and responsibilities one has as a front-line worker is different from that of a manager. It is equally important to consider the constraints that exist within the workplace.

This critical assessment of institutional power needs to be then placed in and linked to their particular social location. For example, social workers who self-identify as TSLGBTQ and work with queer and trans people encounter challenges that are often different from heterosexual and cissexual social workers who work with queer and trans people. Engaging in this kind of critical analysis and reflexivity makes space for social workers to develop context- and site-specific strategies for developing a social work practice that will respond to the needs and respect the realities of TSLGBTQ individuals.

institutional power Refers to the various forms of power that individuals hold based on their social location and position within a particular institution or agency.

Collective Empowerment

Over the course of Canadian history, there have been numerous times in which queer and trans people have participated in advancing social justice and cross-movement solidarity. Advancing TSLGBTQ human rights has always been and continues to be a site of social struggle. An essential component to this struggle has been the role of community organizing and fostering collective empowerment. Social workers have an important role to play in fostering individual and collective empowerment with the TSLGBTQ individuals whom they serve across settings.

A key aspect of collective empowerment is fostering space for queer and trans people to be able to have control over the issues that directly affect them. Social workers can work towards this goal through direct practice activism, policy advocacy, and linking service users to activist groups and community organizations that advance TSLGBTQ human rights. This could mean linking up with any number of initiatives, including the HIV/AIDS movement, trans activism, two-spirited solidarity, LGBTQ refugee rights, queer people of colour organizing, and so forth. This could also mean seeking out organizations that use a peer-support model or incorporate community organizing principles into their work.

Conclusion

This chapter aimed to provide students with the building blocks for social work practice related to issues of sexual and gender diversity, paying close attention to the historical and social dimensions that shape queer and trans peoples' everyday lives. It also engaged with intersectional theory, in order to develop a practice approach that recognizes how multiple systems of oppression shape the complex social identities of queer and trans people. This chapter also identified key barriers that queer and trans people encounter across healthcare and social service settings. Finally, we introduced an anti-oppressive practice model that examines the relationship between social location and institutional power, in order for social workers to engage in social-justice–oriented practice that fosters both individual and collective empowerment.

QUESTIONS FOR CRITICAL THOUGHT

1. Are there aspects of the historical context of sexual and gender diversity in Canada that you didn't know before? If yes, why do you think this was the case?
2. How does heterosexism and cissexism operate across health-care and social service settings?
3. In what ways does disclosure of sexual and/or gender identity and coming out affect TSLGBTQ individuals' access to health-care and social services?
4. What are the ways that intersectionality shape queer and trans people's everyday lives?
5. This chapter described several groups within the TSLGBTQ population that have specific concerns. What are some other TSLGBTQ groups that would benefit from services targeted to their distinct experiences?
6. How might your social location shape the way that you engage in social work practice with TSLGBTQ individuals?

RECOMMENDED READINGS

Brotman, S., & Levy, J.J. (Eds.). (2008). *Homosexualités: Variations linguistiques et culturelles,* (p. 307–338). Québec: Presses de l'Université du Québec, Coll. Santé et Société. This compilation of book chapters in both French and English includes issues related to two-spirited people, queer people of colour, same-sex parenting, and so forth.

Canadian Social Work Review. (2011). Volume 28, Number 1. This specific journal edition includes four journal articles related to incorporating queer theory into social work education, access to shelter services for trans people, the experiences of LGBTQ refugees, and critical race analysis of social work articles related to race and sexuality.

Ezra, J. (2013). *Taking charge: A handbook for health care and social service providers working with trans people.* Action Santé Travesti(e)s et Transsexuel(le)s du Québec. Public Health Agency of Canada. This manual provides specific information and resources for health-care and social service providers working with trans people in Quebec.

Kinsman, G. (1998). Constructing sexual problems: These things may lead to the tragedy of our species. In W. Antony & L. Samuelson (Eds.), *Power and resistance: Critical thinking about Canadian social issues* (2nd ed.) (p. 256–282). Halifax: Fernwood Publishing. This book chapter engages in critical analysis related to the historical context of sexuality within Canada.

RECOMMENDED WEBSITES

2-Spirited People of the 1st Nations
www.2spirits.com
2-Spirited People of the 1st Nations is a non-profit social services organization whose membership consists of Aboriginal gay, lesbian, bisexual, and transgender people in Toronto.

Action LGBTQ with Immigrants and Refugees
www.agirmontreal.org
AGIR is an autonomous non-profit organization in Montreal whose mandate is to develop and offer services, information, programs, and resources, in addition to protecting and defending the legal, social, and economic rights of LGBTQ migrants in the spirit of solidarity.

Action Santé Travesti(e)s et Transsexuel(le)s du Québec
www.astteq.org
Based out of Montreal, ASTT(e)Q aims to promote the health and well-being of trans people through peer support and advocacy, education and outreach, and community empowerment, and mobilization.

The Avenue Community Centre for Gender & Sexual Diversity
www.avenuecommunitycentre.ca
The Avenue Community Centre for Gender & Sexual Diversity is a non-profit agency in Saskatoon working to address health and social issues in the lesbian, gay, bisexual, transgender, two-spirited, and queer (LGBT2Q) community.

Egale Canada Human Rights Trust
www.egale.ca
Egale Canada Human Rights Trust (ECHRT) is Canada's only national charity promoting lesbian, gay, bisexual, and trans (LGBT) human rights through research, education, and community engagement.

Rainbow Health Ontario
www.rainbowhealthontario.ca
Rainbow Health Ontario (RHO) is a province-wide program that works to improve the health and well-being of lesbian, gay, bisexual, and trans people in Ontario through education, research, outreach, and public policy advocacy.

Rainbow Refugee Committee
www.rainbowrefugee.ca
Founded in 2000, Rainbow Refugee Committee (RRC) is a Vancouver-based community group that supports and advocates for people seeking refugee protection because of persecution based on sexual orientation, gender identity, or HIV status. Rainbow Refugee Committee engages in outreach, advocacy, and public education on QLGBT/HIV+ refugee issues.

Trans PULSE Project
www.transpulseproject.ca
The Trans PULSE Project is a community-based research (CBR) project that is investigating the impact of social exclusion and discrimination on the health of trans people in Ontario, Canada.

Disability and Social Work Practice

Carl Ernst, McGill University
Radha MacCulloch, McGill University

LEARNING OBJECTIVES

- To understand how theoretical frameworks inform social work practice.

- To understand how disability emerges through the interaction between bodily impairment and the environment.

- To identify complex social, economic, and physical barriers to the inclusion of persons with disabilities from historical and contemporary perspectives.

- To recognize how policies influence the delivery of health and social services to individuals with disabilities and their families.

- To identify the links among theory, research, policy, and practice and to apply these links to addressing issues facing individuals with disabilities.

Chapter Outline

This chapter describes how disability is defined, categorized, and conceptualized, with particular regard to how this informs social work practice. The prevalence and impact of disability on individuals, caregivers, and society, as well as historical trends in the disability field are discussed. Included within this discussion is the evolution of the disability movement in Canada. Supporting case examples used throughout are grounded in the context of contemporary Canadian health and social services. The chapter concludes with a description of practical tips and guidelines for social workers entering the field.

Defining Disability

What Is Disability? How Is Disability Defined in Canada?

Definitions of disability reveal much about a society and its economy, politics, and values. These concepts and definitions reflect societal expectations of individuals and what activities are valuable or appropriate (Wendell, 1996). As a result, no universal definitions of disability exist in Canada; furthermore, different definitions of disability across various policies, programs, and services can lead to wide variation in care across the country (Marshall, Kendall, Banks, & Gover, 2009). Importantly, slight changes to definitions written into municipal, provincial, or federal laws may result in considerable changes in service.

Different government agencies define disability in various ways, depending on the degree to which that body dispenses resources. Roughly, the more benefits that are available upon request by people with disabilities, the more severe and restrictive the definition of disability. Statistics Canada, which does not provide or offer support for people with disabilities, defines disability following the standards put forward by the World Health Organization. It states that people "have a disability if they (or their parents or guardians, in the case of children 14 and under) report having a physical or mental health condition or a health problem that restricts their ability to engage in activities of daily living" (Human Resources and Skills Development Canada, 2011, p. 3).

Statistics Canada's definition of disability is applied within Canada's national survey on disability, the Canadian Survey on Disability (CSD). Data on rates of disability come directly from self-report questionnaires and delineate severity by the degree and intensity to which activities are restricted in day-to-day life. Degree of disability is categorized as mild, moderate, or severe. Type of disability is divided by age (0–4; 5–14; and 15 and over) into multiple classification categories largely along physical lines, such as "hearing" or "seeing" for children, and "emotional/psychological" or "pain" to name just a few categories for older age groups (Human Resources and Skills Development Canada, 2011).

The Canada Revenue Agency (CRA), which determines tax benefit status, takes a much stricter stance on what constitutes disability. The Disability Tax Credit defines disability as a severe and prolonged impairment in physical or mental functions, certified by a qualified practitioner. Prolonged is defined as continuous over a period greater than 12 months and severity is defined by marked or significant activity restrictions, all or substantially (at least 90 per cent) all of the time. Specifically, the application form reads: "You are unable or it takes you three times the normal time required to perform one or more of the basic activities of daily living even with therapy (other than therapy to support a vital function) and the use of appropriate devices and medication" (Canada Revenue Agency, 2012, form t2201, p. 2). These guidelines themselves, even after certification by a qualified practitioner, are subject to evaluation by an administrator at the CRA.

A consensus definition between Statistics Canada and the Canada Revenue Agency might be the degree of impairment and the extent to which daily life is impeded in performing basic tasks; however, it is clear that many people who would meet the disability criteria for Statistics Canada's Canadian Survey on Disability would not meet the disability criteria stipulated by the CRA. Social workers find these definitions too limited when they attempt to liaise with government agencies in order to access services on behalf of a client. A more useful avenue with which to frame impairment might involve creating new models of disability, models that move away from the more restrictive definitions stipulated by government agencies, and towards a more comprehensive and nuanced perspective.

Theorizing Disability

The Medical Model of Disability

The medical model of disability has a long historical tradition that is predicated on the distinction between the normal and the pathological (Smart, 2001). The **medical model of disability**, also known as the biomedical, disease, clinical, or individual model, views disability as an individual deficit and conceptualizes disability as being fundamentally physiological or anatomical in origin (Smart, 2001). The medical model uses standardized, diagnostic tools and trained "experts" to identify and distinguish pathology or deviance from normality (Rothman, 2010). Medical experts then prescribe a course of treatment that aims to repair or cure the individual of his or her physiological limitations.

> **medical model of disability** Views disability as an individual deficit and identifies disability as being fundamentally biological in origin.

The medical model is challenged by several shortcomings and omissions. First, within this model, disability is viewed as a set of static, uniform, and pathological characteristics. It fails to recognize that the experiences and outcomes of disability vary between individuals across the life course and that many people with disabilities are healthy (Smart, 2001). Furthermore, this model relies on the expert's prescription for treatment and views disability as something to be fixed at one point in time. It consequently fails to take into consideration the individual's assessment of her or his impairment and desired course of treatment and denies that individuals with a disability may not be "cured" and may require different supports throughout their life (Smart, 2001). Second, in identifying disability as an individual deficit, this model serves to objectify the individual (Smart, 2001). The impairment becomes the individual's primary identity (e.g., autistic, quadraplegic), obscuring and denying other aspects of his or her personhood. Third, this model does not consider the social or environmental factors of disability and may thereby medicalize or diminish social problems that cause disability (Marshall et al., 2009; Smart, 2001; Wendell, 1996). While no longer considered the dominant perspective of disability, the influence of the medical model persists today. Medical diagnoses of disability and those who administer them continue to be gatekeepers to service and support.

The Social Model of Disability

The **social model of disability** emerged in the 1970s with the formation of the Union of the Physically Impaired Against Segregation (UPIAS) in Britain (Shakespeare, 2006b). This model emerged in response to the medical model of disability, which, as described above, views disability as an individual deficit and conceptualizes disability as a biological impairment. The social model of disability views individuals with disabilities as an oppressed group and seeks to reconceptualize disability, distinguishing impairment from disability (Shakespeare, 2006a; Shakespeare, 2006b). According to social modelists, impairment is a result of a physical limitation whereas disability is a result of oppression and social exclusion (Shakespeare, 2006a; Shakespeare, 2006b).

> **social model of disability** In contrast to the medical model of disability, this model contends that disability is created or constructed by social and environmental factors only.

ableism Refers to discrimination or prejudice against individuals based on their ability or disability.

According to the social model, disability resides not within the individual but is created or constructed by social factors such as the economy, culture, and language. Early social modelists suggested that disability emerged from the capitalist mode of production, which favoured the able-bodied individual and segregated those with an impairment that impeded their ability to produce (Gustavsson, 2004; Tossebro, 2004). Others suggest that knowledge and discourse are vulnerable to power, thus the concept of disability emerged from the dominant discourse of normality. Therefore the social model overtly challenges **ableist** attitudes and disabling environments, which discriminate against individuals with disabilities.

Like the medical model, the social model also faces challenges in its theoretical assumptions. First, the social model risks discounting the individual entirely. It threatens to deny the individual or personal experience of impairment and reject clinical or individually based intervention. While efforts to distinguish between impairment and disability have been critical to the disability rights movement through locating disability not within the body but within oppressive structures and environments, these efforts have simultaneously led to the separation of chronic illness from disability (Wendell, 2001). This distinction, within disability politics, has subsequently served to diminish the experience of impairment and the realities of individuals with a chronic illness who desire medical intervention to ease their pain or their fatigue (Wendell, 2001). While this chapter has a focus on intellectual and physical disabilities, it is essential to acknowledge that individuals with disabilities may also have ongoing medical needs. In other words, chronic illnesses such as arthritis, fibromyalgia, HIV/AIDS, and multiple sclerosis can cause disability. In fact, in 2005, roughly one third of Canadians reported living with at least one of seven chronic health conditions (Health Council of Canada, 2007) and as with intellectual and physical disabilities, the impact of living with a chronic health condition is pervasive, potentially affecting areas such as employment, education, independent living, and quality of life.

Second, the social model not only assumes that all people with disabilities are oppressed but does not acknowledge that this group differs from other oppressed groups in that they experience both discrimination or oppression as well as impairments in bodily structure and function (Shakespeare, 2006b). Finally, taken to its fullest application, the social model of disability calls for a "barrier-free utopia" which, given the plurality of experiences and abilities, is virtually impossible (Shakespeare, 2006b, p. 201).

Both the medical and social models of disability contribute important elements to how Canada and social work practice view disability. The social model draws attention to the societal and physical barriers faced by people with impairments and promotes social inclusion, while the medical model makes technological and biological advances that improve daily living for people with disabilities. The contribution of both of these models contributed to the World Health Organization's definition of disability, used by many social work practitioners today in Canada.

The World Health Organization's International Classification of Functioning, Disability and Health (ICF)

The World Health Organization (WHO) developed a framework for measuring health and disability, called The International Classification of Functioning, Disability and Health (ICF). The ICF served to bridge the medical and social models to create a biopsychosocial model of functioning, health, and disability. According to the WHO,

Disability is an umbrella term, covering impairments, activity limitations, and participation restrictions. An impairment is a problem in body function or structure; an activity limitation is a difficulty encountered by an individual in executing a task or action; while a participation restriction is a problem experienced by an

TABLE 11.1	Applying the WHO's ICF		
Health Condition	Impairment	Activity Limitation	Participation Restriction
Leprosy	Loss of sensation of extremities	Difficulties in grasping objects	Stigma of leprosy leads to unemployment.
Panic Disorder	Anxiety	Not capable of going out alone	People's reactions leads to diminished social relationships.
Spinal Injury	Paralysis	Not able to use public transportation	Lack of accommodations in public transportation leads to diminished participation in religious or other community activities.
Juvenile Diabetes	Pancreatic dysfunction	None (impairment controlled by medication)	Does not go to school because of stereotypes about disease.
Vitiligo	Facial disfigurement	None	Severely limited participation in social relations owing to fears of contagion.
Person who had a mental health problem and was treated for a psychotic disorder	None	None	Denied employment because of employer's prejudice.

Source: Reproduced, with the permission of the publisher, from Traditional medicine, Geneva, World Health Organization, 2008 (Fact sheet no. 134; http://www.who.int/mediacentre/factsheets/fs134/en/, accessed 13 May 2011).

individual in involvement in life situations. Disability is thus not just a health problem. It is a complex phenomenon, reflecting the interaction between features of a person's body and features of the society in which he or she lives (World Health Organization, n.d.a).

The ICF currently recognizes disability as a "universal experience" that can be experienced by every person who experiences a decrease in their health (World Health Organization, n.d.b). According to the ICF, disability comprises three key components: (1) bodily functions and structures; (2) activity and participation domains; and (3) environmental factors including physical, social, and attitudinal settings. Thus, the ICF states that disability results from the interaction of impairments in bodily functions and structures, limitations in activity, restriction in social participation, and the environments in which people live (See Table 11.1).

This framework is congruent with social work practice; just as the ICF seeks to reconcile the tension between the medical model and the social model of disability, social work practice seeks to reconcile the tension between "social reform and individual change" (Howe, 2009, p. 11).

Categorizing Disability

Ongoing uncertainty around how to describe disability is evident in research and practice addressing disability. In research, some studies describe disability as impairment, using the diagnostic label or broad impairment category only, while others identify disability as only those impairments that cause limitations on activities.

Similarly, in practice, access to services or recognition of having a disability may rely on describing disability as impairment, using the diagnostic label or broad impairment category only, while other services may identify disability as only those impairments that cause limitations on activities and participation. Thus, in Canada, disability may be classified according to two different approaches: (1) the categorical or diagnostic approach or (2) the non-categorical or functional approach. Eligibility for services may be based on providing a specific and formal diagnosis made by a health-care provider through formal assessments of the biological impairment while other services may take a non-categorical approach to disability which focuses on the individual's level of functioning and simply requires evidence of an impairment that impedes certain activities such as employment rather than a diagnostic label (Stein & Jessop, 1982). Perhaps impairment and disability may be better described by level of functioning, captured using *both* a measure of impairment severity *and* a measure of activity limitations (or how that impairment limits the execution of specific tasks).

The Categorical or Diagnostic Approach

The categorical or diagnostic approach is predicated on the identification of the cause and effects of any deviation from normal bodily structures and functions. This approach seeks to identify and classify these deviations based on findings from tests and assessments such as brain scans (MRI/CAT), blood and urine tests, hearing and vision tests, and behavioural assessments and observations.

Benefits of the Categorical Approach

- provides standardized care to individuals across different contexts (e.g., eases clinical discussions and brings consistency to practice and research; Stein & Jessop, 1982);
- allows medicine to specialize and develop expertise in a certain area (e.g., Parkinson's disease, spina bifida);
- allows clinical research to study specific groups with the aim of improving services and individual quality of life;
- permits the collection and tracking of public health statistics;
- permits community-building among those with a shared diagnosis.

Challenges of the Categorical Approach

- may diminish the differences between individuals with a shared diagnosis and the commonalities between individuals with different diagnoses (Stein & Jessop, 1982);
- clinical studies that use a categorical approach cannot explore the experiences of rare disorders (due to small sample sizes).

The Non-categorical or Functional Approach

The non-categorical or functional approach suggests that level of functioning, rather than diagnostic label, has a greater impact on participation and outcomes for individuals with disabilities and can tell us more about how limitations in the body interact with activities associated with certain social roles. According to the WHO's ICF, disability is not only a biological impairment in bodily structure and function but, as noted above, rather the *interaction* of impairment in bodily structure and function, activity limitations, restriction in social participation, and environmental factors such as physical, social, and attitudinal settings (WHO, n.d.b).

Benefits of the Non-categorical Approach

- acknowledges the interaction between the impairment in bodily structure and function and the environment;
- reduces stigma attached to specific diagnoses;
- provides the individual, his or her family, and service providers including social workers with tangible, individualized areas for intervention that are grounded in the day-to-day lives of people with disabilities.

Challenges of the Non-categorical Approach

- complicates classification (medical intervention and clinical research)
- may be time-consuming and difficult to apply in practice (as an awareness and understanding of how the impairment fits within the context of the individual's life is needed).

The 2006 Participation and Activity Limitations Survey outlines 11 different possible types of disabilities among children under 15 years of age and 11 different possible disabilities among adults 15 years of age and older (See Table 11.2).

TABLE 11.2   Types of Disabilities

Types of Disabilities among Children (Less Than 15 Years of Age)		Types of Disabilities among Adults (15 Years of Age and Older)	
Type	Description	Type	Description
Hearing (applicable to all children under 15)	Difficulty hearing.	**Hearing**	Difficulty hearing what is being said in a conversation with one other person, in a conversation with three or more persons, or in a telephone conversation.
Seeing (applicable to all children under 15)	Difficulty seeing.	**Seeing**	Difficulty seeing ordinary newsprint or clearly seeing the face of someone from 4 metres (12 feet).
Speech (applicable to children 5–14)	Difficulty speaking and/or being understood.	**Speech**	Difficulty speaking and/or being understood.
Mobility (applicable to children 5–14)	Difficulty walking. This means walking on a flat firm surface, such as a sidewalk or floor.	**Mobility**	Difficulty walking half a kilometre or up and down a flight of stairs, about 12 steps without resting, moving from one room to another, carrying an object of 5 kilograms (10 pounds) for 10 metres (30 feet), or standing for long periods.
Dexterity (applicable to children 5–14)	Difficulty using hands or fingers to grasp or hold small objects, such as a pencil or scissors.	**Agility**	Difficulty bending, dressing or undressing oneself, getting into and out of bed, cutting own toenails, using fingers to grasp or handle objects, reaching in any direction (for example, above one's head), or cutting own food.

(Continued)

TABLE 11.2   Types of Disabilities (*Continued*)

Types of Disabilities among Children (Less Than 15 Years of Age)		Types of Disabilities among Adults (15 Years of Age and Older)	
Type	Description	Type	Description
Learning (applicable to children 5–14)	Difficulty learning due to the presence of a condition, such as attention problems, hyperactivity, or dyslexia, whether or not the condition was diagnosed by a teacher, doctor, or other health professional.	**Pain**	Limited in the amount or kind of activities that one can do because of a long-term pain that is constant or reoccurs from time to time, for example, recurrent back pain.
Developmental Delay (applicable to children under 5)	Child has a delay in his/her development, either a physical, intellectual, or another type of delay.	**Learning**	Difficulty learning because of a condition, such as attention problems, hyperactivity or dyslexia, whether or not the condition was diagnosed by a teacher, doctor or other health professional.
Developmental disability or disorder (applicable to children 5–14)	Cognitive limitations due to the presence of a developmental disability or disorder, such as Down syndrome, autism, or mental impairment caused by a lack of oxygen at birth.	**Memory**	Limited in the amount or kind of activities that one can do due to frequent periods of confusion or difficulty remembering things. These difficulties may be associated with Alzheimer's disease, brain injuries, or other similar conditions.
Psychological (applicable to children 5–14)	Limited in the amount or kind of activities that one can do due to the presence of an emotional, psychological, or behavioural condition.	**Developmental**	Cognitive limitations due to the presence of a developmental disability or disorder, such as Down syndrome, autism, or mental impairment caused by a lack of oxygen at birth.
Chronic condition (applicable to all children under 15)	Limited in the amount or kind of activities that one can do due to the presence of one or more chronic health conditions that have lasted or are expected to last six months or more and that have been diagnosed by a health professional. Examples of chronic conditions are asthma or severe allergies, heart condition or disease, kidney condition or disease, cancer, epilepsy, cerebral palsy, Spina Bifida, Cystic Fibrosis, Muscular Dystrophy, Fetal Alcohol Syndrome, etc.	**Psychological**	Limited in the amount or kind of activities that one can do due to the presence of an emotional, psychological, or psychiatric condition, such as phobias, depression, schizophrenia, or drinking or drug problems.
Unknown (applicable to all children under 15)	The type of disability is unknown if the respondent answered YES to the general questions on activity limitations, but did not provide any YES to the questions about type of disability that followed.	**Unknown**	The type of disability is unknown if the respondent answered YES to the general questions on activity limitations, but did not provide any YES to the questions about type of disability that followed.

Source: http://www.statcan.gc.ca/pub/89-577-x/4065022-eng.htm

Prevalence of Disability in Canada

In Canada, rates of disability are tracked through a national, cross-sectional survey administered by Statistics Canada and funded by Human Resources and Skills Development Canada (HRSDC). This post-census survey uses self-reporting to collect information about adults and children whose daily activities are limited by physical, mental, or other health-related conditions or problems. This survey, called the Participation and Activity Limitation Survey (PALS), gathered two waves of data in 2001 and 2006 but has since been replaced with the Canadian Survey on Disability (CSD) which conducted its first wave of data collection in 2012. Like its predecessor, the PALS, the sampling frame for the CSD includes all individuals who were 15 years of age or older and living in Canada who responded yes to one of the two questions posed by the National Household Survey (NHS) regarding activity limitations. It is important to note that individuals living in institutions and on First Nations reserves were not included in this survey, as difficulties in accessing or reaching all individuals in these communities hindered the ability to produce accurate statistics. However, the First Nations Regional Longitudinal Health Survey, now with two waves of data collected, fills this gap by providing a snapshot of the health and well-being of those living in First Nations communities across Canada.

Congruent with the WHO's ICF definition of disability, the CSD measures disability according to the severity and frequency of experienced activity limitations. In other words, the CSD defines disability from a functional or non-categorical approach and does not capture specific diagnoses. Using this approach, an individual with an impairment and/or a diagnosis who does not experience activity limitations due to their level of functioning may not be identified as having a disability.

According to the 2012 Canadian Survey on Disability, 3.8 million Canadians (or 13.7 per cent) reported experiencing an activity limitation due to a physical, mental, or other health-related condition (see Table 11.3). The rate of disability varies significantly by age and only marginally by gender. Approximately 15 per cent of women 15 years of age and older reported an activity limitation compared to 13 per cent of men. However,

TABLE 11.3   Prevalence of Disability by Age in Canada

Age Groups	Total Population	Population with Disabilities	Total Disability Rate
Total (15 years of age and older)	27,516,200	3,775,910	13.7
15–64	23,187,350	2,338,240	10.1
15–24	4,462,850	195,720	4.4
25–44	9,159,860	598,680	6.5
45–64	9,564,640	1,543,840	16.1
65 and over	4,328,850	1,437,670	33.2
65–74	2,486,790	653,900	26.3
75 and over	1,842,070	783,770	42.5

Source: The Participation and Activity Limitation Survey 2006 Analytical Report. Ottawa: Statistics Canada, 2007. (Catalogue no. 89-628-XIE — No. 002).

these rates change dramatically when comparing based on age as 33.2 per cent of individuals 65 years of age and older reported an activity limitation compared to 4.4 per cent of individuals between 15 and 24 years of age (Statistics Canada, 2012). It is important to note that informal caregivers provide the majority of the care needed by individuals with disabilities. In fact, the majority of individuals with disabilities identified their main caregivers as family members or friends (83.1 per cent and 13.5 per cent, respectively) while a much smaller group of individuals with disabilities identified organizations and employees (13.4 per cent and 10.7 per cent, respectively) as their primary caregivers (Statistics Canada, 2006).

History of Disability Policy in Canada

Early Beliefs about Individuals with Disabilities

Different cultures at different time periods have had different views on disability. Ancient Greek society viewed lameness, blindness, or other physical impairments as punishment by the gods for sinful acts by ancestors, while similar people were sometimes viewed in medieval times as vessels to encourage charity by the masses. The Enlightenment and pre-industrial eras viewed the same type of individual with disgust, and people with physical impairments were often consigned to the harsh conditions of poorhouses. Physical disabilities have been viewed in diametrically opposite ways, depending on context; people born with physical disabilities were often viewed with pity or contempt, while soldiers with identical impairments were viewed as heroes worthy of state resources (Morton & Wright, 1987). The critical point is that types of disabilities, both physical and mental, have been viewed differently based on societal norms of the time. Prior to the Industrial Revolution for example, before people were described in terms of units of labour, individuals were not necessarily judged on their utility to society. Thus, how we view disability today will likely be very different in the future as societal norms continue to evolve.

Provision of care for individuals with impairments began in churches and other religious entities that provided care for the sick, elderly, or disadvantaged. A classic example is the priories staffed by medical friars in England during the Middle Ages. One of these priories, St. Mary of Bethlehem (called "Bedlam"), became what is now considered the first asylum for the mentally ill in the western world, starting circa 1390. Prior to and including the 1800s, however, there was little state support for people with disabilities worldwide (English Heritage, n.d). Thus, prisons or workhouses became places to house people who looked, acted, or behaved differently. Indeed, the workhouse or almshouse movement was founded on laws such as the English Poor Laws that viewed poverty and urban living as a cause of disability, rather than disability leading to poverty. This was reflected in the harsh conditions of the workhouses mandated to have worse conditions than the lowest paying job available (See Chapter 1 for a discussion of less eligibility). By providing work for all people, government believed that mental illness, immorality, or degeneracy would disappear. In Canada, people with disabilities were either cared for by family, left to survive on the streets, or put in jail (Graham, Swift, & Delaney, 2000).

Prior to the Act of Union of 1867, Canada was divided into three colonies and two of these, Upper and Lower Canada, became what is now Ontario and Quebec, respectively. In the early 1800s, there was no state support for those who were historically termed as "lunatics" or "the insane," despite recognition that people with these problems required some form of protection or safety from society (today's terminology would refer to these individuals as having a psychiatric disorder or an intellectual impairment, differentiated by level of functioning).

Treatment of "the insane" was often harsh, in the absence of state support. While an extreme example, the Salem Witch trials in Massachusetts in 1692, give some idea of how "lunatics" may have been treated in the region of Upper and Lower Canada. People were chained naked to walls in prisons, put in holes or locked in attics of homes, either out of shame or functional necessity for family units. While there were no recorded witch trials in Canada, the treatment of "the insane" was likely similar, and certainly some ended up in jails or hidden in family homes (Chupik & Wright, 2006). To address the issue of providing sanctuary for those considered "insane," the legislature of Upper Canada authorized Charles Duncombe to explore options for caring. Commissioned in 1831, Duncombe and others travelled throughout the United States and reported back to the Upper Canada legislature. Their report and recommendations led to the passage of "An Act to Authorise the Erection of an Asylum within this Province for the Reception of Insane and/or Lunatic Person" in 1839. While the asylum was designed to protect vulnerable individuals from society as a place of refuge (reflected in their architecture, open grounds, and geographical placement away from the community), they quickly took on whole new functions as large places of confinement. Further, asylums rather than prisons, became the last resort for anyone with a disability—whether "insane" or not (Simmons, 1982).

Asylum, Confinement, and Institutionalization

The Provincial Lunatic Asylum opened in the Toronto City jail in 1841 and moved to its permanent home on 999 Queen Street in 1850. Commitment to the asylum could follow two particular routes: (1) designation from two physicians attesting to lunacy (definitions of lunacy varied by a physician), or (2) statement from a justice of the peace saying that the individual was "suspected and believed to be insane and dangerous to be at large" (Ontario, 1887, p. 2592). There was no policy for discharge from asylums (although the Lieutenant Governor could grant this in individual cases), meaning that people could spend their entire lives in an asylum.

Joseph Workman, the first superintendent of the Provincial Lunatic Asylum described the resulting situation at the asylum: "Many people who were mentally retarded, senile, criminal, unemployed, poor or unwanted were deliberately certified as insane . . . certificates of insanity furnished are in 19 cases in 20, entirely fallacious" (Sessions, 1858). This quotation highlights the use of the asylum as a catch-all for unwanted people of any description and the lack of any form of social safety net at the time. Consequently, demands for beds continued to outpace supply and waiting lists were long. From 1850 to the end of the twentieth century, the struggle to keep asylums open to "curables" (those considered to be high functioning "lunatics") and closed to "incurables" (those identified as idiots) persisted. One result of this struggle was the creation of the branch asylum system, which refers to other asylums to house incurables, an example of which is the Orillia Asylum for Idiots in Ontario (renamed the Ontario Hospital School). Asylums in Canada, irrespective of type, were large, housing up to 3,000 inmates, overcrowded, and understaffed. Construction of the buildings was done more with staff or ease of service provision in mind, and led to a gradual medicalization of the housed individual. The use of wire-enmeshed windows, high ceilings, damage-proof furniture, and recessed lights all spoke to poor and dehumanizing conditions. Some lacked recreation facilities (often the first to be cut when construction costs exceeded budgets) and grounds often included money-making schemes in which patients would work unpaid (Simmons, 1982).

At the beginning of the 1900s, the idea of asylums as a place of refuge was almost wholly replaced by the idea of asylums as places to rid society of "unwanted" individuals. Instead of protecting certain people from society, society now required protection from

In the 1900s, asylums were a fearful society's answer to getting rid of individuals with disabilities from the larger community.

© Jerry Cooke/Corbis

eugenics The practice of selecting desired human traits to improve the genetic stock of the population and preventing the breeding of those with undesired traits.

them and this is referred to as custodial care. The knowledge that asylums could house "unwanteds," including the non-disabled elderly or the poor, provided a convenient forum for people in, or connected to, power to impose social controls and project moral judgment on others. The rise of immigration in Canada, the establishment of societal norms, the influence of pseudo-scientific sociological studies (such as the Kallikak and Juke family studies described below), and the misinterpretation of studies on heredity all led to the rise of **eugenics** in Canada and internationally. The lack of oversight on restricting personal freedom, scientifically flawed views of the inheritance of behavioural traits, and the mathematical use of the normal distribution created the perfect storm for the rise of the eugenics movement.

Eugenics was a worldwide phenomenon and had its start prior to the twentieth century. One of the most important concepts leading to the rise of eugenics was heredity, the idea that specific traits are inherited from parents. This concept was first demonstrated by the Russian monk Gregor Mendel (1822–1864), where he described studies of the inheritance of coat color and texture in peas. His study convincingly demonstrated that traits present in one generation can be passed along to the next—in peas. Mendel's work was fodder for social scientists who suggested that this may also be true for undesirable human traits. This is exemplified by the work of researchers Goddard and Dugdale who reported on the Kallikak and Juke families respectively—two families with histories of criminal and antisocial behavior. Their flawed studies (even for the standards of the time) led to the idea that degeneracy is inherited from one generation to the next. These studies, in combination with the work of Quételet (1796–1874), who applied the concept of the statistical norm to human and population characteristics, and Galton, who suggested that selective breeding could improve the quality of the human race (a concept used for thousands of years in agriculture), all contributed to the idea that improving the human stock was not only possible but desirable.

From the early 1900s, social groups such as the Eugenics Society of Canada and the National Council for Women warned of immoral behaviour and criminality and pressured governments to address the problem. The main argument of these groups, based on the work of Dugdale, Goddard, and Galton, was that immoral people have more children than moral people and that complex behavioural traits are faithfully inherited. To better press their case, social reformers created the category of "feeble-mindedness" to medicalize people that did not look or act like them. There was no definition for "feeble-mindedness" except that those considered "feeble minded" did not meet expectations of social norms; "feeble-minded" people could often be non-English speaking immigrants or unwed mothers (Dowbiggin, 1997). In a 1907 report, Dr Helen MacMurchy (1862–1953), Inspector of the Feeble-minded, reported that

> feeble mindedness is difficult to define but not difficult to recognize. They are below those of normal, though small intellect but above actual imbeciles or idiots. They are able to act and may speak fairly well, though usually more or less foolishly. They can partly or even wholly earn their living under supervision, but they are not capable of protecting themselves in the world at large. They lack prudence and self-control. They have no proper will or judgment. Hence we find them in maternity wards, refuges, gaols, and poorhouses (Ontario, 1907, p. 4).

The seriousness with which the government took the menace of the "feeble minded" can be seen in the establishment of a Royal Commission—reserved usually for the most pressing issues of the state—to address "feeble mindedness" (1919). While no buildings were constructed to house "feeble-minded" people, likely because of budgetary constraints, surveys were taken across the country of those individuals who were considered "feeble minded." With the requests to quell the menace of the "feeble minded" running into governmental barriers and fiscal constraints, the idea that sterilization instead of incarceration could also be used to limit the perceived menace emerged. Subsequently, the federal government launched the Royal Commission on Public Welfare in 1929 to appease public mood. The Commission was extremely harsh, even for the day, and most notably recommended compulsory sterilization of people with intellectual impairments (including "feeble mindedness"; McLaren, 1990).

Alberta and British Columbia were the only two Canadian provinces to pass sterilization legislation, in 1928 and 1932, respectively. By this time, over 20 American states had sterilization laws. The Sexual Sterilization Act of Alberta resulted in 516 sterilizations by 1937 and by then the Act was amended to remove the requirement for consent if an individual was "mentally defective." While other provinces did not have explicit legislation related to sterilization, there was significant push from medical and governmental bodies to have one; this is exemplified by a position paper by the lieutenant governor of Ontario at the time (Bruce, 1933). The fear of "defectives" subsided after the discovery of Nazi atrocities in World War II done to people with disabilities (Köbsell, 2006) and the rise of the welfare state in Canada, including social housing, care for veterans, and the beginning of universally accessible and free medical treatment. The post-war awareness of the dangers of segregating individuals by perceived strengths—whether due to ethnicity, religion, IQ, or anything else—was learned, but the same desire to limit reproduction of "retarded" persons persisted. The Alberta Sterilization Act was not repealed until 1972, for example, and sterilization in Alberta continued after the repeal, though now there was a requirement that sterilization be performed by a qualified medical practitioner in adequate facilities, and with informed consent from patient and spouse/guardian (Law Reform Commission of Canada, 1979). This led to sterilization of people with intellectual impairments, evaluated on a case-by-case basis, usually because caregivers could not manage personal hygiene requirements such as those required for menses after puberty (Dyck, 2013). Currently in Canada, sterilization is used only when medically necessary; for example the removal of a diseased organ, for contraception, or to relieve menstrual burden. Importantly, dignity of the individual as well as his or her personal autonomy (i.e., only an individual him- or herself can decide to be sterilized) are the only factors in the decision. For non-competent persons or minors, sterilization is never permitted unless deemed medically essential, as laid out by the Supreme Court of Canada in the *Eve* decision of 1986 (http://scc-csc.lexum.com/scc-csc/scc-csc/en/item/170/index.do).

While people with physical disabilities without cognitive disabilities continued to end up in large asylums, public attitudes and social norms changed for this group as well. Medical research provided an explanation for some impairments and cured others, which led to better understanding of impairments as biological events and not an act of a higher power. Technology and the rise of disease-specific pressure groups in 1920–1960 (e.g., the folding wheelchair in 1932, vaccination) led to more public awareness for disorders, such as polio or cerebral palsy, and to public fundraising campaigns as well as the establishment of specific treatment centres for people with disabilities.

For people with mental illness or cognitive disabilities, large, custodial institutions persisted and continued to be built to meet relentless demand even after 1945, though academic and medical views increasingly challenged the benefits of large asylums. In the early 1960s, two influential documents advocated the integration of people with mental illnesses into the same infrastructure as those used to treat individuals with physical illnesses (CMHA, 1963; RCHS, 1964). These views, in combination with the discovery and increased use of effective medication, set the groundwork for de-institutionalization.

De-institutionalization

The 1970s and 1980s saw significant shifts in the care and support of individuals with disabilities. This shift involved a movement from custodial institutions to units in hospitals and then to community living arrangements. While custodial institutions were vast places of confinement, they did command the expenditure of government revenue as independent organizations. The shifting of patients first to specific hospital wards and then to community care resulted in a drastic decrease of funding for people with disabilities (Kirby, 2004). This lack of service was partially addressed by non-governmental organizations that attempted to address the needs of people with disabilities who abruptly found themselves back in communities. As a social reform, the de-institutionalization movement identified the segregation and institutionalization of individuals as oppressive, harmful, and stigmatizing and acknowledged that the needs and rights of individuals with disabilities could be better met within their home communities.

Using Ontario as an example to highlight these significant shifts, from 1876 to the 1960s, the Ontario government operated a total 16 institutions for individuals with developmental disabilities across rural Ontario (Ontario, 2009). However, by the 1970s, the Walter B. Williston Report entitled "Present Arrangements for the Care and Supervision of Mentally Retarded Persons in Ontario" was one of several reports that informed the 1974 Developmental Services Act, which transferred the responsibility of service provision for individuals with a developmental disability from the Ministry of Health to the Ministry of Community and Social Services (Ontario, 1987), marking the beginning of de-institutionalization. In 1987, the Ontario provincial government committed to closing institutions for individuals with developmental disabilities by 2012, which was achieved in 2009 with the closing of the final three remaining institutions. Such policy reforms were part of the de-institutionalization movement and signalled the beginning of the community living or independent living movement. These shifts did not occur rapidly; rather, they were part of a broader social movement and changing social consciousness that fought for the civil rights of individuals with disabilities.

The transition from custodial to community care was not carefully planned in most cases, and the need for services remained. In some cases, people rarely knew what life was like outside of a large governmental institution, nor were they prepared to address the requirements of everyday life. This was particularly true for people who not only had some form of disability but also were part of a minority group, whether that group was defined by ethnicity, language, sexuality, or geography (e.g., rural). This post–de-institutionalization service vacuum allowed for innovative new strategies of non-governmental service providers, tailored to the needs of certain groups rather than the "one-size-fits-all" model of the large custodial centres. An example of client-tailored care is the Association pour l'integration sociale d'Ottawa (AISO), which is a service to help French speakers with intellectual impairment in the Ottawa region. Beginning in the 1980s, the group had as its initial goal to help the reintegration of French speakers living at the Rideau Regional Centre, a large institution for people with intellectual impairment. Today, the organization runs group homes, offers medical and financial support to individuals, and provides respite care for families. AISO is largely funded by provincial government grants and donations.

The Independent Living Movement and The Dignity of Risk

The Independent Living (IL) movement first emerged in North America in the 1970s at the Berkeley Center for Independent Living in California and was led by a group of students with disabilities (Independent Living Canada, n.d.; Martinez & Duncan, 2003). The IL movement was introduced in Canada by Gerben DeJong, an American IL theorist with a background in social work, at the Coalition of Provincial Organizations of the Handicapped conference in Vancouver in 1980. The IL movement is a philosophy that identifies that individuals with disabilities have the right to live in their communities despite the societal barriers that exist, impeding their full and meaningful participation. DeJong (1979) explained: "The dignity of risk is what the IL movement is all about. Without the possibility of failure, the disabled person is said to lack true independence and the mark of one's humanity—the right to choose for good or evil" (p. 442).

The movement asserts that those who best know the needs of individuals with disabilities and how to address those needs are persons with disabilities themselves. Specifically, this philosophy offers an alternative to traditional medical and rehabilitative service delivery approaches. The IL movement called for integrated, comprehensive, and community-based services, enhanced self-representation and self-determination in making choices about their lives through a de-professionalization of services and the involvement of individuals with disabilities in the administration of services (Centre for Independent Living in Toronto, 2013). Services that foster this approach include peer support and direct funding so that individuals with disabilities can hire, manage, and coordinate their own supports. In Canada, the IL movement operates through Independent Living Resource Centres which are consumer-led, community-based organizations that work to identify gaps in services and other barriers that prevent the full participation of individuals with disabilities in their communities (Martinez, 2003).

Bellwoods Centres for Community Living

The Independent Living movement asserted that disabled individuals have the right to live within their communities and make decisions affecting their own lives.

The de-institutionalization and Independent Living movements were heavily influenced by Bengt Nirje's normalization principle and later by Wolf Wolfensberger's theory of social role valorization. The normalization principle, developed by Bengt Nirje in the 1960s, has served (and by and large continues to serve) as the guiding ideology for service delivery for individuals with disabilities, particularly in Canada and the United States. Nirje (1999) explained that

> the Normalization principle means that you act right when you make available to all persons with intellectual or other impairments or disabilities those patterns of life and conditions of everyday living that are as close as possible to, or indeed the same as, the regular circumstances and ways of life of their communities and their culture (p. 17).

Later, the theory of social role valorization (SRV) informed by Nirje's normalization principle, was developed by psychologist Wolf Wolfensberger. The normalization movement and SRV were influential in key policy and program changes including de-institutionalization, mainstreaming in schools, vocational integration, and independent community living.

Wolfensberger suggested that in every society there are groups of individuals who are at risk of being undervalued or devalued; these groups are, in turn, at risk of being segregated, stigmatized, rejected, or even abused. SRV, he proposed, is a direct response to devaluation; it suggests that access to valued social roles provides access to a number of other "good things in life" such as dignity, respect, participation, belonging, and opportunity (Wolfensberger, 2000, p. 109).

SRV has its roots in social role theory and generally contends that an individual's personal welfare is contingent on the value of the social roles they occupy (Wolfensberger, 2000). In other words, access to valued social roles is dependent upon a feedback loop whereby the perceptions of others influence the development of personal competencies and vice versa (Osburn, 2006). According to SRV, acceptance within society and access to the normal features of life is a prerequisite to access to valued social roles (Wolfensberger, 2000). Thus, within a Canadian context, opportunities for valued social role taking (as opposed to the sick role, the disabled role) are enhanced and sustained through welfare programs that promote inclusion and provide support to individuals with disabilities throughout their life (Marshall, Kendall, Banks, & Gover, 2009). According to Wolfensberger (2000), "society will extend whatever good things it has to offer, to people in valued roles" (p. 109). Thus, the greater the services and supports for individuals with disabilities, the greater their access to socially valued roles and the greater their welfare.

Despite their significant impacts on service delivery, normalization and SRV have been heavily critiqued, particularly within the critical disability scholarship. Disability advocate and author Michael Oliver (1999) challenged the normalization principle:

> Normalization theory offers disabled people the opportunity to be given valued social roles in an unequal society that values some roles more than others. Materialist social theory offers disabled people the opportunity to transform their own lives and in so doing to transform the society in which they live into one in which all roles are valued. As a disabled person, I know which of those choices I prefer, and I also know which most of the disabled people I meet prefer (p. 172).

According to this critique, normalization requires individuals with disabilities to conform to Western capitalist norms. Furthermore, normalization may be critiqued for being grounded in the distinction between normal and abnormal or pathological—a dichotomy that is predicated on the medical model of disability that identifies disability as an individual deficit.

Progress and Development of Disability Rights in Canada

Disability policy in Canada has undergone several major historical shifts that represent evolving and maturing definitions of the causes and impacts of disability (Jongbloed, 2003; see Table 11.4). In the nineteenth and early twentieth centuries, policies reflected a social control or moral approach to disability. At this time, policies regarding institutionalization were designed with the dual goal of protecting vulnerable individuals from society and protecting society from the perceived threat of individuals with disabilities. Shortly after World War I, policies shifted to reflect a more rehabilitative approach to disability. These policies reflected an understanding of disability as a bodily impairment in the individual that required medical intervention in order to rehabilitate him or her to be a contributing member of society. Policies shifted again in the 1970s to reflect a rights-based, social justice approach to disability. These policies reflected a recognition of the rights of individuals with disabilities and the disabling aspects of the social environment, which identified disability as the result of oppression and social exclusion rather than as individual impairment alone.

TABLE 11.4	Notable Events of Progress in the Disability Movement
Vocational Rehabilitation of Disabled Persons Act (1961)	This act was a post-war initiative that aimed to foster a return to work for individuals with disabilities through expanding vocational rehabilitation services for individuals with disabilities and enhancing the coordination of these services. The act involved a cost-sharing agreement between the provincial and federal governments in providing vocational rehabilitation services.
The Canada Pension Plan (1965)	The Canada Pension Plan (CPP), implemented in 1965, is a national, contributory social insurance plan aimed at encouraging individuals to save for their retirement and consequently decreasing poverty in old age. The CPP is a mandatory program based on wage-related contributions deducted from an individual's income. The CPP disability benefit is available to those individuals who have met the minimum qualifying period of contributions and who have a severe and prolonged impairment that prevents them from working (Service Canada, n.d.).
Council of Canadians with Disabilities (1976)	The Council is a human rights organization working towards greater inclusion and accessibility for individuals with disabilities. The council was formed in 1976 by a group of individuals with disabilities and tackles disability issues such as transportation and universal design from a human rights approach.
International Year of Disabled Persons (1981)	The General Assembly of the United Nations declared 1981 as the International Year of Disabled Persons and outlined a series of objectives aimed at improving equality of opportunity and the full participation of individuals with disabilities in society.
Canadian Charter of Rights and Freedoms (1982)	The Canadian Charter of Rights and Freedoms outlines the political and civil rights of all Canadians and is embedded within the Constitution Act of Canada, which became law in 1982. Under the Charter, Every individual is equal before and under the law and has the right to the equal protection and equal benefit of the law without discrimination and, in particular, without discrimination based on race, national or ethnic origin, colour, religion, sex, age, or mental or physical disability (Constitution Act, 1982).
Canadian Human Rights Act (1985)	The Canadian Human Rights Act extends the laws that address discrimination in Canada. Under the Act, the prohibited grounds of discrimination are race, national or ethnic origin, colour, religion, age, sex, sexual orientation, marital status, family status, disability, and conviction for an offence for which a pardon has been granted or in respect of which a record suspension has been ordered (Canadian Human Rights Act, 1985).
Employment Equity Act (1995)	This act was established in Canada in 1986 and then refined in 1995 in order to ensure equality in the workplace after an exploration of participation in the workforce revealed disparities in salaries, occupations, and unemployment across different groups including but not limited to women, Indigenous Peoples, and individuals with disabilities (Employment Equity Act, 1995).
In Unison: A Canadian Approach to Disability Issues (1998)	In 1998, provincial and territorial governments (with the exception of Quebec as they have an independent framework) published this report, identifying a focus on disability as a collective, national priority. The report proposed a framework towards supporting the full and meaningful participation of individuals with disabilities within society (Human Resources and Skills Development Canada, 1998). In 2000, this report was updated to share how individuals with disabilities fare compared to those without disabilities and to highlight effective practices across Canada that have enhanced employment, income, and other disability supports.
United Nations Convention on the Rights of Persons with Disabilities (2010)	The purpose of this convention was to develop a set of universal standards in order to ensure and uphold the human rights of individuals with disabilities. The convention, formally taken up in 2008, re-conceptualized disability, grounding disability issues within a human rights perspective and called for enhanced equality, autonomy, and accessibility and the full participation and inclusion of individuals with disabilities in society. Upon ratifying the convention, a country is legally bound to implement legislation that promotes and ensures the rights of individuals with disabilities. Canada ratified the convention in March 2010.

Social Work Practice with Individuals with a Disability

Today, social workers in the disability field may find themselves in a diversity of roles and environments. In Canada, health and social services are administered provincially and territorially, leading to regional variation in the delivery of services and supports available for individuals with disabilities and their caregivers. Still, while services and supports for individuals with disabilities are embedded within multiple institutions and across different ministries, they share a general orientation towards inclusion, integration, and community living. Services fall under different categories of support, including but not limited to, primary and specialized health care and rehabilitation, income or financial support, case management, respite, specialized therapies, and advocacy and awareness-raising. Within these programs, social workers may provide an equally diverse set of services including counselling and therapy, case management, care coordination, and advocacy.

Health and Social Services for Individuals with Disabilities: Navigating the Systems of Care

Many individuals and disability advocates find accessing and utilizing services a frustrating experience. The multitude of layers of assessment and diagnosis, which allow for access to service, can challenge even the most savvy of logistical strategists. These challenges, though, underline the fact that there is at least the potential for many types of services from different organizations. This contrasts sharply with past history where an "every person for themselves" attitude persisted, or later, where people were treated with a "one-size-fits-all" institutionalization approach. The shift to independence and autonomy brought with it the need to apply for help from different providers, a selection of which are described here.

Federal and Provincial Resource Allocation

Canada has a national health insurance program, which ensures that all residents of Canada are provided with needed services. While provinces and territories are wholly responsible for their health-care plan, they receive funding from the federal government in the form of transfers. Provinces and territories receive three major transfers from the federal government each year: (1) Canada Health Transfer (CHT); (2) Canada Social Transfer (CST); and (3) Equalization and Territorial Formula Financing. In 2013–14, these transfers will amount to a total of $62.3 billion. The Canada Health Transfer is the largest of the three transfers and the amount allocated to each province and territory is designed to ensure that comparable services are available across the country. While each province and territory must include some features in their health insurance plan that are standard across the country, they may also offer additional benefits, often to specific populations such as seniors or children. As a result, depending on individual needs, some provinces or territories may provide more advantageous services and supports than others.

Universality of Equivalent Care

While efforts are made to ensure comparable access to needed medical services across the country, issues of jurisdiction (*where* services are delivered and *by whom*) and access (*eligibility for* and *availability of* services and supports) may complicate care for individuals with disabilities. First, not all services, particularly specialized services, are available across all regions in each province and territory. Instead, specialized services are usually offered in large urban centres requiring individuals and families to move to the care. Second,

Case STUDY

Jordan's Principle

JORDAN'S PRINCIPLE IS A CHILD-FIRST principle, implemented in 2007 following a jurisdictional dispute between the federal government and the government of Manitoba over who was responsible for providing care for Jordan River Anderson, a young child with complex medical needs. Jordan, from the Norway House Cree Nation in Manitoba, died in hospital while the federal and provincial governments tried to come to an agreement over who would cover the costs of his transfer to and care within his home community. Jordan's Principle applies not only to health but also to all government services such as education and recreation and requires that services be delivered to a child in medical need without delay or disruption. The principle requires that if a dispute occurs, the government of first contact is to pay for service and reimbursement is to be worked out between governments following service provision. Since its creation, little has been done towards its actual implementation between and across federal and provincial governments (Blackstock, 2008; MacDonald, 2012; MacDonald & Attaran, 2007). However, in 2013 the Federal Court of Canada found that Jordan's Principle is binding on the Government of Canada. As a result, for example, the Office of Aboriginal Affairs and Northern Development was directed to reimburse the Pictou Landing Band for care costs incurred for a disabled youth living on the reserve.

jurisdictional disputes between federal and provincial governments regarding responsibility for health-care provision may impede timely decisions related to health care (see "Case Study" above on Jordan's Principle). Lastly, while an individual may be eligible for particular services and supports, in reality, long wait lists or lack of resources in rural areas may limit access to these services.

In each province and territory, private supplemental health insurance, often available through employers, is available through private companies to cover, either fully or partially, non-essential medical services or elective medical procedures such as dental or vision services and pharmaceutical drugs. Thus, some health care in Canada is funded outside of the national insurance program, through private insurance companies or out-of-pocket payments.

Income Support

Publicly funded federal and provincial income support programs offer financial assistance to individuals who are not able to work due to impairment or disability. For these programs, disability must be prolonged and severe, preventing the individual from being able to earn a living. Eligibility for income support programs, such as the Canada Pension Plan Disability Benefit (a federal program), the Ontario Disability Support Program or the Assured Income for the Severely Handicapped in Alberta (provincial programs), usually involves a detailed application that may require supporting documentation regarding the individual's work history, financial status, disability status or medical condition, and family status.

Income support may also include programs such as the Saskatchewan Rental Housing Supplement (SRHS). The Saskatchewan provincial government has a number of income supplement support programs for people with disabilities. One of these, the SRHS, provides financial support to people with a disability that produces a recognized housing impact (for example, stair-only access for people in a wheelchair). This supplement is designed to support rental costs where supports (elevators, grab bars, intercoms) are already in place, and not the construction of such supports.

Specialized Services

Specialized services such as the Autism Intervention Program in Ontario for children with autism spectrum disorder and services offered through the Family Support for Children with Disabilities (FSCD) program in Alberta usually require medical documentation of the child's impairment or condition and may conduct a broader assessment of child and family needs. These programs are publicly funded provincial programs and may differ in their approach to service provision. Some programs offer direct service, others offer direct funding, and some offer parents and caregivers either option. Direct service offers children and families direct service to publicly funded programs run by the province. Direct funding options provide families with the funding to be able to arrange for their own services, often through private agencies.

Educational Services

Disability rights campaigners fought hard for the right to send children with special needs to schools designed for "typical" children (also known as the mainstreaming movement of the 1980s). In adopting this policy, most school boards across Canada are required to provide exceptional students with the services needed to meet their needs. This approach, as suggested, seeks to integrate students into classrooms according to their age cohort, irrespective of their level of functioning. Children with special needs might be accompanied by a full- or part-time aid or educational assistant whose job it is to facilitate learning and inclusion in collaboration with the classroom teacher. In many cases they might follow an Individualized Education Plan (IEP), which outlines the unique needs and learning goals for each student in conjunction with the overall learning goals of the class. The integration approach in schools was considered a major step in the disability rights movement (although access to needed supports can be challenging at times due to financial constraints) and has had benefits extending far beyond the original scope, namely, the sensitization of children without disabilities in classrooms.

Non-governmental Organizations (NGOs)

A major provider of support to people with disabilities in Canada comes not from municipal, provincial, or federal governments but from NGOs. These vary in size and scope, are often designed with particular types of disability in mind, and tend to be founded by parents or people with a particular interest in a particular area. One example is Recreation Integration Victoria (See "In Their Own Words" box below). Notably, many NGOs receive government grants to function, but are managed independently.

In Their Own Words

RECREATION INTEGRATION VICTORIA (RIV)

THE VISION OF RECREATION INTEGRATION Victoria (RIV) in Victoria, British Columbia, is that all people should have equal opportunities to participate fully in the life of the community, and our mission is to facilitate active lifestyles for people with disabilities. Beyond the physical benefits, people who lead active lives experience improved self-esteem, a reduced sense of loneliness, improved social and life skills, community participation, and a better self-image.

We assist people with disabilities to pursue their leisure interests through generic programs and services in the community. This entails identifying the closest location to their home where they can pursue their interest(s) at a time that complements
(Continued)

their schedule. The final consideration we address is how their disability impinges on their ability to participate. This is where we might identify the need for a 1:1 volunteer, adapted equipment, staff education on adapting the activity to include the person with a disability, and/or addressing transportation issues. Choice is a fundamental component in establishing an active lifestyle, so participating at a local recreation centre, pursuing an interest with a friend, family member, or volunteer or joining a disability sport organization are all options that are available to the individual.

RIV is a unique partnership between the inter-municipally funded Recreation Integration Victoria (formerly Integrated Recreation Services), the Victoria Integration Society (VIS), and the Disabled Sailing Association of BC, Victoria Branch (DSABC, Victoria). Our three-sector partnership allows us to take advantage of a cross-section of funding sources available to NGOs, the private sector, and local government. Through our collaboration, each partner's contribution is leveraged. Each of our local municipalities contributes a percentage of our total budget, based on their population as it relates to the population of our total catchment area. In this way a municipality with a small population can offer a full range of services to their citizens, which they would not otherwise be able to afford. Similarly, provincial government sources of funding get a bigger bang for their buck as their funding increases our capacity to do what we do, without the expectation that they should fund the entire service. This is the reason partnerships work; everyone contributes to the larger service without having to foot the whole bill. Efficiencies realized through the partnership ensure maximum benefit is being provided to the consumer, costly duplication of services is avoided, and resources, including capital, physical, and human, are being shared to all partners' mutual benefit.

Doug Nutting is the Director of Recreation Integration Victoria (RIV).

© Matthew Kerr

Thanks to organizations such as Recreation Integration Victoria (RIV), people with disabilities have more opportunity to explore and participate in activities within their communities.

Settings for Social Workers in a Disability Context

Historically, social work practice with individuals with disabilities has been embedded within medicine and health care, a field that firmly adhered to the medical model of disability. Conversely, the disability rights movement and the more recent field of disability studies have challenged the medical model of disability, which views disability as an individual deficit, instead exploring the social, political, economic, and cultural factors that create and influence disability. Even today, social work practice with individuals with disabilities may continue to be seen as embedded within practices that seek to rehabilitate or cure the individual of their impairment through medical intervention alone.

Acknowledgement of this historical tension is crucial to critical and reflexive social work practice. Today, however, social workers practise *across* and *within* this dichotomy, working towards both individual change and social reform, according to the unique needs of the individual and his or her family. Grounded in a social justice perspective, social workers seek to understand how vulnerable populations are at risk of marginalization and oppression and work within and across systems to uphold human rights. Social workers are "dedicated to the welfare and self-realization of all people . . . [particularly those] who are vulnerable, oppressed, and/or living in poverty"

Practical TIP

Working in a Disability Context

SOCIAL WORKERS MAY BE INVOLVED in multiple settings when working in a disability context:

- health and rehabilitation in clinical settings;
- health and rehabilitation in community settings (see the Program for Assertive Community Treatment below);
- schools;
- residential settings (short- and long-term respite, camps);
- youth protection;
- shelters;
- mentorship programs;
- recreation and leisure programs;
- government (municipal, provincial/territorial, federal);
- research;
- advocacy and human rights organizations;
- social policy think tanks.

The Program for Assertive Community Treatment (PACT) team is an example of a program that offers health and rehabilitation services in a community setting. The PACT team is an intensive community-based program supporting individuals with severe mental illness such as schizophrenia or bipolar disorder to live independently in the community. The program is composed of a multidisciplinary team of professionals including but not limited to psychiatry, nursing, and social work. The team provides psychiatric care, case management, vocational supports, crisis management, and assistance with activities of daily living on a 24/7 basis in order to support community integration and self-management of illness, reduce hospitalizations, and foster quality of life.

(Canadian Association of Social Workers, 2005, p. 3). Three of social work's core values include: (1) "respect for the inherent dignity and worth of persons"; (2) "pursuit of social justice" and; (3) "service to humanity" and highlight the profession's dedication to human rights and social fairness (CASW, 2005; see Chapter 3 for a more detailed discussion of the CASW Code of Ethics core values). Social workers find themselves in a diverse array of settings, working towards both individual change (such as special education and rehabilitation) and social reform (such as advocacy), an approach that is also highly congruent with the WHO's International Classification of Functioning, Disability and Health.

Promoting Inclusion: Roles for Social Workers in a Disability Context

Promoting Access to Specialized Health, Rehabilitative, and Social Services for People with Disabilities or their Families

Social workers are involved in supporting people with disabilities and their families in accessing specialized care. Social workers may be involved in intake and eligibility assessments required for access to specialized services or therapies such as intensive behavioural intervention for children with autism spectrum disorders. In these settings, social workers meet with the individual and her or his family to assess the individual's level of functioning and the psychosocial needs of both the individual and the family. Social workers may also work as part of an inter-professional team in providing case management and care coordination for those individuals with chronic or multiple impairments who receive care across a number of different settings.

Supporting the Transition to Adulthood

The transition to adulthood for youth with disabilities involves both institutional and developmental transitions. Youth experience the transition from paediatric to adult health and rehabilitative care and from the school system to the community. Many institutional settings offer services and supports aimed at fostering a positive transition between institutions while simultaneously addressing key psychosocial or developmental goals. Social workers may be involved in these programs, which prepare youth to begin to manage their own health care, practise independent living skills, become involved in the community, and identify both short- and long-term life goals. At this juncture in the lives of individuals with disabilities, social workers play a key role in partnering with the individual and his or her family in negotiating the multiple systems in which the youth is embedded in order to foster meaningful outcomes in young adulthood.

Promoting Access to Educational Services, Employment, and Independent Living

Social workers work with people with disabilities towards enhancing their meaningful participation in society. Depending on the needs, strengths, and interests of the individual, this may broadly include (but is not limited to) supporting access to education, employment, and independent living. First, social workers may work within elementary and secondary schools to ensure that students are provided the necessary modifications or accommodations in order to succeed in school. Post-secondary school institutions such as colleges and universities often have a centre for students with disabilities where social workers partner with students to identify and implement the supports needed to enhance learning and foster participation in the academic community. Second, social workers work with people with disabilities in both accessing meaningful employment opportunities and supporting their ongoing participation in the workforce. These programs may include vocational assessments, job preparation, job coaching, mentoring and supervision, and environmental modifications or assistive technologies within the workplace. However, workplace programs and supports that are based on an understanding of disability as permanent and predictable may not fit the needs of individuals with chronic illness. Susan Wendell, Professor Emerita from Simon Fraser University in British Columbia, suggests that many current programs and supports for individuals with disabilities are largely predicated on the definition of the "healthy disabled"—those individuals who have permanent, stable, and predictable disabilities (Wendell, 2001, p. 19). This definition of disability does not necessarily reflect the nature and/or experience of chronic illness. Chronic illness (and the accompanying perception of illness), on the other hand, often shifts or fluctuates as the individual experiences periods of acute illness or periods of temporary relief from symptoms (Paterson, 2001). In terms of workplace supports for individuals with chronic illness, social workers may play an important role within the health-care team in both identifying and advocating for unique and individualized accommodations. As Wendell (2001) suggests, these may include increased flexibility in the expected speed or pace in which work is performed and the scheduling of work activities or deadlines. Third, social workers also work with people with disabilities in fostering opportunities for independence. This can mean different things for different people, depending on their level of functioning and identified needs. For some, independence involves the opportunity for autonomous decision-making and for others it means living completely independently in the community. As a result, social workers foster independence in a number of ways—from ensuring that the individual with a disability is involved in key discussions and decisions regarding his or her life to working with the individual with a disability in identifying and coordinating the supports necessary for living independently in the community such as accessible housing, transportation, and supports for daily living activities.

Addressing Poverty: Access to Income Support for People with Disabilities and their Families

In Canada, poverty is determined using the low-income cut-off (LICO) which is established by determining if an individual spends more than 20 per cent of her or his after-tax income than the average individual on food, shelter, and clothing. Family size and geographic location are also taken into consideration (Statistics Canada, n.d.).

According to the 2006 PALS, children with disabilities are more likely to live in low-income households than children without disabilities, largely due to the negative impact of caregiving on family employment (Human Resources and Skills Development Canada, 2011). Younger working-age adults with disabilities (25–54 years of age) had lower employment incomes than working-age adults without disabilities. Employment income also varies by gender and by type of disability, with women with disabilities earning less than men with disabilities and individuals with developmental disabilities earning the lowest average total income of all disability types. Older working-age adults with disabilities (55–64 years of age) have lower household incomes than their peers without disabilities. Furthermore, more individuals with disabilities and families with children with disabilities live below the LICO than those individuals without disabilities and those families without children with disabilities. A number of government-funded income support programs exist for individuals with disabilities who are unable to work or work full-time and to buffer the costs of specialized services or respite care. Social workers may work with individuals and their families in identifying and applying for key income support programs for which they are eligible (see the Saskatchewan Rental Housing Supplement). However, as the statistics indicate, individuals with disabilities are more likely to live below the low-income cut-off than those without disabilities. Therefore, social workers also act as advocates in practice, policy, and research, campaigning for the individuals with whom they work for large-scale policy reform and conducting research to explore the impact of poverty on individuals with disabilities in order to provide recommendations for reform.

Fostering Quality of Life

Quality of life is generally understood to be a multifaceted construct comprising both objective and subjective dimensions including but not limited to (1) interpersonal relations; (2) social inclusion; (3) personal development; (4) physical well-being; (5) self-determination; (6) material well-being; (7) emotional well-being; and (8) rights (Schalock, 2004). Quality of life, as a construct, promotes the importance of considering personal choice and subjectivity in determining goals and measuring outcome success. In a broader sense, social workers work from a critical ecological systems perspective (Bronfenbrenner, 1979; Ungar, 2002) and acknowledge that individuals' strengths, needs, and the opportunities available to them emerge through an interplay of systems—between an individual, family, community, and greater society (See Chapter 2, Social Work Theories). Therefore, social workers work within and across systems to address sites of oppression and marginalization and may work in ways that address not only physical and material well-being but also life satisfaction, self-determination, agency, citizenship, and social participation.

Addressing Caregiver Well-Being

Informal caregivers such as family and friends provide the majority of care for individuals with disabilities. Providing care for a loved one with a disability—a partner, a parent, or a child—can have a significant impact on the caregiver's overall well-being. Caregivers may experience financial strain, negative impacts on employment (job loss, job instability, or change in employment status), marital or relationship difficulties, role changes, and feelings of grief or loss. Social workers may work with both the individual with the disability as well as his or her primary caregiver and family in providing supports. Caregiver supports may include respite, which provides the caregiver with a short- or long-term break from daily care that can be offered either in and out of the family home. Other supports might involve counselling and therapy to address role changes within the family system, feelings of grief and loss, and mental health issues such as depression and anxiety.

For example, the Respite Program for Local Communities (RPLC) in the Northwest Territories (NWT) offers a creative respite care program for caregivers of children with disabilities. The Northwest Territories Disability Council, with funding provided by the NWT government, offers respite care to people outside of Yellowknife. Northern communities can pose unique challenges for social workers, particularly outside of urban centres. The RPLC responds to these unique challenges in a number of ways. The eligibility criteria for respite are few. Care recipients must be between 0 and 18 years of age, live at home with their family or legal guardian, and have a permanent impairment or health condition that requires ongoing support. Importantly, self-referrals are accepted and the definition of disability is relatively wide. Some unique features of the program are that respite workers can be selected by the family and trained by the program. This can be a friend or other family member not living in the same house as the care recipient. Training and salary for the respite care worker is provided by the NWT Disability Council. This program emphasizes both the community- and family-centred approach to care.

Social Work Practice Guidelines

As discussed, social workers in the disability field may work in a variety of different settings. The following broad guidelines may be useful in informing social work practice across settings and in fostering individualized partnerships with those with whom we work to address the biological, social, and environmental factors that affect the meaningful inclusion of people with different abilities in Canadian society.

Understand the Interaction between Impairment and the Environment

Developing an understanding of the individual's particular bodily impairment and how it facilitates or impedes the execution of certain activities and participation in society are fundamental to understanding what supports and services are needed and why. Consider the following cases:

- If a particular impairment does not impede certain activities relevant to the individual or his or her participation in society, does he or she require support?
- If that person experiences discrimination despite having no functional limitations, how might you intervene?
- An individual with cerebral palsy is able to walk without the aid of a mobility device when she is assessed at the rehabilitation centre; however, she tells you that she cannot hold down a job because of mobility and transportation issues. What might be going on?

Understand the Concept of Ableism and Its Impact on Individuals with Disabilities and their Families

In practice, social workers must be aware of how ableist attitudes and disabling environments can serve to marginalize individuals with disabilities and restrict their full participation in society. Therefore, critically reflecting on how both micro- and macro-social relationships can create oppression is an integral component of social work practice with people with disabilities. For example, critical, reflexive social work practice involves anything from being mindful of how a diagnosis and prognosis is shared with individuals and their families to examining the physical barriers preventing people with mobility impairments from getting to work in the winter.

Challenge Disability Stereotypes and Recognize the Lived Experiences of People with Disabilities

Challenging disability dichotomies and stereotypes and identifying the nuances of the lived experiences of people with disabilities is critical to social work practice that addresses individual and family needs of the person with whom you are working and acknowledges how inequalities and marginalization occur. Consider the following questions that address disability stereotypes:

- Are all parents and caregivers of individuals with disabilities stressed, overwhelmed, and burnt out all of the time? Are all parents and caregivers "super heroes," going above and beyond?
- Are all caregivers women?

- Would all people with disabilities describe themselves as brave and courageous? Are all people with disabilities oppressed, isolated, and marginalized?
- Are all disabilities visible, stable, and long-term?
- Are all individuals with disabilities healthy?
- Is an individual with a specific health condition disabled across all contexts and situations?

Listening to the lived experiences of people with disabilities and chronic health conditions allows social workers to understand their unique experiences of living with a particular disability or chronic illness and the impact it has had on their lives. This allows for tailored supports that address the individual's unique needs, whether that be therapy and rehabilitation or advocacy for better transportation services. As Michael J. Prince (2009), disability advocate and Professor of Social Policy in British Columbia, explains

> In terms of recognition politics, the project of enabling citizenship entails deconstructing the dominant image of the "disabled" person as someone with a visible, long-term physical impairment; pluralizing the image with the realities of diverse forms of disablements; and connecting the differences in relation to power relations and systems of inequalities (p. 48).

Work in Partnership with Individuals and their Families

Working in partnership with individuals, their families, and their social networks is fundamental to social work practice. First, working in partnership is necessary in identifying and addressing outcomes and goals that are relevant to the person with whom you are working—goals that fit with his or her strengths, needs, and interests. Second, the individual is embedded within his or her family system and both influences and is influenced by family members and other family and social variables. Thus, inviting those identified as important to the person with whom you are working to be involved in care, support, or rehabilitation is not only necessary in order to consider the needs of both the individual and the family (e.g., long-term planning) but may also enhance desired outcomes. Furthermore, the dichotomous conceptualization of dependence–independence and the assumption that successful rehabilitation requires movement from one to the other is false. Complete independence from family or friends and colleagues is not necessarily practical nor realistic for individuals with disabilities, their families, and service providers. Rather, the notion of interdependence may be more applicable, as it suggests that individuals are interdependent with other people and individuals fulfill their personal potential through relationship-building, reciprocity, and mutual support (Kim & Turnbull, 2004; Yeung, Passmore, & Packer 2008).

Identify Case Management and Care Coordination Needs

Individuals with disabilities may have complex needs that require the involvement of multiple service providers across different institutions. Needs may differ from person to person, therefore individualized discussion of how care is managed and coordinated is critical to putting together a program of supports that work together in fostering opportunity and meaningful inclusion in society.

Consider the Life Course of the Individual

Individuals with disabilities and their families may experience a rupture in their life course due to the disability—whether congenital or acquired later in life. An understanding and awareness of the life course or the normative order or sequence of life is important in developing relevant goals and identifying potential sources of hope, strength, worry, frustration, or stress.

In other words, it is important to take into account how developmental tasks fit with the individual's chronological age, biological development, and personal characteristics (agency and choice) as well as the culture and social institutions of the time if one is to properly understand the lived experiences of individuals with disabilities and their families.

Conclusion

Definitions of disability reflect societal norms and values. While Canada does not have a universal definition of disability, current policies and programs reflect a definition of disability that addresses biological, social, and environmental components. The history of disability services in Canada began with large custodial institutions and shifted to the Independent Living movement in the mid- to late 1970s. This shift was accompanied by a changing social consciousness that fought for the civil rights of individuals with disabilities and an increased number of policies, programs, and services aimed at fostering community inclusion and enhancing quality of life made available by both government and non-government bodies. Social workers play an important role in supporting individuals with a disability and their families across all settings, particularly in navigating the system of care and coordinating an individualized program of services and supports that addresses biopsychosocial needs and identifies the strengths and abilities of the individual.

QUESTIONS FOR CRITICAL THOUGHT

1. Describe the key differences between the terms "impairment" and "disability."
2. How do different conceptualizations of disability (e.g., medical versus social model) influence the types of interventions and supports that may be made available to an individual with a disability?
3. Identify a specific impairment (e.g., cerebral palsy, schizophrenia, spinal cord injury). Describe how the bodily impairment may hinder activities of daily living and participation in society and identify the potential social, cultural, and environmental barriers that individuals with this impairment may experience in living in their community. Discuss how you might address each of these barriers in practice.
4. Identify both the potential benefits and challenges of the diagnostic approach to categorizing disability. How does having a specific diagnosis, such as autism spectrum disorder, affect the individual? What are the implications of receiving a specific diagnosis?
5. Describe how de-institutionalization led to the current systems of support for people with disabilities. How well do these systems work together?
6. How do client-, family-, and community-centred approaches differ for social workers in practice? What are some examples of programs that exemplify these strategies?
7. Compare and contrast services that are available for people with disabilities or their caregivers when clients are under 18 compared to when they are adults.

RECOMMENDED READINGS

Barrow, F.H. (2006). The International Classification of Functioning, Disability, and Health (ICF): A new tool for social workers. *Journal of Social Work in Disability & Rehabilitation*, 5, 1, 65–73. doi: 10.1300/J198v05n01_04. This article offers a description of the World Health Organization's International Classification of Functioning, Disability, and Health and offers insight into its applicability to social work practice with people with disabilities.

Davis, L.J. (2010). *The disability studies reader* (3rd ed.). New York: Routledge. The Disability Studies Reader offers a comprehensive introduction to disability studies with contributions that address the historical perspectives of disability, relevant theoretical frameworks, and identity politics, among other topics.

Kovacs Burns, K., & Gordon, G.L. (2010). Analyzing the impact of disability legislation in Canada and the United States. *Journal of Disability Policy Studies, 20,* 4, 205–218. doi: 10.1177/1044207309344562. This article offers an exploration of disability legislation in both Canada and the United States, identifying the similarities and differences between the two countries, best practices, and areas for improvement.

Mackelprang, R.W. (2010). Disability controversies: Past, present, and future. *Journal of Social Work in Disability & Rehabilitation, 9,* 2, 87–98. doi: 10.1080/1536710X .2010.493475. This article identifies contentious issues involving disability and current social work practice and highlights how evolving disability definitions and language have influenced the role and perceptions of social workers in the disability field.

Prince, M.J. (2009). *Absent citizens: Disability politics and policy in Canada.* Toronto: University of Toronto Press Inc. This book offers a critical examination of Canadian social policies that affect persons with disabilities and explores how the legal, political, cultural, economic, and social aspects of Canadian society shape the citizenship and participation experiences of individuals with disabilities.

RECOMMENDED WEBSITES

Canadian Centre on Disability Studies
http://disabilitystudies.ca/
The CCDS is a university-affiliated centre based in Manitoba that discusses research, education, and key disability issues.

Council of Canadians with Disabilities
http://www.ccdonline.ca/en/
The Council of Canadians with Disabilities is a human rights organization working towards greater inclusion and accessibility for individuals with disabilities. The website presents discussions around current research, policies, and programs that affect individuals with disabilities.

Independent Living Canada
http://www.ilcanada.ca/article/home-125.asp
The Independent Living Canada website provides comprehensive information about the IL movement in Canada as well as a number of other initiatives aimed at enhancing the quality of life of individuals with disabilities.

Office for Disability Issues, Human Resources, and Skills Development Canada
http://www.hrsdc.gc.ca/eng/disability_issues/mandate/index.shtml
The ODI website shares information about current Canadian disability legislation and policies, provides a list of disability-related non-governmental organizations, and includes an Accessibility Resource Centre, which lists a number of tools and resources, including those for improving accessibility to employment, housing, and services.

The World Health Organization's International Classification of Functioning, Disability and Health (ICF)
http://www.who.int/classifications/icf/en/
This website offers a comprehensive description of the WHO's tool for classifying functioning, disability, and health (the ICF). The ICF checklist, a tool for clinicians to use in assessing impairment in bodily structures and functions, activity limitations, participation restrictions, and other contextual factors (personal and environmental), is available for download.

Social Work with Aging Populations

LEARNING OBJECTIVES

- To appreciate how assumptions and frameworks about aging shape policy, practice, and experiences of aging.

- To recognize how Canadian policies and services affect experiences of aging.

- To consider how social locations, such as ethnicity/race, gender, ability, sexual orientation, and economic status can affect older adults' experiences of aging and access to aging services.

- To appreciate the ways in which practitioners' cultural values, beliefs, and attitudes about aging influence their work with older adults.

- To consider alternate ways of thinking about and intervening with older adults facing a variety of issues or challenges.

Chapter Outline

This chapter introduces dominant paradigms in aging and explores how these understandings have shaped policy, practice, and aging experiences. Different ways of knowing, delivering services, and practising with older adults facing a variety of challenges are presented. Particular groups requiring distinct supports within the Canadian aging population are identified.

Issues of aging and older adults are linked with all fields of social work practice including but not limited to—child welfare (e.g., grandparents as primary caregivers to grandchildren), corrections (e.g., the graying of the inmate population), community development and activism (e.g., the Raging Grannies), substance use, mental health, health care, homelessness, and interpersonal violence. Given that the population is rapidly aging and that social workers in any setting will find themselves working with older adults and their families, all social workers should have some general knowledge about aging processes and services and their impact on older adults and families.

Overview of Canada's Aging Population

Canada, like most Organisation for Economic Co-Operation and Development (OECD) countries, is experiencing a demographic shift, with citizens 65 and older representing the fastest growing cohort. In 2011, Canadians 65 and older represented 14.4 per cent of the population and that number is expected to double within the next 25 years. The aging of the Canadian population is due to a combination of an increasing life expectancy, a declining birth rate, and the aging of the **baby boom generation**. The populations of Nunavut, Yukon, and Northwest Territories are also aging; however, percentages of the population 65 and older are significantly lower in these territories than the rest of Canada due in part to lower life expectancies of Indigenous Peoples in these areas.

baby boom generation
Refers to individuals born post-World War II (1946–1965) when there was a significant increase in births. The oldest baby boomers turned 65 in 2011.

Within the population of Canadians 65 and older, the greatest growth is amongst those 85 and up. This group of older adults is sometimes referred to as "old-old" because of their marked differences in living arrangements, health, and health-care utilization than those older adults 65–84 years of age. For example, according to 2011 Census data, only 1 per cent of adults between the ages of 65 and 69 lived in some form of collective living facility compared to 29.6 per cent of those 85 and older. Furthermore, according to the General Social Survey (2012) only 4 per cent of older adults between 65 and 74 years were dependent on others for some form of assistance with **activities of daily living** compared to 21.5 per cent of older adults 85 and older.

activities of daily living
A term used in health care to refer to daily self-care activities such as feeding, bathing, dressing, and grooming.

Aging is often discussed in terms of decline and loss. For example, when presenting statistics on the aging of the Canadian population, researchers, politicians, and members of the social media emphasize anticipated fiscal crises due to the projected overburdening of the health-care or pension systems (see Canadian Institute for Health Information, 2011; Echenberg, Gauthier, & Léonard, 2011). While it is true that advanced age is associated with an increased risk of chronic disease and that age is often accompanied by loss such as death of close friends and partners, it is also true that older adults make major contributions to society in the form of tangible assistance to spouses, children, grandchildren, friends, and neighbours and voluntarism (Fast et al., 2006; Gee & Gutman, 2000). Additionally, older adulthood can be associated with gains and opportunities such as increased time for leisure and

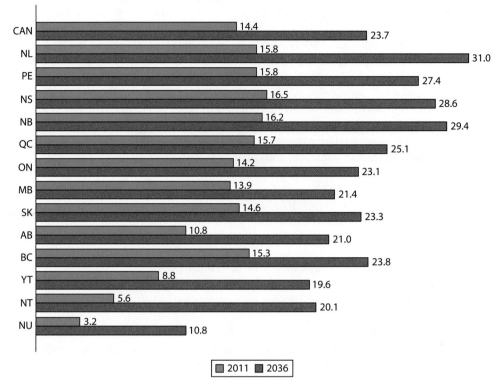

Population 65 years and over, by region, 2011 and projected 2036 (percent)

Region	2011	2036
CAN	14.4	23.7
NL	15.8	31.0
PE	15.8	27.4
NS	16.5	28.6
NB	16.2	29.4
QC	15.7	25.1
ON	14.2	23.1
MB	13.9	21.4
SK	14.6	23.3
AB	10.8	21.0
BC	15.3	23.8
YT	8.8	19.6
NT	5.6	20.1
NU	3.2	10.8

2011 2036

FIGURE 12.1 // Aging Population by Regions in Canada

Source: HRSDC calculations based on Statistics Canada. *Estimates of population, by age group and sex for July 1, Canada, provinces and territories, annual* (CANSIM Table 051–0001); and Statistics Canada. *Projected population, by projection scenario, sex and age group as of July 1, Canada, provinces and territories, annual* (CANSIM table 052–0005). Ottawa: Statistics Canada, 2011.

personal growth. The predominantly negative discussions prevalent in research, policy statements, and social media precipitate **ageism**. This results in attitudes, behaviours, and institutional policies and practices that function to subordinate or exclude people based on their advanced age. For example, when older adults are accompanied to a medical appointment by a younger family member, it is not uncommon for allied health professionals to speak directly to the family member because they assume the family member will be more likely to understand and follow what they are saying.

Social workers are not immune to negative attitudes and beliefs about aging. Research has documented that despite the growing need, social worker students view work with older adults as less prestigious, challenging, or rewarding than other areas of social work practice (Wang, Chonody, & Krase, 2013). Recent efforts to address ageist attitudes in social work trainees has found that experience with and exposure to older adults and opportunities to reflect on and challenge negative feelings and perceptions associated with age are effective mechanisms for improving social work students' perceptions of practice with older adults.

ageism A form of stereotyping about older people that associates aging with decline and results in exclusion and marginalization.

Practical TIP

Test Your Knowledge about Aging

TEST YOUR KNOWLEDGE ABOUT AGING by answering True or False to the following selection of questions from *The Facts on Aging Quiz* (Breytspraak, Kendall, & Halpert, n.d.).

- It is very difficult for older adults to learn new things.
- As adults grow older, reaction time increases.
- Older adults have the highest suicide rate of any age group.
- Most old people lose interest in and capacity for sexual relations.
- As people live longer, they face fewer acute conditions and more chronic health conditions.
- Retirement is often detrimental to health—that is, people frequently seem to become ill or die soon after retirement.
- Older adults are less anxious about death than are younger and middle-aged adults.
- The modern family no longer takes care of its elderly.
- Most older drivers are quite capable of safely operating a motor vehicle.
- Most old people are set in their ways and unable to change.

Go to http://cas.umkc.edu/agingstudies/AgingFactsQuiz.asp to check your answers and reflect on how common "myths" about aging have shaped your beliefs about older adults.

Ethnic and Racial Diversity among Older Adults in Canada

Like the rest of Canada, Canada's population of older adults is increasingly ethnically and racially diverse. Just over 9 per cent of older adults in Canada are members of a visible minority group (Durst, 2010). Part of this ethnic and racial diversity is a consequence of a growth in the aging immigrant population from non-European countries, particularly Asia and the Middle East which now comprises 22.8 per cent of Canadian immigrants 65 and over. Older immigrants who have lived in Canada for less than 20 years are at significantly higher risk of living in poverty than Canadian-born older adults (Kaida & Boyd, 2011). Furthermore, although the Indigenous Canadian population is still relatively young, the vast majority of older adults in Nunavut (91 per cent) and the Northwest Territories (65 per cent) are Indigenous. Indigenous older adults self-report double to triple the rate of certain chronic conditions such as heart problems, hypertension, diabetes, and arthritis suggesting that this group of older adults experiences more barriers to aging well. The differential aging experiences of older adults are important to consider when examining policies, service provision, and practices. For example, given the shorter life expectancy and diminished health of Indigenous older adults as a group it could be argued that lowering the age of access to public pensions for this population would be equitable. This would provide Indigenous older adults with better income security and access to subsidized medications thereby improving their opportunities to age well.

Aging of Minority French-Speaking Canadians

Thirteen per cent of French-speaking Canadians (both native born and those who immigrated) live outside of Quebec with the largest proportions residing in Ontario, New Brunswick, and British Columbia (Statistics Canada, 2010). Older French-speaking Canadians residing outside of Quebec appear to be more vulnerable to challenges associated with aging such as poverty, poor health, and poor access to health services than their English-speaking counterparts (Bouchard, Sedigh, Batal, Imbeault, Makvandi, & Silva de la Vega, 2012). Despite the documented risks associated with the intersection of age and official language minority status, this group of Canadians is virtually absent from provincial and federal reports and strategies targeting older Canadians (Special Senate Committee on Aging, 2009).

Theorizing Aging

Micro Theories of Aging

There are a number of theories of aging that focus on how individuals positively adjust to the aging process. Rather than seeing old age as a passive stage of life associated with debilitation and decline, these theorists have looked to define positive adaptation in old age. **Activity theory**, for example, (Havighurst & Albrecht, 1953) posits that remaining active and engaged in social roles helps to preserve self-worth and satisfaction in old age. More recently **Successful Aging** (Rowe & Khan, 1997) advances that individuals have the capacity to prevent disease and minimize functional decline through diet, exercise, and active engagement in life. From these perspectives, keeping active, healthy, and positive in later life can prevent the onset of illness and decline and support positive mental health in old age. The notion that individuals have an important role to play in ensuring

activity theory Proposes that positive aging occurs when older adults stay active and maintain social connections.

Successful Aging Views positive aging as the prevention of functional decline and engagement in meaningful activities.

© Kali Nine LLC/iStockphoto

Research suggests that, by remaining social and engaging in activities, older adults can remain highly satisfied in old age, while at the same time reduce the risk of negative health.

positive aging is prevalent in social policy, media, and front-line practice. For example, the 2006 Seniors Health Report Card issued by the National Advisory Council on Aging (now called the National Seniors Council) looked to examine how "successful" Canada has been in promoting a healthy senior population by analyzing the general health and activity levels of older Canadians. Further, Rosanova (2010), who reviewed 146 newspaper articles featuring older adults in the *Globe and Mail* from 2004–2006, found that older adults featured as aging successfully were portrayed as choosing to be active and engaged, whether with aerobics exercises, dating, volunteering in Iraq, building retirement communities, or fighting for social justice. Finally, a frequent practice intervention in home or institutional settings is to offer older adults opportunities for engagement in social and recreational activities, which are believed to reduce isolation and prevent cognitive and physical decline (Park, 2009).

selective optimization with compensation A positive coping process of aging.

Recognizing the inevitability of decline in advanced age, Baltes and Baltes (1990) offer a model of **selective optimization with compensation**. From their perspective positive adjustment to aging includes a process of accepting and compensating for functional limitations by being selective about the activities on which to focus. According to the theory, focusing on fewer most-valued activities will allow for optimization (i.e., doing things as well as possible) and compensation (i.e., allowing for more time to accomplish things). This perspective can inform practice with older adults who have experienced functional decline by providing social workers and older adults with a modified lens from which to judge success. A. Rubenstein, a famous concert pianist shared how he compensated for his decline in speed, agility, and memory by practising fewer pieces (selection); practising more often (optimization), and deliberately slowing down before reaching a fast section of a musical piece to make it appear faster than it is (compensation).

traditional developmental psychology Views aging as one of a series of life stages with associated tasks.

Traditional developmental psychology also offers a theoretical perspective on aging by presenting two stages of development for older adults (Erickson, 1982). Later adulthood, which spans ages 60–75 years, is identified as a developmental stage where individuals grapple between achieving integrity (i.e., looking back on life with happiness, contentment, and meaning) or despair (i.e., seeing only a series of failures and wondering what life has really amounted to). Introspection is considered to be the central process for resolving this psychosocial crisis. Elderhood, which spans 75 years and older, is identified as a developmental stage where individuals grapple between accepting immortality (i.e., passing on ideas, thoughts, and traditions to the next generation) or experiencing extinction (i.e., lack of faith in connection with the next generation). Social support is considered the key to resolving this psychosocial crisis because individuals must be socially engaged to pass on their ideas, thoughts, and lessons learned (Lang & Carstensen, 2002). While these stages of development have been critiqued for their focus on past accomplishments, decline, and loss, similar to activity theory, successful aging, and the theory of selective optimization with compensation, the stages highlight how older adults can positively shape their own aging experiences and adjust to the psychological and social challenges of aging. However, by focusing predominantly on individual **agency**, micro theories of aging tend to negate how structural realities, such as inequitable access to health care and education, and personal histories and preferences, contribute to aging experiences. Taken alone these theories can lead us to blame individuals and lead individuals to blame themselves for their lack of "success" in aging.

agency The power individuals have to act and make decisions.

Macro Theories of Aging

life-course perspective Views aging as a process that spans the life course.

Macro theories of aging look beyond the individual to examine how social structures shape individual experiences of aging. The most dominant structural perspective in aging is the **life-course perspective**, which examines how the combination of developmental stages (Later Adulthood, 60–75 years; Elderhood, 75 years and older), personal life events (loss of a spouse, retirement), social locations (ethnicity, socio-economic status), and historical or social events (the Great Depression) work in combination to shape people's experiences and opportunities in old age. While the life-course perspective does not reject the basic tenets of developmental psychology, it recognizes that historical events experienced by **cohorts** may call into question the relevance and achievement of the developmental tasks for particular groups of people. For example, Indigenous older adults, who were children during the residential school system, may have a difficult time resolving the developmental conflict between integrity and despair because this form of racism and oppression experienced at a younger age can severely and irreparably challenge one's view of the world. The perspective also acknowledges that the **cumulative advantage** or **cumulative disadvantage** afforded by one's social location over time shapes aging experiences such that those advantaged or disadvantaged by social location in early life will experience multiplying advantage or disadvantage in later life. For example, a single middle-aged woman who exits the workforce to provide care to her aging mother will not only experience economic hardship during her caring years, she will be further economically disadvantaged in older age because her pension will be significantly reduced due to her exit from the workforce and inability to contribute to a pension plan during mid-life. She may also have trouble re-entering the workforce especially if work conditions and skills required have significantly changed during her exit. By acknowledging how individual-life histories are shaped over time by the combination of personal challenges, historical events, and social location, the life-course perspective calls on social workers to consider the intersection of age, gender, socio-economic status, sexual orientation, ability, race/ethnicity, and cohort effects when attempting to understand the aging experiences of older adults.

While the life-course perspective provides some aspects of a framework for researching social inequities, it does not look to uncover the structural conditions that contribute to the ways in which older adults are defined, define themselves, and are treated. In this way it helps to explain or describe how the social order may affect an individual, but does not provide avenues for uncovering that which is taken for granted (Katz, 2000). To fill this gap, perspectives in critical gerontology have emerged, which aim to expose how our thinking about aging came to be and how this in turn has created an ideal of aging that is only available to a select few (Pike, 2011; Wild, Wiles, & Allen, 2013). Among these critical perspectives is the **political economy of aging** which posits that the experience of old age can only be understood within the context of the economy, the state, the labour market, and the intersections of class, gender, and racial/ethnic divisions in society (Estes, 1991; McDonald, 1996. This theory argues that the onset of dependency and diminished socio-economic status and self-esteem in later life are an outcome of public policies, economic trends, and changing social structures. The theory seeks to uncover how economic and political forces create age inequalities in the way older adults are defined and treated. For example, because paid labour is associated with success and independence in most OECD countries, older adults who eventually retire from paid labour are challenged to continue to be seen and see themselves as productive citizens who contribute to society. This becomes even more challenging for older adults experiencing frailty who by virtue of their physical or cognitive decline become more visibly dependent on others. Likely because of this pressure to be seen as productive and independent, older adults most commonly express the fear of becoming a burden to others (Graham & Stephenson, 2010).

Macro theories of aging are useful to social workers because they help to highlight how the intersections of race, gender, socio-economic status, sexual orientation, and ability may work together to differentially shape the aging experiences of Canadians. By providing a lens from which to examine issues of equity and access for different groups of older adults, macro theories arm social workers with the ability to identify issues of inequity and work towards more socially just policies, programs, and services.

cohort Group of persons who were born at the same historical time and who experience particular social changes within a given culture in the same sequence and at the same age.

cumulative advantage The tendency of one's social location to have an enduring and increasingly positive impact over the life course.

cumulative disadvantage The tendency of one's social location to have an enduring and increasingly negative impact over the life course.

political economy of aging A theory that emphasizes the broad implications of political and economic forces that contribute to constructions of old age and aging.

Practical TIP

Creating a Timeline

ONE WAY TO INCORPORATE THE life-course perspective into direct social work practice is to conduct a timeline with clients. Start by drawing a horizontal line and dividing it into life stages such as childhood, adolescence, young adulthood, adulthood, and late adulthood. For each life stage, ask clients to recount personal life events, decisions, turning points (e.g., events seen as opening or closing opportunities), and historical life events. Record both the personal and historical events that happened to clients directly (e.g., the onset of an illness or the death of a family member) and indirectly (e.g., historical events that happened to a previous generation such as the Holocaust), whose impact they inherited. By drawing a timeline of a person's life, one can create a visual tool that can help social workers and clients see the connection between current challenges and significant life events. Asking clients how they managed to overcome particular hardships can reorient them to the strength and resilience they have developed over the course of their lives.

Policies that Have an Impact on Older Adults

Retirement Policies and Programs

Older adults' economic security is heavily determined by pension policy. An analysis of the rules and regulations governing Canada's three-tiered pension system clearly reveals how work history, social location, and the timing and circumstances surrounding retirement work together to differentially shape older adults' financial security in late life. By understanding the pension system in Canada, social workers can both help clients to access appropriate benefits and challenge inequitable pension policies.

Old Age Security (OAS) and the Guaranteed Income Supplement (GIS) represent programs in the first tier of Canada's three-tiered system. These programs provide basic income security to older adults independent of their participation in the workforce. Eligibility for OAS is based solely on age and not workforce exit. Eligibility for GIS is based on a means test. Hence pensioners with low incomes who receive OAS may also qualify for GIS to top up their retirement income. To be eligible for both OAS and GIS, older adults must have resided in Canada as adults (from the age of 18) for 40 + years. Older adults who have resided in Canada for at least 10 years in adulthood can receive partial benefits, while those residing in Canada for less than 10 years receive nothing. This requirement of residency in adulthood is based in part on the premise that those benefitting from this social good must have contributed to Canadian society as independent adults. Meant as a form of basic income security, OAS is clawed back from individuals whose income exceeds $69,562 from other sources (at 2012 rates).

The increase in average life expectancy combined with the aging of the Canadian population has given rise to much debate about the legitimacy of allowing Canadians to access retirement benefits at the age of 65. Many economists and policy-makers have argued for an age increase for all pension benefits to mitigate a growth in the **dependency ratio** and prevent working-age Canadians from carrying a greater tax burden to support retirees

dependency ratio The ratio of retirees to the working-age population.

(MacKewan, 2012). After years of debate, the Government of Canada announced in their 2012 budget plans to increase the age of eligibility for OAS and GIS from 65 to 67 by April 2023. Those who will bear the greater burden of this policy decision are older single women, persons with disabilities, and people from Indigenous communities who often rely heavily on OAS and GIS for their retirement income (National Seniors Council, 2011; Uppal, Wannell, & Imbeau, 2009). Those who will not be affected are older adults with high income whose OAS benefits are clawed back anyway.

The dependency ratio is based on the assumption that those individuals outside of the paid labour market represent a social burden to those individuals inside the paid labour market. This assumption overlooks the important contributions people outside of paid labour make to both the formal and informal economies (Dosman, Fast, Chapman, & Keating, 2006). Justifying a raised retirement age by suggesting that society cannot economically afford a high portion of non-productive citizens serves to reinforce the notion that older adults are dependent and burdensome when they do not work in paid labour. As stated above, it also disproportionately disadvantages groups of older adults whose economic security in old age is likely to be precarious.

The Canadian Pension Plan (CPP) or the Quebec Pension Plan in Quebec (QPP) represents the second tier in Canada's three-tiered pension system. These programs are mandatory public pension plans funded by the combination of contributions from employees and employers. As a social insurance scheme, the CPP/QPP is meant to protect Canadian workers and their spouses/partners from lost income upon retirement from the workforce. The amount of CPP/QPP older adults receive depends on the level of contributions made during the contributory period and the age one draws on the benefits. Older adults whose partners were CPP/QPP contributors and who are deceased receive survivor's benefits to support them in their retirement. In keeping with the motivation to increase the standard retirement age of Canadians, recent amendments to CPP/QPP policy have resulted in penalizing older adults for retiring early and rewarding them for retiring later (McDonald & Donahue, 2011). For example, as of 2013 older adults who wait until 70 years to collect their CPP will benefit from an increase in CPP earnings of up to 42 per cent. Further, as of 2012, older adults 65 and older can draw on their benefits and continue working rather than exit the workforce. Finally, older adults who draw CPP/QPP benefits between the ages of 60 and 65 experience a reduction in benefits. This backdoor method of increasing the retirement age will differentially affect low-to-middle income earners who depend heavily on CPP earnings to support their income security in retirement (Townson, 2010).

Prior to 2000, eligibility for spousal benefits attached to CPP was limited to spouses and common-law heterosexual couples living in a conjugal relationship for more than one year. This threatened older same-sex couples' economic security in retirement and widowhood. Since 2000, eligibility was extended to same-sex couples retroactive to January 1998 and following a class action lawsuit (*Hislop v. Canada*), eligibility was extended in 2006 to everyone eligible from the time the Canadian Charter of Rights and Freedoms came into force (1985). While the recognition of older gay and lesbian couples' rights to pension access is an important move forward in pension policy, as in other instances in Canadian social policy, the task of fully dismantling this form of institutional discrimination fell on individual gay and lesbian men and women who challenged the original amendment (Egale Canada, 2012, 2004). Social workers must not lose sight of the fact that many older clients, particularly those 85 and older are reticent to disclose their sexual orientation due to years of discrimination and may, by virtue of this legitimate fear, forgo their rightful pension benefits (Fredriksen-Goldsen & Muraco, 2010).

Private pension plans represent the third tier of Canada's pension system. Private plans consist of either workplace plans or Registered Retirement Savings Plans (RRSPs). These private arrangements receive tax subsidies from federal and provincial governments. The assumption behind the public pension system in Canada has always been that most Canadians would and should generate an adequate retirement income for themselves by supplementing public pension programs with their own savings or through membership of a workplace pension plan. Despite the individualist assumption that Canadians should save for their own retirement, it is notable that only 38 per cent of workers have a workplace pension plan and only 31 per cent of Canadians have private retirement savings through RRSPs (Townson, 2010).

From Forced Retirement to Non-retirement

In recent years the Canadian parliament has passed a series of acts and amendments to protect the right of older workers to remain in the workforce. The Keeping Canada's Economy and Jobs Growing Act (2011) amended the Canada Labour Code to ensure that all employees regardless of age receive severance pay upon involuntary termination regardless of age and pension eligibility. Further, on December 16, 2012, the amendments to the Canadian Human Rights Act and the Canada Labour Code were brought into force to prohibit federally regulated employers from setting a **mandatory retirement** age. These workers were the last of Canadian workers still subject to forced exit from the workforce due solely to age.

mandatory retirement
A policy that forces workers to terminate employment based only on the criteria of age.

J.D. Pooley/Getty Images

While mandatory retirement at a certain age is prohibited, many older adults must continue to work in order to support themselves.

Given the societal importance attributed to paid labour, these types of policies have been commended for allowing older adults, still capable of remaining in the workforce, to retain their status as useful and productive citizens rather than retreating from the workforce to make way for younger cohorts. However, other pathways of forced retirement still exist in Canada. Among them are older adults forced to leave the workforce due to poor health or familial caregiving responsibilities (McDonald & Donahue, 2000; McDonald, Sussman, & Donahue, 2002) and those who feel implicit pressure to retire early from their workplace to make room for younger workers (McPherson & Wister, 2008; Schellenberg et al., 2005). These forced exits are often accompanied by precarious economic security during retirement years.

On the other end of the spectrum, some older adults with work histories in **non-standard employment** such as part-time and temporary work may not be able to retire at all because they lack access to private pension plans (RRSPs), employer-sponsored pensions, and pensions from the Canada Pension Plan (Townson, 2006; Vosko, MacDonald, & Campbell, 2009). Many non-standard employment situations are also precarious because they offer low wages, low job security, limited control over workplace conditions, little protection from health and safety risks in the workplace, and less opportunity for training and career progression. The group of older adults in non-standard employment contexts represented 38 per cent of the Canadian working population in 2001 (Kapsalis & Tourigny, 2004; Townson, 2006; Vosko, Zukewich, & Cranford, 2003). The pathway to retirement for these precarious workers may be non-retirement. Older adults who are either forced to retire early due to unforeseen circumstances or forced to remain in the workforce due to precarious employment histories may benefit from social work interventions to cope with their challenging circumstances.

non-standard employment
Refers to forms of employment that lack job-stability, entitlement to fringe benefits, and pension security.

Long-Term Care Policies and Programs

While many older adults are well enough to care for themselves, older adults represent a significant majority of the clientele utilizing long-term care services, for example, approximately 75 per cent of home-care recipients (Health Council of Canada, 2012) and 92 per cent of facility-based long-term care residents are over the age of 65 (Canadian Healthcare Association, 2009b). Consequently, long-term care policies and programs have a significant impact on older adults' and their families' experiences with aging and social work practice with older adults.

Long-term care typically refers to ongoing, indefinite support for individuals who require assistance caring for themselves. While there is great variability in access to and provision of long-term care services across provinces and territories, Canadian long-term care services typically include a continuum of four key services: home care, community support services, supportive/assisted living arrangements, and facility-based long-term care (Canadian Healthcare Association, 2009b).

Home Care

Home-care services encompass an array of publically funded health and social services delivered to individuals in their homes or other community settings such as rent-geared-to-income apartment complexes and retirement homes. It includes professional health services (i.e., nursing, occupational therapy, or physical therapy), assessment and referral to community support services, and personal-care services (i.e., bathing, feeding, transferring). Despite federal influence, there is no federal legislation or national standards for the provision of home care in Canada. Instead, provincial and regional authorities determine service eligibility, levels of care, and budget allocations. All provinces and territories

Case STUDY

Living on the Margins

THE AGING OF THE POPULATION, the scarcity of social housing, the rising cost of living, and the continued devolution of responsibility for financial security from the state to the individual has resulted in projections of a six-fold increase in the number of older homeless adults in Canada in the coming decades (Hulchanski, 2009; Laird, 2007). Currently in Canada approximately 18 per cent of the homeless population are over 51 years, an age considered to represent "old" because homeless adults have a lower life expectancy and experience health-related issues at an earlier age than non-homeless older adults (Shelter, Support and Housing Administration, 2006). Despite the growing incidence of the homelessness in old age, policies and programs addressing issues of the homeless in Canada are typically geared towards youth (Burns, Grenier, Lavoie, Rothwell, & Sussman, 2013).

Although homelessness in older age is beginning to receive some research attention, few scholars have differentiated between people who become homeless in old age (recent older homeless adults) and those whose homelessness spans the adult life course (chronic older homeless adults) (Crane et al., 2005; McDonald, Dergal, & Cleghorn, 2007). Filling this important gap in knowledge, McDonald and colleagues (2007) compared recent and older homeless adults in a major city in Canada to identify possible differences in causes of homelessness, service use, and needs for support and programming. The results suggest important distinctions that social workers and policy-makers should consider when delivering services to or designing programs for older homeless adults.

This multi-method, Toronto-based descriptive study used four sources of data: secondary data collected by homeless shelters, structured face-to-face interviews with 68 older homeless persons, 30 in-depth, semi-structured interviews with recently and at-risk homeless adults, and focus group data informed by 27 service providers.

The following reviews key findings that highlight significant and meaningful differences in demographic profiles, service use, and psychosocial events triggering homelessness that must be considered.

currently have some form of standardized assessment process to determine older adults' eligibility for home-care services and connect them with other relevant services in the continuum of care such as community-based services (meals on wheels, transportation services, adult day programs, and volunteer visiting) and residential-care options. In some provinces access to home-care programs is needs-based with no user fees attached (e.g., Quebec, Ontario, Manitoba, Prince Edward Island, and the three territories) while other provinces institute a means test and fees for some services based on income (British Columbia, Alberta, Saskatchewan, New Brunswick, Nova Scotia, and Newfoundland and Labrador; Canadian Healthcare Association, 2009a).

Although the task-based nature of home support (e.g., the provision of a bath or a bandage change) is typically underscored in service descriptions and funding formulas, research has repeatedly highlighted the importance of the relational aspects of the care provided by allied health professionals and home support workers to older adults' experiences with home-care services (Bourgeault, 2010). When workers are consistent and

Demographic differences: Recently homeless older adults are more likely to be women and to be immigrants to Canada than chronic homeless older adults. This may in part be reflective of inequities in pension access experienced by women who may have exited the work force to support and care for family members and immigrants who may not meet the residency requirement for OAS.

Differences in access to services targeting homeless populations: Recently homeless older adults are more likely to lack information about the homeless service system, are less likely to stay in a homeless shelter, and are less likely to report having enough to eat than chronically homeless older adults. This suggests that traditional aging services such as home care and long-term community services may represent the first point of entry for recently homeless older adults. Information on homeless shelters, food banks, and community kitchens should be offered through these channels.

Differences in access to health services: Recently homeless older adults report more barriers to health-care utilization than chronically homeless older adults including lack of a health card, inability to afford prescribed medications, and lack of confidence in the health-care system. This suggests that social service workers coming into contact with recently homeless older adults should provide information specific to accessing health care including the process of seeking health services without a medical card and the locations of health clinics and practitioners considered to be particularly sensitive to the health needs of homeless adults.

Differences in psychosocial needs: Recently homeless older adults are more likely to attribute imminent crises as causes of their homelessness such as the loss of a job, family conflict, and widowhood than chronically homeless older adults. These psychosocial needs should be considered when offering support and intervention to older homeless adults. They may also be considered when planning for the prevention of late-life homelessness.

become acquainted with the likes/dislikes and routines of older people, care is considered of high quality. Conversely when workers are constantly changing and work is framed solely around the completion of an assigned task, home care is seen as impersonal, bureaucratic, and stressful (Sussman, 2009; Sussman & Regehr, 2009). Social workers therefore have an important role to play in advocating for service consistency and in working alongside interdisciplinary team members to recognize and acknowledge the personhood of their clientele.

Ironically, although provincial and territorial governments emphasize their commitment to aging in place, funding for home care has increasingly been allocated to short-term acute services at the expense of long-term, ongoing preventative home care (Cohen, Hall, Murphy, & Priest, 2009). Further, despite older adults' expressed needs for assistance with household and house maintenance tasks such as light cleaning, shopping, and yard work, by 2000, most home-care programs across the country limited in-home support to personal/medical care only. This restriction to service provision began to distinguish "optional" from "essential" services (Ceci & Purkis, 2011). Both trends have been justi-fied by politicians, health-care administrators, and service providers as imperative due to the anticipated health-care burden expected from an aging population. Most affected by these decisions in service allocation are older adults with low incomes who cannot afford to supplement their care and informal support networks such as family or friends who are becoming increasingly expected to supplement for inadequate publically funded services (Fast, Keating, Otfinowski, & Derksen, 2004). According to Statistics Canada's General Social Survey (2007), 70 per cent of community-residing older adults receiving some form of long-term care rely solely on family and friends for this assistance. Further, 30 per cent of family and friends providing this care report social and economic costs and 13 per cent report health costs, underscoring that limited home care bears important consequences for both older adults and their family members.

Community Support Services

Community support services are not-for-profit, locally run health and social services that supplement home-care services by providing transportation, meals on wheels, adult day programs, friendly visiting services, and in-home support for housekeeping and mainten-ance (Denton, Ploeg, Tindale, Hutchison, Brazil, Akhtar-Danesh, Lillie, & Plenderleith, 2010). While some base funding is usually provided by provincial or territorial govern-ments, the combination of fundraising, user fees, and volunteerism allow these services to operate. According to Canadian research, older adults' awareness of community sup-port services appears to be shaped in part by their place of birth and level of education. Canadian-born and adults with higher levels of education are more likely to be aware of community support services than those born outside of Canada or with less education (Chappell, MacDonald, & Stones, 2008; Denton et al., 2010). Given the multiplicity of small agencies providing these services, social workers are pivotal in raising older adults' and families' awareness of these services and their potential for providing supplemental support.

Supportive/Assisted Living Arrangements

Supportive/assisted living arrangements (sometimes termed retirement homes, assisted living facilities, or intermediate care) are congregate living facilities for older adults who require minimal personal assistance and can direct their own care (i.e., are cognitively intact). Services typically provided are communal meals, weekly housekeeping, social pro-gramming, and at least one on-site staff person 24 hours per day. Unlike traditional nursing homes, residents typically occupy individual apartments with small kitchenettes rather than hospital-style rooms. In some Canadian provinces and territories, these intermediate congregate living environments have been integrated into the public system as some desig-nated spots within these facilities are available through a centralized assessment process with standardized fees set by local health authorities (e.g., Alberta, British Columbia, and Quebec). In other provinces, these services are completely outside of the public system, and access is restricted to those who can afford the fees and who apply directly to a facility of their choice (e.g., Ontario). With limited home and community support services and an increase of the level of care requirements for entry into nursing homes across Canada, social workers will be increasingly called on to help older adults and their families under-stand and access intermediate congregate living options. This is particularly true in British Columbia and Alberta where provincial governments have attempted to control antici-pated growing health-care costs by reducing the number of beds and facilities funded in

© Paul Doyle/Alamy

Through assisted living care, older adults are able to maintain a level of independence while having access to on-site support for meals, medication, and activities.

the facility-based long-term care sector and increasing the number of spaces and facilities funded in assisted living environments (Canadian Health Care Association, 2009b).

Facility-Based Long-Term Care

Facility-based long-term care services (sometimes referred to as residential-care facilities, nursing homes, or long-term care homes) are publically funded and regulated facilities provided to people who need high levels of nursing or personal care. Older Canadians in all provinces and territories access facility-based long-term care through a single entry point where a care coordinator administers a standardized assessment to determine eligibility. Individuals considered eligible for admission typically require between 2.5–3.5 hours of daily personal care (depending on the province/territory), 24-hour supervision, and a secure environment (Berta et al., 2006). Despite preferences for community care, between 18 and 33 per cent of older adults living in Canada 85 or older relocate to a nursing home (Banerjee, 2009). While there are fees attached to facility-based living, low-income adults who cannot afford monthly fees are subsidized.

The negative perceptions and stigma attached to facility-based living are prevalent and affect older adults' and families' acceptance of and adjustment to long-term care (Caouette, 2005; Leggett, Davies, Hiskey, & Erskin, 2011; Rowles, 2000). While community care is associated with quality of life and independence, facility-based living conjures images of deterioration and death (Castle & Engberg, 2007; Smith, 2004). These images are exacerbated in research, policy, and social media. For example, the following headlines were the results of a simple Internet search using the key words "newspaper" and "nursing home" in spring 2013: *If you send your parents to a nursing home, you are sending them to die*

Theory in Practice

POST-CAREGIVING

BETWEEN 80–90 PER CENT OF THE CARE provided to older adults in need of support in the community is provided by family and friends (Health Council of Canada, 2012). Although caregiving has been conceptualized as a career with varying phases punctuated by key events or transitions such as the transition from family member or friend to active caregiver (Aneshensel, Pearlin, Mullan, Zarit, & Whitlatch, 1995), theory development and service provision have been devoted to identifying and responding to the tasks and challenges caregivers face when the care recipient is alive. Post-caregiving, a transition faced by caregivers when the care recipient dies, has only recently been described as a distinct stage in the career or life course of caregivers (Ghesquiere, Yamile & Katherine, 2011; Orzeck & Silverman, 2008). Linked to but distinct from active caregiving, this stage propels former caregivers into a period of reflection, questioning, and adjustment.

Combined with the challenges of acute and sometimes complicated mourning, this phase can involve a loss of purpose and a need to redefine self after being consumed by the caregiving role. The long-term care system in its current form typically abandons caregivers at this critical stage of their trajectory because service delivery is either designed around the older adult requiring care (e.g., home care) or the active caregiver (e.g., caregiver support groups). For example, when an older adult is a home-care recipient, case management services provide both the older adult and their family and friends with assistance by assessing their needs, linking them to appropriate resources, and providing guidance and recommendations as circumstances change and more care is required. When direct services are no longer required due to the death of the primary recipient of services—the older adult—services are

(Globe & Mail, Sept 23, 2010); *Nursing home residents are neglected* (Toronto Star Nov 11, 2011); *Woman, 87, trapped in nursing home elevator for 29 hours* (Toronto Sun January 1, 2013); and *Families say Canada's largest veterans facility neglects vets* (Globe & Mail November 8, 2012). Using the terms "newspaper" and "home care" revealed nothing.

The dramatic adjustments to facility-based living such as imposed routines and regulations undoubtedly challenge older adults' adjustment to long-term care home living (Wiersma & Dupuis, 2010). However, some older adults have also expressed feelings of relief and improved quality of life following relocation (Hersch, Spencer, & Kapoor, 2003; Jungers, 2010; Newson, 2008; Walker, Currey, & Hogstel, 2007). This suggests that distress, deterioration, and hopelessness can be minimized by supportive practices (Castle, 2001; Jolley, Jefferys, Katona, & Lennon, 2011).

The Special Senate Committee on Aging created in 2006 to examine implications of an aging society in Canada noted that facility-based living environments usually provide services in the dominant language and culture of the region only. As a result, official language minority older adults and older adults who speak neither English nor French experience a greater degree of social isolation, sadness, and anxiety when facing relocation than older adults who speak the official language of the region (Special Senate Committee on Aging, 2009).

immediately withdrawn and caregivers are left to manage the emotional demands of post-caregiving on their own (Larkin, 2009). In fact the immediate retreat of services that have sometimes been a part of the weekly routine of caregivers for years can represent an abandonment for caregivers that further complicates their mourning and challenges their reflections of purpose and meaning.

In an effort to prevent abandonment and offer appropriate services to post-caregivers, Cavendish Health and Social Service Centre, a Montreal-based health network has adapted their services to identify and respond to post-caregivers at risk of psychosocial challenges. In addition to offering caregiver-specific bereavement groups through their innovative Caregiver Support Centre, the Health and Social Service Centre is piloting an informational tree that guides all front-line workers in home care and long-term residential care to consider risk factors and intervention protocols for caregivers once a care recipient is deceased. More specifically when the primary recipient of services, the older adult with care needs, dies, the front-line workers charged with overseeing and monitoring the case will complete a form prompting them to consider possible risk factors for post-caregiving complications such as the quality of the caregiver-care receiver relationship during the course of caregiving, the type of relationship (spouse, adult child, friend), the caregiver's health and mental health history, and the circumstances surrounding the care recipient's death. Pending the degree of risk identified, workers will be prompted to provide a home visit to the caregiver one month following the death of a care recipient, signal the caregiver as a priority for short-term counselling through the Caregiver Support Centre, or refer them to other services within or outside of the Health and Social Service Centre such as vocational counselling services. This initiative is an exemplary example of the innovation that can transpire when organizations translate theoretical and empirical knowledge into service delivery.

Supporting Positive Relocations to Facility-Based Long-Term Care

Relocation to facility-based long-term care is a multi-phased process that involves a decision-making stage, a moving stage, and an initial adjustment stage (Smith & Crome, 2000; Sussman & Dupuis, 2012). Research suggests that social workers can be instrumental in facilitating older adults' and family members' adjustment to long-term care by providing them with opportunities to explore their options, express their emotions, and access good information at all stages of the relocation process. Practices found to be supportive during the decision-making period include providing families and older adults with opportunities to process their reactions and feelings about facility-based long-term care, and providing opportunities to visit available facilities and talk to residents and families who have relocated to challenge societal stigmas (Davies & Nolan, 2006). Specific interventions found to be helpful during moving include greeting new residents and spending time orienting them to their environment on moving day and speaking to older adults and families in advance of the move to provide them with specific information about what to bring and what to expect. Supportive interventions post-adjustment include treating family members as partners in the care of their relatives by honouring their knowledge and keeping them informed and involved in decisions and maximizing residents' abilities to continue to practise valued routines and rituals (e.g., late bed times; Caron, Ducharme, & Griffith, 2006; Sussman & Dupuis, 2014, 2012).

Elder Abuse: A Global Issue

Elder abuse is an important social issue that began to receive international recognition approximately 10 years ago when it was defined by the World Health Organization (2002) as "a single or repeated act, or lack of appropriate action, occurring in any relationship where there is an expectation of trust that causes harm or distress to an older person" (p. 3). Four years following, it gained further ground as a global issue (2006), when the World Health Organization and the International Network for the Prevention of Elder Abuse jointly enacted World Elder Abuse Awareness Day (WEAAD), held annually on June 15. Alongside many other OECD countries, the Canadian government and all provincial/territorial governments have participated in WEAAD since its inception by providing funding for local initiatives and developing posters and information kits to be distributed across the country.

Most research and practice in the area of elder abuse has focused on abuse that takes place in the community by a family member or friend. However, elder abuse can also take place in residential settings, or in the community by paid, in-home care-givers (McDonald, 2011). Commonly recognized types of elder abuse include physical, psychological, financial, and sexual. However, medication, spiritual, or human rights violations have also been considered forms of elder abuse. Often, more than one type of abuse occurs at the same time (Walsh, Ploeg, Lohfeld, Horne, MacMillan, & Lai, 2007). For example, financial or property abuse is typically accompanied by psychological and emotional abuse.

Elder Abuse in Canada

It is estimated that between 4 and 10 per cent of Canadian seniors experience some type of abuse (National Seniors Council, 2007). The two most frequently identified and reported types of elder abuse in Canada are financial and emotional. These two forms of abuse represent 40 to 70 per cent of all reported cases (Beaulieu, Gordon, & Spencer, 2003).

In Canada most aspects of family life lie within the jurisdiction of the provincial and territorial governments. As a consequence formal responses to incidences of mistreatment and neglect, including legislation and programs, are unique in each province or territory. For example, the province of Quebec, which developed the Governmental Action Plan to Combat Elder Abuse (2010–2015) proclaimed the establishment of a province-wide confidential telephone line offering support and information to older adults, their family members, and professionals. Other provinces with similar provincial lines specific to elder abuse include British Columbia and Ontario. The province of Alberta took a different approach in their *Strategy for Collective Action* (Alberta Health, 2010), streamlining older adults in abusive situations to use a family violence information line. Other provinces/territories use a more generalized approach include Northwest Territories and Manitoba, which offer confidential elder abuse advice and information alongside other information relevant to older adults through an information line for older adults.

adult protection legislation
Gives a specific provincial health or social service department the responsibility to respond to the abuse or neglect cases that are brought to its attention.

Some provinces/territories have also developed **adult protection legislation** (examples include Manitoba, Alberta, Nova Scotia, Newfoundland Labrador, Prince Edward Island and Yukon). In most cases, adult protection staff strive to help abused or neglected adults by having them voluntarily accept services. However, government

TABLE 12.1	Possible Signs of Different Forms of Abuse
Physical abuse	Bruises, injuries, defensive or evasive responses to questions about accidents, history of family violence or assaults, changes in behaviour, weight loss, uncleanliness of physical surroundings
Psychological or emotional abuse	Dependency, depression, poor personal hygiene, cognitive dysfunctions (particularly rapid onset dysfunctions)
Sexual abuse	Genital or anal wounds or lacerations, genital infections, genital or vesicle irritations, sleep disturbances, excessive anxiety during changing or bathing, aggressive or depressive behaviour and mistrust of others
Financial or property abuse	Rise in number of bank transactions, unusual real estate transactions, accumulation of unnecessary goods, disappearance of objects of value
Rights violations	Denial of an individual's right of consent or right of refusal regarding care and medical treatment, breach of confidentiality, denial of an individual's right to manage his or her own assets either independently or with minimal assistance
Negligence	Poor personal hygiene, malnutrition, skin sores, constipation or urinary tract problems, social isolation

Source: Adapted from p. 17 of Ministry of Families & Older Adults (2010). *Government action plan to counter elder abuse 2010–2015.* Ministry of Families & Older Adults: Quebec.

services may go to family court for an order imposing the health- and personal-care services on older adults deemed incapable of making health or financial decisions for themselves. This occurs as a last resort, and for a limited period of time (usually up to 12 months). Because adult protection legislation was modelled on the legislation used to protect children it has been critiqued for infantilizing older adults. Hence mistreated or neglected older adults may be further marginalized by legal interventions, which by their very nature are paternalistic.

In an effort to take more federal leadership, the Canadian Network for the Prevention of Elder Abuse was established in 2000. The network consists of stakeholders from professional, provincial/governmental, academic, and older adults' organizations. At present the network receives no direct sustaining funding from the federal government. Hence it has limited capacity to direct provincial/territorial strategies (Harbison, Coughlan, Beaulieu, Karabanow, VanderPlaat, Wildeman, & Wexler, 2012).

Theorizing Elder Abuse

There are a number of perspectives purported to enhance our understanding of the causes and consequences of elder abuse and neglect. From a micro perspective, elder abuse has been understood as either a consequence of caregiver stress or dysfunctional familial dynamics. In the caregiver stress understanding, elder abuse is seen in part as a direct consequence of the increased pressures placed on family members or friends to provide care to older relatives who, by virtue of the caregiving demands placed on them, project their frustration and distress on the older adults under their care. This caregiver stress conceptualization has led to risk assessments and interventions that focus on identifying caregiver distress and providing supportive services to relieve over-burdened caregivers from the sole responsibility of care (Reis & Nahmiash, 1998; Straka & Montminy, 2006). From the dysfunctional familial dynamics perspective, elder abuse is seen either as conjugal violence

In Their Own Words

ELDER ABUSE PREVENTION

AS A FEMINIST ORGANIZATION WE struggled with how to approach elder abuse prevention among newcomer families in a manner that was respectful, supportive, and useful. The work would have to grapple with the overriding stigma of hidden fear and shame. In many traditional cultures, it is unthinkable for adult children to physically abuse their elders, deny medical treatment, or sell their belongings without consent. But it is common. The intersections between language barriers, immigration status, economic uncertainty, and social isolation create a hostile breeding ground for violating the rights of seniors.

We chose to take a community development and feminist approach in elder abuse prevention. This was not simply a "family matter." As a responsible service provider we needed to look at the social and personal power dynamics as newcomer women are marginalized by migration and aging. We entered the work with much trepidation. After all, we would violate the ultimate taboo: adult parents naming their own children as abusers.

To break the shame and silence, we needed to (1) focus on elders' rights and (2) facilitate a safe, elder-led space. Two of the women approached me and suggested we host seniors-only yoga classes. We made that happen; an instructor was brought in and we built personal relationships. A few months later we invited elders in the community to join the Sister to Sister project. After a weekend leadership training, the agency would hire local elders to host sharing circles, or peer discussion circles in their homes, malls, and places of workshop.

Word of mouth spread faster than social media, and within a few days 45 women had joined. In the first 6 months, these leaders organized 25 circles held in Vietnamese,

---

grown old or as a reverse form of abuse where an adult child faced with the responsibility of supporting an aging parent is abusive as a consequence of the childhood abuse he/she experienced (Walsh, Ploeg, Lohfeld, Horne, MacMillan, & Lai, 2007). This conceptualization has led to enhancing services typically offered to adults living with family violence for an older population (such as shelters specific to older adults or hotlines specializing in family violence at all stages of the life cycle). Both micro perspectives attempt to explain the emotional and physical abuse experienced by older adults at the hand of adult children and spouses. Less clear is their relationship to financial abuse, the most common form of elder abuse reported by older adults.

From a macro perspective, ageism has been found to play a role in elder abuse. The societal notions that associate aging with decline and render older adults to be less worthy and more dependent than other persons has been most influential in informing understandings of the causes of **institutional abuse** where poor quality of care, poor enforcement of standards, and lack of well-trained staff all contribute to instances of abuse. These factors have a direct relationship to the value placed on older adults within these institutions. Interestingly, higher rates of elder abuse tend to be found in societies with a high prevalence of ageism suggesting an important connection between societal values and maltreatment and neglect of older adults (Angus & Reeve, 2006; Phelan, 2008). Despite this reality, most services, programs, and interventions are informed by micro perspectives of elder abuse.

institutional abuse Any act or omission directed at a resident of a congregate living facility that causes the person harm.

Spanish, Bengali, Mandarin, and Hindi. The sharing circle shifted to whatever safe space it needed to be: a home-cooked meal, a henna session in the park, or a formal seminar that included the local imam reinforcing the unethical nature of elder abuse. Each circle started with the presumption that knowledge is power and the foundation for shifting attitudes and behaviours. Examples of physical, sexual, emotional, and financial abuse were circulated, women exchanged support, made referrals, and strategized around how to create change—all in their mother tongue. Strategies ranged from providing individual supports around housing, legal aid, and health care to advocating for broader policy changes around pensions and immigration regulations.

Feeling ambitious, a few months later a conference at a local university was organized with 120 seniors and service providers. Two years later, we formed a Council of Elders who created their own communications plan and YouTube channel.

As an organization, we learned much from the Council of Elders. They defined elder abuse much broader than our narrow definition. Seniors described how the role reversal caused by migration renders them "useless" to their own children and the sadness they feel when they cannot communicate with their own grandchildren. As proud, independent seniors "back home" they are rendered vitally powerless and are imprisoned by language barriers and social isolation. We realized as service providers we had to think about elder abuse prevention also in terms of access to ESL classes and advocating for accessible transit. In response, we started a women-only newcomer seniors ESL class. Not long after, a senior marched up to her instructor and said, "I have lived here for many years, but now . . . I know where I stand in this country."

Maya Roy, BSW, MSc, is the executive director at Newcomer Women's Services Toronto.

Social Location and Elder Abuse

Most existing definitions of elder abuse have been conceptualized by professionals without the input of older adults. In recent years these professionally constructed definitions of elder abuse and neglect have been shown to lack particular relevance to older adults in general and to older adults from divergent social locations in particular. For example, Tam and Neysmith (2006), who studied Chinese immigrant older adults' experiences of elder abuse, identified disrespect and shame from adult children as pivotal forms of emotional abuse. These women did not necessarily identify with the categories of abuse more typically acknowledged in current social work practice. Walsh and colleagues (2007) who conducted 16 focus groups with older adults representing myriad social and economic locations such as older immigrant adults, gay, lesbian, and transgender adults, and Indigenous older adults noted that commonly identified types of elder abuse expressed amongst participants included structural and societal abuse (e.g., inadequate government policies, health-care cuts, and inadequate pensions), disrespect and ageist attitudes, and legal abuse (e.g., violation of human, legal, and medical rights). These forms of abuse are rarely named in awareness campaigns, government documents, and elder abuse screening tools. Social workers are well positioned to identify policies and practices that render groups of older adults vulnerable to abuse and advocate for macro-level interventions because of their commitment to marginalized groups.

Conclusion

Older adults are a diverse group whose experiences of aging are shaped by the combination of social location, beliefs, and assumptions about aging, and policies and services. This chapter has reviewed the diversity of Canada's aging population, and drawn attention to groups of older adults more or less advantaged by current policies and programs. Also presented was the rationale for social workers in all contexts to learn more about the issues, challenges, and opportunities associated with aging.

QUESTIONS FOR CRITICAL THOUGHT

1. What biases do you have about aging? How might these beliefs affect your view of yourself when you are older?
2. How have your beliefs and assumptions about aging been influenced by social media?
3. Describe the ways in which economic concerns, the aging of the population, and general public opinion have shaped Canadian pension policy.
4. What programs are delivered through Canada's long-term care services? What are some of the provincial differences in service delivery? How might these differences affect older adults' and their families' experiences with service access?
5. If you were a social worker helping an older adult contemplating relocation to a long-term care home, what would you think about asking or exploring? Provide a rationale for your approach based on content from the chapter.
6. What is adult protective legislation? Discuss the pros and cons of this legal approach to elder abuse with a classmate.
7. Think about the area of social work practice in which you are most interested. What issues associated with aging might you face working in this area? What do you need to know to feel competent working with those issues?

RECOMMENDED READINGS

Armstrong, P., Boscoe, M., Clow, B., Grant, K., Harworth-Brockman, M., Jackson, B., Pederson, A., Selley, M., & Springer J. (Eds,). (2009). *A place to call home: Long-term care in Canada*. Toronto: Fernwood. This edited collection of scholars and practitioners provides an overview of Canada's long-term care system and offers a vision for delivering alternate forms of long-term care that address issues of equity and access.

Chappell, N., McDonald, L., & Stones, M. (2007). *Aging in contemporary Canada* (2nd ed.). Toronto: Pearson Education Canada. This book provides a comprehensive overview of how our understandings and approaches to aging have changed based on demographic shifts in Canada's aging population.

McPherson, B.D., & Wister, A. (2008). *Aging as a social process: Canadian perspectives*. Oxford: Oxford University Press. This book introduces students to a wide variety of theoretical perspectives and methodological approaches to aging. It encourages students to deepen their critical thinking and observational skills through reflective questions and real-life illustrations.

RECOMMENDED WEBSITES

The National Initiative for the Care of the Elderly
www.nicenet.ca
The National Initiative for the Care of the Elderly is an international network of researchers, practitioners, and students dedicated to improving the care of older adults, both in Canada and abroad. The site is devoted to disseminating knowledge of research-informed best practices in aging.

The Seniors Council of Canada
www.seniorscouncil.gc.ca
The Seniors Council of Canada (formerly named the National Advisory Council on Aging) advises the Government of Canada on all matters related to Canada's aging population. The website provides a series of publications on a variety of challenges and opportunities faced by Canada's aging population. Recent national reports commissioned by the Council include aging experiences and profiles amongst older adults with low incomes, aging and the voluntary sector, elder abuse in contemporary Canada, and labour force participation amongst older adults. The Seniors Council of Canada was formerly named the National Advisory Council on Aging.

The Canadian Longitudinal Study on Aging
www.clsa-elcv.ca
The Canadian Longitudinal Study on Aging is a large, national, long-term study that will follow approximately 50,000 men and women between the ages of 45 and 85 for at least 20 years. The study site includes information on the study, the researchers, and published findings that are relevant to informing policy and practice with older adults.

International Social Work

LEARNING OBJECTIVES

- To highlight the role and importance of international social work practice in our diverse and rapidly evolving global context.

- To trace the "internationalization" of the social work profession and historical patterns of expansion.

- To address the multiple meanings and definition(s) of "international social work."

- To identify the roles and functions of international welfare organizations.

- To examine the values and ethics inherent to international social work practice.

- To demonstrate the link between social work practice and issues of global importance.

Chapter Outline

This chapter begins by addressing the need for and importance of international social work as well as the profession's historical pattern of expansion. Over the past several decades, interest in the realm of international social work has grown, bringing forth both opportunities and challenges. One of the challenges the chapter explores is adequately defining international social work, as well as the changing definition of the concept over time. This is followed by a discussion of the role and functions of international welfare organizations, including the United Nations, government agencies, non-government organizations, and faith-based organizations in the delivery of services, policy-making, and advocacy. Given the complexities inherent to international social work practice, whether domestic or international, issues of knowledge, values, and ethics are addressed. The chapter then examines the problem of child soldiers to demonstrate the link between social work practice and issues of global importance, and concludes with a discussion of the future opportunities and challenges in the realm of international social work.

Why International Social Work?

We live and practise in rapidly changing contexts where our connections, exchanges, responsibilities, and knowledge bases are no longer simply local, provincial, or national in nature, but increasingly international. As Link and Ramanathan (2011) have noted, "local and national borders are no longer sufficient limits for our information sources and ethical practice" (p. 1). **Globalization**—a concept that refers to an analysis of the contemporary world that sees the national economic, political, social, and cultural systems as having become increasingly integrated—is thought by many to have had a pivotal impact on social work theory and practice (Hugman, 2010; Lawrence et al., 2009). Globalization has continued to alter and transform the everyday lives of communities and the individuals within them on an international scale. It has also worked to reshape the environment in which social workers practise and have introduced new responsibilities, challenges, and novel opportunities for social workers and the profession as a whole. Below are some key reasons why international social work practice and a broader global knowledge base are becoming increasingly vital for emerging as well as highly experienced social workers.

First, international social forces and events, especially the movement of populations, have changed the makeup of social work agency caseloads and have affected domestic practice in many countries, including Canada. Canada's metropolitan centres increasingly reflect an array of cultures, religions, and languages, which have an important impact on political, economic, cultural, and social life. Social workers are increasingly engaging with clients affected by international events and realities, leading to a growing number of social workers that undertake internationally related domestic practice.

Second, more than ever, social problems and issues are shared by both more and less economically developed countries, making mutual work and exchange increasingly important and desirable. Global alliances concerning issues such as the environment, poverty, hunger, and health require international research and practice, and necessitate the development of global citizenship. Despite the so-called **North–South divide**—a term used to connote the socio-economic and political divisions that exist between the wealthy developed countries, known collectively as Global North, and the poorer developing or transitional countries known as Global South—countries are increasingly joining forces on key socio-economic and political issues. Most nations comprising the "North" are located in the Northern Hemisphere (nations of North American and Europe). Notable

globalization A mainly economic process including the breaking down of borders and barriers to international trade but can also describe economic, political, social, technological, culture transformations that lead to greater interconnectedness of people and systems around the world.

North–South divide A distinction based on the main developmental division between countries being that of the highly developed countries and the developing countries that are almost all located to the south.

exceptions include Australia and New Zealand, illustrating that the divide is not wholly defined by geography.

Third, the actions of one country, whether political, cultural, economic, or social, directly and indirectly have an impact upon the social and economic well-being of others. Examples such as the world economy, natural disasters, armed conflicts, the environment, the HIV/AIDS pandemic, and the world arms race are just a few examples that highlight the difficulty in establishing a clear division between what is "foreign" and what is "domestic."

Fourth, advances in technology and communications have created enhanced opportunities for international and community sharing and exchanges. As Hugman (2010) notes, "the revolution in communications, the ability to travel readily to remote parts of the world, the increasing cultural diversity of national populations, enhanced global trade and economic activities as well as greater international political cooperation, have all fostered the globalization of the human experience" (p. 22).

Fifth, social justice and **human rights** are a global necessity and concern. The effects of social injustice are having powerful consequences around the world. Globalization and capitalistic expansion have intensified social and economic inequality. One half of the world's population is living in severe poverty. In fact, world poverty is responsible for one third of all human deaths (50,000 deaths per day, 18 million deaths per year), and yet eradication would only require 1 per cent of the global product (Pogge, 2008). The World Health Organization released a report addressing the determinants of health that concluded that social justice is a matter of life and death, and that social injustice is killing people on an alarming scale (WHO, 2008). Human rights are basic rights and freedoms that all people are entitled to regardless of nationality, sex, national or ethnic origin, ability, race, sexual orientation, gender identity, religion, language, or other status. Human rights include civil and political rights, such as the right to freedom of speech, expression, or peaceful assembly; and social, cultural, and economic rights including the right to participate in culture, the right to food, the right to work, and the right to receive an education. Human rights are protected and upheld by international and national laws and treaties.

human rights Basic rights and freedoms that all people are entitled to regardless of nationality, sex, national or ethnic origin, ability, sexual orientation, gender identity, race, religion, language, or other status.

Developments in international law and human rights have established broad, universal standards to which all countries and governments must comply. Citizens of the globe, regardless of their originating country or hemisphere, deserve to be protected from violations of their basic human rights and dignity. However, addressing human rights and social justice around the globe continues to be an ongoing challenge. Social work holds a rich history of social justice and human rights as part of its fundamental values and concerns. In fact, the commitment to social justice and human rights permeates the mandates and codes of ethics of provincial, national, and international social work organizations (Lundy, 2011). The profession is unquestionably needed in the fight to address poverty, social justice, and human rights locally, nationally, and internationally, and to practise on a broader structural and global scale. At the same time, the profession must also act in a self-critical and reflexive manner, cognizant of its own role within histories of oppression and marginalization.

These above-noted global realities and trends inevitably shape contemporary social work theory, research, and practice and thus require the establishment of greater global professional awareness, new knowledge(s), and approaches.

Social Work beyond Borders: International Social Work Organizations, Historical Patterns of Expansion, and the Canadian Connection

Historical research has uncovered the profession's strong interest in international exchange and development. In 1928, the First International Conference of Social Work drew 2,500 participants from 42 countries, representing six continents. Educators at the 1928 meeting discussed plans for an international school of social work to further the goal of cross-national exchange of ideas and practices. Although never realized, the commitment to an international vision and collaboration was evident. Out of these meetings emerged three significant international bodies, all founded in 1928, which continue their work today. The International Association of Schools of Social Work (IASSW) is an international community of schools and educators in social work, promoting quality education, training, and research for the theory and practice of social work, administration of social services, and formulation of social policies. The International Council on Social Welfare (ICSW) is an international non-governmental organization operating throughout the world for the cause of social welfare, social justice, and **social development**, working actively with the UN. The secretariat is located in Utrecht, The Netherlands. The International Federation of Social Workers (IFSW) is a global organization striving for social justice, human rights, and social development through the promotion of social work, best practice models, and the facilitation of international cooperation. The IFSW has special consultative status with the United Nations Economic and Social Council. They are also accredited by the International Labour Organization, UNICEF, the Council of Europe, and the European Union. The organization currently represents over 750,000 social workers around the globe.

The growth of the profession internationally has been significant. In 1929, the first organized efforts at international collaboration were made through the IASSW, which had at the time 46 member schools in 10 countries (Midgley, 2001). In 1950, the United Nations undertook its first survey of social work education. During this period, there were 373 schools in 46 countries. Twenty-five years later, the IASSW had 459 members in 66 countries (Midgley, 2001). The profession is now in its second century and social work has been established on every continent, and organized educational programs in social work have existed for more than half a century, emphasizing the profession's global reach.

While there have been efforts at building and expanding the profession across the globe, several patterns in the evolution of social work internationally are evident. In the first pattern, around 1900, a number of social work schools emerged almost concurrently in London, Amsterdam, New York, and Berlin. Much of the social services at that time were being developed to address the emerging needs arising from the Industrial Revolution in Northern Europe and America. Social work thus emerged in these contexts as a local and national response to emerging social problems in late nineteenth-century life, particularly to the harsh employment conditions. Services thus focused upon families, settlement houses, and assistance to orphans, widows, young women, and immigrants. International exchanges of ideas and knowledge within the field of social work did exist during the early half of the twentieth century through collaborative activities such as "charity visiting" and "settlement work," which largely occurred between the UK, US, Denmark, and Canada (Healy, 2001; Midgley, 2001, p. 22).

In contrast to the above, the second pattern in the evolution and expansion of social work did not emerge as a result of local responses to local or national problems. Instead, social work was largely introduced into Asian, African, and Caribbean countries by American and European "experts" (often in the form of missionaries and by officials of colonial governments) to address issues related to underdevelopment (Midgley, 2001). In other cases, social work arrived in newly independent nations under UN auspices or through aid projects. Writing in 1972, de Jongh notes: "I do not know of any developing country in which social work education was an original product of national development; the origins can always be traced back to strong foreign influences" (Midgley, 2001, p. 23). Midgley (1981) provides an analysis of such "professional imperialism." In what has become a classic work, Midgley argues that the reality of international social work was far

social development
Concerned with processes of change that lead to improvements in human well-being, social relations, and social institutions that are equitable, sustainable, and compatible with principles of democratic governance and social justice.

from being a process of "transmission" or "exchange," implying equality or openness of relationship. Instead, Midgley notes that the spread of the social work profession from countries of the Global North to other countries reflected the colonial and post-colonial political and economic structures within which it was practised. This pattern and its legacy have profound implications for current and future practice, which will be addressed later in the chapter. A third and similar pattern has been the introduction of social work in the countries of the former Soviet Union and Eastern Bloc, including Russia, Eastern European nations, China and Viet Nam—a process that has also involved substantial foreign influence.

Canada has played a prominent role within international social work initiatives. Drover and Rogers (2009) note that Canada has been actively involved in the International Federation of Social Workers (IFSW), the International Association of Schools of Social Work (IASSW) and the UN Interregional Consultation on Developmental Social Welfare Policies and Programs. Canadian social work educators have also played an important role in IASSW's international endeavors by serving on committees and collaborating in research and intervention activities. Canadians have also assisted in locating resources for promoting social work education and social development in the Global South (Hiranandani, 2011). Canada's leadership role in international organizations has been evident in founding the United Nations Relief and Rehabilitation Administration in 1943, the World Health Organization, and United Nations in 1945, and drafting the Universal Declaration of Human Rights in 1948 (Drover & Rogers, 2009).

Defining International Social Work: An Ongoing Challenge

In some ways, the notion of "international social work" challenges traditional notions and conceptualizations of social work as well as the role and responsibilities of the profession. Historically, social work emerged as a profession that worked primarily to address the needs of "citizens" of a nation-state, demarcating clear boundaries in terms of client populations, service users and professional responsibilities. International social work, which moves "beyond borders," fundamentally challenges this traditional conceptualization and re-defines "citizenship" to include a global dimension. The reality of international social work raises the issue of the profession's responsibility and commitment to marginalized and oppressed populations outside of traditional territorial borders.

What is international social work? is a question that has been an area of discussion among scholars and practitioners over the last century. The use of the term "international social work" dates back to the 1920s. In a 1928 speech written for the First International Conference of Social Work, Eglantyne Jebb, founder of Save the Children UK, declared that there had been a "rapid and surprising increase in actual international social work since the Great War" and that "international social work demands constant contact between social workers on an international intellectual basis" (cited in Healy and Link, 2012, p. 10). Since then, myriad definitions of international social work have been proposed, with scholarship on the topic intensifying in the early twenty-first century. However, despite the increased discussion and debate, there is no singular, accepted definition of "international social work" or a universal use of the concept. Some of the definitions and conceptualizations of the term that have emerged over the past 20 years are highlighted below. Definitions of international social work tend to fall within the realms of direct practice with international populations (broadly defined), as well as to serve as a lens through which to view and guide one's work and practice.

Hokenstad et al. (1992) maintained that "international social work" could be defined as focusing "on the profession and practice in different countries, the different roles that social workers perform, the practice methods they use, the problems they deal with, and the many challenges they face" (p. 4). Healy (2001) proposed that international social work has four dimensions and areas for action: (1) internationally informed domestic practice; (2) participation in and international exchange; (3) international practice; and (4) international policy formulation and advocacy. The first two potentially involve all social workers; the third tend to involve only a small percentage of social workers, and the fourth, while involving all social workers indirectly as part of the profession, may directly involve relatively few. These four dimensions are addressed in greater detail below:

1. *Internationally Related Domestic Practice and Advocacy*: Social workers are increasingly being called upon to deal with problems that have an international dimension—meaning that two or more countries are involved in some way in a particular case or policy issue. Areas of practice and policy that have an international dimension include refugee resettlement, international adoption work, and social work in border areas. Such contexts require that social workers have in-depth knowledge of all of the countries and contexts at play. Healy also suggests that as part of international advocacy, social workers take stances and act as advocates on aspects of their own country's foreign and national policy that affects peoples in other countries, such as legislation on immigration.
2. *Professional Exchange*: This refers to the capacity to exchange social work information and experiences internationally and to use the knowledge and experience to improve social work practice at home. This can include reading periodicals from other countries and regions, and participating in professional interchange at international meetings to enrich one's own practice.
3. *International Practice*: This refers to the preparation of professional social workers to contribute directly to international development work through employment or volunteer work in international development agencies.
4. *International Policy Development and Advocacy*: This refers to the capacity of the social work profession to act as a global movement to formulate and promulgate positions on important social issues and make a contribution to the resolution of global problems related to its sphere of expertise.

Cox and Pawar (2006) defined international social work within the context of a globalized world emphasizing an integrated approach that addresses human rights and ecological and social development perspectives. They articulate international social work to be

> the promotion of social work education and practice globally and locally, with the purpose of building a truly integrated international profession that reflects social work's capacity to respond appropriately and effectively, in education and practice terms, to the various global challenges that are having a significant impact on the well-being of large sections of the world's population. This global and local promotion of social work education and practice is based on an integrated-perspectives approach that synthesizes global, human rights, ecological, and social development perspectives of international situations and responses to them (p. 20).

Hugman (2010) asserted that crossing borders is key to any definition of international social work. He defined international social work as

> practice and policy concerning situations in which professionals, those who benefit from their services or the causes of the problems that bring these two actors together have travelled in some way across the borders between nations. That is,

social work is international when the social worker, the service user, or the social issue moves between or connects two or more countries (p. 20).

Drawing upon this notion of "crossing borders," Hugman et al. (2010, p. 632–633) identified five key dimensions of international social work:

1. International social work can be seen as the practice of social work in a country other than the home country of the social worker.
2. In the second part of the twentieth century, international social work also came to mean working with individuals, families, or communities whose origins are in a country other than that where the social worker is practising (for example, social work with refugees or other migrants).
3. Working with international organizations, such as international non-government organizations such as International Committee of the Red Cross (ICRC) or quasi-governmental organizations, such as the United Nations.
4. Exchanges or collaborations between countries in which social workers share ideas or work together on projects that cross national borders.
5. International social work has begun to incorporate the notion of **glocalization**. This idea refers to an understanding of the local context in terms of the impact of economic and cultural globalization on the local socio-cultural area as well as the impact of the local on the global.

> **glocalization** A term popularized by Bauman (1998) who argued that globalization should be understood as linking global and local processes.

International social work has been described as a *lens through which to view practice* (Lyons et al., 2006). Given current trends in demography and migration, alongside conditions of globalization that have altered everyday life at the individual, community, and societal levels, social workers are compelled to develop an "international perspective" on practice. In the words of Dominelli (2005), embracing such a perspective emphasizes international social work as "a form of practice that localizes the global and globalizes the local" (p. 505). Lawrence et al. (2009) argue that developing an international perspective can be achieved by increasing our knowledge about comparative social welfare, exploring social work practice in other countries, and by enhancing our skills in cross-cultural work. In particular, they maintain that developing an international social work perspective or lens requires social workers to acquire and adopt *knowledge* of social welfare beyond one's immediate context; of different cultures and contexts for social work practice; *skills* in working with people from different countries and contexts; and *values* which respect difference and promote principles of human rights and social justice. An international perspective can not only act as a tool to inform social workers what happens elsewhere, but it allows workers to think about their own situation differently (Lawrence et al., 2009), thus encouraging critical thinking and reflexivity.

Perhaps in an attempt to merge the practical with the conceptual and theoretical, Healy and Link (2012) provide a definition of international social work that is both practice oriented and value based. They provide seven bullet points to encapsulate the breadth of their definition:

* a way of looking at and appreciating the world (worldview) and acknowledging the impact of globalization on human well-being;
* practice, including locally based practice, informed by international knowledge;
* practice, concern, and action on globally experienced social issues;
* participation in international professional organizations and dialogue;
* understanding of the global profession;
* promotion of development and human rights;
* a future and action-oriented movement for global change.

In Their Own Words

INTERNATIONAL SOCIAL WORK

IN A WORLD THAT SEEMS to be getting smaller and smaller, international social work has earned a prominent and exciting place within our profession. Now more than ever, social workers are faced with opportunities to cross oceans and borders to address social injustice in research, developmental, and humanitarian capacities. Yet with these opportunities come important ethical considerations around the impact of exporting this kind of "help." Good intentions alone do not necessarily make for good practice. Given our history of colonialism, and the harmful relations that were formed in the name of "goodwill" and "humanitarianism," it is necessary to unpack and critically reflect on our methods of helping in communities of the South.

Our role as social workers should not be to import and impose our own idea of what communities need, but rather to help equip communities with the tools they need to decide for themselves. In my experience conducting research with war-affected children in Uganda and working with the Red Cross, I have seen first-hand the wealth of knowledge and talent that lies at the grassroots level. Despite the rhetoric of "vulnerability" and "helplessness" that is so often attached to war-affected communities, I have seen a strong capacity to cope and survive despite great adversity. To offer assistance that undermines local capacity sends a message of Western superiority and arrogance that is both irresponsible and counterproductive. As social workers in communities that are not our own, we must begin with the understanding that we have far more to learn than we have to offer and that we can best serve communities by helping to restore confidence and promote self-determination above all. Through our professional practice we have an opportunity and responsibility to set a standard for international assistance that is founded upon collaboration and respect for local ways of knowing and doing.

Lindsay Jones, MSW, is a psychosocial delegate for the Emergency Response Unit of the Canadian Red Cross, Ottawa, Ontario.

The challenge of defining "international social work" is far from settled, and the discussions and debates surrounding the practices, worldviews, and outlooks tied to the concept will likely continue. Nonetheless, given the relatively recent efforts to define the concept as well as the growing interest in the field of international social work, our understanding and knowledge regarding its meaning and implications will likely expand and solidify over the coming years.

International Social Welfare Organizations and Their Functions

Most international social welfare organizations are involved in the development or promotion of human rights and social justice. Organizations include the United Nations, government agencies, non-governmental organizations, and faith-based organizations. Within these organizations, social workers undertake a wide variety of tasks including the organization of relief and humanitarian aid, needs assessments, advocacy, research, or training and support of local social welfare personnel as well as the direct provision of services including counselling, casework, and community development (Cox & Pawar, 2006).

The United Nations and Its Agencies

Since its inception, the United Nations (UN) has served as the primary institution for nations to work towards peace and development based on the principles of justice, human dignity, and the well-being for all as well as the provision of multilateral assistance. Formed in 1945 at the end of World War II, with an initial membership of 51 nation states, the UN sought to serve as a structure to oversee international laws and to protect future generations from the atrocities of war. One of its first tasks was to develop international human rights. The UN is where governments meet to discuss issues of global concern and make decisions on a collective scale. When decisions are made (through the creation of conventions, treaties, resolutions, and declarations) **civil society**, including **non-governmental organizations** (NGOs) and **international non-governmental organizations** (INGOs) are tasked with implementing those decisions and making them a reality (Mama, 2012). Civil society refers to the wide array of non-governmental and not-for-profit organizations that have a presence in public life, expressing the interests and values of their members, based on ethical, cultural, political, scientific, religious, or philanthropic considerations. Civil society organizations include community groups, NGOs, labour unions, Indigenous groups, charitable organizations, faith-based organizations, professional associations, and foundations. Non-governmental organizations are private organizations that pursue activities to relieve suffering, promote the interests of the poor, protect the environment, provide basic social services, or undertake community development. International non-governmental organizations normally have a similar mission to NGOs, but are international in scope and may have offices around the world to deal with specific issues in many countries.

civil society Refers to the wide array of non-governmental and not-for-profit organizations that have a presence in public life, expressing the interests and values of their members.

non-governmental organizations (NGOs) Private organizations that pursue activities to relieve suffering, promote the interests of the poor, protect the environment, provide basic social services, or undertake community development.

international non-governmental organizations (INGOs) Normally have a similar mission to an NGO, but it is international in scope and may have offices around the world to deal with specific issues in many countries.

© xenotar/iStockphoto

Today, the United Nations consists of 193 member states striving towards global peace and development.

Social work played a strong role in the emergence of the UN in the 1940s and its subsequent development (Healy & Link, 2012). Social work's history with the UN has included social activism, pacifism, policy advocacy, and research and program development. As the UN continued to grow, social workers were involved in the development of the United Nations Children's Fund (UNICEF), the United Nations Development Programme (UNDP), the United Nations Fund for Population Activities (UNFPA), the Office of the United Nations High Commissioner for Refugees (UNHCR), the World Health Organization (WHO), and the World Food Programme (WFP). All these agencies come under the umbrella of the Economic and Social Council (ECOSOC), which reports to the UN General Assembly.

International policy advocacy forms the major part of the work undertaken by social workers who work for an NGO that is affiliated with the UN (Healy & Link, 2012). Typically, these social workers are engaged in global social issues that are fundamental to social work: poverty, human rights, health, migration, and the status of women and children and other historically marginalized populations. Social work representatives work to understand the circumstances and forces that affect various groups and populations and then bring these conditions to light at the UN, advocating for change where possible. This work is accomplished by working with UN staff, NGO committees, and other social work leaders within the UN system. Social workers not affiliated with the UN, but who have a vested interest in global social policy are able to attend the Annual Social Work Day at the UN, which is sponsored by the IFSW and the IASSW. Thousands of social work practitioners and students come to the annual event to meet other social workers who hold similar international interests.

Government Agencies

multilateral organizations Organizations formed between three or more nations to work on issues that relate to all of the countries in the organization. Examples of multilateral organizations include UNICEF and the World Bank.

Governments, including the Canadian government, carry out international programs through their national agencies and through participation in **multilateral organizations** which are formed between three or more nations to work on issues that relate to all of the countries in the organization. Examples of multilateral organizations include UNICEF and the World Bank. International social welfare functions of governments include humanitarian assistance, professional and educational exchange in social welfare, research on comparative social welfare, direct services to international populations, such as refugee assistance, and participation in various international programs and conferences.

The Department of Foreign Affairs, Trade and Development Canada (DFATD) is Canada's lead agency for development assistance, and heads Canada's international effort to help people living in poverty. DFATD's current priorities are increasing food security, securing the future of children and youth, and stimulating sustainable economic growth. DFATD aims to manage Canada's support and resources effectively and accountably to achieve meaningful, sustainable results and engage in policy development in Canada and internationally, enabling Canada's effort to realize its development objectives. A unique feature of government aid in Canada is that provincial governments also provide aid. The federal government permits provinces to sponsor aid projects as long as they are consistent with overall Canadian social and foreign policies.

Non-governmental Organizations

The World Bank defines NGOs as "private organizations that pursue activities to relieve suffering, promote the interests of the poor, protect the environment, provide basic social services, or undertake community development" (cited in the World Association of Non-Governmental Organizations, 2009). Since the 1970s, NGOs have been critical actors in local, national, and international processes to promote social development, welfare, and human rights (Libal & Harding, 2012). Some NGOs are primarily service organizations, while others provide no services, but are primarily focused on advocacy. Increasingly, NGOs have identified the need to serve as voices for more effective international assistance programs and for responsible international policies. NGOs vary widely in terms of size, purpose, scope, and type of work as well as in terms of their relationships with communities, states, and other organizations (Fisher, 1997).

Social workers increasingly staff national and local NGOs, whether they are providing direct or indirect services, working as community organizers, or serving in advocacy or policy-making roles. These organizations are critical in generating "community-led, issue driven efforts toward social change" (Roff, 2004, p. 203) that are in line with social work values of promoting community participation and advocacy for social justice and human rights. In Canada, key NGOs that work on international social work issues include InterPares, Equitas, and the Canadian Council for Refugees.

International Non-governmental Organizations

An international non-governmental organization (INGO) normally has a similar mission to an NGO, but it is international in scope and may have offices around the world to deal with specific issues in many countries. In terms of services, they range from those that provide micro-level services to those that have a macro approach to international social work. For example, International Social Service (ISS) provides micro-level services. Located in Geneva with branches in numerous countries around the globe, ISS specializes in cross-national casework involving migration, refugees, family law, and children's rights. An example of an INGO that focuses on macro-level services (social development, research, policy) is Oxfam. Other INGOs, such as Save the Children, the International Committee of the Red Cross, the International Rescue Committee, or Care International, have broad types of interventions at both micro and macro levels of intervention and programming. For the most part, INGOs focus on social development and humanitarian aid.

Following World War II, 41 international NGOs were accorded consultative status with the UN Economic and Social Council (ECOSOC). This gave INGOs access to intergovernmental advocacy processes and allowed them to work alongside UN agencies in implementing human rights, development, and humanitarian relief programs. In 1992, the number of NGOs with consultative status to the UN had risen to more than 700, and in 2009 to nearly 3,200 (Mama, 2012). The expansion of NGOs in development and relief efforts has been linked to several factors. First are the increases in armed conflicts, humanitarian disasters, and the failure of nation states to ensure social development and human rights for their people. Second, some argue that the proliferation of NGOs is linked to **neo-liberal** models of economic growth that stress the need to cut taxes and public spending and to reduce state-run programs that promote social development and social welfare (Libal & Harding, 2012). **Neo-liberalism** is a set of economic policies whereby the control of economic factors is shifted from the public sector to the private sector. Neo-liberalism advocates that governments reduce deficit spending, limit subsidies, reform tax law to broaden the tax base, open up markets to trade by limiting protectionism, and privatize state-run businesses. Hugman (2010) maintains that social workers are not particularly well represented within INGOs. He states that this may be related to the low visibility of social work for these organizations and the fact that social work may be perceived as being focused upon clinical approaches, casework, and child protection. This, however, may shift over time as more social workers become employed in these organizations.

neo-liberalism A set of economic policies whereby the control of economic factors is shifted from the public sector to the private sector.

In Their Own Words

APPRECIATING THE WORLD FROM A GLOBAL PERSPECTIVE

FOR OVER 10 YEARS, I HAVE been living and working in international settings with populations affected by war, disaster, and abject poverty, to all of whom I am extremely grateful for sharing their lives and experiences with me. I have also been fortunate enough to meet some amazing social workers from different cultures, who have influenced my view of international social work. As a social worker from North America working in Europe, Asia, Africa, and the Middle East, my role is less about practising traditional social work (i.e., counselling, case management, etc.) and more about complementing and building upon the existing capacity of indigenous social work mechanisms.

For me, international social work is not necessarily about practising social work abroad or with people from other cultures here in Canada. Rather, it's a way of looking at and appreciating the world from a global perspective. Practically, it is the integration of multiple forms of knowledge—from a range of contexts and populations—to inform current social work practice. Taking a global perspective of social work is tough, because our own local knowledge is often deeply ingrained in our practice, making it difficult to always be open to a range of other (sometimes unfamiliar) ideas, notions, and theories. Yet, herein lies one of the challenges and opportunities that makes international social work so stimulating.

Working as a social worker in international settings also poses many physical and personal challenges. For example, how can social workers fight for social justice in conditions of political oppression and adversity, when their own safety and freedom may be compromised? Working in the often extreme circumstances posed by international settings tests social workers and their guiding principles. But social workers can also be enriched by these experiences, especially if one stays true to the social work principle of meeting human needs shaped by a commitment to social justice.

I also view sharing experiences as a means for peace-building and reconciliation. I have discovered that an "us-versus-them" mentality is a prevalent feature in many of the conflict-ridden areas that I work in. In these situations, Charles Lamb's words echo in my mind: "Don't introduce me to that man, because I want to go on hating him. If I meet him, I can't hate him." Therefore, in my work with war-affected populations, I stress the importance of hearing from a wide range of voices, exchanging stories and experiences, and ultimately contributing to a global community that is more tolerant of others, as one vital step towards building global social justice.

Bree Akesson, LMSW, MPH.

Faith-Based Organizations

A faith-based organization is one where there is "*religious integration*—the notion that religion is not an independent attribute but a dynamic that is incorporated into the organization in a variety of ways and intensities" (Sider & Unruh, 2004, p. 116, emphasis in original). It runs on a continuum, based on the extent to which the organization is connected to "religion as it is expressed in observable and explicit phenomena such as language, symbols, policies, and activities. Such manifestations of religion may include mission statements, selection criteria for personnel and resources, administrative practices, programmatic activities, and service methodologies" (p. 117). Faith-based organizations that focus on the provision of international social welfare are shaped by political, social and economic forces similar to secular agencies, but are different in that "they are motivated by their faith and they have a constituency which is broader than humanitarian concerns" whereby their constituents feel "a duty to respond to the needs of the poor and the marginalized" based on their faith (Ferris, 2005, p. 316).

Faith-based and religiously affiliated service agencies can range from large national and multinational organizations with multimillion-dollar budgets and thousands of employees to organizations with limited budgets and restricted staff resources (Sinha, 2013). These entities work internationally in hospitals and schools, with poverty prevention programs and broader community development initiatives, as social justice advocates, and to provide humanitarian assistance (Ferris, 2005). Faith-based organizations working internationally and based in Canada include Islamic Relief Canada, World Vision Canada, Canadian Jewish Humanitarian and Relief Committee, and Canadian Lutheran World Relief.

Values and Ethics in International Social Work

The complexities surrounding the Canadian Association of Social Workers *Code of Ethics* have been addressed in Chapter 3. An interesting issue to reflect upon is whether the values and principles found in the *Code of Ethics* are similar to those in other countries. Banks (2006) provides a review of codes of ethics from 31 national social work associations around the world. Banks found several commonalities among them including statements concerning the overarching values of the profession (notably "integrity," "rights," and "justice"), the appropriate application of these values as well as the moral qualities ("virtues") that should be demonstrated by social workers. Banks (2006) asserts that social work around the world can be regarded as having a "common morality approach" (p. 41).

Other social work organizations have attempted to develop and address common ethical principles. In particular, the IFSW has produced a Statement of Ethical Principles (http://ifsw.org/policies/statement-of-ethical-principles) that aim to promote ethical debate and reflection in the member organizations, among the providers of social work in member countries as well as in Schools of Social Work and among social work students. It is noted in the Preface that

> some ethical challenges and problems facing social workers are specific to particular countries; others are common. By staying at the level of general principles, the . . . IFSW statement [of ethical principles] aims to encourage social workers across the world to reflect on the challenges and dilemmas that face them and make ethically informed decisions about how to act in each particular case.

However, when considering international practice issues, what are the opportunities and challenges in establishing a code of ethics that covers ethical practice for social workers around the globe? Can a universal set of social work values be defined that apply to professional work in every country? This raises philosophical issues with very practical consequences for social workers working in multicultural as well as international settings. This debate is frequently understood as two competing schools of thought—**universalism** versus **cultural relativism**. Universalism is the position that states that core values apply to all human beings, irrespective of their identity (including cultural background or personal

universalism The position that states that core values apply to all human beings, irrespective of their identity (including cultural background or personal preferences).

cultural relativism Advocates that culture is the sole source for the validity of a moral right or rule and that members of one society may not legitimately condemn the practices of societies with different traditions, especially practices considered culturally based.

preferences). Proponents of this view argue that "all members of the human family share the same inalienable rights" (Mayer, 1995, p. 176) and that "culture is irrelevant to the validity of moral rights and rules" (Donnelly, 1984, p. 400). Gray and Fook (2004) have suggested that while there are practical and conceptual challenges in understanding social work in universal terms, there are some important reasons why we might choose to do so. They argue that universal principles enable us to increase "our knowledge and understanding of human problems, strengthen practice and further [develop] the profession in raising its profile" (p. 637).

On the other hand, proponents of cultural relativism argue that "culture is the sole source for the validity of a moral right or rule" (Donnelly, 1984, p. 400) and that "members of one society may not legitimately condemn the practices of societies with different traditions," especially practices considered culturally based (Mayer, 1995, p. 176). Criticisms of universalist approaches (and international codes of ethics like the one emerging from the IFSW) have come from social workers from Africa, Asia, and Pacific Islands (Mafile'o, 2006; Silavwe, 1995; Yip, 2004) as well as indigenous social workers in Australia, Canada, New Zealand, and the US (Weaver, 1997). In particular, these critics view such "universal" ethical principles as inherently "Eurocentric" and essentially reflecting the dominance of the Global North in ideas about social work theory and practice.

These realities have given rise to the concepts and practices of **indigenization** and **authenization**. Indigenization refers to the adoption and adaptation of theories and practices in social work in ways that are relevant to the local (indigenous) context. Authentization refers to a process of developing theories and practices for social work that are derived out of the realities of the local context (Walton & El Nasr, 1988).

indigenization Refers to the adoption and adaptation of theories and practices in social work in ways that are relevant to the local (indigenous) context.

authentization Refers to a process of developing theories and practices for social work that are derived out of the realities of the local context.

© Maciej Dakowicz/Alamy

Global North social work practices may not always be internationally applicable. Social workers in different settings must take care to adapt to theories that are relevant to that local context.

Theory in Practice

IN A CULTURAL CONTEXT

PRACTITIONERS IN THE FIELD OFTEN encounter situations that raise profound ethical dilemmas as they interact with multiple cultures and contexts. Social workers may struggle, at the practical level, with the universalism–relativism debate. Here is an example:

> A social worker trained in Canada returns to Zambia, his country of origin. As part of his newly established role, the social worker was assigned to bring a boy from a police station back to his rural village. The child had committed a minor theft in the city. When returning with the child to the village, the social worker met with a local community member and elder who inquired about the boy's welfare, how he was doing. The social worker responded: "I cannot tell you what happened. His situation is confidential. I need to speak with his parents." The community member was shocked and bewildered. The social worker felt shame and confusion at his own response.

This case example addresses the issues raised by Silavwe (1995) in his discussion of "universal" social work values. He argues that the espoused international professional values of "confidentiality" and "self-determination," which have emerged largely from an individualistic framework, have been imported into Zambia. He highlights that these values conflict with traditional Zambian values of cooperation, shared responsibility, mutuality, and openness in defining what is "good" and "right." He notes that individualistic notions of client confidentiality and self-determination make little sense in a Zambian context where decision-making is made collectively at open gatherings where local families and community members, social workers, clergy, traditional healers, and political leaders are all present. Silavwe recommends that group determination should replace self-determination as the dominant value in African social work.

The above case example demonstrates that confidentiality can take on vastly different meanings in multiple contexts, and when used inappropriately and out of context, can actually be harmful. In the case example of the Zambian boy, the strict use of confidentiality as typically drawn upon in the Global North, and the deliberate exclusion of key and caring community members in the boy's life, may actually eliminate existing protective mechanisms that have the capacity to support the client in question.

International Social Work Practice: The Implications of the "Export Model"

As part of a study-abroad program, a Canadian social work student travels to Colombia for the first time as part of her field placement with a local Colombian NGO that provides support to marginalized women within Indigenous communities. While working with local women, the student implicitly draws upon cognitive-behavioral models of practice that emphasize "faulty thinking" and individualized models of client interactions that she learned in her course work at university. Her local field supervisor, having

Case STUDY

Ongoing Tensions in International Social Work Practice: Intervention in Post-war Sierra Leone and Conflicting Professional Paradigms

A SMALL COUNTRY IN WEST AFRICA, Sierra Leone was engulfed in a brutal decade-long civil war between 1991 and 2002 that led to the death of an estimated 70,000 people, the displacement of more than 2 million people, the amputations of more than 10,000 people, and the destruction of the country's limited infrastructure (Denov, 2010). At the height of post-war humanitarian interventions, there were approximately 250 NGOs operating in the country, more than half of which were international (Coulter, 2009). Given their strong and powerful presence in post-conflict Sierra Leone, international initiatives have tended to dominate the scholarly, policy, and practice literature on the country's post-war recovery (Gupta & Zimmer, 2008). In contrast, little attention has been paid to local forms of post-conflict interventions and, in particular, their impact on women and girls (who experienced brutal forms of gender-based violence and gross human rights violations during the armed conflict).

Doucet and Denov (2012) conducted a study that explored the interventions and approaches used by local social workers targeting women in the aftermath of the war. Drawing on interviews with a small sample of local Sierra Leonean social workers, Doucet and Denov found that these social workers used unique and context-specific approaches in their post-war work and practice with war-affected women. Practice techniques included the use of religious references and instilling a fear of God in clients, giving specific and directive advice to clients, the use of self-disclosure as a fundamental aspect of practice, and the importance of "forgetting" the war-time abuses and human rights violations that they had experienced. These local helpers utilized a variety of skill sets and focused heavily on principles of solidarity and spirituality rather than clinical diagnostics and psychology.

The study ultimately highlighted the inherent tensions between local Sierra Leonean approaches to practice and those typically used in the context of the Global North. In relation to professional boundaries and self-disclosure, the Canadian Association of Social Workers (CASW) *Code of Ethics* stipulates that social workers should: "strive for impartiality in their professional practice, and refrain from imposing their personal values, views and preferences on clients" (CASW, 2005, p. 9). However, this professional value addressed in the CASW *Code of Ethics* appears to contradict local

observed her interactions with women, comments that such models and frameworks are not well-suited for her work with the local women. The student, who had good intentions, realizes she is largely ill-equipped and unprepared for her ongoing work in the field.

Efforts to internationalize social work education in Canada have expanded substantially in recent years (Drover & Rogers, 2009). Globalization has increased international collaborations leading to an increase in exchange programs, joint research ventures, and study-abroad programs (Healy, Asamoah, & Hokenstad, 2003). At the same time, the social work profession in colonized countries has been subject to a steady influx of international influences, often uninvited and unwanted. Given the history of international relations more generally, social workers that seek to broaden the reach of their work across practices in Sierra Leone, whereby social workers often provided directive advice. All the social workers in the study reported that impartiality is intentionally avoided and self-disclosure is deemed a core element of practice.

The inclusion of religious references when providing counselling to women represented another area of tension. The CASW *Code of Ethics* highlights the importance of client self-determination: "[Self-determination is] a core social work value that refers to the right to self-direction and freedom of choice without interference from others" (CASW, 2005, p. 11). Instilling the fear of God or suggesting a religious figure as a source of comfort, as was reported by the Sierra Leonean social workers, would not be perceived as acceptable professional practice in the context of the Global North. Finally, the notion of "forgetting" may be highly counter-intuitive to social work practitioners from the Global North who tend to emphasize the use of "talk therapy," whereby in the "retelling" of events, an individual is said to gain insight into his or her own personality, ultimately aiming to alter individual behaviour (Bracken & Petty, 1998).

These realities point to a deep-seated tension in the field of post-conflict social work and international practice—that of conflicting professional paradigms. Social workers from the Global North working in post-conflict settings may enter into therapeutic relationships with war-affected individuals using their own professional templates, worldviews, values, and paradigms. These paradigms, as we have seen here, may conflict with local understandings and ways of seeing and doing.

In emergency settings such as war and disaster, social workers may have limited time to reflect upon the intricacies involved in cross-cultural practice and the unintended consequences and negative effects that such interventions may bring. When dealing with cultural and symbolic issues such as healing, grief, and trauma, the complexities grow further. In addition, histories of colonization, hierarchies of power, and divergent social locations make ongoing critical reflection and analyses of power relations intrinsic to working relationships with war-affected individuals and communities.

Such findings point to a need to advocate for supporting local capacities and the inclusion of local social workers in internationally funded programs, which will not only benefit service users, but also, in the context of post-war recovery, can help rebuild the social capital networks that may have been damaged by the conflict.

international boundaries must be especially cognizant of the potential to reproduce oppressive, imperialistic relationships, especially with regards to Northern and Southern countries whose relationships over the last two centuries have been shaped and formed by colonial practices and interventions. Given the historic roots of social work's expansion as a profession (particularly in the Global South), there is an inherent danger that social workers will perpetuate such relationships and legacies of colonialism. As Healy and Link (2012) note, international exchange has often been characterized by

> unselective imposition of foreign models of education and practice. Uncritical export of social work concepts and relationships based on superior-inferior status has

created distrust of internationalism, much as the negative effects of globalization on poorer peoples and countries have created resistance. The legacy of the export model remains a barrier to support for internationalizing the profession (p. 13).

Issues of power, within historical, cultural, and political frameworks must be critically examined by all social workers working in contexts and cultures that are not their own, but particularly those in which there has been a history of colonialism, in order to ensure to preserve the principles and ethical standards of the profession, particularly the most fundamental of which is the principle of "do no harm." Moreover, social workers working outside of their countries and contexts of origin have a professional obligation to meticulously research the contexts in which they will be working.

Importantly, when engaging in international forms of practice, all social workers need to ask themselves, does international practice ultimately bring forth a good or desirable outcome? Does it promote the empowerment and the best interests of those it serves? Before engaging in international social work practice, Long (2009) suggests that students ask themselves: "Why here?" "Why now?" He writes:

> Involvement in international social work practice should be intentional, meaningful, centred on using one's talents for the benefit of consumer groups. A conscious and concerted effort should be made to ensure that international practice is advantageous to the identified client populations, not a vacation-like adventure in a foreign land (p. 11).

In a similar vein, Hiranandani (2011) notes that international social workers from Canada must engage in a deeper analysis of the construction of their own national identity and nation-building practices before embarking upon international social justice work. She asserts that "it is imperative that we set our own house in order first and connect the dots between our own ideologies, domestic, and foreign policies, and the fate of the 'Third World' if we wish to make a lasting impact on poverty and injustice around the globe" (p. 96).

Social Work and International Issues: The Global Reality of Child Soldiers

A key imperative of this chapter is to highlight the link between social work practice and issues of global importance. Drawing upon the phenomenon of child soldiers as an example, this section will examine the role(s) played by social workers at various local, national, and international levels and in a variety of organizations in responding to this important international issue.

Violence and armed conflict are commonplace in the everyday lives of many of the world's children. In countries around the globe, children have been first-hand victims and witnesses of war, and the atrocities that invariably accompany armed aggression. In addition, children continue to be drawn into conflict as active participants. Hundreds of thousands of child soldiers, both boys and girls, are currently associated with armed groups around the world (Coalition to Stop the Use of Child Soldiers, 2008). A child soldier is defined as

> Any person below 18 years of age who is or who has been recruited or used by an armed force or armed group in any capacity, including but not limited to children,

boys and girls, used as fighters, cooks, porters, messengers, spies or for sexual purposes. It does not only refer to a child who is taking or has taken a direct part in hostilities (Paris Principles, 2007, p. 7).

Hundreds of thousands of soldiers under the age of 18 are estimated to be part of fighting forces around the globe (Coalition to Stop the Use of Child Soldiers). In fact, child soldiers are said to exist in all regions of the world and, inevitably, wherever there is conflict (Coalition to Stop the Use of Child Soldiers, 2008).

While there is growing evidence of the conditions and factors underlying the phenomenon of child soldiery in the developing world, much of the scholarly and policy literature have portrayed child soldiery as a uniquely male phenomenon and failed to include gender perspectives on armed conflict. Informed largely by traditional perceptions of armed conflict as a phenomenon occurring between males—perceptions reinforced by popular media images of boys armed with AK47s—girls are frequently deemed peripheral and rendered invisible within fighting forces (Denov, 2008). Despite their relative invisibility, girls are currently used in fighting forces far more widely than is reported. Between 1990 and 2003, girls were associated with fighting forces in 55 countries and were active participants in conflict in 38 countries around the globe (McKay & Mazurana, 2004). Girls appear to be most often present in armed opposition groups, paramilitaries, and militias, yet they are also present in government forces. While the proportion of females in armed groups and forces varies according to geographic region, it generally ranges from 10 per cent to 30 per cent of all combatants (Bouta, 2005). In recent conflicts in Africa, girls are said to have comprised 30–40 per cent of all child combatants (Mazurana et al., 2002, p. 105).

© Mike Goldwater/Alamy

Many global organizations against the use of child soldiers aim to protect children, such as this boy, from military recruitment and allow them to reclaim their right to a proper childhood.

The UN System

In response to the problem of child soldiers, the UN has addressed the issue of children implicated in armed conflict and the prevention of child recruitment into armed groups through a variety of conventions, treaties, protocols, and resolutions. These include the United Nations Convention on the Rights of the Child (1989), the Optional Protocol of Convention on the Rights of the Child on the Involvement of Children in Armed Conflict (2000), and UN Security Council Resolutions 1261, 1314, 1379, 1460, 1539, 1612, all of which aim to protect children from the scourge of war. In 2005, the UN Security Council established an unprecedented monitoring and reporting mechanism (MRM) on grave violations against children in armed conflict under its resolution 1612. The purpose of the MRM is to provide for the systematic gathering of accurate, timely, and objective information on grave violations committed against children in armed conflict. Such information is used to foster accountability and compliance of parties to conflict with international child protection standards. The United Nations reports on six grave violations against children in armed conflict including killing or maiming of children, recruitment or use of children by armed forces and groups, sexual violence against children, attacks against schools or hospitals, abduction of children, and denial of humanitarian access for children. The information is included in the annual report of the Secretary-General on children and armed conflict and country-specific reports. These reports trigger action by the Security Council and other actors.

In addition, through its programming, UN agencies such as UNICEF have been actively involved in the protection of children in situations of armed violence, the prevention of underage recruitment, and the creation of **demobilization** and **reintegration** initiatives to support former child soldiers in the aftermath of war. Reintegration is the process by which ex-combatants acquire civilian status and gain sustainable employment and income. Reintegration is a social and economic process with an open timeframe, primarily taking place in communities at the local level. It is part of the general development of a country and a national responsibility, and often requires long-term, external assistance. Moreover, UNICEF, when working on the ground, often monitors and reports on grave violations committed against children, establishes dialogue with parties in conflict, and develops action plans to end violations committed against children if parties are committed to do so. They are also involved in national or regional advocacy efforts.

The UN has a Special Representative on Children and Armed Conflict. The Special Representative serves as a moral voice and independent advocate for the protection and well-being of boys and girls affected by armed conflict; works with partners to propose ideas and approaches to enhance the protection of children in armed conflict and to promote a more concerted protection response; builds awareness and gives prominence to the rights and protection of children in armed conflict; and undertakes humanitarian and diplomatic initiatives to facilitate the work of operational actors on the ground with regard to children in armed conflict. Social work representatives, whether working directly at the UN or working alongside the UN through representative NGOs, are thus able to contribute to advocacy, policy-making, and on-the-ground programming for children affected by war.

Non-government Organizations

Several INGOs and NGOs have been involved in advocating for greater international awareness in terms of prevention strategies for child recruitment into armed groups and implementing support strategies for children following their demobilization. International non-governmental organizations include Child Soldiers International, an international human rights research and advocacy organization that seeks to end the military recruitment

demobilization Refers to the formal and controlled discharge of active combatants from armed forces or other armed groups.

reintegration The process by which ex-combatants acquire civilian status and gain sustainable employment and income.

and the use in hostilities, in any capacity, of any person under the age of 18 by state armed forces or non-state armed groups. This INGO advocates for the release of unlawfully recruited children, promotes their successful reintegration into civilian life, and calls for accountability for those who unlawfully recruit or use them. Other INGOs that advocate for children in armed conflict include Human Rights Watch and Watchlist.

National and local NGOs have also played critical roles, at the societal, community, and individual levels, in addressing various issues relating to former child soldiers. At the societal level, NGOs have sought to address issues of governance, poverty, education, employment, the implementation of children's rights, and other structural factors that may be critical to understanding the participation and recruitment of children in armed conflict. At the community level, social workers working within national and local NGOs have been involved with reintegration initiatives. Reintegration of former child soldiers is a complex and long-term undertaking. It often begins with negotiating the release of children and their physical separation from armed forces and groups. The family tracing and reunification phase that follows is a time-consuming and resource-intensive effort. Beyond the practical challenge of locating the families and communities of lost children, successful reunification must also address the challenge of reconciling children, their families, and their communities, especially when children may have committed atrocities within their own communities (Denov & Maclure, 2007; Denov, 2010). At the individual level, local social workers have provided support to children affected by war in the provision of employment and educational opportunities, health care, recreation activities, and individual forms of psychosocial support and assistance.

Canadian Government Agencies

In the past, Canada has played an important role in issues related to children in armed conflict. Canada hosted the first International Conference on War-Affected Children in 2000, established a formal agenda on the issue, and took a lead role in advocating for children in armed conflict to the UN Security Council (Government of Canada, 2008). In addition, the Canadian government, through DFATD, has provided funding to support rehabilitation and reintegration programs for former child soldiers and supported research initiatives that have studied the lives, needs, and realities of former child soldiers (Denov, 2008). Canada played a strong role in the creation and negotiation of the Optional Protocol to the Convention on the Rights of the Child on the Involvement of Children in Armed Conflict and was an early supporter of the Office of the Special Representative for Children and Armed Conflict. During its tenure on the Security Council in 1999–2000, Canada introduced the first thematic debate on children in armed conflict. In 2006, Canada established and continues to chair the Group of Friends on Children and Armed Conflict, an informal New York-based network of over 38 member states. This group provides a venue to discuss a variety of issues and provides for a united front for advocacy petitions to the United Nations Security Council to take stronger measures aimed at those who commit grave violations. Social workers working for DFATD continue to be involved in policy and programming in the area of children affected by armed conflict.

Canadian NGOs and Agencies

Canadian NGOs, such as War Child and the Child Soldier Initiative, have played important roles in advocating on behalf of child soldiers and children affected by war, both in Canada and abroad. War Child's mission is to work with war-affected communities to help children reclaim their childhood through access to education, opportunity, and justice. War Child takes an active role in raising public awareness around the impact of war on communities and the shared responsibility to act. The Child Soldier Initiative aims to develop and implement new strategies and tactical guidance with the aim to gradually eradicate the use and recruitment of child soldiers around the world.

In addition to NGOs, children affected by war and their families may become refugees or seek asylum in Canada. As such, former child soldiers may come into contact with Canadian agencies working with refugees and thus become part of the caseload of social workers across the country. Therefore, in their daily work, social workers working within these agencies are assisting children affected by war in their resettlement to Canada.

Social work, as a profession, has a potentially important contribution to make to the issue of child soldiers, both within and outside Canada, particularly given the profession's ongoing commitment to empowerment, advocacy, marginalized communities, youth protection, anti-oppressive practice, and cultural competence. Yet while social work has made important contributions to the issue, its presence within international debates, discussions, and advocacy concerning war, political violence, and related global trends and processes could be vastly improved. Given the turbulent life histories of innumerable children affected by war, to ignore their needs is to risk a continuation of marginality, instability, and violence.

Practical TIP

Training and Preparing for International Social Work Practice

IN HER DISCUSSION OF INTERNATIONAL social work, Healy (2001) emphasizes the need for emerging and seasoned social workers to develop an awareness and understanding of the opportunities for social work in community and international relief and development. Drawing on Healy's work, below are some key areas, which can help to guide social workers in their *training and preparation* for international practice, whether domestic or international, theoretical or practical.

Developing Cross-Cultural Knowledge, Values, and Ethics

Social workers would benefit by developing

- knowledge of the role of culture and context in understanding human behaviour;
- knowledge of cultures other than one's own and the principles for learning about cultures;
- an understanding of the process and impact of voluntary and involuntary migration;
- knowledge of cross-cultural practice principles;
- an ongoing reflexivity concerning the theoretical, ethical, and value dilemmas in international practice—whether domestic or international;
- knowledge of the major forces of human oppression internationally;
- knowledge of the policy impact on communities and individuals locally, nationally, and internationally.

Practice Issues

When engaging in international practice (whether "foreign" or "domestic"), social workers must

- engage in ethical, critical, and respectful practice, being aware of diversity, difference, and the implications of social location;

- enhance their skills to work within a complex and interdisciplinary context within local, national, and international frameworks;
- develop knowledge of how past, current, and future theoretical perspectives and values inform the lived experience of communities and individuals locally, nationally, and internationally;
- develop technical skills for managing local, national, and international projects.

Understanding of Major Global Social Issues and the Efforts to Address Them

Social workers would benefit from the following areas of study and reflection:

- an understanding of power and how globalization shapes and mediates the relationships between the Global South and the Global North;
- knowledge of selected global problems;
- knowledge of the social welfare activities of major world organizations including the UN;
- knowledge of basic concepts of social development;
- an understanding of the social impacts of global interdependence.

The International Profession

Social workers should be encouraged to develop

- knowledge of the profession in an international context, including familiarity with the functions of social work in other countries;
- knowledge of the roles of international social work organizations.

Resources for Future Learning

Ongoing learning and exploration through academic literature, government sources, and community organizations are key to developing one's knowledge and skills. Social workers can actively develop

- knowledge of some of the major sources of global and cross-national social welfare data;
- familiarity with social work scholarship in one or more other countries or regions, especially in one's area of professional interest and expertise.

Conclusion

Professional social work originated in Europe and North America at the end of the nineteenth century—a period characterized by the vast imperialist expansion and domination of Africa, much of Asia, and the Caribbean by the US and European powers. Domination was far-reaching, disrupting patterns of family life, culture, and religion, powering the expropriation of natural and human resources, and drawing boundaries for the convenience of the colonizers with little or no regard for local culture, understandings, and knowledge. The effects have been enduring and are replicated in newer forms of domination by the international economic order. The "internationalization" of the social work profession, while important and valuable, may create and perpetuate dominant paradigms and "ways of knowing" that may marginalize or silence local sources of knowledge and indigenous forms of practice. A key future challenge of international social work is to address the "tension between establishing universal principles of social work through international collaboration in research and practice, while respecting indigenous uniqueness, distinct local traditions and cultural strength" (Link & Ramanathan, 2011, p. 10). It should be noted, however, that indigenous forms of knowledge and practice are not entirely a panacea. Research and practice has highlighted that social injustice, inequality, and forms of exploitation and oppression may, at times, permeate indigenous practices and local interventions (Baingana et al., 2005). Nonetheless, local knowledges must be carefully, rigorously, and respectfully included in order to ensure relevant and effective practice.

Some make the argument that the field of international social work has not adequately responded to the challenges and opportunities of the new global era, specifically noting that the activities are haphazard and uncoordinated and that "the absence of a systematic attempt to internationalize the profession has seriously impeded its ability to contribute meaningfully at the international level" (Midgley, 2001, p. 23). While indeed a future challenge, Herbert-Boyd (2007) has argued that working in extreme circumstances and crisis situations test social workers and their guiding theories and practice to their limits. At the same time, however, she notes that social work can be "enriched by catastrophe" if it is adaptable, dynamic, geared to meet human need, and shaped by a commitment to social justice.

International social work practice in the twenty-first century demands "equality, mutuality, reciprocal benefits and a true exchange of ideas around the globe" (Elliott & Segal, 2008, p. 355). While the profession must acknowledge the negative realities of its history, it can also celebrate the "transnational dimension of social work and movement of individuals and exchange of ideas about practice that contributed to its founding" (Healy & Link, 2012, p. 13). Indeed, the profession has the capacity to create a new and rich history of active engagement with the critical issues of our time.

QUESTIONS FOR CRITICAL THOUGHT

1. To what extent do you think social work values are universally applicable? What are the strengths and limitations and points of tension in attempting to define universal social work values?
2. Reflect upon the multiple definitions of "international social work." What are the strengths and limitations of the current definitions? What do you feel should be added to the growing and changing definition?
3. Do social workers have a responsibility to campaign to influence policies in countries other than their own? If so, how should they do this? If not, why not?
4. Why do you think that social workers may be underrepresented in INGOs? What are the implications for the profession?
5. Identify a global issue of concern. Drawing upon the themes highlighted in the chapter, how can social work as a profession contribute to addressing the issue at societal, community, and individual levels?

RECOMMENDED READINGS

Gilchrist James, G., Ramsay, R., & Drover, G. (Eds.). (2009). *International social work: Canadian perspectives*. Toronto: Thompson Educational Publishing. This book outlines the ways in which Canadian social workers are, or have been, involved in international social work. Each contributor has been involved in international social work practice—some in developing countries, some in developed countries, and some in both.

Hugman, R. (2010). *Understanding international social work: A critical analysis*. New York: Palgrave Macmillan. This text provides an analysis of international social work. Each chapter includes case studies to illustrate practice issues in different geographical locations.

Healy, L., & Link, R. (Eds.). (2012). *Handbook of international social work*. Oxford: Oxford University Press. This collection addresses the integral nature of international social work knowledge to all areas of practice, policy, and research. Chapters map the key issues, organizations, competencies, training and research needs, and ethical guidelines central to international social work practice today, emphasizing the linkages among social work, development, and human rights practice.

Lavalette, M., & Ioakimidis, V. (Eds.). (2011). *Social work in extremis: Lessons for social work internationally*. Bristol: The Policy Press. This book contains a collection of articles from a variety of countries that explores the nature and role of social work and its relationship to communities in extreme circumstances. These circumstances vary from wars, national conflicts, and emergencies, to natural disasters and other calamities where urgent responses are required.

RECOMMENDED WEBSITES

Canadian International Development Agency (CIDA)
www.acdi-cida.gc.ca
This site provides news, background, and resources about global issues and sustainable economic development from Canada's lead agency for development assistance.

Child Soldiers International
http://www.child-soldiers.org/
This website outlines key issues concerning child soldiers.

International Association of Schools of Social Work (IASSW)
http://www.iassw-aiets.org/
The IASSW is a worldwide association of schools of social work. The website provides information about their role, membership, task forces, global standards, news, resources, and structure.

International Federation of Social Workers (IFSW)
www.ifsw.org
The website of the IFSW addresses the role, governance, membership, and resources of this international organization representing social work practitioners, faculty, and students.

United Nations (UN)
www.un.org
This website addresses the themes of international peace and security, development, human rights, humanitarian affairs, and international law.

Appendix:
Code of Ethics, 2005

Acknowledgements

The Canadian Association of Social Workers (CASW) acknowledges with thanks the National Association of Social Workers (NASW) for permission to use sections of the copyrighted NASW 1999 *Code of Ethics* in the development of the CASW 2005 *Code of Ethics* and CASW 2005 *Guidelines for Ethical Practice*. The CASW also acknowledges that other codes of ethics and resources were used in the development of this *Code* and the *Guidelines for Ethical Practice*, in particular the *Code of Ethics* of the Australian Association of Social Workers (AASW). These resources can be found in the Reference section of each document.

Purpose of the CASW Code of Ethics

Ethical behaviour lies at the core of every profession. The Canadian Association of Social Workers (CASW) *Code of Ethics* sets forth values and principles to guide social workers' professional conduct. A code of ethics cannot guarantee ethical behaviour. Ethical behaviour comes from a social worker's individual commitment to engage in ethical practice. Both the spirit and the letter of this *Code of Ethics* will guide social workers as they act in good faith and with a genuine desire to make sound judgements.

This *Code of Ethics* is consistent with the International Federation of Social Workers (IFSW) *International Declaration of Ethical Principles of Social Work* (1994, 2004), which requires members of the CASW to uphold the values and principles established by both the CASW and the IFSW. Other individuals, organizations, and bodies (such as regulatory boards, professional liability insurance providers, courts of law, boards of directors of organizations employing social workers and government agencies) may also choose to adopt this *Code of Ethics* or use it as a basis for evaluating professional conduct. In Canada, each province and territory is responsible for regulating the professional conduct of social workers to ensure the protection of the public. Social workers are advised to contact the regulatory body in their province or territory to determine whether it has adopted this *Code of Ethics*.[1]

---

1 To find the IFSW declarations or information about your relevant regulatory body, visit the CASW web site: http://www.casw-acts.ca

Recognition of Individual and Professional Diversity

The CASW *Code of Ethics* does not provide a set of rules that prescribe how social workers should act in all situations. Further, the *Code of Ethics* does not specify which values and principles are most important and which outweigh others in instances of conflict. Reasonable differences of opinion exist among social workers with respect to which values and principles should be given priority in a particular situation. Further, a social worker's personal values, culture, religious beliefs, practices and/or other important distinctions, such as age, ability, gender, or sexual orientation can affect his/her ethical choices. Thus, social workers need to be aware of any conflicts between personal and professional values and deal with them responsibly.

Ethical Behaviour Requires Due Consideration of Issues and Judgement

Social work is a multifaceted profession. As professionals, social workers are educated to exercise judgment in the face of complex and competing interests and claims. Ethical decision-making in a given situation will involve the informed judgment of the individual social worker. Instances may arise when social workers' ethical obligations conflict with agency policies, or relevant laws or regulations. When such conflicts occur, social workers shall make a responsible effort to resolve the conflicts in a manner that is consistent with the values and principles expressed in this *Code of Ethics*. If a reasonable resolution of the conflict does not appear possible, social workers shall seek appropriate consultation before making a decision. This may involve consultation with an ethics committee, a regulatory body, a knowledgeable colleague, supervisor or legal counsel.

Preamble

The social work profession is dedicated to the welfare and self-realization of all people; the development and disciplined use of scientific and professional knowledge; the development of resources and skills to meet individual, group, national and international changing needs and aspirations; and the achievement of social justice for all. The profession has a particular interest in the needs and empowerment of people who are vulnerable, oppressed, and/or living in poverty. Social workers are committed to human rights as enshrined in Canadian law, as well as in international conventions on human rights created or supported by the United Nations.

As professionals in a country that upholds respect for diversity, and in keeping with democratic rights and freedoms, social workers respect the distinct systems of beliefs and lifestyles of individuals, families, groups, communities and nations without prejudice (United Nations Centre for Human Rights, 1992). Specifically, social workers do not tolerate discrimination[2] based on age, abilities, ethnic background, gender, language, marital status, national ancestry, political affiliation, race, religion, sexual orientation or socio-economic status.

---

2   Throughout this document the term "discrimination" refers to treating people unfavourably or holding negative or prejudicial attitudes based on discernable differences or stereotypes. It does not refer to the positive intent behind programs, such as affirmative action, where one group may be given preferential treatment to address inequities created by discrimination.

Core Social Work Values and Principles

Social workers uphold the following core social work values:

Value 1: Respect for Inherent Dignity and Worth of Persons

Value 2: Pursuit of Social Justice

Value 3: Service to Humanity

Value 4: Integrity in Professional Practice

Value 5: Confidentiality in Professional Practice

Value 6: Competence in Professional Practice

The following section describes each of these values and discusses their underlying principles.

Value 1: Respect for the Inherent Dignity and Worth of Persons

Social work is founded on a long-standing commitment to respect the inherent dignity and individual worth of all persons. When required by law to override a client's wishes, social workers take care to use the minimum coercion required. Social workers recognize and respect the diversity of Canadian society, taking into account the breadth of differences that exist among individuals, families, groups and communities. Social workers uphold the human rights of individuals and groups as expressed in The *Canadian Charter of Rights and Freedoms* (1982) and the United Nations *Universal Declaration of Human Rights* (1948).

Principles:

- Social workers respect the unique worth and inherent dignity of all people and uphold human rights.
- Social workers uphold each person's right to self-determination, consistent with that person's capacity and with the rights of others.
- Social workers respect the diversity among individuals in Canadian society and the right of individuals to their unique beliefs consistent with the rights of others.
- Social workers respect the client's right to make choices based on voluntary, informed consent.
- Social workers who have children as clients determine the child's ability to consent and where appropriate, explain to the child and to the child's parents/guardians, the nature of the social worker's relationship to the child.
- Social workers uphold the right of society to impose limitations on the self-determination of individuals, when such limitations protect individuals from self-harm and from harming others.
- Social workers uphold the right of every person to be free from violence and threat of violence.

Value 2: Pursuit of Social Justice

Social workers believe in the obligation of people, individually and collectively, to provide resources, services and opportunities for the overall benefit of humanity and to afford them protection from harm. Social workers promote social fairness and the equitable distribution of resources, and act to reduce barriers and expand choice for all persons, with special regard for those who are marginalized, disadvantaged, vulnerable, and/or have exceptional needs. Social workers oppose prejudice and discrimination against any person or group of persons, on any grounds, and specifically challenge views and actions that stereotype particular persons or groups.

Principles:
- Social workers uphold the right of people to have access to resources to meet basic human needs.
- Social workers advocate for fair and equitable access to public services and benefits.
- Social workers advocate for equal treatment and protection under the law and challenge injustices, especially injustices that affect the vulnerable and disadvantaged.
- Social workers promote social development and environmental management in the interests of all people.

Value 3: Service to Humanity

The social work profession upholds service in the interests of others, consistent with social justice, as a core professional objective. In professional practice, social workers balance individual needs, and rights and freedoms with collective interests in the service of humanity. When acting in a professional capacity, social workers place professional service before personal goals or advantage, and use their power and authority in disciplined and responsible ways that serve society. The social work profession contributes to knowledge and skills that assist in the management of conflicts and the wide-ranging consequences of conflict.

Principles:
- Social workers place the needs of others above self-interest when acting in a professional capacity.
- Social workers strive to use the power and authority vested in them as professionals in responsible ways that serve the needs of clients and the promotion of social justice.
- Social workers promote individual development and pursuit of individual goals, as well as the development of a just society.
- Social workers use their knowledge and skills in bringing about fair resolutions to conflict and in assisting those affected by conflict.

Value 4: Integrity in Professional Practice

Social workers demonstrate respect for the profession's purpose, values and ethical principles relevant to their field of practice. Social workers maintain a high level of professional conduct by acting honestly and responsibly, and promoting the values of the profession. Social workers strive for impartiality in their professional practice, and refrain from imposing their personal values, views and preferences on clients. It is the responsibility of social workers to establish the tenor of their professional relationship with clients, and others to whom they have a professional duty, and to maintain professional boundaries. As individuals, social workers take care in their actions to not bring the reputation of the profession into disrepute. An essential element of integrity in professional practice is ethical accountability based on this *Code of Ethics*, the IFSW *International Declaration of Ethical Principles of Social Work*, and other relevant provincial/territorial standards and guidelines. Where conflicts exist with respect to these sources of ethical guidance, social workers are encouraged to seek advice, including consultation with their regulatory body.

Principles:

- Social workers demonstrate and promote the qualities of honesty, reliability, impartiality and diligence in their professional practice.
- Social workers demonstrate adherence to the values and ethical principles of the profession and promote respect for the profession's values and principles in organizations where they work or with which they have a professional affiliation.
- Social workers establish appropriate boundaries in relationships with clients and ensure that the relationship serves the needs of clients.
- Social workers value openness and transparency in professional practice and avoid relationships where their integrity or impartiality may be compromised, ensuring that should a conflict of interest be unavoidable, the nature of the conflict is fully disclosed.

Value 5: Confidentiality in Professional Practice

A cornerstone of professional social work relationships is confidentiality with respect to all matters associated with professional services to clients. Social workers demonstrate respect for the trust and confidence placed in them by clients, communities and other professionals by protecting the privacy of client information and respecting the client's right to control when or whether this information will be shared with third parties. Social workers only disclose confidential information to other parties (including family members) with the informed consent of clients, clients' legally authorized representatives or when required by law or court order. The general expectation that social workers will keep information confidential does not apply when disclosure is necessary to prevent serious, foreseeable and imminent harm to a client or others. In all instances, social workers disclose the least amount of confidential information necessary to achieve the desired purpose.

Principles:

- Social workers respect the importance of the trust and confidence placed in the professional relationship by clients and members of the public.
- Social workers respect the client's right to confidentiality of information shared in a professional context.
- Social workers only disclose confidential information with the informed consent of the client or permission of client's legal representative.
- Social workers may break confidentiality and communicate client information without permission when required or permitted by relevant laws, court order or this *Code*.
- Social workers demonstrate transparency with respect to limits to confidentiality that apply to their professional practice by clearly communicating these limitations to clients early in their relationship.

Value 6: Competence in Professional Practice

Social workers respect a client's right to competent social worker services. Social workers analyze the nature of social needs and problems, and encourage innovative, effective strategies and techniques to meet both new and existing needs and, where possible, contribute to the knowledge base of the profession. Social workers have a responsibility to maintain professional proficiency, to continually strive to increase their professional knowledge and skills, and to apply new knowledge in practice commensurate with their level of professional education, skill and competency, seeking consultation and supervision as appropriate.

Principles:

- Social workers uphold the right of clients to be offered the highest quality service possible.
- Social workers strive to maintain and increase their professional knowledge and skill.
- Social workers demonstrate due care for client's interests and safety by limiting professional practice to areas of demonstrated competence.
- Social workers contribute to the ongoing development of the profession and its ability to serve humanity, where possible, by participating in the development of current and future social workers and the development of new professional knowledge.
- Social workers who engage in research minimize risks to participants, ensure informed consent, maintain confidentiality and accurately report the results of their studies.

Glossary

Capacity

The ability to understand information relevant to a decision and to appreciate the reasonably foreseeable consequences of choosing to act or not to act. Capacity is specific to each decision and thus a person may be capable of deciding about a place of residence, for example, but not capable with respect to deciding about a treatment. Capacity can change over time (Etchells, Sharpe, Elliot and Singer, 1996).

Recent references in law point to the concept of "a mature minor," which Rozovsky and Rozovsky (1990) define as ". . . one with capacity to understand the nature and consequences of medical treatment. Such a person has the power to consent to medical treatment and parental consent is not necessary" (p 55). They quote the comments by The Honorable Justice Lambert in *Van Mol v. Ashmore*, which help clarify common law with respect to a minor's capacity to consent. He states:

> At common law, without reference to statute law, a young person, still a minor, may give, on his or her own behalf, a fully informed consent to medical treatment if he or she has sufficient maturity, intelligence and capacity of understanding what is involved in making informed choices about the proposed medical treatment . . . once the capacity to consent has been achieved by the young person reaching sufficient maturity, intelligence and capability of understanding, the discussions about the nature of the treatment, its gravity, the material risks and any special and unusual risks, and the decisions about undergoing treatment, and about the form of the treatment, must all take place with and be made by the young person whose bodily integrity is to be invaded and whose life and health will be affected by the outcome.

Child

The *Convention on the Rights of the Child* passed by the United Nations in 1959 and ratified by Canada in 1990, define a child as a person under the age of 18 years unless national law recognizes an earlier age of majority (Alberta Law Reform Institute, 1991). The age of majority differs in provinces and territories in Canada. Under the *Criminal Code of Canada*, the age of consent is held to be over the age of 14 years; age in the context of the criminal code frequently refers to capacity to consent to sexual relations. All jurisdictions in Canada have legislation regarding child protection, which defines the age of a child for the purposes of protection. In Canada, in the absence of provincial or territorial legislation, courts are governed by common law. Social workers are encouraged to maintain current knowledge with respect to legislation on the age of a child, as well as capacity and consent in their jurisdiction.

Client

A person, family, group of persons, incorporated body, association or community on whose behalf a social worker provides or agrees to provide a service or to whom the social worker is legally obligated to provide a service. Examples of legal obligation to provide service include a legislated responsibility (such as in child welfare) or a valid court order. In the case of a valid court order, the judge/court is the client and the person(s) who is ordered by the court to participate in assessment is recognized as an involuntary client.

Conduct Unbecoming

Behaviour or conduct that does not meet social work standard of care requirements and is, therefore, subject to discipline. In reaching a decision in Matthews and Board of Directors of Physiotherapy (1986) 54 O.R. (2d) 375, Saunders J. makes three important statements regarding standards of practice, and by implication, professional codes of ethics:

1. Standards of practice are inherent characteristics of any profession.
2. Standards of practice may be written or unwritten.
3. Some conduct is clearly regarded as misconduct and need not be written down, whereas other conduct may be the subject of dispute within a profession. (See "Standard of Practice.")

Confidentiality

A professional value that demands that professionally acquired information be kept private and not shared with third parties unless the client provides informed consent or a professional or legal obligation exists to share such information without client informed consent.

Discrimination

Treating people unfavourably or holding negative or prejudicial attitudes based on discernable differences or stereotypes (AASW, 1999).

Informed Consent

Voluntary agreement reached by a capable client based on information about foreseeable risks and benefits associated with the agreement (e.g., participation in counselling or agreement to disclose social work report to a third party).

Human Rights

The rights of an individual that are considered the basis for freedom and justice, and serve to protect people from discrimination and harassment. Social workers may refer to the *Canadian Charter of Rights and Freedoms* enacted as Schedule B to the *Canada Act* 1982 (U.K.) 1982, c. 11, which came into force on April 17, 1982, as well as the *Universal Declaration of Human Rights* (1948) proclaimed by the United Nations General Assembly December 10, 1948.

Malpractice and Negligence

Behaviour that is included in "conduct unbecoming" and relates to social work practice behaviour within the parameters of the professional relationship that falls below the standard of practice and results in, or aggravation of, injury to a client. It includes behaviour that results in assault, deceit, fraudulent misrepresentations, defamation of character, breach of contract, violation of human rights, malicious prosecution, false imprisonment or criminal conviction.

Self-Determination

A core social work value that refers to the right to self-direction and freedom of choice without interference from others. Self-determination is codified in practice through mechanisms of informed consent. Social workers may be obligated to limit self-determination when a client lacks capacity or in order to prevent harm (Regehr and Antle, 1997).

Social Worker

A person who is duly registered to practise social work in a province or territory; or where mandatory registration does not exist, a person with social work education from an institution recognized by the Canadian Association of Schools of Social Work (CASSW) or an institution from outside of Canada that has been approved by the CASW, who is practising social work and who voluntarily agrees to be subject to this *Code of Ethics*. **Note:** Social workers living in Quebec and British Columbia, whose social work education was obtained outside of Canada, follow a separate approval process within their respective provinces.

Standard of Practice

The standard of care ordinarily expected of a competent social worker. It means that the public is assured that a social worker has the training, the skill and the diligence to provide them with social work services. Social workers are urged to refer to standards of practice that have been set by their provincial or territorial regulatory body or relevant professional association (see "Conduct Unbecoming").

Voluntary

"In the context of consent, 'voluntariness' refers to a patient's right to make treatment decisions free of any undue influence, such as ability of others to exert control over a patient by force, coercion or manipulation. . . . The requirement for voluntariness does not imply that clinicians should refrain from persuading patients to accept advice. Persuasion involves appealing to the patient's reason in an attempt to convince him or her of the merits of a recommendation. In attempting to persuade the patient to follow a particular course of action, the clinician still leaves the patient free to accept or reject this advice." (Etchells, Sharpe, Dykeman, Meslin and Singer, 1996, p. 1083).

References

AASW. (1999). *AASW code of ethics*. Kingston: Australian Association of Social Workers (AASW).

Alberta Law Reform Institute. (1991). *Status of the child: Revised report* (Report No. 60). Edmonton, Alberta: Law Reform Institute.

BASW. (2002). *BASW: A code of ethics for social workers.* British Association of Social Workers (BASW).

Canadian Charter of Rights and Freedoms Enacted as Schedule B to the *Canada Act 1982,* c.11 (1982). [http://laws.justice.gc.ca/en/charter/]

CASW. (1994). *Social Work Code of Ethics.* Ottawa: Canadian Association of Social Workers (CASW).

Criminal Code, R.S., c. C-34, s.1. (1985). [http://laws.justice.gc.ca/en/C-46/40670.html]

Etchells, E., G. Sharpe, C. Elliott, and P. Singer. (1996). Bioethics for clinicians: 3: Capacity. *Canadian Medical Association Journal,* 155, 657–661.

Etchells, E., G. Sharpe, M.J. Dykeman, and P. Singer. (1996). Bioethics for clinicians: 4: Voluntariness. *Canadian Medical Association Journal,* 155, 1083–1086.

IFSW. (1994). *The ethics of social work: Principles and standards.* Geneva, Switzerland: International Federation of Social Workers (IFSW). (2004). *Ethics in social work: Statement of principles.* Geneva, Switzerland: International Federation of Social Workers (IFSW).

Lens, V. (2000). Protecting the confidentiality of the therapeutic relationship: Jaffe v. Redmond. *Social Work,* 45(3), 273–276.

Matthews and Board of Directors of Physiotherapy (1986) 54 O.R. (2d) 375.

NASW. (1999). *Code of Ethics.* Washington: National Association of Social Workers (NASW).

Regehr, C. and B.J. Antle. (1997). Coercive influences: Informed consent and court-mandated social work practice. *Social Work,* 42(3), 300–306.

Rozovsky, L.E. and F.A. Rozovsky. (1990). *The Canadian law of consent to treatment.* Toronto: Butterworths.

United Nations. (1948). *Universal Declaration of Human Rights.* New York: United Nations. [http://www.unhchr.ch/udhr/]

United Nations Centre for Human Rights. (1992). Teaching and learning about human rights: A manual for schools of social work and the social work profession (Developed in co-operation with International Federation of Social Workers and International Association of Schools of Social Workers). New York: United Nations.

383 Parkdale Avenue, Suite 402
Ottawa, Ontario, Canada
K1Y 4R4
Telephone: (613) 729–6668
Fax: (613) 729–9608
Email: casw@casw-acts.ca
Website: www.casw-acts.ca

Glossary

ableism Refers to discrimination or prejudice against individuals based on their ability or disability.

Aboriginal A term used to describe the original people of Canada. It is an umbrella term encompassing the three legally defined groups: First Nations, Métis, and Inuit.

acculturation A process of adaptation between two cultures, particularly how traditions, values, language, and beliefs change as they come into contact with a new (usually dominant) culture.

actions, activities, and responsibilities The negotiated expectations workers and clients establish for the work they will do together.

activities of daily living A term used in health care to refer to daily self-care activities such as feeding, bathing, dressing, and grooming.

activity theory Proposes that positive aging occurs when older adults stay active and maintain social connections.

adult protection legislation Gives a specific provincial health or social service department the responsibility to respond to the abuse or neglect cases that are brought to its attention.

ageism A form of stereotyping about older people that associates aging with decline and results in exclusion and marginalization.

agency The power individuals have to act and make decisions.

Anishnaabe The people who originally lived in central and northern Ontario and Manitoba.

anonymous data Data provided by a participant that no one, including the researcher, can trace back to the participant who provided it.

anti-oppression social work Acknowledges oppression in societies, economies, cultures, and groups and attempts to remove or negate it.

assimilation A process by which individuals' cultural identities are minimized or eliminated, replaced by the cultural identities of the larger society.

authentization Refers to a process of developing theories and practices for social work that are derived out of the realities of the local context.

baby boom generation A group of individuals born post-World War II (1946–1965) when there was a significant increase in births. The oldest baby boomers turned 65 in 2011.

Badgley Report Published in 1984, it shed light on the prevalence of sexual abuse of children across Canada. The report was pivotal in raising awareness of child sexual abuse and shedding light on a previously under-explored issue.

Battered Child Syndrome A term coined by C. Henry Kempe that refers to injuries sustained by a child as a result of physical abuse, usually inflicted by an adult caregiver.

behaviour therapy Refers to techniques that alter an individual's maladaptive reactions to particular stimuli. It involves the most basic methods of altering human behaviour, such as reward and punishment, reinforcement, and even biofeedback, using conditioning techniques, with an emphasis on life skills.

best interest of the child Refers to the principle that the best interests of the child must be the primary consideration in all actions concerning children.

Black feminism Points to the diversity of women and the different forms of oppression by which they are affected. Given that Black women are oppressed in many areas of social and domestic life, their experience of oppression is heightened as compared to white women.

Canadian Charter of Rights and Freedoms A bill of rights entrenched in the Canadian constitution that guarantees certain political rights to Canadian citizens and civil rights of everyone in Canada from the policies and actions of all areas and levels of government. It is designed to unify Canadians around a set of principles that embody those rights.

Canadian Multiculturalism Act Enacted in 1988, this act provided recognition of Canada's diversity with regard to "race, national or ethnic origin, colour and religion [as] a fundamental characteristic of Canadian society" and committed "to a policy of multiculturalism designed to preserve and enhance the multicultural heritage of Canadians."

care and concern Expressed when the social worker seeks to understand an individual and family out of a genuine desire to help.

case management Focuses on helping individuals and families navigate their way to resources.

catharsis Release of emotional tension through an activity or experience.

child abuse The physical or psychological mistreatment of a child by an adult (biological or adoptive parents, step-parents, guardians or other adults). This includes physical abuse, sexual abuse, emotional maltreatment, and exposure to domestic violence.

child savers Middle-class philanthropists who saw the state, society's moral decline, deficient parenting, and the hazards of urban life as "evils" from which children required saving.

cissexism The belief that cissexuality is natural and the norm and that any other form of gender identity and expression is inferior.

civil society Refers to the wide array of non-governmental and not-for-profit organizations that have a presence in public life, expressing the interests and values of their members, based on ethical, cultural, political, scientific, religious, or philanthropic considerations. Civil society organizations include community groups, NGOs, labour unions, indigenous groups, charitable organizations, faith-based organizations, professional associations, and foundations.

clan Groups of families that have the same inherited social and political roles.

client-centred An approach that places individuals and families at the centre of the helping relationship honouring their perceptions and experiences and supporting their active involvement in solutions.

clinical work Focuses on working with thoughts, interactions, behaviours, and emotions of an individual or family.

closed groups Group where membership does not change during the life of the group.

cohort Group of persons who were born at the same historical time and who experience particular social changes within a given culture in the same sequence and at the same age.

collaboration The development of mutually agreed on goals and tasks between social worker and individuals and families.

colonization Invasion or taking over sovereignty of another nation.

common factors A term used to emphasize the common relational elements in all approaches and techniques informing direct practice with individuals and families.

concepts Building blocks of theory and tend to have two parts, a symbol (representing a word or term) and a definition. Concepts also contain built-in assumptions of the nature of human beings, social reality, or a particular phenomenon.

confidential data Data that could be linked with a particular participant; however, it is the researcher's responsibility to ensure that these connections are not made public.

consolidating gains Involves reinforcing the capacities within clients that led to positive change.

co-occurring disorders Refers to an individual having co-existing mental health and substance abuse issues. Dual diagnosis is also a term used describing the situation of the same individual.

counter-transference Refers to therapists' emotional reaction to a client, whether conscious or unconscious. Examples of countertransference during practice include unusual interest, admiration, boredom, anger, hatred, anxiety, or dread in relation to a client that become an obstacle to effective clinical work.

crowding Defined as more than one person per room (bathrooms, halls, vestibules, and rooms used solely for business purposes are not counted as rooms).

culturagram An assessment to understand multiple facets of a client's migration experience (Congress, 2004). Tools used for assessment with migrant clients such as the culturagram can also be used by social workers themselves to help uncover and understand their own cultural contexts and how those contexts shape their world views and thus interactions with clients.

cultural genocide Processes that intend to destroy the cultures of a group of people.

cultural relativism Advocates that culture is the sole source for the validity of a moral right or rule and that members of one society may not legitimately condemn the practices of societies with different traditions, especially practices considered culturally based.

cumulative advantage The tendency of one's social location to have an enduring and increasingly positive impact over the life course.

cumulative disadvantage The tendency of one's social location to have an enduring and increasingly negative impact over the life course.

cumulative effects Long-term effects of material and social deprivation that make children more likely to show adverse health and developmental outcomes.

decolonization Indigenous and non-Indigenous people working together to dismantle the attitudes, powers, and institutions that keep practices of colonization alive.

demobilization Refers to the formal and controlled discharge of active combatants from armed forces or other armed groups.

deontological theories Maintain that certain acts are intrinsically good or bad in and of themselves, irrespective of their consequences.

dependency ratio The ratio of retirees to the working-age population.

descriptive studies Use systematic, intentional data collection in order to describe a population, organization, and so forth to provide an accurate portrait of various characteristics of populations.

"deserving" poor Individuals in poverty assessed as being poor through no fault of their own.

doli incapax A defense developed under English common law. Children under the age of 7 were deemed incapable of committing a criminal act. For children between 7 and 13 years, this defense could be rebutted if there was evidence to establish that the child had sufficient intelligence and experience to know the nature and consequences of the conduct and to appreciate that it was wrong.

duty to report Refers to a professional's obligation, in the course of his or her duties, to report any suspected child abuse or neglect when there are reasonable grounds for believing a child may be in need of protection.

eclectic approach An approach a social worker uses drawing upon a range theories and techniques from different theoretical perspectives, not specifically favouring one theory but uses theory flexibly.

eco-map A pictorial representation of a person's connections to other persons or systems in his or her environment.

ecosystem theories A way to think about the fundamental interactions between people and their social and physical environments.

egalitarianism A belief that all people should share equal social, political, and economic rights and opportunities.

ego Balances and mediates the desires of the id and the external demands of the superego.

Eighth Fire According to Anishnaabe prophesies, this is a time in the future when non-Aboriginal people will turn to Aboriginal people for help.

empathy The capacity to understand and respond to another person's subjective experience.

enfranchisement A process whereby "Indians" could become Canadian citizens, gaining the right to vote but only by relinquishing their ties to their communities, which included any land rights.

eugenics The practice of selecting desired human traits to improve the genetic stock of the population and preventing the breeding of those with undesired traits.

evaluation studies The use of any of the approaches from exploratory, descriptive, and explanatory research to assess a program, an intervention, or a service.

evidence-based practice An approach that "bring[s] practice and research together so as to strengthen the scientific knowledge base supporting social work intervention" (Mullen, Bledsoe, & Bellamy, 2008, p. 326).

explanatory studies Seek to answer the "why" question by testing hypotheses, expanding a theory's explanation for a particular phenomenon, or assessing which explanation, such as an intervention, is most effective for particular populations.

exploratory research Focuses on a "new" topic about which the researcher wants to learn more and seeks to build a foundation of general knowledge about a topic and provide support to initial theory-making.

family ethic A perspective that began in the colonial era defining a woman's role solely as a wife and mother.

Family Group Conferences Processes involving extended family in decisions regarding the protection and care of children while strengthening and supporting families.

family structure Refers to the way the family is organized including the roles family members play, and closeness and distance between members.

faulty-engine theories Shift the focus of practice attention not to the past, but to the here and now. These sets of theories aim to alter faulty or distorted thinking that impede optimal functioning.

gender dysphoria Identified within the DSM as a psychiatric disorder for those whose gender assigned at birth differs from their gender identity (Ezra, 2013).

genogram A visual representation of family that illustrates a family's history, structure, demographics, functioning, and patterns of relating to one another.

genuineness Being open, real, and sincere with individuals and families.

globalization Often referred to as mainly an economic process including the breaking down of borders and barriers to international trade. However, the concept can describe a multitude of economic, political, social, technological, or cultural transformations which lead to greater interconnectedness of people and systems across the world.

glocalization A term popularized by Bauman (1998) who argued that globalization should be understood as linking global and local processes.

goals Future, desired end states for the client.

Haudenosaunee The people whose traditional territory is now called southern Quebec and Ontario.

heterosexism The assumption that heterosexuality is natural and the norm and that any other form of sexual identity or expression is inferior.

holistic Recognition of the whole person including spiritual, physical, emotional, and psychological.

homelessness Refers to a situation of an individual or family without stable, permanent, appropriate housing, or the immediate prospect, means, and ability of acquiring it.

homophobia The irrational fear, hatred, and intolerance of lesbian, gay, and bisexual people.

human rights Basic rights and freedoms that all people are entitled to regardless of nationality, sex, national or ethnic origin, race, religion, language, or other status. Human rights include civil and political rights, such as the right to freedom of speech, expression, or peaceful assembly; and social, cultural, and economic rights including the right to participate in culture, the right to food, and the right to work and receive an education. Human rights are protected and upheld by international and national laws and treaties.

id Refers to one's unconscious and is composed of powerful forces of drives, instincts, and desires.

immigrant A person admitted to the Canada as a lawful permanent resident.

income inequality The extent to which income is unequally distributed in a population.

Indian Act An act created by the Parliament of Canada in 1876 to define "Indian" status and outline the administration of "Indian" rights although it does not grant Indian rights.

Indian Agent White government officials who displaced traditional Aboriginal leadership and held the power to enforce the Indian Act, including deciding who would be considered status and acting as arresting officers, prosecutors, and judges all in one.

Indians A Canadian government term used to refer to Aboriginal people who have status according to the Indian Act.

indigenization Refers to the adoption and adaptation of theories and practices in social work in ways that are relevant to the local (indigenous) context.

Indigenous Peoples Peoples who are native to the area in which they live. Usually refers to these people groups internationally and is a term used by the United Nations.

indoor relief Assistance provided in an institutional setting, such as a poorhouse, almshouse, or workhouse.

in-home services Services that aim to assist and support families to live together harmoniously in a safe and secure environment. Services include family counselling, parental support, in-home child care, homemaker services, and educational services for parents and families.

institutional abuse Any act or omission directed at a resident of a congregate living facility that causes the person harm.

institutional power Refers to the various forms of power that individuals hold based on their social location and position within a particular institution or agency.

integration The outcome of settlement regarded by settlement programs as the optimal mode for migrant well-being; defined as participation in economic, social, cultural, and political areas of life of a settlement country while retaining connections to one's country of origin.

interactional model A model where leadership is not the exclusive domain of the leader but is shared among members as an empowering function.

intergenerational trauma Refers to trauma passed down from generation to generation in Aboriginal communities, resulting in unhealthy family relationships such as violence, mental health challenges, such as depression, and internalized oppression sometimes manifested as substance misuse.

international non-governmental organizations Normally have a similar mission to NGOs, but are international in scope and may have offices around the world to deal with specific issues in many countries.

intersectionality Defined as systems of oppression based on race, class, gender, ability, religion, citizenship status, and sexual/gender identity that intersect with each other.

Inuit The people who traditionally occupied the most northern parts of Canada. There are four regions in Canada that comprise Inuit Nunangat—Inuit homeland: Inuvialuit, Nunatsiavut, Nunavik, and Nunavut. Two of these four regions have achieved regional government: Nunavut in 1999 and Nunatsiavut in 2005.

Inuit Qaujimajatuqangit The Inuktitut (Inuit language) term for traditional or Indigenous knowledge of the Inuit.

involuntary Requests for services wherein clients have been pressured to seek the services of a social worker either by a court mandate or by facing a sanction for not seeking service.

labour force participation rate The percentage of the population identified as either employed or unemployed and seeking employment relative to the entire population.

latency effects Effects of early childhood experiences that predispose children to either good or poor health regardless of their experiences in later life.

least intrusive measures Meant to ensure that child welfare interventions are at the least intrusive level, while nonetheless protecting children from abuse and neglect.

less eligibility Principle requiring that the standard of living of an individual receiving public assistance or the conditions of work (e.g., workhouse conditions) had to be less favorable than what a labourer would receive who worked the lowest-paying labour market job.

liberal feminists Seek equality between men and women, particularly in the workplace and caring and family responsibilities.

LICOs (Low-income cut-offs) An estimate of poverty, are income thresholds below which a family will likely devote a larger portion of its income on the necessities of food, shelter, and clothing than the average family.

life course perspective Views aging as a process that spans the life course.

linking Defined as "the practitioner's conscious attempt to make connections between similarities in feelings or experiences that exist among members" (Kosoff, 2003, p. 35).

mandatory retirement A policy that forces workers to terminate employment based only on the criteria of age.

manifest destiny A force that predetermines an inevitable series of events for the future.

Marxist feminists Highlights the unequal distribution of power as the critical component of women's oppression, elevating women's oppression from an individual to a collective level.

matriarchal A system of social and political inheritance through female lineage.

medical model of disability Views disability as an individual deficit and identifies disability as being fundamentally biological in origin.

Medicine Wheel An ancient symbol that signifies a holistic method of helping and healing individuals, families, and communities.

Métis Those of mixed ancestry of First Nations and European descent who do not have status as defined by the Indian Act. The Métis have a distinct culture, history, and language.

microaggressions Brief and constant verbal, behavioural, or environmental indignities, whether intentional or unintentional, that communicate hostile, derogatory, or negative slights and insults (Sue et al., 2007).

migrant A person who has moved from one country to another either temporarily or permanently.

mountain-moving theories Theories that seek to eliminate disadvantage and empower people to realize their hopes for themselves, their families, and their communities. These theories, which include feminist, anti-oppressive, Indigenous, structural social work, and critical social work, connect the personal with the political and shift the focus from individual blame to collective solutions across social, economic, and political domains.

multilateral organizations Organizations formed between three or more nations to work on issues that relate to all of the countries in the organization. Examples of multilateral organizations include UNICEF and the World Bank.

narrative "A story which performs social functions" (Fook, 2002:132). Narratives are said to have particular structures, which serve to provide some kind of meaning for the teller. Most narratives contain a temporal ordering of events, or an incident and a consequence that follows.

neglect Refers to situations in which a child's caregiver fails to provide adequate clothing, food, or shelter, deliberately or otherwise. The term "neglect" can also apply to the abandonment of a child or the omission of basic care such as medical or dental care.

neo-liberalism A set of economic policies whereby the control of economic factors is shifted from the public sector to the private sector. Neo-liberalism advocates that governments reduce deficit spending, limit subsidies, reform tax law to broaden the tax base, open up markets to trade by limiting protectionism, and privatize state-run businesses.

non-governmental organizations Private organizations that pursue activities to relieve suffering, promote the interests of the poor, protect the environment, provide basic social services, or undertake community development.

nonrefoulement (literally meaning no return) Prohibits the return of persons—no matter what their crime or suspected activity—to a place where they would be at risk of torture and other ill treatment.

non-standard employment Refers to forms of employment that lack job stability and entitlement to fringe benefits and pension security.

non-status The opposite of status. Non-status Aboriginal people are not registered under the Indian Act and, therefore, cannot access any of their rights under this Act.

North–South divide A distinction based on an understanding of the main developmental division between countries being that of the highly developed countries and the developing countries that are almost all located to the south. Most nations comprising the "North" are located in the Northern Hemisphere (nations of North American and Europe). Notable exceptions include Australia and New Zealand, illustrating that the divide is not wholly defined by geography.

onion-peeling theories Theories that focus on peeling back the layers of past experiences in order for people can gain insight and awareness into what prevents them from moving forward in their lives.

open groups Groups that experience changes in membership throughout the life of the group as members can come and go.

otherness The condition of being viewed as strange or different.

outdoor relief Material assistance given to individuals and families in their own homes.

out-of-home services Services that are implemented when the home situation is deemed unsuitable for the child. Such services include placement in day-care centres, foster care, group homes, institutional care, family housing assistance, and adoption.

pathway effects Refer to a situation when children's exposures to risk factors at one point do not have immediate health effects but later lead to situations that do have health consequences.

patriarchy A social system characterized by men's power and privilege.

planning next steps A process of exploring and anticipating future needs and potential resources to address them

The Political Economy of Aging Emphasizes the broad implications of political and economic forces that contribute to constructions of old age and aging.

post-colonial A theory that examines colonial literature and history through the eyes of those who have been colonized which debunks the notion of European racial superiority and works towards decolonization.

postmodern An understanding that reality only comes into being through how one interprets the world around him- or herself. Thus, there is no one truth, but rather, there are many truths.

post-modern feminism A theory that highlights the complexity of social relations that involve women by focusing on how discourse shapes how women are and should be treated. This perspective seeks to interrogate and throw into question discourses and categories, rather than accepting them.

practice-based evidence Calls upon practitioners to think about the outcome they and their clients hope to achieve during the course of their interactions, and implement a means of representing the outcome in a measurable way.

process Refers to the manner in which a social worker gathers information.

processing the emotional bond Refers to facilitating the expression of emotion associated with ending the work between worker and client.

product Refers to the written assessment.

purist approach A practice when a particular theory or theoretical perspective is regularly drawn upon regardless of the nature of a client's presenting issues.

purpose The rationale for service.

qualitative approach A way to "study things in their natural settings, attempting to make sense of, or interpret, phenomena in terms of the meanings that people bring to them" (Denzin & Lincoln, 2005, p. 3). Ways of collecting data typically include in-depth interviews, field observations, and reviews of written documents and data are expressed as words, images, objects, or sounds (Neuman & Robson, 2012).

quantitative approach Focuses on the production of numerical findings that can be statistically interpreted in order to generalize them to populations beyond the study sample. Ways of collecting data typically include questionnaires, experiments and using data collected previously (called secondary data).

radical feminists Assert that women's freedom depends upon the elimination of patriarchy. This view seeks to promote separate women's structures within existing organizations and women's own social structures.

reflexivity A process by which the worker's thinking influences the action, ensuring a more sophisticated analysis of practice. Reflexivity moves beyond reflection by introducing an analysis of power and the dynamics of power and critical thought.

refugee Any person who is outside his or her country of nationality who is unable or unwilling to return to that country because of persecution or a well-founded fear of persecution.

refugee claimant A temporary resident in the humanitarian population category who requests refugee protection upon or after arrival in Canada but whose claim has not yet been decided.

reintegration The process by which ex-combatants acquire civilian status and gain sustainable employment and income. Reintegration is essentially a social and economic process with an open timeframe, primarily taking place in communities at the local level. It is part of the general development of a country and a national responsibility, and often necessitates long-term external assistance.

repatriate The process of locating an Aboriginal person's First Nation community and reuniting him or her with the birth family as well as registering him or her as status Indians under the Indian Act.

reserve The reserve system was set up to restrict Aboriginal people registered under the Indian Act to particular areas of Canada that were considered unattractive to settlers.

resettlement The process by which refugees are given permanent legal residency in a host country.

residential school An institution that housed Aboriginal children who were forcibly removed from their families and communities and deprived of their cultures, languages, and spirituality while exposing them to abuse and illness.

restorative justice A process whereby the parties with a stake in a particular offence come together to resolve collectively how to deal with the aftermath of the offence and its implications for the future. Within Indigenous communities, restorative justice practices aim to restore the balance after harm has been committed. Some of these methods are, for example, sentencing circles which involve the person who has done the harm, the victim, and community members such as Elders and family members.

reviewing progress A process facilitated by the worker to help clients reflect back on their initial concerns to elicit insights about progress made.

risk assessment An activity designed to determine the likelihood of future abuse or neglect so that action can be taken to prevent it.

Safe Third Country A provision of IRPA that designated the USA as a "safe third country," which effectively closed the land border to most refugee claimants.

selective optimization with compensation A positive coping process of aging.

self-awareness Refers to a social worker's insight into how he/she affects and/or is affected by others.

self-determination The ability to make decisions and choices for oneself.

self-disclosure An intentional attempt at revealing something about the self of the worker to the client.

separated minors Children who may be with an adult who is not a parent or previous primary caregiver. Even though in the presence of an adult, a separated minor can still be considered a "person of concern" as the accompanying adult may not be able to adequately provide for the child or might be a trafficker.

Sixties Scoop Refers to the practice that occurred from the 1960s to the 1980s of apprehending unusually high numbers of Indigenous children and fostering or adopting them, largely to non-Indigenous families. This removal led to further loss of cultural identity, contact with their families and communities of origin, and, in some cases, loss of their status under the Indian Act.

social capital Refers to "features of social organizations such as networks, norms, and social trust that facilitate coordination and cooperation for mutual benefit" (Putnam, 1995, p. 67).

social casework Addressing an issue by systematically gathering detailed data regarding an individual's environment and analyzing the data, followed by making a data-based diagnosis and treatment plan.

Social Darwinism As related to poverty, the belief that indiscriminate relief would weaken a person's moral character, leading to the weakening of society and those who were poor were "unfit" while those who were wealthy were not only "fit" but possessed higher moral character.

social determinants of health A model that encompasses the economic and social conditions that shape individuals, communities, and jurisdictions' health overall; the primary determinants of whether an individual stays healthy or becomes ill; the extent to which a person has the physical, social, and personal resources to identify and achieve personal aspirations, meet needs, and cope with his or her environment; and the quantity and quality of resources that a society makes available and accessible to its members (Raphael, 2009, p. 2).

social development The processes of change that lead to improvements in human well-being, social relations, and social institutions, and that are equitable, sustainable, and compatible with principles of democratic governance and social justice.

Social Gospel Movement An integrated theological and social movement centred on social development and change.

socialist feminists A theory that emphasizes the interpersonal and relationship aspects of women's oppression as created by patriarchy. It also broadened the analysis of feminist theory to include questions of sexuality and identity.

social location Refers to someone's affiliation as a member of a group based on race, ethnicity, gender, ability, class, religion, citizenship status, sexual/gender identity, and so forth. An individual's social location includes the particular geographic and socio-historical context into which one is born (Rich, 1984).

social model of disability In contrast to the medical model of disability, this model contends that disability is created or constructed by social and environmental factors only.

social welfare An organized system which provides social services and programs to assist individuals and families.

stage A distinct period in a process of a group's growth and development.

status First Nations people who are registered under the Indian Act based on blood quantum and historical policy.

story-telling theories The ways that stories can be reinterpreted to enable more positive and rewarding life-outcomes. Building on notions of strengths-based practice, story-telling theories focus on externalizing problems and finding narrative solutions that lead to a greater sense of well-being.

strength-based social work An approach asserting that people have inherent strengths and are motivated towards well-being and optimal functioning.

structural social work Focuses on the structural significance of social problems rather than viewing them as personal issues and analyzes the impacts that structures in society have upon people.

Successful Aging Views positive aging as the prevention of functional decline and engagement in meaningful activities.

superego Acts as "the conscience" and develops during one's childhood through socialization. It is the internalization of the values and norms of society, taught by parents and caregivers. The superego is meant to control the drives and desires of the id.

target problems Issues or challenges clients face that they wish to change.

task group A group that focuses on completing a specific assignment or goal for a clientele, organization, or community.

temporary foreign worker Someone who has been hired by a Canadian employer to fill temporary labour or skill shortages.

theory Represents an explanatory framework that aims to help make sense of the complexity of human lives and behaviour. In aiming to help "make sense," theories help structure and organize thinking, and establish an explanation for what we think is going on.

time limits The time parameters social workers and clients establish for the work they will do together.

tracking Involves observing patterns of interaction between family members while listening to the issues they are discussing.

traditional developmental psychology Views aging as one of a series of life stages with associated tasks.

transference Refers to the translocation of past experiences to the present without conscious awareness. Transference reactions involve attitudes, fantasies, desires, and conflicts from historically significant object relationships to the therapist.

transfer payments Refer to federal funds used to help cover a portion of the costs of a provincial program (Maioni, 2004).

transitioning Refers to the process through which trans people start to move away from their gender assigned at birth to their preferred gender expression and identity (Ezra, 2013).

transphobia The irrational fear, hatred, and intolerance of trans people.

treatment group A group that focuses primarily on socio-emotive or behavioural needs of participants.

Turtle Island A phrase originally coined by the Haudenosaunee to refer to the continent now known as North America.

unaccompanied minors Children under 18 years of age who arrive in a potential settlement country without the presence of an adult.

"undeserving" poor Those assessed to be physically capable of work in some form or another but are unemployed.

undocumented migrant Refers to someone who has come to Canada as a visitor, student, or temporary worker and then continued residence in Canada after his or her visa has expired or a refugee claimant whose claim for asylum is denied (Elrick, 2007).

United Nations Convention on the Rights of the Child (CRC) Applies to "every human being below the age of eighteen years." A hallmark of the CRC is its integration of broad categories of rights, including civil and political rights and economic, social, and cultural rights. The only two nation states that have not ratified the CRC are Somalia and the US.

universalism The position that states that core values apply to all human beings, irrespective of their identity (including cultural background or personal preferences).

universal truths Beliefs that are accepted by the entire world.

utilitarian theories Theories that suggest actions are right and wrong according to their outcomes rather than their intrinsic features.

voluntary Requests for services wherein clients have self-referred or agree with those referring them that social work services are warranted.

welfare state A country in which the government assumes responsibility for ensuring that its citizens' basic needs are met.

worldview The lens through which a group of people sees the world around them, their values, and relationships.

References

Chapter 1

Abramovitz, M. (1996). *Regulating the lives of women: Social welfare policy from colonial times to the present.* Cambridge, MA: South End.

Allen, R. (2007). The Social Gospel. In J. Coates, J.R. Graham, & B. Swartzen-truber, with B. Ouellette (Eds.), *Spirituality and social work: Selected Canadian readings* (pp. 299–322). Toronto, ON: Canadian Scholars' Press Inc.

Ambrosino, R., Ambrosino, R., Heffernan, J., & Shuttlesworth, G. (2012). *Social work and social welfare,* (7th ed.). Belmont, CA: Brooks/Cole.

Arnakak, J. (2002). Incorporation of Inuit Qaujimatatuqangit or Inuit traditional knowledge, into the government of Nunavut. *Journal of Aboriginal Economic Development, 3,* 1, 33–39.

Arnakak, J. (2000). Commentary: What is *Inuit Qaujimajatuqangit?* Using Inuit family and kinship relationships to apply *Inuit Qaujimajatuqangit. Nunatsiaq News,* 25 August.

Axinn, J., & Levin, H. (1992). *Social welfare: A history of the American response to need* (3rd ed.). New York: Longman.

Axinn, J., & Stern, M. (2007). *Social welfare: A history of the American response to need,* (7th ed.). New Jersey: Allyn & Bacon.

Barnes, S. (2005). Black church culture and community action. *Social Forces, 84,* 2, 967–994.

Baskin, C. (2011). *Strong helpers' teachings: The value of Indigenous knowledges in the helping professions.* Toronto: Canadian Scholars' Press.

Berton, P. (2001). *The Great Depression, 1929–1939.* Toronto: Anchor Canada.

Bickley, J.B. (1998). Care for the caregiver: The art of self-care. *Seminars in Perioperative Nursing, 7,* 2, 114–121.

Billingsley, A. (1995). The Black church as a social service institution. *Black Caucus: Journal of the NABSW, 1,* 4, 1–5.

Blondin, G. (1999). As an Indian I love my Indian culture. I still am in love with the land, I am still in love with my history. In P. Kulchyski, D. McCaskill, & D. Newhouse, *In the words of Elders: Aboriginal cultures in transition* (pp. 377–413). Toronto: University of Toronto Press.

Bradbury, B. (2007). *Age, gender and daily survival in industrializing Montreal.* Toronto: McClelland & Stewart, 1993.

Breton, M. (2002). Empowerment practice in Canada and the United States. *The Social Policy Journal, 1,* 19–34.

Chaves, M., & Higgins, L.M. (1992). Comparing the community involvement of Black and White congregations. *Journal for the Scientific Study of Religion, 31,* 425–440.

Collin, C., & Jensen, H. (2009). *A statistical profile of poverty in Canada.* Parliamentary Information and Research Service, Library of Parliament. Available at http://www.parl.gc.ca/Content/LOP/ResearchPublications/prb0917-e.pdf.

Collins, W.L. (2005). Embracing spirituality as an element of professional self-care. *Social Work & Christianity, 32,* 3, 263–274.

Dane, B. (2002). Duty to inform: Preparing social work students to understand vicarious traumatization. *Journal of Teaching in Social Work, 22,* 3/4, pp. 3–19.

Este, D. (2007). Black churches in Canada: Vehicles for fostering community development in African-Canadian communities—a historical analysis. In J. Coates, J.R. Graham, B. Swartzen-truber, & B. Ouellette (Eds.), *Spirituality and Social Work: Selected Canadian readings* (pp. 299–322). Toronto: Canadian Scholars' Press Inc.

Este, D. (2004). The Black church as a social welfare institution: Union united church and the development of Montreal's Black community, 1907–1940. *The Journal of Black Studies, 35,* 3, 3–22.

Fingard, J. (1974). The winter's tale: The seasonal contours of pre-industrial poverty in British North America, 1815–1860. *Historical Papers/Communications historiques, 9,* 1, 65–94.

Graham, J., Coholic, D., & Coates, J. (2007). Spirituality as a guiding construct in the development of Canadian social work. In John Coates, John R. Graham, and Barbara Swartzentruber (Eds.), *Spirituality and social work: Selected Canadian readings* (pp. 23–46). Toronto: Canadian Scholars' Press.

Guest, D. (1997). *The emergence of social security in Canada* (3rd ed.). Vancouver: UBC Press.

Hart, M.A. (2009). For Indigenous People, by Indigenous People, with Indigenous People: Towards an Indigenous research paradigm. In R. Sinclair, M.A. Hart, & G. Bruyere (Eds.), *Wicihitowin: Aboriginal social work in Canada* (pp. 153–169). Halifax, NS: Fernwood.

Hart, M.A. (2002). *Seeking Mino-Pimatisiwin: An Aboriginal approach to helping.* Halifax: Fernwood.

Henry, F. (1973). *Forgotten Canadians: The Blacks of Nova Scotia.* Toronto: Longmans.

Hiemstra, J.L. (2002). Government relations with faith-based non-profit social agencies in Alberta. *Journal of Church & State, 44,* 19–44.

Hill, D. (1981). *The freedom seekers: Blacks in early Canada.* Agincourt: ON: The Book Society of Canada.

Hoefer, R. (1996). A conceptual model for studying social welfare policy comparatively. *Journal of Social Work Education, 32,* 1, 101–113.

Irving, A. (1992). The scientific imperative in Canadian social work: Social work and social welfare research in Canada, 1897–1945. *Canadian Social Work Review/Revue canadienne de service social, 9,* 1, 9–27.

Ives, N., & Aitken, O. (2009). From colonized region to globalized region? Challenges to addressing social issues in Nunavik in the transition to regional government. *Indigenous Policy Journal, 20,* 3. http://ipjournal.wordpress.com/2009/12/16/from-colonized-region-to-globalized-region/

Jameson, A. (1859). *Sisters of charity and the communion of labour: Two lectures on the social employments of women.* London: Longman, Brown, Green, Longmans, & Roberts.

Jennissen, T., & Lundy, C. (2011). *One hundred years of social work: A history of the profession in English Canada, 1900–2000.* Ontario: Wilfrid Laurier University Press.

Katz, M. (1996). *In the shadow of the poorhouse: A social history of welfare in America* (rev. ed.). New York: Basic.

Keller, R.S., & Ruether, R.R. (2006). (Eds.). *Encyclopedia of women and religion in North America.* Bloomington, Indiana: Indiana University Press.

Kulchyski, P., McCaskill, D., & Newhouse, D. (Eds). (1999). *In the words of Elders: Aboriginal cultures in transition.* Toronto: University of Toronto Press.

Lessard, R. (1987). Le Bureau des pauvres de Sainte-Famille: Île d'Orléans (1698–1700). *Cap-aux-Diamants: La revue d'histoire du Québec, 3,* 3, 65. Available at http://id.erudit.org/iderudit/6771ac.

Linteau, P.-A., Durocher, R., & Robert, J.-C. (1983). *Quebec: A history, 1867–1929.* Translated by Robert Chodos. Originally published as Histoire du Québec contemporain: De la Confédération à la crise. Toronto : James Lorimer.

Marks, L. (1995). Indigent committees and Ladies Benevolent Societies: Intersections of public and private poor relief in late nineteenth century small town Ontario. *Studies in Political Economy, 47,* 61–87.

Mason, M.A. (1999). That's why I figure, well, this is a chance for me to tell. It was a tough life. In P. Kulchyski, D. McCaskill, & D. Newhouse, *In the words of Elders: Aboriginal cultures in transition* (pp. 417–441). Toronto: University of Toronto Press.

Midgley, J. (1995). *Social development: The developmental perspective in social welfare.* London: Sage.

Minville, E. (1939). The Church and social welfare–assistance (Works of Mercy). In *Labour legislation and social services in the province of Quebec. A study prepared for the Royal Commission on Dominion-Provincial relations* (pp. 47–49). Ottawa.

Mooney, M.A. (2009). *Faith makes us live; Surviving and thriving in the Haitian diaspora.* Berkeley, CA: University of California Press.

Mortin, I. (1953). *Program development at the University Settlement of Montreal.* Unpublished Master of Social Work thesis, McGill University School of Social Work, Montreal.

Mosley, J. (2013). Recognizing new opportunities: Reconceptualizing policy advocacy in everyday organizational practice. *Social Work, 58,* 3, 231–239.

Nitsch, T.H. (1999). My heritage was so ingrained in me that I knew I would never lose it. In P. Kulchyski, D. McCaskill, & D. Newhouse, *In the words of Elders: Aboriginal cultures in transition* (pp. 67–93). Toronto: University of Toronto Press.

Osbourne, J.E. (1985). *The evolution of the Canada Assistance Plan.* Development National Health and Welfare, Service to the Public—Canada Assistance Plan, Government of Canada.

Pauktuutit Inuit Women of Canada. (2006). The Inuit way: A guide to Inuit culture. Available at http://www.uqar .ca/files/boreas/inuitway_e.pdf.

Rabesca, M. (1999). Our culture will not die because our culture is nature through God, that's the way it's always going to be. It will never die. In P. Kulchyski, D. McCaskill, and D. Newhouse, *In the words of Elders: Aboriginal cultures in transition* (pp. 363–376). Toronto: University of Toronto Press.

Radey, M., & Figley, C.R. (2007). The social psychology of compassion. *Clinical Social Work Journal, 35,* 207–214.

Reid, M. (2009). Kaxlaya Gvilas: Upholding traditional Heiltsuk laws, values and practices as Aboriginal Peoples and allies. In R. Sinclair, M.A. Hart, & G. Bruyere (Eds.), *Wícihitowin: Aboriginal social work in Canada* (pp. 200–221). Halifax, NS: Fernwood.

Richmond, M. (1917). *Social diagnosis.* New York: Russell Sage Foundation.

Salamon, L.M. (1995). *Partners in public service: Government-nonprofit relations in the modern welfare state.* Baltimore: Johns Hopkins University Press.

Schneider, R. (2002). Influencing "state" policy. *The Social Policy Journal, 1,* 113–116.

Spitzer, A., Bar-Tal, Y. & Ziv, L. (1996). The moderating effect of age on self-care. *Western Journal of Nursing Research, 18,* 2, 136–140.

St. Vincent de Paul Societies. *Vincentian Life, History.* Available at http://www.ssvp.ca/Vincentian-Life.

Tagalik, S. (2009). *Inuit Qaujimajatuqangit:* The role of Indigenous knowledge in supporting wellness in Inuit communities in Nunavut. *Inuit Child & Youth Health.* National Collaborating Centre for Aboriginal Health. Available at http://www.nccah-ccnsa.ca/docs/fact%20sheets/child%20and%20youth/Inuit%20IQ%20EN%20web.pdf.

Titmuss, R.M. (1958). *Essays on the welfare state.* London: Allen & Unwin.

Urdang, E. (2010). Awareness of self—A critical tool. *Social Work Education, 29,* 523–538.

Walker, J. (1995). African Canadians. In M. Magocsi (Ed.), *Encyclopedia of Canada's people* (pp. 139–176). Toronto, ON: University of Toronto Press.

Wall, S. (2001). *To become a human being: The message of Tadodaho Chief Leon Shenandoah.* Charlottesville, VA: Hampton Roads.

Ward, N., Billingsley, A., Simon, A., & Burris, J.C. (1994). Black churches in Atlanta reach out to the community. *National Journal of Sociology, 8,* 49–74.

White, G. (2009). Governance in Nunavut: Capacity vs. Culture? *Journal of Canadian Studies/Revue d'études canadiennes, 43,* 2, 57–81.

Williams, D. (1997). *The road to now: A history of Blacks in Montreal.* Montreal, PQ: Vehicule Press.

Winks, R. (1971). *The Blacks in Canada: A history.* Montreal, QC: McGill-Queen's University Press.

Woodsworth, J.S. (1911). *My neighbour: A study of city conditions, a plea for social service.* Toronto: The Missionary Society of the Methodist Church.

Young, B. (1994). *The Politics of codification: The Lower Canadian Civil Code of 1866.* Montreal, QC: McGill-Queen's University Press.

Chapter 2

Allan, J. (2009). Theorising new developments in critical social work. In J. Allan, L. Briskman, and B. Pease (Eds.), *Critical social work: Theories and practices for a socially just world.* Crows Nest, New South Wales: Allen & Unwin.

Andrae, D. (2011). General systems theory: Contributions to social work theory and practice. In F. Turner, *Social work treatment: Interlocking theoretical approaches* (pp. 242–254). Oxford: Oxford University Press.

Baikie, G. (2009). Indigenous-centred social work. In R. Sinclair, M. Hart, and G. Bruyere, (Eds.), *Wícihitowin: Aboriginal social work in Canada*. Winnipeg: Fernwood.

Baines, D. (2011). *Doing anti-oppressive practice: Social justice social work*. Halifax: Fernwood.

Baskin, C. (2011). *Strong helpers' teachings: The value of Indigenous knowledges in the helping professions*. Toronto, ON: Canadian Scholars' Press.

Bopp, M., & Bopp, J. (2001). *Recreating the world: A practical guide to building sustainable communities*. Calgary, AB: Four Worlds Press.

Borden, W. (Ed.). (2010). *Reshaping theory in contemporary social work*. New York: Columbia University Press.

Borg, D., Brownlee, K., & Delaney, R. (1995). Postmodern social work practice with Aboriginal people. In R. Delaney & K. Brownlee (Eds.), *Northern social work practice*. Thunder Bay, ON: Lakehead University.

Bowlby, J. (1984). *Attachment and Loss*. New York: Penguin.

Briskman, L. (2007). *Social Work with indigenous communities*. Annandale, New South Wales: Federation Press.

Bronfenbrenner, U. (1979). *The Ecology of Human Development: Experiments by Nature and Design*. Boston: Harvard University Press.

Bruyere, G. (2010). The decolonization wheel: An Aboriginal perspective on social work practice with Aboriginal peoples. In K. Brownlee, R. Neckoway, R. Delaney, & D. Durst, (Eds.), *Social work & Aboriginal Peoples: Perspectives from Canada's rural and provincial Norths* (pp. 1–11). Thunder Bay, ON: Centre for Northern Studies, Lakehead University.

Bruyere, G. (1998). Living in another man's house: Supporting Aboriginal learners in social work education. *Canadian Social Work Review, 15, 2,* 169–176.

Connolly, M., & Harms, L. (2012). *Social work: From theory to practice*. Cambridge: Cambridge University Press.

Connolly, M. & Healy, K. (2009). Social work practice theories and frameworks. In M. Connolly and L. Harms (Eds.), *Social work: Contexts and practice* (pp. 19–36). Melbourne: Oxford University Press.

Dominelli, L. (2002). *Feminist social work theory and practice*. Basingstoke, UK: Palgrave.

Drucker, D. (2003). Whither international social work? A reflection. *International Social Work, 46,* 1, 53–81. DOI: 10.1177/0020872803046001596

Fook, J. (2002). *Social work: Critical theory and practice*. London: Sage.

Gibney, P. (2003). *The pragmatics of therapeutic practice*. Melbourne: Psychoz Publications.

Gray, M., & Webb, S. (2009). Critical social work. In *Social Work Theories and Methods* (pp. 99–109). London: Sage.

Gray, M., Yellow Bird, M., & Coates, J. (2008). Towards an understanding of Indigenous social work, in M. Gray, J. Coates, & M. Yellow Bird (Eds.), *Indigenous social work around the world: Towards culturally relevant education and practice* (pp. 49–58). Hampshire, England: Ashgate.

Healy, K. (2005). *Social work theories in context: Creating frameworks for practice*. Basingstoke: Palgrave Macmillan.

Howe, D. (2009). *A brief introduction to social work theory* (pp. 1–8). New York, NY: Palgrave MacMillan.

Howe, D. (1987). *An introduction to social work theory*. Aldershot: Wildwood House.

Hudson, C. (2000). A the edge of chaos: A new paradigm for social work? *Journal of Social Work Education, 36,* 2, 215–230.

Ives, N., & Loft, M. (2013). Building bridges with Indigenous communities through social work education. In M. Gray., J. Coates, M. Yellow Bird, and T. Hetherington (Eds.), *Decolonising social work* (pp. 239–255). London: Ashgate.

Kreuger, L., & Newman, W. (2006). *Social work research methods: Qualitative and quantitative applications*. Boston: Pearson.

Lorde, A. (2007). *Sister outsider: Essays and speeches*. Berkeley, CA: The Crossing Press Feminist Series.

Martinez-Brawley, E. (1999). Social work, postmodernism and higher education. *International Social Work, 42,* 3, 333–46.

Mullaly, B. (2010). *Challenging oppression and confronting privilege* (2nd ed.). Oxford: Oxford University Press.

Mullaly, B. (2007). *The New Structural Social Work*. Oxford: Oxford University Press.

Oko, J. (2011). *Understanding and using theory in social work*. Exeter: Learning Matters Ltd.

Orme, J. (2009). Feminist social work. In M. Gray and S. Webb, (Eds.), *Social work theories and methods* (pp. 65–75). London: Sage.

Orme, J. (2002). Feminist social work. In R. Adams, L. Dominelli, & M. Payne (Eds.), *Social work: Themes, issues and critical debates* (2nd ed.) (pp. 218–226). Basingstoke, UK: Palgrave.

Owen, I. (1999). Exploring the similarities and differences between person-centred and psychodynamic therapy. *British Journal of Guidance & Counselling, 27,* 2, 165–178.

Parrot, L. (2010). *Values and ethics in social work practice*. Exeter: Learning Matters Ltd.

Payne, M. (2005) *Modern social work theory*. Chicago: Lyceum.

Richmond, M. (1917). *Social diagnosis*. New York: Russell Sage Foundation.

Riley, A. (1996). Murder and social work. *Australian Social Work, 49,* 2, 37–43.

Schriver, J. (1998). *Human behaviour and the social environment: Shifting paradigms in essential knowledge for social work practice*. Boston: Allyn & Bacon.

Sheldon, B. (1995). *Cognitive-behavioral theory: Research, practice and philosophy*. London: Tavistock.

Sinclair, R. (2009). Bridging the past and future: An introduction to Indigenous social work issues. In R. Sinclair, M. Hart, and G. Bruyere, (Eds.), *Wícihitowin: Aboriginal social work in Canada*. Winnipeg: Fernwood.

Sinclair, R., Hart, M.A., & Bruyere, G. (2009). *Wícihitowin: Aboriginal social work in Canada*. Halifax: Fernwood Publishing

Teater, B. (2010). *An introduction to applying social work theories and methods*. Maidenhead: Open University Press.

Trocmé, N., Knoke, D., & Blackstock, C. (2004). Pathways to the overrepresentation of Aboriginal children in Canada's child welfare system. *Social Service Review, 78,* 4, 577–600.

Watzlawick, P., Weakland, J., & Fisch, E. (1974). *Change: principles of problem formulation and problem resolution*. New York: Norton and Co.

Yellow Bird, M. & Gray, M. (2010). Indigenous people and the language of social work. In M. Gray, J. Coates, and M. Yellow Bird, (Eds.), *Indigenous social work around the world: Towards culturally relevant education and practice*. Surrey: Ashgate.

Chapter 3

Baines, D. (Ed.). (2011*). Doing anti-oppressive practice: Social justice social work*. Halifax, NS: Fernwood.

Betan, E.J. (1997). Toward a hermeneutic model of ethical decision making in clinical practice. *Ethics & Behavior, 7*, 4, 347–365.

Brant Castellano, M. (2004, January). The ethics of Aboriginal research. *Journal of Aboriginal Health*, 98–114.

Briskman, L. (2001). A moral crisis for social work: Critical practice & codes of ethics. *Critical Social Work, 2*, 1, 1–9.

Brown, M. (2005). Research, respect and responsibility: A critical review of the Tri-Council Policy Statement in Aboriginal community-based research. *Pimatisiwin, 3*, 2, 79–100.

Canadian Association of Social Workers (CASW). (2005a). *Code of ethics*. CASW. Available at http://casw-acts.ca/sites/default/files/attachements/CASW_Code%20of%20Ethics.pdf.

Canadian Association of Social Workers (CASW). (2005b). *Guidelines for ethical practice*. CASW. Available at http://casw-acts.ca/sites/default/files/attachements/CASW_Guidelines%20for%20Ethical%20Practice.pdf.

Delaney, R., & Brownlee, K. (Eds.). (2009). *Northern and rural social work practice: A Canadian perspective*. Thunder Bay, Ontario: Centre for Northern Studies, Lakehead University.

Denzin, N. (2008). IRBs and the turn to Indigenous research ethics. In Brinda Jegatheesen (ed.), *Advances in program evaluation, vol. 12. Access: A zone of comprehension and intrusion* (pp. 97–123). Bingley, England: Emerald Group.

Denzin, N.K., & Lincoln, Y.S. (2005). *The sage handbook of qualitative research* (3rd ed.). Thousand Oaks, CA: Sage.

Epstein, E. (1987). Pedagogy of the preturbed. *Journal of Teaching in Social Work, 1*, 1, 71–89.

First Nations Centre (2007). *OCAP: Ownership, control, access and possession*. Sanctioned by the First Nations Information Governance Committee, Assembly of First Nations. Ottawa: National Aboriginal Health Organization.

Gambrill, E. (2006). Evidence-based practice and policy: Choices ahead. *Research on Social Work Practice, 16*, 338–357.

Gray, M., & Gibbons, J. (2007). There are no answers, only choices: Teaching ethical decision making in social work. *Australian Social Work, 60*, 2, 222–238.

Halverson, G., & Brownlee, K. (2010). Managing ethical considerations around dual relationships in small rural and remote Canadian communities. *International Social Work, 53*, 2, 247–260.

Horn, O.K., Jacobs-Whyte, H., Ing, A., Bruegl, A., Paradis, G., & Macaulay, A.C. (2007). Incidence and prevalence of type 2 diabetes in the First Nation community of Kahnawa:ke, Quebec, Canada, 1986–2003. *Canadian Journal of Public Health, 98*, 6, 438–43.

IFSW. (2004). *Ethics in social work, statement of principles*, Preface. Available at http://ethics.iit.edu/ecodes/node/3934 accessed on December 3, 2012.

Ives, N., & Loft, M. (2013). Building bridges with Indigenous communities through social work education. In M. Gray., J. Coates, M. Yellow Bird, and T. Hetherington (Eds.), *Decolonising social work* (pp. 239–255). London: Ashgate.

Kahnawake Schools Diabetes Prevention Project (KSDPP). (2007). *Code of research ethics*. KSDPP. Available at www.ksdpp.org.

King, T. (Ed.). (1990). *All my relations: An anthology of contemporary Canadian Native fiction*. Toronto: McClelland & Stewart.

Kovach, M. (2009). *Indigenous methodologies: Characteristics, conversations, and contexts*. Toronto: University of Toronto Press.

Loewenberg, F.M., & Dolgoff, R. (1996). *Ethical decisions for social work practices*. Itasca, IL: Peacock.

Macaulay, A.C., Cargo, M., Bisset, S., Delormier, T., Lévesque, L., Potvin, L., & McComber, A.M. (2006). Community empowerment for the primary prevention of Type 2 diabetes: Kanien'kehá:ka (Mohawk) ways for the Kahnawake Schools Diabetes Prevention Project (pp 407–458). In M.L. Ferreira, & G.C. Lang, (Eds.), *Indigenous Peoples and diabetes: Community empowerment and wellness*. Durham, NC: Carolina Academic Press.

Maschi, T., Probst, B., & Bradley, C. (2009). Mapping social work students' perceptions of the research process: A qualitative follow-up study. *The Journal of Baccalaureate Social Work, 14*, 2, 63–78.

Mattison, M. (2000). Ethical decision making: The person in the process. *Social Work, 45*, 3, 201–212.

McCracken, S.G., & Marsh, J.C. (2008). Practitioner expertise in evidence-based practice decision making. *Research on Social Work Practice, 18*(4), 301–310.

Michell, H. (1999, Fall). Pakitinâsowin: Tobacco offerings in exchange for stories and the ethic of reciprocity in First Nations research. *Journal of Indigenous Thought*. Regina: SIFC-Department of Indian Studies.

Montour, L.T., & Macaulay, A.C. (1985). High prevalence rates of diabetes mellitus and hypertension on a North American Indian reservation. *Canadian Medical Association Journal, 132*, 1110–1112.

Mullaly, B. (2010). *Challenging oppression and confronting privilege* (2nd ed.). Oxford: Oxford University Press.

Mullen, E.J., Bledsoe, S.E., & Bellamy, J.L. (2008). Implementing evidence-based social work practice. *Research on Social Work Practice, 18*, 4, 325–338.

Neuman, L.W., & Robson, K. (2012). *Basics of social research: Qualitative and quantitative approaches* (2nd ed.). Toronto: Pearson.

Noble, C., & Briskman, L. (1996). Social work ethics: The challenge to moral consensus. *New Zealand Social Work Review, 8*, 3, 2–8.

Padgett, D. (2008). *Qualitative methods in social work research* (2nd ed.). Thousand Oaks, CA: Sage.

Perlman, D. (2004, May). Ethics in clinical research: A history of human subject protections and practical implementation of ethical standards. *SoCRA Source*, 38–41.

Proctor, E.K., & Rosen, A. (2008). From knowledge production to implementation: Research challenges and imperatives. *Research on Social Work Practice, 18*, 285–291.

Reamer, F. (2012, May). The dark side of social work: Ethical misconduct. *Social Work Today* [digital edition]. http://www.socialworktoday.com/news/eoe_051712.shtml.

Reamer, F. (1998). The evolution of social work ethics. *Social Work, 43*, 6, 488–500.

Rubin, A., & Babbie, E.R. (2005). *Research methods for social work*. Toronto: Nelson.

Sackett, D.L., Straus, S.E., Richardson, W.S., Rosenberg, W., & Haynes, R.B. (2000). *Evidence based medicine: How* to practice and teach EBM. New York: Churchill Livingstone.

Schnarch, B. (2004). Ownership, control, access, and possession (OCAP) or self-determination applied to research: A critical analysis of contemporary First Nations research and some options for First Nations communities. *Journal of Aboriginal Health, 1,* 1, 80–95.

Secret, M., Ford, J., & Rompf, E.L. (2003). Undergraduate research courses: A closer look reveals complex social work student attitudes. *Journal of Social Work Education, 39,* 3, 411–422.

Shuster, E. (1997). Fifty years later: The significance of the Nuremberg Code. *The New England Journal of Medicine, 337,* 20, 1436–1440.

Tuhiwai Smith, L. (1999). *Decolonizing methodologies: Research and Indigenous Peoples.* New York: Zed Books.

Wade, K., & Neuman, K. (2007). Practice-based research: Changing the professional culture and language of social work. *Social Work in Health Care, 44,* 4, 49–64.

Wiwchar, D. (2005). Nuu-chah-nulth blood returns to the West coast. *Ha-Shilth-Sa, 31,* 25, 1–4.

Chapter 4

Biestek, F. (1957). *The casework relationship.* Chicago: Loyola University Press.

Bogo, M. (2006). *Social work practice concepts, processes & interviewing.* New York: Columbia University Press.

Bowen, M. (1961). Family psychotherapy. *American Journal of Orthopsychiatry, 31,* 40–60.

Dias, P., & Paré, A. (2000). *Transitions: Writing in academic and workplace settings.* Cresskill, NJ: Hampton Press.

Duncan, B.L., Miller, S.D., & Sparks, J.A. (2004). *The heroic client.* New York: Jossey-Bass.

Epstein, L., & Brown, L. (2002). *Brief treatment and a new look at the task-centred approach* (4th ed.). Boston, MA: Allyn & Bacon.

Fantus, S., & Mishna, F. (2013). The ethical and clinical implications of using cyber-communication in face-to-face therapy. *Smith College Studies in Social Work, 83,* 466–480.

Farber, B.A. (2006). *Self-disclosure in therapy.* New York, NY: Guilford Press.

Finn, J. (2006). An exploratory study of email use by direct social work

practitioners. *Journal of Technology in Human Services, 24,* 1–20.

Flaskas, C. (2007). Holding hope and hopelessness: Therapeutic engagements with the balance of hope. *Journal of Family Therapy, 29,* 186–202.

Gelman, C.R. (2009). MSW students' experience with termination. Implications and suggestions for classroom and field instruction. *Journal of Teaching in Social Work, 29,* 169–187.

Germain, C.B., & Gitterman, A. (1996). The ecological perspective. In C.B. Germain & A. Gitterman, *The life model of social work practice: Advances in theory and practice* (2nd ed.). New York: Columbia University Press.

Gibson, M.F. (2012). Opening up: Therapist self-disclosure in theory, research and practice. *Clinical Social Work Journal, 40,* 287–296.

Hepworth, D.H., Rooney, R.H., Rooney, G.D., Strom-Gottfried, K., & Larsen, J. (2010). *Direct social work practice: Theory & skills.* Belmont, CA: Brooks/Cole.

Hodge, D.R., & Limb, G.E. (2011). Spiritual assessment and Native Americans: Establishing social validity of a contemporary set of assessment tools. *Social Work, 56,* 3, 213–223.

Horvath, A.O., & Bedi, R.P. (2002). The alliance. In J.C. Norcross (Ed.). *Psychotherapy relationships that work: Therapist contributions and responsiveness to patients* (pp. 37–69). New York: Oxford University Press.

Howe, D. (2009). *A brief introduction to social work theory.* Houndsmills, Hampshire: Palgrave MacMillan.

Iverson, R.R., Gergen, K.J., & Fairbanks, R.P. (2005). Assessment and social construction: Conflict or co-creation? *British journal of social work, 35,* 689–708.

Keefler, J. (2006). *Recording psychosocial assessments in social work: Problems and solutions.* Unpublished doctoral thesis, McGill University.

Keefler, J., Bond, S., & Sussman, T. (2013). L'évaluation psychosociale (translation: Psychosocial assessment). In E. Harper & H. Dorvil (Eds.), *Le travail social: Théories, méthodologies et pratiques* (pp. 267–290) (translation: Social work: Theories, methodologies and practices). Montreal: Les presses de l'Université du Québec à Montreal, Québec.

Kilpatrick, A.C., & Holland, T.P. (2006). *Working with families: An integrative*

model by level of need. Boston, MA: Allyn & Bacon.

Lemma, A. (2010). The power of relationship: A study of key working as an intervention with traumatised young people. *Journal of Social Work Practice, 24,* 4, 409–427.

Maiter, S., Palmer, S., & Manji, S. (2006). Strengthening social worker–client relationships in child protective services: Addressing power imbalances and "ruptured" relationships. *Qualitative Social Work, 5,* 2, 167–186.

Mattaini, M., & Meyer, C. (2002). *Foundations of social work practice: A graduate text.* Washington, D.C: National Association of Social Workers Press.

Mattison, M. (2012). Social work practice in the digital age: Therapeutic e-mail as a direct practice methodology. *Social Work, 57,* 3, 249–258.

McGoldrick, M., Gerson, R., & Shellenberger, S. (1999) *Genograms: Assessment and intervention.* New York, W.W. Norton.

Miley, K.K., O'Melia, M., & Dubois, B. (2011). *Generalist social work practice. An empowering approach* (6th ed.). Don Mills, ON: Pearson.

Mishna, F., Bogo, M., Root, J., Sawyer, J.L., & Khoury-Kassabri, M. (2012). "It just crept in": The digital age and implications for social work practice. *Clinical Social Work Journal, 40,* 277–286.

Murdoch, J.W., & Connor-Greene, P.A. (2000). Enhancing therapeutic impact and therapeutic alliance through electronic mail homework assignments. *Journal of Psychotherapy Practice and Research, 9,* 232–237.

Nichols, M.P. (2011). *The essentials of family therapy* (5th ed.). Boston, MA: Allyn & Bacon.

Pace, K., & Pizana, D. (2004). *Qualities of authentic relationships across differences.* Michigan: Michigan State University Extension.

Perlman, H. (1957). *Social casework. A problem solving process.* Chicago: The University of Chicago Press.

Poulin, J., & Young, T. (1997). Developments of a helping relationship inventory for social work practice. *Research on Social Work Practice, 7,* 4, 463–489.

Reamer, F.G. (2013). Social work practice in a digital age: Ethical and risk management challenges. *Social Work, 58,* 2, 163–172.

Salabeey, D. (2009). *The strengths perspective in social work practice* (5th ed.). New York: Pearson.

Seabury, B.A., Seabury, B.H., & Garvin, C. (2011) *Foundations of interpersonal practice in social work: Promoting competence in generalist practice* (3rd ed.). Thousand Oaks, CA: Sage.

Tribe, R., & Thompson, K. (2009). Exploring the three-way relationship in therapeutic work with interpreters. *International Journal of Migration, Health and Social Care, 5*, 2, 13–21.

Turner, L. (2005). Social work practice in Canada's officially bilingual province: Challenges and opportunities. *Canadian Social Work Review, 22*, 2, 131–154.

Ungar, M. (2011). *Counselling in challenging contexts: Working with individuals and families across clinical and community settings* (8th ed.). Belmont, CA: Brooks/Cole.

Ward, B. (2012). The cultural genogram: Enhancing the cultural competence of social work students. *Social Work Education, 31*, 5, 570–586.

Whitlock, J., Lader, W., & Conterio, K. (2007). The Internet and self-injury: What psychotherapists should know. *Journal of Clinical Psychology, 63*, 1135–1143.

Zur, O. (2007). *Boundaries in psychotherapy: Ethical and clinical explorations.* Washington, DC: American Psychological Association.

Chapter 5

Alinsky, S. (1971). *Rules for radicals.* New York: Random House.

Alinsky, S. (1941). Community analysis and organization. *American Journal of Sociology, 46*, 6, 798–808.

Barlow, C., Rogers, G., & Coleman, H. (2004). Peer collaboration: A model for field instructor development and support. *The Clinical Supervisor, 22*, 2, 173–190.

Bens, I. (2012). *Facilitating with ease: Core skills for facilitators, team leaders and members, managers, consultants, and trainers* (3rd ed.). San Francisco, CA: John Wiley & Sons.

Boehm, A., & Cnaan, R.A. (2012). Towards a practice-based model for community practice: Linking theory and practice. *Journal of Sociology & Social Welfare, 39, 1*, 141–168.

Brabender, V., Smolar, A.I., & Fallon, A.E. (2004). *Essentials of group therapy.* Hoboken, NJ: Wiley, 2004.

Bronstein, L.R. (2003). A model for interdisciplinary collaboration. *Social Work, 48*, 3, 297–306.

City of Calgary (n.d.). Community Assessment Handbook. Available at http://www.calgary.ca/CSPS/CNS/Pages/Publications-guides-and-directories/Community-Assessment-Handbook/Community-Assessment-Handbook.aspx.

Coholic, D., Lougheed, S., & Lebreton, J. (2009). The helpfulness of holistic arts-based group work with children living in foster care. *Social Work With Groups, 32*, 1–2, 29–46.

Connors, J.V., & Caple, R.B. (2005). A review of group systems theory. *Journal for Specialists in Group Work, 30*, 2, 93–110.

Cooke, D., McNally, L., Mulligan, M., Harrison, J., & Newman, S. (2001). Psychosocial interventions for caregivers of people with dementia: A systematic review. *Aging and Mental Health, 5*, 2, 120–135.

Coyle, G.L. (1930). *Social process in organized groups.* New York: Richard R. Smith.

Dando, H., & Finlon, C. (2003). Social work in an interdisciplinary HIV/AIDS program. In B. Willinger & A. Rice (Eds.), *A history of AIDS social work in hospitals: A daring response to an epidemic.* New York: Haworth.

DiNitto, D.M., & McNeece, C.A. (2008). *Social work issues and opportunities in a challenging profession.* Chicago, IL: Lyceum Books.

Dylan, A. (2003). Talking circles: A traditional form of group work. In N. Sullivan et al. (Eds.), *Social work with groups: Social justice through personal, community and societal change* (pp. 119–134). NY: Haworth Press.

Fall, K. A., & Wejnert, T. J. (2005). Co-leader stages of development: An application of Tuckman and Jensen (1977). *The Journal for Specialists in Group Work, 30*, 4, 309–327.

Fellin, P. (1995). Understanding American communities. In J. Rothman, J.L. Erlich, and J.E. Tropman (Eds.), *Strategies of community intervention* (5th ed.) (pp. 114–128). Itasca, Illinois: F.E. Peacock Publishers.

Forsyth, D. (2010). *Group dynamics* (5th ed.). Belmont, CA: Wadsworth, Cengage Learning.

Freire, P. (1993). *Pedagogy of the oppressed* (1970) (M.B. Ramos, Trans.). New York: Continuum.

Garland, J.A., Jones, E., & Kolodny, R.L. (1976). A model for stages of development in social work groups. In S. Bernstein (ed.), *Explorations in group work: Essays in theory and practice* (pp. 17–71). Boston, MA: Charles River.

Gebbie, K. (1995). A holistic look at the human immunodeficiency virus pandemic. *Holistic Nursing Practice, 10*, 1, 1–9.

Greeley, A.T., Garcia, V.L., Kessler, B.L., & Gilchrest, G. (1992). Training effective multicultural group counselors: Issues for a group training course. *Journal for Specialists in Group Work, 17*, 4, 196–209.

Hales, S., & Cowels, J. (2009). Psycho-educational groups. In I. Soderbick (Ed.), *International Handbook of Occupational Therapy Interventions* (pp. 255–260). New York: Springer.

Hall, J.C. (2011). A Narrative approach to group work for men who batter. *Social Work with Groups, 34*, 2, 175–189.

Hart, M. (2002). *Seeking mino-pimatisiwin: An Aboriginal approach to helping.* Halifax: Fernwood Publishing.

Hartford, M.E. (1971). *Groups in social work.* New York: Columbia University Press.

Hinshaw, A.S., & DeLeon, P. (1995). Toward achieving multidisciplinary professional collaboration. *Professional Psychology: Research and Practice, 26*, 2, 115–116.

Jones, A., & Meier, A. (2011). Growing www.parentsofsuicide: A case study of an online support community. *Social Work with Groups, 34*, 101–120.

Klein, A. (1972). *Effective group work: An introduction to principle and method.* New York: Association Press.

Korazim-Kőrösy, Y., Mizrahi, T., Katz, C., Karmon, A., Garcia, M.L., & Bayne Smith, M. (2007). Towards interdisciplinary community collaboration and development. *Journal of Community Practice, 15*, 1/2, 13–44.

Kosoff, S. (2003). Single session groups: Applications and areas of expertise. *Social Work with Groups, 26*, 1, 29–45.

Kurland, R. (2006). Debunking the "blood theory" of social work with groups: Group workers are made not born. *Social Work with Groups, 30*, 1, 11–24.

Lasker, R.D., & Weiss, E.S. (2003). Creating partnership synergy: The critical role of community stakeholders. *Journal of Health and Human Services Administration, Summer,* 119–139.

Lifshitz, J. (1996). Developing the role of a social worker within a multidisciplinary team in an HIV/AIDS outpatient clinic. *The Social Worker, 64,* 4, 34–42.

Lindsay, J., Roy, V., Montminy, L., Turcotte, D., & Genest-Dufault, S. (2008). The emergence and the effects of therapeutic factors in groups. *Social Work with Groups, 31,* 3–4, 255–271.

Mah, H., & Ives, N. (2011). It takes a village: Perspectives from a multidisciplinary team addressing the needs of HIV+ refugees in Canada. *Refuge, 27,* 75–88.

Marbley, A.F. (2004). His eye is on the sparrow. A counselor of color's perception of facilitating groups with predominantly white members. *The Journal of Specialists in Group Work, 29,* 3, 247–268.

Ohmer, M.L., & DeMasi, K. (2009). *Consensus organizing: A community development workbook: A comprehensive guide to designing, implementing, and evaluating community change initiatives.* Thousand Oaks, CA: Sage.

Palloff, R.M., & Pratt, K. (2001). *Lessons from the cyberspace classroom: The realities of online teaching.* San Francisco, CA: Jossey-Bass.

Parker-Oliver, D., Bronstein, L.R., & Kurzejeski, L. (2005). Examining variables related to successful collaboration on the hospice team. *Health and Social Work, 30,* 4, 279–286.

Pinching, A.J. (1989). Models of clinical care. *AIDS, 3,* Supplement 1, S209–S213.

Poole, J., Gardner, P., Flower, M.C., & Cooper, C. (2009). Narrative therapy, older adults and group work?: Practice, research and recommendations. *Social Work with Groups, 32,* 4, 288–302.

Putnam, R.D. (2000). *Bowling alone: The collapse and revival of American community.* New York: Simon and Schuster.

Putnam, R.D. (1995). Bowling alone: America's declining social capital. *Journal of Democracy, 6,* 1, 65–78.

Rothman, J. (2001). Approaches to community intervention. *Strategies of Community Intervention, 6,* 27–63.

Rothman, J. (1995). Approaches to community intervention. In J. Rothman,
J.L. Erlich, and J.E. Tropman (Eds.), *Strategies of community intervention* (5th ed.) (pp. 26–63). Itasca, Illinois: F.E. Peacock Publishers.

Rothman, J. (1968). *Three models of community organization practice.* New York: Columbia University Press.

Rubin, S. (2011). Tackling taboo topics: Case studies in group work. *Social Work with Groups, 34,* 3–4, 257–269.

Runkel, P.J., Lawrence, M., Oldfield, S., Rider, M., & Clark, C. (1971). Stages of group development: An empirical test of Tuckman's hypothesis. *Journal of Applied Behavioral Science, 7,* 2, 180–193.

Schiller, L.Y. (2007). Not for women only. Applying the relational model of group development with vulnerable populations. *Social Work with Groups, 30,* 2, 11–26.

Shechtman, Z., & Perl-dekel, O. (2008). A comparison of therapeutic factors in two group treatment modalities. Verbal & Art Therapy. *The Journal for Specialists in Group Work, 25,* 3, 288–304.

Smock, K. (2004). *Democracy in action: Community organizing and urban change.* New York: Columbia University Press.

Staples, L. (2012). Community organizing for social justice. Grassroots groups for power. *Social Work with Groups, 35,* 287–96.

Szreter, S., & Woolcock, M. (2004). Health by association? Social capital, social theory and the political economy of public health. *International Journal of Epidemiology, 33,* 4, 650–67.

Teater, B. (2010). *An introduction to applying social work theories and methods.* Maidenhead: Open University Press.

Toseland, R.W., Palmer-Ganeles, J., & Chapman, D. (1986). Teamwork in psychiatric settings. *Social work, 31,* 1, 46–52.

Toseland, R.W., & Rivas, R.F. (2012). Chapter 1 Introduction. The knowledge base of group work practice. *An Introduction to Group Work Practice* (7th ed.) (pp. 11–43). Boston: Allyn & Bacon.

Tuckman, B.W. (1965). Developmental sequence in small groups. *Psychological Bulletin, 63,* 6, 384.

Tuckman, B.W., & Jensen, M.A.C. (1977). Stages of group development revisited. *Group & Organization Management, 2,* 419–427.

Turner, H. (2011). Concepts of effective facilitation of open groups. *Social Work with Groups, 34,* 3–4, 246–256.

Wayne, J. & Gitterman, A. (2004). Offensive behavior in groups: Challenges and opportunities. *Social Work with Groups, 26,* 2, 23–34.

Weil, M., & Ohmer, M.L. (2013). Applying practice theories in community work. In M. Weil, M. Reisch, & M.L. Ohmer (Eds.), *The handbook of community practice* (2nd ed.)(pp. 123–161). Los Angeles, CA: Sage.

Yalom, I.D. (1995). *The theory and practice of group psychotherapy.* Basic Books.

Yalom, I., & Leszcz, M. (2005). *The theory and practice of group psychotherapy* (5th ed.) New York: Basic Books.

Yu, A., & Gregg, C.H. (1993). Asians in groups: More than a matter of cultural awareness. *Journal for Specialists in Group Work, 18,* 2, 86–93.

Chapter 6

Abada, T., Hou, F., & Ram, B. (2008). The effects of harassment and victimization on self-rated health and mental health among Canadian adolescents. *Social Science & Medicine, 67,* 557–567.

Abramovich. I.A. (2012). No safe place to go—LGBTQ youth homelessness in Canada: Reviewing the literature. *Canadian Journal of Family and Youth, 4,* 1, 29–51.

Ahnquist, J., Wamala, S.P., & Lindstrom, M. (2012). Social determinants of health: A question of social or economic capital? *Social Science & Medicine, 74,* 930–939.

Andersen, R.M., Rice, T.H., & Kominski, G.F. (2011). *Changing the US health care system: Key issues in health services policy and management.* Hoboken, NJ: John Wiley & Sons.

Armstrong, P., & Armstrong, H. (2010). *The wasting away of care: The undermining of Canadian health care* (2nd ed.). Oxford: Oxford University Press.

Baker, C.K., Billhardt, K.A., Warren, J., Rollins, C., & Glass, N.E. (2010). Domestic violence, housing instability, and homelessness: A review of housing policies and program practices for meeting the needs of survivors. *Aggression and Violent Behavior, 15,* 430–439.

Baum, A., & Grunberg, N.E. (1991). Gender, stress, and health. *Health Psychology, 10,* 2, 80.

Benzeval, M., Judge, K., & Shuls, S. (2001). Understanding the relationship between income and health: How much can be gleaned from cross-sectional data? *Social Policy & Administration, 35,* 4, 376–396.

Block, S. & Galabuzi, G.-E. (2011). *Canada's colour coded labour market: The gap for racialized workers.* Ottawa: Canadian Centre for Policy Alternatives.

Bouchard, L., Batal, M., Imbeault, P., Gagnon-Arpin, I., Makvandi, E., & Sedigh, G. (2012). La santé des francophones de l'Ontario: Un portrait régional tiré des Enquêtes sur la santé dans les collectivités canadiennes (ESCC). Rapport préparé pour le Bureau des services de santé en français, Ministère de la Santé et des Soins de longue durée. Available at http://www.rrasfo.ca/images/docs/publications/2012/rapport_escc_ontario-final.pdf.

Brunner, E., & Marmot, M. (2005). Social organisation, stress and health. In M. Marmot & R. Wilkinson (Eds.), *Social determinants of health* (2nd ed.) (pp. 17–43). Oxford: Oxford University Press.

Burke, M., & Silver, S. (2013). Canadian health care: Reclaiming universal legacies. In A. Westhues & B. Wharf (Eds.), *Canadian social policy: Issues and Perspectives* (pp. 371–400). Waterloo, ON: Wilfrid Laurier Press.

Cadell, S., Johnson, M., Bosma, H., & Wainright, W. (2010). An overview of contemporary social work practice in palliative care. *Progress in Palliative Care, 18,* 4, 205–211.

Canada Mortgage and Housing Corporation. (2010). *2006 Census housing series: Issue 8—Households in core housing need and spending at least 50% of their income on shelter, research highlight.* Ottawa: CMHC.

Canadian Association of Social Workers. (n.d.). *The role of social work in mental health.* Available at http://www.casw-acts.ca/en/role-social-work-mental-health.

Canadian Council on Learning. (2008, March). *Lessons in learning.* Bullying in Canada: How intimidation affects learning. Available at http://www.ccl-cca.ca/pdfs/LessonsInLearning/Mar-20-08-Bullying-in-Canad.pdf.

Canadian Home Care Association (2008). *Portraits of home care in Canada.*

Ottawa: The Canadian Association of Home Care.

Canadian Homeless Research Network (CHRN). (2012). *The Canadian definition of homelessness.* CHRN. Available at http://www.homelesshub.ca/Library/Canadian-Definition-of-Homelessness-54225.aspx.

Canadian Institute for Health Information (CIHI). (2009). *National Health Expenditure Trends, 1975 to 2009.* ON: CIHI.

Canadian Mental Health Association (CMHA). (n.d.). *What is mental illness?* Available at http://www.cmha.ca/mental_health/what-is-mental-illness/#.Upejk3fWbK1.

Canadian Teacher's Federation. (2009). *Supporting education…building Canada: Child poverty and schools.* Available at http://www.ctf-fce.ca/Research-Library/FINAL_Hilldayleavebehind_eng.pdf.

Canadian Women's Foundation. (n.d.). *Fact sheet: Moving women out of poverty.* Available at http://www.canadian-women.org/sites/canadianwomen.org/files/PDF-FactSheet-EndPoverty-Jan2013.pdf.

Carter, T.S., & Osborne, J. (2009). Housing and neighbourhood challenges of refugee resettlement in declining inner city neighbourhoods: A Winnipeg case study. *Journal of Immigrant & Refugee Studies, 7,* 3, 308–327.

Citizens for Public Justice (CPJ). (2012). *Poverty trends scorecard.* CPJ. Available at www.cpj.ca

Collin, C., & Jensen, H. (2009). *A statistical profile of poverty in Canada, PRB 09-17E.* Social Affairs Division, Library of Parliament.

Community Foundations of Canada (CFC). (2013). *Fertile ground: Sowing the seeds of change in Canada's food system.* Community Foundations of Canada.

Cornish, P.A., Church, E., Callanan, T., Bethune, C., Robbins, C., & Miller, R. (2003). *Telemedicine Journal and e-Health, 9,* 1, 63–71.

Craig, S.L., & Muskat, B. (2013). Bouncers, brokers and glue: The self-described practices of social workers in urban hospitals. *Health & Social Work, 38,* 1, 7–16.

Crompton, S. (2011). What's stressing the stressed? Main sources of stress among workers. *Canadian Social Trends.* Statistics Canada, Catalogue no. 11-008-X.

D'Addario, S., Hiebert, D., & Sherrell, K. (2007). Restricted access: The role of social capital in mitigating absolute homelessness among immigrants and refugees in the GRVD. *Refuge, 24,* 1, 107–115.

Danso, R. (2002). From "There" to "Here": An investigation of the initial settlement experiences of Ethiopian and Somali refugees in Toronto. *GeoJournal, 56,* 1, 3–14.

DeMiglio, L., & Williams, A. (2012). Shared care: the barriers encountered by community based palliative care teams in Ontario. *Health and Social Care in the Community, 20,* 4, 420–429.

Denton, M., Prus, S., & Walters, V. (2004). Gender differences in health: A Canadian study of the psychosocial, structural and behavioural determinants of health. *Social Science & Medicine, 58,* 2585–2600.

Disabled Persons Commission. (2009). *Employment statistics for people with disabilities in Nova Scotia: A statistical report.* Dartmouth, NS: Disabled Persons Commission.

Drake, R.E., Szmukler, G., Mueser K.T., & Thornicroft, (2011). Introduction to community mental health care. In G. Thornicroft, G. Szmukler, & K.T. Mueser (Eds.), *Oxford textbook of community mental health.* Oxford: Oxford University Press.

Due, P., Holstein, B., Lynch, J., Diderichsen, F., Gabhain, S., Scheidt, P., Currie, C., & The Health Behaviour in School-Aged Children Bullying Working Group (2005). Bullying and symptoms among school-aged children: international comparative cross sectional study in 28 countries. *The European Journal of Public Health, 15,* 2, 128–132.

Esposito, T., Trocmé, T., Chabot, M., Shlonsky, A., Collin-Vézina, C., & Sinha, V. (2013). Placement of children in out-of-home care in Québec, Canada: When and for whom initial out-of-home placement is most likely to occur. *Children and Youth Services Review, 25,* 2031–2039.

Evans, P.M. (1997). Divided citizenship? Gender, income security, and the welfare state. In P. M. Evans, & S. Poirier, (Eds.), *Women and the Canadian welfare state: Challenges and changes* (pp 91–115). Toronto: University of Toronto Press.

Forest, P.-G., Marchildon, G.P., & McIntosh, T. (Eds.). (2004). *The governance of health care in Canada: The Romanow Papers, Volume 3.* Toronto: University of Toronto Press.

Freeman, S., Heckman, G., Naus, P.J., & Marston, H.R. (2013). Breaking down barriers. Hospice care as a human right in Canada. *Educational Gerontology, 39,* 4, 241–249.

Friedman-Krauss, A., & Barnett, W.S. (2013). Early childhood education: Pathways to better health. *NIEER Policy Brief, 25.* National Institute for Early Education Research, Rutgers University.

Gaetz, S., Donaldson, J., Richter, T., & Gulliver, T. (2013). *The state of homelessness in Canada 2013.* Toronto: Canadian Homelessness Research Network Press.

Galabuzi, G.E. (2006). *Canada's economic apartheid: The social exclusion of racialized groups in the new century.* Toronto: Canadian Scholars' Press.

Galea, S., & Vlahov, D. (2002). Social determinants and the health of drug users: Socioeconomic status, homelessness, and incarceration. *Public Health Reports, 117,* S135–S145.

Gaumer, B., & Desrosiers, G. (2004). L'histoire des CLSC au Québec: Reflet des contradictions et des luttes à l'intérieur du Réseau. *Ruptures, 10,* 1, 52–70.

Gaumer, B., & Fleury, M.-J. (2008). CLSCs in Quebec: Thirty years of community action. *Social Work in Public Health, 23,* 4, 89–106.

Government of Canada. (2006). *The human face of mental health and mental illness in Canada.* Minister of Public Works and Government Services Canada.

Guest, D. (1997). *The emergence of social security in Canada* (3rd ed.). Vancouver: UBC Press.

Guttmann, A., Shipman, S.A., Lam, K., Goodman, D.C., & Stukel, T.A. (2010). Primary care physician supply and children's health care use, access, and outcomes: Findings from Canada. *Pediatrics, 125,* 1119–1126.

Health Canada. (2012). Canada's Health Care System. Available at http://www .hc-sc.gc.ca/hcs-sss/pubs/system-regime/2011-hcs-sss/index-eng .php#a3

Health Council of Canada. (2013). Canada's most vulnerable: Improving health care for First Nations, Inuit and Metis seniors. Health Council of Canada. Available at http://www .healthcouncilcanada.ca/content_bh .php?mnu=2&mnu1=48&mnu2=30& mnu3=55.

Hiebert, D.J., Germain, A., Murdie, R., Preston, V., Renaud, J., Rose, D., Wyly, E., Ferreira,V., Mendez, P., & Murnaghan, A.M. (2006). *The housing situation and needs of recent immigrants in the Montréal, Toronto, and Vancouver CMAs: An overview.* Ottawa, ON: Canada Mortgage and Housing Corporation.

Human Resources and Skills Development Canada. (2012). *The National Shelter Study 2005–2009.* Homelessness partnership strategy, HRSDC. Available at http://www.esdc.gc.ca/eng/ communities/homelessness/reports/ shelter_study.shtml.

Human Resources and Skills Development Canada. (2011). *Disability in Canada: A 2006 Profile.* Available at http://www .esdc.gc.ca/eng/disability/arc/disability_ 2006.pdf.

Human Resources and Skills Development Canada. (n.d.). Indicators of well-being in Canada: Work—Unemployment rate. Available at http://www4.hrsdc .gc.ca/.3ndic.1t.4r@-eng.jsp?iid=16.

Hurrelmann, K., & Richter, M. (2006). Risk behaviour in adolescence: The relationship between developmental and health problems. *Journal of Public Health, 14,* 20–28.

Ives, N., Sinha, V., Leman, D., Goren, A., Levy-Powell, R., & Thomson, W. (2012). Exploring the intersection of culture and education in Nunavik. *Journal of Comparative Social Work, 1.* http://jcsw.no/local/media/jcsw/docs/ jcsw_issue_2012_1_3_article.pdf.

Johnson, M.E., Brems, C., & Burke, S. (2002). Recognizing comorbidity among drug users in treatment. *American Journal of Drug and Alcohol Abuse, 28,* 2, 243–261.

Kidd, S.A. (2007). Youth homelessness and social stigma. *Journal of Youth and Adolescence, 36,* 3, 291–299.

Kirmayer, L.J., Tait, C.L., & Simpson, C. (2009). The mental health of Aboriginal Peoples in Canada: Transformations of identity and community. In L.J. Kirmayer & G.G. Valaskakis (Eds.), *Healing traditions: The mental health of Aboriginal Peoples in Canada* (pp. 3–35). Vancouver: UBC Press.

Kosteniuk, J.G., & Dickinson, H.D. (2003). Tracing the social gradient in the health of Canadians: Primary and secondary determinants. *Social Science & Medicine, 57,* 263–276.

Lasser, K.E., Himmelstein, D.U., & Woolhandler, S. (2006). Access to care, health status, and health disparities in the United States and Canada: Results of a cross-national population-based survey. *American Journal of Public Health, 96,* 7, 1300–1307.

Lawlor, D. A., Davey Smith, G., Patel, R., & Ebrahim, S. (2005). Life-course socioeconomic position, area deprivation, and coronary heart disease: Findings from the British Women's Heart and Health Study. *American Journal of Public Health, 95,* 91–97.

Leloup, X., &. Zhu, N. (2006). Différence dans la qualite; de logement: Immigrants et non-immigrants à Montréal, Toronto et Vancouver. *Journal of International Migration and Integration, 7,* 2, 134–166.

Lenon, S. (2000). Living on the edge: Women, poverty, and homelessness in Canada. *Canadian Women's Studies/Les cahiers de la femme, 20,* 3, 123–126.

Link, B., & Phelan, J.C. (1996). Understanding sociodemographic differences in health: The role of fundamental social causes [editorial]. *American Journal of Public Health, 86,* 4, 471–2.

Macdonald, D., & Wilson, D. (2013). *Poverty or prosperity: Indigenous children in Canada.* Canadian Centre for Policy Alternatives. Available at http://www .policyalternatives.ca/publications/ reports/poverty-or-prosperity.

Madore, O. (2005). *The Canada Health Act: Overview and options.* Parliamentary Information and Research Service, Issue 94-4E, Library of Parliament.

Maioni, A. (2010). Citizenship and health care in Canada. *International Journal of Canadian Studies/Revue internationale d'études canadiennes, 42,* 225–242.

Maioni, A. (2004). Roles and responsibilities in health care policy. In T. McIntosh, P.G. Forest, & G.P. Marchildon (Eds.), *The governance of health care in Canada: The Romanow papers* (pp. 169–198). Toronto: University of Toronto Press.

Marchildon, G.P. (2009). The policy history of Medicare. *Canadian Bulletin of Medical History/Bulletin canadien d'histoire de la médecine, 26,* 2, 247–260.

Marchildon G.P., & Torgerson, R. (2013). *Nunavut: A health system profile*. Montreal: McGill-Queen's University Press.

Marmot, M. (2005). Social determinants of health inequalities. *The Lancet, 365*, 1099–104.

Marmot, M., & Wilkinson, R.G. (2005). (Eds.). *Social determinants of health* (2nd ed.). Oxford: Oxford University Press.

McDonough, P., & Walters, V. (2001). Gender and health: Reassessing patterns and explanations. *Social Science & Medicine, 52*, 4, 547–559.

McDonough, P., Walters, V., & Strohschein, L. (2002). Chronic stress and the social patterning of women's health in Canada. *Social Science & Medicine, 54*, 5, 767–782.

Meshesha, L.Z., Tsui, J. I., Liebschutz, J.M., Crooks, D., Anderson, B. J., Herman, D.S., & Stein, M.D. (2013). Days of heroin use predict poor self-reported health in hospitalized heroin users. *Addictive Behaviors, 38*, 12, 2884–2887.

Mikkonen, J., & Raphael, D. (2010). *Social determinants of health: The Canadian facts*. Toronto, ON: York University School of Health Policy and Management.

Mirowsky, J., & Ross, C.E. (2003). *Education, social status and health*. Hawthorne, New York: Walter de Gruyter.

Muennig, P., Schweinhart, L., Montie, J., & Neidell, M. (2009). Effects of a prekindergarten educational intervention on adult health: 37-year follow-up results of a randomized controlled trial. *American Journal of Public Health, 99*, 8, 1431–1437.

Ontario Association of Social Workers. (2004). *Social work in hospital-based health care*. Toronto: OASW.

Organisation for Economic Co-operation and Development. (OECD). (2008). *Growing unequal: Income distribution and poverty in OECD nations*. Paris: Organisation for Economic Co-operation and Development. Available at http://www.oecd-ilibrary.org/social-issues-migration-health/growing-unequal_9789264044197-en.

OECD. (2003). *Transforming disability into ability: Policies to promote work and income security for disabled people*. Paris: Organisation for Economic Co-operation and Development.

OECD. (2002). *OECD territorial reviews: Canada*. Paris: Organisation for Economic Co-operation and Development.

Parliament of Canada. (n.d.). *The health of Canadians—the federal role*. Final report, Vol. 6: Recommendations for Reform. Available at http://www.parl.gc.ca/content/sen/committee/372/soci/rep/repoct02vol6part7-e.htm.

Patton, G.C., Coffey, C., Carlin, J.B., Degenhardt, L., Lynskey, M., & Hall, W. (2002). Cannabis use and mental health in young people: Cohort study. *British Medical Journal, 325*, 1195–1198.

Pearson, C., Janz, T., & Ali, J. (2013, September). Mental and substance use disorders in Canada. *Health at a Glance*, Statistics Canada Catalogue no. 82-624-X.

Phipps, S. (2003). *The impact of poverty on health: A scan of research literature*. Ottawa, ON: Canadian Population Health Initiative.

Plourde, C. (2007). *Psychoactive substance use among Nunavik youths: Results of the survey*. Summary Report presented to Canadian Institutes of Health Research (CIHR). Nunavik Regional Board of Health and Social Services.

Quan, H., Fong, A., De Coster, C., Wang, J., Musto, R., Noseworthy, T.M., & Ghali, W.A. (2006). Variation in health services utilization among ethnic populations. *Canadian Medical Association Journal, 174*, 6, 787–791.

Ramji, S., & Quiñonez, C. (2012). Public preferences for government spending in Canada. *International Journal for Equity in Health, 11*, 1, 64–73.

Randall, G.E. (2008). The impact of managed competitions on diversity, innovation and creativity in home care services. *Health and Social Care in the Community, 16*, 4, 347–353.

Raphael, D. (2011). *Poverty in Canada: Implications for health and quality of life* (2nd ed.). Toronto: Canadian Scholars' Press.

Raphael, D. (2009). *Social determinants of health* (2nd ed.). Toronto: Canadian Scholars' Press.

Ray, B. & Preston, V. (2009). Are immigrants socially isolated? An assessment of neighbours and neighboring in Canadian cities. *Journal of International Migration & Integration, 10*, 3, 217–244.

Romanow, R.J. (2002). *Building on values: The future of health care in Canada*.

Final report to the Commission on the Future of Health Care in Canada. National Library of Canada CP32-85/2002E.

Rose, D. (2001). The housing situation of refugees in Montreal three years after arrival: The case of asylum seekers who obtained permanent residence. *Journal of International Migration and Integration/ Revue de l'integration et de la migration internationale, 2*, 4, 493–529.

Schmid, H., & Nic Gabhain, S. (2004). Alcohol use. In C. Currie, C. Roberts, A. Morgan, R. Smith, W. Settertobulte, O. Samdal, V. Barnekow Rasmussen (eds.), *Young people's health in context— Health behaviour in school-aged children (HBSC) study: International report from the 2001/02 survey (pp. 73–83)*. WHO-Europe, Copenhagen.

Selye, H. (1973). The evolution of the stress concept: The originator of the concept traces its development from the discovery in 1936 of the alarm reaction to modern therapeutic applications of syntoxic and catatoxic hormones. *American Scientist, 61*, 6, 692–699.

Sharif, N., Dar, A.A., & Amaratunga, C. (2000). *Ethnicity, income and access to health care in the Atlantic region: A synthesis of the literature*. Dalhousie University/IWK Health Centre: Maritime Centre of Excellence for Women's Health.

Sibley, L.M., & Weiner, J.P. (2011). An evaluation of access to health care services along the rural-urban continuum in Canada. *BMC Health Services Research* (online), 11, 20.

Smye, V., & Mussell, B. (2001). *Aboriginal mental health: "What works best." A discussion paper*. University of British Columbia Mental Health Evaluation & Community Consultation Unit.

Statistics Canada. (2013). Statistics Canada, *Table 202-0102—Average female and male earnings, and female-to-male earnings ratio, by work activity, 2007 constant dollars, annual*, CANSIM database.

Statistics Canada. (2006). *Aboriginal Peoples in Canada in 2006: Inuit, Métis and First Nations, 2006 Census*. Catalogue no. 97-558-XIE.

Tait, H. (2008). *Aboriginal Peoples Survey, 2006: Inuit health and social conditions*. Social and Aboriginal Statistics Division. Ottawa, ON: Statistics Canada. Catalogue no. 89-637-X—No. 001.

Tester, F.J., & McNicoll, P. (2004). Isumagijaksaq: Mindful of the state: Social constructions of Inuit suicide. *Social Science & Medicine, 58,* 2625–2636.

Timony, P.E., Gauthier, A.P., Hogenbirk, J.C., & Wenghofer, E.F. (2013). Promising quantities, disappointing distribution. Investigating the presence of French-speaking physicians in Ontario's rural Francophone communities. *Rural and Remote Health, 13,* 2543.

United Nations Development Programme (UNDP). (2010). *The real wealth of nations: Pathways to human development. Human Development Report 2010.* UNDP.

UNICEF Office of Research (2013). Child well-being in rich countries: A comparative overview, *Innocenti Report Card 11.* Florence, Italy: UNICEF Office of Research.

Veenstra, G. (2009). Racialized identity and health in Canada: Results from a nationally representative survey. *Social Science & Medicine, 69,* 4, 538–542.

Verbrugge, L.M. (1985). Gender and health: An update on hypotheses and evidence. *Journal of Health and Social Behavior, 26,* 3, 156–182.

Vosko, L. (2006). *Precarious employment: Understanding labour market insecurity in Canada.* Montreal, McGill-Queen's. University Press.

Waldram, J.B., Herring, A.D., & Young, T.K. (2006). Aboriginal peoples and the health transition. In *Aboriginal Health in Canada* (2nd ed.)(pp. 73–125). Toronto: University of Toronto Press.

Watkins, K.E., Hunter, S.B., Wenzel, S.L., Tu, W., Paddock, S.M., Griffin, A., & Ebener, P. (2004). Prevalence and characteristics of clients with co-occurring disorders in outpatient substance abuse treatment. *American Journal of Drug and Alcohol Abuse, 30,* 4, 749–764.

Wilder Craig, R. (2007). A day in the life of a hospital social worker: Presenting our role through the personal narrative. *Qualitative Social Work, 6,* 431–447.

Wilkinson, R., & Marmot, M. (2003). *Social determinants of health: The solid facts* (2nd ed.). Copenhagen, WHO Regional Office for Europe: World Health Organization.

Williams, A.M., Crooks, V.A., Whitfield, K., Kelley, M.L., Richards, J.L., DeMiglio, L., & Dykeman, S. (2010). Tracking the evolution of hospice palliative care in Canada: A comparative case study analysis of seven provinces. *BMC Health Services Research, 10,* 1, 147.

Williams, C. (2010). Economic well-being. In *Women in Canada: A gender-based statistical report.* Statistics Canada. Available at http://www.statcan.gc.ca/pub/89-503-x/2010001/article/11388-eng.pdf.

Williams, C. (2006). Disability in the workplace. *Perspectives, February,* 17–24. Statistics Canada—Catalogue no. 75-001-XIE.

Wilson, D., & Macdonald, D. (2010). *The income gap between Aboriginal Peoples and the rest of Canada.* Ottawa, ON: Canadian Centre for Policy Alternatives. Available at http://mail.policyalternatives.org/sites/default/files/uploads/publications/reports/docs/Aboriginal%20Income%20Gap.pdf.

Wilson, K., & Rosenberg, M.W. (2002). Exploring the determinants of health for First Nations peoples in Canada: Can existing frameworks accommodate traditional activities? *Social Science & Medicine, 55,* 11, 2017–2031.

Zhang, X. (2009). Earnings of women with and without children. *Perspectives on Labour and Income, 10,* 3, 9.

Chapter 7

Alvi, S. (2002). A criminal justice history of children and youth in Canada. In B. Schissel & C. Brooks, (Eds.). *Marginality and condemnation.* Halifax: Fernwood.

Angus Reid Group. (1998). *Canadian attitudes toward the Young Offenders Act.* Ottawa, Canada: Author.

Baker, K., Kelly, G., & Wilkinson, B. (2011). *Assessment in youth justice.* Bristol: Policy Press.

Bala, N. (2011). Setting the context: Child welfare law in Canada. In K. Kufeldt & B. McKenzie, (Eds.), *Child welfare: Connecting research, policy and practice.* Waterloo: Wilfred Laurier University Press.

Bala, N. (2005). The development of Canada's youth justice law. In K. Campbell, (Ed.), *Understanding youth justice in Canada.* Toronto: Pearson Education.

Brade, C. (2007). Have we really come that far? Child welfare legislation in Ontario. *OACAS Journal, 51,* 4, 1–18.

Brennan, S. (2012) *Youth court statistics in Canada, 2010/2011.* Statistics Canada. Retrieved from http://www.statcan.gc.ca/pub/85-002-x/2012001/article/11645-eng.pdf.

Cameron, G., Freymond, N., Cornfield, D., & Palmer, S. (2007). Positive possibilities for child and family welfare: Expanding the Anglo-American Child Protection Paradigm. In G. Cameron & G. Adams (Eds.), *Moving toward positive systems of child and family welfare: Current Issues and Future Directions.* Waterloo: Wilfrid Laurier University Press.

Canadian Association of Social Workers. (2012). *Social work practice in child welfare.* Available at http://www.casw-acts.ca/en/social-work-practice-child-welfare.

Calverly, D., Cotter, A., & Halla, E. (2010) Youth custody and community service in Canada, 2008/2009, *Juristat, 30,* 1.

Cash, S. (2001) Risk assessment in child welfare: The art and the science. *Children and Youth Services Review, 23,* 11, 811–830.

Chartrand, L. (2005). Aboriginal youth and the criminal justice system. In K. Campbell, (Ed.), *Understanding youth justice in Canada.* Toronto: Pearson Education.

Chartrand, L., & McKay, C. (2006). *A review of research on criminal victimization and First Nations, Metis and Inuit Peoples 1990–2001.* Policy Centre for Victim Services, Department of Justice Services.

Covell, K., & Howe, B. (2001). *The challenge of children's rights for Canada.* Waterloo: Wilfred Laurier University Press.

Denov, M. (2005). Children's rights, juvenile justice and the UN convention on the rights of the child: Implications for Canada. In K. Campbell (Ed.), *Understanding Youth Justice in Canada.* Toronto: Pearson Education.

Freeman, M. (1997). *The moral status of children.* The Hague: Martinus Nijhoff.

Galloway, G., & Séguin, R. (2012, September 10). Harper's promise fulfilled as House passes crime bill. *The Globe and Mail.* Available at: http://www.theglobeandmail.com/news/politics/ottawa-notebook/harpers-promise-fulfilled-as-house-passes-crime-bill/article535802/.

Goldson, B. (2001). A rational youth justice? Some critical reflection on the research, policy and practice relation. *Probation Journal, 48*, 2, 76–85.

Green, G., & Healy, K. (2003). *Tough on kids: Rethinking approaches to youth justice.* Saskatoon, SK: Purich Publishing.

Hogeveen, B. (2005). History, development, and transformations in Canadian juvenile justice, 1800–1984. In K. Campbell (Ed.), *Understanding youth justice in Canada.* Toronto: Pearson Education.

Johnston, P. (1983). *Native children and the child welfare system.* Toronto: Canadian Council on Social Development in association with James Lorimer & Co.

Kemper, Y. 2005. *Youth in war to peace transitions.* Berlin: Berghof Research Center for Constructive Conflict Management.

Kufeldt, K., & McKenzie, B. (Eds.). (2011). *Child welfare: Connecting research, policy and practice.* Waterloo: Wilfred Laurier University Press.

Latimer, J. (2001). A meta-analytic examination of youth delinquency, family treatment, and recidivism. *Canadian Journal of Criminology, 43,* 237–253.

Leahy, R. (2003). *Cognitive therapy techniques: A practitioner's guide.* London: Guilford Press.

Mallea, P. (1999). *Getting tough on kids: Young offenders and the "law and order" agenda.* Winnipeg: Canadian Centre for Policy Alternatives.

McLellan, A. (1999, May 12). [Press Release]. Remarks by [then] federal Justice Minister, Department of Justice.

National Council of Welfare. (2007). *Poverty Profile 2007.*

Parliament of Canada. (1997). *13th Report of the Standing Committee on Justice and Legal Affairs.*

Pickford, D., & Dugmore, P. (2012). *Youth justice and social work.* London: Sage.

Pilote, A., & Magnan, M. (2012) La construction identitaire des jeunes francophones en situation minoritaire au canada: négociation des frontières linguistiques au fil du parcours universitaire et de la mobilité géographique. *Canadian Journal of Sociology, 37,* 2, 169–195.

Public Health Agency of Canada. (2010). *Canadian incidence study of reported child abuse and neglect, 2008: Major findings.* Retrieved from http://www.phac-aspc.gc.ca/ncfv-cnivf/pdfs/nfnts-cis-2008-rprt-eng.pdf.

Roberts, J. (2003). Sentencing juvenile offenders in Canada: An analysis of recent reform legislation. *Journal of Contemporary Criminal Justice, 19,* 4, 413–434.

Royal Commission on Aboriginal Peoples. (1996). *Aboriginal peoples and the criminal justice system.* Report of the National Round Table on Justice Issues. Ottawa: Canada Communications Group.

Schissel, B. (2011). *About Canada: Children and youth.* Winnipeg: Fernwood Publishing.

Sinha, M. (2012). *Family violence in Canada: A statistical profile, 2010.* Statistics Canada. Retrieved from http://www.statcan.gc.ca/pub/85-002-x/2012001/article/11643-eng.pdf.

Sinha, V., Trocmé, N., Blackstock, C., MacLaurin, B., & Fallon, B. (2011). Understanding the overrepresentation of Indigenous children in Canada's child welfare system. In K. Kufeldt & B. McKenzie, B. (Eds.), *Child welfare: Connecting research, policy and practice.* Waterloo: Wilfred Laurier University Press.

Smith, G., Dorling, D., Gordon, D. and Shaw, M. (1999). The widening health gap: What are the solutions? *Critical Public Health, 9,* 2, 151–70.

Sprott, J. (1998). Understanding public opposition to a separate youth justice system. *Crime and Delinquency, 44,* 399–411.

Statistics Canada. (2011). *Family violence in Canada: A statistical profile.* Ottawa: Minister of Industry.

Statistics Canada. (2007). *Youth custody and community services.* http://www.statcan.ca/Daily/English/070314/d070314d.htm.

Statistics Canada (2001). *Aboriginal peoples in Canada: Canadian Centre for Justice statistics profile series.* Ottawa: Ministry of Industry.

Swift, K., & Callahan, M. (2006), Problems and potential of Canadian child welfare. In N. Freymond & G. Cameron, (Eds.), *Towards positive systems of child and family welfare.* Toronto: University of Toronto Press.

Todres, J. (1998). Emerging limitations on the rights of the child: The U.N. Convention on the Rights of the Child and its early case law. *Columbia Human Rights Law Review, 30,* 159–200.

Tufts, J., & Roberts, J. (2002). Sentencing juvenile offenders: Comparing public preferences and judicial practice. *Criminal Justice Policy Review, 13,* 1, 46–64.

UNICEF. (2012). *Measuring child poverty: Report Card 10.* UNICEF Innocenti Research Centre.

White, R., & Graham, H. (2010). Working with offenders: A guide to concepts and practices. New York: Willan.

Wiig, J., & Tuell. J. (2008). *Guidebook for juvenile justice & child welfare system coordination and integration: A Framework for improved outcomes.* Arlington VA: Child Welfare League of America.

Chapter 8

Aboriginal Healing and Wellness Strategy. (2012). *Goal of the Aboriginal healing and wellness strategy.* Retrieved from http://www.mcss.gov.on.ca/en/mcss/programs/community/ahws/goal_strategy.aspx.

Aboriginal Healing Foundation. (2008). *From truth to reconciliation: Transforming the legacy of residential schools.* Retrieved from http://www.ahf.ca/downloads/from-truth-to-reconciliation-transforming-the-legacy-of-residential-schools.pdf.

Aboriginal Healing Foundation. (2006). *Métis history and experience and residential schools in Canada* (pp. 9–30). Ottawa, ON: Aboriginal Healing Foundation.

Andersen, C. (2011). Moya 'Tipimsook ("The People Who Aren't Their Own Bosses"): Racialization and the misrecognition of "Métis" in Upper Great Lakes. *Ethnohistory, 58,* 1, 37–63. doi: 10.1215/00141801-2010-063.

Anderson, K. (2011). *Life stages and Native women: Memory, teachings and story medicine.* Winnipeg: University of Manitoba Press.

Annett, K.D., & Lawless, L. (Producers). (2007). Unrepentant [DVD]. Available from http://www.hiddenfromhistory.org/.

Archibald, L., Dewar, J., Reid, C., & Stevens, V. (2012). *Dancing, singing, painting, and speaking the healing story: Healing through creative arts.* Ottawa, ON: Aboriginal Healing Foundation.

Baskin, C. (2012). The Seven Fires Prophesies: Pre-contact, colonization and today. Power Point Presentation.

Baskin, C. (2011). *Strong helpers' teachings: The value of Indigenous knowledges in the helping professions.* Toronto: Canadian Scholars' Press Inc.

Baskin, C. (2002). Circles of resistance: Spirituality in social work practice, education and transformative change. *Currents: New scholarship in the human services, 1,* 1. http://fsw.ucalgary.ca/currents/articles/cyndy_baskin/baskin_main.htm.

Baskin, C., Strike, C., & McPherson, B. (In press). Women of the shining light: A story from the southern direction. In R. Sinclair (Ed.), *Kiskeyihtamowin: Aboriginal social work theory, praxis and critique.* Winnipeg: Brunswick Press.

Baskin, C., Strike, C. & McPherson, B. (2012). Using the Seven Sacred Teachings to improve services for Aboriginal mothers experiencing drug and alcohol misuse problems and involvement with child welfare. In D. Newhouse, K. FitzMaurice, T. McGuire-Adams, & D. Jette (Eds.), *Well-being in the urban Aboriginal community: Fostering biimaadiziwin, a national research conference on urban Aboriginal Peoples.* Toronto: Thompson Educational Publishing Inc.

Bishop, A. (2005). *Beyond token change: Breaking the cycle of oppression in institutions.* Halifax, Canada: Fernwood Publishing.

Bishop, A. (1994). *Becoming an ally: Breaking the cycle of oppression.* Halifax: Fernwood Publishing.

Blackstock, C. (2012). Moving forward in hope. In D. Fuchs, S. McKay, & I. Brown (Eds.), *Awakening the spirit: Moving forward in child welfare, voices from the prairies* (pp. xvii-xxiv). Regina, SK: Canadian Plains Research Centre.

Blackstock, C. (2011). Wanted: Moral courage in Canadian child welfare. *First Peoples Child & Family Review 6,* 35–46.

Blackstock, C. (2008). *Rooting mental health in an Aboriginal worldview.* Ottawa:

The Centre of Excellence for Child and Youth Mental Health at CHEO.

Brave Heart, M.Y.H. (2004). The historical trauma response among Natives and its relationship to substance abuse. In E. Nebelkoph & M. Phillips (Eds.), *Healing and mental health for Native Americans: Speaking in red* (pp. 7–18). Lanham, MD: AltaMira Press. Also in *Journal of Psychoactive Drugs 35, 1,* 7–13.

Brave Heart, M.Y.H. (2000). Wakiksuyapi: Carrying the historical trauma of the Lakota. *Tulane Studies in Social Welfare, 21–22,* 245–266.

Brave Heart, M.Y.H. (1999). Oyate Ptayela: Rebuilding the Lakota Nation through addressing historical trauma among Lakota parents. *Journal of Human Behavior and the Social Environment, 2,* 1/2, 109–126.

Brave Heart, M.Y.H. (1998). The return to the Sacred Path: Healing the historical trauma response among the Lakota. *Smith College Studies in Social Work, 68,* 3, 287–305.

Canadian Association of Social Workers (2013). *Joint statement supporting Indigenous Peoples.* Retrieved from www.casw-acts.ca/en/news/press-release.

Canadian Association of Social Workers. (2005). *What is social work?* And *Code of Ethics: The preamble.* Ottawa, Canada: Canadian Association of Social Workers.

Canadian Roots Exchange. (2012). About Canadian Roots: Who are the Canadian Roots Exchange? Retrieved from http://www.canadianroots.ca/.

Canda, E. (1989). Religious content in social work education: A comparative approach. *Journal of Social Work Education, 25,* 1, 36–45.

Carniol, B. (2005). Analysis of social location and change: Practice implications. In S. Hick, R. Pozzuto, & J. Fook, (Eds.), *Social work: A critical turn* (pp. 153–166). Toronto, Canada: Thompson Educational Publishing.

Castellano, M. Brant. (2006). *Final report of the Aboriginal Healing Foundation, Volume I: A healing journey: Reclaiming wellness.* Ottawa, ON: Aboriginal Healing Foundation.

CBC Learning (2012a). *8th fire: At the crossroads.* Toronto: CBC.

CBC Learning (2012b). *8th fire: It's time.* Toronto: CBC.

Crichlow, W. (2002). Western colonization as disease: Native adoption and cultural

genocide. *Critical Social Work, 3,* 1. Retrieved from http://www.uwindsor.ca/criticalsocialwork.

Dion Stout, M. & Kipling, G. (2003). *Aboriginal people, resilience and the residential school legacy.* Ottawa, ON: Aboriginal Healing Foundation.

Duran, E., (2006*). Healing the soul wound: Counseling with American Indians and other NativePeoples.* New York: Teachers College Press.

Duran, E., & Duran, B. (1995). *Native American postcolonial psychology.* Albany, NY: State University of New York Press.

Fiske, J. (2008). Making the intangible manifest: Healing practices of the Qul-Aun Trauma Program. In J.B. Waldram (Ed.), *Aboriginal healing in Canada: Studies in therapeutic meaning and practice.* Ottawa, ON: Aboriginal Healing Foundation.

Fletcher, C., & Denham, A. (2008). Moving toward healing: A Nunavut case study. In J.B. Waldram (Ed.), *Aboriginal healing in Canada: Studies in therapeutic meaning and practice.* Ottawa, ON: Aboriginal Healing Foundation.

Fontaine, T. (2010). *Broken circle: The dark legacy of Indian residential schools, a memoir.* Surrey, BC: Heritage House Publishing.

Fournier, S., & Crey, E. (1997). *Stolen from our embrace: The abduction of First Nations children and the restoration of Aboriginal communities.* Vancouver: Douglas & McIntyre.

General Synod Archives. (2008). *Anglican Church of Canada: Mission and justice relationships.* Retrieved from http://www.anglican.ca/relationships/trc/histories/gordons-school-punnichy.

Gone, J.P. (2008). The Pisimweyapiy Counselling Centre: Paving the red road to wellness in Northern Manitoba. In J.B. Waldram (Ed.), *Aboriginal healing in Canada: Studies in therapeutic meaning and practice.* Ottawa, ON: Aboriginal Healing Foundation.

Gordon, J. (2013). *History of Idle No More grassroots movement.* Retrieved from http://idlenomore.ca/index.php/about-us/item/1-history-of-idle-no-more-grassroots-movement.

Gosek, G. & Bennett, M. (2012). A day's discourse among Aboriginal scholars and practitioners about child welfare work in Canada. *Awakening the spirit: Moving forward in child welfare, voices from the prairies* (pp. 23–26). Regina, SK: Canadian Plains Research Centre.

Gray, L. (2011). *First Nations 101.* Vancouver: Adaawx Publishing.

Hart, M. (2002). *Seeking mino-pimatisiwin: An Aboriginal approach to helping.* Halifax: Fernwood Publishing.

Haudenosaunee Grand Council (2012). Haudenosaunee Grand Council position on Canada's Bill C-45, press release. NY: Onondaga Nation Territory.

Indian and Northern Affairs Canada (2004). *Residential Schools.* Retrieved from http://www.ainc-inac.gc.ca/ach/lr/ks/plhst/plhst_rsscl-eng.asp.

Jacobs, B., & Williams, A. (2008). *From truth to reconciliation: Transforming the legacy of residential schools. Missing and murdered Aboriginal women* (pp. 119–142). Ottawa: Dollco Printing.

Kirmayer, L.J., Fletcher, C., & Watt, R. (2009). Locating the ecocentric self: Inuit concepts of mental health and illness. In Kirmayer, L. & Valaskakis, G. (Eds.), *Healing traditions: The mental health of Aboriginal peoples in Canada* (pp. 289–314). Vancouver: University of British Columbia Press.

Kral, M.J. (1998). Suicide and the internalization of culture: Three questions. *Transcultural Psychiatry, 35,* 2, 221–233.

Kral, M.J. (1994). Suicide as social logic. *Suicide and Life-threatening Behavior 24,* 3, 245–255.

Kral, M.J., & Idlout, L. (2009). Community wellness and social action in the Canadian Arctic: Collective agency as subjective well-being. In L. Kirmayer, & G. Valaskakis, (Eds.). *Healing traditions: The mental health of Aboriginal peoples in Canada* (pp. 315–334). Vancouver: University of British Columbia Press.

Laprairie, C. (2005). Aboriginal peoples and the Canadian criminal justice system. In D. R. Newhouse, C. J. Voyageur, & D. Beavon (Eds.), *Hidden in plain sight: Contributions of Aboriginal peoples to Canadian identity and culture* (pp. 236–245). Toronto: University of Toronto Press.

Mawhiney, A., & Nabigon, H, (2011). Aboriginal theory: A Cree medicine wheel guide for healing first nations. In. F.J. Turner (Ed.), *Social work treatment: Interlocking theoretical approaches* (5th ed., pp. 15–29). New York: Oxford University Press.

McFarlane, C. (February 2013). Idle No More is for everyone. *Native Canadian Centre of Toronto Newsletter,* p. 3.

Milloy, J. (1999). A national crime: The Canadian Government and the residential school system, 1879–1986. Winnipeg: University of Manitoba Press.

Morrissette, V., McKenzie, B., & Morrissette, L. (1993). Towards an Aboriginal model of social work practice. *Canadian Social Work Review, 10,* 1, 91–108.

Mullaly, R. (2002). *Challenging oppression: A critical social work approach.* Toronto: Oxford University Press.

Mullaly, R. (1997). *Structural social work.* Toronto: Oxford University Press.

Mullaly, B. (2010). *Challenging oppression and confronting privilege.* Don Mills, Canada: Oxford University Press.

Nabigon, H.C., & Wenger-Nabigon, A. (2012). *"Wise practices":* Integrating traditional teachings with mainstream treatment approaches. *Native Social Work Journal 8,* 43–55.

Neal, A.G. (1998). *National trauma and collective memory: Major events in the American century.* New York: M.E. Sharpe Publishing.

Ontario Association of Children's Aid Societies. (2011). *First Canadian conference on family group conferencing: Honouring the circle, connections and wisdom.* Toronto: OACAS.

Pannekoek, F. (2001). Métis studies: The development of a field and new directions. In T. Binnema, G.J. Ens, & R.C. Macleod (Eds.). *From Rupert's Land to Canada: Essays in honour of John E. Foster* (pp. 111–128). Edmonton, Alberta: University of Alberta Press.

Regan, P. (2010). *Unsettling the settler within: Indian residential schools, truth telling and reconciliation in Canada.* Vancouver: University of British Columbia Press.

Reimer, G., & Chartrand, J. (2004). Documenting historic Métis in Ontario. *Ethnohistory 5,* 3, 567–607. doi: 10.1215/00141801-51-3-(3)

Royal Commission on Aboriginal Peoples. (2004). *Perspectives and realities: The search for belonging, perspectives of youth.* Ottawa: Indian and Northern Affairs Canada.

Royal Commission on Aboriginal Peoples. (1996). *Aboriginal peoples and the criminal justice system.* Report of the National Round Table on Justice Issues. Ottawa: Canada Communications Group.

Sherwin, C. (2010). *Experiences with family group decision making in rural Ontario.*

(Unpublished doctoral dissertation). University of Victoria, Victoria, BC.

Sinclair, R. (2009). Identity or racism? Aboriginal transracial adoption. In R. Sinclair, M. A. Hart, & G. Bruyere (Eds.), *Wicihitowin: Aboriginal social work in Canada* (pp. 89–113). Winnipeg: Fernwood Publishing.

Statistics Canada. (2008). *Aboriginal peoples highlight tables, 2006 census.* (97-558-XIE) Retrieved from http://www12.statcan.ca.

Thunderbird, S. (2012). Indian Act–1876. Retrieved from http://www.shannon-thunderbird.com/indian_act.htm.

Truth and Reconciliation Commission of Canada. (2012). *Truth and Reconciliation Commission of Canada interim report.* Winnipeg: Truth and Reconciliation Commission of Canada.

Wahbung Abinoonjiiag Inc. (2011). *Wahbung Abinoonjiiag Inc.* Retrieved from http://wahbung.org/.

Waldram, J.B., Innes, R., Kaweski, M., & Redman, C. (2008). Building a Nation: Healing in an urban context. In J.B. Waldram (Ed.), *Aboriginal healing in Canada: Studies in therapeutic meaning and practice.* Ottawa, ON: Aboriginal Healing Foundation.

Warriors Against Violence. (2010). *Warriors against Violence.* Retrieved from http://www.kiwassa.bc.ca/wav/.

Wesley-Esquimaux, C.C., & Smolewski, M. (2004). *Historic trauma and Aboriginal healing.* Ottawa: Aboriginal Healing Foundation. Retrieved from www.ahf.ca/downloads/historic-trauma.pdf.

Chapter 9

Abella, I., & Troper, H. (2010). *None is too many: Canada and the Jews of Europe.* Toronto: University of Toronto Press.

Ahearn, F.L. (Ed.). (2000). *Psychosocial wellness of refugees: Issues in qualitative and quantitative research.* New York: Berghahn Books.

Ali, M.A. (2006). Children alone, seeking refuge in Canada. *Refuge, 23,* 2, 68–80.

Baines, D. (Ed) (2007). *Doing anti-oppressive practice: Building transformative politicized social work.* Black Point: Fernwood.

Beiser, M., & Hou, F. (2006). Ethnic identity, resettlement stress and depressive affect among Southeast Asian refugees in Canada. *Social Science & Medicine, 63,* 137–150.

Berg, L., & Millbank, J. (2009). Constructing the personal narratives of lesbian, gay and bisexual asylum claimants. *Journal of Refugee Studies, 22,* 195–222.

Berry, J.W. (2002). Conceptual approaches to acculturation. In K.M. Chun, P. B. Organista, & G. Marin (Eds.), *Acculturation: Advances in theory, measurement, and applied research* (pp.17–37). Washington, DC: American Psychological Association.

Biles, J., Burstein, M., & Frideres, J. (Eds.), (2008) *Immigration and integration in Canada in the twenty-first century.* Montreal: McGill-Queen's University Press.

Bloch, A., Galvin, T., & Harrell-Bond, B. (2000). Refugee women in Europe: Some aspects of the legal and policy dimensions. *International Migration, 38,* 2, 169–190.

Boyd, M. (2011). Immigrants in Canada: Trends and issues. In B. Edmonston & E. Fong, *The Changing Canadian Population* (pp. 207–231). Montreal: McGill-Queen's University Press.

Boyd, M. (2006). *Gender aspects of international migration to Canada and the United States.* International Symposium on International Migration and Development, Population Division, Department of Economic and Social Affairs, United Nations Secretariat.

Boyd, M., & Cao, X. (2009). Immigrant language proficiency, earnings, and language policies. *Canadian Studies in Population, 36,* 63–86.

Bronfenbrenner, U. (1979). *The ecology of human development.* Cambridge, MA: Harvard University Press.

Canadian Council for Refugees (CCR). (n.d.). *A hundred years of immigration to Canada, 1900–1999: A chronology focusing on refugees and discrimination.* Canadian Council for Refugees.

Canadian Human Rights Commission. (2001). *Race, colour, national or ethnic origin: Anti-discrimination casebook.* Ottawa, ON: Minister of Public Works and Government Services. Retrieved from www.chrc-ccdp.ca/pdf/publications/adceng.pdf.

Centre d'encadrement pour jeunes filles immigrantes (CEFJI). (2004). *Pour une journée Québecoise des filles immigrantes.* Montreal, Quebec.

Chenoweth, J., & Burdick, L. (2001). The path to integration: Meeting the special needs of refugee elders in resettlement. *Refuge, 20,* 20–30.

Cho, M. (1996). Immigrant women are more often victims of family violence. In D.L. Bender, B. Leone, S. Barbour, B. Stalcup, & A.E. Sadler (Eds.), *Family violence* (pp. 132–138). San Diego, CA: Greenhaven.

Choudry, A., Hanley, J., Jordan, S., Shragge, E., & Stiegman, M. (2009). *Fight back: Workplace justice for immigrants.* Halifax: Fernwood.

Chui, T. (2011). *Immigrant women: A gender-based statistical report.* Component of Statistics Canada Catalogue no. 89-503-X, Statistics Canada.

Citizenship and Immigration Canada (2012). *Facts and figures 2012—Immigration overview: Total entry of foreign students by category.* Available at http://www.cic.gc.ca/english/resources/statistics/facts2012/temporary/17.asp.

Citizenship and Immigration Canada. (2011a). *Backgrounder—Facts in Canada's immigration history.* Available at http://www.cic.gc.ca/english/department/media/backgrounders/2011/2011-06-27.asp.

Citizenship and Immigration Canada. (2011b). *Facts and figures 2011—Immigration overview: Permanent and temporary residents, permanent residents by category.* Available at http://www.cic.gc.ca/english/resources/statistics/facts2011/permanent/02.asp.

Citizenship and Immigration Canada. (2011c). *Facts and figures 2011—Immigration overview: Permanent and temporary residents, total entries of refugee claimants by top source countries.* Available at http://www.cic.gc.ca/english/resources/statistics/facts2011/temporary/25.asp.

Citizenship and Immigration Canada. (2011d). *Facts and figures 2011—Immigration overview: Permanent and temporary residents, total entries of refugee claimants by gender and age.* Available at http://www.cic.gc.ca/english/resources/statistics/facts2011/temporary/29.asp.

Citizenship and Immigration Canada. (2009). *Facts and figures 2009.* Available at http://www.cic.gc.ca/english/resources/statistics/facts2009/permanent/16.asp.

Citizenship and Immigration Canada. (2005). *Recent immigrants in metropolitan areas: Canada—A comparative profile based on the 2001 Census.* Available at http://www.cic.gc.ca/english/resources/research/census2001/canada/intro.asp.

Citizenship and Immigration Canada. (n.d.) *Protection and assistance for victims of human trafficking.* Available at http://www.cic.gc.ca/english/information/applications/trp.asp.

Congress, E. (2004). Cultural and ethical issues in working with culturally diverse patients and their families; the use of the culturagram to promote cultural competent practice in health care settings. *Social Work in Health Care, 39,* 249–262.

Dane, B. (2002). Duty to inform: Preparing social work students to understand vicarious traumatization. *Journal of Teaching in Social Work, 22,* 3/4, pp. 3–19.

Dauvergne, C. (2012). International human rights in Canadian immigration law: The case of the Immigration and Refugee Board of Canada. *Indiana Journal of Global Legal Studies, 19,* 1, 305–326.

Dempsey, C. (2005). *Elderly immigrants in Canada: Income sources and self-sufficiency.* Strategic Research and Statistics, Citizenship and Immigration Canada.

Drachman, D. (1992). A stage-of-migration framework for service to immigrant populations. *Social Work, 37,* 1, 68–72.

Elgersma, S. (2007). *Unaccompanied and separated minors as refugee claimants* (No. PRB 07-15E). Ottawa, ON: Parliamentary Information and Research Services, Library of Parliament.

Elrick, J. (2007). Country profile: Canada. *focus Migration, 8,* 1–11. Available at http://focus-migration.hwwi.de/uploads/tx_wilpubdb/CP_08_Canada.pdf.

Fadiman, A. (1997). *The spirit catches you and you fall down.* New York: Farrar, Straus, and Giroux.

Folson, R.B., (Ed.). (2004). *Calculated kindness: Global restructuring, immigration, and settlement in Canada.* Halifax, NS: Fernwood.

Furuto, S.B.C.L. (2004). Theoretical perspectives for culturally competent practice with immigrant children and families. In R. Fong (ed.), *Culturally competent practice with immigrant and refugee children and families* (pp. 19–38). New York: Guilford.

Hanes, R. (2011). *None is still too many: An historical exploration of Canadian immigration legislation as it pertains to people with disabilities*. Council of Canadians with Disabilities. Available at http://www.ccdonline.ca/en/socialpolicy/access-inclusion/none-still-too-many.

Hugman, R. (2010). *Understanding international social work: A critical analysis*. London, UK: Palgrave Macmillan.

Ighodaro, M.E. (2006). A critical anti-racist exploration of Canadian immigration and refugee policy practice. In *Living the experience: Migration, exclusion, and anti-racist practice* (pp. 42–61). Halifax: Fernwood.

Immigration and Refugee Protection Act (IRPA). (2001). Available at http://laws-lois.justice.gc.ca/eng/acts/I-2.5/index.html.

Kopinak, J.K. (1999). The health of Bosnian refugees in Canada. *Ethnicity and Health, 4*, 65–82.

Korac, M. (2001). Cross-ethnic networks, self-reception system, and functional integration of refugees from the Former Yugoslavia in Rome. *Journal of International Migration and Integration, 2*, 1–26.

Krahn, H., Derwing, T., Mulder, M., & Wilkinson, L. (2000). Educated and underemployed: Refugee integration into the Canadian labour market. *Journal of International Migration and Integration, 1*, 59–84.

Lam, L. (1996). *From being uprooted to surviving: Resettlement of Vietnamese-Chinese "boat people" in Montreal, 1980–1990*. Toronto: York Lanes Press.

LaViolette, N. (2009). Independent human rights documentation and sexual minorities: An ongoing challenge for the Canadian refugee determination process. *International Journal of Human Rights, 13*, 2, 437–476.

Lee, E.O.J., & Brotman, S. (2011). Identity, refugeeness, belonging: Experiences of sexual minority refugees in Canada. *Canadian Review of Sociology, 48*, 3, 243–274.

Lehrer, W., & Sloan, J. (2003). *Crossing the boulevard: Strangers, neighbors, aliens in a new America*. New York: W. W. Norton.

Lie, B. (2002). A 3-year follow-up study of psychosocial functioning and general symptoms in settled refugees. *Acta Psychiatrica Scandinavica, 106*, 6, 415–425.

Lum, D. (2007). *Culturally competent practice: A framework for understanding diverse groups and justice issues*. Belmont, CA: Thomson Brooks/Cole.

Lyons, K., & Stathopoulos, P. (2001). Migration and refugees in Europe: Greek and British perspectives on implications for social work practice and education. *European Journal of Social Work, 4*, 55–63.

Magalhaes, L., Carrasco, C., & Gastaldo, D. (2011). Undocumented migrants in Canada: A scope literature review on health, access to services, and working conditions. *Journal of Immigrant and Minority Health, 12*, 1, 132–151.

Mah, H., & Ives, N. (2010). It takes a village: Perspectives from a multidisciplinary team addressing the needs of HIV+ refugees in Canada. *Refuge, 27*, 75–88.

McGregor, J. (1993). Refugees and the environment. In R. Black & V. Robinson (Eds.), *Geography and refugees* (pp. 157–170). London, UK: Belhaven Press.

Miller, K.E., Muzurovic, J., Worthington, G.J., Tipping, S., & Goldman, A. (2002). Bosnian refugees and the stressors of exile: A narrative study. *American Journal of Orthopsychiatry, 72*, 141–154.

Montgomery, C. (2002). The "brown paper syndrome": Unaccompanied minors and questions of status. *Refuge, 20*, 2, 56–67.

Montgomery, E. (2008). Long-term effects of organized violence on young Middle Eastern refugees' mental health. *Social Science & Medicine, 67*, 1596–1603.

Mortland, C. A. (2001). Cambodian adaptation & community response. In David W. Haines & Carol A. Mortland (Eds.), *Manifest destinies: Americanizing immigrants and internationalizing Americans* (pp. 71–88). Westport, CT: Praeger.

Mullaly, B. (2010). *Challenging oppression and confronting privilege* (2nd ed.). Don Mills: Oxford University Press.

Parrott, L. (2009) Constructive marginality: Conflicts and dilemmas in cultural competence and anti-oppressive practice, *Social Work Education, 28*, 6, 617–630.

Posadski, A. (2012, August 23). "Government says high number of immigrants will help economic recovery." *The Globe & Mail*. Accessed on October 29, 2012 at http://m.theglobeandmail.com/news/politics/government-says-high-number-of-immigrants-will-help-economic-recovery/article1905529/?service=mobile.

Potocky-Tripodi, M. (2002). *Best practices for social work with refugees and immigrants*. New York: Columbia University Press.

Profitt, N.J. (2008). Who cares for us? Opening paths to a critical, collective notion of self-care. *Canadian Social Work Review, 25*, 147–168.

Radey, M., & Figley, C.R. (2007). The social psychology of compassion. *Clinical Social Work Journal, 35*, 207–214.

Rehaag, S. (2009). Bisexuals need not apply: A comparative appraisal of refugee law and policy in Canada, the United States, and Australia. *International Journal of Human Rights, 13*, 2–3, 415–436.

Roy, G., & Montgomery, C. (2003). Practice with immigrants in Quebec. In A. Al-Krenawi and J. R. Graham (Eds.), *Multicultural social work in Canada* (pp. 122–145). Oxford: Oxford University Press.

Russell, M.N., & White, B. (2001). Practice with immigrants and refugees. *Journal of Ethnic and Cultural Diversity in Social Work, 9*, 3, 73–92.

Salaff, J.W., & Greve, A. (2004). Can women's social networks migrate? *Women's Studies International Forum, 27*, 2, 149–162.

Shakya, Y.B., Guruge, S., Hynie, M., Akbari, A., Malik, M., Htoo, S., Khogali, A., Mona, S.A., Murtaza, R., & Alley, S. (2010). Aspirations for higher education among newcomer refugee youth in Toronto: Expectations, challenges, and strategies. *Refuge, 27*, 2, 65–78.

Simmons, A.B. (2010). *Immigration and Canada: Global and transnational perspectives*. Toronto: Canadian Scholars' Press.

Smith, J. (2003). *L'Intervention et les femmes immigrantes*. Auberge Madeline. Montreal, QC.

Stewart, M.J., Neufeld, A., Harrison, M.J., Spitzer, D., Hughes, K., & Makwarimba, E. (2006). Immigrant women family caregivers in Canada: Implications for policies and programmes in health and social sectors. *Health & Social Care in the Community, 14*, 4, 329–340.

Torres, S., Spitzer, D., Hughes, K., & Hanley, J. (2012). From temporary worker to resident: The LCP and its impact through an intersectional lens. In C. Straehle and P. Lenard (Eds.), *Legislated inequality* (pp. 227–244). Toronto: University of Toronto Press.

UNHCR. (2012). *2011 Global Trends: A year of crises*. Division of Operational Services, Field Information and Coordination Support Section, UNHCR.

UNHCR. (2011). *Working with persons with disabilities in forced displacement*. Division of International Protection, UNHCR.

University of Ottawa Human Rights Research and Education Centre (2012). *IRB Refugee status determinations*. Available at http://www.cdp-hrc .uottawa.ca/projects/refugee-forum/ projects/documents/REFUGEESTATS-COMPREHENSIVE1999–2011.pdf.

Urdang, E. (2010). Awareness of self—A critical tool. *Social Work Education, 29*, 523–538.

US Department of State. (2012). *Trafficking in persons report. Country narratives: Canada*. Available at http://www .state.gov/j/tip/rls/tiprpt/2012/.

Valtonen, K. (1999). The societal participation of Vietnamese refugees: Case studies in Finland and Canada. *Journal of Ethnic and Migration Studies, 25*, 469–491.

Walsh, C., Hanley, J., Ives, N., Hordyk, S.-R., & Mahano, B. (2011). *Uncovering Invisibilities: Understanding Experiences of Newcomer Women Across the Homelessness Spectrum*, funded by the Homeless Partnership Strategy, Human Resources and Skills Development Canada.

Warde, B. (2012). The cultural genogram: Enhancing the cultural competency of social work students. *Social Work Education, 31*, 5, 570–586.

Weber, L. (2006). The shifting frontiers of migration control. In S. Pickering & L. Weber (Eds.), *Borders, mobility and technologies of control*. Dordrecht, Netherlands: Springer.

Women's Refugee Commission. (n.d.). *Disabilities*. Accessed on February 17, 2014 at http://womensrefugeecommis-sion.org/programs/disabilities.

World Health Organization. (2011). *World report on disability*. Accessed on November 14, 2013 at http:// whqlibdoc.who.int/publica-tions/2011/9789240685215_eng.pdf.

Wouk, J., Yu, S., Roach, L., Thomson, J., & Harris, A. (2006). Unaccompanied/ separated minors and refugee protection in Canada. *Refuge, 23, 2*, 125.

Chapter 10

Anderson, K. (2003). *A recognition of being: Reconstructing Native woman-hood*. Toronto, Ontario: Sumach Press.

Baines, D. (2011). *Doing anti-oppressive practice: Building transformative politicized social work* (2nd ed.). Halifax: Fernwood Publishing.

Berg, L., & Millbank, J. (2009). Constructing the personal narratives of lesbian, gay and bisexual asylum claimants. *Journal of Refugee Studies, 22*, 195–222.

Bleys, R. (1995). *The geography of perversion: Male to male sexual behaviour outside the west and the ethnographic imagination, 1750–1918*. New York: New York University.

Brotman, S., & Kraniou, S. (1999). Ethnic and lesbian: Understanding identity through the life-history approach. *Affilia, 14, 4*, 417–438.

Brotman, S., & Levy, J.J. (Eds.). (2008). *Homosexualités: variations linguistiques et culturelles*. Québec: Presses de l'Université du Québec, Coll. Santé et Société.

Brotman, S., & Ryan, B. (2001). *Critical issues in practice with gay, lesbian, bisexual and two-spirit people and communities: Educational module*. McGill School of Social Work. Montreal, QC. ISBN 077170590-5 (44 pp.)

Brotman, S., Ryan, B., & Cormier, R. (2003). The Health and social service needs of gay and lesbian elders and their families in Canada. *The Gerontologist, 43, 2*, 192–202.

Brotman, S., Ryan, B., Jalbert, Y., & Rowe, B. (2002). The Impact of coming out on health and health care access: The Experiences of gay, lesbian, bisexual and two-spirit people. *Journal of Health and Social Policy, 15, 1*, 1–29.

Carter, S. (2008). *The importance of being monogamous: Marriage and nation building in Western Canada to 1915*. Edmonton: The University of Alberta Press.

Crenshaw, K. (1991). Mapping the margins: Intersectionality, identity politics and violence against women of color. *Stanford Law Review, 43, 6*, 1241–1299.

Cronin, A., Ward, R., Pugh, S., King, A., & Price, E. (2011). Categories and their consequences: Understanding and supporting the caring relationships of older lesbian, gay and bisexual people. *International Social Work, 54, 3*, 421–435.

D'Emilio, J. (1998). Capitalism and gay identity. In W.B. Rubenstein, C.A. Ball, & J.S. Schacter (Eds.), *Cases and materials on sexual orientation and the law: Lesbians, gay men and the law*. New York: New Press.

Driskell, Q.–L., Finley, C., Gilley, B.J., & Morgensen, S.L. (2011). *Queer indigenous studies: Critical interventions in theory, politics and literature*. Tucson: The University of Arizona Press.

Ezra, J. (2013). *Taking charge: A handbook for health care and social service providers working with trans people*. Action santé travesti(e)s et transsexuel(le)s du Québec. Public Health Agency of Canada.

Finney, S., Dean, M., Loiselle, E., & Saraceno, J. (2011). Some children are equal, but some are more equal than others: Minoritization, structural inequities and social justice praxis in residential care. *International Journal of Child, Youth and Family Studies, 3–4*, 361–384.

Goldberg, A.E. (2010). *Lesbian and gay parents and their children: Research on the family life cycle*. American Psychological Association.

Grenier, A., & Brotman, S. (2010). Les multiples vieillissements et leurs representations. In M. Charpentier, N. Guberman, V. Billette, J.P. Lavoie, A. Grenier, & I. Olazabal, I. (Eds.), *Vieillir au pluriel: Perspectives sociales* (pp. 23–34). Quebec: Presses de l'Université du Québec.

Gupta, A. (2008). *This alien legacy: The origins of "sodomy" laws in British colonialism*. Human Rights Watch. New York: New York.

Harper, G.W., Jernewall, N., & Zea, M.C. (2004). Giving voice to emerging science and theory for lesbian, gay and bisexual people of color. *Cultural diversity and ethnic minority psychology.* 10 (3), 187–199.

Ingram, G. (2003). Returning to the scene of the crime: Uses of trial dossiers on consensual male homosexuality for urban research, with examples from twentieth-century British Columbia. *GLQ: A Journal of Lesbian and Gay Studies, 10, 1*, 77–110.

Janoff, D. (2005). *Pink blood: Homophobic violence in Canada.* Toronto: University of Toronto Press.

Jenicek, A., Lee, E., & Wong, A. (2009). "Dangerous Shortcuts": Representations of LGBT refugees in the post 9/11 Canadian press. *Canadian Journal of Communications: Special Issue—Race, Ethnicity, and Intercultural Communication, 34,* 4, 635–658.

Kinsman, G. (1998). Constructing sexual problems: These things may lead to the tragedy of our species. In W. Antony & L. Samuelson (Eds.), *Power and resistance: Critical thinking about Canadian social issues* (2nd ed.)(pp. 256–282). Halifax: Fernwood Publishing.

Kleiss, K. (2012). *Homosexuality no longer classed as "mental illness" in Alberta billing code.* Retrieved from http://www.edmontonjournal.com/news/Homosexuality+longer+classed+mental+illness+Alberta+billing+code/6778104/story.html.

Kovach, M. (2005). Emerging from the margins: Indigenous methodologies. In L. Brown & S. Strega (Eds.), *Research as resistance–Critical, indigenous and anti-oppressive approaches* (pp. 19–36). Toronto, Ontario: Canadian Scholars' Press.

Kundouqk & Qwul'sih'yah'maht. (2009). Children at the centre: Indigenous perspectives on anti-oppressive child welfare practice. In S. Strega & S.A. Esquao (Eds.). *Walking this path together: Anti-racist and anti-oppressive child welfare practice* (pp. 29–44). Halifax: Fernwood Publishing.

Lavergne, C., Dufour, S., Trocmé, N., & Larrivee, M. (2008). Visible minority, aboriginal and caucasian children investigated by Canadian protective services. *Child Welfare, 87,* 2, 59–76.

Lee, E.O., & Brotman, S. (2011). Identity, refugeeness, belonging: Experiences of sexual minority refugees in Canada. *Canadian Review of Sociology, 48,* 3, 241–274.

Meyer-Cook, F. (2008). Two-spirit people: Traditional pluralism and human rights. In S. Brotman & J. J. Lévy, *Intersections: Cultures, sexualités et genres* (pp. 245–280). Montréal: Presses de l'Université du Québec.

Meyer-Cook, F., & Labelle, D. (2004). Namaji: Two-spirit organizing in Montreal, Canada. *Journal of Gay and Lesbian Social Services, 16,* 1, 29–51.

Mullaly, B. (2010). *Challenging oppression and confronting privilege* (2nd ed.). Oxford University Press: Oxford.

Munoz, J. E. (1999). *Disidentifications: Queers of color and the performance of politics.* Minneapolis: University of Minnesota Press.

Pyne, J. (2012). Unsuitable bodies: Trans people and cisnormativity in shelter services. *Canadian Social Work Review, 28,* 1, 129–137.

Rich, A. (1984). Notes towards a politics of location. In M. Diaz-Diocaretz & I. Zavala (Eds.), *Women feminist identity and society in the 1980s.* John Benjamins Publishing Company.

Ristock, J. (2008). Same-sex relationship violence and the need for intersectionality: Hearing the voices of women at the margins. In S. Brotman & J. J. Levy (Eds.), *Homosexualités: variations linguistiques et culturelles* (pp. 439–456). Québec: Presses de l'Université du Québec, Coll. Santé et Société.

Ristock, J., & Pennell, J. (1996). *Community research as empowerment: Feminist links, postmodern interruptions.* New York: Oxford.

Ristock, J., Zoccole, A., & Passante, L. (2010). *Aboriginal Two-Spirit and LGBTQ Migration, Mobility and Health Research Project: Winnipeg, Final Report.* November 2010.

River, L. (2006). *A feasibility study of the needs of older lesbians in Camden and surrounding boroughs.* Report to Age Concern Camden. Retrieved February 4, 2007, from http://www.ac-communities.org.uk/documents//POLARI%20REPORT.pdf.

Ryan, B. (1999). The continuum of attitudes towards homosexuality. Course notes for Critical Issues in Social Work with Gay, Lesbian, Bisexual and Two-Spirit People. In S. Brotman and B. Ryan (2001, March), *Critical issues in practice with gay, lesbian, bisexual and two-spirit people and communities: Educational module.* McGill School of Social Work. Montreal, QC. ISBN 077170590-5 (44 pp.)

Ryan, B., Brotman, S., Baradaran, A., & Lee, E. (2008). The colour of queer health care: Experiences of multiple oppression in the lives of queer people of colour in Canada. In S. Brotman & J.J. Levy, (Eds.), *Homosexualités: variations linguistiques et culturelles*

(pp. 307–338). Québec: Presses de l'Université du Québec, Coll. Santé et Société.

Serano, J. (2007). *Whipping girl: A transsexual woman on sexism and the scapegoating of femininity.* Emeryville, CA: Seal.

Smith, A. (1997). Cultural diversity and the coming-out process: Implications for clinical practice. In B. Greene (Ed.), *Ethnic and cultural diversity among lesbians and gay men. Psychological perspectives on lesbian and gay issues* (pp. 279–300). Thousand Oaks, CA: Sage Publications.

Statistics Canada (2012). *Police-reported hate crimes 2010.* The Daily.

Strong-Boag, V. (2007). Children of adversity: Disabilities and child welfare in Canada from the nineteenth to the twenty-first century. *Journal of Family History, 32,* 4, 413–432.

Sue, D.W., Capodilupo, C.M., Torino, G.C., Bucceri, J.M., Holder, A.M.B, Nadal, K.L., & Esquilin, M. (2007). Racial microaggressions in everyday life: Implications for clinical practice. *American Psychologist, 62,* 4, 271–286.

Sussman, T., Churchill, M., Brotman, S., Chamberland, L., Daley, A., Dumas, J., MacDonell, J., MacIntosh, H., Ryan, B., Enriquez, M.C., Heffernan, D., Henriques, A., & Singh, S. (2013). *Identifying barriers, developing solutions: Addressing the health and social needs of gay, lesbian, bisexual and transgender older adults who reside in long-term care homes: An Environmental Scan.* McGill School of Social Work, Montreal.

Tremble, B., Schneider, M., & Appathurai, C. (1989). Growing up gay or lesbian in a multicultural context. *Journal of Homosexuality, 22,* 253–267. Toronto: The Haworth Press.

Valverde, M. (2008). *The age of light, soap and water: Moral reform in English Canada, 1885–1925.* University of Toronto Press: Toronto, ON.

Wallach, I., & Brotman, S. (2012) Ageing with HIV/AIDS: a scoping study among people aged 50 and over living in Quebec. *Ageing and Society, 10,* 1–31.

Warner, T. (2002). *Never going back: A history of queer activism in Canada.* Toronto: University of Toronto Press.

Weston, K. (1991). *Lesbians, gays, kinship.* Columbia University Press: New York.

White, M.A. (2010). *Intimate archives, migrant negotiations: Affective governance and the recognition of "same-sex" family class migration in Canada*. Dissertation submission. York University: Toronto.

Chapter 11

Blackstock, C. (2008). Jordan's Principle: An editorial. *Paediatric Child Health*, 13(7), 589–590.

Bronfenbrenner, U. (1979). *The Ecology of human development: Experiments by nature and design*. Boston: Harvard University Press.

Bruce, H.A. (1933). The sterilization of the feeble-minded. *Canadian Medical Association Journal, 29*, 3, 260–263.

Canada Revenue Agency. (2012). Disability Tax Credit Certificate, form t2201. Available at http://www.cra-arc.gc.ca/E/pbg/tf/t2201/t2201-12e.pdf.

Canadian Association of Social Workers. (2005). *Code of ethics*. Retrieved January 31, 2013, from http://www.casw-acts.ca/en/what-social-work/casw-code-ethics.

Canadian Human Rights Act. (1985). Retrieved February 5, 2013 from http://laws-lois.justice.gc.ca/eng/acts/h-6/page-1.html#h-1.

Canadian Mental Health Association. (1963). *More for the Mind—A Study of Psychiatric Services in Canada*, Toronto.

Centre for Independent Living in Toronto. (2013). *What is IL?* Retrieved February 7, 2013, from http://www.cilt.ca/default.aspx.

Chupik, J. & Wright, D. (2006). Treating the idiot child in early 20th century Ontario. *Disability and Society, 21*, 1, 77–90.

Constitution Act. (1982). Retrieved February 5, 2013 from http://laws-lois.justice.gc.ca/eng/Const/page-15.html.

Davis, L.J. (2010). *The Disability Studies Reader*, (3rd ed.). New York: Routledge.

DeJong, G. (1979). Independent living: From social movement to analytic paradigm. *Archives of Physical Medicine and Rehabilitation, 60*, 435–446.

Dowbiggin, I.R. (1997). *Keeping America sane: Psychiatry and eugenics in the United States and Canada 1880–1940*. Ithaca, NY Cornell University Press.

Dyck, E. (2013). *Facing eugenics: Reproduction, sterilization, and the politics of choice*. Toronto: University of Toronto Press.

Employment Equity Act. (1995). Retrieved February 7, 2013 from http://laws-lois.justice.gc.ca/eng/acts/e-5.401/index.html.

English Heritage. (n.d.). *A history of disability: From 1050 to the present day*. Retrieved from https://www.english-heritage.org.uk/discover/people-and-places/disability-history/.

Graham, J., Swift, K., & Delaney, R. (2000). Historical influences. *Canadian Social Policy: An Introduction* (pp. 19–38). Scarborough, ON: Prentice Hall, Canada.

Gustavsson, A. (2004). The role of theory in disability research—springboard or strait-jacket? *Scandinavian Journal of Disability Research, 6*, 1, 55–70.

Health Council of Canada. (2007). *Population patterns of chronic health conditions in Canada: A data supplement to why health care renewal matters: Learning from Canadians with chronic health conditions*. Toronto: Health Council. www.healthcouncilcanada.ca.

Howe, D. (2009). *A brief introduction to social work theory*. London: Palgrave MacMillan.

Human Resources and Skills Development Canada. (2011). *Disability in Canada: A 2006 Profile*. Retrieved from http://www.esdc.gc.ca/eng/disability/arc/disability_2006.pdf.

Human Resources and Skills Development Canada. (1998). *In unison: A Canadian approach to disability issues*. (MP43-390/1998E). Retrieved from http://www.publications.gc.ca/site/eng/79880/publication.html.

Independent Living Canada. (n.d.). *What is IL?* Retrieved February 7, 2013, from http://www.ilcanada.ca/article/what-is-il-148.asp.

Jongbloed, L. (2003). Disability Policy in Canada: An Overview. *Journal of Disability Policy Studies, 13*, 4, 203–209.

Kim, K.H., & Turnbull, A. (2004). Transition to adulthood for students with severe intellectual disabilities: Shifting toward person-family interdependent planning. *Research and Practice for Persons with Severe Disabilities, 29*, 1, 53–57.

Kirby, M.J.L. (2004). Mental health, mental illness and addiction: Overview of policies and programs in Canada, interim report of The Standing Senate Committee On Social Affairs, Science and Technology (section 7.2.3).

Köbsell, S. (2006). Towards self-determination and equalization: A short history of the German disability rights movement. *Disability Studies Quarterly, 26*, 2.

Law Reform Commission of Canada. (1979). *Sterilization: Implications for mentally retarded and mentally ill persons*. Ottawa: Minister of Supply and Services. Retrieved from http://archive.org/stream/sterilizationimp00lawr#page/102/mode/2up/search/102.

MacDonald, N. (2012). Aboriginal children suffer while governments ignore Jordan's Principle. *Canadian Medical Association Journal*, Early Release.

MacDonald, N. & Attaran, A. (2007). Jordan's Principle, governments' paralysis. *Canadian Medical Association Journal, 177*, 4, 321.

Marshall, C.A., Kendall, E., Banks, M.E., & Gover, R.M.S. (Eds.). (2009). *Disabilities: The Experience: Definitions, Causes, and Consequences*. Westport, Connecticut: Praeger Publishers.

Martinez, K. (2003). *Independent Living in the U.S. & Canada*. Retrieved from http://www.independentliving.org/docs6/martinez2003.html.

Martinez, K., & Duncan, B. (2003). The road to independent living in the USA: an historical perspective and contemporary challenges. *Disability World, A bimonthly web-zine of international disability news and views, 20*.

McLaren, A. (1990). *Our own master race: Eugenics in Canada, 1885–1945*. Toronto: Oxford Press.

Morton, D., & Wright, G.T. (1987). *Winning the second battle: Canadian veterans and the return to civilian life 1915–1930*. Toronto; London: University of Toronto Press.

Nirje, B. (1999). How I came to formulate the Normalization principle. In R.J. Flynn & R.A. Lemay (Eds.), *A quarter-century of normalization and social role valorization: Evolution and impact*. Ottawa: University of Ottawa Press.

Oliver, M.J. (1999). Capitalism, disability, and ideology: A materialist critique of the normalization principle. In R.J. Flynn & R.A. Lemay (Eds.), *A quarter-century of normalization and social role valorization: Evolution and impact*. Ottawa: University of Ottawa Press.

Ontario. (2009). *Closing institutions for people with a developmental disability*.

Retrieved February 5, 2013, from http://news.ontario.ca/mcss/en/2009/03/closing-institutions-for-people-with-a-developmental-disability.html.

Ontario. (1987). *Challenges and opportunities: Community living for people with developmental handicaps.* Toronto: Queen's Printer for Ontario.

Ontario. (1907). Sessional Papers—Legislature of the Province of Ontario, *9*, 63.

Ontario. (1887). An act respecting lunatic asylums and the custody of insane persons. *The revised statutes of Ontario, 1887.* Toronto: John Notman, Law Printer to the Queen.

Osburn, J. (2006). An overview of social role valorization. *The SRV Journal, 1*, 1, 4–13.

Paterson, B.L. (2001). The shifting perspectives model of chronic illness. *Journal of Nursing Scholarship, 33*, 1, 21–26.

Prince, M.J. (2009). *Absent citizens: Disability politics and policy in Canada.* Toronto: University of Toronto Press Inc.

Rothman, J.C. (2010). The challenge of disability and access: Reconceptualizing the role of the medical model. *Journal of Social Work in Disability & Rehabilitation, 9*, 2–3, 194–222.

Royal Commission on Health Services (Hall Report). (1964). Queens Printer: Ottawa, Catalogue No. Z1-1961/3-1.

Schalock, R.L. (2004). The concept of quality of life: what we know and do not know. *Journal of Intellectual Disability Research, 48*, 3, 203–216.

Service Canada. (n.d.). *CPP Disability—Summary.* Retrieved February 5, 2013, from http://www.servicecanada.gc.ca/eng/isp/cpp/summary.shtml.

Sessions, Province of Canada, Journals. (1858). Volume 16, Appendix 4 (9), p. 6.

Shakespeare, T. (2006a). *Disability rights and wrongs.* London; New York: Routledge.

Shakespeare, T. (2006b). The social model of disability. In L.J. Davis (Ed.), *The disability studies reader* (pp. 197–204). New York: Routledge.

Simmons, H.G. (1982). *From asylum to welfare.* Ontario: National Institute on Mental Retardation.

Smart, J. (2001). *Disability, society, and the individual.* Gaithersburg, Maryland: Aspen Publishers Inc.

Statistics Canada. (n.d.). *Low income cut-offs.* Retrieved January 31, 2012,

from http://www.statcan.gc.ca/pub/75f0002m/2009002/s2-eng.htm.

Statistics Canada. (2012). Canadian Survey on Disability 2012. Data Tables: Table 1.1 *Prevalence of disability for adults by sex and age group, Canada, 2012.* Statistics Canada Online Catalogue 89-654-X. Last updated December 3, 2013. Retrieved August 13, 2014, from http://www.statcan.gc.ca/pub/89-654-x/2013001/tbl/tbl1.1-eng.htm.

Statistics Canada. (2006). *The Participation and Activity Limitation Survey 2006 Tables (Part IV).* Ottawa: Statistics Canada, 2010. (Catalogue no. 89-628-X no. 015).

Stein, R.E.K., & Jessop, D.J. (1982). A non-categorical approach to chronic childhood illness. *Public Health Reports, 97*, 354–362.

Tossebro, J. (2004). Introduction to the special issue: Understanding disability. *Scandinavian Journal of Disability Research, 6*(1), 3–7.

Ungar, M. (2002). A deeper, more social ecological social work practice. *Social Service Review, 76*, 3, 480–497.

Wendell, S. (2001). Unhealthy disabled: Treating chronic illnesses as disabilities. *Hypatia, 16*, 4, 17–33.

Wendell, S. (1996). *The rejected body: Feminist philosophical reflections on disability.* New York: Routledge.

Wolfensberger, W. (2000). A brief overview of social role valorization. *Mental Retardation, 38*, 2, 105–123.

World Health Organization. (n.d.a). *Health topics: Disabilities.* Retrieved January 31, 2013, from http://www.who.int/topics/disabilities/en/.

World Health Organization. (n.d.b). *International classification of functioning, disability and health (ICF).* Retrieved January 31, 2013, from http://www.who.int/classifications/icf/en/.

Yeung, P.H.Y., Passmore, A.E., & Packer, T.L. (2008). Active citizens or passive recipients: How Australian young adults with cerebral palsy define citizenship. *Journal of Intellectual & Developmental Disability, 33*, 1, 65–75.

Chapter 12

Alberta Health (2010). *Addressing elder abuse in Alberta. A strategy for collective action.* Government of Alberta.

Aneshensel, C., Pearlin, L.I., Mullan, J.T., Zarit, S. H., & Whitlatch, C.J. (1995). *Profiles in caregiving: The unexpected career.* New York: Academic Press.

Angus, J., & Reeve, P. (2006). Ageism: A threat to "aging well" in the 21st century. *Journal of Applied Gerontology, 25*, 2, 137–152.

Baltes, P.B., & Baltes, M.M. (1990). Psychological perspectives on successful aging: The model of selective optimization with compensation. In P.B. Baltes & M.M. Baltes (Eds.), *Successful aging: Perspectives from the behavioral sciences* (pp. 1–34). New York: Cambridge University Press.

Banerjee, A. (2009). Long-term care in Canada. An overview. In P. Armstrong, M. Boscoe, B. Clow, K. Grant, M. Haworth-Brockman, B. Jackson, A. Pederson, M. Seeley, and J. Springer (Eds.), *A place to call home: Long-term care in Canada* (pp. 29–57). Halifax: Fernwood Publishing.

Beaulieu, M., Gordon, R.M., & Spencer, C. (2003). *An environmental scan of abuse and neglect of older adults in Canada: What's working and why.* Report prepared for Federal/Provincial/Territorial Committee of Officials of Seniors.

Berta, W., Laporte, A., Zarnett, D., Valdmanis, V., & Anderson, G. (2006). A pan-Canadian perspective on institutional long-term care. *Health Policy, 79*, 175–194.

Bouchard, L., Sedigh, G., Batal, M., Imbeault, P., Makvandi, E., & Silva de la Vega, E. (2012). Language as an important determinant of poverty in the aging Francophone minority population in Canada. *The International Journal of Aging & Society, 2*, 4, 61–76.

Bourgeault, I.L. (2010). Chapter twelve: The provision of care: Professions, politics and profit. In T. Bryant, D. Raphael, & M. Rioux (Eds.), *Staying alive: Critical perspectives on health, illness and health care* (2nd ed.) (pp. 309–326). Toronto: Canadian Scholars Press. Retrieved from http://site.ebrary.com/lib/mcgill/docDetail.action?docID=10541213.

Breytspraak, L., Kendall, L., & Halpert, B. (n.d.). *Facts on aging quiz.* University of Missouri-Kansas City Gerontology Program. Available at http://cas.umkc.edu/agingstudies/AgingFactsQuiz.asp.

Burns, V., Grenier, A., Lavoie, J.P., Rothwell, D., & Sussman, T. (2013).

Les personnes âgées itinérantes. Invisibles et exclues. Une analyse de trois stratégies pour contrer l'itinérantes. (translation: Older homeless people. Invisible and excluded. An analysis of three strategies to address homelessness). *Frontière, 25*, 1, 31–56.

Canadian Healthcare Association. (2009a). *Home care in Canada: From the margins to the mainstream.* Canadian Healthcare Association, Ottawa. ISBN 978-1-896151-33-5.

Canadian Healthcare Association (2009b). *New directions for facility based long term care.* Ottawa: Canadian Healthcare Association. ISBN 978-1-896151-35-9.

Canadian Institute for Health Information (2011). *Health care in Canada. A focus on seniors and aging.* Canadian Institute for Health Information. Ottawa.

Caouette, E. (2005). The image of nursing homes and its impact on the meaning of home for elders. In G.D. Rowles & H. Chaudhury (Eds.), *Home and identity in later life: International perspectives* (pp. 251–275). NY: Springer Publishing.

Caron, C.D., Ducharme, F., & Griffith, J. (2006). Deciding on institutionalization for a relative with dementia: The most difficult decision for caregivers. *Canadian Journal on Aging, 25*, 2, 193–205.

Castle, N.G. (2001). Relocation of the elderly. *Medical Care Research Review, 58*, 291–333.

Castle, N.G., & Engberg, J. (2007). Nursing home deficiency citations for medication use. *Journal of Applied Gerontology, 26*, 208–232.

Ceci, C., & Purkis, M.E. (2011). Means without ends: justifying supportive home care for frail older people in Canada, 1990–2010. *Sociology of Health & Illness, 33*, 7, 1066–1080.

Chappell, N.L., MacDonald, L., & Stones, M. (2008). *Aging in contemporary Canada* (2nd ed.). Toronto, ON: Pearson Educational.

Cohen, M., Hall, N., Murphy, J., & Priest, A. (2009). *Innovations in community care. From pilot projects to system change.* Vancouver: Canadian Centre for Policy Alternatives. ISBN 978-1-897569-33-7.

Crane, M., Byrne, K., Ruby, F., Lipmann, B., Mirabelli, F., Rota-Bartelink, A., Ryan, M., Shea, R., Watt, H., & Warnes, M. (2005). The causes of homelessness in later life: Findings from a 3-nation study. *Journal of Gerontology: Social Sciences, 60*, 3, 152–159.

Davies, S., & Nolan, M. (2006). "Making it better": Self-perceived roles of family caregivers of older people living in care homes: A qualitative study. *International Journal of Nursing Studies, 43*, 281–291.

Denton, M., Ploeg, J., Tindale, J., Hutchison, B., Brazil, K., Akhtar-Danesh, N., Lillie, J., & Plenderleith, J.M. (2010). Would older adults turn to community support services for help to maintain their independence? *Journal of Applied Gerontology, 29*, 5, 554–578.

Dosman, D., Fast, J., Chapman, S.A., & Keating, N. (2006). Retirement and productive activity in later life. *Journal of Family and Economic Issues, 27*, 401–419.

Durst, D. (2010). Elderly immigrants in Canada: Changing faces and greying temples. In D. Durst & M. MacLean (Eds.), *Diversity and aging among immigrant seniors in Canada: Changing faces and greying temples* (pp. 15–35). Edmonton: Brush Education.

Echenberg, H., Gauthier, J., & Léonard, A. (2011). Some public policy implications of an aging population. *Current and Emerging Issues—41st Parliament.* Library of Parliament, Ottawa.

Egale Canada (2012). 2013 UPR Submission. Toronto, ON: Egale Canada. Available at http://archive.egale.ca/extra%5CUPR%20Submission.pdf.

Egale Canada (2004). *Outlaws & inlaws: Your guide to LBGT rights, same-sex relationships and Canadian law.* Ottawa: Egale Canada.

Erickson, E.H. (1982). *The life cycle completed.* New York, Norton.

Estes, C.L. (1991). The new political economy of aging: Introduction and critique. In *Critical perspectives on aging: The political and moral economy of growing old.* (pp. 19–36). Amityville, NY: Baywood.

Fast, J., Charchuk, M., Keating, N., Dosman, D., & Moran, L. (2006, March). *Participation, roles and contributions of seniors.* Final report to Human Resources and Skills Development Canada (formerly Social Development Canada) Knowledge and Research Directorate, Ottawa, ON.

Fast, J.E., Dosman, D., & Moran, L. (2006). Productive activity in later life: Stability and change across three decades. *Research on Aging, 28*, 691–712.

Fast, J., Keating, N., Otfinowski, P., & Derksen, L. (2004). Characteristics

of family/friend care networks of frail seniors. *Canadian Journal on Aging, 23*, 1, 5–19

Fredriksen-Goldsen, K.I., & Muraco, A. (2010). Aging and sexual orientation: A 25-year review of the literature. *Research on Aging, 32*, 3, 372–13.

Gee, E., & Gutman, G. (2000). *The overselling of population aging. Apocalyptic demography, intergenerational challenges and social policy.* Don Mills, Ontario: Oxford University Press.

Ghesquiere, A., Yamile, M.M.H., & Katherine, M. (2011). Risks of complicated grief in family caregivers. *Journal of Social Work in End-Of-Life & Palliative Care, 7*, 2–3, 216–240.

Graham, J.E., & Stepheson, P.H. (Eds). (2010). *Contesting aging and loss.* Toronto: University of Toronto Press.

Harbison, J., Coughlan, S., Beaulieu, M., Karabanow, J., VanderPlaat, M., Wildeman, S., & Wexler, E. (2012). Understanding "elder abuse and neglect": A critique of assumptions underpinning responses to the mistreatment and neglect of older people. *Journal of Elder Abuse and Neglect, 24*, 2, 88–103.

Havighurst, R.J., & Albrecht, R. (1953). *Older people.* New York, NY: Longmans, Green.

Health Council of Canada. (2012). *Seniors in need, caregivers in distress: What are the home care priorities for seniors in Canada?* Toronto: Health Council of Canada. ISBN 978-1-926961-38-5 PDF.

Hersch, G., Spencer, J., & Kapoor, T. (2003). Adaptation by elders to new living arrangements following hospitalization: A qualitative, retrospective, analysis. *Journal of Applied Gerontology, 22*, 3, 315–339.

HRSDC. (2011). *Estimates of population, by age group and sex for July 1, Canada, provinces and territories, annual* (CANSIM Table 051-0001). Ottawa: Statistics Canada.

HRSDC. (2011). *Projected population, by projection scenario, sex and age group as of July 1, Canada, provinces and territories, annual* (CANSIM table 052-0005). Ottawa: Statistics Canada.

HRSDC. (n.d.). *Indicators of well-being in Canada: Canadians in Context—Aging Population.* Retrieved on May 14, 2013, from http://www4.hrsdc.gc.ca/.3ndic.1t.4r@-eng.jsp?iid=33.

Hulchanski, D. (2009). *Homelessness in Canada: Past, present, future.* Paper presented at the Growing Home, Housing and Homelessness in Canada, University of Calgary. http://www.cprn.org/documents/51110_EN.pdf.

Jolley, D., Jefferys, P., Katona, C., & Lennon, S. (2011). Enforced relocation of older people when care homes close: A question of life and death? *Age & Ageing, 40*, 534–537.

Jungers, C.M. (2010). Leaving home: An examination of late-life relocation among older adults. *Journal of Counseling & Development, 88*, 416–423.

Kaida, L., & Boyd, M. (2011). Poverty variations among the elderly. The roles of income security policies and family co-residence. *Canadian Journal on Aging, 30*, 1, 83–100.

Kapsalis, C., & Tourigny, P. (2004). Duration of non-standard employment. *Perspectives on Labour and Income, 5*, 12, online edition.

Katz, S. (2000). Busy bodies. Activities, aging and the management of everyday life. *Journal of Aging Studies, 14*, 20, 135–152.

Laird, G. (2007). *Shelter: Homelessness in a growth economy. Canada's 21st century paradox.* Calgary, Alberta: Chumir Ethics Foundation.

Lang, L., & Carstensen, L.L. (2002). Time counts: Future time, perspective and social relationships. *Psychology & Aging, 17*, 1, 125–139.

Larkin, M. (2009). *Vulnerable groups in health and social care.* UK: Sage Publications.

Leggett, S., Davies, S., Hiskey, S., & Erskin, J.A.K. (2011). The psychological effects of considering a move into residential care: An age-related study. *Journal of Housing for the Elderly, 25*, 31–49.

MacKewan, A. (2012). *Working after age 65. What is at stake?* Alternative federal budget technical paper. Canadian Centre for Policy Alternatives. Available at http://www.policyalternatives.ca/sites/default/files/uploads/publications/National%20Office/2012/04/WorkingAfter65.pdf.

McDonald, L. (2013). The evolution of retirement as systematic ageism. In P. Brownell and J. J. Kelly (Eds.), *Ageism and mistreatment of older workers* (pp. 69–90). Netherlands: Springer.

McDonald, L. (2011). Elder abuse and neglect in Canada: The glass is still half full. *Canadian Journal on Aging, 30*, 3, 437–466.

McDonald, L. (1996). *Transitions into retirement: A time for retirement.*

Toronto. Centre for Applied Social Research, Faculty of Social Work, University of Toronto.

McDonald, L., Dergal, J., Cleghorn, L. (2007). Living on the margins. *Journal of Gerontological Social Work, 49*, 1/2, 19–46.

McDonald, L., & Donahue, P. (2011). Retirement lost? *Canadian Journal on Aging, 30*, 3, 401–422.

McDonald, L., & Donahue, P. (2000). Poor health and retirement: The Canadian case. *Ageing and Society, 20*, 493–522.

McDonald, L., Sussman, T., & Donahue, P. (2002, October). *The economic consequences when the caregiving is over.* Paper presented at the Canadian Association on Gerontology 31st Annual Scientific and Educational Meeting, Montreal, Quebec, Canada.

McPherson, B.D., & Wister, A. (2008). *Aging as a social process: Canadian perspectives* (5th ed.). Oxford: Oxford University Press.

Ministry of Families & Older Adults. (2010). *Government action plan to counter elder abuse 2010–2015.* Ministry of Families & Older Adults: Quebec.

National Advisory Council on Aging. (2006). *Seniors in Canada 2006 Report Card.* Public Health Agency of Canada. Cat HP30-1/2006E.

National Seniors Council. (2011). *Report of the National Seniors Council on low income among seniors.* Available at http://www.seniorscouncil.gc.ca/eng/research_publications/low_income/2009/hs1_9/page05.shtml.

National Seniors Council. (2007). *Report from the National Seniors Council on elder abuse.* Available at http://www.seniorscouncil.gc.ca/eng/research_publications/elder_abuse/2007/hs4_38/hs4_38.pdf.

Newson, P. (2008). Relocation to a care home part one: Exploring reactions. *Nursing and Residential Care, 10*, 7, 321–324.

Orzeck, P., & Silverman, M. (2008). Recognizing post-caregiving as part of the caregiving career: Implications for practice. *Journal of Social Work Practice: Psychotherapuetic Approaches in Health, Welfare and Community, 22*, 2, 211–220.

Park, N.S. (2009). The relationship of social engagement to psychological well-being of older adults in assisted

living facilities. *Journal of Applied Gerontology, 28*, 4, 461–481.

Phelan, A. (2008). Elder abuse, ageism, human rights and citizenship: Implications for nursing discourse. *Nursing Inquiry, 15*, 4, 320–329.

Pike, E.C.J. (2011). The active aging agenda: Old folk devils and new moral panic. *Sociology of Sport Journal, 28*, 209–225.

Reis, M., & Nahmiash, D. (1998). Validation of the Indicators of Abuse (IOA) screen. *The Gerontologist, 38*, 4, 471–480.

Rosanova, J. (2010). Discourse of successful aging in the Globe & Mail. Insights from critical gerontology. *Journal of Aging Studies, 24*, 213–222.

Rowe, J.W., & Kahn, R.L. (1997). Successful aging. *Gerontologist, 37*, 4, 433–440.

Rowles, G.D. (2000). Habituation and being in place. *The Occupational Therapy Journal of Research, 20* (Suppl.), 52S–66S.

Schellenberg, G., Turcotte, M., & Ram, B. (2005). Preparing for retirement. *Canadian Social Trends, 78*, 8–11.

Shelter, Support and Housing Administration. (2006). *Street needs assessment: Results and key findings.* Shelter, Support and Housing Administration. Toronto, Ontario: Toronto City Council.

Smith, A.E., & Crome, P. (2000). Relocation mosaic: A review of 40 years of resettlement literature. *Reviews in Clinical Gerontology, 10*, 81–95.

Smith, M. (2004, Spring). *Commitment to care: A plan for LTC in Ontario.* Final report prepared for the Ministry of Health and LTC. Toronto, Ontario.

Special Senate Committee on Aging (2009). *Canada's aging population: Seizing the opportunity.* Final Report of the Special Senate Committee on Aging, Ottawa.

Statistics Canada (2010). *Statistical portrait of the French speaking immigrant population outside of Quebec (1991 to 2006).* 89-641-X.

Statistics Canada. (2007). *General social survey, care tables.* Catalogue no. 89-633-X. Retrieved June 14, 2013 from http://www.statcan.gc.ca/pub/89-633-x/89-633-x2008001-eng.pdf.

Statistics Canada. (2006). Aboriginal seniors in Canada. In *A portrait of seniors in Canada* (pp. 221–268). Available at http://www.statcan.gc.ca/pub/89-519-x/89-519-x2006001-eng.pdf.

Straka, S.M., & Montminy, L. (2006). Responding to the needs of older women experiencing domestic violence. *Violence Against Women, 12*, 3, 251–67.

Sussman, T. (2009). The influence of service factors on spousal caregivers' perceptions of community services. *Journal of Gerontological Social Work, 52*, 4, 406–422.

Sussman, T., & Dupuis, S. (2012). Supporting a relative's move into a long-term care home: The role of starting point in shaping family members' transition experiences. *Canadian Journal on Aging, 31*, 4, 395–410.

Sussman, T., & Regehr, C. (2009). The influence of community based services on the burden of spouses caring for their partners with dementia. *Health and Social Work, 34*, 1, 29–40.

Tam, S., & Neysmith, S. (2006). Disrespect and isolation: Elder abuse in Chinese communities. *Canadian Journal on Aging, 25*, 2, 141–151. doi:10.1353/cja.2006.0043.

Townson, M. (2010). *Options for pension reform. Expanding the Canada Pension Plan* (Policy brief). Canadian Centre for Policy Alternatives. Available at http://www.policyalternatives.ca/sites/default/files/uploads/publications/reports/docs/Options%20for%20Pension%20Reform.pdf.

Townson, M. (2006). *Growing older, working longer.* Ottawa, Ontario, Canada: Canadian Centre for Policy Alternatives.

Uppal, S., Wannell, T., & Imbeau, E. (2009, August). Pathways into the GIS. *Perspectives on Labour and Income.* Statistics Canada—Catalogue No. 75-001-X, pp. 5–14.

Vosko, L.F., MacDonald, M., & Campbell, I. (Eds.). (2009). *Gender and the contours of precarious employment.* London: Routledge.

Vosko, L.F., Zukewich, N., & Cranford, C. (2003). Precarious jobs: A new typology of employment. *Perspectives on Labour and Income, 4,* 10.

Walker, C.S., Currey, L.C., & Hogstel, M. (2007). Relocation stress syndrome for older adults transitioning from home to long-term care facility. Myth or reality? *Journal of Psychosocial Nursing and Mental Health Services, 45,* 1, 1–8.

Walsh, C.A., Ploeg, J., Lohfeld, L., Horne, J., MacMillan, H., & Lai, D. (2007). Violence across the lifespan: Interconnections among forms of abuse as described by marginalized Canadian elders and their caregivers.

British Journal of Social Work, 37, 3, 491–514.

Wang, D.S., Chonody, J., & Krase, K. (2013). Social work faculty's knowledge of aging: Results of a national sample. *Educational Gerontology, 39,* 6, 428–440.

Wiersma, E., & Dupuis, S.L. (2010). Becoming institutional bodies. Socialization into a long term care home. *Journal of Aging Studies, 24,* 278–291.

Wild, K., Wiles, J.L., & Allen, R.E.S. (2013). Resilience: Thoughts on the value of the concept from critical gerontology. *Ageing & Society, 33,* Special issue 01, 137–158.

World Health Organization (2002). *Aging and life course: Elder abuse.* Available at www.who.int/ageing/projects/elder_abuse/en/.

Chapter 13

Baingana, F., Fannon, I., & Thomas, R. (2005). *Mental health and conflicts: Conceptual framework and approach.* Washington: World Bank.

Banks, S. (2006) *Ethics and values in social work.* Basingstoke: Macmillan.

Bauman, Z. (1998). *Globalization: The human consequences.* Cambridge, MA: Polity Press.

Bouta, T. (2005). *Gender and disarmament, demobilization and reintegration: Building blocks for Dutch policy.* Netherlands: Clingendael Conflict Research Unit.

Bracken, P., & Petty, C. (1998). *Rethinking the trauma of war.* Michigan: Free Association Books.

CASW. (2005). *CASW: Code of ethics.* Ottawa, Ontario: Canadian Association of Social Workers.

Coalition to Stop the Use of Child Soldiers (2008) *Global Report.* London: Coalition to Stop the Use of Child Soldiers.

Coulter, C. (2009). *Bush wives and girl soldiers: women's lives through war and peace in Sierra Leone.* Ithaca, New York: Cornell University Press.

Cox, D., & Pawar, M. (2006). *International social work: Issues, strategies and programs.* London: Sage.

Denov, M. (2010). *Child soldiers: Sierra Leone's Revolutionary United Front.* Cambridge: Cambridge University Press.

Denov, M. (2008). Girl soldiers and human rights: Lessons from Angola, Mozambique, Northern Uganda and Sierra Leone. *International Journal of Human Rights, 12,* 5, 811–833.

Denov, M., & Maclure, R. (2007). Turnings and epiphanies: Militarization, life histories and the making and unmaking of two child soldiers in Sierra Leone. *Journal of Youth Studies, 10,* 2, 243–261.

Dominelli, L. (2005). International social work: Themes and issues for the 21th century. *International Social Work, 48,* 4, 504–507.

Donnelly, J. (1984). Cultural relativism and universal human rights. *Human Rights Quarterly, 6,* 400–419.

Doucet, D., & Denov, M. (2012). The power of sweet words: Local forms of intervention with war-affected women in rural post-conflict Sierra Leone. *International Social Work, 55,* 612–628.

Drover, G., & Rogers, G. (2009). Canadians and international social work. In G. Gilchrist James, R. Ramsay, and G. Drover (Eds.), *International social work: Canadian perspectives* (pp. 2–21). Toronto, ON: Thompson Education Publishing.

Elliott, D., & Segal, U. (2008). International social work. In B. White, K. Sowers, and C. Dulmus (Eds.), *Comprehensive handbook of social work and social welfare.* Hoboken, NJ: Wiley.

Ferris, E. (2005). Faith-based and secular humanitarian organizations. *International Review of the Red Cross, 87,* 311–325.

Fisher, W. (1997). Doing good? The politics and antipolitics of NGO practices. *Annual Review of Anthropology, 26,* 439–464.

Government of Canada. (2008). *Statement by Ambassador John McNee to the Security Council Open Debate on Children and Armed Conflict.* Retrieved August 15, 2010 at http://www.canadainternational.gc.ca/prmny-mponu/canada_un-canada_onu/statements-declarations/security_council-conseil_securite/11768.aspx?lang=eng.

Gray, M., & Fook, J. (2004). The quest for a universal social work: Some issues and implications. *Social Work Education, 23,* 5, 625–644.

Gupta, L., & Zimmer, C. (2008). Psychosocial intervention of war-affected children in Sierra Leone. *British Journal of Psychiatry, 192,* 3, 212–216.

Healy, L. (2001). *International social work: Professional action in an interdependent world.* Oxford: Oxford University Press.

Healy, L.M., Asamoah, Y., & Hokenstad, M.C. (2003). *Models of international collaboration in social work education*. Alexandria, VA: Council on Social Work Education.

Healy, L., & Link, R. (Eds.). (2012). *Handbook of international social work*. Oxford: Oxford University Press.

Herbert-Boyd, M. (2007). *Enriched by catastrophe: Social work and social conflict after the Halifax explosion*. Halifax: Fernwood Publishing.

Hiranandani, V. (2011). Canadian identity: Implications for international social work by Canadians. *Critical Social Work, 12*, 87–100.

Hokenstad, M., Khinduka, S., & Midgley, J. (1992). *Profiles in international social work*. Washington, DC: National Association of Social Work.

Hugman, R. (2010). *Understanding international social work: A critical analysis*. New York: Palgrave Macmillan.

Hugman, R., Moosa-Mitha, M., & Moyo, O. (2010). Towards a borderless social work: Reconsidering notions of international social work. *International Social Work, 53*, 5, 629–643.

Lawrence, S., Lyons, K., Simpson, G., & Huegler, N. (Eds.). (2009). *Introducing international social work*. Exeter: Learning Matters.

Libal, K., & Harding, S. (2012). Nongovernmental organizations and global social change. In L. Healy and R. Link (Eds.), *Handbook of international social work*. Oxford: Oxford University Press.

Link, R., & Ramanathan, C. (2011). *Human behaviour in a just world: Reaching for a common ground*. Lanham, MD: Rowman and Littlefield.

Long, D. (2009). International social work education and practice. In C. Tice and D. Long (Eds.), *International social work: Policy and Practice*. London: Wiley.

Lundy, C. (2011). *Social work, social justice and human rights: A Structural approach to practice*. Toronto: University of Toronto Press.

Lyons, K., Manion, K., & Carlsen, M. (2006). *International perspectives on social work*. New York: Palgrave.

Mafile'o, T. (2006). "Matakainga" (behaving like family): The social work client relationship in Pasifika social work. *Social Work Review, 18*, 1, 31–36.

Mama, R. (2012). Representing social work at the United Nations and other international bodies. In L. Healy and R. Link (Eds.), *Handbook of international social work*. Oxford: Oxford University Press.

Mayer, A. (1995). Cultural particularism as a bar to women's rights: Reflections on the Middle Eastern experience. In J. Peters and A. Wolper (Eds.), *Women rights, human rights: International feminist perspectives*. New York: Routledge.

Mazurana, D., McKay, S., Carlson, K., & Kasper, J. (2002). Girls in fighting forces and groups: Their recruitment, participation, demobilization and reintegration. *Peace and Conflict: Journal of Peace Psychology, 8*, 2, 97–123.

McKay, S., & Mazurana, D. (2004). *Where are the girls? Girls in fighting forces in Northern Uganda, Sierra Leone, and Mozambique: Their lives during and after war*. Montreal: International Centre for Human Rights and Democratic Development.

Midgley, J. (2001). Issues in International Social Work: Resolving Critical Debates in the Profession. *Journal of Social Work, 1*, 1, 21–35.

Midgley, J. (1981) *Professional imperialism*. London: Heinemann.

Pogge, T. (2008). *World poverty and human rights*. Cambridge: Cambridge University Press.

Roff, S. (2004). Nongovernmental organizations: The strengths-based perspective at work. *International Social Work, 47*, 2, 202v212.

Sider, R.J., & Unruh, H.R. (2004). Typology of religious characteristics of social service and educational organizations and programs. *Nonprofit and Voluntary Sector Quarterly, 33*, 109–134.

Silavwe, G. (1995). The need for a new social work perspective in an African setting: the case of social work in Zambia. *British Journal of Social Work, 25*, 1, 71–84.

Sinha, J.W. (2013). Unintended consequence of the faith-based initiative: Organizational practices and religious identity within faith-based human service organizations. *Nonprofit and Voluntary Sector Quarterly, 42*, 3, 563–583.

Walton, R., & El Nasr, M. (1988). The indigenization and authentization of social work in Egypt. *The Community Development Journal, 23*, 3, 148–155.

Weaver, H. (1997). Which canoe are you in? A view from a First Nations person. *Reflections, 3*, 4, 12–17.

World Association of Non-Governmental Organizations. (2009). *What are nongovernmental organizations?* Retrieved June 10, 2009, from www.ngohandbook.org/index.php?title=What_are_Non-Governmental_Organizations_(NGOs)%3F.

World Health Organization. (2008). *Closing the gap in a generation: Health equity through action on social determinants of health*. Geneva: Author.

Yip, K. (2004). A Chinese cultural critique of global qualifying standards for social work education. *Social Work Education, 23*, 5, 597–612.

Index